THE LAW OF
CONTRACTS
AND THE UNIFORM
COMMERCIAL CODE

THE LAW OF CONTRACTS AND THE UNIFORM COMMERCIAL CODE

Pamela Tepper

WEST PUBLISHING

an International Thomson Publishing company IP®

Albany • Bonn • Boston • Cincinnati • Detroit • London • Madrid
Melbourne • Mexico City • Minneapolis/St. Paul • New York • Pacific Grove
Paris • San Francisco • Singapore • Tokyo • Toronto • Washington

Cover photo courtesy of the The Gallery at Market East Philadelphia, PA
Cover Design: Essinger Design Associates

Delmar Staff
Administrative Editor: Jay Whitney
Developmental Editor: Christopher Anzalone
Project Editor: Theresa M. Bobear
Production Coordinator: Jennifer Gaines
Art & Design Coordinator: Douglas Hyldelund

COPYRIGHT © 1995
West Legal Studies is an imprint of Delmar, a division of Thomson Learning. The Thomson Learning logo is a registered trademark used herein under license.

Printed in the United States of America
    8 9 10 XXX 05 04 03 02

For more information, contact Delmar, 5 Maxwell Drive, P.O. Box 8007, Clifton Park, NY 12065-8007; or find us on the World Wide Web at http://www.delmar.com

International Division List

Japan:
Thomson Learning
Palaceside Building 5F
1-1-1 Hitotsubashi, Chiyoda-ku
Tokyo 100 0003 Japan
Tel: 813 5218 6544
Fax: 813 5218 6551

Australia/New Zealand:
Nelson/Thomson Learning
102 Dodds Street
South Melbourne, Victoria 3205
Australia
Tel: 61 39 685 4111
Fax: 61 39 685 4199

UK/Europe/Middle East:
Thomson Learning
Berkshire House
168-173 High Holborn
London
WC1V 7AA United Kingdom
Tel: 44 171 497 1422
Fax: 44 171 497 1426

Latin America:
Thomson Learning
Seneca, 53
Colonia Polanco
11560 Mexico D.F. Mexico
Tel: 525-281-2906
Fax: 525-281-2656

Canada:
Nelson/Thomson Learning
1120 Birchmount Road
Scarborough, Ontario
Canada M1K 5G4
Tel: 416-752-9100
Fax: 416-752-8102

Asia:
Thomson Learning
60 Albert Street, #15-01
Albert Complex
Singapore 189969
Tel: 65 336 6411
Fax: 65 336 7411

Library of Congress Cataloging-in-Publication Data:
Tepper, Pamela R. 1957-
        The law of contracts and the uniform commercial code / Pamela Tepper. —1st ed.
            p.   cm.
        Includes index.
        ISBN 0-8273-6324-9
        1. Contracts—United States   2. Commercial law—United States
        3. Legal assistants—United States—Handbooks, manuals, etc.
    1. Title.
    KF801.Z9T415   1995
    346.73′02 — dc20   94-30039
    [347.3062]   CIP

To my parents, Martin and Irene,
thanks for giving me the opportunities and believing in me.
And to my brothers, Marc and Andy,
for just being the best.

CONTENTS

CHAPTER 2: Formation of a Contract: Offer and Acceptance   20

CHAPTER 3: Mutual Assent of the Parties   41

CHAPTER 4:   Consideration: The Value for
the Promise   **67**

CHAPTER 5: Capacity: The Ability to Contract   86

CHAPTER 9:   Remedies in Contract Law   188

CHAPTER 10: Third-Party Contracts   216

CHAPTER 14: Seller and Buyer Remedies   336

PREFACE

For whatever reasons, contracts is one of those subjects which students fear—and assume—will be boring. However, during more than six years of teaching, I have seen my students realize that contracts could be fun as well as intellectually challenging.

When given the opportunity to write a contracts textbook, I was faced with the task of putting my teaching practices into a readable text. Because I am a firm believer in students learning **case law**, each chapter of this book includes a number of cases to illustrate the legal concepts in the text. Both instructor and student should note that these cases have been heavily edited for teaching purposes. Finding illustrative cases that students enjoy and find interesting can be a challenge, but these cases have been classroom-tested and approved. The cases chosen are current, or at least of current interest. When I could find cases about familiar personalities or products, I used them. Also, to illustrate many of the legal concepts, I used comics from the daily newspapers. Even Peanuts and Blondie have contract problems! Consequently, I wanted students to know that contracts is a subject that touches their everyday lives, not just something taught by stuffy law professors.

To follow that concept, each chapter has a section entitled **Practical Application**, which includes real-life examples of the concepts presented in that chapter. My goal was not only to show the students the legal theories behind a concept, but also then to each them how to draft the corresponding legal documents. When appropriate, examples of language used in an actual contract are cited, or examples of documents paralegals would be asked to draft are identified in this section. The intent of this section was both to show practical examples and also to provide a guide for students in their daily practice after the contracts course is over. In a sense, the Practical Application section is a permanent desk reference for students.

Learning legal terminology can be a drain on students. Running to a dictionary to look up new words takes time and diverts attention from learning the subject. To alleviate this problem, this text has the dictionary definitions for all legal terminology in the margins from *Ballentine's*

Law Dictionary: Legal Assistant Edition (Handler, Delmar/LCP 1994). This feature is new and unique and is a time-saver for all students.

Because this text deals with both the common law of contracts and the Uniform Commercial Code, most of the referenced portions of the Restatements or Code are cited in the text. This feature minimizes the need to purchase additional texts or materials to accompany this book.

The basic text consists of 16 chapters. The first 10 chapters discuss the basic common law of contracts. The elements of contracts are addressed in the earlier chapters, with later chapters dealing with the *Statute of Frauds,* the *parol evidence rule, damages,* and *assignments.* Chapters 11 through 14 focus on *Article 2 of the Uniform Commercial Code (Sales).* The student is introduced to the concepts of the code and differences between the common law and the Code are noted. The final two chapters, 15 and 16, illustrate *how to draft a contract.* Chapter 15 presents an overview of some grammar concepts and some general drafting tips; Chapter 16 illustrates the general provisions found in many contracts and gives examples of completed contracts for student use.

Finally, each chapter has section *summaries* for quick reference, as well as *questions for review* and *exercises.* Each section is designed to assist the student in reinforcing the concepts learned in the chapter.

ACKNOWLEDGMENTS

With an undertaking of this size, there are always a number of people to thank. My paralegal, LeAnn Morehouse, was invaluable. She was always there for me and a real source of strength when things got a bit crazy. Without her, this book would have been difficult to complete, but with her, it all fell into place. Thank you for being the best paralegal that I could ever have.

Next to my paralegal, Jay Whitney, my editor, deserves the highest of praise. He made this project a joy. Jay let me write the book I envisioned and was the most supportive editor. I cannot thank him enough. The assistance of Glenna Stansfield and Chris Anzalone of Delmar Publishers was invaluable. Both were always there to lend encouraging words when it was difficult to envision the final product. They always offered insightful suggestions, which I know made this text better.

Perhaps some of the most important people to acknowledge are all my former students at Southeastern Paralegal Institute in Dallas, Texas. They gave me the inspiration for this book and challenged me to make contracts interesting. I will always be grateful for their contribution in making me a better contracts instructor.

To all the reviewers who spent the time to evaluate my manuscript, I greatly appreciate all your suggestions. Thank you to:

Finally, this book would have never been written had my family not been so supportive. When I could not see the final product, they always reminded me of my goals. Thank you.

P.T.

REVIEWERS

Dianna Murphy
Midway College and Eastern Kentucky University

John DeLeo
Central Pennsylvania Business School

Clark Wheeler
Santa Fe Community College

Kay Zumwalt
Alaska Jr. College

Tunney S. Robison
Center for Advanced Legal Studies

Sandra K. Stratton
William Woods University

Marjorie Fishman
Athens Area Technical Institute

Joan Gress Stevens
Loyola University, Institute of Paralegal Studies

Jim Caffrey
Bentley College

Harry Pascuzzi

Paul Baldovin
Florida Atlantic University

C. Suzanne Bailey
Lansing Community College

Chapter Cartoons

Chapter 1 Laugh Parade. (c) 1993; Reprinted courtesy of Bunny Hoest and Parade Magazine

Chapters 2, 11, and 13 Farcus. (c) 1993 Farcus Cartoons/Distributed by Universal Press Syndicate

Chapter 3 (c) 1993 Creator's Syndicate, Inc.

Chapters 4, 9, 10, and 14 Courtesy of George B. Abbott

Chapter 5 Family Circus. (c) 1993 Bil Keane, Inc. Distributed by Cowles Syndicate, Inc.

Chapter 6 The Quigmans. Copyright 1994, Los Angeles Times Syndicate. Reprinted with permission.

Chapter 7 The Wizard of Id. (c) 1993 Creator's Syndicate, Inc.

Chapter 8 Ziggy. (c) 1993 Ziggy and Friends, Inc./Distributed by Universal Press Syndicate

Chapter 12 Blondie. Reprinted with special permission of King Features Syndicate

Chapter 15 Non Sequitur. Courtesy of (c) 1994, The Washington Post Writers Group. Reprinted with permission.

Chapter 16 Peanuts reprinted by permission of UFS, Inc.

PART I

An Introduction to Contracts

CHAPTER 1
Contract Law:
A General Introduction

1.1 THE LAW OF CONTRACTS

For many, mention of the word "contracts" sends chills and fear through their bodies. Most think of contracts as elusive, unapproachable, and even boring. Not so! When approached with an open mind, contracts can be eye-opening and, yes, entertaining.

Because the law of contracts affects virtually all aspects of daily life, it is important to understand its importance as well as its significance. The simplest task involves contract law. For example, when you purchase groceries at the food market, contract law governs the action. When you look for a new car or new apartment, contract law applies. That is why it is important to have a working knowledge of contract law. In this chapter, contract law is discussed generally; later chapters delve into more details.

Before the detail can be discussed, an understanding of the laws that govern contract transactions is paramount. Contract law can be divided into two broad categories: common law contracts and statutory contract law, specifically that of the Uniform Commercial Code (U.C.C.). Each area is equally significant in contract law.

The Common Law of Contracts

Prior to the creation of statutes, the law developed primarily from behavior and later through judge-made law. Disputes were brought before a tribunal where judges analyzed behavior and the rules of a community to determine how the behavior should be judged. Eventually, through the development of a formal court system, judges handed down decisions creating standards for future judges (and citizens) to follow, called **precedents**. Setting and following precedents became the foundation of what now is known as the **common law**. The common law of contracts is, therefore, the law created by judges to settle disputes arising out of contractual relationships. The first half of this book focuses primarily on the common law of contracts and the *Restatement of Contracts.*

The Restatements of Contracts

As a response to the volume of case law being decided in this country, a group of lawyers, judges, and law professors formed the American Law Institute (ALI) in 1923. The purpose of the ALI was to gather the law to create a guide for legal professionals, called the Restatements. The ALI initially produced Restatements in nine areas, including torts, property, and contracts.

The Restatements consist of chapters and subsections which state generally accepted legal rules and principles known as **black-letter law**. Each section is followed by comments by the ALI and illustrations. Although the Restatements are acknowledged and used by courts, they have never received formal judicial recognition and do not carry the weight of case law or statutes. Consequently, their value is debated and many have mixed views on their importance. Nevertheless, the Restatements have played an integral part in the development of contract law.

Presently, the ALI has published a *Restatement (First) of Contracts* and a *Restatement (Second) of Contracts,* which are divided into 16 general chapters. The Restatements of Contracts provide a detailed account of the law of contracts. The Restatements are sometimes adopted by state legislatures, making them part of the statutory law, but this is the exception and not the rule. As the Supreme Court of Oregon observed:

> although this court frequently quotes sections of the Restatements of the American Law Institute, it does not literally adopt them in the matter of legislative enacting . . . . The Restatements themselves purport to be just that, "restatements" of law found in other sources, although at times they candidly report that the law is in flux and offer a formula preferred on policy grounds.

Brewer v. Erwin, 600 P.2d 398, 410 (Or. 1979). However, the Restatements are a good guide to understanding general principles of law and are referenced throughout the chapters of this book.

TERMS

precedent
Prior decisions of the same court, or a higher court, which a judge must follow in deciding a subsequent case presenting similar facts and the same legal problem, even though different parties are involved and many years have elapsed.

common law
Law found in the decisions of the courts rather than in statutes; judge-made law.

black-letter law
Fundamental and well-established rules of law.

The Uniform Commercial Code

As society became more mobile, difficulties arose in doing business from state to state; there was a need for uniformity of commercial law among the states. To deal with this problem, the National Conference of Commissioners on Uniform State Laws was created. The Conference's task was to develop uniform standards of practice in commercial law.

The earliest Acts passed by the Conference were the Negotiable Instruments Act, the Sales Act, and the Bill of Lading Act. Unfortunately, these acts did not fulfill the needs of the commercial marketplace. The older acts were the prelude to the Conference's most notable achievement, the Uniform Commercial Code (U.C.C.).

The U.C.C. consists of nine articles, which are outlined in Figure 1-1. Because it has been adopted in whole or in part by all fifty states, including

Article	Purpose
Article 1 General Provisions	Sets out the general purposes of the U.C.C. and the definitions used in the Code.
Article 2 Sales	Applies to all transactions involving the sale of goods.
Article 3 Commercial Paper	Governs presentment of checks and transactions relating to banks.
Article 4 Bank Deposits and Collections	Read in conjunction with Article 3, focuses on the rules and regulations of bank deposits and collections of commercial paper.
Article 5 Letters of Credit	Sets out requirements for commercial transactions involving credit arrangements between banks and their customers.
Article 6 Bulk Transfers	Governs the sale and transfer of business assets and notice requirements to creditors.
Article 7 Warehouse Receipts, Bills of Lading, and Other Documents of Title	Governs transactions regarding documents of title and when title passes to a party.
Article 8 Investment Securities	Sets out requirements for security transactions and investment in registered form.
Article 9 Secured Transactions; Sales of Account and Chattel Paper	Governs any transaction that creates a security interest in personal property or fixtures, chattel paper, or accounts.

FIGURE 1-1 Articles of the Uniform Commercial Code

the District of Columbia and the U.S. Virgin Islands, the U.C.C. is considered statutory law. With the adoption of the U.C.C. in the United States, merchants and business people can construct their contractual arrangements with higher degrees of certainty and reliability. The U.C.C. is an important source of contract law and governs commercial contract law. Thus, the second half of this book is devoted to the U.C.C.'s Article 2, Sales, the statutory counterpart to the common law of contracts.

1.2 THE CONTRACT DEFINED

The age-old question is: What is a contract? Simply stated, a *contract* is an agreement between parties for value which is legally enforceable. Although the preceding statement generally defines a contract, the most widely cited definition is from the *Restatement (Second) of Contracts* § 1:

> A contract is a promise or set of promises for the breach of which the law gives a remedy, or the performance of which the law in some way recognizes as a duty.

The law has formal names for the parties to a contract. The person who initiates the contract—namely, the one who makes the promise—is referred to as the **promisor**. The person to whom the promise is made is the **promisee**. Frequently, these terms are used when setting forth the parties' contractual obligations. Knowing and understanding the terminology is half the battle to learning contract law. Take the time to learn it.

To have a binding contract, there must be two competent parties who intend to be bound by their promises. Critical to the definition of contracts is

Laugh Parade®
BY BUNNY HOEST AND JOHN REINER

"It's not going to be easy to learn their language."

TERMS

promisor
  A person who makes a promise.
promisee
  A person to whom a promise is made.

the necessity of intent. The parties must desire to be bound to a contract, or the contract may fail. If the requisite intent is present and the promises are broken, the law may enforce the promise, usually through a lawsuit.

The law goes beyond mere intent, however. It also provides that a contract must meet certain elements to be enforceable. Those elements are offer, acceptance, mutual assent, consideration, capacity, and legality. Another requirement that needs to be considered is whether the contract must be in writing. Although contracts can be either oral or written, the law requires that certain types of contracts must be in writing to be enforceable; this suggests that some contracts may not be binding and enforceable unless written. (See Figure 1-2.) This complex area is discussed in greater detail in Chapter 7.

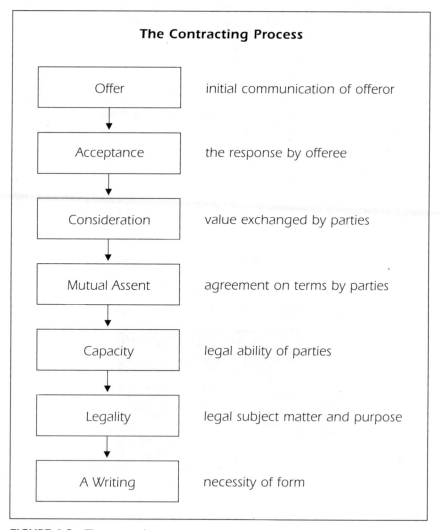

FIGURE 1-2 The contracting process

TERMS

offer
    A proposal made with the purpose of obtaining an acceptance, thereby creating a contract.

The Elements of Contract

Important to all who enter into contracts is their enforceability. Without reasonable assurances that the promises of parties are enforceable, contract law would be chaotic. An understanding of the general elements needed to bind parties to a contract is necessary.

The Offer An **offer** is a communication to a party of a desire to enter into a contract. The party initiating the offer is the **offeror** and the party to whom the offer is directed is the **offeree**. The offeree has the power to accept the offer, beginning the process of contracting. This concept is discussed more fully in Chapter 2.

The Acceptance The **acceptance** is the response by the offeree to the offeror of an intent to contract. Unless an acceptance occurs, the contracting process ends. The offer and acceptance are basic necessities if a contract is to evolve. Chapter 2 also delves into this area.

Mutual Assent Critical to contracting is the element of **mutual assent**. Each party must have the same understanding of the terms and conditions of the contract. If one party withholds vital information which induces a party to contract, then mutual assent does not exist and there is no contract. This area of law is discussed in Chapter 3.

Consideration Every contract must have **consideration**, which is the value paid for the promise. There must be an exchange of value between the contracting parties, such as money, property, or services. All contracts must have consideration to be enforceable. Look to Chapter 4 for a detailed discussion.

Capacity The parties to the contract must have the legal ability to enter into a contract. Under the law, **capacity** constitutes being over the age of 18 and of sound mind. Persons who are under 18 (minors), drunkards, or mentally insane generally do not have the capacity to contract. Incapacity is difficult to show and presents unique problems in contract law. Chapter 5 focuses on capacity as an issue in contract.

Legality All contracts must be legal to be enforceable. They must have a legal purpose and legal subject matter. Although the element of **legality** seems clear, under society's changing needs and mores, new issues are analyzed every day. Is a surrogate motherhood contract legal? Can you contract to have your body frozen or to commit suicide? Issues like these are addressed in Chapter 5.

The Legal Form Although the law states that there are six elements to create a binding contract, one additional element may exist: the need for a

---

offeror
A person who makes an offer.

offeree
A person to whom an offer is made.

acceptance
[T]he assent by the person to whom an offer is made to the offer as made by the person making it. Acceptance is a fundamental element of a binding contract. . . . In general terms, the receipt and retention of that which is offered. . . . Unspoken consent to or concurrence in a transaction by virtue of failure to reject it. . . . Agreement; approval; assent.

mutual assent
A meeting of the minds; consent; agreement.

consideration
The reason a person enters into a contract; that which is given in exchange for performance or the promise to perform; the price bargained and paid; the inducement. Consideration is an essential element of a valid and enforceable contract. A promise to refrain from doing something one is entitled to do also constitutes consideration.

capacity
1. Competency in law.
2. A person's ability to understand the nature and effect of the act in which he or she is engaged.

legality
The condition of conformity with the law; lawfulness.

writing. The statute that guides parties in making this determination is the **Statute of Frauds**, which suggests that certain contracts must be in writing to be enforceable. Sometimes parties may think they have a contract, but unless it is in a suitable written form, it may not be enforceable. This element is critical to the contracting process and is further discussed in Chapter 7.

Therefore, all the elements must be present for a contract to be binding and the contracting process to work. A discussion of the elements of contract is found in *Gray v. Reynolds,* 514 So. 2d 973 (Ala. 1987). Mr. Gray sued Mr. Reynolds for not fulfilling his obligations under a contract. Pay particular attention to the court's analysis of the elements of contract and the result.

GRAY v. REYNOLDS

Supreme Court of Alabama
Sept. 25, 1987

The plaintiff, Van Gray, appeals the judgment entered in favor of the defendants, James M. Reynolds and J. Eugene Garrison, in a breach of contract action. Gray contracted with Reynolds and Garrison (both hereinafter referred to as "Reynolds") to purchase sawdust at $.50 per ton. However, before Gray could complete his contract, Reynolds sold 6000 tons of the same sawdust to a third party for $1.00 per ton. Gray then sued Reynolds for breach of contract. The trial court ruled in favor of Reynolds, holding that the writing sued upon was insufficient to support a judgment in favor of Gray and that the writing constituted a standing offer from Reynolds to Gray for Gray to purchase sawdust at a set price. We disagree with the judgment of the trial court and reverse.

On March 2, 1984, Gray and Reynolds entered into the following agreement, written by Reynolds:

CONTRACT OF SALE
AGREEMENT DATE *MARCH 2, 1984*
This agreement is a contract for the sale and removal of approximately 9,000 tons of sawdust being sold by J. Eugene Garrison and James M. Reynolds. The purchaser of said sawdust will be Van Gray.
It is hereby agreed that the above stated owners will convey said sawdust to Van Gray for cash payment at the rate of $0.50 per ton. It is further agreed that Van Gray will remove the entire sawdust pile, leaving the real property

level and drainable. Payments for this sawdust will be made on a weekly basis.

After the contract was signed, Gray spent $4,000 improving a road located on the property so that he could use heavy equipment to remove the sawdust. Gray removed sawdust for several weeks in March and April. After this period, due to equipment problems, Gray did not haul away any sawdust for a period of several weeks. When Gray returned to the property to resume hauling the sawdust, Reynolds called Gray and told him he was allowing a Mr. Brown to haul away sawdust for $1.00 per ton. Soon thereafter, Gray returned to the property and noticed a loader parked near the sawdust pile and saw that someone other than himself had removed sawdust. He also noticed damage to the road that he had improved. At this time, Gray considered the contract breached, and he contacted his attorney.

The elements of a contract are: (1) an agreement, (2) with consideration, (3) between two or more contracting parties, (4) with a legal object, and (5) legal capacity. No argument is made between the parties concerning the last three elements.

First, there must be an agreement. In order to determine the nature of a contract, the court should look at the contract's terms and conditions. In order to determine the contract's nature and meaning, the trial court must construe the contract as a whole.

The contract plainly states that Gray is to buy 9,000 tons of sawdust from Reynolds for $.50 a ton. It also states that Gray is to remove the entire sawdust pile. Both parties agreed that the pile was estimated at 9,000 tons. It is clear that Gray was to purchase the whole pile. The contract gives the location of the property and states that Gray is to make cash payments on a weekly basis.

The agreement in this case is supported by consideration.

> Adequate consideration exists, or is implied, if it arises from any act of the plaintiff from which the defendant derived a pecuniary benefit . . . if such act was performed by the plaintiff to the desired end, with the expressed or implied assent of the defendant. That which creates and carries a benefit to the party promising, or causes trouble, injury, inconvenience, prejudice, or detriment to the other party, is sufficient consideration.

In this case, Gray spent $4,000 improving the road in order to be able to remove the sawdust. Reynolds sold Gray all the sawdust at $.50 per ton, and Reynolds further received a benefit by the promised removal of the sawdust. Reynolds testified that one of his main concerns was the complete removal of the sawdust from the property so that he could build a convenience store. It is apparent that Reynolds was to receive a benefit at Gray's detriment.

Where a contract, from its terms, is plain and free from ambiguity, it must be enforced as written. It is clear that Gray purchased the sawdust pile from Reynolds and that Reynolds breached the contract when he sold some of the sawdust to a third party at a higher price. Therefore, the trial court erred when it ruled that the contract was nothing more than a standing offer, and its judgment is reversed.

QUESTIONS FOR ANALYSIS

Did the court reach the correct conclusion, or should the trial court's decision stand? State the basis for your answer. Identify the elements of a valid contract from the case decision.

1.3 CONTRACTS CLASSIFIED

Contracts are classified in a variety of ways. Some classifications focus on the method of contract formation and others focus on the contract's legal effect. The classifications discussed in this section are not mutually exclusive.

Contracts are classified as: (1) bilateral and unilateral; (2) express and implied; (3) executed and executory; (4) valid, void, voidable, and enforceable; and (5) formal and informal. A contract can belong to more than one of these classifications; for instance, a contract can be bilateral, express, and executed. This can become confusing, but closer review will clear up any confusion.

Bilateral and Unilateral Contracts

A **bilateral contract** is a common type of contract in which each party exchanges a promise for a promise, binding the parties to a contract. This usually occurs when someone makes an offer and an acceptance follows. For

TERMS

Statute of Frauds
A statute, existing in one or another form in every state, that requires certain classes of contracts to be in writing and signed by the parties. Its purpose is to prevent fraud or reduce the opportunities for fraud.

bilateral contract
A contract in which each party promises performance to the other, the promise by the one furnishing the consideration for the promise from the other.

example, if Mr. Hartman asks Ms. Greyson, "Will you come paint my garage tomorrow for $200?" and Ms. Greyson replies, "Yes, I will paint your garage tomorrow for $200," a bilateral contract is created. Each party has made a promise to the other. Through the exchange of mutual promises, a bilateral contract is created. If one of the parties does not fulfill its promise, then the harmed party can enforce the contract in court through a breach of contract action, discussed in Chapter 8.

In contrast, a **unilateral contract** does not involve an exchange of promises. Only one party makes a promise, with the other party required to do some act in return. In a unilateral contract, the act of performing is the acceptance. There is no exchange of promises nor an exchange of communication. Let's modify the garage example: Assume that Mr. Hartman went to Ms. Greyson's house and knocked on her door to make his offer. Getting no response, Mr. Hartman leaves Ms. Greyson a note: "Will you come paint my garage for $200 tomorrow? [signed by] Mr. Hartman." No more communication occurs between the parties. The next day, Ms. Greyson shows up to paint Mr. Hartman's garage. A unilateral contract has been formed.

A distinguishing characteristic between bilateral and unilateral contracts is timing. In a bilateral contract, the exchange of promises binds the parties almost immediately. The offeror cannot take back the offer (revoke it), as the acceptance has already occurred. However, with a unilateral contract, the acceptance does not take effect until performance begins. Until performance commences, the offeror can revoke the initial offer.

Review *White v. Hugh Chatham Memorial Hospital,* 97 N.C. App. 130, 387 S.E.2d 80 (1990), which analyzes the concept of unilateral contracts. In this case, the court had to determine whether an employer had offered its employee a unilateral contract for group health insurance.

TERMS

unilateral contract
A contract in which there is a promise on one side only, the consideration being an act or something other than another promise. . . . [A] unilateral contract is an offer that is accepted not by another promise, but by performance.

WHITE v. HUGH CHATHAM MEMORIAL HOSPITAL, INC.

Court of Appeals of North Carolina
Jan. 16, 1990

Plaintiff was employed by defendant as a full time nurses' assistant from March, 1951 to December, 1985 when she was discharged because of a disabling illness. The parties never had a written contract covering the employment. For several years before her discharge plaintiff was covered by the company's low cost group medical insurance plan that had limits of $1,000,000. In January, 1983 defendant distributed to its employees, including plaintiff, a "Personnel Policies Handbook," which stated that: "A full time employee who becomes disabled during his employment will be able to maintain his group insurance." Plaintiff knew of the statement and became disabled while a full time employee but was not permitted to continue her group medical insurance, as the policy of defendant's group carrier did not permit disabled former employees to continue under it. The individual policy that plaintiff was able to obtain costs more than the group policy, though its limits are only $100,000. Defendant's representation as to disabled employees being able to continue the group coverage was not withdrawn or disavowed before plaintiff became disabled. In denying that it was legally bound to make the coverage available and in discussing the matter with plaintiff defendant's were neither abusive nor demeaning but, as plaintiff testified in her deposition, were kind and considerate.

It is equally clear, however, that the evidence does raise a genuine issue of fact as to plaintiff's claim for breach of contract. For the contract that plaintiff alleged and that her materials support is not a mutually binding bilateral employment contract, as the court and defendant mistakenly assumed, but a unilateral contract based upon defendant's offer of extra benefits to employees who continued in employment until disabled and upon plaintiff accepting that offer by remaining in defendant's employment until she was disabled. Defendant's argument that the record contains no indication that after receiving the handbook plaintiff promised to continue her employment is irrelevant, since unilateral contracts are not based upon mutual promises or obligations as bilateral contracts are.

A unilateral contract is one in which there is a promise on one side only, the consideration on the other side being executed . . . It has also been defined as a promise by one party or an offer by him to do a certain thing in the event the other party performs a certain act. . . . As is deducible from the foregoing, the distinctive features of an unilateral contract are that the offeror is the master of his offer and can withdraw it at any time before it is accepted by performance, and that while the offer is still outstanding the offeree can accept it by meeting its conditions. Such contracts have been enforced by our courts in many cases involving circumstances similar to those recorded here.

The statement in defendant's personnel book concerning the additional benefits that disabled employees could enjoy if they remained in its full time employment until they became disabled—seriously and responsibly made from all appearances—is evidence that it was an offer to make its group insurance available to any employee who met the conditions stated; and that plaintiff knew about the offer and continued in defendant's employment until she became disabled is evidence enough that she accepted the offer. If the contract was made it was certainly breached and defendant is obligated to pay the difference between the cost of the substitute coverage obtained and the cost of defendant's group coverage of $1,000,000 for one employee, which is the benefit that it stated would be available. That the substitute coverage obtained has limits less than $1,000,000 would not increase defendant's obligation as long as those limits cover her medical and hospital expenses, but upon the lesser limits ceasing to cover her medical expenses defendant's obligation would increase accordingly up to the difference between the limits and $1,000,000.

QUESTIONS FOR ANALYSIS

Did the court find that a bilateral or unilateral contract existed? What was the court's decision and its definition of a unilateral contract?

Express and Implied Contracts

An **express contract** is one that is specifically stated. Each party knows the terms and conditions of the contract, whether oral or written. It is prudent to reduce an oral express contract to writing, lest Statute of Frauds issues arise (see Chapter 7). Using the previous example with Ms. Greyson and Mr. Hartman, the oral communication between them to paint the garage for $200 could be an oral express contract; the example involving the note to Ms.

express contract
A contract whose terms are stated by the parties.

Greyson from Mr. Hartman would be a written express contract. Each is an express contract with a difference in form.

Implied contracts are different. An implied contract is created by the acts of the parties involved. It is inferred from the facts and circumstances surrounding the transaction. Behavior dictates the terms of the contract. Assume you go into a cafeteria whose rules require you to pay after you have eaten. The cafeteria has given you the food that you ate and it is implied that you will pay. This type of contract is also referred to as an **implied in fact contract**. Each party to the contract expects something from the exchange, even though no formal agreement was expressed. Both express and implied contracts are enforceable.

Another type of implied contract is an **implied in law contract** or **quasi contract**. This kind of contract focuses on the need for fairness.

Quasi Contracts

A contract that is created by a court is an *implied in law contract* or a *quasi contract*. It is a type of contract that promotes fairness and prevents injustice. A quasi contract is based upon the premise that although the parties may not have intended a contract, if one party benefits unjustly to the detriment of the other party, the court will compensate the party who did not benefit, to avoid unjust enrichment. **Unjust enrichment** occurs when the circumstances surrounding a situation create a benefit to a party, even though no formal contract was created. If the benefiting party does not pay for what was received, another party will be harmed. To prevent this unfairness, courts compensate for the reasonable value of the benefit so that no one will be "unjustly enriched." There are a number of instances in which the theory of quasi contract is applied:

Mistake When a party benefits from another's mistake, the court will impose a contract and compensate the injured party. The court will not allow a party to benefit or profit from another's misfortune.

Emergency Aid Courts will award compensation to a physician who aids in an emergency. If a doctor renders assistance to an unconscious victim, a court will award the doctor a reasonable value for the services performed. Again, the court is preventing unjust enrichment.

Necessity When a doctor aids a sick minor, even after the parents refuse treatment, the doctor will be compensated for the services. The basis of recovery is quasi contract. (However, this example often involves religious beliefs, which is another matter entirely.)

Work Performed under Unenforceable Contract When certain oral contracts are not enforceable because a writing is necessary, some courts will use the quasi-contract doctrine to prevent an unfair result. The court will look to the benefit received and place a reasonable value on that benefit. Compensation is based upon the principles of quasi contract and unjust enrichment.

Now, using the earlier example, where Ms. Greyson painted Mr. Hartman's garage, let's change the example and create a quasi-contract situation. Assume that Mr. Hartman left Ms. Greyson a note requesting that his garage be painted tomorrow and stating, "Let me know by 8:00 o'clock P.M." Ms. Greyson never contacted Mr. Hartman, so Mr. Hartman then asks Mr. Bernard to paint the garage. Mr. Bernard agrees to paint the garage for $200 and agrees to show up at 9:00 A.M. the next day. When Ms. Greyson sees the note that evening, she decides she will paint the garage, but because it is late, she doesn't contact Mr. Hartman. Instead, she shows up at 8:30 A.M. the next day and begins painting. Mr. Hartman sees Ms. Greyson from the window but does not stop her. At 9:00 A.M., Mr. Bernard begins assisting Ms. Greyson and paints the other half of the garage. Although the contract between Hartman and Greyson was invalid, because the offer had expired, the court would probably award Ms. Greyson a reasonable amount of money for her services, since Mr. Hartman did benefit from her work. This is a quasi contract.

Care should be taken not to confuse an implied in fact contract and an implied in law contract. The former is a contract created by the acts and intentions of the parties, whereas the latter is one created by the courts. That distinction is critical to any analysis as to type of contract.

A difficult question to answer under the quasi-contract theory is "How much compensation is just?" The answer, unfortunately, is, "It depends." Generally, courts look at the reasonable value of the benefit and the cost of the benefit. That does not mean, however, that the reasonable amount is that which is ordinarily charged. The courts normally look to the prices charged in a community to determine a fair value. Consequently, under quasi contract, a benefit received may not be paid under a party's usual fee, as the court will determine what is reasonable and just.

Executed and Executory Contracts

Executed contracts are fully performed contracts. No further performance is necessary by the parties, as there is a completed contract. The only issue that may arise when a contract has been executed is the performance itself and whether the agreement has been fully performed. This raises issues regarding remedies, which are discussed in Chapter 9.

Note that the term *executed* has another meaning in contracts. It also means "to sign an agreement." Here, no performance has occurred, and only the intentions of the parties are set out. Consequently, be careful with terminology, as a word may have several meanings.

When parties sign a contract, there often are future obligations to perform. When nothing has been done, or the duties have been only partially performed, the contract is said to be *executory*. An **executory contract** is a contract under which a condition or promise has not been performed by one

---

TERMS

implied in fact contract
[Contract which the] law infers from the circumstances, conduct, acts, or relationship of the parties rather than from their spoken words.

implied in law contracts
Quasi contracts or constructive contracts imposed by the law, usually to prevent unjust enrichment.

quasi contract
An obligation imposed by law to achieve equity, usually to prevent unjust enrichment. A quasi contract is a legal fiction that a contract exists where there has been no express contract.

unjust enrichment
The equitable doctrine that a person who unjustly receives property, money, or other benefits that belong to another may not retain them and is obligated to return them. The remedy of restitution is based upon the principle that equity will not permit unjust enrichment.

executed contract
A contract whose terms have been fully performed.

executory contract
A contract yet to be performed, each party having bound himself or herself to do or not to do a particular thing.

or all parties to the contract. A typical type of executory contract is a real estate contract for the sale and purchase of a home. Although each party signs the contract (executes it), there usually are obligations that must be completed before the sale is final. Assume that in the real estate contract the buyer must qualify for financing. At the time the contract is signed, the contract is executory. When the buyer gains the financing, the seller will tender the deed and other documents to consummate the sale. After this occurs, then the contract will be executed.

Valid, Void, Voidable, and Enforceable Contracts

To have a valid contract, all the elements of a contract must be present, making it legally binding and enforceable. Not all contracts are valid, however.

A **void** contract is one that never has any legal effect. Even at the contract's attempted inception, it can never come into existence. For example, a contract to kill someone is void. A person who contracts to kill someone and does not get paid cannot request a court to enforce the contract for nonpayment; its subject matter is illegal and the attempted contract is therefore void.

A **voidable** contract is one that may be avoided or cancelled by one of the parties. Usually a voidable contract occurs with minors, intoxicated, or insane persons. A contract also may be voidable when one party to the contract fails to act honestly, such as by committing fraud or misrepresentation. The person who has been harmed has the right to cancel the contract. Unless a party attempts to avoid the contract, the contract is presumed valid. Unlike void contracts, which are automatically invalid, in a voidable contract, someone has to disaffirm or reject the contract. Until the act of **disaffirmance** happens, the contract may be valid.

Unenforceable contracts are different. Because of some intervening factor, a contract that appears to have all the necessary elements may not be enforceable. This occurs when a statute, such as the Statute of Frauds, dictates the necessity for a contract to be in writing, or a law is passed which makes a contract unenforceable. For example, let's say you have a terminal illness and you contract for someone's services to assist in a suicide. If, after the contract is consummated but prior to the suicide, a law is passed which outlaws assisted suicides, the contract would be unenforceable by a court. Consequently, parties to a contract may not always have control over their destinies.

Formal and Informal Contracts

In earlier days, the common law required the parties to engage in certain formalities when contracting. For example, the law required that certain contracts be under **seal**. This formality required persons to affix a wax imprint or insignia to the document. For the contract to be valid, these

TERMS

void
Null; without legal effect. . . . [A] transaction that is void is a transaction that, in law, never happened.

voidable
Avoidable; subject to disaffirmance; defective but not invalid unless disaffirmed by the person entitled to disaffirm.

disaffirmance
Refusal to fulfill a voidable contract. . . . Disclaimer; repudiation; disavowal; renunciation.

seal
An imprint made upon an instrument by a device such as an engraved metallic plate, or upon wax affixed to the instrument. The seal symbolizes authority or authenticity. Modern law does not commonly require that instruments be under seal. In instances where it does, the abbreviation "LS" is universally accepted as a legal seal.

formalities had to be followed, therefore creating **formal contracts**. Additionally, formal contracts had to be in writing, signed, and often witnessed.

Many of these formalities have been eliminated, but one notable exception is in the real estate area. Contracts for the transfer of real estate require adherence to certain formalities. A general warranty deed requires such things as identity of all parties, a description of the real property, signatures of the parties, notarization, delivery, and filing.

Informal contracts or **simple contracts** have become the standard today. With less formality, the focus is on the parties' intent. No special language is required. All that is required is that the parties' obligations be expressed in the agreement. Most standardized forms will do, and even a handwritten document signed by the parties will suffice. The key to informal contracts is expression of the parties' intent. Thus, informal contracts may be oral or written or implied from the parties' actions. They regulate many of our daily activities, which shows the importance of contract law to our lives.

1.4 PRACTICAL APPLICATION

Under the law, contracts take on many different forms. When drafting a contract, keep in mind the concepts discussed in this chapter. One of the best examples of the concepts discussed is a real estate contract. Review Figure 1-3 for a practical application of the legal issues in this chapter.

formal contract
1. A signed, written contract, as opposed to an oral contract. 2. A contract that must be in a certain form to be valid.

informal contract
A contract not in the customary form, often an oral contract.

simple contract
1. A parol contract. 2. At common law, any contract not under seal.

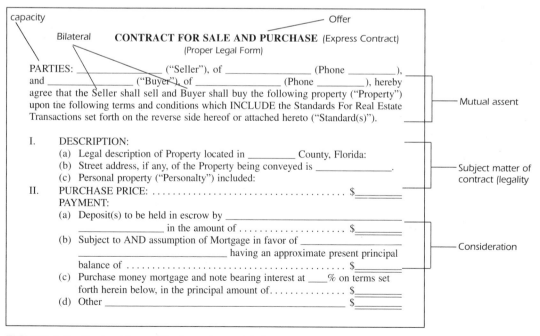

FIGURE 1-3 Contract form with elements annotated

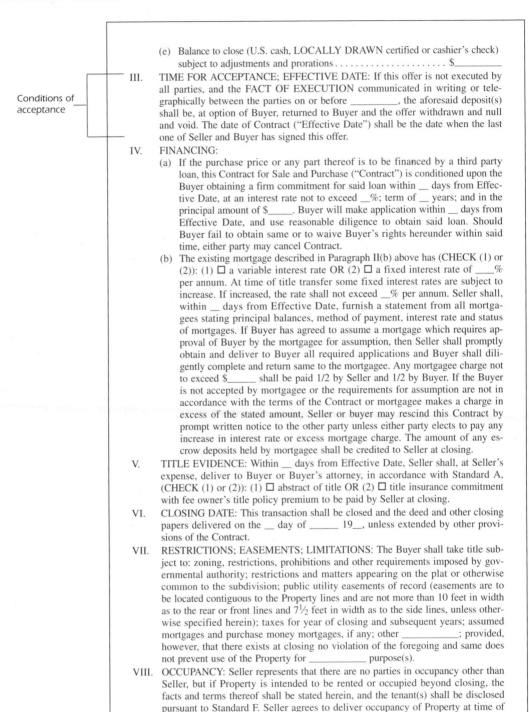

Conditions of acceptance

(e) Balance to close (U.S. cash, LOCALLY DRAWN certified or cashier's check) subject to adjustments and prorations . . . . $_____

III. TIME FOR ACCEPTANCE; EFFECTIVE DATE: If this offer is not executed by all parties, and the FACT OF EXECUTION communicated in writing or telegraphically between the parties on or before _____, the aforesaid deposit(s) shall be, at option of Buyer, returned to Buyer and the offer withdrawn and null and void. The date of Contract ("Effective Date") shall be the date when the last one of Seller and Buyer has signed this offer.

IV. FINANCING:
(a) If the purchase price or any part thereof is to be financed by a third party loan, this Contract for Sale and Purchase ("Contract") is conditioned upon the Buyer obtaining a firm commitment for said loan within __ days from Effective Date, at an interest rate not to exceed __%; term of __ years; and in the principal amount of $_____. Buyer will make application within __ days from Effective Date, and use reasonable diligence to obtain said loan. Should Buyer fail to obtain same or to waive Buyer's rights hereunder within said time, either party may cancel Contract.
(b) The existing mortgage described in Paragraph II(b) above has (CHECK (1) or (2)): (1) ☐ a variable interest rate OR (2) ☐ a fixed interest rate of ___% per annum. At time of title transfer some fixed interest rates are subject to increase. If increased, the rate shall not exceed __% per annum. Seller shall, within __ days from Effective Date, furnish a statement from all mortgagees stating principal balances, method of payment, interest rate and status of mortgages. If Buyer has agreed to assume a mortgage which requires approval of Buyer by the mortgagee for assumption, then Seller shall promptly obtain and deliver to Buyer all required applications and Buyer shall diligently complete and return same to the mortgagee. Any mortgagee charge not to exceed $_____ shall be paid 1/2 by Seller and 1/2 by Buyer. If the Buyer is not accepted by mortgagee or the requirements for assumption are not in accordance with the terms of the Contract or mortgagee makes a charge in excess of the stated amount, Seller or buyer may rescind this Contract by prompt written notice to the other party unless either party elects to pay any increase in interest rate or excess mortgage charge. The amount of any escrow deposits held by mortgagee shall be credited to Seller at closing.

V. TITLE EVIDENCE: Within __ days from Effective Date, Seller shall, at Seller's expense, deliver to Buyer or Buyer's attorney, in accordance with Standard A, (CHECK (1) or (2)): (1) ☐ abstract of title OR (2) ☐ title insurance commitment with fee owner's title policy premium to be paid by Seller at closing.

VI. CLOSING DATE: This transaction shall be closed and the deed and other closing papers delivered on the __ day of _____ 19__, unless extended by other provisions of the Contract.

VII. RESTRICTIONS; EASEMENTS; LIMITATIONS: The Buyer shall take title subject to: zoning, restrictions, prohibitions and other requirements imposed by governmental authority; restrictions and matters appearing on the plat or otherwise common to the subdivision; public utility easements of record (easements are to be located contiguous to the Property lines and are not more than 10 feet in width as to the rear or front lines and $7\frac{1}{2}$ feet in width as to the side lines, unless otherwise specified herein); taxes for year of closing and subsequent years; assumed mortgages and purchase money mortgages, if any; other _____; provided, however, that there exists at closing no violation of the foregoing and same does not prevent use of the Property for _____ purpose(s).

VIII. OCCUPANCY: Seller represents that there are no parties in occupancy other than Seller, but if Property is intended to be rented or occupied beyond closing, the facts and terms thereof shall be stated herein, and the tenant(s) shall be disclosed pursuant to Standard F. Seller agrees to deliver occupancy of Property at time of

FIGURE 1-3 *(Continued)*

closing unless otherwise stated herein. If occupancy is to be delivered prior to closing, Buyer assumes all risk of loss to Property and Personalty from date of occupancy, shall be responsible and liable for maintenance thereof from said date, and shall be deemed to have accepted the Property and Personalty in their existing condition as of time of taking occupancy unless otherwise stated herein or in separate writing.

IX.   ASSIGNABILITY: (CHECK (1) or (2)): Buyer (1) ☐ may assign OR (2) ☐ may not assign, Contract.

X.   TYPEWRITTEN OR HANDWRITTEN PROVISIONS: Typewritten or handwritten provisions inserted herein or attached hereto as addenda shall control all printed provisions of Contract in conflict therewith.

XI.   INSULATION RIDER: If Contract is utilized for the sale of a new residence, the Insulation Rider shall be attached hereto and made part hereof.

XII.   SPECIAL CLAUSES: (utilize space below)

THIS IS INTENDED TO BE A LEGALLY BINDING CONTRACT.
IF NOT FULLY UNDERSTOOD, SEEK THE ADVICE OF AN ATTORNEY
PRIOR TO SIGNING.

THIS FORM HAS BEEN APPROVED BY THE FLORIDA ASSOCIATION
OF REALTORS AND THE FLORIDA BAR.

Approval does not constitute an opinion that any of the terms and conditions in this Contract should be accepted by the parties in a particular transaction. Terms and conditions should be negotiated based upon the respective interests, objectives and bargaining positions of all interested persons.

Copyright 1985 by The Florida Bar and the
Florida Association of REALTORS, Inc.
- - - - - - - - - -

Acceptance
signed by parties

Executed by Buyer on _____

WITNESSES: (Two recommended but NOT required)

_____   _____
                                                  (Buyer)

_____   _____
                                                  (Buyer)

Executed by Seller on _____

Executed
(fully performed)

WITNESSES: (Two recommended but NOT required)

_____   _____
                                                  (Seller)

_____   _____
                                                  (Seller)

Deposit(s) under Paragraph II received; if other than cash, then subject to clearance.

By: _____   (Escrow Agent)

BROKER'S FEE: (CHECK & COMPLETE THE ONE APPLICABLE)

FIGURE 1-3   *(Continued)*

SUMMARY

1.1   Contract law is divided into two categories: common law contracts and the Uniform Commercial Code. Common law contract law developed from decisions by judges, whereas the U.C.C. is statutory law adopted individually by each state.

1.2   A contract is an agreement between two or more parties for value which is legally enforceable. All contracts must have six elements to be binding. The elements are offer, acceptance, consideration, mutual assent, capacity, and legality. Another element to consider is proper form, such as under the Statute of Frauds.

1.3   Contracts can have different classifications: (1) bilateral and unilateral; (2) express and implied; (3) executed and executory; (4) valid, void, voidable, and enforceable; and (5) formal and informal. In a bilateral contract, the parties exchange a promise for a promise, whereas in a unilateral contract only one party makes a promise, with the other party required to do some act in return. An express contract is one that is specifically stated. It can be oral or written. An implied contract, however, may be one of two types. There is an implied in fact contract, which is inferred from the facts and circumstances of the transaction, or an implied in law contract, which is court-created. Contracts may be executed contracts, which are fully performed contracts, or executory contracts, in which a condition or promise has not been performed by one or all of the parties. Another classification distinguishes void and voidable contracts. A void contract has no legal effect and can never become a contract, whereas a voidable contract can be canceled or avoided by one of the parties. The final category is formal and informal contracts, with a formal contract requiring the parties to fulfill certain legal formalities. An informal contract, in contrast, has no special legal requirements. It focuses on the intention of the parties.

REVIEW QUESTIONS

1. Distinguish between the common law of contracts and the Uniform Commercial Code.
2. What are the Restatements of Contracts?
3. State the definition of a contract.
4. What are the terms for the parties to a contract?
5. List the elements of a contract.
6. Define a bilateral contract and a unilateral contract.
7. What is an implied contract? Distinguish it from a quasi contract.
8. What is the difference between a void contract and a voidable contract?

9. How are formal contracts different from informal contracts?
10. List the classifications of contracts.

EXERCISES

1. List five examples of an implied contract from your daily life.
2. Review *Marvin v. Marvin*, 557 P.2d 106 (Cal. 1976) and list the contract issues found in the case.
3. Locate some contract forms, identify the elements of a contract, and then classify the contracts.
4. In the letter in Figure 1-4, identify:
    a. Is it a valid contract? Why or why not?
    b. Who are the parties?
    c. Are all the elements of the contracting process (Figure 1-2) present?
    d. What do you think will happen to the agreement if Wood sells the garage?

1760 Eastern Pky.
Sept. 30, 1985

Dear Mr. Whitney,
    Please feel free to store your Olds in the left side of the garage at any time and for as long as you wish free of any charge what-so-ever. Am enjoying your lovely and handy TV stand.
    Will give you key to garage so if you wish to start car or work on same you can do it. There's a light switch on left near door.
    Kindest regards to you both.

              Ericson L. Wood

FIGURE 1-4

CHAPTER 2
Formation of a Contract: Offer and Acceptance

2.1 PRELIMINARY ISSUES: AN OFFER OR PRELIMINARY NEGOTIATION

The contracting process develops in stages, with the first stage being the offer. An **offer** is a communication by the **offeror** to another party, the **offeree**, of an intent to be bound to a contract. The *Restatement (Second) of Contracts* § 24 defines an *offer* as:

> the manifestation of willingness to enter into a bargain, so made as to justify another person in understanding that his assent to the bargain is invited and will conclude the bargain.

Critical to the definition is the intent of the party making the initial offer. Unless the offeror has the requisite intent to be bound to the proposed bargain, an offer will not follow.

Offeror Must Have Intent

The first question that must be asked is whether the offeror has serious intent or is simply testing the waters through preliminary negotiations.

Preliminary negotiation is discussed in the *Restatement (Second) of Contracts* § 26 as follows:

> A manifestation of willingness to enter into a bargain is not an offer if the person to whom it is addressed knows or has reason to know that the person making it does not intend to conclude a bargain.

Preliminary negotiations are considered a form of solicitation and normally will not constitute an offer. Lacking is the commitment of a promise by the offeror to be bound to an offer. Assume that a student is considering selling some old textbooks. She places a sign on a kiosk saying, "Am interested in selling my old textbooks, would consider $10 a book." A second student contacts the first student and says, "I will take all your books for $10 a book." This situation does not create an offer. The first student was only soliciting bids from people. A firm promise or commitment does not exist; there is no intent.

Common law rules suggest that an offeror must intend to be bound to the contract. If the intent of the offeror is lacking, the assumption is that an offer did not exist. The tricky part is determining a party's serious intent to make a contract, as opposed to a mere proposal or even making an offer in jest. The court will apply an objective standard rather than a subjective standard to determine whether an offer exists. The test is based upon a reasonable person test: Would a reasonable person in the offeree's position believe that the offeror intended to be bound to a contract? The key to this test is not what the offeror considers reasonable, or even the offeree's impression of the seriousness of the offer. It is the third party's impression of the intent communicated by the offer. An illustration of this situation is *City of Everett v. Estate of Sumstad*, 95 Wash. 2d 853, 631 P.2d 366 (1981). There, the contents of a "mysterious" safe were at issue. The court had to determine whether the contents of the safe had been sold at an auction and whether a contract existed.

TERMS

offer
A proposal made with the purpose of obtaining an acceptance, thereby creating a contract. 2. A tender of performance. 3. A statement of intention or willingness to do something.

offeror
A person who makes an offer.

offeree
A person to whom an offer is made.

THE CITY OF EVERETT v. ESTATE OF SUMSTAD

Supreme Court of Washington, En Banc
July 23, 1981

Petitioners, Mr. and Mrs. Mitchell, are the proprietors of a small secondhand store. On August 12, 1978, the Mitchells attended Alexander's Auction, where they frequently had shopped to obtain merchandise for their own use and for use as inventory in their business. At the auction the Mitchells purchased a used safe with an inside compartment for $50. As they were told by the auctioneer when they purchased the safe, the Mitchell's found that the inside compartment of the safe was locked. The safe was part of the Sumstad Estate.

Several days after the auction, the Mitchell's took the safe to a locksmith to have the locked compartment opened. The locksmith found $32,207 inside. The Everett Police Department, notified by the locksmith, impounded the money.

We agree with the Court of Appeals that the question is not whether the Estate, through its agent, entrusted the safe and its contents to the auctioneer who sold it in the ordinary course of business. Clearly the entrustment did occur. The issue is whether there was in fact a sale of the safe and its unknown contents at the auction. In contrast to the Court of Appeals, we find that there was.

A sale is a consensual transaction. The subject matter which passes is to be determined by the intent of the parties as revealed by the terms of their agreement in light of the surrounding circumstances. The objective manifestation theory of contracts, which is followed in this state, lays stress on the outward manifestation of assent made by each party to the other. The subjective intention of the parties is irrelevant.

> A contract has, strictly speaking, nothing to do with the personal, or individual, intent of the parties. A contract is an obligation attached by the mere force of law to certain acts of the parties, usually words, which ordinarily accompany and represent a known intent. If, however, it were proved by twenty bishops that either party, when he used the words, intended something else than the usual meaning which the law imposes upon them, he would still be held, unless there were some mutual mistake, or something else of the sort.
>
> The apparent mutual assent of the parties, essential to the formation of a contract, must be gathered from their outward expressions and acts, and not from an unexpressed intention.

The inquiry, then, is into the outward manifestations of intent by a party to enter into a contract.

We impute an intention corresponding to the reasonable meaning of a person's words and acts. If the offeror, judged by a reasonable standard, manifests an intention to agree in regard to the matter in question, that agreement is established.

[T]he Mitchells were aware of the rule of the auction that all sales were final. Furthermore, the auctioneer made no statement reserving rights to any contents of the safe to the Estate. Under these circumstances, we hold reasonable persons would conclude that the auctioneer manifested an objective intent to sell the safe and its contents and that the parties mutually assented to enter into that sale of the safe and the contents of the locked compartment.

> The unique facts of this case make it one of those apparently rare instances in history in which the objective manifestations of the contracting parties reflected a mutual assent to the sale of the unknown contents of the object sold. The function of a safe is to provide a place for storing one's money or other valuables. When a locked safe is sold without the key, under all of the circumstances present in this case, the reasonable expectations of the buyer should be protected.

We concur in this view.

QUESTIONS FOR ANALYSIS

Was the court's decision fair? Why did the court reach the result it did? Do you believe the court's judgment is correct? Why?

Use caution in making offers that you do not intend to be taken seriously. As in the *City of Everett* case, the court will enforce a contract based upon the objective intent, and may enforce an agreement even if that was not your true intention. It is the effect upon the offeree's understanding of the communication, along with a court's application of the objective test, which determines whether an offer exists.

Terms of Offer Must Be Definite

Not only must an offeror have intent, but also the terms of the offer must be sufficiently certain and definite so that the offeree knows what to accept. The more specific the terms, the higher the likelihood that an offer will exist. If terms are left out or the parties are still haggling over terms, the transaction will probably constitute a preliminary negotiation rather than an offer.

Unfortunately, what constitutes definite, clear, and certain terms is a question of fact for a judge or a jury. Sometimes the law sets out specific requirements, such as for real estate contracts, as to how definite an offer must be to be effective, but this is the exception and not the rule.

To be safe, an offer should specify, at a minimum, the material terms, which are considered to be: (1) the parties; (2) the price; (3) the subject matter of the contract; and (4) the time of performance of the contract.

Parties The persons intending to be bound to a contract should be clearly identified. There should be no question as to who the offeror and the offeree are and thus who will ultimately be responsible under the contract. Failure to identify the parties in an offer is fatal to the process.

Price The specific price the parties intend to pay for the subject matter of the contract is important. Under the common law of contracts, the law does not permit the price term to be uncertain and negotiated at a later date. The offer must contain the specific price, or the offer will be considered merely an invitation to negotiate or a preliminary negotiation, but not an offer.

Note that price terms under the Uniform Commercial Code (U.C.C.) need not be certain for a definite offer to exist. Distinctions between the common law and the U.C.C. are essential when determining whether an offer exists. For example, the paralegal and attorney will determine whether the transaction is a sale of goods. If so, then the U.C.C. applies; otherwise, the rules of common law will apply to the transaction.

Subject Matter Certainty of the subject matter is a requirement for an effective offer. The subject matter must be easily identifiable and not subject to question. How specific the identity of the subject matter must be depends on the subject matter itself. Real estate requires substantial detail, whereas an offer for the purchase of a compact disc player would probably require less. Statutes may dictate how definite the subject matter of the offer must be, so the best rule to follow is to be detailed enough so that reasonable persons could not differ on the subject matter of the offer.

Time of Performance When the parties perform their obligations could be critical to the transaction, such as in a construction contractor-real estate transaction. Often parties will specify a date for performance and set conditions if the performance is not met. Under common law contracts, if the time of performance is not specified, a reasonable time period will be implied. Each transaction will dictate what is considered reasonable, or the time will be determined by case law.

Offeror Must Communicate Offer

An offer cannot be valid unless it is communicated to the offeree. The offeree must know of the offer in order for there to be a power of acceptance. This observation may seem inane, but look at it in the context of a reward. Assume that there has been a surge of bank robberies in a small town. The local city council posts a reward of $10,000 for anyone who catches the bank robber. One afternoon, a tourist, who knows nothing about the robberies, is walking up Main Street and spots a man with a ski mask running out of the bank holding a bag. The tourist grabs the bank robber as the police run to aid in the arrest. Can the tourist claim the $10,000? Probably not, because he knew nothing of the offer, which makes him ineligible to receive the reward. The law requires that the offeror communicate the offer *and* that the offeree know of the offer's existence for there to be a valid power of acceptance.

Advertisements and Solicitations

Some offers appear to be offers, but are treated as invitations to make offers. An advertisement is a typical example of an invitation to make an offer, also known as a *preliminary negotiation*. An advertisement is not generally found to be an offer, because it lacks specificity and definiteness of terms. On the surface, an advertisement suggests a desire to enter into a contract, but the law has construed advertisements as mere **solicitations** or invitations to negotiate.

Typical advertisements lack certainty as to quantity and the number of intended offerees. With the advent of consumer protection legislation in many states, however, advertisements are becoming more specific and closer to real offers. Today's advertisements often state a specific item; limit quantity, price, and model number; and set a time period for the ad's effect. Any question as to whether the advertisement has the needed material terms to constitute an offer is erased. An early case dealing with the advertisement problem is *Lefkowitz v. Great Minneapolis Surplus Store, Inc.*, 251 Minn. 188, 86 N.W.2d 689 (1957).

LEFKOWITZ v. GREAT MINNEAPOLIS SURPLUS STORE, INC.

Supreme Court of Minnesota
Dec. 20, 1957

This case grows out of the alleged refusal of the defendant to sell to the plaintiff a certain fur piece which it had offered for sale in a newspaper advertisement. It appears from the record that on April 6, 1956, the defendant published the following advertisement in a Minneapolis newspaper:

"Saturday 9 A.M. Sharp
3 Brand New Fur Coats Worth to $100.00
First Come First Served
$1 Each"

On April 13, the defendant again published an advertisement in the same newspaper as follows:

"Saturday 9 A.M.
2 Brand New Pastel Mink 3-Skin Scarfs
Selling for $89.50
Out they go Saturday. Each $1.00
1 Black Lapin Stole Beautiful,
worth $139.50 . . . . $1.00
First Come First Served"

The record supports the findings of the court that on each of the Saturdays following the publication of the above-described ads the plaintiff was the first to present himself at the appropriate counter in the defendant's store and on each occasion demanded the coat and the stole so advertised and indicated his readiness to pay the sale price of $1. On both occasions, the defendant refused to sell the merchandise to the plaintiff, stating on the first occasion that by a "house rule" the offer was intended for women only and sales would not be made to men, and on the second visit that the plaintiff knew the defendant's house rules.

The defendant contends that a newspaper advertisement offering items of merchandise for sale at a named price is a "unilateral offer" which may be withdrawn without notice. He relies upon authorities which hold that, where an advertiser publishes in a newspaper that he has a certain quantity or quality of goods which he wants to dispose of at certain prices and on certain terms, such advertisements are not offers which become contracts as soon as any person to whose notice they may come signifies his acceptance by notifying the other that he will take

a certain quantity of them. Such advertisements have been construed as an invitation for an offer of sale on the terms stated, which offer, when received, may be accepted or rejected and which therefore does not become a contract of sale until accepted by the seller; and until a contract has been so made, the seller may modify or revoke such prices or terms. On the facts before us we are concerned with whether the advertisement constituted an offer, and, if so, whether the plaintiff's conduct constituted an acceptance.

There are numerous authorities which hold that a particular advertisement in a newspaper or circular letter relating to a sale of articles may be construed by the court as constituting an offer, acceptance of which would complete a contract. The test of whether a binding obligation may originate in advertisements addressed to the general public is "whether the facts show that some performance was promised in positive terms in return for something requested."

Whether in any individual instance a newspaper advertisement is an offer rather than an invitation to make an offer depends on the legal intention of the parties and the surrounding circumstances. We are of the view on the facts before us that the offer by the defendant of the sale of the Lapin fur was clear, definite, and explicit, and left nothing open for negotiation. The plaintiff having successfully managed to be the first one to appear at the seller's place of business to be served, as requested by the advertisement, and having offered the stated purchase price of the article, he was entitled to performance on the part of the defendant. We think the trial court was correct in holding that there was in the conduct of the parties a sufficient mutuality of obligation to constitute a contract of sale.

Affirmed.

QUESTIONS FOR ANALYSIS

Did the court determine that Great Minneapolis Surplus Store had made a valid offer? What was the result of the case? What rationale did the court use in reaching its conclusion?

Now, compare the advertisements in Figure 2-1 and determine which one is a solicitation for an offer and which one could be construed as an offer. Which advertisement would be construed as an offer? What terms could be

TERMS

solicitation
Invitation of a business transaction.

added to each advertisement to make it a valid offer? Who are the offerees in the advertisement? What kind of contract is created if an offeree accepts?

Advertisement A	Advertisement B
MIDNIGHT MADNESS SALE Microwave Ovens $79.95 Quantities Limited First Come - First Served	Midnight Madness Sale American Brand Microwave Ovens $79.95 Watt 650; 2 Cubic Turn Style Model #A1263B2124 Quantities Limited to 10 Hurry While Supplies Last

FIGURE 2-1 Advertisements for comparison

Advertisement A from Figure 2-1 may be a result of a common sales practice called **bait and switch**. A seller offers a product, which it often does not intend to sell, to lure a customer into the place of business. The advertisement is the "bait" to get customers in; when they request the merchandise in the advertisement, the seller states that the item is no longer available and offers a similar item that is usually more expensive (the "switch"). The goal of the advertisement is to gain leads on persons who are interested in the product advertised. Laws have been enacted federally and in many states to guard against these practices. Such statutes are often known as Deceptive Trade Practices Acts, which prevent unfair conduct by businesses against consumers. These laws have made this type of practice illegal and often punishable by civil or criminal penalties. An advertisement must contain a true or "bona fide" offer to sell the advertised product.

To guard against allegations of bait and switch and consumer fraud, many stores place limitations in their advertisements and put conditions on the offers. Invariably, these limitations are in the fine print in an unobtrusive corner. These limitations may appear to be protection, but when deceptiveness is involved, the law tends to fall on the side of the consumer.

Review Figure 2-2 for some advertising restrictions that appear to limit the power of acceptance and raise the question as to when a true offer is created. Are any of the advertisements offers? Why? Are the limitations valid to constitute a solicitation or a preliminary negotiation? The qualifications placed upon the offers by the language in Figure 2-2 reflect a growing concern over an offeree's interpretation of the word *offer*. Detail has become the rule to avoid even the hint of deceptiveness on the part of an offeror.

2.2 ACCEPTANCE OF THE OFFER

Once an offer is communicated, it can be accepted. The **acceptance** is the response by the offeree to the offeror of an intent to be bound to the terms set out in the offer. Only the person to whom the offer is directed has the power to accept. Unless a party knows of the offer, that party has no power of acceptance.

1. Notice: Some products in this ad may be slightly different from illustrations. Some quantities are limited and subject to prior sale. Rainchecks are available on most advertised stock items. We reserve the right to limit quantities. Any typographical, photographic, or production error in products, pricing or offers is subject to correction in pricing and description.
2. Quantities limited. No rain checks.
3. Prices and offers good through April 1, 1994.
4. Items not described as reduced or as special purchases are at regular price. Special purchases are not reduced, and are limited in quantity. Prices do not include delivery, unless specified. We try to have adequate stock of advertised items. When out of stocks occur, you have a choice: 1) a "raincheck", or 2) a substitute item at the same percentage discount if the item was reduced, or 3) an equal or better item at the advertised price if the item was not reduced. Excludes limited offers, special orders and items not normally available.
5. Our firm intention is to have every advertised item in stock on our shelves. If an advertised item is not available for purchase due to any unforeseen reason, a RainCheck will be issued on request for the merchandise (one item or reasonable family quantity) to be purchased at the sale price whenever available, or will sell you a comparable quantity item at a comparable reduction price.

FIGURE 2-2 Limitations in advertising language

An acceptance by the offeree of the offer may be written, oral, or implied. Each mode of communication has a common thread: it must be **unconditional** and unequivocal—there can be no question as to the offeree's intent.

Written Acceptance

The offeree may respond to the offeror in a written communication. This form may be an appropriate method of acceptance, but a caveat arises when an offer states a specific manner of acceptance. If the offer states a particular manner of acceptance, then, to be effective, the acceptance must comply with the terms of the offer. This is a **stipulation** which effectively sets limitations on the acceptance. For example, assume that Mr. Williams has made the following offer to Ms. Henson:

> January 5, 1994
>
> Dear Ms. Henson:
>
> I need 10 paralegals to work on a special project for a thirty (30) day period beginning March 1, 1994. I will pay $10.00 per hour. Please respond to me by facsimile (FAX) or certified mail only.
>
> Sincerely,
> Mr. Williams

This example limits the mode of acceptance. If Ms. Henson replied through another method, such as express mail or telegram, the acceptance would be ineffective.

TERMS

bait and switch
A form of fraud in which a merchant advertises an item at a low price to entice customers into the store and then, claiming that the advertised article is no longer in stock, attempts to persuade the customer to purchase a higher priced item. Most states have made this practice a criminal offense.

acceptance
[T]he assent by the person to whom an offer is made to the offer as made by the person making it. Acceptance is a fundamental element of a binding contract. . . . In general terms, the receipt and retention of that which is offered. . . . Unspoken consent to or concurrence in a transaction by virtue of failure to reject it. . . . Agreement; approval; assent.

unconditional
Without conditions; without restrictions; absolute.

stipulation
A mandate; a requirement; a condition.

Let's change the Williams example. If the offer by Mr. Williams ended by stating only, "please respond," this would allow the offeree to communicate the acceptance in whatever method she chose. Because no time for the response is stated, a reasonable time period would be implied. The best tactic for Mr. Williams to use to avoid any ambiguity is to specify both the mode of acceptance and the time period for acceptance. Otherwise, the offer is open for an indefinite period of time, with no specific medium for acceptance, and the offeror is clearly placed at a disadvantage.

The Mailbox Rule

When an offer is communicated by mail, the acceptance can be made through the same medium—the mail. The **mailbox rule** states that when an offer is communicated in the mail, the acceptance is effective upon deposit in the mail, regardless of receipt by the offeror. This rule can have chaotic results, as the offeror may not know that any offer has been accepted and revoke the offer prior to receiving the acceptance. The **revocation** is effective upon receipt by the offeree, but the acceptance is effective upon deposit in the mail, regardless of receipt by the offeror. Therein lies the problem with the mailbox rule.

Because the mail is often an unpredictable mode of communication, it is wise for the offeror to set out conditions or a stipulation for the acceptance. A better method to control or obviate the mailbox rule is to state in your offer a time period for acceptance. For example, state in your offer, "The acceptance must be received by the offeror by 5:00 p.m. on March 1, 1994." Review *American Heritage Life v. Koch,* 721 S.W.2d 611 (Tex. Ct. App.–Tyler 1986) and observe how the court treated the mailbox rule. The results may surprise you.

AMERICAN HERITAGE LIFE INSURANCE COMPANY v. KOCH

Court of Appeals of Texas, Tyler
Dec. 19, 1986

On September 23, 1985, the plaintiff/appellee, Virginia Koch (Mrs. Koch), the widow and beneficiary of Alfred R. Koch (Koch), instituted this suit against defendant/appellant, American Heritage Life Insurance Company (American Heritage), to recover $50,000 additional proceeds of an accidental death insurance policy issued to Koch by American Heritage. The facts of this case are not in dispute. On February 24, 1984, Koch enrolled in a group insurance policy that provided for $100,000 accidental death benefits. In 1985, American Heritage sent Koch a premium notice that included an application to increase his accidental death benefits to $150,000. Koch signed the application on March 26, 1985, and on March 29, 1985, Mrs. Koch mailed the application and a check for the additional premiums to American Heritage's agent, Kirk-Van Orsdel, Inc. (Orsdel). Orsdel received the application and additional premiums on April 3, 1985, and negotiated the check the following

day. On April 16, 1985, Koch died in an automobile accident. American Heritage paid $100,000,
representing the proceeds of the policy, to Mrs.
Koch on August 6, 1985.

The sole question we must determine is whether
the increased coverage became effective prior to
Koch's death. The application provided that the increased coverage would "become effective upon
the first day of the month following the receipt of
my premium payment." (Emphasis added.) Mrs.
Koch argues that by sending its offer for increased
benefits by mail, American Heritage has made the
post office its agent to receive and carry the acceptance, and accordingly, American Heritage received the premiums on March 29, 1985. Under
this theory, the additional coverage would have become effective on April 1, 1985, prior to Koch's
death.

Mrs. Koch's argument is unsound. The "mailbox rule" actually provides that when a party makes
an offer through the mail, the contract is created
when a written acceptance by the offerree, properly addressed and stamped, is deposited with the
post office. This rule does not apply, however, if
the offer contains a stipulation that the acceptance
must be received before the contract is completed.
The plain language of this offer requires that the
acceptance be actually received before calculating
when Coverage began. Since Koch's application
and additional premiums were not received by
Orsdel until April 3, 1985, the increased coverage
would not have become effective until May 1, 1985,
after Koch's death.

The judgment of the trial court is reversed, and
the judgment is rendered that Mrs. Koch take
nothing from American Heritage.

QUESTIONS FOR ANALYSIS

Why did the mailbox rule not apply in the *Koch* case? Can you reconcile the case decision with the mailbox rule? What is the critical difference between the mailbox rule and the case result?

Communication of the acceptance by the same mode used by the offeror is effective when delivered through that same medium (e.g., if the offer
is by telegram and the acceptance is by telegram, the acceptance is effective
when transmitted). However, if the acceptance is by a different medium than
that used by the offeror, the acceptance is effective upon receipt by the offeror. Using the Williams example again, suppose the offer did not stipulate
a manner of acceptance. If the offer was faxed and the acceptance was
mailed, the mailbox rule would not apply, and the acceptance would be effective only upon receipt by the offeror, not upon dispatch. For an offeror,
controlling the method of acceptance is critical, and it can later also avert
headaches and legal hassles.

Oral Acceptance

An acceptance may be communicated orally as well as in writing.
When negotiating face-to-face, a verbal acceptance of an offer is effective.
When the offeror hears the words "I accept" or a similar expression of assent, the acceptance is effective. This proposition applies when the telephone
is used as well. When the offeree utters words of assent, the acceptance is

TERMS

mailbox rule
 Rule in contract law
 that acceptance of an
 offer is effective upon
 dispatch (i.e., mailing)
 by the offeree and not
 upon receipt by the
 offeror. Sometimes
 called the implied
 agency rule because the
 Post Office is deemed
 to be the agent of
 the offeror. This
 rule applies to the
 acceptance of an offer,
 but not to the making,
 rejection, or revocation
 of an offer.

revocation
 A nullification,
 cancellation, or
 withdrawal of a power,
 privilege, or act.

effective at that moment. Suppose that an offer is communicated by telephone and the offeree contacts the offeror within the time period specified and responds affirmatively to an answering machine or voice mail. Is that considered the same mode of communication? The courts have not decided this issue, but arguably it is the same mode of acceptance.

Implied Acceptance

An offeree's actions or conduct can indicate acceptance of an offer. This is often accomplished by performance by the offeree. Some believe that lack of communication or silence is assent to an offer. This is not the case. Unless both parties agree, silence is not normally considered an acceptance of an offer. If that were the case, imagine how the law of contracts would be turned upside down! This would place too much burden on the offeror.

There are exceptions to the rule, however. The *Restatement (Second) of Contracts* § 69 sets out three situations in which silence constitutes acceptance:

1. Where an offeree fails to reply to an offer, his silence and inaction operate as an acceptance in the following cases only:
   a. Where an offeree takes the benefit of a offered service with reasonable opportunity to reject them and reason to know that they were offered with the expectation of compensation.
   b. Where the offeror has stated or given the offeree reason to understand assent may be manifested by silence or inaction, and the offeree in remaining silent and inactive intends to accept the offer.
   c. Where because of previous dealings or otherwise, it is reasonable that the offeree should notify the offeror if he does not intend to accept.

But review *First Texas Savings Association v. Jergins,* 705 S.W.2d 390 (Tex. Ct. App.–2d Dist. 1986), which focuses on the terms of an offer and when an acceptance occurs. Here silence does not constitute acceptance by the offeree.

FIRST TEXAS SAVINGS ASSOCIATION v. JERGINS

Court of Appeals of Texas, Fort Worth
March 22, 1986

The undisputed evidence shows that First conducted a contest designated as "$5,000 Scoreboard Challenge". The contest provided that contestants were to complete an entry form and deposit same with First. A random drawing of the entry forms would provide the winner with an $80 savings account with First, plus four tickets to a Dallas Mavericks home basketball game chosen by First. Another provision of the was that if the Mavericks held their opponent in the chosen game to 89 or fewer points, the recipient of the tickets would be awarded an additional $5,000 money market certificate. Drawings were conducted monthly from October 1982 through March 1983.

On or about October 13, 1982, Jergins completed and deposited her entry form with First. On or about November 1, 1982, First attempted to amend the contest provisions by posting a notice at its branches specifying that to win the $5,000 it would be necessary for the Mavericks to hold their opponent to 85 or fewer points. Shortly prior to December 29, 1982, Jergins' entry form was drawn and she was notified she had won the $80 savings account and four tickets to the Mavericks' January 22, 1983 game against the Utah Jazz. The notice advertised Jergins that if the Jazz scored 85 or fewer points, First would award her the $5,000 money market certificate. Jergins claimed her prize and used the tickets to attend the game. The Jazz scored 88 points. Jergins requested the $5,000 and First refused, stating the Jazz had scored more than 85 points in the game. Jergins filed suit and both parties filed motions for summary judgment. The trial court denied First's motion and granted summary judgment for Jergins.

Both parties agree the matter of whether there was a contract and, if so, the terms constituting the contract are proper subjects for a summary judgment. [The] issue before this Court is to determine at what point in time the contract was formulated. If an offer is made, a contract is formulated when the offer is unconditionally accepted. In order to be entitled to the rewards of the offer, it is necessary that the party accepting same perform any and all obligations or requirements contained in the offer. In the instant case, the only obligation or requirement of performance placed on Jergins was to complete and deposit the entry form provided by First. From that point forward the requirements of performance rested solely with First. Essentially the contract terms were (1) if Jergins would complete the entry and deposit same with First, (2) First would include the entry with others for a random drawing. First also contracted to conduct monthly drawings. The winner was to receive (a) $80 saving account, (b) four game tickets and (c) a chance to win $5,000 if the Mavericks'

opponent scored 89 or fewer points. The contract was formulated at the time Jergins completed and deposited the entry form. There was nothing further required of Jergins and she had no control over the outcome of the contest. She had completed her part of the contract. When First drew her entry form, she was entitled to the $80, four tickets and to have a game assigned to her in which she had a chance to win $5,000. First partially completed its obligations under the contract. It (1) placed Jergins entry with the others for a random drawing, (2) conducted the promised drawing, (3) awarded the winner of the drawing $80 plus four tickets, and (4) assigned a Mavericks' home game. The only portion of the contract that went unperformed was the obligation to award $5,000 in the event the opponent scored 89 or fewer points. First's first point of error is overruled.

The second point of error alleging acceptance of a modification of the contract is without merit. First seems to contend that upon receipt of the notification by Jergins that she had won $80 and four tickets that she should have refused same and protested that First was attempting to change the contract agreement by reducing the point total from 89 to 85. We disagree.

In its brief, First correctly argues, "[a] party asserting modification 'must prove that his proposed modification was made known to the plaintiff and that the plaintiff accepted the terms of his proposed modification. . . . [I]n order to prove a new contract. . . it [is] necessary to show that notice thereof was given directly or indirectly, and that plaintiff accepted.' "Jergins accepted what she was entitled to receive under the contract and patiently waited to see if she would be entitled to any further award. She in no way indicated an acceptance of the attempted modification of the contract. She was entitled to the $80 and four tickets when her name was drawn and First would have had no valid reason to refuse the award regardless of whether Jergins protested the attempted modification. The law requires and acceptance, not a protest.

The judgment of the trial court is affirmed.

QUESTIONS FOR ANALYSIS

How did the court define an offer? When was the offer accepted? What terms did Mrs. Jergins agree to? What type of contract was consummated between the parties?

Notice in the *Jergins* case that once Mrs. Jergins had deposited her entry form, her acceptance was effective. A later change in the terms of the offer did not affect her, and for good reason. Imagine if an offeror did not like the terms of an offer created and decided to change those terms after an acceptance. If the law permitted this kind of conduct, the law of contracts would be in a constant state of chaos. The *Jergins* court had to enforce the original offer to preserve the integrity of contract law.

Unilateral and Bilateral Contracts Distinguished

When all that is required of the offeree is performance, a **unilateral** contract is formed upon performance. The mode of acceptance is the conduct or actions of the offeree. No exchange of responses is necessary to indicate assent to the offer; rather, performance indicates the acceptance. Acceptance of an offer through performance causes uncertainty, as in the earlier reward example. Courts favor a clear assent by the offeree to the offeror, creating a **bilateral** contract. An exchange between the parties is clear. Until communicated, an acceptance is ineffective, which leaves less room for uncertainty about the offeree's actions.

Mirror Image Rule

Whether an acceptance is communicated through a writing, orally, or impliedly, under common law the acceptance must match the offer exactly. The rule is known as the *mirror image rule.* The rule states that an offer and acceptance must be exact. They must mirror each other, and any deviation from the terms of the offer is a counteroffer. A **counteroffer** is a new offer. Under the mirror image rule, it does not matter how slight the deviation or qualification is between the acceptance and the offer. The rule is interpreted strictly and, unless the counteroffer is accepted by the original offeror, an agreement is not formed.

2.3 TERMINATION OF THE OFFER

There are a number of ways to end the contract formation process, thereby terminating the offer. Depending on the circumstances, offers can terminate upon the happening of certain events, by the action of the parties, or by operation of law. Each method results in the same thing: termination of the offer.

Action of the Parties

Various actions of the parties can terminate an offer. Typical actions terminating an offer are a counteroffer, rejection, revocation, and expiration of time.

The Counteroffer

A change in the terms, however slight, of the original offer creates a counteroffer. The power of acceptance is now switched, with the offeror having the power to accept the new offer. The formation process begins again, thus terminating the original offer. The common law is strict in its interpretation of deviations from the original offer. As previously discussed, any change in the terms of the original offer terminates the offer. Virtually no exceptions exist under this common law rule.

Rejection

In effect, a counteroffer is a rejection of the offer. **Rejection** occurs when an offeree does not accept the stated terms of an offer. The negotiating terminates unless a new offer is communicated.

Rejection is a typical method to terminate an offer. An acceptance can be written, oral, or implied, and so can the rejection. Using the earlier Williams example, if Ms. Henson faxed a letter which stated, "I am in receipt of your offer, however, at this time, I must reject it," this response would terminate the original offer.

FARCUS

"Okay, fellas, I have a counter-offer ..."

TERMS

unilateral
1. Affecting the interests of only one party or one side.
2. One-sided; having only one side.

bilateral
1. Involving two interests. 2. Having two sides.

counteroffer
A position taken in response to an offer, proposing a different deal.

rejection
Any act or word of an offeree, communicated to an offeror, conveying his or her refusal of an offer.

A rejection can also be verbally communicated, either face-to-face or by telephone. Finally, a rejection may occur when the offeree's behavior suggests nonacceptance. This is a more difficult and ambiguous situation. Suppose that an attorney offers to sell you his desk and chair for $500. You, however, go out and purchase a new desk and chair. That action would, in effect, be an implied rejection.

Revocation

Prior to an offer being accepted, an offeror may withdraw the offer at any time. This act is known as *revocation*. Some acts or events invite revocation. Presume that an offer is communicated and that no acceptance has been received by the offeror. The offeror withdraws the offer by mail and the offeree receives the withdrawal prior to acceptance. This constitutes revocation. The exception is when the acceptance has been mailed and the revocation has not been received by the offeree. Assume that Marc mails an offer to James on the 15th of the month. It arrives on the 16th. On the 25th, Marc mails a revocation which does not arrive until the 28th. James mails his acceptance on the 27th. Because James mailed his acceptance before he received Marc's revocation, the acceptance stands. This illustrates another aspect of the mailbox rule.

Exception to Revocation: The Option Contract When an offeree pays the offeror money to keep an offer open for a specified period of time, an **option contract** is created. The offeror cannot revoke the offer, as the payment creates an **irrevocable offer**. The value paid restricts the rights of the offeror and enhances the power of the offeree. As long as the option is in effect, the offeror cannot revoke the offer, even if someone makes a better offer. Assume that you have been reading the advertisements for cars and you find a 1989 Jaguar for only $10,000. After viewing the car and having a service person check it out, you decide you want it. Unfortunately, you are short of cash and cannot afford $10,000 at this time. You ask the seller, if you pay $1,000, will he hold the offer open only to you for 15 days? The seller agrees and you tender the $1,000. An option contract is created. The offer is irrevocable, because you paid for the power to accept within that period of time and for the seller not to make any offers on the car to anyone else during the 15-day period. Any attempted revocation by the offeror would be ineffective.

Expiration or Lapse of Time

Another means of revocation occurs automatically when a time limit has been set on the offer. If the offeror states in the offer that the acceptance must be received by a specific date, the offer automatically terminates unless acceptance is received by that specific time. An offeror may set time limits in which the offeree must accept the offer. If the offeree does not accept within the specified time period, the offer is automatically revoked and expires or lapses due to the time limitation. This method of revocation is very useful, as it sets restraints on an offeree's power to accept. An offeror does not want to leave an offer open indefinitely.

Although case law suggests that an offer that does not have a specific time deadline will expire upon the reasonable passage of time, this rule leaves open the age-old question of what is "reasonable." The courts will review each circumstance to determine reasonableness. When time appears to be important factor, the court will imply a shorter time period. Unfortunately, there is no exact time period for "reasonable period of time." Therefore, to be safe, a definite termination date is the best protection.

Operation of Law

Offers can also be revoked due to some intervening factor over which neither party has control. Under the law, a party making the offer will not be held to the offer. Typical methods of terminating an offer by operation of law are (1) legality; (2) death; (3) insanity; and (4) destruction of the subject matter.

Legality

When legislation is enacted that makes the subject of the offer illegal, the offer is terminated. Suppose that a winery offers to a supplier a container of Chilean red wine. The U.S. government then determined that Chile has many human rights violations and an embargo on Chilean goods imported into this country is passed by the U.S. Congress. The offer would not stand because it would be illegal to import the goods into this country. The offer would be terminated by a superseding illegality. Neither party has control over the circumstances and therefore it would be inappropriate to hold the offeror to the offer.

Death

Death of the offeror automatically terminates the offer. No communication is necessary to the offeree, but, as a practical matter, it makes good business sense to let an offeree know that an offeror has died. Note that if the offeree dies, the power to accept by that intended offeree is terminated.

Insanity

Persons who have been declared by a court to be of unsound mind or insane do not have the power to create an offer. The basis behind this mode

TERMS

option contract
1. An offer, combined with an agreement supported by consideration not to revoke the offer for a specified period of time; a future contract in which one of the parties has the right to insist on compliance with the contract, or to cancel it, at his or her election.

irrevocable offer
Under the Uniform Commercial Code, an offer to buy or sell goods made in a signed writing which, by its terms, gives assurance that it will be held open. A firm offer is not revocable for want of consideration during the time it states it will be held open, or, if no time is state, for up to three months.

of termination is that the offeror does not have the legal capacity to make the offer. This area is treated in more depth in Chapter 6.

Destruction of the Subject Matter

When an offer is communicated and the subject matter of that offer is then destroyed, the offer is terminated. This often occurs when acts are out of the offeror's control. For example, a farmer in Florida offers to a national grocery chain her entire crop of oranges for that season. While the grocery chain is evaluating the offer, a hurricane destroys the crop. The offer is terminated.

Destruction of the subject matter often occurs because of acts of God, such as tornadoes, earthquakes, hurricanes, and floods. Termination, under these circumstances, occurs because the thing or entity essential to the contract—the subject of the contract—is destroyed.

2.4 PRACTICAL APPLICATION

Most paralegals will find themselves involved in the formation stage of contracts when drafting an offer to purchase, a letter proposing an offer, or a letter of acceptance. Each form memorializes the intentions of the parties and begins the contracting process. To assist in this task, some examples of documents putting the offer and acceptance into practical effect are shown in Figures 2-3 to 2-7.

July 1, 1994

Mr. Chase Brown
134 Main Street
Chicago, Illinois

Dear Mr. Brown:

I offer to sell you my 1990 Jaguar if you agree to pay me $30,000.00. You need to pay me $10,000.00 down and the remainder in payments of $600.00 per month until paid. Please notify me on or before the close of business on July 15, 1994 by return mail if you wish to accept the terms and conditions of this offer. Your acceptance shall not be effective until actually received by me on that date.

Very truly yours,

A.C. Granger

FIGURE 2-3 Offer specifying manner of acceptance

July 1, 1994

Mr. Chase Brown
134 Main Street
Chicago, Illinois

Dear Mr. Brown:

We have discussed the sale of my 1990 Jaguar to you. It is my understanding that you have agreed to pay $30,000.00 with $10,000.00 down. The remaining balance shall be paid out monthly at $600.00 per month.

If this letter expresses all of the terms of our agreement in a manner satisfactory to you, please indicate your acknowledgment by signing one copy of this letter in the space designated below, and returning the signed copy to me by July 10, 1994. Your signature will make this agreement effective and binding between us.

_____
Signature of offeror, A.C. Granger

_____
Typed name of offeror

Accepted on this ____ day of _____, 19____.

_____
Signature of offeree, Chase Brown

_____
Typed name of offeree

FIGURE 2-4 Offer containing form of acceptance

STATE OF NEW JERSEY   §
                                       §
COUNTY OF SALEM   §

KNOW ALL MEN BY THESE PRESENTS:

That Anna Webb, of the County of Salem and State of New Jersey, of and in consideration of the sum of $1000,00, receipt of which is acknowledged, grants to Harvey Little, of the County of Cumberland and State of New Jersey, the option and right to puchase for the sum of Fifty Thousand Dollars ($50,000.00), Block Two, Woodland Subdivision, Salem County, New Jersey. The option must be exercised by the close of business on June 15, 1994 by giving written notice of the exercise of the option to me by fax at (609) 426-1883, accompanied by a payment of $2,000.00 earnest money, and the execution and delivery within ten (10) days after the exercise of the option of a note and mortgage securing payment of the remaining balance.

In the event that this option is not exercised by June 15, 1994, it shall automatically and immediately terminate without further notice, and all your rights under this option agreement will then terminate.

SIGNED this ____ day of _____, 19____.

_____
Signature of grantor of option
Anna Webb

_____
Typed name of grantor of option

FIGURE 2-5 Option agreement

The undersigned exercises the option granted by Anna Webb on May 31, 1994, and accepts the terms and conditions of the offer.

Dated this ____ day of _____, 19____.

_____
Signature of grantee of option
Harvey Little

_____
Typed name of grantee of option.

FIGURE 2-6 Exercising of option

July 15, 1994

Dear Mr. Brown:

My offer to you dated July 1, 1994, in which I offered to you a 1990 Jaguar, is withdrawn and revoked. Any acceptance attempted after receipt of this notice shall be of no force or effect.

_____
Signature of offeror, A.C. Granger

_____
Typed name of offeree

FIGURE 2-7 Revocation of offer

SUMMARY

2.1 An offer is a communication by the offeror to an offeree of an intent to be bound to a contract. The offeror must have intent to be bound to a contract, must communicate it, and must create specific terms. An offer should include the material terms, such as the parties, the price, the subject matter, and the time of performance. Advertisements may be an invitation or an offer, if definite enough.

2.2 The acceptance is the response by the offeree to the offeror of an intent to be bound to the terms of the contract. The acceptance can be written, oral, or implied. If an offer is communicated in the mail and the response is communicated through the mail, the mailbox rule applies. An acceptance must match the offer exactly. This is the common law rule referred to as the mirror image rule.

2.3 There are a number of methods to terminate an offer. An offer can be terminated by the actions of the parties or by operation of law. Through the actions of the parties, an offer can be terminated by a counteroffer, rejection, revocation, or expiration of time. Other methods to terminate are by operation of law, including illegality, death, insanity, or destruction of the subject matter.

REVIEW QUESTIONS

1. What is an offer?
2. What elements must an offer include to be valid?
3. Are advertisements offers? Why or why not?
4. How are bait and switch transactions created?
5. Define *acceptance*.
6. How can an acceptance be communicated to the offeror?
7. Define the mailbox rule.
8. What is the mirror image rule?
9. What are ways to terminate an offer by the actions of the parties? By operation of law?
10. What is an option contract?

EXERCISES

1. Review your local newspaper for its advertisements. Pick four or five and determine if the advertisements are invitations to offer or offers. Discuss the basis of your conclusions.
2. Read *DeSantis v. Sears, Roebuck & Co.*, 543 N.Y.S.2d 228 (1989) and answer the following questions:
   a. What are the facts of the case?
   b. What is the rule of law from this case?
   c. Did the court find that a valid offer existed?
3. At precisely 11:00 a.m., the Driftwood, a bar in the lower Greenville area, opens its doors. At 11:03 a.m. Donald Trumptup, a well-known real estate developer, enters the Driftwood and orders a beer from the bartender. Donald is a likeable chap who enjoys good conversation and good drink. As the day passes, Donald leisurely drinks beer after beer, never getting wasted but maintaining a "good buzz."

   At 4:55 p.m., J.R. Reynolds enters the Driftwood and sits down next to Trumptup. They have the following conversation:

   J.R. What a day! [sigh] Hey, could you pass the pretzels? Yo, Bartender, let's have a beer down here!

   D.T. Had a rough day, have you?

   J.R. Nag, nag, nag. That's all my wife does is nag. All day she's been on my back about moving out of our apartment. She knows I've been busting my butt trying to find an affordable house but, as you may know, good real estate isn't easy to find. I just can't take her pressure much longer.

D.T. [in his stupor, he decides to have some fun with this pathetic soul.] Sir, this may be your lucky day. You see, I'm a real estate agent, and I can offer to sell you this beautiful two-bedroom two-bath house for the low, low price of $25,000. [D.T. takes a picture out of his breast pocket and shows J.R. a luxurious home. In reality, this is Donald's own home and it has a fair market value of $250,000.] It is located on 123 Greenville Avenue.

J.R. [with genuine excitement in his voice] Oh my goodness, what a deal. I must have it! What must I do?

D.T. Well, a lawyer friend of mine once told me that all transactions in land must be in writing, so we draw up a contract.

D.T. grabs a napkin and writes the following:

CONTRACT

I, Donald Trumptup, hereby agree to sell the house located at 123 Greenville to J.R. Reynolds upon payment of $25,000.00. This agreement is meant to be a final and binding contract between the two parties.

Sincerely,

Donald Trumptup

J.R. ecstatically takes the napkin contract and rushes out the door, saying he must go home and break the good news to his wife. As soon as he leaves, Donald bursts into laughter and shares this story with his barroom buddies.

Did D.T. sell his house? Is there an offer?

3.1 MUTUAL ASSENT DEFINED

One of the most important parts of a contract is the parties' agreement to the terms and conditions set forth in the offer and acceptance. The parties must willingly and genuinely assent to the terms of contract or the contract may be invalid. This is known as **mutual assent**.

Mutual assent is "the meeting of the minds." Under the law, this concept signifies that all parties have been open and honest in their dealings and that all understand the basis of the bargain. There are no hidden terms or meanings; each term is stated and is what it is. The communication of the

TERMS

mutual assent
   A meeting of the minds; consent; agreement.

offer and the acceptance leads to an agreement between the parties and thus is a necessary element to a contract.

To determine whether mutual assent exists, a court will apply an objective standard. Did the parties to the contract act in such a way that it could reasonably be concluded that the parties agreed to the same terms and conditions, or did the acts of the parties show a contrary intent? The essence of mutual assent hinges on the parties having a mutual understanding of the terms and conditions of the contract. As with an offer, critical to the concept of mutual assent is the intent, viewed objectively by a third party. Most terms must be clearly identified so that, objectively, a conclusion can be reached that a contract was consummated. Consequently, when the offer is communicated to and accepted by the offeree, an agreement is reached between the parties known as mutual assent.

3.2 METHODS OF DESTROYING MUTUAL ASSENT

A problem arises when parties are not honest and genuine or make mistakes in their contractual negotiations. When terms are deliberately omitted, or mistakes occur, or parties are placed under undue pressure, the contracting process suffers. When these problems occur, mutual assent does not exist and the contract will fail. The most common ways to destroy mutual assent are fraud, misrepresentation, mistake, duress, and undue influence. If one of these things is proven, the contract will terminate.

Another method of destroying mutual assent, which has developed over the years, is embedded in public policy. Protecting the public from unfair contracts is a basis fo **rescission** of a contract because of lack of mutual assent. A common public policy argument used by attorneys and courts is that the contract is **unconscionable**. Often this occurs when a party to a contract takes advantage of the other party by using terms that are patently unjust or unfair.

Whatever the means, all these methods (see Figure 3-1) destroy the meeting of the minds and thus terminate a contract.

Destroying Mutual Assent	
Fraud	Duress
Misrepresentation	Undue influence
Mistake	Unconscionability

FIGURE 3-1 Means of destroying mutual assent

Fraud

Fraud is a common method of destroying mutual assent. By definition, it is a wrongful statement of fact or omission of fact knowingly made by one party with the intent to induce another party into entering a contract. Although fraud has many definitions, critical to establishing fraud as a basis for destroying mutual assent is that the party *knew* that his or her representation or statement was false. To understand fraud, we need to dissect its elements.

Misstatement of Fact

To establish fraud, a party must show that the party initiating the contract misstated a fact or failed to state a fact. Assume that a car buyer asks whether the mileage on the odometer is accurate. A few days before, the salesperson watched the mechanic roll back the odometer. If the salesperson tells the buyer that the odometer is accurate, then a misstatement of fact occurs. Similarly, if the salesperson omits telling the buyer that the odometer is inaccurate, even though he or she knows it is, that constitutes an omission of fact.

Fact Is Material

Simply misstating a fact is insufficient. The misstatement or omission of fact be material to the contract, that is, it must be critical to a party's decision to enter into the transaction. It goes to the heart of the contract. Following the car example, had the buyer known that the mileage was inaccurate, the buyer probably would not have purchased the car. The mileage was important to the buyer in rendering a decision. Inaccurately representing the fact that the odometer had been rolled back and the mileage misstated is material to the contract.

Knowledge of False Statement

Central to proving fraud is proving that the party making the statement had knowledge of its falsity. At the time the statement is made, the party must know it is false. Using the same example, the salesperson knew that the odometer had been rolled back, but still represented that the mileage was accurate. Making this statement with the knowledge that it was false was an element of the fraud. Knowledge is critical to establishing a case of fraud.

Intent to Deceive

A person claiming fraud must prove not only that the statement was made falsely, but also that the person who made the statement had the intent to deceive the party to whom the statement was made. The intent must be deliberate and with total disregard of the actual facts. To establish a claim for fraud, the party making any statement or omission must be shown to have had the intent to deceive the person into entering into a contract. This is critical to a fraud claim. Again, in the odometer example, the salesperson clearly had the intent to deceive the perspective buyer into purchasing the

TERMS

rescission
The abrogation, annulment, or cancellation of a contract by the act of a party. Rescission may occur by mutual consent of the parties, pursuant to a condition contained in the contract, or for fraud, failure of consideration, material breach, or default. It is also a remedy available to parties by a judgment or decree of the court. More than mere termination, rescission restores the parties to the status quo existing before the contract was entered into.

unconscionable
Morally offensive, reprehensible, or repugnant. An unconscionable contract is a contract in which a dominant party has taken unfair advantage of a weaker party, who has little or no bargaining power, and has imposed terms and conditions that are unreasonable and one-sided. A court may refuse to enforce an unconscionable contract. What is or is not "unconscionable" often depends upon the contract's commercial setting.

fraud
Deceit, deception, or trickery that is intended to induce, and does induce, another to part with anything of value or surrender some legal right.

car, as the sales person knew about the odometer rollback. By showing an intentional misstatement of a material fact, a case of fraud is almost complete.

Reliance on Misstated Fact or Representation

In addition to showing the representations made by the person committing the fraud, it must be shown that the person to whom the communication was made relied to his or her detriment on the false representations of that party. If it can be shown that the person accepted the contract, that the person relied on the representations made, and that the representations proved to be deceptive, a case for fraud is virtually assured. Continuing with the odometer case, the salesperson represented that the lower mileage count was accurate; there is no doubt that the buyer relied on this deception, which became part of the basis for the buyer's entering into the contract. The reliance element is established.

Representation Caused Damage

The final element of fraud is that damage resulted because the defrauded party relied to his or her detriment on the misstatement or omission of fact. This element directly goes to the issue of injury. To successfully establish a case for fraud, a party must show that it has been injured or damaged by the other party's representation and that the representation caused harm. This element is usually easy to show when the other elements are present. Finishing the odometer example, the demonstrable injury or detriment is that the purchaser lost substantial value in the car, because he or she did not pay on the basis of the car's true mileage. As the true mileage was much higher, the value of the car is substantially diminished, causing injury or harm to the purchaser. Therefore, the damage would be the difference between the actual value of the car (with the true mileage) and the amount actually paid by the purchaser.

Effect of Fraud

When a person can prove fraud, the contract is usually voidable by the person who has been injured. The reason the contract is voidable is because a critical element of the contract has been destroyed: the mutual assent. To this end, a court will award a party damages (money) or rescind the contract (cancel it) and place the parties back in the same position they would have occupied prior to consummating the contract. The damages and remedies that a court can award are discussed more fully in Chapter 9. For a discussion of fraud, examine *Oettinger v. Lakeview Motors, Inc.*, 675 F. Supp. 1488 (E.D. Va. 1988). Notice what the court considered in determining whether fraud was present (see also Figure 3-2).

OETTINGER v. LAKEVIEW MOTORS, INC.
United States Distric Court, E.D. Virginia
Jan 7, 1988

This case was tried to the Court without a jury on the plaintiff's claims of odometer fraud, alleging violations of both federal and state statutes. At the conclusion of the trial, the Court found the defendant Lakeview Motors, Inc., liable to the plaintiff for a violation of 15 U.S.C. § 1989, the federal Motor Vehicle Information and Cost Savings Act.

Mrs. Oettinger brings her claim under 15 U.S.C. §§ 1988 and 1989, the liability provisions of the federal odometer fraud statute. 15 U.S.C. § 1988(b) states that "no transferor shall violate any rule prescribed under this section or give a false statement to a transferee in making any disclosure required by such rule." Therefore, a dealer who gives a false odometer statement to a customer violates § 1988; if he does so with intent to defraud, then he is civilly liable under § 1989.

On July 30, 1984, Lakeview Motors sold one 1981 Buick Century bearing VIN 1G4AL69A6BH122906 to the plaintiff, Mary Ann Boyd Oettinger. The sale price was $7,000.

At the time of sale, the odometer reading on the car was 40,141 miles. Lakeview completed an odometer mileage statement, certifying to the plaintiff in writing that, to the best of its knowledge, this reading showed the actual mileage on the car. This mileage certification was required by law.

At the time of sale, the actual mileage on the car was some 35,000 miles higher than that shown on the odometer. This meant the actual mileage the car had traveled was in excess of 75,000 miles.

Lakeview Motors was a "transferor" within the meaning of 15 U.S.C. § 1988(a).

In purchasing the car, the plaintiff relied upon the odometer's mileage reading and Lakeview's certification that it was accurate. She would not have purchased this 1981 Buick had she known that it actually traveled over 75,000 miles; nor would she have paid $7,000 for the car.

The mileage number written on the title certificate was irregular and suspicious in appearance. It appears to have been physically altered from an original number of "72521" miles to a forged number of "37,252.1" miles. As investigators testified, several features indicate that the mileage number on the rear of [the] title had been altered . . . . The defendant Lakeview took possession of the title documents when it purchased the car at N.C. auction. In addition, there is a large discrepancy between the mileage figures shown on the reassignment documents and those shown on the official odometer statements.

From this documented sequence of figures, two suspicious facts immediately stand out for any observer: *First,* the mileage reading shown on the reassignment documents actually dropped by nearly 5000 miles between the purchase by Johnny's Used Cars and its sale to Lakeview Motors.

Second, the official odometer statements reflect far higher mileage numbers than those figures shown on the reassignment documents. These figures would have put any observer on notice of the mileage gap and the likelihood of odometer fraud. On the basis of all the evidence introduced at trial, the Court concludes that Lakeview acted with fraudulent intent when it certified to the plaintiff that the car's odometer reading was accurate. Once it purchased the car, Lakeview was or should have been aware of the facts indicating odometer tampering. Having received through the title documents a reason to suspect the odometer of fraudulent tampering, Lakeview is deemed to have known all that a minimal inspection would have revealed. Finally, the inference of intent to defraud is made all the more compelling by Lakeview's behavior in the face of suspicious circumstances: it displayed willful ignorance and reckless disregard of the truth when it certified to the plaintiff that, "to the best of its knowledge," the odometer reading was correct. Even the faintest effort at ascertaining the true facts would have told Lakeview otherwise.

Once a dealer has notice of grounds for suspecting an odometer's inaccuracy, the law imposes on him a duty of further inquiry. The dealer must then investigate the facts in order to ascertain whether the odometer's mileage reading is reliable, before certifying it as such; or if he chooses not to do this, then he is legally bound to inform the customer that he suspects the odometer is incorrect and that it should not be relied upon. Thus, a dealer is subject to liability where he recklessly disregards the truth as to a car's actual mileage. The defendant Lakeview was under a duty to have the knowledge in question before it certified the odometer reading; the information was peculiarly available to Lakeview as a dealer, and not readily accessible to the buying public; and, very probably, the odometer statement was made in part to induce the sale of the car. Consequently, under these conditions, it is fair to infer from Lakeview's recklessness that it acted with intent to defraud some purchasers. In this case, the evidence showed that had the Lakeview dealers paid even passing honest scrutiny to the title documents for the 1981 Buick,

they would have become suspicious of the number purporting to state the car's actual mileage. Lakeview's agents possessed reason to know; they were on notice that something could well be wrong with the mileage reading, and yet they failed to act. The law does not and cannot tolerate such willful ignorance in the face of obvious warning signs—signs that would have moved reasonable people to undertake further inquiry.

Under these circumstances, this Court is led to conclude that Lakeview's failure to investigate and its reckless disregard for making accurate odometer statements "stemmed from an intent to defraud purchasers" in general, if not the plaintiff in particular. In summary, the facts proven at trial convincingly show that Lakeview acted with reckless disregard of the car's actual mileage and with fraudulent intent when it sold the car to the plaintiff and certified the odometer's reading as reflecting the car's actual mileage.

QUESTIONS FOR ANALYSIS

What definition of fraud is used by the *Oettinger* court? What was the critical factor in the court's decision? What is the court's holding?

Fraud			
1. Mistatement of fact		4. Reliance on deception	
2. Fact is material		5. Representation caused damage	
3. Knowledge and intent to deceive			

FIGURE 3-2 Elements of fraud

Misrepresentation

Fraud and misrepresentation have similar characteristics. **Misrepresentation** is defined as a misstatement of fact or omission of fact made innocently without the intent to deceive. The key difference between fraud and misrepresentation is the element of intent. In misrepresentation, the statement is made innocently without the knowledge necessary to establish deliberate conduct.

Using the odometer example from the previous section, assume that the salesperson had no reason to suspect odometer tampering. When asked whether the odometer was an accurate reflection of the mileage, the salesperson answered yes, and misrepresentation occurred. This clearly is a false statement of fact, but in this instance, it is not made knowingly with the intent to deceive—it is made innocently. That is the distinguishing characteristic between fraud and misrepresentation.

The Duty to Disclose

An issue that is a constant source of debate is how far a party's duty to disclose extends. Must all facts be disclosed? Must a party correct a false assumption? The answer, unfortunately, is that it depends. The law requires that parties act honestly in their dealings. Withholding vital or material information can give rise to a claim of misrepresentation. For example, assume a seller puts a house on the market. Prior to placing the house on the market, the seller notices that some of the wood in the house has rotted and as a precaution has a pesticide company spray for termites. While walking through the house, prospective buyers ask whether the house has termites. Does the seller have a duty to disclose that the house was sprayed for termites? The answer is probably yes, because the seller suspected termites in the house. Would a negative response to the buyer's question result in a claim for representation? The answer is probably yes.

Understanding the duty to disclose means understanding what constitutes a material fact. If the matter affects a basic assumption in the contract, the duty to disclose exists. Here the issue is not only the materiality of the information, but also that one party is relying on a misplaced assumption. Did the misrepresentation induce the party to enter into the contract? If so, misrepresentation exists.

With the advent of many consumer protection laws, full and complete disclosure is the trend. The old doctrine of *caveat emptor*—"let the buyer beware"—is no longer a safe haven for the dishonest or even the innocent. The law has made a 180-degree turn, from placing limited responsibility on sellers for nondisclosure to placing heavy burdens on sellers for full and complete disclosure. Compare a famous early case, *Swinton v. Whitinsville Savings Bank*, 42 N.E.2d 808 (Mass. 1942) with *Zimmerman v. Northfield Real Estate, Inc.*, 156 Ill. App. 3d 154, 510 N.E.2d 409 (1986). Notice how the law has substantially changed. The courts place a higher burden on the party with the knowledge rather than the unsuspecting innocent party.

TERMS

misrepresentation
The statement of an untruth; a misstatement of fact designed to lead one to believe that something is other than it is; a false statement of fact designed to deceive.

SWINTON v. WHITINSVILLE SAV. BANK

Supreme Judicial Court of Massachusetts
June 22, 1942

The declaration alleges that on or about September 12, 1938, the defendant sold the plaintiff a house in Newton to be occupied by the plaintiff and his family as a dwelling; that at the time of the sale the house "was infested with termites, an insect that is most dangerous and destructive to buildings"; that the defendant knew the house was so infested; that the plaintiff could not readily observe this condition upon inspection; that "knowing the internal destruction that these insects were creating in said house", the defendant falsely and fraudulently concealed from the plaintiff its true condition; that the plaintiff at the time of his purchase had no knowledge of the termites, exercised due care thereafter, and learned of them about August 30, 1940; and that, because of the destruction that was being done and the dangerous condition that was being created by the termites, the plaintiff was put to great expense for repairs and for the installation of termite control in order to prevent the loss and destruction of said house.

The charge is concealment and nothing more; and it is concealment in the simple sense of mere failure to reveal, with nothing to show any peculiar duty to speak. The characterization of the concealment as false and fraudulent of course adds nothing in the absence of further allegations of fact.

If this defendant is liable on this declaration, every seller is liable who fails to disclose any nonapparent defect known to him in the subject of the sale which materially reduces its value and which the buyer fails to discover. Similarly it would seem that every buyer would be liable who fails to disclose any nonapparent virtue known to him in the subject of the purchase which materially enhances its value and of which the seller is ignorant. The law has not yet, we believe, reached the point of imposing upon the frailties of human nature a standard so idealistic as this. That the particular case here stated by the plaintiff possesses a certain appeal to the moral sense is scarcely to be denied. Probably the reason is to be found in the facts that the infestation of buildings by termites has not been common in Massachusetts and constitutes a concealed risk against which buyers are off their guard. But the law cannot provide special rules for termites and can hardly attempt to determine liability according to the varying probabilities of the existence and discovery of different possible defects in the subjects of trade. The rule of nonliability for bare nondisclosure has been stated and followed by this court.

ZIMMERMAN v. NORTHFIELD REAL ESTATE, INC.

Illinois Appellate Court
December 31, 1986

Plaintiffs Irving R. and Geraldine C. Zimmerman purchased a single family residence and later discovered that the lot size was smaller than they had thought, and that the house had numerous defects. Plaintiffs filed this action, alleging fraud, negligent misrepresentation, and certain statutory violations, against defendants Northfield Real Estate, Inc. and its agent Ellen A. Reed (brokers), and sellers William Dunn and Mary Lou Dunn, who is now known as Mary Lou Steinbach.

The complaint alleges that during the period of April to October 1983, plaintiffs visited the sellers' home in Northfield, Illinois several times. In October 1983, plaintiffs signed a contract with the sellers agreeing to pay $325,000 for the home. The contract included an exculpatory clause:

"10(j). Purchaser acknowledges for the benefit of Seller and for the benefit of third parties that neither the Seller, broker nor any of their agents have made any representations with respect to any material fact relating to the real estate, its improvements and included personal property unless such representations are in writing and further that Purchaser has made such investigations as Purchaser deems necessary or appropriate to satisfy Purchaser that there has been no deception, fraud, false pretenses, misrepresentations, concealments, suppressions or omission of any material fact by the Seller, the Broker, or any of their agents relating to the real estate, its improvements and included personal property."

The requisite elements of a common law fraud case of action are that a false statement of material fact was intentionally made; that the party to whom the statement was made had a right to rely on it and did so; that the statement was made for the purpose of inducing the other party to act; and that reliance by the person to whom the statement was made led to his injury. Intentional concealment of a material fact is the equivalent of a false statement of material fact. Where a person has a duty to speak, his failure to disclose material information constitutes fraudulent concealment.

The complaint alleges that defendants intentionally concealed, or made statements in regard to, material facts. The complaint alleges that defendant knew the lot size was less than one acre; knew the bathtubs and plumbing drain tile system did not work properly; knew the basement had four or five leaks; knew the south and east walls were badly deteriorated by moisture; knew the living room wall contained a substantial hole; and knew the basement had suffered massive flooding of up to four feet of water.

The complaint alleged that the brokers had a duty to speak regarding material information of which they had knowledge. Realtors have a duty to disclose material facts under the Real Estate Brokers and Salesmen License Act. Real estate brokers and salespersons occupy a position of trust with respect to purchasers with whom they are negotiating and owe a duty to exercise good faith in their dealing with such purchasers even absent the existence of an agency relationship. Thus, the brokers' silence may constitute fraudulent concealment of material facts. The broker defendants had a duty to disclose the massive flooding problems and the actual lot size. Concealment or misrepresentation of these material facts was fraudulent. Whether the brokers had knowledge of other claimed patent defects may be adduced at trial.

Plaintiffs allege that the omissions and false statements were of material facts. A misrepresentation is material and therefore actionable if it relates to a matter upon which plaintiff could be expected to rely in determining whether to engage in the conduct in question. Here, in deciding whether to buy the home, plaintiffs could be expected to rely upon representations and omissions regarding matters relating to lot size, flooding, leaks and other defects in the home, and thus the matters are material. Defendants refer to the massive flooding

which neighbors call "Dunn's Lake" as a mere "puddling." Defendants also refer to the 40% lot size difference as "somewhat smaller' and as being "not incorrect by much." We find defendants' characterizations unpersuasive.

The complaint alleges that plaintiffs relied on the statements or silence and thereby acted to their detriment. Plaintiffs discovered the defects after signing a contract of sale, making a downpayment, and taking possession. Plaintiffs also sufficiently allege that the statements were made for the purpose of inducing them to buy the house. A party is considered to intend the necessary consequences of his own acts. As a proximate result of these affirmative misrepresentations, concealments and omissions, plaintiffs allege they were required to spend large sums to cure the physical defects and that they now own a lot worth considerably less than the sale price because of the lot size which measured 40% less than the one acre advertised. Thus, we find the complaint states a cause of action for fraud against both the broker defendants and seller defendants.

A plaintiff may recover solely economic losses in tort against those in the business of supplying information for the guidance of others in their business transactions. Realtors are in the business of supplying such information. Consequently, plaintiffs may recover economic losses from the broker defendants.

Defendants maintain, in regard to the fraud count, that plaintiffs' reliance was unreasonable. Steinbach contends that her statement to plaintiffs that the basement had one leak "effectively disclosed the existence of the flooding problem." Using the Titanic as an example, she argues that it is the quantity of water leakage, not the number of leaks, which is important. The statement, that only one leak existed, however, may have left the buyers with a false sense of security. Where a plaintiff's inquiries are inhibited by a defendant's statements which create a false sense of security, the plaintiff's failure to investigate further is not fatal. A person may not enter into a transaction with his eyes closed to available information. Steinbach argues that plaintiffs did not "seek to look behind the [basement wall] panelling which covered the disclosed defects." We find these arguments to be without merit. We cannot say as a matter of law that plaintiffs closed their eyes to available information by not ripping down the panelling in an effort to discover the true extent of the leakage and flooding damage after defendant told them there was only one leak. Furthermore, even if plaintiffs were guilty of failing to insist on verification of the size of the lot an condition of the home, the cause of action stated in court I is for fraud, an intention tort, and defendants' liability generally cannot be defeated by an assertion of plaintiffs' negligence once plaintiffs show they had a right to rely on the misrepresentations.

Defendants argue further that plaintiffs were not justified in relying on the statements and omissions at issue in regard to the negligence count. Whether an injured party justifiably relied upon defendants' words or silence depends on the surrounding circumstances. A party is not justified in relying on representations made when he had an ample opportunity to ascertain the truth of the representations. The question of whether defendants had a right to rely on the broker defendants' representations and omissions regarding the size of the lot and the defects in the home must be answered in light of all of the facts which plaintiffs had actual knowledge of as well as those which

they might have discovered by the exercise of ordinary prudence. Under the circumstances presented here, the issue of reasonable reliance is for the trier of fact. Reasonable inferences from the complaint are insufficient to find that an ordinary inspection would not have disclosed the defects at issue here.

We acknowledge defendants' contention that plaintiffs had a copy of the property survey. The survey, however, tells a purchaser very little because it does not give square foot information, and a typical buyer cannot read the survey language. Furthermore, defendants' argument that plaintiffs received the lot they sought, according to the property's legal description of the boundaries, is a matter for the trier of fact.

[W]e hold that plaintiffs have pleaded legally recognized causes of action against the broker defendants for common law fraud; common law negligence; violations of the Consumer Fraud Act; and violations of the Broker Licensing Act. The trial court erred in dismissing counts I, II, III and IV as to the broker defendants. Plaintiffs have pleaded a legally recognized cause of action against the seller defendants for common law fraud, and the trial court properly denied the motion to dismiss that count.

QUESTIONS FOR ANALYSIS

What is the rule of law in *Swinton?* In *Zimmerman?* Can you reconcile the results in the cases? Why do you think the decisions are so diametrically opposed? Do you agree with both courts' opinions? Why?

Giving part of the truth creates a misleading impression and will constitute misrepresentation. The duty to disclose is clear.

Duty to Disclose: Fiduciaries

The duty to disclose is imposed on persons who are in **fiduciary relationships**. Persons who are in positions of trust, where other persons rely upon them to be truthful and honest, are required to disclose all information known to them. This relationship arises between partners, attorney and client, and trustee and beneficiary. A duty of utmost good faith and loyalty exists in a fiduciary relationship. In an ordinary situation, the duty to disclose certain information may not arise, but the reliance of a person on the fiduciary creates a special duty under these circumstances. Therefore, failure to disclose information will lay the foundation for a claim of misrepresentation.

A showing of misrepresentation forms the basis of recovery by a wronged party, the **plaintiff**, against the alleged wrongdoer, the **defendant**. The recovery can be in the form of money (legal damages), or in the form of an equitable remedy such as recission. When a contract is rescinded, the court basically turns back the hands of time and places the parties in the position they were in before the misrepresentation. In effect, by rescinding the contract, a court erases the obligations and duties of the parties—with one notable exception: the Defendant often pays for the injustice caused.

Because the element of intent can be difficult to prove, parties who are alleging that a contract lacks mutual assent because of fraud also often allege misrepresentation. If a party cannot prove the intent element necessary for a fraud case, that party may resort to showing that the statement was made innocently and prove misrepresentation. In this situation, recovery can be awarded by a court.

Mistake

Mistake is another common means to destroy mutual assent. **Mistake** occurs when the parties to a contract are wrong about some act or event that is material to the transaction. As with fraud or misrepresentation, one of the critical elements is the materiality of the mistaken facts. Ignorance of the law or illiteracy will not form a basis of mistake. The courts will hold such parties to the content of the agreement.

Courts distinguish between two types of mistakes: mutual mistake and unilateral mistake. For a contract to be set aside or rescinded, a mistake normally has to be mutual. In a unilateral mistake situation, courts normally will not rescind the contract, but will hold the parties to their duties and obligations.

Mutual Mistake

In a **mutual mistake**, both parties are wrong about a material fact of the transaction, and thus the court will often rescind the contract. Because there has not been a meeting of the minds, in that the parties to the contract have not agreed on the terms and conditions of the contract, a contract cannot be consummated. When mutual mistake is asserted, either party may renounce the contract, thus making the contract voidable. The *Restatement (Second) of Contracts* § 152 sets out three basic requirements to prove mutual mistake:

> (1) mistake must be made as to a basic assumption of the contract; (2) the mistake must have a material effect on the contract; and (3) the party requesting relief cannot bear the risk of the mistake in the contract.

TERMS

fiduciary relationship
A relationship between two persons in which one is obligated to act with the utmost good faith, honesty, and loyalty on behalf of the other.

plaintiff
A person who brings a lawsuit.

defendant
The person against whom an action is brought.

mistake
1. An erroneous mental conception that influences a person to act or to decline to act; an unintentional act, omission, or error arising from ignorance, surprise, imposition, or misplaced confidence. "Mistake" is a legal concept especially significant in contract law because, depending upon the circumstances, it may warrant reformation or rescission of a contract. 2. An error, a misunderstanding; an inaccuracy.

mutual mistake
A mistake of fact that is reciprocal and common to both parties to an agreement, each laboring under the same misconception with respect to a material fact. Such a mistake will justify reformation of the contract, and may warrant its rescission.

Taking each of the elements from the *Restatement* separately, the following should be analyzed in a mistake case.

1. *Mistake as to basic assumption of contract.* The legal requirement that the mistake must be made as to a basic assumption of the contract focuses on the subject matter of the contract and the parties' intentions. For example, if the parties are contracting for sale of a condominium in a Florida resort and the buyer assumes that the condominuim is on the beach and the seller assumes that the condominium at issue overlooks the parking lot, a basic assumption of the contract is misunderstood, creating the basis for a mistake.

2. *Mistake must have material effect on contract.* The next legal requirement, that the mistake must have a material effect on the contract, suggests that if the mistake does not go to the heart of the contract, a mistake will not be found. Continuing with the condominium example, if the buyer assumed that of the condominium was on the beach, whereas the seller thought a parking lot view was the subject of the sale, the mistake would have a direct effect on the contract. However, if two beachfront condominiums were for sale and the only difference between the units was the unit numbers, a mistake would not be found which would set aside the contract.

3. *Party requesting relief cannot bear risk of mistake in contract.* The final element is that the party requesting relief cannot bear the risk of the mistake in the contract. In this situation, the mistake cannot be by the party bringing the lawsuit. For example, if the buyer never looked at the condominiums and wrongfully assumed that the condominium was on the beach, then a mistake has not occurred.

If these elements are proven, mutual mistake exists. One of the most famous cases dealing with mutual mistake involves two men contracting for the sale of a cow. *Sherwood v. Walker,* 66 Mich. 568, 33 N.W. 919 (1887) illustrates the concept of mutual mistake.

SHERWOOD v. WALKER

Supreme Court of Michigan
July 7, 1887

The main controversy depends upon the construction of a contract for the sale of the cow. The Walkers are importers and breeders of polled Angus cattle. The plaintiff is a bankers living at Plymouth, in Wayne county. Meeting one of the defendants, he was informed that they had a few head upon their Greenfield farm. He was asked to go out and look at them, with the statement at the time that they were probably barren, and would not breed. May 5, 1886, plaintiff went out to Greenfield, and saw the cattle. A few days thereafter, he called upon one of the defendants with the view of purchasing a cow, known as "Rose 2d of Aberlone." After considerable talk, it was agreed that defendants would telephone Sherwood at his home in Plymouth in reference to the price. The second morning after this talk he was called up by telephone, and the terms of the sale were finally agreed upon. He was to pay five and one-half cents per pound, live weight, fifty pounds shrinkage. He was asked how he intended to take the cow home, and replied that he might ship her from King's cattle-yard. He requested defendants to confirm the sale in writing, which they did by sending him a letter.

On the twenty-first of the same month the plaintiff went to defendants' farm at Greenfield, and presented the order and letter to Graham, who informed him that the defendants had instructed him not to deliver the cow. Soon after, the plaintiff tendered to Hiram Walker, one of the defendants, $80, and demanded the cow. Walker refused to take the money or deliver the cow. The plaintiff then instituted this suit. After he had secured possession of the cow under the writ of replevin, the plaintiff caused her to be weighed by the constable who served the writ, at a place other than King's cattle-yard. She weighed 1,420 pounds. The defendants then introduced evidence tending to show that at the time of the alleged sale it was believed by both the plaintiff and themselves that the cow was barren and would not breed; that she cost $850, and if not barren would be worth from $750 to $1,000; that after the date of the letter, and the order to Graham, the defendants were informed by said Graham that in his judgment the cow was with calf, and therefore they instructed him not to deliver her to plaintiff, and on the twentieth of May, 1886, telegraphed plaintiff what Graham thought about the cow being with calf, and that consequently they could not sell her.

Plaintiff explained the mention of the two cows in [his own] letter by testifying that, when he wrote this letter, the order and letter of defendants was at his home, and, writing in a hurry, and being uncertain as to the name of the cow, and not wishing his cow watered, he thought it would do no harm to name them both, as his bill of sale would show which one he had purchased. Plaintiff also testified that he asked defendants to give him a price on the balance of their herd at Greenfield, as a friend thought of buying some, and received a letter dated May 17, 1886, in which they named the price of five cattle, including Lucy, at $90, and

Rose 2d at $80. When he received the letter he called defendants up by telephone, and asked them why they put Rose 2d in the list, as he had already purchased her. They replied that they knew he had, but thought it would make no difference if plaintiff and his friend concluded to take the whole herd.

It appears from the record that both parties supposed this cow was barren and would not breed, and she was sold by the pound for an insignificant sum as compared with her real value if a breeder. She was evidently sold and purchased on the relation of her value for beef, unless the plaintiff had learned of her true condition, and concealed such knowledge from the defendants. Before the plaintiff secured the possession of the animal, the defendants learned that she was with calf, and therefore of great value, and undertook to rescind the sale by refusing to deliver her.

It must be considered as well settled that a party who has given an apparent consent to a contract of sale may refuse to execute it, or he may avoid it after it has been completed, if the assent was founded, or the contract made, upon the mistake of a material fact,—such as the subject-matter of the sale, the price, or some collateral fact materially inducing the agreement; and this can be done when the mistake is mutual.

If there is a difference or misapprehension as to the substance of the thing bargained for; if the thing actually delivered or received is different in substance from the thing bargained for, and intended to be sold,—then there is no contract; but if it be only a difference in some quality or accident, even though the mistake may have been the actuating motive to the purchaser or seller, or both of them, yet the contract remains binding. "The difficulty in every case is to determine whether the mistake or misapprehension is as to the substance of the whole contract, going, as it were, to the root of the matter, or only to some point, even though a material point, an error as to which does not affect the substance of the whole consideration."

[In] the case made by this record, the mistake or misapprehension of the parties went to the whole substance of the agreement. If the cow was a breeder, she was worth at least $750; if barren, she was worth not over $80. The parties would not have made the contract of sale except upon the understanding and belief that she was incapable of breeding, and of no use as a cow. It is true she is now the identical animal that they thought her to be when the contract was made; there is no mistake as to the identity of the creature. Yet the mistake was not of the mere quality of the animal, but went to the very nature of the thing. A barren cow is substantially a different creature than a breeding one. If the mutual mistake had simply related to the fact whether she was with calf or not for one season, then it might have been a good sale, but the mistake affected the character of the animal for all time, and for its present and ultimate use. She was not in fact the animal, or the kind of animal, the defendants intended to sell or the plaintiff to buy. She was not a barren cow, and, if this fact had been known, there would have been no contract. The mistake affected the substance of the whole consideration, and it must be considered that there was no contract to sell or sale of the cow as she actually was. The thing sold and bought had in fact no existence. She was sold as a beef creature would be sold; she is in fact a breeding cow, and a valuable one. The court should have instructed the jury that if they found that the cow was sold, or contracted to be sold, upon the understanding of both parties that she was barren, and useless for the purpose of breeding, and that in fact she was not barren, but capable of breeding, then the defendants had a right to rescind, and to refuse to deliver, and the verdict should be in their favor.

QUESTIONS FOR ANALYSIS

What is the definition of *mutual mistake?* Did the parties have a true understanding of the transaction and have a meeting of the minds? If not, what was the basis of the mistake?

Unilateral Mistake

The situation is different for a **unilateral mistake**, a common basis for wishing to set aside a contract. In a unilateral mistake case, only one party is mistaken about a material fact to the transaction. Traditionally, a court will not rescind a contract based on unilateral mistake. There are some exceptions to this rule, but courts rescind contracts based upon unilateral mistakes sparingly.

For unilateral mistake, *Restatement (Second) of Contracts* § 153 adds requirement to those set out under mutual mistake: "enforcement of the contract would be unconscionable *or* the other party (the one not claiming mistake) had reason to know of the mistake *or* the noncomplaining party caused the mistake." If a party can prove all the requirements under § 153 of the *Restatement,* a contract can be voidable based upon unilateral mistake.

Proving unilateral mistake is difficult and, as a result, courts take care in using unilateral mistake as a basis to cancel contracts. A few years ago, a controversy arose when a leading food manufacturer ran a contest for the general public. Coupons were printed up with different prizes, with one of the grand prizes being a van. To win, a contestant needed to match a front half of a van to a back of the van. Supposedly, only a limited number of cards made a complete van. Unbeknownst to the manufacturer, the printer mistakenly printed too many winning tickets. When numerous contestants won and attempted to claim the prizes, the company refused, stating that there had been a mistake and offered small sums of cash instead. Was a contract created? Yes. Was there a basis to void the contract? No. The manufacturer could allege mistake, but it would have been unilateral.

Duress

Duress is another means to avoid a contract. Duress is wrongful pressure placed upon a person so as to deprive him or her of free will. For a duress action to be sustained, specific elements must be proven. The party alleging duress must show that the pressure or force asserted was extreme and that, had the pressure not been exerted, the party would not have entered into the transaction.

Coercion

Duress is difficult to prove, as it must go beyond a mere threat or overcoming of a party's free will. In a duress case, the pressure must be such that the conduct is extreme and not merely that the party was vulnerable. Coercion is a key element to a duress case.

Assume that you visit your dentist to have a tooth capped and you receive an injection of an anesthetic. You have an allergic reaction to the anesthetic which later causes dizziness and blotching on your skin. The doctor caps your tooth and you leave. You find out from a friend that other people have had similar reactions to and symptoms from such injections. Two months later, you bite into a candy bar and crack the dental work so that the cap falls out. You do not want to go back to the same dentist, but you cannot afford to go to another dentist. You contact the dentist and ask for a refund of the payment. The dentist refuses unless you sign a release of liability. Because you do not have the money and you want to go to another dentist, you sign the document. This may be a case of duress, if it can be shown that the doctor placed undue pressure on you to sign the release to get a refund and have the dental work repaired.

Four situations generally give rise to a duress case (Figure 3-3). First, when a party threatens another party with violence, duress exists. If you are a parent and someone holds a gun to your child's head and states, "Unless you sign this contract, I will shoot your child," duress exists. Secondly, threats of imprisonment can create inordinate pressure on someone, destroying free will. For example, your spouse threatens that if you do not sign this decree of divorce giving up custody of the children, assault charges will be filed. This form of coercion may create duress. Thirdly, a claim for duress arises when a party threatens to take or keep another person's property. Here one party wrongfully asserts a claim against a person's property to extract a contractual advantage.

Finally, duress can be alleged when a party threatens to breach a contract. This may occur when a party is dissatisfied with a contract and attempts to use leverage to modify or change the contract terms by threatening

TERMS

unilateral mistake
A misconception by one, but not both, parties to a contract with respect to the terms of the contract.

duress
Coercion applied for the purpose of compelling a person to do, or to refrain from doing, some act.

Duress
1. Threat of violence
2. Threat of physical imprisonment
3. Threat to take/keep personal property
4. Threat to breach contract

FIGURE 3-3 Elements of duress

a breach. A California case illustrates this issue. One of the stars of the movie *Problem Child II* demanded, during shooting, that his salary for starring in the role be raised from $80,000 to $500,000. The actor threatened to walk off the set and stop production if the contract price was not raised. The studio agreed, but later sued alleging duress. The studio won. The jury returned a verdict of duress; the studio only had to pay the original contract terms, and the young actor had to repay the excess amount.

A new form of duress, known as *economic duress* has developed, but it is *very* difficult to prove. Economic duress occurs when:

1. wrongful or unlawful conduct exists;
2. causing financial hardship;
3. when an injured party acts against his or her free will;
4. causing economic detriment to himself or herself; and
5. no immediate legal remedy exists.

Courts find economic duress in limited situations. This defense should be used sparingly. See if you agree with the court's decision as to whether economic duress existed in *St. Louis Park Investment Co. v. R.L. Johnson Investment Co.*, 411 N.W.2d 288 (Minn. 1987).

ST. LOUIS PARK INVESTMENT CO. v. R.L. JOHNSON INVESTMENT COMPANY, INC.

Court of Appeals of Minnesota
Sept. 1, 1987

In July 1984, Twinco Automotive Warehouse, Inc. and respondent R.L. Johnson Investment Company entered into a purchase agreement. Shortly thereafter, appellant St. Louis Park Investment Company received an assignment of Twinco's interest in the purchase agreement. The parties agreed to convey the property by a contract for deed and to close on August 31, 1984.

Office space located on the property totalled approximately 5000 square feet, with a tenant, SPS Companies, occupying about 2750 square feet. During negotiations, appellant stressed that its then current lease ended September 30, 1984, and that it required the full 5000 square feet of office space by the closing date.

As a result, the parties included a provision in the purchase agreement requiring respondent to obtain SPS Company's early release from the lease. If respondent failed to obtain the release, it was obligated under the provision to construct an additional 2750 square feet of office space to accommodate appellant. The provision did not state the exact date respondent was required to obtain the early release. The provision further specified that no tenant other than SPS Companies could occupy the property at the time of closing. One day before the eventual September 6, 1984 closing date, respondent obtained a release from SPS Companies terminating its lease as of October 31, 1984.

Prior to closing, appellant's counsel had sent respondent's counsel a proposed draft of the contract for deed, which included language stating that the purchase agreement and its provisions would survive the contract for deed and continue in full effect during the contract for deed term. Respondent's counsel objected to those terms, and executed and delivered at closing a contract that excluded the survival language.

At closing, appellant's counsel objected to the delayed termination of the SPS lease on October 31 as opposed to the August 31, 1984 closing date. He claimed that because the SPS lease did not terminate as of August 31, 1984, respondent was required under the purchase agreement to construct the additional office space. Respondent and its counsel claimed they were not obligated because they had complied with the purchase agreement by terminating the SPS lease early. Respondent refused to close under the terms sought by appellant. After consultation, appellant and its counsel decided to close, and executed the contract for deed drafter by respondent's attorney. No additional terms were preserved except as set forth in the contract for deed. The contract for deed thus contained no language regarding the construction of additional office space, or any language extending the effect of the purchase agreement. Respondent asserts that at no time did appellant or its counsel that they were closing under protest. Appellant, on the other hand, claims it was forced to close under protest because of the need to take possession of the property before it was required to move from its then current location by September 30, 1984.

A few days after the closing, appellant again demanded that respondent construct the additional office space. After respondent refused, appellant constructed the additional office space and initiated this action, claiming economic duress in connection with the purchase and sale of the property.

Appellant claims there is a genuine issue of material fact that it was subject to economic duress. Economic duress or business compulsion generally is defined as wrongful or unlawful conduct resulting in the pressure of a business necessity or financial hardship, which compels the injured party to execute an agreement against their will and to their economic detriment. The injured party must have no immediate legal remedy. Merely driving a hard bargain or wresting advantage of another's financial difficulty is not duress.

Although a significant number of jurisdictions have recognized duress under the more specific categories of "economic durress" or "business compulsion," Minnesota has yet to address the theory. Minnesota courts only recognize duress as a defense to a contract when there is coercion by means of physical force or unlawful threats, which destroys one's free will and compels compliance with the demands of the party exerting the coercion. In addition, a claim of duress will not be sustained when the claimant entered into the contract with full knowledge of all the facts, advice from an attorney, and ample time for reflection. Because appellant executed the deed willingly after consultation with an attorney and was not subjected to physical force or unlawful threats, we find there is no issue of material fact relating to duress as defined by the Minnesota Supreme Court.

QUESTIONS FOR ANALYSIS

How did the court define *economic duress?* Do you believe that the decision was fair? What facts were critical to the court's decision?

Undue Influence

Undue influence is yet another method of destroying mutual assent. Closely related to duress, the significant difference is that undue influence arises out of a confidential relationship. Undue influence occurs when a party who is in a position of trust unduly uses that position to gain advantages over a person who is in a weakened position. Undue influence can be a common problem with the sick and elderly. Quite often, caretakers unduly influence weakened persons and extract monetary advantages from them. This can also occur within family relationships, as when one sibling influences a parent to disinherit another sibling in an attempt to extract inordinant monetary gain in the parent's will. When undue influence is alleged, courts look very closely at the method used by the dominant person and the circumstances surrounding the contract. How weakened or susceptible was the person? What is the relationship between the parties?

Another area in which undue influence cases are common is fiduciary relationships. As with a misrepresentation case, this often occurs between a trustee and beneficiaries, partners in a partnership, officers and shareholders in a corporation, and even in the legal profession between lawyers and clients. When these types of legal relationships are created, courts pay close attention to the acts of the fiduciary. What the court normally looks for is an unnatural disposition by a beneficiary to a trustee or to a person who is in a clearly controlling position, like an attorney; or by a sickly person. When an individual can show that undue influence occurred, the court can set aside the contract and void it. Look at *Russo v. Jaydan Associates,* 559 A.2d 354 (Me. 1989), in which the central issue was undue influence.

TERMS

undue influence
Inappropriate pressure exerted on a person for the purpose of causing him or her to substitute his or her will for he will or wishes of another. Undue influence is a form of coercion to which the aged or infirm are particularly vulnerable, especially at the hands of a person whom they feel they have reason to trust.

RUSSO v. JAYDAN ASSOCIATES

Supreme Judicial Court of Maine
June 1, 1989

In 1958 or 1959, seller's parents purchased property consisting of approximately 12 acres of land in Scarborough. Seller acquired title to the property over ten years ago. A structure consisting of two rooms and a bath, is situated on the property and has served as a residence either for seller's parents or for seller since the property was purchased. Seller has a long history of psychiatric illness. She has suffered from fear and depression for at least twenty years and has manifested suicidal tendencies for at least ten years. In 1987, she was diagnosed as a manic depressive personality. Seller's

psychiatrist testified that seller's personality structure and coping skills might render her particularly susceptible to a neighbor's plea.

Seller was admitted to Jackson Brook Institute on September 26, 1985 after she had intentionally taken an overdose of Valium and an anti-anxiety medication. During her stay at Jackson Brook, seller met a patient named Barry Salaman with whom she shared certain interests. Both had always wanted to live on a farm and raise horses. Salaman told seller he knew of a farm "way up north." As a result of those conversations, seller, for the first time, considered selling her property in order to put a down payment on that farm.

Seller was discharged from Jackson Brook on October 9, 1985 and returned home. During the two weeks immediately following her discharge from the hospital, seller was visited four or five times by Marlis Goldschmidt, a neighbor and acquaintance who was aware of seller's psychiatric problems. During one of the visits, Marlis mentioned that she desperately needed to purchase a piece of land. Seller was sympathetic and ultimately agreed to sell Marlis two and one half acres of her property for $5000. Marlis's husband, Donald, worked with James Miller, one of the buyers, in the painting business. In the fall of 1985, James and Daniel Miller formed a real estate partnership known as Jaydan Associates. Marlis had suggested to seller that she sell the remaining land to make a "good life" for herself and Salaman had continued to call seller to discuss the possibility of purchasing a farm "up north." Marlis told seller that her remaining land was worth approximately $25,000 to $30,000.

On November 7, 1985, buyers met seller through Marlis and Donald Goldschmidt. James Miller knew that seller had problems and that she had been hospitalized at Jackson Brook, although he didn't realize the extent of her difficulties. Buyers and seller signed a handwritten contract drafted by Daniel Miller the very day they met. Seller set the terms of the sale and insisted that the parties conclude the agreement immediately. The contract reflects a purchase price of $25,000, with $1000 payable upon the signing of the contract and $9000 payable at closing which was to occur on or before December 1, 1985. The balance was payable in monthly installments of $300. The parties also agreed that seller might remain on the property until May of 1986. On November 9, the parties executed a typewritten contract, the terms of which were identical to those in the original contract. The parties closed the transaction on November 15, 1985. After receiving the $10,000 payment, seller gave Salaman $3200 which he told her he needed to make a down payment on the horse farm up state. With the balance of the money she paid off a bank loan, and "blew" the rest.

At no point in these transactions did seller consult an attorney, a real estate broker, or an appraiser. In fact, she discussed the sales and the value of the land with Marlis Goldschmidt only. When asked, seller told counsel she was signing the deed of her own free will. After the transaction was concluded, buyers paid the Goldschmidts a finder's fee of $500.

The trial justice found that the conveyance of the eight acre parcel from seller to buyer resulting from undue influence. The justice stated as follows:

> Ms. Russo, given her longstanding psychological problems, frequent commitments and heavy medication, was subject to undue influence by a combination of the person she met at Jackson Brook, the Goldschmidts, and, to a much lesser extent, James and Daniel Miller. She was the victim of people who had an opportunity and good position to exercise undue influence over her for a clearly improper purpose. The result of this undue influence is dramatically evidenced by the sale of her property for an unusually low price.

A party asserting undue influence must prove that claim by clear and convincing evidence. Thus far, claims of undue influence in Maine have arisen in the context of will disputes. We defined the doctrine in the following terms:

> By undue influence . . . is meant influence, in connection with the execution of the will and operating at the time the will is made, amounting to moral coercion, destroying free agency, or importunity which could not be resisted, so that the testator, unable to withstand the influence, or too weak to resist it, was constrained to do that which was not his actual will but against it.
> Undue influence often closely resembles and is near akin to actual fraud. But strictly speaking it is not synonomous with fraud. In the making of a will, undue influence is exerted, where the mind of the nominal maker of the document, in yielding to the dominancy and supervision of another's designing mind, does what otherwise the ostensible actor would not have done. . . . The influence must arise either from proof or presumption of law. It is never inferred from mere opportunity or interest,

though these facts if shown should weigh with other facts. But kindness, entreaty, the offer of inducement to gain the making of a will in one's favor, is legitimate, so long as he who made the will had the free choice to make it or not.

We have previously identified a number of factors that bear upon the question of undue influence. [W]e stated that the existence of a confidential relationship between the testator and the individual who allegedly influenced him and the fact that the testator disposed of his property in an unnatural or unexpected manner are "prominent among the circumstances which have been taken as evidence of undue influence." Proof of such circumstances permits an inference of undue influence. This inference may be strengthened by evidence of mental infirmity. In addition, whether or not the testator had independent legal advice is a factor to consider in evaluating whether the will was the product of undue influence.

The Restatement of Contracts has comprehensively defined the doctrine as follows:

(1) Undue influence is unfair persuasion of a party who is under the domination of the person exercising the persuasion or who by virtue of the relation between them is justified in assuming that that person will not act in a manner inconsistent with his welfare.

(2) If a party's manifestation of assent is induced by undue influence by the other party, the contract is voidable by the victim.

(3) If a party's manifestation of assent is induced by one who is not a party to the transaction, the contract is voidable by the victim unless the other party to the transaction in good faith and without reason to know of the undue influence either gives value or relies materially on the transaction.

We adopt the Restatement formulation and find sufficient evidence to support the application of the doctrine in this case. [W]e conclude that the record supports findings (1) that on the basis of the relation between seller and Marlis Goldschmidt, seller was justified in assuming that the Goldschmidts would not act in a manner inconsistent with her welfare, and (2) that the Goldschmidts acted as the undisclosed agents of the buyers. Given the existence of the required relationship between buyers and seller, the record provides evidence of circumstances supporting the Superior Court's assumed finding that the sale was "produced by means that seriously impaired the free and competent exercise of judgment." In this regard, the court appropriately considered the unfairness of the sale price, the absence of independent advice and counsel, and the susceptibility of seller as heightened by her mental infirmity. Although none of these circumstances standing alone is determinative, taken together, they amply support the judgment of the Superior Court.

QUESTIONS FOR ANALYSIS

What definition of undue influence was relied upon? What facts were central to the court's decision? Was the court's holding fair? Why or why not?

Unconscionability

All contracts impose upon each party the duty to act in good faith and to deal fairly. When contracts are grossly unfair as to the performance or enforcement of one party, the issue of unconscionability may arise. An *unconscionable contract* is one that shocks public sensibilities and is unreasonably oppressive. Basically, such a contract results when the parties' bargaining positions are so unequal that the public is best protected by invalidating the contract, due to the oppressive and shocking nature of the bargain.

Although the doctrine of unconscionability dates back hundreds of years, the defense of unconscionability gained new momentum in the 1970s, as a movement to protect consumers grew. The key element to proving that a contract is unconscionable is the showing of a lack of meaningful assent to the contract by a party claiming the defense and showing that the party affected truly did not understand the terms and conditions of the contract or had no choice, destroying mutual assent.

Unconscionability has been segmented into two areas: procedural unconscionability and substantive unconscionability. Each type deals with the contract process.

Procedural Unconscionability

When there is no meaningful choice by one party who enters into a contract, procedural unconscionability may exist. The key is in the party's assent to the contract. In forming the contract, the party is forced to enter into the contract without the ability to change, alter, or modify its terms. Nonnegotiable clauses, often referred to an **boilerplate** provisions, are tucked away in the contract, and the contracting party is in a "take it or leave it" position. Sometimes procedural unconscionability can occur when a high-pressure salesperson misleads consumers.

Restatement Second § 208 gives some guidance in determining procedural unconscionability. The *Restatement* suggests that unconscionability can be found if there is:

1. A belief by the stronger party that there is no reasonable probability that the weaker party will fully perform;
2. Knowledge of the stronger party that the weaker will be unable to receive substantial benefits from the contract;
3. Knowledge of the stronger party that the weaker party is unable reasonably to protect his or her interest by reason of physical or mental infirmities, ignorance, illiteracy, or inability to understand the language of the agreement.

As with most reasons for destroying mutual assent, a judge or jury will have to determine whether procedural unconscionability exists. Courts will look at the effect of the contract on the party who was restricted in contributing to the bargaining process.

Adhesion Contracts   Some courts have termed unconscionable contracts to be contracts of adhesion. **Adhesion contracts** are ones where one party to the contract is able to impose its will on another party, leaving no mutuality of assent between the parties. Some have termed this a kind of **overreaching**. These kinds of contracts violate public policy and are usually set aside to protect the public good. What is key in understanding adhesion contracts is that these types of contracts are not open to negotiation. The offeree must take the terms as they are or forgo entering into the contract. This

TERMS

boilerplate
Language common to all legal documents of the same type. Attorneys maintain files of such standardized language for use where appropriate.

adhesion contract
A contract prepared by the dominant party (usually a form contract) and presented on a take-it-or-leave-it basis to the weaker party, who has no real opportunity to bargain about its terms.

overreaching
Taking unfair advantage in bargaining.

clearly puts the offeror at an unfair advantage and basically takes all aspects of mutual assent away from the contract.

Often adhesion contracts are standardized. They are preprinted, non-negotiated contracts whose terms are set in stone except for the parties, price, quantity, and length of payment. Otherwise, each term is set. Characteristics found in some adhesion contracts are *very* small type (the "fine print"), unclear or ambiguous terminology, or overly complex language that clearly favors the drafter.

Not all adhesion contracts are unconscionable, however. The court will review the totality of the circumstances surrounding the contract. Was there a gross disparity of bargaining powers? Did the party claiming an adhesion contract make any contribution to the bargaining process? Was there really mutual assent? If courts respond negatively to such questions, a contract of adhesion may be found.

The common thread winding through adhesion and unconscionability in contracts is the courts' attempt to protect the public welfare. Public policy is served by not allowing one party to unfairly benefit from a contract when the other party could not really participate in the contracting process.

Substantive Unconscionability

Oppressive or overly harsh contracts are *substantively unconscionable*. This type of unconscionability often occurs with excessive price terms or unfair alterations in a party's remedies for breach of contract.

Substantive unconscionability is prevalent in **installment contracts**. Here a party pays, over a period of time, a purchase price with accrued interest and charges on an item bought. Often the interest charges and fees are three to four times the actual price paid or the actual value of the items purchased. Courts have held that this is unconscionable and a basis for voiding the contract.

The other area where substantive unconscionability becomes a factor is in the remedies afforded a purchaser upon default under a contract. Here the individual or entity controlling contract terms expands its rights while diminishing the other party's rights. Courts have deemed this unfair and often refuse to enforce such contracts. Courts also have the option of excising the unconscionable clause to balance the contract's effect on the parties. The focus of the court's actions is always principles of fairness.

3.3 PRACTICAL APPLICATION

Questions as to fraud and misrepresentation do not often jump off the pages of a contract, crying for investigation. Rather, facts develop which suggest that parties have not been honest in their dealings. As a paralegal, you may be asked to investigate circumstances in which fraud or misrepresentation may have occurred. Similarly, in a duress or undue influence case, the issues do not jump out at you—they require analysis and examination.

Along with your attorney, always ask questions and probe into the minds of the parties to the contract to determine if the mutual assent has been destroyed. Often, it is a slow, deliberate process.

Mistake is a bit different. Mistake often appears on the face of the contract, such as in the price or quantity term; these are usually clerical errors. To avoid this problem, thoroughly check contracts for mathematical, typographical, and spelling errors. If it is your job to check figures and proofread, do so carefully. Any legal professional's nightmare is missing a critical word (like omitting the "not" from "shall not") and thus changing the entire meaning of the contract.

The paralegal should pay special attention to provisions that appear too one-sided and thus might be unconscionable. Provisions that should be closely watched are default, remedy, and interest provisions. Courts scrutinize these provisions closely, and they are often litigated. This section gives some examples of provisions that have been determined ineffective by some courts. The key in evaluating a provision is whether its effect is a punishment and whether the parties had freedom in the negotiating process.

Default Provisions

When a party does not perform its obligations under a contract, that party is in default. Virtually all contracts have default provisions. To analyze the validity of a default provision, determine what effect the provision has on the defaulting party. Is the provision harsh and offensive and therefore unconscionable?

Examine the following default provisions.

---

1.   In the event of a default of any kind, I hereby agree that the entire lease shall be accelerated and I shall be liable thereon for all past due principal payments, all accelerated payments, interest thereon at the rate of fifteen 15% per annum, costs, and all other related charges, together with attorney's fees in the amount of one-third of the total accelerated amount under the lease.

2.   Upon the occurrence of an event of default and at any time thereafter, Lessor, in addition to any other rights and remedies he may have, shall have the right to take possession of the equipment, whereupon Lessee's right to use the same under and subject to the terms and provision of this Lease, and any other right or interest of Lessee to or in the equipment, shall absolutely cease, but *such taking by Lessor shall not relieve Lessee of its obligations and liabilities hereunder.*

The effect is that a default, no matter how minor, will have an unconscionable result. Courts have held that such default provisions are invalid. When drafting, pay close attention to the cumulative effects of default provisions.

Also, review provisions for excessive fees and charges. Again, courts will look to the cumulative effect of the clause: if it is clearly oppressive,

TERMS

installment contract
A contract that requires or authorizes the delivery of goods in separate lots.

and if accumulated could surpass the amount of the money borrowed and interest charged, the clause would probably be rendered unconscionable.

Interest Provisions

Provisions charging interest are very standard in contracts. The interest charged or the cumulative effect of an interest charge must be analyzed closely to determine if the interest charged is too high. Laws set limits on interest, and excessive rates are usurious and unenforceable. Review interest provisions carefully and look at their total effect. For a more in-depth discussion on interest, see Chapter 6.

Remedy Provisions

When one party's remedies are too limited, courts often hold the limiting provisions unconscionable. In such cases, one party excludes all possible remedies for another party that has been unable to perform its contractual obligations, rendering the contract too one-sided and invalid. Examine the following provisions:

---

1. The buyer's limit for breach of performance by the seller shall be limited to the difference between the contract price and the fair market value at the time of the breach, and in no event is the buyer entitled to lost profits, consequential or punitive damages of any kind.

2. In the event of a breach of performance, the party shall only be entitled to the purchase price of the product purchased. This shall be the buyer's sole remedy and shall be in lieu of any other claims for incidental or consequential damages.

3. In no event shall the harmed party be entitled to recover for incidental or consequential damages, including but not limited to loss of profits, inconvenience, replacement of the product, or other loss thereof.

Most of these provisions limit the possible recovery for one party in a contract and could be held unconscionable by a court. When provisions are too oppressive, the party preparing the contract will suffer the consequence, which is often rescission.

This section presents a small sampling of provisions that might be deemed unconscionable. As a paralegal, your job will be to assist your attorney in making sure that the contract provisions drafted are enforceable by a court, if challenged, and that the contract is not unfair or overly harsh.

SUMMARY

3.1   Mutual assent is a necessary element of a contract. It is found when the parties have the same understanding of the terms and conditions of the contract. Mutual assent can be destroyed by fraud, misrepresentation, mistake, duress, undue influence, and unconscionability.

3.2   One of the ways to destroy mutual assent is fraud. The main elements needed to prove a fraud case is that one party made a (1) misstatement of fact; (2) the fact was material to the contract; (3) the party had knowledge of the statement's falsity; (4) the party intended to deceive; (5) the other party relied on the misstatement of fact; and (6) the misstatement caused damage.

Closely related to fraud is misrepresentation, which is an innocent misstatement of fact not intended to deceive. Under misrepresentation cases, there may be a duty to disclose.

Mistake is another method to destroy mutual assent. There are two types of mistake: mutual and unilateral. Contracts can also be set aside based upon duress and undue influence. In either situation, a party is not acting freely when entering into the contract. Finally, unconscionable contracts, in which the terms are unfair and oppressive, may be set aside based upon public policy arguments. Adhesion contracts are types of unconscionable contracts.

REVIEW QUESTIONS

1. Define mutual assent.
2. How is mutual assent destroyed?
3. What is the definition of fraud?
4. What are the critical elements in proving a fraud case?
5. What is the distinguishing characteristic between fraud and misrepresentation?
6. Upon whom is the duty to disclose imposed?
7. List the different types of mistakes and their definitions.
8. What must be proven to avoid a contract in a duress case?
9. Identify the types of relationships that are scrutinized when the defense of undue influence is raised.
10. What are some of the instances in which court will set aside a contract based upon unconscionability? List the types of unconscionability.

EXERCISES

1. Locate a retail installment contract and review its contents to determine if all the provisions are fair. Write down any provisions that might be deemed unconscionable.
2. Review *Williams v. Walker-Thomas Furniture Co.,* 350 F.2d 445 (D.C. Cir. 1965).

    a. Identify the facts of the *Williams* case.

    b. What is the issue before the court?

    c. What is the rule of law from the case?

    d. Summarize the dissent.

3. Lenny lives in Dallas and owns a 1985 Porsche 911. Lenny just got word that he is being transferred to New York City in two weeks. As everyone knows, owning a car in Manhattan is simply unbearable. With this in mind, Lenny places the following advertisement in the newspaper:

Must Sell Immediately—1985 Red Porsche 911.
Asking around $2,000.
Please call at 974-5060 or stop
by at 90125 Sunset Boulevard.

The following day, George, an auto mechanic, goes to Lenny's house with $2,000 cash. Upon arrival, George says, before Lenny has a chance to say anything, "Here's $2,000 cash; give me the keys to the car."

Lenny courteously replies, "I apologize for misleading you, but I inadvertently looked up the wrong price for my Porsche. What I accidently did was put the 1975 Blue Book price in my advertisement instead of the 1985 price. It was quite careless of me." Lenny continues, "The 1985 Blue Book price for a Porsche is $10,000, but since you came all the way down here and seem interested in the car, I will offer it to you for only $8,000."

George then grumbles defiantly, "No way, you said $2,000 in your advertisement and that is what I got right here. You are legally obligated to sell me that car for $2,000." Lenny declines to take the $2,000. Disgusted, George drives straight to his attorney's office seeking legal advice. It just so happens that George's attorney is also a senior partner in the firm in which you are a paralegal. Write a memo analyzing the legal issues in this case.

CHAPTER 4
Consideration: The Value for the Promise

4.1 THE NATURE OF CONSIDERATION

In any discussion of contracts, invariably the concept of consideration is debated. Everyone thinks they know what consideration is, but, as will be seen, it may not be what you think. In understanding consideration, let's establish a few ground rules. First, rid yourself of the notion that consideration is only money. It is *not* only money, as will be seen later in this chapter. Second, consideration deals with value; it is what the parties think is valuable, even if others do not. Consequently, think of consideration as something personal between the parties and look at the concept objectively. Finally, consideration may be something of great value or little value: *the amount does not matter.* The most important point to keep in mind while learning about consideration is that it is a necessary element in a valid contract and courts often will do whatever is necessary to find it. With few exceptions, consideration must exist for there to be a binding contract.

Putting all the myths aside, a working definition of **consideration** is necessary. *Consideration* is a benefit to the promisor or a detriment to the promisee which is bargained for and given in exchange for a promise. For consideration to exist in a contract, there must be an exchange of something of value. **Value** is defined as something of worth to the parties. In addition, there must be a bargained exchange between the parties. The parties must suffer a legal benefit or legal detriment; that is, something must be given up in exchange for the promise. Also, the consideration must be legal. Therefore, for consideration to exist, there must be (1) a detriment or benefit; (2) that is a bargained exchange of the parties (3) for value (4) of a promise and (5) that is legal. Dissecting the elements will assist in understanding consideration.

4.2   THE ELEMENTS OF CONSIDERATION

The required existence of consideration proves the serious intent of the parties to bind themselves to the promises exchanged. If consideration was not needed, many could walk away from contracts, suggesting that the promise was merely a **gift** and therefore unenforceable. This would allow persons to abandon their contracts and probably promote even more lawsuits than presently exist. Consequently, consideration is a valuable part of the process.

A Detriment or Benefit

The first part of the definition of consideration states that there must be a benefit or detriment to the parties. Each party to the contract gains something or gives up something in the contracting process. When a gain to a party is found, a legal **benefit** will exist; when a sacrifice occurs by one of the parties, a legal **detriment** exists. Legal detriment is usually found when parties do something or act in some way that they do not legally have to or refrain (forbear) from doing something that they have a legal right to do. For example, assume that a friend offers you $100 for not eating chocolate for one month. You have a legal right to eat chocolate, but if you want to earn the $100, you must give up chocolate (that is, "forbear" from eating it). That is a valid detriment and a benefit to the parties. Your friend benefits from your eating healthy and your detriment is not eating the chocolate you love.

Bargained Exchange of the Parties

Not only must a benefit or detriment be involved, but there also must be a bargained-for exchange by the parties. Here, a promise is exchanged for another promise, as in a bilateral contract; or a promise is exchanged for an act, as in a unilateral contract; or a promise is exchanged for the forbearance of an act. The focus is on the exchange of promises between the parties of benefits and detriments. This concept is known as **mutuality**. Mutuality exists between the parties, furnishing each with some form of detriment or benefit. Using the chocolate example, the exchange is that one party promises to give the other party $100 for not eating chocolate. Examine *Jennings v. KSCS,* 708 S.W.2d 60 (Tex. Ct. App.–Fort Worth 1986). Notice what issue the court focused on to find that consideration may have existed between the parties.

mutuality
Two persons having the same relationship toward each other with respect to a particular right, obligation, burden, or benefit; the condition of being mutual. Mutuality is essential to the existence of a binding contract.

JENNINGS v. RADIO STATION KSCS

Court of Appeals of Texas, Fort Worth
May 8, 1986

Appellant, a prisoner in the texas Department of Corrections, brought suit pro se against appellees for breach of an oral contract. The trial court granted appellees' motion for summary judgment denying appellant's right to recovery. We reverse and remand.

Appellant's first amended original petition alleges that his only contact with the outside world is the radio and that he regularly listens to appellee radio station. The petition further alleges: that it is the appellees' policy to regularly state that they play "at least three-in-a-row, or we pay you $25,000. No bull, more music on KSCS;" that each time appellee plays "five-in-a-row" they actually play only three songs, followed by a brief commercial, and then *two* songs; and that appellant contracted appellee on specific occasions after the station failed to play at least three consecutive songs but appellee refused to pay him $25,000.

Appellees filed a motion for summary judgment which was granted by the trial court. Appellant did not respond to the motion for summary judgment.

It is elementary contract law that a valuable and sufficient consideration for a contract may consist of either a benefit to the promisor or a loss or detriment to the promisee. Thus when a promisee acts to his detriment in reliance upon a promise, there is sufficient consideration to bind the promisor to his promise. In the instant case, appellant's petition alleged that he stopped listening to KSCS when appellee refused to pay him $25,000. Implicit in this statement is an allegation by appellant that he listened to KSCS *because* appellee promised to pay him $25,000 if he could catch the radio station playing fewer than three songs in a row. Appellant thus relied to his detriment. He could have listened to *any* station, but he listened to KSCS because of the promise. Appellee also benefitted by the promise. KSCS gained new listeners, like appellant, who listened in the hope of winning $25,000. We hold that appellant's petition sufficiently alleges a cause of action sounding in breach of contract to necessitate a trial on the merits.

We reverse the summary judgement and remand the cause to the trial court.

QUESTIONS FOR ANALYSIS

How did the court define consideration? What was the benefit to the promisor (KSCS) and the detriment to the promisee (Jennings)? What is the court's rationale for its decision?

For Value

Critical to the concept of consideration is that the exchange must be something of value to the parties. Note that the parties decide on the value—

it need not be what you or I would deem value. Value may consist of money, services, property, or the act of forbearing. Each type of value is valid as consideration.

Money

The most typical kind of value (or consideration) is money. In most contracts, the consideration bargained for is the exchange of money. For example, a contractor offers $5,000 to an electrician for installing all the electrical wiring in a house. The exchange of promises is that the electrician will provide wiring in exchange for $5,000 of money from the contractor.

Property

Exchanges of property between the parties also constitute value and, therefore, consideration. For example, assume Henry owns only a computer and needs the use of a printer. He finds Mike, who has a printer but no computer. The parties could contract as follows:

I promise to allow you to use my printer three times a week in exchange for the use of your computer every morning from 9:00 a.m. to 11:00 a.m., Monday through Friday.

The consideration is the exchange of property, and therefore value, to each party.

Services

Another thing of value to parties is services. An exchange of services between parties is also considered valid consideration. A court will look merely for an exchange, not necessarily what the exchange is. Suppose a farmer needs workers but does not have much money to pay wages. The farmer requests that the workers work 30 hours per week in exchange for free food and lodging. The value is the exchange of services for property. Courts have held this to be value, as it is a bargained-for exchange between the parties.

Acts of Forbearance

Requesting persons to refrain from doing something that they have a legal right to do also is considered value. Here, the value may be unique or personal to the parties, but it is nevertheless something of value. Suppose a friend states, "If you stop smoking, I will give you my 1992 Honda." An outsider might look at this exchange and ask, "Where is the value?" The value is in the giving up of something of value—a Honda—for the detriment of not smoking. Courts have held such exchanges to be valid, and thus they constitute consideration.

A Promise Between the Parties

The parties must have made a promise to each other for something of value, or consideration will not be found. For example, I promise to give you my ring. You take it. What is the promise between the parties? There is none. Giving up a ring in exchange for nothing is gratuitous and, therefore, a gift. There is no promise between the parties; no exchange, no benefit or detriment, no value. If I promise to give you a ring in exchange for $300, then that is a promise between the parties and enforceable.

Value Must Be Legal

The value exchanged must be legal. If the parties exchange something that they do not have the legal right to exchange, the consideration is nonexistent. For example, Lillie offers to sell her child to Rachel, who is childless, for $25,000. The consideration here would be illegal and unenforceable in a court.

Review *Hamer v. Sidway,* 27 N.E.2d 256 (N.Y. App. Div. 1891), which analyzes what constitutes consideration (see also Figure 4-1).

HAMER v. SIDWAY

Court of Appeals of New York
April 14, 1891

William E. Story, Sr., was the uncle of William E. Story, 2d. At the celebration of the golden wedding of Samuel Story and wife, father and mother of William E. Story, Sr., on the 20th day of March, 1869, in the presence of the family and invited guests, he promised his nephew that if he would refrain from drinking, using tobacco, swearing, and playing cards or billiards for money until he became 21 years of age, he would pay him the sum of $5,000. The nephew assented thereto, and fully performed the conditions inducing the promise. When the nephew arrived at the age of 21 years, and on the 31st day of January, 1875, he wrote to his uncle, informing him that he had performed his part of the agreement, and had thereby become entitled to the sum of $5,000. The uncle received the letter, and a few days later, and on the 6th day of February, he wrote and mailed to his nephew the following letter: Buffalo, Feb. 6, 1875. W. E. Story, Jr.—Dear Nephew: Your letter of the 31st ult. came to hand all right, saying that you had lived up to the promise made to me several years ago. I have no doubt but you have, for which you shall have five thousand dollars, as I promised you. I had the money in the bank the day you was twenty-one years old that I intend for you, and you shall have the money certain. Now, Willie, I do not intend to interfere with this money in any way till I think you are capable of taking care of it, and the sooner that time comes the better it will please me. Willie, you are twenty-one, and you have many a thing to learn yet. This money you have earned much easier than I did, besides acquiring good habits at the same time, and you are quite welcome to the money. Truly yours, W. E. STORY. P. S. You can consider this money on interest." The nephew received the letter, and thereafter consented that the money should remain with his uncle in accordance with the terms and conditions of the letter. The uncle died on the 29th day of January, 1887, without having paid over to his nephew any portion of the said $5,000 and interest.

[The question] which lies at the foundation of plaintiff's asserted right of recovery, is whether by virtue of a contract defendant's testator, William E. Story, became indebted to his nephew, William E. Story, 2d, on his twenty-first birthday in the sum of $5,000.

[Consideration is defined] as follows: "A valuable consideration, in the sense of the law, may consist either in some right, interest, profit, or benefit accruing to the one party, or some forbearance, detriment, loss, or responsibility given, suffered, or undertaken by the other." Courts "will not ask whether the thing which forms the consideration does in fact benefit the promisee or a third party, or is of any substantial value to any one. It is enough that something is promised, done, forborne, or suffered by the party to whom the promise is made as consideration for the promise made to him." In general a waiver of any legal right at the request of another party is a sufficient consideration for a promise." "Any damage, or suspension, or forbearance of a right will be sufficient to sustain a promise." 'Consideration' means not so much that one party is profiting as that the other abandons some legal right in the present, or limits his legal freedom of action in the future, as an inducement for the promise of the first." Now, applying this rule to the facts before us, the promisee used tobacco, occasionally drank liquor, and he had a legal right to do so. That right he abandoned for a period of years upon the strength of the prom-ise of the testator that for such forbearance he would give him $5,000. [H]e restricted his lawful freedom of action within certain prescribed limits upon the faith of his uncle's agreement, and now, having fully performed the conditions imposed, it is of no moment whether such performance actually proved a benefit to the promisor, and the court will not inquire into it; but were it a proper subject of inquiry, we see nothing in this record that would permit a determination that the uncle was not benefited in a legal sense. "[T]he right to use and enjoy the use of tobacco was a right that belonged to the plaintiff, and not forbidden by law. The abandonment of its use may have saved him money, or contributed to his health; nevertheless, the surrender of that right caused the promise, and having the right to contract with reference to the subject-matter, the abandonment of the use was a sufficient consideration to uphold the promise."

QUESTIONS FOR ANALYSIS

What did the court find to be the consideration? How did the court define *consideration?* Was the court's decision justified? Why or why not?

Consideration
1. Legal benefit/detriment
2. Bargained exchange (mutuality)
3. Exchange must be of value to the parties —Money —Property —Services —Acts of forbearance
4. A promise between parties
5. Value must be legal

FIGURE 4-1 Elements of consideration

4.3 THE ADEQUACY OF CONSIDERATION

Oddly enough, courts do not have a predetermined set of rules to decide how much consideration is enough to bind a contract. In fact, courts shy away from inquiring into the adequacy of the consideration bargained for in a contract. The reason behind this arm's-length approach is that courts encourage freedom of the bargaining process and believe that the responsibility of how much consideration is sufficient rests with the parties to the contract. Even if the value bargained for seems inadequate or unfair, courts generally will not inquire into the reasons why parties agreed on a particular amount or type of consideration.

As a result, consideration may be for $10 or some other small sum, even though an outsider looking in may wonder why the consideration exchanged is so small. Sometimes in contracts, parties will use a minimal sum to complete the formalities of the contracting process, as shown in the following examples:

> For and in consideration of the sum of $10.00, the parties do hereby agree to sell the property located at 184 Main Street, New City, U.S.A.
>
> For and in consideration of the mutual promises and agreements . . .

These samples demonstrate that although the stated value is often minimal, it shows that there was an exchange between the parties, no matter how small. Courts, will however, inquire into adequacy if the consideration appears to be nominal and perpetuating a sham. The indication in those situations is that there was no bargain at all and therefore no consideration. When sham consideration is found, the courts will not enforce the promises between the parties.

Exceptions to every rule exist, even though inquiries into the adequacy of the consideration are few. When issues of fraud, misrepresentation,

mistake, duress, undue influence, and unconscionability (the defenses discussed in Chapter 3) are raised, the adequacy of the consideration may also become an issue. However, such instances are unusual.

4.4 ABSENCE OF CONSIDERATION

When consideration is absent, a courts will not enforce the contract made between the parties. Because consideration is a necessary element in contract formation, the lack of it will render the contract invalid, unless an exception exists. Instances in which courts have found consideration lacking or absent involve gifts, illusory promises, moral consideration, past consideration, and contracts under the preexisting duty rule (see Figure 4-2).

Gifts

The promise of a gift is unenforceable, as it lacks adequate consideration. If someone promises to bequeath a gift in a **will** and does not fulfill that promise, courts will not find that a contract existed between the parties, because there was no consideration. In a gift situation, there is no bargained-for exchange nor a benefit or detriment to the parties. The exchange is one-sided, with only one party benefiting and no legal detriment being suffered. No expectation of a bargained-for exchange occurs, and therefore there is no enforceable contract. Assume that a relative states, "I will give you my diamond ring when I die." If she dies and gives the ring to someone else, can you go to court and have the promise enforced? No. There is no bargained-for exchange and therefore no contract.

Illusory Promises

Promises based upon a party's wishes, desires, or hopes are not an adequate basis for a contract. Expressions that create such indefiniteness are considered illusory and create illusory promises. An **illusory promise** is one that gives a false impression of a contract and in reality does not obligate the party making the promise to anything. There is no bargained-for exchange between the parties. Words that suggest an illusory promise are:

We will order your products when we need them.
We will order the product as demand dictates.
We will request shipment of your product when we wish.

None of these promises creates a *mutuality of obligation* between the parties; therefore, they lack the necessary consideration to be binding. Because, illusory promises lack consideration, they are unenforceable contracts.

TERMS

will
1. An instrument by which a person (the testator) makes a disposition of his or her property, to take effect after his or her death. A will is ambulatory and revocable during the testator's lifetime.

Moral Consideration

A promise to compensate for a past moral obligation is unsupported by consideration and unenforceable. There is no bargained-for exchange between the parties, as one performs the act gratuitously without regard to contractual considerations. Courts generally will not find consideration for a past moral obligation. *Miller v. Miller,* 664 P.2d 39 (Wy. 1983), is a good illustration of a case in which the issue of moral consideration was raised. The case involves whether a son was obligated on his deceased mother's debt.

illusory promise
A promise whose performance is completely up to the promisor. Because the carrying out of such a promise is optional, there is no mutuality, and therefore the promise cannot form the basis of a valid contract.

MILLER v. MILLER

Supreme Court of Wyoming
May 20, 1983

The First National Bank in Wheatland filed suit against the estate of Freda Miller, deceased. The amended complaint alleged that G.O. Miller, Vivian Miller Hytrek, and Cecil Miller, as executors of the estate, owed payment on a promissory note executed by Freda Miller. The defendants, appellees herein, confessed judgment on the note and proceeded to trial on an amended third-party complaint against appellant Cecil Miller, contending that the obligation was his. The district court ruled in favor of appellees. Although appellant urges five issues on appeal, we need only address the issue of whether the evidence was sufficient to support the judgment.

We reverse.

On January 27, 1966, appellant and his wife entered into a real estate contract with his mother, Freda Miller, which provided that appellant buy the family farm. The purchase price was $75,000; purchasers also assumed a mortgage to Travelers Insurance Company of approximately $82,000. The $75,000 due Freda Miller was to be paid in 30 years and was not to bear interest.

On April 17, 1978, Freda Miller and appellant co-signed a promissory note for $60,000 to the First National Bank in Wheatland. The loan proceeds went to appellant. On June 14, 1978, Freda Miller, appellant and his wife refinanced the farm through Travelers Insurance Company and increased the mortgage to Travelers to $210,000. The proceeds which resulted from this refinancing, $91,823.67, went from Travelers Insurance Company to Freda Miller. On

July 14, 1978, she paid in full the April 17, 1978 note to the First National Bank in Wheatland.

On October 31, 1978, Freda Miller executed a promissory note for $60,000 in favor of First National Bank in Wheatland. This loan was to purchase a modular home for Freda Miller. The October 31, 1978, promissory note is the note sued on by the bank against appellees.

On November 3, 1978, appellant, his wife and their son entered into a contract with Freda Miller. They agreed to assume the $210,000 Travelers Insurance Company loan, and to pay Freda Miller $100,000 in installments without interest. Freda Miller died around the middle of November, 1978.

It is well established that an offer, acceptance, and consideration are the basic elements of a contract. The burden of proving a contract is on the one seeking to recover on it. This includes the burden of proving consideration.

Consideration is a necessary element for a valid agreement and the burden of showing it is on the one claiming the benefit of the agreement. Lack of consideration to support the agreement would be a failure of that party's burden.

A generally accepted definition of consideration is that a legal detriment has been bargained for and exchanged for a promise. The Restatement of Contracts says that a performance or a returned promise must be bargained for. "* * * The performance may consist of an act, other than a promise, or a forbearance, or the creation, modification or destruction of a legal relation." Lack of consideration goes to the validity of contract formation. Absent some indicia of actual consideration, a contract will be held invalid by the courts.

The question whether an oral contract exists is one of fact. Nevertheless, as with any question of fact, the decision of the finder of fact will be reversed if there is little or no evidence to support the finding. Appellees failed to prove that there was any consideration for appellant's alleged promise to pay.

Appellees contended that appellant entered into the November 3, 1978, contract because it covered different land than the 1966 contract. The proof was apparently presented to show that appellant received more value from Freda Miller than he had agreed to pay for in formal contracts, and that therefore he must have intended and agreed to pay the $60,000 note for the modular home to the bank to even things out between his mother and himself. Appellees seem to be arguing that appellant had a motive for offering to pay the note on the modular home, but evidence of motive does not substitute the necessary element of consideration in a contract. Perhaps appellant had a moral obligation to pay the note, but moral obligation alone is not a valid consideration for a promise to pay. A moral obligation is not necessarily a legal one.

Appellant did tell his mother and others that he would pay off the October 31, 1978, loan, if and when he could. Appellees argue that this statement by appellant that he would pay the note shows a contract. However, "the mere fact that one man promises something to another creates no legal duty and makes no legal remedy available in case of non-performance."

Appellees will probably remain convinced that they should be paid. Nevertheless, they failed to meet their burden of proof; perhaps, because of the confused state of affairs, they never could. Regardless, this court will not find a contract where one has not been proved to exist.

QUESTIONS FOR ANALYSIS

What was the court's holding? Did the court find consideration to bind the son to his deceased mother's debt? What was the basis of the court's decision.

Past Consideration

When an obligation already exists and a promise is made for some future act previously suffered by the promisee, there is no consideration. A pretext appears to exist for a contractual relationship, but mutuality is lacking. The key is that a promise to give value for goods or services previously rendered is **past consideration** and does not create the basis of a new, enforceable contract.

The Preexisting Duty

Closely related to past consideration is the *preexisting duty rule*. When a person has a preexisting responsibility to act or to refrain from doing something, there is no bargained-for exchange. The obligation exists either by law or prior agreement, and therefore the law will not infer consideration, as no detriment is suffered. Under this rule, consideration cannot be bargained for between the parties, as the responsibility to act or refrain from acting is already a duty.

The preexisting duty rule has been heavily litigated in the public service area. People such as firefighters, elected officials, and particularly law enforcement officers cannot extract benefits from a citizen for a task they are already obligated to perform. Let's assume that there has been a rash of burglaries in your neighborhood. A police officer knocks on your door and states that for $100 the police will patrol your area and watch for any burglars. You agree. Later you find out that you should not have had to pay the additional money, as patrolling was the officer's job anyway. If you were sued by the police officer, the court would find in your favor, as the contract is not supported by consideration. The officer had a preexisting duty to patrol; it was part of the job.

The preexisting duty rule also often arises with regard to construction contracts. Typically, a contractor agrees to provide services for a specific amount. While performing the service, the contractor realizes that the sum contracted for is insufficient to complete the job. The contractor threatens to quit work unless a higher price is paid for the service. The other party usually pays the additional sum to avoid a walk-off. The courts will not enforce payment of the additional sum, however, because a preexisting duty exists.

Similarly, in entertainment contracts, actors can threaten to walk off a movie set unless a higher salary is given. Remember the *Problem Child II* example from Chapter 3? The young star threatened to walk off unless the studio gave him $420,000 more to play the role. When the studio sued and won, the court found duress, but it also could have reasoned that the young actor had a preexisting duty and that no new contract had been formed.

Absence of Consideration	
1. Gifts	4. Past consideration
2. Illusory promises	5. Preexisting duty
3. Moral consideration	

FIGURE 4-2 Situations in which consideration is absent

4.5 THE EXCEPTIONS: CONTRACTS ENFORCEABLE WITHOUT CONSIDERATION

In the law, there are exceptions to every rule. Under certain circumstances, contracts will be enforceable even though there is no consideration. Some of these exceptions are found in the (1) doctrine of promissory estoppel, (2) promises made after the statute of limitations has run, (3) discharge in bankruptcy, and (4) promises to pay for benefits received.

Promissory Estoppel

The concept of **promissory estoppel** focuses on principles of justice and fairness. Although no consideration is apparent from the promises, if a

TERMS

past consideration
Consideration given prior to entering into a contract. Past consideration is not sufficient consideration to support a contract.

promissory estoppel
The principle that a promisor will be bound to a promise (that is, estopped to deny the promise), even though it is without consideration, if he or she intended that the promise should be relied upon and it was in fact relied upon, and if a refusal to enforce the promise would result in an injustice.

party changes his or her position in reliance on a promise, courts may imply that consideration exists and find that a contract was created. This concept was articulated in *Restatement (First) of Contracts* § 90:

> A promise which the promisor should reasonably expect to induce action or forbearance on the part of the promisee or a third person and which does induce such action or forbearance is binding if injustice can be avoided only by enforcement of the promise.

As the *Restatement* suggests, promissory estoppel focuses on the need for fairness and the avoidance of injustice in the contracting process. Promissory estoppel has been applied not only when consideration is challenged, but also in other areas of contract law. *Feinberg v. Pfeiffer Co.*, 322 S.W.2d 163 (Mo. Ct. App. 1959) illustrates the application of promissory estoppel when the consideration was questionable.

FEINBERG v. PFEIFFER COMPANY
St. Louis Court of Appeals, Missouri
March 17, 1959

Plaintiff began working for the defendant, a manufacturer of pharmaceuticals, in 1910, when she was but 17 years of age. By 1947 she had attained the position of bookkeeper, office manager, and assistant treasurer of the defendant, and owned 70 shares of its stock out of a total of 6,503 shares issued and outstanding. Twenty shares had been given to her by the defendant or its then president, she had purchased 20, and the remaining 30 she had acquired by a stock split or stock dividend. Over the years she received substantial dividends on the stock she owned, as did all of the other stockholders. Also, in addition to her salary, plaintiff from 1937 to 1949, inclusive, received each year a bonus varying in amount from $300 in the beginning to $2,000 in the later years.

On December 27, 1947, the annual meeting of the defendant's Board of Directors was held at the Company's offices in St. Louis. At that meeting the Board of Directors adopted the following resolution, which, because it is the crux of the case, we quote in full:

"The Chairman thereupon pointed out that the Assistant Treasurer, Mrs. Anna Sacks Feinberg, has given the corporation many years of long and faithful service. Not only has she served the corporation devotedly, but with exceptional ability and skill. The President pointed out that although all of the officers and directors sincerely hoped and desired that Mrs. Feinberg would continue in her present position for as long as she felt able, nevertheless, in view of the length of service which she has contributed provision should be made to afford her retirement privileges and benefits which should become a firm obligation of the corporation to be available to her whenever she should see fit to retire from active duty, however many years in the future such retirement may become effective. It was, accordingly, proposed that Mrs. Feinberg's salary which is presently $350.00 per month, be increased to $400.00 per month, and that Mrs. Feinberg would be given the privilege of retiring from active duty at any time she may elect to see fit so to do upon a retirement pay of $200.00 per month for life, with the distinct understanding that the retirement plan is merely being adopted at the present time in order to afford Mrs. Feinberg security for the future and in the hope that her active services will continue with the corporation for many years to come. After due discussion and consideration, and upon motion duly made and seconded, it was—

"Resolved, that the salary of Anna Sacks Feinberg be increased from $350.00 to $400.00 per month and that she be afforded the privilege of retiring from active duty in the corporation at any time she may elect to see fit so to do upon retirement pay of $200.00 per month, for the remainder of her life."

Plaintiff testified on cross-examination that she had no prior information that such a pension plan was contemplated, that it came as a surprise to her, and that she would have continued in her employment whether or not such a resolution had been adopted. It is clear from the evidence that there was no contract, oral or written, as to plaintiff's length of employment, and that she was free to quit, and the defendant to discharge her, at any time.

Plaintiff did continue to work for the defendant through June 30, 1949, on which date she retired. In accordance with the foregoing resolution, the defendant began paying her the sum of $200 on the first of each month. [The president] died on November 18, 1949, and was succeeded as president of the company by his widow. Because of an illness, she retired from that office and was succeeded in October, 1953, by her son-in-law, Sidney M. Harris. After his election, he stated, a new accounting firm employed by the defendant questioned the validity of the payments to plaintiff on several occasions, and in the Spring of 1956, upon its recommendation, he consulted the Company's then attorney, Mr. Ralph Kalish. Harris testified that both Ernst and Ernst, the accounting firm, and Kalish told him there was no need of giving plaintiff the money. He also stated that he had concurred in the view that the payments to plaintiff were mere gratuities rather than amounts due under a contractual obligation, and that following his discussion with the Company's attorney plaintiff was sent a check for $100 on April 1, 1956. Plaintiff declined to accept the reduced amount, and this action followed.

[The] basic issue in the case [is] whether plaintiff has proved that she has a right to recover from defendant based upon a legally binding contractual obligation to pay her $200 per month for life.

It is defendant's contention, in essence, that the resolution adopted by its Board of Directors was a mere promise to make a gift, and that no contract resulted either thereby, or when plaintiff retired, because there was no consideration given or paid by the plaintiff. It urges that a promise to make a gift is not binding unless supported by a legal consideration; that the only apparent consideration for the adoption of the foregoing resolution was the "many years of long and faithful service" expressed therein; and that past services are not a valid consideration for a promise. Defendant argues further that there is nothing in the resolution which made its effectiveness conditional upon plaintiff's continued employment, that she was not under contract to work for any length of time but was free to quit whenever she wished, and that she had no contractual right to her position and could have been discharged at any time.

Plaintiff concedes that a promise based upon past services would be without consideration, but contends that there were two other elements which supplied the required element: First, the continuation by plaintiff in the employ of the defendant for the period from December 27, 1947, the date when the resolution was adopted, until the date of her retirement on June 30, 1949. And, second, her change of position, i.e., her retirement, and the abandonment by her of her opportunity to continue in gainful employment, made in reliance on defendant's promise to pay her $200 per month for life.

We must agree with the defendant that the evidence does not support the first of these contentions. There is no language in the resolution predicating plaintiff's right to a pension upon her continued employment. She was not required to work for the defendant for any period of time as a condition to gaining such retirement benefits. She was told that she could quit the day upon which the resolution was adopted, as she herself testified, and it is clear from her own testimony that she made no promise or agreement to continue in the employ of the defendant in return for its promise to pay her a pension. Hence there was lacking that mutuality of obligation which is essential to the validity of a contract.

But as to the second of these contentions we must agree with plaintiff. By the terms of the resolution defendant promised to pay plaintiff the sum of $200 a month upon her retirement. Consideration for a promise has been defined in the Restatement of the Law of Contracts, Section 75, as:

"(1) Consideration for a promise is
 (a) an act other than a promise, or
 (b) a forbearance, or
 (c) the creation, modification or destruction of a legal relation, or
 (d) a return promise, bargained for and given in exchange for the promise."

As the parties agree, the consideration sufficient to support a contract may be either a benefit to the promisor or a loss or detriment to the promisee.

Section 90 of the Restatement of the Law of Contracts states that: "A promise which the promisor should reasonably expect to induce action or forbearance of a definite and substantial character on the part of the promisee and which does induce such action or forbearance is binding if injustice can be avoided only by enforcement of the promise." This doctrine has been described as that of "promissory estoppel."

"It is generally true that one who has led another to act in reasonable reliance on his representations of fact cannot afterwards in litigation between the two deny the truth of the representa-tions, and some courts have sought to apply this principle to the formation of contracts, where, relying on a gratuitous promise, the promisee has suf-fered detriment. It is to be noticed, however, that such a case does not come within the ordinary definition of estoppel. If there is any representation of an existing fact, it is only that the promisor at the time of making the promise intends to fulfill it. As to such intention there is usually no misrepresentation and if there is, it is not that which has injured the promisee. In other words, he relies on a promise and not on a misstatement of fact; and the term 'promissory' estoppel or something equivalent should be used to make the distinction."

Was there such an act on the part of plaintiff, in reliance upon the promise contained in the resolution, as will estop the defendant, and therefore create an enforceable contract under the doctrine of promissory estoppel? We think there was.

QUESTIONS FOR ANALYSIS

Did the court find a contract? If so, what was the basis for the court's findings? What was the consideration in this case? Explain the court's reasoning.

The doctrine of promissory estoppel focuses not only on the fact that the promisee relied to his or her detriment, but that the reliance was reasonably foreseeable by the promisor. Foreseeability is one of the keys in finding promissory estoppel.

Promissory estoppel has also been used as a means to enforce contracts when charities are involved. Often individuals or entities make charitable pledges but fail to fulfill them. Because charities rely on contributions, courts have held that a contract exists based upon the principles of promissory estoppel. Although a convincing argument can be made that a charitable pledge is merely a gift, charitable organizations rely to their detriment on pledges. They plan their organizations' functions, such as staff and expenses, around pledges. Courts have thus used promissory estoppel as a means to enforce otherwise invalid contracts.

Statute of Limitations

State statutes impose time periods, known as **statutes of limitations**, in which a party must file a lawsuit; otherwise that party loses the right to sue.

Once a statute of limitation passes, a party cannot validly exercise a right to pursue the claim. Statutes of limitations vary from state to state depending on the **cause of action**. What is clear, though, is that a party cannot attempt to enforce a prior obligation, such as a debt, once the statute of limitations has passed, unless the party owing the debt puts the promise in writing. Simply saying "I will pay the debt I owe you" after the statute of limitations has passed fails because there is no consideration.

Bankruptcy

When a party files bankruptcy, creditors have real difficulty in collecting on contracts made prior to the bankruptcy. Debtors, however, through the laws in the Bankruptcy Code, have the opportunity to reaffirm debts. If the court accepts the new promise by the debtor, the contract will be enforceable pursuant to the Bankruptcy Reform Act of 1978, even though no consideration exists between the parties.

Benefits Received

When a party has received a benefit, such as emergency medical care, whether a contract exists between the parties depends upon whether consideration is found. If the party did not agree to pay for the medical treatment, is there consideration for an enforceable contract? The answer depends upon whether the services were requested by the party. When the answer is yes, consideration often will be found to bind the parties to a contract; but if the services were not requested, courts will not find that consideration was present.

This raises an issue when emergency medical care services are rendered but not requested. Should the doctor have to be the good samaritan and not receive payment for the services performed? Although consideration may not exist, recall from Chapter 1 the doctrine of quasi-contract (implied-in-law contracts). Here, the court would create a contract based upon principles of fairness and justice, even though no consideration exists.

4.6 CONSIDERATION IN DISPUTE

Often disputes arise as to the amount of consideration due under a contract. When this happens, a settlement between the parties may occur. However, for a settlement to result, courts distinguish between whether the disputed amount is a liquidated or an unliquidated claim.

Liquidated Claims

A **liquidated claim** is a specific sum owed to a party. The amount owed is undisputed and known by all the parties to the contract. If the person who owes the amount attempts to tender part payment of the amount

TERMS

statute of limitations
Federal and state statutes prescribing the maximum period of time during which various types of civil actions and criminal prosecutions can be brought after the occurrence of the injury or the offense.

cause of action
Circumstances that give a person the right to bring a lawsuit and to receive relief from a court.

liquidated claim
A claim the amount of which is agreed upon by the parties or which can be determined by applying rules of law or by mathematical calculation.

as full payment of the obligation, does new consideration exist to discharge the prior debt? No. The party has a preexisting duty to pay the entire debt and part payment will not constitute new consideration for a new contract to cancel the claim.

Unliquidated Claims

The counterpart of a liquidated claim is an **unliquidated claim**, where the sum is either not specifically known or is disputed. Suppose Angela agrees to pay $75 to get a haircut and have highlights put in her hair. When she gets home, a chemical reaction to the highlighting gives her rashes and peeling of the scalp. She quickly runs to her bank and stops payment on the check she wrote to the hair stylist. Now, the amount due is unliquidated and disputed.

To remedy the situation, the parties may agree to a specific amount to satisfy the amount owed or in dispute. This is known as a **compromise and settlement agreement**. When disputes arise between parties, it is not uncommon for parties to agree on a compromise amount (usually a lesser amount). The parties in effect are executing what is known as an *accord and satisfaction*. The compromise or agreement between the parties is known as the **accord** and the payment of the agreed amount is known as the **satisfaction**. This solves the problem of consideration. (*Note:* The accord and satisfaction always are prepared together and are treated as one document.)

4.7 PRACTICAL APPLICATION

Paralegals will assist their attorneys in analyzing contracts for consideration. Is consideration present? If consideration is not found, does an exception apply? Case law will be your guide in answering these questions.

Contracts are full of provisions showing the element of consideration which binds the agreement between the parties. Examples of such provisions are found in Figure 4-3.

TERMS

unliquidated claim
A claim whose existence or amount is not agreed upon by the parties; a claim whose amount cannot be determined by applying rules of law or by mathematical calculation.

compromise and settlement agreement
An agreement to settle a dispute, followed by performance of the promises contained in the agreement.

accord
An agreement.

satisfaction
1. The discharge of an obligation by the payment of a debt.
2. The performance of a contract according to its terms.

General Consideration Provisions

General Form

In consideration of the sum of TEN THOUSAND DOLLARS AND NO CENTS ($10,000.00) paid to Marjorie Hight by Howard Brown, the receipt of which is acknowledged, Hight agrees as follows:

For Value Received

For value received, Harvey Brownwood agrees with Daniel Charleston to do the following:

FIGURE 4-3 General consideration provisions

Mutual Promises

The parties in consideration of their mutual promises to each other agree as follows:

Services Rendered

In consideration of the performance by Harvey Brownwood of Lawn Care Services, Daniel Charleston agrees to pay the total sum of $400.00 (Four Hundred Dollars and No Cents).

Love and Affection

In consideration of the natural love and affection that Mary Ann Michaels has for Joan Smith, Mary Ann Michaels agrees to:

Release of Claim Provision

In consideration of the release of the claim brought by Marjorie Hight against Howard Brown regarding the alleged defects in construction of her garage, Howard Brown to pay the amount of $4,000.00 to Marjorie Hight on or before June 15, 1994, as full and final payment of all claims.

Settlement Provision

In consideration of the mutual promises, covenants, and agreements set forth in this settlement agreement, the parties agree as follows:

Real Estate Provision

Purchase and sale of property

In consideration of the mutual promises and covenants set out, Marjorie Hight agrees to sell and does sell, and Howard Brown agrees to buy and pay for, and does buy, the property located at:

Conveyance of real property

In consideration of the conveyance by Marjorie Hight to Howard Brown of the real property situated in _____, Howard Brown agrees to pay FIVE HUNDRED THOUSAND DOLLARS AND NO CENTS ($500,000.00) for the property located at:

Devise of real property

In consideration of the agreement by Marjorie Hight, contemporaneously with this agreement, to make a will and provide therein for the devise to Howard Brown of the real property more particularly described below, and the agreement not to revoke the devise contained in such will, and further agreement not to sell, transfer, convey, mortgage, or otherwise dispose of such property to any other person, Howard Brown agrees as follows:

Provision for a Gift

Gift of Household Goods

Know all men by these presents, that I, Anna Morris of Chicago, Illinois, in consideration of natural love and affection, give to my daughter, Jenna Morris, all the household furniture and effects, books, pictures, and all other tangible personal property whatsoever in my dwelling house at 128 Main Street, Chicago, Illinois.

Gift of Real Property

Witnesseth, that the Donor, in consideration of his natural love and affection for the Donee, does hereby give, grant, and convey to the Donee, her heirs and assigns, all the following described real property:

FIGURE 4-3 *(Continued)*

SUMMARY

4.1 Consideration is a necessary element in a contract. It is defined as a benefit to the promisor or a detriment to the promisee, bargained for and given in exchange for a promise. For consideration to exist, there must be an exchange between the parties where a legal benefit and legal detriment occur.

4.2 Certain elements must be fulfilled for consideration to exist: (1) a detriment or benefit; (2) a bargained exchange of the parties; (3) for value; and (4) a promise between the parties; (5) that is legal. Value can be money, services, property, or the act of forbearing.

4.3 Courts do not have absolute rules to determine the adequacy of consideration. Whether the consideration is adequate depends upon the value placed on the promises by the parties.

4.4 When consideration is absent, the contract between the parties will not be enforced. Gifts lack consideration because there is no exchange between the parties. Similarly, with an illusory promise, there is no exchange between the parties; only a desire or wish is communicated. A past moral obligation will not be enforced, as consideration is lacking. When a past contractual relationship exists, no new consideration will be found to bind the new promises. The preexisting duty rule provides a basis for the prior contract's enforcement.

4.5 Exceptions exist when a contract will be enforced even though there is no consideration. These situations are under the doctrine of promissory estoppel; promises made after the running of the statute of limitations; discharge in bankruptcy; and promises to pay for benefits received.

4.6 Sometimes consideration may be in dispute. When this occurs, distinguish between liquidated and unliquidated claims. If claims can be settled, the parties may enter into an accord and satisfaction.

REVIEW QUESTIONS

1. How is consideration defined?
2. What are the basic elements of consideration?
3. Identify the different types of value which may constitute consideration.
4. How do courts determine the adequacy of consideration?
5. List some situations in which consideration is absent.
6. What is an illusory promise?
7. Define the preexisting duty rule.
8. What are the exceptions to enforcement of a contract that lacks consideration?
9. Under what doctrine have courts enforced charitable pledges? Why?
10. Distinguish between a liquidated and an unliquidated claim.

EXERCISES

1. Listen to a local radio station that runs contests, like the one in *Jennings v. KSCS* cited in this chapter. Bring to class the proposed contest rules and discuss what the consideration is in the contest. Consider writing your local radio station for copies of the rules.

2. Brief *Worner Agency, Inc. v. Doyle,* 479 N.W.2d 468 (Ill. 1985) and answer the following questions:
   a. What are the facts of the case?
   b. What is the court's decision in the case?
   c. Did the court find sufficient consideration to bind the parties to a contract? Explain your answer.

3. Find examples in your daily life where consideration might become an issue. Look for contracts, deeds, tickets and family bequests as situations where consideration is a focal point.

CHAPTER 5
Capacity: The Ability to Contract

5.1 DEFINING LEGAL CAPACITY

In contract law, agreeing or understanding the terms and conditions of a contract is not sufficient to bind the parties. An additional element must be present: capacity. **Capacity** is the legal ability to enter into a contract. This concept is easily defined as being over the legal age (which means 18 or 21 years of age, depending on your state statute) and being of sound mind (which means mentally competent).

Most individuals who enter into a contract have capacity, and it does not become an issue, but the occasion does arise when the parties to a contract lack the legal capacity to bind themselves to the contract. Persons who fall into this category are minors, mentally handicapped, legally insane, intoxicated, and drugged persons. In some instances, aliens and convicted felons also lack capacity. Depending upon how the law views the person, those who lack capacity create either void or voidable contracts. (Remember from Chapter 1 that a void contract is never valid; a voidable contract is one that may be avoided by the person with the disability, but it may become valid.) Capacity is essential to the validity of a contract. This chapter focuses on parties whose capacity may be challenged (see Figure 5-1).

Capacity			
1. Adult by law		4. Legal resident	
2. Legally sane and mentally healthy		5. Not a felon	
3. Sober/not addicted to drugs			

FIGURE 5-1   Persons with legal capacity

5.2   A MINOR'S CONTRACTUAL CAPACITY

State statutes determine when a person legally becomes an adult. Usually majority is defined as somewhere between 18 and 21 years of age. Prior to reaching the age of majority, **minors**, or *infants* as the law sometimes refers to them, lack the capacity to create binding contracts. *Restatement (Second) of Contracts* § 14 states the following as to minors:

> Unless a statute provides otherwise, a natural person has the capacity to incur only voidable contractual duties until the beginning of the day before that person's eighteenth birthday. Not only must a person be of legal age, but [he or she] must also be competent mentally. Persons who are mentally disabled or incapacitated generally do not have the full legal ability to contract.

Under the law, minors create voidable contracts, in that they generally are not be held responsible for the contracts they create. Minors who contract with adults can avoid contracts they enter into by disaffirming those contracts. **Disaffirmance** is a method of rejecting a contract through cancellation. Basically, a minor can disaffirm a contract prior to reaching majority and for a reasonable time after reaching majority. Courts differ, though, as to what is considered a reasonable time to disaffirm a contract. Consequently, courts look to the subject matter, the parties, and when the disaffirmance took place to determine if it is reasonable. However, the adult who contracts with a minor does not have the same luxury. When an adult contracts with a minor, the contract is binding unless the minor disaffirms or the minor lets the adult out of the contract. The law clearly protects the minor.

A method of holding a minor to a contract is to insist that an adult co-sign the contract. This effectively eliminates the minor's ability to disaffirm the contract, as the adult will remain responsible for the contract. In addition, if a minor's **guardian** enters into a contract on the minor's behalf, that contract will generally be valid as well. Contracts made by a guardian often have a court's approval, negating the minor's right of disaffirmance and thus making them enforceable.

Simmons v. Parkette National Gymnastics Training Center, 670 F. Supp. 140 (E.D. Pa. 1987) focused not only on the disaffirmance issue, but also on the general capacity issue. This case posed some interesting questions, as a parent was involved in the contractual arrangement.

TERMS

capacity
1. Competency in law.
2. A person's ability to understand the nature and effect of the act in which he or she is engaged. . . . 4. Ability or capability generally.

minor
A person who has not yet attained his or her majority; a person who has not reached legal age; a person who has not acquired the capacity to contract.

disaffirmance
1. The refusal to fulfill a voidable contract.
2. Disclaimer; repudiation; disavowal; renunciation.

guardian
A person empowered by the law to care for another who, by virtue of age or lack of mental capacity, is legally unable to care for himself or herself. Guardianship may also involve the duty of managing the estate of the incompetent person.

SIMMONS v. PARKETTE NATIONAL GYMNASTIC TRAINING CENTER
United States District Court, E.D. Pennsylvania
July 9, 1987

The plaintiffs instituted this action claiming that the minor plaintiff, Tara A. Simmons, suffered personal injury as a result of the negligent acts and/or omissions of one or more of the defendants' employees. The minor plaintiff's mother asserts causes of action against the defendants in her own right and on behalf of her minor daughter as the child's parent and natural guardian.

The defendants assert as an affirmative defense a "release" alleged to have been executed by the plaintiffs on February 12, 1984. The defendants seek judgment on the ground that the release absolves them from all liability for the damages allegedly suffered by the plaintiffs.

The "release" asserted by the defendants provides as follows:

> In consideration of my participation in Parkettes, I, intending to be legally bound, do hereby, for myself, my heirs, executors, and administrators, waive and release any and all right and claims for damages which I may hereafter accrue to me against the United States Gymnastic Federation, the Parkette National Gymnastic Team, their officers, representatives, successors, and/or assigns for any and all damages which may be sustained and suffered by me in connection with my association with the above gymnastic program, or which may arise out of my travelling to or participating in and returning from any activity associated with the program.

As can be seen, the release is prospective in nature, *i.e.,* it purports to exculpate the defendants from future liability, as opposed to a release compromising and settling an already existing claim for damages. It is axiomatic under Pennsylvania law that,

> A valid release is an absolute bar to recovery for everything included in the release, and it can only be set aside *as any contract* . . . in the

presence of clear, precise and indubitable evidence of fraud, accidental means or *incompetence of the party who is alleged to have signed it.*

As to the minor plaintiff's mother's claim, we conclude that her cause of action is indeed barred by the exculpatory agreement she signed. She does not argue and has presented no evidence that the release was the product of fraud, duress, incompetence or other factor which would invalidate it. Further, the fact that her minor daughter has purported to disaffirm the release has no effect on her own, personal claim for damages.

The effect of the exculpatory agreement upon the minor plaintiff's claim for damages presents a somewhat more difficult question. It is hornbook contract law that a minor, with certain exceptions, is not competent to enter into a "valid" contract. Where a minor executes a contract, however, the agreement is not "void," but rather, "voidable." After reaching the age of majority, the minor may disaffirm the contract, thereby rendering it a nullity. An exculpatory agreement such as that involved herein is simply a specific type of contract. Syllogistically, therefore, one would assume that the minor plaintiff may nullify the release by disaffirming it and, apparently in response to the defendants' motion, this is what she has purported to do.

[T]he minor plaintiff in this case herself executed the purported release in addition to her mother. Our research has failed to disclose a single instance in which a Pennsylvania court, a district court applying Pennsylvania law or the Third Circuit Court of Appeals has addressed the precise question whether a minor may disavow a prospective, exculpatory contract which he or she has signed. Similar cases have only dealt with the question of whether a minor may disaffirm a release which she has signed compromising and settling a claim that has already accrued to the minor.

As noted earlier, this case does not involve a release executed pursuant to a compromise and settlement of an already existing claim, but rather, a release which purportedly prospectively exculpated the defendant from liability for the claim the minor plaintiff asserts here. Here, it can be argued that the "benefit" received by the minor plaintiff in consideration for her execution of the release was the defendants' allowing her to participate in their organization. We do not believe, however, that this was the type of "benefit" the courts had in mind. The common law rule that minors, with certain exceptions, may disaffirm their contracts has as its basis the public policy concern that minors should not be bound by mistakes resulting from their immaturity or the overbearance of unscrupulous adults.

In the case before us there was no court involvement in the transaction which occurred between the minor plaintiff and the defendants. Thus, she received none of the protections provided by the special rules of procedure which apply to the settlement of minors' claims. Further, the public policy concern of the effective settlement of litigation is not involved here because of the very nature of the exculpatory agreement which the minor plaintiff executed. For these reasons, we do not believe that the Pennsylvania courts would bind the minor plaintiff to the agreement which she signed. Thus, we will deny the defendants' summary judgment motion as to those claims asserted by the minor plaintiff.

QUESTIONS FOR ANALYSIS

Upon what two central issues did the court focus? What was the court's decision? What was the basis of the court's decision? What facts were important to the court in rendering its decision?

Necessities

Exceptions exist to every rule. When minors contract for **necessities**, such as food, clothing, shelter, and medical services, they, along with their parents, will be responsible for the reasonable value of those services and charges. For example, if a physician provides medical services and the minor does not pay, the parents will be responsible for paying for the services. Note that the law states that the minor or parents will be responsible for the *reasonable value* of those services. If someone attempts to take advantage of a minor and charge an exorbitant fee for a service, a court will determine what the customary and standard charge is for the service rendered and impose only a fair charge. The courts will not allow people to take advantage of minors.

Further, the Courts consider the ability to pay. Generally, courts look to parents to pay for contracts for necessities. If the parents cannot afford to pay, courts have held the children responsible for such contracts. The basis for this liability is often rooted in quasi contract (see Chapter 1).

The more difficult question is what is a *necessity*. How do courts define this word, which imposes liability on minors or their families? Courts look to a child's needs, social status, and economic ability. Determining exactly what a child needs is very difficult and is usually analyzed on a case-by-case basis. Is a car a necessity? A boat? A stereo system? Although a stereo system appears clearly not to be a necessity, assume that a minor is a linguist

TERMS

necessaries (necessities)
Things reasonably necessary for maintaining a person in accordance with his or her position in life. Thus, depending upon the person's economic circumstances, "necessaries" may not be limited simply to those things required to maintain existence, i.e., shelter, food, clothing, and medical care.

and needs a stereo system to practice languages and speech patterns. Perhaps then a stereo would be a necessity. Courts look closely at each situation. However, it should be noted that parents are normally responsible only for necessities; if the minor contracts for something other than a necessity, a parent will not be responsible, unless he or she is a co-signor. Compare *Webster Street Partnership, Ltd. v. Sheridan,* 220 Neb. 9, 368 N.W.2d 439 (1985) with *University of Cincinnati Hospital v. Cohen,* 57 Ohio App. 3d 30, 566 N.E.2d 187 (1989). Determine if the courts' holdings are appropriate for the situations presented.

WEBSTER STREET PARTNERSHIP, LTD. v. SHERIDAN

Supreme Court of Nebraska
May 17, 1985

Webster Street is a partnership owning real estate in Omaha, Nebraska. On September 18, 1982, Webster Street, through one of its agents, Norman Sargent, entered into a written lease with Sheridan and Wilwerding for an apartment. The lease provided that Sheridan and Wilwerding would pay to Webster Street by way of monthly rental the sum of $250 due on the first day of each month until August 15, 1983. The lease also required the payment of a security deposit in the amount of $150 and a payment of $20 per month for utilities during the months of December, January, February, and March. Liquidated damages in the amount of $5 per day for each day the rent was late were also provided for by the lease. The evidence conclusively establishes that at the time the lease was executed both tenants were minors and, further, that Webster Street knew that fact.

The tenants paid the $150 security deposit, $100 rent for the remaining portion of September 1982, and $250 rent for October 1982. They did not pay rent for the month of November 1982, and on November 5 Sargent advised Wilwerding that unless the rent was paid immediately, both boys would be required to vacate the premises. The tenants both testified that, being unable to pay the rent, they moved from the premises on November 12.

In a letter dated January 7, 1983, Webster Street's attorney made written demand upon the tenants for damages in the amount of $630.94. On January 12, 1983, the tenants' attorney denied any liability, refused to pay any portion of the amount demanded, stated that neither tenant was of legal age at the time the lease was executed, and demanded return of $150 security deposit.

Webster Street thereafter commenced suit against the tenants and sought judgment in the amount of $630.94. To this petition the tenants filed an answer alleging that they were minors at the time they signed the lease, that the lease was therefore voidable, and that the rental property did not constitute a necessary for which they were otherwise liable. In addition, Sheridan cross-petitioned for the return of the security deposit, and Wilwerding filed a cross-petition seeking the return of all moneys paid to Webster Street. Following trial, the municipal court of the city of Omaha found in favor of Webster Street and against both tenants in the amount of $630.94

The tenants appealed to the district court for Douglas County. The district court found that the tenants had vacated the premises on November 12, 1982, and therefore were only liable for the 12 days in which they actually occupied the apartment and did not pay rent. The district court also permitted Webster Street to recover $46.79 for cleanup and repairs. The tenants, however, were given credit for their $150 security deposit, resulting in an order that Webster Street was indebted to the tenants in the amount of $3.25.

It appears to be Webster Street's position that the district court erred in failing to find that Sheridan had ratified the lease within a reasonable time after obtaining majority, and was therefore responsible for the lease, and that the minors had become emancipated and were therefore liable, even though Wilwerding had not reached majority.

As a general rule, an infant does not have the capacity to bind himself absolutely by contract. The right of the infant to avoid his contract is one conferred by law for his protection against his own improvidence and the designs of others. The policy of the law is to discourage adults from contracting with an infant; they cannot complain if, as a consequence of violating that rule, they are unable to enforce their contracts.

However, the privilege of infancy will not enable an infant to escape liability in all cases and under all circumstances. For example, it is well established that an infant is liable for the value of necessaries furnished him. An infant's liability for necessaries is based not upon his actual contract to pay for them but upon a contract implied by law, or, in other words, a quasi-contract.

Just what are necessaries, however, has no exact definition. The term is flexible and varies according to the facts of each individual case. The meaning of the term "necessaries" cannot be defined by a general rule applicable to all cases; the question is a mixed one of law and fact, to be determined in each case from the particular facts and circumstances in such case. A number of factors must be considered before a court can conclude whether a particular product or service is a necessary. The particular infant must have an actual need for the articles furnished; not for mere ornament or pleasure. The articles must be useful and suitable, but they are not necessaries merely because useful or beneficial. Concerning the general character of the things furnished, to be necessaries the articles must supply the infant's personal needs, either those of his body or those of his mind. However, the term "necessaries" is not confined to merely such things as are required for a bare subsistence. There is no positive rule by means of which it may be determined what are or what are not necessaries, for what may be considered necessary for one infant may not be necessaries for another infant

whose state is different as to rank, social position, fortune, health, or other circumstances, the question being one to be determined from the particular facts and circumstances of each case.

This undisputed testimony is that both tenants were living away from home, apparently with the understanding that they could return home at any time. It would therefore appear that in the present case neither Sheridan nor Wilwerding was in need of shelter but, rather, had chosen to voluntarily leave home, with the understanding that they could return whenever they desired. One may at first blush believe that such a rule is unfair. Yet, on further consideration, the wisdom of the rule is apparent. If, indeed, landlords may not contract with minors, except at their peril, they may refuse to do so. In that event, minors who voluntarily leave home but who are free to return will be compelled to return to their parents' home—a result which is desirable. We therefore find that both the municipal court and the district court erred in finding that the apartment, under the facts in this case, was a necessary.

Because the rental of the apartment was not a necessary, the minors had the right to avoid the contract, either during their minority or within a reasonable time after reaching their majority. Disaffirmance by an infant completely puts an end to the contract's existence, both as to him and as to the adult with whom he contracted. Because the parties then stand as if no contract had ever existed, the infant can recover payments made to the adult, and the adult is entitled to the return of whatever was received by the infant.

The record shows that Wilwerding clearly disaffirmed the contract during his minority. Moreover, the record supports the view that when the agent for Webster Street ordered the minors out for failure to pay rent and they vacated the premises, Sheridan likewise disaffirmed the contract. The record indicates that Sheridan reached majority on November 5. To suggest that a lapse of 7 days was not disaffirmance within a reasonable time would be foolish. Once disaffirmed, the contract became void; therefore, no contract existed between the parties, and the minors were entitled to recover all of the moneys which they paid and to be relieved of any further obligation under the contract.

UNIVERSITY OF CINCINNATI HOSPITAL v. COHEN

Court of Appeals of Ohio
April 5, 1989

The defendant-appellant, Jennifer Cohen, appeals from an order granting summary judgment in which the trial court awarded $245,206.50 in favor of the plaintiff-appellee, University of Cincinnati Hospital, but against Jennifer's parents and her for medical services furnished. Although not reflected in a journal entry, the amount claimed by the hospital under its judgment has been reduced to $221,274.17 since counsel agree that there was a mathematical miscalculation. Jennifer's assignment of error presents two issues; (1) whether her minority absolves her from liability for emergency medical services furnished to her by the hospital, and (2) whether her parents' agreement with the hospital to pay her medical expenses was an accord and satisfaction as to her. The answer is "no" to both questions.

Jennifer, who was seventeen at the time and supported by her parents, sustained serious injuries in an automobile collision. A helicopter transported her from the scene to the hospital for emergency treatment and care. Between September 14, 1985 and December 3, 1985, she accumulated charges of $221,274.17. Subsequently, Jennifer's mother executed an assignment to the hospital of all rights and benefits under her employer's hospital insurance plan.

After Jennifer reached the age of majority, the hospital brought this action against Jennifer and her parents, jointly. Counsel for the hospital informed the trial judge that the parents and the hospital had entered into a settlement agreement, but that the hospital would proceed against Jennifer, who denied liability. Counsel for Jennifer argued that she did not contract with the hospital for the services furnished her, and that as a minor, she was not liable. Jennifer's parents have not joined in this appeal.

Ohio follows that common-law rule which provides that a minor's contracts, except for necessaries, are voidable at his or her option. The liability-for-necessaries exception is not based on contract principles; rather, it stems from quasi-contract and unjust enrichment imposed at the time an implied

contract for the reasonable value of necessaries furnished to the minor arises. Since medical services constitute necessaries, a parent having custody of a child is likewise liable for the debt under an implied contract for the minor child's medical care because of the duty to support. If the parents fail or refuse to pay for emergency medical care furnished to save the minor's life, the provider hospital or physician may then look to the child for payment.

Jennifer also contends that if she is liable for the hospital's charges for medical services despite her minority, her parents' settlement agreement with the hospital was an accord and satisfaction as to the debt. A presumption that the hospital relied on the parents' credit for payment exists since Jennifer lived with her parents. Therefore, the relationship between Jennifer and her parents creates primary and secondary liability and the hospital must first look to the parents for payment. A compromise and settlement by parents, who are primarily liable, resulting from payment of a lesser amount in full satisfaction of an unliquidated claim constitutes an accord and satisfaction and discharges the debt of the minor who is secondarily liable.

The terms of the parents' settlement agreement with the hospital negate an accord and satisfaction. Obviously, Jennifer did not intend to join in the settlement agreement with her parents since she consistently maintained that she was not liable to the hospital. More significant, however, is the rule that a liquidated debt or claim cannot be compromised by payment of a lesser sum unless there is consideration separate from the terms of the compromise and settlement. Jennifer did not challenge the accuracy or reasonableness of the hospital's charges. Therefore, it is a liquidated debt. Furthermore, her parents' agreement with the hospital was not for payment of a lesser amount in satisfaction of its $221,274.17 claim.

Finally, Jennifer did not satisfy her burden of proof for an accord and satisfaction since there is no evidence that her parents actually performed the terms of the agreement. Nothing was offered to suggest that the hospital intended to discharge Jennifer's debt in return for her parents' promise.

Therefore, the trial judge correctly granted the hospital's motion for summary judgment.

QUESTIONS FOR ANALYSIS

How can these cases be reconciled? What facts distinguish these cases? Did either of the courts define *necessity?* If so, what is the definition?

Misrepresenting Age

More than ever, minors look and act like adults. It is difficult to distinguish a 15-year-old from a 20-year-old—and with fake identification easy to acquire, misrepresenting one's true age is not difficult. Granted, adults should investigate a "suspected" minor, but that is not always possible. When a minor misleads another party into entering into a contract, both parties can often disaffirm the contract.

Ordinarily, an adult cannot disaffirm a contract made with a minor, but when allegations of misrepresentation are involved, the law will not hold the unsuspecting party to the contract. The rules vary from state to state, but one thing appears to be clear: minors cannot benefit from their own wrongdoing.

To even out the rules, although courts firmly maintain a minor's right to disaffirm a contract, they also require the minor to put the adult back in the same position the adult occupied prior to the contract and the misrepresentation. The courts attempt to prevent unjust enrichment and act in a fair and equitable manner. Consequently, when contracts are voided based upon misrepresentation, the law will force minors to return the property gained by their acts and not allow them to profit from their wrongdoing.

Although courts try to be fair, the tendency is still to lean heavily toward the side of the minor. If the minor cannot return the item, or the item is damaged, it is highly likely that the minor will be afforded the opportunity to disaffirm the contract, with virtually no consequences. The reason behind this policy is that adults should know better! *Gillis v. Whitley's Discount Auto Sales, Inc.,* 319 S.E.2d 661 (N.C. Ct. App. 1984) illustrates the misrepresentation issue.

GILLIS v. WHITLEY'S DISCOUNT AUTO SALES, INC.

Court of Appeals of North Carolina
Sept. 4, 1984

On 21 August 1981, William Todd Wallace purchased a 1977 Datsun automobile from Whitley's Discount Auto Sales, Inc. (Whitley's) for $3080. At the time, Wallace had just turned sixteen years old. Wallace paid $1200 in cash from Social Security benefits and financed the remaining $1880 with a car loan from Richmond County Bank. According to the credit application, Wallace was eighteen years old. Whitley's endorsed Wallace's credit application. After Wallace and the Datsun had been involved in two car accidents, Wallace returned the Datsun to Whitley's on 5 May 1982 and demanded payment of all monies paid.

When Whitley's did not return any of the purchase money, plaintiff, Mary Gillis, Wallace's guardian ad litem, brought this action on 15 June 1982 to disaffirm Wallace's contract with Whitley's, since it was entered into while Wallace was an unemancipated minor. Whitley's argues that the trial court erred in granting summary judgment on the issue of liability when there were legitimate issues of fact as to (1) whether the car was a necessity, and (2) whether Wallace perpetrated a fraud on Whitley's by misrepresenting his age. We affirm.

Under the common-law rule, the conventional contracts of a minor are voidable, except those for necessaries and those authorized by statute. The minor or his legal representative is free to disaffirm the minor's contract either during his minority or within a reasonable time after the minor reaches majority. Whitley's did not plead the affirmative defense that the car was a necessary. Since the affirmative defense that the car was a necessity was not pleaded or effectively argued before the trial court, it cannot be raised for the first time on appeal.

Whitley's second argument for vacating the summary judgment, Wallace's fraudulent misrepresentation of his age, also fails. A minor's representation of his age does not bar him from disaffirming his contract. Therefore, Wallace's allegedly fraudulent misrepresentation of his age was not a valid defense to Wallace's action to disaffirm his contract.

We hold that the trial court did not err in in granting summary judgment on the issue of liability.

When a minor disaffirms a contract, he may recover the consideration he has paid, if he restores whatever part he still has of the benefit he received under the contract. Wallace is entitled to the consideration he personally has paid, since he has returned the damaged car to Whitley's. As a minor, Wallace is only entitled to recover the consideration he personally has paid or is continuing to pay under a valid loan agreement; he is not entitled, as a matter of law, to the total loan liability he originally incurred. A minor is not entitled to a windfall. He is merely to be made whole.

QUESTIONS FOR ANALYSIS

Did the court allow the minor to disaffirm the contract? What conditions did the court set out for the minor in voiding the contract? Was misrepresentation of age by a minor a valid defense? Why or why not?

Ratification: Validating a Contract

When a minor accepts benefits from a contract, **ratification** occurs. The key to ratification is when it happens. For ratification to be effective, a minor must show some act of approval or benefit in some way from the contract after majority. Any other result would not protect the minor.

Ratification can elevate a once voidable contract to the status of a valid one. When a minor becomes an adult and shows a willingness to abide by the terms of a contract made as a minor, ratification may be found. Ratification can be found from a subtle act, such as continuing to make payments on a car upon reaching majority. This is known as *implied ratification.* Ratification may also occur from an express act, which may be oral or written, such as a written letter. No matter what the form of ratification, attaining majority will effect the enforceability of the contract and erase any prior disability. Consequently, minors should pay close attention to their actions when the age of majority approaches.

FAMILY CIRCUS   By Bil Keane

"A penny for your thoughts, Billy."

"Make it a quarter and we've got a deal."

5.3 THE CAPACITY OF INSANE AND MENTALLY ILL PERSONS

Much of the law deals with gray areas. The analysis and evaluation of a case depend on a particular set of facts and circumstances. This is particularly true when dealing with the issue of capacity and how it relates to a person's mental abilities. The *Restatement (Second) of Contract*'s view of mental incapacity is found in § 15, which states:

(1) a person incurs only voidable contractual duties by entering into a transaction if, by reason of mental illness or defect:
    (a) he is unable to understand in a reasonable manner the nature and consequences of the transaction; or
    (b) he is unable to act in a reasonable manner in relation to the transaction and the other party has reason to know of his condition.

Persons who lack mental capacity generally create voidable contracts or void contracts. The law makes distinctions as to a person's capacity based on

TERMS

ratification
The act of giving one's approval to a previous act, whether one's own or someone else's, which, without such confirmation, would be nonbinding. A person may ratify a contract by expressly promising to be bound by it. Ratification may be implied from a person's conduct; it may also take place as a result of accepting the benefits of a transaction. Ratification is the confirmation of an act that has already been performed, as opposed to the authorization of an act that is yet to be performed.

the degree of mental inability. Suppose that an individual's mental ability is impaired only temporarily. In that instance, the mentally infirm person may have moments of lucidity and thus can understand the terms of a contract. If it can be proven that the person understood the contract and was competent, the contract may be enforced; but if the party was not competent or was mentally insane *at the time the contract was created,* a voidable contract is formed. If the mental infirmity worsens, the party may disaffirm the contract just as a minor could.

Determining whether a contract by a mentally disabled person is voidable or enforceable is a very difficult task. Each situation has to be evaluated independently to determine whether the person truly understood the terms of the contract and the consequences of those acts in the contract. Review *Butler v. Harrison,* 578 A.2d 1098 (D. C. 1990) for a good example of a court's analysis of mental incapacity. Pay close attention to the court's rationale.

BUTLER v. HARRISON

District of Columbia Court of Appeals
July 13, 1990

Mrs. Harrison, her husband, and her son, Edward C. Calhoun, acquired 1426 C Street, N.E., as joint tenants in 1946. By quitclaim deeds dated December 7, 1973 and January 31, 1974, Mr. Harrison and Mr. Calhoun conveyed their interests in the property to Mrs. Harrison as sole owner. On April 8, 1982, Mrs. Harrison conveyed title to Mr. Harrison and herself as tenants by the entirety by a quitclaim deed recorded April 12, 1982. Mrs. Harrison died testate on November 27, 1984, at the age of 74. Pursuant to her will, executed on January 22, 1974, appellants, Mrs. Harrison's son and her grandchildren, were to receive the C Street property subject to a life estate in Mr. Harrison. Mr. Harrison died testate on March 4, 1985, devising all of his property, including the C street property, to appellees, Luther Harrison and Jessier Mae Price, his brother and sister. Appellants filed a complaint to set aside the April 8, 1982, quitclaim deed on the ground that Mrs. Harrison suffered from senile dementia when she executed the deed and consequently lacked the mental capacity to execute it.

At trial, Mr. Calhoun testified that sometime in 1980 his mother began to lose her concentration during conversations, would forget who he was,

and would be forgetful and withdrawn. He also testified, however, that Mrs. Harrison's confusion would "come and go." Mrs. Harrison's granddaughters offered similar testimony. Evidence also showed that Mrs. Harrison was hospitalized from May 27, 1982, to June 5, 1982, when she was diagnosed as suffering from an "altered mental state" and "probably senile dementia," and again in October 1982, when her diagnosis as suffering from a noncorrectable form of dementia was confirmed.

Dr. Josephine King, the attending physician during Mrs. Harrison's first hospitalization, who supervised Mrs. Harrison's treating physicians but had no personal contact with her, testified that Mrs. Harrison's condition prevented her from thinking in an analytical, coordinated fashion and that she suffered from a loss of recent and distant memory. Dr. King interpreted the medical records from the first hospitalization as showing that Mrs. Harrison was disoriented as to person, place, and time, and totally confused throughout her initial hospital stay, and noted that a CAT scan demonstrated some atrophy of her brain which is commonly associated with such symptoms. She testified however, that in May 1982, Mrs. Harrison, although totally confused, could carry on a conversation with her family and the doctors. Dr. King did not think that she was qualified to comment on Mrs. Harrison's mental capacity prior to her hospital admission and offered no opinion.

Dr. Samuel Scott, Mrs. Harrison's treating physician during her second hospitalization, five months after she executed the deed at issue, found Mrs. Harrison to be totally disoriented as to time and place, that she did not know what season of the year or what year it was, and that she was unable to concentrate or engage in intellectual functions. Dr. Scott concluded that when he saw her in October 1982, she lacked the mental capacity to understand the legal nature of a document and deduced, based on her then present condition, that her mental capacity to understand such a document back in April 1982 was "doubtful" at best.

Appellees offered the evidence of Mr. Harrison's brother, Luther, who testified about visiting Mrs. Harrison at her home several times a week in 1982 and at the hospitals. According to him, Mrs. Harrison always knew who he was and asked how he was doing and otherwise seemed all right. Sterling W. Perry, Esquire, who had provided legal services for Mr. and Mrs. Harrison, remembered nothing unusual about Mrs. Harrison's behavior on the day she executed the deed and testified that she had explained the contents of the deed to Mrs. Harrison and advised her about the deed's legal effect. Ms. Perry testified that while she had no medical training, she thought, based on her regular office procedure, that Mrs. Harrison was "fit" to sign the deed, since otherwise she would not have allowed her to sign it. Neither witness had been aware of Mrs. Harrison's dementia condition.

The trial judge declined to set aside the April 8, 1982, quitclaim deed, ruling that appellants had failed to meet their burden of proof to show by a preponderance of the evidence that Mrs. Harrison lacked the mental capacity to execute the deed. The judge found that the only evidence relating to

her lack of mental capacity was the medical opinion of two doctors.

Further, the trial judge ruled that appellants' lay opinion about Mrs. Harrison's mental condition during the time she executed the deed was insufficient to prove her lack of mental capacity. While there was consistent testimony that Mrs. Harrison's alertness was deteriorating as of December 1981 and thereafter, there also was evidence, the judge noted, that she had both good and bad days.

The test of mental capacity to contract is whether the person in question possesses sufficient mind to understand, in a reasonable manner, the nature, extent, character, and effect of the particular transaction in which she is engaged, whether or not she is competent in transacting business generally. It is presumed that an adult is competent to enter into an agreement and the burden of proof is on the party asserting incompetency. Further, the party asserting incompetency must show not merely that the person suffers from some mental disease or defect such as dementia, but that such mental infirmity rendered the person incompetent to execute the particular transaction according to the standard set forth above.

While a person's prior and subsequent condition may be inquired into for the purpose of reflecting on her mental state at the time in question, and lay opinion testimony is admissible on the issue of mental capacity, there was no direct evidence concerning Mrs. Harrison's mental condition on the date she executed the quitclaim deed other than Ms. Perry's recollection that nothing unusual happened. Although there was evidence that Mrs. Harrison suffered from a disease resulting in progressive mental incompetency and that her mental capacity around April 1982 was marked by alternating periods of confusion and lucidity, the trial judge could properly give greater credence to the testimony of lay persons who saw Mrs. Harrison at the relevant time than to medical testimony regarding her condition five months later.

QUESTIONS FOR ANALYSIS

What was the court's test for mental incapacity? Did the court find mental incompetence? What facts support the court's holdings?

An easier issue arises when a person has been legally declared by a court to be insane or *non compos mentis*. Those who are declared by a court to be insane are denied the right to contract, and thus any contract they create is void. The court appoints a guardian to act on the person's behalf, and the guardian's acts must always be with court approval. The only person who can enter into contracts for the declared incompetent person is the guardian. There are no exceptions to this rule, as courts will protect insane persons from themselves and society.

As with minors, society is also protected when necessities are provided to mentally incapacitated persons. A mentally incapacitated person is liable for contracts created for necessities, under the theory of quasi contract. Only the reasonable value of the services will be allowed, however; as with minors, courts do not allow the mentally incapacitated to be taken advantage of.

5.4 OTHER PERSONS LACKING CAPACITY

There are other situations in which persons are legally incapable to contract. This incapacity occurs when a person is intoxicated or drugged, is an alien, or is a convicted felon.

Intoxicated or Drugged Persons

Persons who are under the influence of alcohol or drugs often lack the capacity to contract. Capacity is determined by the degree of intoxication. If the intoxication is to such a degree that the party has no ability to understand the nature of the contract, the court may not enforce the contract. The contract created is voidable.

As with mentally incapacitated persons, courts have to evaluate these situations on a case-by-case basis. Unless the facts are clear, courts generally do not like to avoid contracts based upon intoxication by alcohol or drugs.

Persons who are intoxicated may disaffirm or ratify a contract when sobriety returns. If disaffirmance is desired, it must be total and complete, that is, the party must return all consideration. Unless disaffirmance occurs soon after the disability is removed (i.e., upon sobriety), the assumption will be that the party has ratified the contract and thus it will be enforced.

Aliens

TERMS

alien
   Any person present
   within the borders
   of the United States
   who is not a U.S. citizen. . . . Any foreigner.

Persons who are not citizens of the United States are known as **aliens**. As a general rule, aliens have the capacity to contract and have very few restrictions on that ability to contract. Exceptions include contracting with an alien whose country is at war with the United States. While hostilities are continuing, such aliens lack the capacity to contract and may create a voidable contract. This situation does not occur that often.

Convicted Felons

Upon imprisonment, many prisoners have restrictions placed not only on their freedom, but also on their ability to contract. Consequently, contracts created by incarcerated persons are unenforceable and void. However, once prisoners are freed, their contractual rights are restored and they enjoy virtually the same rights they had prior to imprisonment.

Figure 5-2 sets forth the types of contracts minors, insane persons, intoxicated persons, aliens, and convicts can create.

Classification	Status of Contract
Minors	Voidable
Mentally incapacitated a. Lucid moment b. Competent but not judicially c. Declared incompetent by court	Valid Voidable Void
Intoxicated persons (alcohol or drugs)	Voidable
Aliens	Voidable
Convicts a. Imprisonment b. Release	Voidable Valid

FIGURE 5-2   Status of contract by person with questionable capacity

5.5 PRACTICAL APPLICATION

As with mutual assent, issues of capacity do not often jump off the pages of a contract. In many circumstances, investigation will determine if a legally incapacitated person's rights were violated. But one area where capacity is a clear issue involves the preparation of **affidavits**. Many paralegals are asked to draft affidavits for a variety of reasons. For example, an affidavit may accompany a **pleading**, such as a **complaint**, or a **motion**, such as a motion for summary judgment. Most affidavits begin with a paragraph that specifically deals with the capacity issue. A sample introductory paragraph might read:

My name is Joseph Simms. I am over the age of eighteen and of sound mind. I have never been convicted of a felony nor a crime involving moral turpitude. I have personal knowledge of the facts herein and know the purposes for which this affidavit is being made.

affidavit
Any voluntary statement reduced to writing and sworn to or affirmed before a person legally authorized to administer an oath or affirmation; a sworn statement.

pleadings
Formal statements by the parties to an action setting forth their claims or defenses. The various kinds of pleadings, and the rules governing them, are set forth in detail in the Federal Rules of Civil Procedure and, with respect to pleading in state courts, by the rules of civil procedure of the several states.

complaint
The initial pleading in a civil action, in which the plaintiff alleges a cause of action and asks that the wrong done be remedied by the court.

motion
An application made to a court for the purpose of obtaining an order or rule directing something to be done in favor of the applicant. The types of motions available to litigants, as well as their form and the matters they appropriately address, are set forth in detail in the Federal Rules of Civil Procedure and the rules of civil procedure of the various states, as well as in the Federal Rules of Criminal Procedure and the various states' rules of criminal procedure. Motions may be written or oral, depending on the type of relief sought and on the court in which they are made.

There are variations on such paragraphs such as:

My name is Joseph Simms. I am competent to make this affidavit and have personal knowledge of the facts herein.

Notice that such paragraphs focus on the issue of capacity by stating that the **affiant** has reached majority, is not insane, and has not been convicted of a crime. These representations are critical to the validity of an affidavit and should not be overlooked in drafting.

A paralegal may also encounter the capacity issue when a party disaffirms or ratifies a contract. Ordinarily, your task will be to assist in drafting a letter to a service provider or merchant, such as a car dealership, an electronics store, or even a hospital. Figure 5-3 shows a letter disaffirming a contract. The letter could be revised so that Cheryl Hargrove, the minor, could sign the letter.

Mr. Richard Simon   March 31, 1994
ABC Cars
2154 Chestnut Street
New City, U.S.A. 81176

     Re: Disaffirmance of Car Purchase

Dear Mr. Simon:

     On March 11, 1994, my daughter, Cheryl Hargrove, purchased a car from your establishment. She was sixteen (16) years old at the time of the transaction, a minor.

     At the time of the transaction, she tendered Five Hundred Dollars and No Cents ($500.00) as a down payment when she signed the contract. I demand the return of the $500.00 prior to returning the car.

     I will have her return the car and keys on April 14, 1994, if the check is sent to us by April 7, 1994.

     Thank you for your cooperation.

                                Sincerely,

                                Sally Hargrove

FIGURE 5-3 Letter disaffirming contract

The minor, upon reaching the age of legal adulthood, may also reaffirm the once-voidable contract (see the ratification letter in Figure 5-4).

Mr. Richard Simon
ABC Cars
2154 Chestnut Street
New City, U.S.A. 81176

September 17, 1994

Re: 1990 Toyota Corolla

Dear Mr. Simon:

On March 11, 1994, I purchased a 1990 Toyota Corolla. At the time I signed the contract I was seventeen (17) years old. I turned eighteen (18) years old on July 31, 1994, and want to continue my obligations under the contract. I therefore affirm my obligations under the contract.

Sincerely,

Cheryl Hargrove

FIGURE 5-4 Letter ratifying contract

SUMMARY

5.1   Parties must have capacity to enter into contracts. To have capacity, a party must be over the legal age and of sound mind. Persons who lack capacity create void or voidable contracts.

5.2   Minors lack the capacity to contract. Depending upon the timing of the transaction, a minor can either disaffirm or ratify a contract. When minors contract for necessities, their parents will be held responsible for the reasonable value of the necessities provided. In addition, if a minor misrepresents his or her age, the adult will not be held to the contract.

5.3   Persons who are mentally incapacitated create either void or voidable contracts. Whether the contract is void or voidable depends upon whether the court has declared a person incompetent. Mentally incompetent parties are responsible for paying for necessities.

5.4   Individuals who are intoxicated or drugged may lack mental capacity. The contracts they create are voidable. Generally, aliens have the capacity to contract and convicted felons lack capacity to contract while imprisoned.

REVIEW QUESTIONS

1. How is *capacity* defined?
2. How can a minor legally reject a contract?
3. What is one method of holding a minor responsible for a contract?
4. How is *necessity* defined?

TERMS

affiant
    A person who makes a sworn written statement or affidavit.

5. Who is responsible for a minor's contract when it involves a necessity?
6. Are minors responsible for their contracts when they misrepresent their age? Why or why not?
7. Define *ratification* and when it applies.
8. What types of contracts do the mentally incapacitated create?
9. Can intoxicated persons create a valid contract? Why or why not?
10. When can a convicted felon create a valid contract?

EXERCISES

1. Draft an introductory paragraph for an affidavit which complies with your state statutes.
2. A minor, Jennifer Owens, has purchased a 1991 Mustang convertible from the local used car dealership, ABC Motors, Inc. Prepare a letter disaffirming the purchase of the car.
3. Brief *Kargar v. Sorrentino*, 788 S.W.2d 189 (Tex. Ct. App.–Houston [14th Dist.] 1990).
   a. What are the facts of the case?
   b. Determine the court's holding.
   c. What was the basis of the court's reasoning?

CHAPTER 6
Legality in Contracts

6.1 LEGALITY: A NECESSITY FOR ENFORCEABILITY

Even after competent parties have accepted an offer, provided the consideration, and understood the terms for mutual assent, one more element must be present for a contract to be enforceable. This final necessary element is **legality**. The contract must have a legal purpose and legal subject matter to be enforceable between the parties. If a contract is deemed illegal, it is void.

Sometimes contracts that appear to be legal are later deemed by a court to be illegal. This causes concern for those creating contracts. Parties do not know that the contract they created was illegal and therefore unenforceable. The illegality may be the result of a court challenge during which the decision strikes down the contract. Consequently, the parties may not have been able to predict the outcome of their contractual agreement. Legality can be difficult to identify when no clear legal guidance exists.

In addition, an illegal contract can be formed when a party violates a statute or public policy. These very common occurences will void a contract. The *Restatement (Second) of Contracts* § 178 discusses legality as follows:

TERMS

legality
The condition of conformity with the law; lawfulness.

A promise or other term of an agreement is unenforceable on grounds of public policy if legislation provides that it is unenforceable or the interest in its enforcement is clearly outweighed in the circumstances by a public policy against the enforcement of such terms.

When such violations occur, the contract will be deemed illegal. Consequently, contracts may be illegal if they violate statutes or public policy.

6.2 CONTRACTS VIOLATING A STATUTE

A common type of illegal contract occurs when the parties' agreement or conduct is prohibited by law. The most obvious situation that violates a statute is a contract for hire (an agreement to kill someone for money). Common sense tells us that if you hire someone to kill your parents, promise the killer the proceeds of a life insurance policy as payment, and then renege on the agreement, no court in this country will enforce the contract. That kind of activity is criminal and an agreement to engage in unlawful activity is void and unenforceable. So are agreements to engage in tortious activity, such as a deliberate scheme to defraud unsuspecting investors. These acts would be regarded as illegal and a contract involving such acts would be illegal and unenforceable.

Illegal agreements go beyond a person's activities. Illegal agreements are also found in contractual terminology that violates laws on usury, wagering, Sunday laws, and unlicensed persons. Each has a common measure, in that they violate specific state statutory provisions.

Usury Laws

States regulate the amount of interest individuals and business entities can charge in a loan or credit transaction. These statutes are known as **usury** laws. A usurious contract exists when money is loaned at a higher interest rate than a state statute permits. To protect the public from the greedy excesses of business, states put a ceiling on the amount of interest that may be charged in a lending situation. An example of a Texas usury statute is reprinted in Figure 6-1.

Interest rates may vary according to the risk involved in a transaction. Private lending companies and pawn shops, whose customers often have poor credit histories and represent a high risk, can charge a higher interest rate than a banking institution. Again, the interest rate is regulated by statute.

Another area in which interest rates are monitored closely is in retail installment contracts, such as for credit cards or the purchase of any consumer item like a computer, stereo, or refrigerator. The rates companies can charge are regulated by the states. Figure 6-2 examines provisions for charging interest in retail installment contracts. Note how specific the language in the contracts is and also how small the print is. Such agreements are used every day and are legally enforceable.

TERMS

usury
Charging a rate of interest that exceeds the rate permitted by law.

Art. 5069–1.02. Maximum rates of interest

Except as otherwise fixed by law, the maximum rate of interest shall be ten percent per annum. A greater rate of interest than ten percent per annum unless otherwise authorized by law shall be deemed usurious. All contracts for usury are contrary to public policy and shall be subject to the appropriate penalties perscribed in Article 1.06 of this Subtitle.

Art. 5069–1.06. Penalties

(1) Any person who contracts for, charges or receives interest which is greater than the amount authorized by this Subtitle, shall forfeit to the obligor three times the amount of usurious interest contracted for, charged or received, such usurious interest being the amount the total interest contracted for, charged, or received exceeds the amount of interest allowed by law, and reasonable attorney fees fixed by the court except that in no event shall the amount forfeited by less than Two Thousand Dollars or twenty percent of the principal, whichever is the smaller sum; provided, that there shall be no penalty for any usurious interest which results from an accidental and bona fide error.

(2) Any person who contracts for, charges or receives interest which is in excess of double the amount of interest allowed by this Subtitle shall forfeit as an additional penalty, all principal as well as interest and all other charges and shall pay reasonable attorney fees set by the court; provided further that any such person violating the provisions of this section shall be guilty of a misdemeanor and upon conviction thereof shall be punished by fine of not more than One Thousand Dollars. Each contract or transaction in violation of this section shall constitute a separate offense punishable hereunder.

FIGURE 6-1 Sample usury statute (Texas)

_____ CHARGE ACCOUNT AGREEMENT

I apply for credit with _____ (_____). The information on the back of this agreement is true. I authorize _____ to investigate my credit record including my references and statements, and to report my performance of this agreement to any consumer reporting agency or other credit grantor.

The monthly statement from _____ will show my account balance (the amount I owe) at the bill closing date by which payment must be made. If my account is not a 30 Day Account, the statement will also show a minimum payment due (the amount which must be paid by the next bill closing date), and finance charge, and the "average daily balance" on which it was calculated. The time between closing dates is referred to as a billing period. I understand that I will have either a 30 Day or an Option Account. I may also have an Extended Payment Account, but _____ may limit the types of goods and services which I may purchase under the Extended Payment Account.

30-DAY ACCOUNT: I agree to pay _____ the full amount of my new balance on or before my next bill closing date. If I do not pay the full amount of my account balance on or before my next bill closing date, I agree that _____ may, upon notice to me, convert my 30 Day Account to an Option Account.

OPTION ACCOUNT: Whenever I have an account balance, I agree to pay _____ on or before my next bill closing date whichever of the following is greater. (a) 20% of my account balance or (b) $10.

EXTENDED PAYMENT ACCOUNT: Whenever I have an account balance, I agree to pay _____ on or before my next bill closing date, whichever of the following is the greatest: (a) 5% of my highest account balance since the last time I had a zero balance; (b) $50; or (c) a monthly amount agreed to in writing by _____ and me.

FIGURE 6-2 Sample retail installment contract

I agree that _____ shall retain a security interest in each item purchased, until it is fully paid for; may repossess any merchandise for which _____ has not been paid in full; may dispose of the merchandise at public or private sale, and hold me responsible for any unpaid balance of my account and may exercise all other rights and remedies of a secured party under the _____ Uniform Commercial Code and any other applicable laws.

I may pay the full balance of my Option or Extended Payment Account at any time to avoid additional finance charge.

A finance charge will be applied to Option and Extended Payment Accounts. _____ figures the finance charge on my account by applying the periodic rate of $1\frac{1}{2}\%$ per month (ANNUAL PERCENTAGE RATE OF 18%) to the "average daily balance" of my account (including current transactions). To get the "average daily balance" _____ takes the beginning balance of my account each day, adds any new purchases or miscellaneous debits, and subtracts any payments or credits. This gives _____ the daily balance. Then, _____ adds all the daily balances for the billing cycle and divides the total by the number of days in the billing cycle. This gives _____ the "average daily balance".

No finance charge will be assessed for a billing period in which there is no previous balance or during which payments and credits equal or exceed the previous balance. Earlier receipt of payments, during a billing period will lower the finance charge for that period. _____ may revise the terms of this agreement after notifying me, but the changes may not increase the payments required for previous purchases. Revisions in the calculation of finance charge or annual percentage rate may not exceed the legal limits.

I apply for 30 Day ☐ Option ☐ Extended Payment ☐

Payments are not considered made until received by _____. If I fail to make payments when due, all sums owed by me to _____ immediately become due. If I fail to pay the amount owed in full and you give my account to an attorney (who is not one of your salaried employees) for collection, I will pay you a reasonable amount to cover the attorney's fee and court costs.

I may be liable for the unauthorized use of my _____ charge indentification card. I will not be liable for unauthorized use that occurs after I notify _____ credit office where my account was opened, at the address shown on the back of my bill, of the loss, theft of possible unauthorized use. Notice may be oral or written. In any case my liability will not exceed $50.

NOTICE: SEE OTHER SIDE FOR INFORMATION ABOUT YOUR RIGHTS TO DISPUTE BILLING ERRORS.

NOTICE: ANY HOLDER OF THIS CONSUMER CREDIT CONTRACT IS SUBJECT TO ALL CLAIMS AND DEFENSES WHICH THE DEBTOR COULD ASSERT AGAINST THE SELLER OF GOODS OR SERVICES OBTAINED PURSUANT HERETO OR WITH THE PROCEEDS HEREOF. RECOVERY HEREUNDER BY THE DEBTOR SHALL NOT EXCEED AMOUNTS PAID BY THE DEBTOR HEREUNDER.

NOTICE TO THE BUYER: DO NOT SIGN THIS AGREEMENT BEFORE YOU READ IT OR IF IT CONTAINS BLANK SPACES, YOU ARE ENTITLED TO AN EXACT COPY OF THE AGREEMENT YOU SIGN.

I AGREE TO THE ABOVE TERMS AND ACKNOWLEDGE RECEIPT OF A COPY OF THIS AGREEMENT AND A COPY OF NOTICE OF RIGHTS TO DISPUTE BILLING ERRORS.

Applicant Signature _____ Joint Applicant or _____ Date _____
Co-Signature

Address _____ Address _____

FIGURE 6-2 *(Continued)*

When violation of a state's usury law is proved, the contract is void. The sanctions for violating usury laws range from a lender's being able to collect the interest charged on the principal amount loaned to the lender's receiving no payment at all for either the principal or the interest charged. Each state has its own penalties.

Wagering Laws

Most states prohibit their citizens from gambling, betting, or participating in games of chance. Unless condoned by a state, any agreement or scheme that promises prizes or money is illegal.

There are exceptions. For example, Nevada and New Jersey allow casino gambling, and Louisiana allows betting on horse racing. A new trend permitted in many states is wagering in state-sponsored lotteries; many states now permit such wagering because it produces revenue and avoids higher taxes.

Sunday Laws

Many states prohibit the formation and performance of contracts on Sunday. These laws are known as *Sunday laws* or *blue laws.* (Note: The term "blue law" is derived from the fact that the first laws banning Sunday contracts were written on blue paper.) The logic behind Sunday laws is that persons should have a day of rest. Sunday laws have been repealed or eased in many states to allow the sale of merchandise and the making of contracts on Sunday. Many states still do prohibit certain transactions, however, such as the sale of alcoholic beverages on Sunday.

Where Sunday laws still exist, a contract made on a Sunday may be deemed void. There are definite ways to avoid the deathknell for such a contract; a party might claim either (1) that the contract was not actually accepted on a Sunday, or (2) lack of knowledge that the contract was executed on a Sunday.

Undoubtedly, the trend is to relax Sunday laws. Issues of First Amendment rights have been raised by groups challenging such laws. Many states have left the option of observing Sunday laws to local governments. Consequently, one county may observe a Sunday law even though an adjoining county may not. Check state restrictions for Sunday law prohibitions.

Unlicensed Performance Laws

Many laws require certain businesses and professionals be licensed. Licensing requirements stem from the need for public protection; professions such as law, medicine, accountancy, and architecture have such requirements to protect the public from persons who do not meet standard educational and testing criteria for licensing. Most of us realize that attorneys must have a minimum legal education and pass a state bar to become licensed to practice law. Practicing law without a license is illegal and violates most states' statutes. The purpose for the licenses is regulatory, not economic. A contract involving an unlicensed professional would probably be unenforceable.

However, other licensing requirements for businesses or professions exist for purely economic reasons. Licensing provides needed revenue for state and local governments. When persons fail to obtain the requisite revenue-based licenses, contracts made by them may still be enforceable. Courts examine these contracts closely, but when the legislative intent is economic, such contracts will usually be enforced. The approach to licensing as set out in *Restatement (Second)* § 181 has been adopted by many states:

> If a party is prohibited from doing an act because of his failure to comply with a licensing, registration, or similar requirement, a promise in consideration of his doing that act or of his promise to do it is unenforceable on grounds of public policy if:
> a. the requirement has a regulatory purpose; and
> b. the interest in the enforcement of the promise is clearly outweighed by the public policy behind the requirement.

Licensing requirements should be reviewed before undertaking a commercial transaction with a professional who is regulated by state statute. Enforceability of the contract will depend on whether the professional licensing is for public protection or revenue.

6.3 CONTRACTS VIOLATING PUBLIC POLICY

Courts have the discretion to void a contract if it is unfair, offends the public's moral sensibilities, or is oppressive. Unconscionable contracts fall into the category of oppressive and unfair transactions. An unconscionable contract can be avoided based upon lack of mutual assent, as we learned in Chapter 3, and also on the basis of legality. The focus for a court is the public good and public interest.

One type of contract that has received much public attention and court scrutiny are **surrogate motherhood** contracts. A surrogacy contract involves the hiring of a woman to bear another woman's or couple's child for a fee. These contracts usually provide a substantial fee to the surrogate for the service, as well as the payment of medical expenses. Upon the birth of the child, the surrogate gives the child to the biological parents and terminates all her rights to the child. Unfortunately, as they say, easier said than done. Cases have developed on this issue all over the country, with the two most publicized cases from California and New Jersey. Each focuses on the surrogacy issue, but the facts of the cases are different and so are the results. Review *In re Baby M,* 109 N.J. 396, 537 A.2d 1227 (1988) and *Johnson v. Calvert,* 5 Cal. 484, 851 P.2d 776, 19 Cal. Rptr. 2d 494 (1993) paying close attention to each court's analysis of the legality of the contract issue.

TERMS

surrogate motherhood
The status of a woman who "hosts" the fertilized egg of another woman in her womb or who is artificially inseminated with the sperm of a man who is married to someone else and to whom (with his wife) she has agreed to assign her parental rights if the child is delivered.

IN RE BABY M

Supreme Court of New Jersey
Decided Feb. 3, 1988

In this matter the Court is asked to determine the validity of a contract that purports to provide a new way of bringing children into a family. We invalidate the surrogacy contract because it conflicts with the law and public policy of this State. While we recognize the depth of the yearning of infertile couples to have their own children, we find the payment of money to a "surrogate" mother illegal, perhaps criminal, and potentially degrading to women. Although in this case we grant custody to the natural father, the evidence having clearly proved such custody to be in the best interests of the infant, we void both the termination of the surrogate mother's parental rights and the adoption of the child by the wife/stepparent. We thus restore the "surrogate" as the mother of the child.

In February 1985, William Stern and Mary Beth Whitehead entered into a surrogacy contract. It recited that Stern's wife, Elizabeth, was infertile, that they wanted a child, and that Mrs. Whitehead was willing to provide that child as the mother with Mr. Stern as the father.

The contract provided that through artificial insemination using Mr. Stern's sperm, Mrs. Whitehead would become pregnant, carry the child to term, bear it, deliver it to the Sterns, and thereafter do whatever was necessary to terminate her maternal rights so that Mrs. Stern could thereafter adopt the child. Mr. Stern, on his part, agreed to attempt the artificial insemination and to pay Mrs. Whitehead $10,000 after the child's birth, on its delivery to him.

[T]he Sterns learned of the Infertility Center, the possibilities of surrogacy, and of Mary Beth Whitehead. On February 6, 1985, Mr. Stern and Mr. and Mrs. Whitehead executed the surrogate parenting agreement. After several artificial inseminations over a period of months, Mrs. Whitehead became pregnant. On March 27, 1986, Baby M was born.

Mrs. Whitehead realized, almost from the moment of birth, that she could not part with this child. She had felt a bond with it even during pregnancy. Despite powerful inclinations to the contrary, she turned her child over to the Sterns on March 30 at the Whiteheads' home. Later in the evening of March 30, Mrs. Whitehead became deeply disturbed, disconsolate, stricken with unbearable sadness. The next day she went to the Sterns' home and told them how much she was suffering.

The depth of Mrs. Whitehead's despair surprised and frightened the Sterns. She told them that she could not live without her baby, that she must have her, even if only for one week, that thereafter she would surrender her child. The Sterns, concerned that Mrs. Whitehead might indeed commit suicide, not wanting under any circumstances to risk that, and in any event believing that Mrs. Whitehead would keep her word, turned the child over to her. It was not until four months later, after a series of attempts to regain possession of the child, that Melissa was returned to the Sterns.

Due to Mrs. Whitehead's refusal to relinquish the baby, Mr. Stern filed a complaint seeking enforcement of the surrogacy contract. He alleged, accurately, that Mrs. Whitehead had not only refused to comply with the surrogacy contract but had threatened to flee from New Jersey with the child in order to avoid even the possibility of his obtaining custody.

The Sterns' complaint, in addition to seeking possession and ultimately custody of the child, sought enforcement of the surrogacy contract. Pursuant to the contract, it asked that the child be permanently placed in their custody, that Mrs. Whitehead's parental rights be terminated, and that Mrs. Stern be allowed to adopt the child, *i.e.*, that, for all purposes, Melissa become the Sterns' child.

We have concluded that this surrogacy contract is invalid. Our conclusion has two bases: direct conflict with existing statutes and conflict with the public policies of this State, as expressed in its statutory and decisional law.

One of the surrogacy contract's basic purposes, to achieve the adoption of a child through private placement, though permitted in New Jersey "is very much disfavored." Its use of money for this purpose is illegal and perhaps criminal. In addition to the inducement of money, there is the coercion of contract: the natural mother's irrevocable agreement, prior to birth, even prior to conception, to surrender the child to the adoptive couple. Such an agreement is totally unenforceable in private placement adoption. Even where the adoption is through an approved agency, the formal agreement to surrender occurs only after birth, and then, by regulation, only after the birth mother has been offered counseling.

The surrogacy contract conflicts with: (1) laws prohibiting the use of money in connection with adoptions; (2) laws requiring proof of parental unfitness or abandonment before termination of parental rights is ordered or an adoption is granted; and (3) laws that make surrender of custody and consent to adoption revocable in private placement adoptions.

As the trial court recognized, without a valid termination there can be no adoption. This requirement applies to all adoptions, whether they be private placements or agency adoptions. In this case a termination of parental rights was obtained not by proving the statutory prerequisites but by claiming the benefit of contractual provisions. [I]t is clear that contractual agreement to abandon one's parental rights, or not to contest a termination action, will not be enforced in our courts.

The surrogacy contract's invalidity, resulting from its direct conflict with the statutory provisions, is further underlined when its goals and means are measured against New Jersey's public policy. The contract's basic premise, that the natural parents can decide in advance of birth which one is to have custody of the child, bears no relationship to the settled law that the child's best interests shall determine custody.

The surrogacy contract guarantees permanent separation of the child from one of its natural parents. Our policy, however, has long been that to the extent possible, children should remain with and be brought up by both of their natural parents.

The whole purpose and effect of the surrogacy contract was to give the father the exclusive right to the child by destroying the rights of the mother.

Under the contract, the natural mother is irrevocably committed before she knows the strength of her bond with her child. She never makes a totally voluntary, informed decision, for quite clearly any decision prior to the baby's birth is, in the most important sense, uninformed, and any decision after that, compelled by a pre-existing contractual commitment, the threat of a lawsuit, and the inducement of a $10,000 payment, is less than totally voluntary. Her interests are of little concern to those who controlled this transaction.

This is the sale of a child, or, at the very least, the sale of a mother's right to her child, the only mitigating factor being that one of the purchasers is the father. Almost every evil that prompted the prohibition on the payment of money in connection with adoptions exists here.

In America, we decided long ago that merely because conduct purchased by money was "voluntary" did not mean that it was good or beyond regulation and prohibition. There are, in short, values that society deems more important than granting to wealth whatever it can buy, be it labor, love, or life. Whether this principle recommends prohibition of surrogacy, which presumably sometimes results in great satisfaction to all of the parties, is not for us to say. We note here only that, under existing law, the fact that Mrs. Whitehead "agreed" to the arrangement is not dispositive.

In sum, the harmful consequences of this surrogacy arrangement appear to us all too palpable. In new Jersey the surrogate mother's agreement to sell her child is void. Its irrevocability infects the entire contract, as does the money that purports to buy it.

JOHNSON v. CALVERT

California Supreme Court
Date decided May 20, 1993

In this case we address several of the legal questions raised by recent advances in reproductive technology. When, pursuant to a surrogacy agreement, a zygote formed of the gametes of a husband

and wife is implanted in the uterus of another woman, who carries the resulting fetus to term and gives birth to a child not genetically related to her, who is the child's "natural mother" under California law? Does a determination that the wife is the child's natural mother work a deprivation of the gestating woman's constitutional rights? And is such an agreement barred by any public policy of this state?

We conclude that the husband and wife are the child's natural parents, and that this result does not offend the state or federal Constitution or public policy.

Mark and Crispina Calvert are a married couple who desired to have a child. Crispina was forced to undergo a hysterectomy in 1984. Her ovaries remained capable of producing eggs, however, and the couple eventually considered surrogacy. In 1989 Anna Johnson heard about Crispina's plight from a coworker and offered to serve as a surrogate for the Calverts.

On January 15, 1990, Mark, Crispina, and Anna signed a contract providing that an embryo created by the sperm of Mark and the egg of Crispina would be implanted in Anna and the child born would be taken into Mark and Crispina's home "as their child." Anna agreed she would relinquish "all parental rights" to the child in favor of Mark and Crispina. In return, Mark and Crispina would pay Anna $10,000 in a series of installments, the last to be paid six weeks after the child's birth. Mark and Crispina were also to pay for a $200,000 life insurance policy on Anna's life. The zygote was implanted on January 19, 1990. Less than a month later, an ultrasound test confirmed Anna was pregnant.

In July 1990, Anna sent Mark and Crispina a letter demanding the balance of payments due her or else she would refuse to give up the child. The following month, Mark and Crispina responded with a lawsuit, seeking a declaration they are the legal parents of the unborn child. Anna filed her own action to be declared the mother of the child, and the two cases were eventually consolidated. The parties agreed to an independent guardian ad litem for the purposes of the suit.

The child was born on September 19, 1990, and blood samples were obtained from both Anna and the child for analysis. The blood test results excluded Anna as the genetic mother. The parties agreed to a court order providing that the child would remain with Mark and Crispina on a temporary basis with visits by Anna.

The "parent and child relationship" means "the legal relationship existing between a child and his natural or adoptive parents incident to which the law confers or imposes rights, privileges, duties, and obligations. It includes the mother and child relationship and the father and child relationship." "The parent and child relationship extends equally to every child and to every parent, regardless of the marital status of the parents." The "parent and child relationship" is thus a legal relationship encompassing two kinds of parents, "natural" and "adoptive."

Passage of the [Uniform Parentage] Act clearly was not motivated by the need to resolve surrogacy disputes, which were virtually unknown in 1975. Yet it facially applies to any parentage determination, including the rare case in which a child's maternity is in issue. In deciding the issue of maternity under the Act we have felt free to take into account the parties' intentions, as expressed in the surrogacy contract, because in our view the agreement is not, on its face, inconsistent with public policy.

Preliminarily, Mark and Crispina urge us to interpret the Legislature's 1992 passage of a bill that would have regulated surrogacy as an expression of this state's public policy despite the fact that Governor Wilson's veto prevented the bill from becoming law. Senate Bill No. 937 contained a finding that surrogate contracts are not against sound public and social policy. Had Senate Bill No. 937 become law, there would be no room for argument to the contrary. The veto, however, raises a question whether the legislative declaration truly expresses California's public policy.

Anna urges that surrogacy contracts violate several social policies. Relying on her contention that she is the child's legal, natural mother, she cites the public policy embodied in Penal Code § 273, prohibiting the payment for consent to adoption of a child. She argues further that the policies underlying the adoption laws of this state are violated by the surrogacy contract because it in effect constitutes a prebirth waiver of her parental rights.

We disagree. Gestational surrogacy differs in crucial respects from adoption and so is not subject to the adoption statutes. The parties voluntarily agreed to participate in in vitro fertilization and related medical procedures before the child was conceived; at the time when Anna entered into the contract, therefore, she was not vulnerable to financial inducements to part with her own expected offspring. As discussed above, Anna ws not the genetic mother of the child. The payments to Anna under the contract were meant to compensate her for her services in gestating the fetus and undergoing labor, rather than for giving up "parental" rights to the child. Payments were due both during the pregnancy and after the child's birth. We are, accordingly, unpersuaded that the contract used in this case violates the public policies. For the same reasons, we conclude that these contracts do not implicate the policies underlying the statutes governing termination of parental rights.

It has been suggested that gestational surrogacy may run afoul of prohibitions on involuntary servitude. We see no potential for that evil in the contract at issue here, and extrinsic evidence of coercion or duress is utterly lacking. We note that although at one point the contract purports to give Mark and Crispina the sole right to determine whether to abort the pregnancy, at another point it acknowledges: "All parties understand that a pregnant woman has the absolute right to abort or not abort any fetus she is carrying. Any promise to the contrary is unenforceable." We therefore need not determine the validity of a surrogacy contract purporting to deprive the gestator or her freedom to terminate the pregnancy.

Finally, Anna and some commentators have expressed concern that surrogacy contracts tend to exploit or dehumanize women, especially women of lower economic status. Anna's objections center around the psychological harm she asserts may result from the gestator's relinquishing the child to whom she has given birth. Some have also cautioned that the practice of surrogacy may encourage society to view children as commodities, subject to trade at their parents' will.

We are unpersuaded that gestational surrogacy arrangements are so likely to cause the untoward results Anna cited as to demand their invalidation on public policy grounds. Although common sense suggests that women of lesser means serve as surrogate mothers more often than do wealthy women, there has been no proof that surrogacy contracts exploit poor women to any greater degree than economic necessity in general exploits them by inducing them to accept lower-paid or otherwise undesirable employment. We are likewise unpersuaded by the claim that surrogacy will foster the attitude that children are mere commodities; no evidence is offered to support it. The limited data available seem to reflect an absence of significant adverse effects of surrogacy on all participants.

The argument that a woman cannot knowingly and intelligently agree to gestate and deliver a baby for intending parents carries overtones of the reasoning that for centuries prevented women from attaining equal economic rights and professional status under the law. To resurrect this view is both to foreclose a personal and economic choice on the part of the surrogate mother, and to deny intending parents what may be their only means of procreating a child of their own genetic stock. Certainly in the present case it cannot seriously be argued that Anna, a licensed vocational nurse who had done well in school and who had previously borne a child, lacked the intellectual wherewithal or life experience necessary to make an informed decision to enter into the surrogacy contract.

QUESTIONS FOR ANALYSIS

What is the court's holding in the *Baby M* case? In the *Johnson* case? Identify the basis for the New Jersey court's setting aside the surrogacy contract. What were the critical differences between the cases?

Now, suppose you live in a state where neither statute nor case law prohibits a party from entering into a surrogacy contract. You prepare a surrogacy contract and then the surrogate refuses to perform. Is the contract legal or illegal? What are your rights? There is no answer until a court or legislature sets the standard. You could be entering into a contract that is seemingly legal but may be deemed illegal if challenged. The area of surrogacy contracts is still developing and may garner different results in every state.

A new type of contract that has received some publicity lately is that developed by a men's group in the New York City area which requires a woman to sign a contract showing consent to sexual intercourse. The contract was developed to protect men from allegations of rape. Obviously, many issues can be debated on the legality of the contract or the effectiveness of the mutual assent. Was the contract signed under duress? Was there mutual assent? This type of contract will undoubtedly produce conflict based upon questions of public policy.

Public debate was also precipitated by the movie *Indecent Proposal*. In the story, a wealthy businessman offered a young couple $1 million in exchange for his spending 24 hours with the wife. (This undoubtedly included some intimate relations.) If the wife spent the 24 hours with the businessman, she would be entitled to $1 million. Is this legal prostitution? Is the contract between the parties legal? What would happen if the businessman decided not to pay the $1 million dollars? Could the couple enforce the contract in a court?

THE QUIGMANS   By Buddy Hickerson

Covenants Not to Compete

In many circumstances, parties will agree not to engage in competition for a period of time and within a specific geographical area. Such provisions are frequently included in contracts for the sale of a business. Because we live in a free market economy where competition is encouraged, restricting competition raises questions of unfairness. The *Restatement (Second)* § 187 states:

> A promise to refrain from competition that imposes a restraint that is not ancillary to an otherwise valid transaction or relationship is unreasonably in restraint of trade.

Often in business relationships, contract provisions restrict the right to compete. These provisions protect one party when there is a high likelihood that the other party's competition could substantially and negatively affect its business. These provisions are known as **restrictive covenants** or **covenants not to compete**. Restrictive covenants can be categorized into covenants incident to the sale of a business and covenants incident to an employment relationship. Each restricts the ability to compete under very specific circumstances.

Restatement (Second) § 188 has been adopted by many states as a basis for analyzing the validity of a noncompetition provision. The provision provides:

> (1) A promise to refrain from competition that imposes a restraint that is ancillary to an otherwise valid transaction or relationship is unreasonably in restraint of trade if:
>   (a) the restraint is greater than is needed to protect the promisee's legitimate interest, or
>   (b) the promisee's need is outweighed by the hardship to the promisor and the likely injury to the public.
> (2) Promises imposing restraints that are ancillary to a valid transaction or relationship include the following:
>   (a) promise by the seller of a business not to compete with the buyer in such a way as to injure the value of the business sold;
>   (b) promise by an employee or other agent not to compete with his employer or other principal;
>   (c) promise by a partner not to compete with partnership.

Courts have used the *Restatement* definitions in determining the enforceability of noncompetition agreements.

Covenants Incident to Sale of a Business

It is common, as part of the conditions for sale of a business, to restrict or limit the seller's ability to compete in the same field for a specified period of time within a specified geographical area. This contractual provision is important because it effectively prohibits a seller from going into the same business, using the same contacts and suppliers, and, in effect, selling the prospective buyer nothing. Laws allow for reasonable restrictions and reasonable restraints on competition when the provision is incident to the sale of a business. Whether a covenant not to compete is enforceable depends on the scope of the covenant.

Most courts set restrictions as to the geographical area and time period in which a covenant may be enforced. The court will look to the type of business involved, the general geographical area in which the business performs, and the overall impact of the restriction on a person's right to engage in business. If the covenant goes beyond what is reasonable and necessary, the court may either excise the provision and enforce the contract without the noncompetition provision, or reform the provision to limit the geographical area and make it reasonable. For example, suppose that you are in the market to sell a business in the state of New Jersey. Your business involves the sale of seashell art. Your business is limited to the counties of Atlantic and Ocean in the southern portion of New Jersey. However, the covenant as drafted provides that the seller is restricted from selling seashell art in the entire state of New Jersey for a period of seven years. This would likely be considered an unreasonable restraint of trade and competition. The provision would probably be declared void, because it extends for too long a time and covers a larger geographical area than is reasonable and necessary. Critical to the analysis of a noncompetition clause is its reasonableness.

Many states have statutes regulating the reasonableness of covenants not to compete, but the statutes have strict requirements. Courts do not look kindly upon contracts that restrict trade, and will do whatever is necessary to allow free competition in a market economy.

Covenants Incident to Employment

Similarly, employers may restrict the right of employees to compete in the same business after their employment has terminated. The same standards of reasonableness apply as for covenants not to compete. The restrictions may include geographical and time constraints. Covenants in employment contracts are very common, especially in industries such as computers, high technology, and manufacturing. Employers attempt thereby to protect the investment they have in their employees, especially when employees are exposed to confidential, proprietary information and trade secrets. As a method of protection for employers, courts have enforced restrictions in employment contracts. Again, what courts look for is the extent of the provision and its effect on the employee. In *New Haven Tobacco Co. v. Perrelli,* 559 A.2d 715 (Conn. 1989) the court analyzed an employment restrictive covenant. See if the court reached an appropriate resolution to the dispute.

Exculpatory Clauses

Clauses that limit one's liability are known as **exculpatory clauses**. Exculpatory clauses are closely monitored by the courts and undergo basically the same analysis as for unconscionable and adhesion contracts. Courts will determine (1) whether the bargaining powers of the parties were equal and

TERMS

covenant not to compete (restrictive covenant)
   A provision in an employment contract in which the employee promises that, upon leaving the employer he or she will not engage in the same business, as an employee or otherwise, in competition with the former employer. Such a covenant, which is also found in partnership agreements and agreements for the sale of a business, must be reasonable with respect to its duration and geographical scope.
exculpatory clause
   A clause in a contract or other legal document excusing a party from liability for his or her wrongful act.

NEW HAVEN TOBACCO COMPANY v. PERRELLI

Appellate Court of Connecticut
June 6, 1989

DuPONT, Chief Judge.

The plaintiff appeals from the judgment of the trial court invalidating as unreasonable a restrictive covenant contained in an employment contract signed by the plaintiff and the defendant. We find error.

The following facts are undisputed. In December, 1980, the plaintiff, a wholesale tobacco business, and the defendant entered into an employment contract that contained the following covenant: "Because of the importance and value of the information disclosed to the Employee, as part of the consideration for his employment, the Employee agrees that he will not directly or indirectly sell products similar to those of the Employer to any of the customers that he has dealt with or has discovered and become aware of while in the employ of the Employer for a period of twenty-four months from the termination of his employment."

The defendant voluntarily terminated his employment relationship with the plaintiff in November, 1981. Shortly thereafter, the defendant opened his own wholesale tobacco business and sold "products similar to those of the Employer" to certain customers of the plaintiff within the twenty-four month period of the restrictive covenant.

A covenant that restricts the activities of an employee following the termination of his employment is valid and enforceable if the restraint is reasonable. There are five criteria by which the reasonableness of a restrictive covenant must be evaluated: (1) the length of time the restriction is to be in effect; (2) the geographic area covered by the restriction; (3) the degree of protection afforded to the party in whose favor the covenant is made; (4) the restrictions on the employee's ability to pursue his occupation; and (5) the extent of interference with the public's interests. [A] finding of unreasonableness in any one of the criteria is enough to render the covenant unenforceable.

The application of a restrictive covenant must be confined to a geographic area that is reasonable in view of the particular situation. "A restrictive covenant which protects the employer in areas in which he does not do business or is unlikely to do business is unreasonable with respect to the area."

The covenant is not an anticompetitive covenant that restricts an employee from engaging in the same business as the employer in a given geographical area and prohibits the employee from doing business with all consumers of the service located in that area. Instead, the covenant at issue imposes an antisales restriction that prevents the employee from transacting business with only a specified group of consumers, namely, the customers of the former employer.

An antisales restriction, as opposed to an anticompetitive restriction, is by its nature limited to a definite geographic area. The geographic area affected by an antisales covenant is limited to that area in which the customers of the former employer are located, and the restriction, even within that area, applies only to those customers.

In the present case, the plaintiff's market, and thus its protected customer list, are local and limited to the greater New Haven area. Thus, although the covenant does not contain an explicit geographic limitation, the covenant is in fact limited to a reasonable geographic area.

In determining whether a restrictive covenant unreasonbly deprives the public of essential goods and services, the reasonableness of the scope and severity of the covenant's effect on the public and the probability of the restriction's creating a monopoly in the area of trade must be examined.

We also must evaluate the reasonableness of the covenant with respect to the time limitation of the covenant, the restriction imposed on the employee's ability to pursue his occupation and the degree of protection afforded to the employer by the covenant. We conclude that the covenant is also reasonable with respect to these criteria. The covenant prevents the defendant from transacting business with customers of the plaintiff for a period of two years after leaving the plaintiff's employ. Such a two year restriction is clearly reasonable.

As to the remaining criteria, the protection of an employer's interest in his customers through the use of similar covenants restricting an employee from entry into the employ of or selling to or soliciting an employer's customers, has been held reasonable with respect to both the degree of protection afforded an employer and the restriction placed on an employee's pursuit of his or her occupation.

Because the restrictive employment covenant at issue is reasonable with respect the five criteria, and thus valid and enforceable, we conclude that the plaintiff is entitled to enforcement of the covenant and that the trial court erred in rendering judgment for the defendant.

QUESTIONS FOR ANALYSIS

Did the appellate court agree with the trial court's application of the law? What is the rule of law in the *Perrelli* case? What fact was critical to the court's analysis? What criteria did the court apply in evaluating the reasonableness of the restrictive covenant?

(2) whether the parties had any bargaining powers at all. Many of us see exculpatory clauses daily. For example, when you park your car in a parking lot, a limitation of liabilityis often printed on the claim ticket. Usually the claim ticket states that management will not be held responsible for any items stolen or for damage to the car while it is in the possession of the garage. Lift tickets for ski resorts also have printed exculpatory clauses which attempt to absolve the ski resorts from any liability for their negligence. The list can go on and on, but whether the exculpatory clause is valid is determined by comparing the bargaining powers of the parties and analyzing how offensive and oppressive the contract is. Review *Harris v. Walker*, 119 Ill. 2d 542, 519 N.E.2d 917 (1988), where the main focus is the validity of an exculpatory clause.

HARRIS v. WALKER

Supreme Court of Illinois
Feb. 11, 1988

Justice SIMON

Plaintiff, Ronald K. Harris, Jr., was injured when he fell off a horse he had rented from the Ky-Wa Acres riding stables, owned and operated by the defendant, Al Walker. Plaintiff rented the horse from defendant's stable and claimed to fully understand and accept the risks of horseback riding.

Though the plaintiff apparently conceded that exculpatory contracts generally insulate defendants from liability on common law negligence claims, we reaffirm that under certain circumstances

exculpatory contracts may act as a total bar to a plaintiff's negligence claim. We start from our often-repeated axiom that "[p]ublic policy strongly favors freedom to contract as is manifest in both the United States Constitution and our constitution." Regarding contracts that shift the risks of one's own negligence to another contracting party, the general rule is to enforce exculpatory contracts "unless (1) it would be against a settled public policy of the State to do so, or (2) there is something in the social relationship of the parties militating against upholding the agreement." More recently, we observed that exculpatory clauses are not favored and must be strictly construed against the benefitting party, particularly one who drafted the release.

In this case, defendant's sign-in sheet contained the following release agreement:

Your signature below indicates that you have read the posted rules and will abide by them. Also, your signature shall release Ky-Wa Acres and employees of any liabilities you may incur while on the premises or for any injury which may result from horseback riding. If your signature is not reliable please do not sign or ride.

In addition, the prominently posted rules stated that riders rode at their own risk. Plaintiff stated in his deposition that he was an experienced rider and that he understood the release he signed.

Horseback riding involves various risks of injury that are plain to experienced riders. As the court stated, "[t]he parties may not have contemplated the precise occurrence which resulted in plaintiff's accident, but this does not render the exculpatory clause inoperable." When the parties adopt broad language in a release, it is reasonable to interpret the intended coverage to be as broad as the risks that are obvious to experienced participants. Even if the release in this case is strictly construed

against the defendant, its terms are broad enough to cover the situation at issue here. We believe that only the most inexperienced of horseback riders would not understand that under certain circumstances a horse may become spooked or "side-shocked" and cause a rider to fall from the horse. Yet plaintiff was an experienced rider who claimed to understand the release he signed.

Our review of the record and search for public policies that might be violated by the enforcement of this release have failed to uncover any policy reasons not to hold this release effective. In sum, we do not find any public policy in conflict with upholding the defendant's contractual release from negligence liability.

In addition to finding no public policy that is offended by enforcing the exculpatory contract here, we see nothing in the relationship between the contracting parties that suggests that the exculpatory agreement should not be enforced. This is not a case where the plaintiff is in an unequal bargaining position. This plaintiff voluntarily chose to enter into a relationship with the defendant whereby plaintiff agreed to accept the risks associated with horseback riding. Therefore, the plaintiff will not be heard to complain of a risk which he has encountered voluntarily, or brought upon himself with full knowledge and appreciation of the danger.

QUESTION FOR ANALYSIS

Did the court enforce the exculpatory clause against the defendant? What facts support the court's decision? What analysis did the court use in evaluating the exculpatory clause?

6.4 EXCEPTIONS TO ILLEGALITY

There is a limited exception to nonenforceability of illegal contracts. Court's may use the concept known as *pari delicto* (equally at fault), which focuses on the illegal acts of the parties. A court will not reward one party for its illegal acts in order to prove a case against another illegal actor. If the court finds that the parties to the contract were not equally blameworthy of an illegal act or that one party was not guilty of moral turpitude, the court may enforce the contract against the person who is less guilty; in this instance, the parties are not in pari delicto. This situation is infrequent. An example of the pari delicto doctrine is found in an early case, *Liebman v. Rosenthal,* 57 N.Y.S.2d 875 (1945).

LIEBMAN v. ROSENTHAL

Supreme Court, Kings County
Sept. 7, 1945

HOOLEY, Justice.

[T]he complaint is that plaintiff Liebman and his family, who were residents of Paris, France, and the defendant Rosenthal, who is also a resident of Paris, France, were sojourning at Bayonne, France, in the month of May, 1941, that the plaintiff was desirous of getting his family and himself to Portugal in order to escape the oncoming German army, that the defendant represented that he was an intimate friend of the Portuguese Consul in Bayonne and the he, defendant, could and would obtain visas to Portugal for the plaintiff and his family but that he would have to give such Consul the equivalent of $30,000. The complaint further alleges that the plaintiff thereupon handed over to the defendant six diamond bracelets and six diamond brooches of the value of $28,000 and went with the defendant to the office of the Portuguese Consul for the purpose of making an application for the visas to Portugal, that defendant made no application of any kind for said visas to the Portuguese Consul but instead absconded with the jewelry, and that he subsequently appeared in the City of New York where plaintiff met him and demanded the return of said jewelry.

The basis of his application here is that, as a matter of law, the alleged agreement between plaintiff and defendant was criminal, immoral and illegal in that it provided that the defendant bribe the Portuguese Consul. Defendant contends that where parties enter into an illegal agreement, they are deemed in part in pari delicto and plaintiff is not entitled to recover any consideration paid or transferred in furtherance of the illegal object.

Where money has been paid on an illegal contract which has been executed, and both the parties are in pari delicto, neither of them can recover from the other the money so paid; but if the contract is executory, and party paying the money is desirous of rescinding the contract, he may do so, and recover back his money. While the law will not enforce the prohibited contract, it will take notice of the circumstances, and if justice and equity require a restoration of money or property received by either party thereunder, it will, and in many cases has, given relief.

From the complaint in the case at bar it appears that this contract was wholly unexecuted and that the action is not brought to enforce the contract but rather to obtain moneys paid to one who is alleged to have defrauded the plaintiff by false representations.

Moreover, it sufficiently appears from the complaint that the plaintiff's actions were motivated by the desire of saving the lives of himself and his family from the Hitlerian army. If it be true that in such a situation this plaintiff delivered property in a large amount to the defendant, it may not be successfully contended that, acting under such pressure, the plaintiff was in pari delicto with the defendant upon whose representations and promises of action the plaintiff alleges he relied. There is no question of public policy involved in a case like this where a man is attempting to save himself from an enemy who has violated all the laws of civilization. Protection of one's self and one's family is among the first laws of nature and this court can appreciate that under similar conditions the most law-abiding man would enter into such an agreement as this plaintiff is alleged to have made. Rather it may be said that public policy should not permit the defendant to profit by what plaintiff maintains happened here.

QUESTIONS FOR ANALYSIS

For whom did the court find, and why? What was the basis of the court's analysis? What facts were central to the court's holding?

Connected to the concept of in pari delicto is *locus poenitentiae* (a time in which to repent). Here, a party can withdraw from a contemplated illegal act before liability results. Thus, courts will allow a party to an illegal contract time to repudiate the contract before the illegal act is performed. As a result of this act of repentance, the court will allow recovery in the form of **restitution** from the party who has rescinded an illegal bargain, if that is appropriate.

Divisible Contracts

To avoid the injustice that voiding an illegal contract may cause, courts can apply the *doctrine of divisibility.* By dividing a contract into sections, courts can remove an illegal provision and enforce the remaining legal provisions of the contract.

Before the doctrine can be applied, the contract and the circumstances surrounding its formation must meet certain requirements. First, the contract must be **divisible** into corresponding pairs of performances which the parties treated as equivalent exchanges. If the illegal performance is severable, the remainder of the contract will be enforced. Second, the illegality cannot affect the entire contract. If the entire contract is illegal, it cannot be divisible. Lastly, the party seeking enforcement of the contract must not have engaged in serious misconduct.

If a case meets these requirements, the doctrine of divisibility applies and the illegal part will be severed from the contract. Courts find this to be a more equitable result when illegality is raised.

6.5 PRACTICAL APPLICATIONS

When drafting contract provisions, always check the status of the law. Research will be critical to determining the enforceability of many contract provisions. When statutes or case law do not provide guidance, common sense is advised as the key to understanding legality.

The following are some examples of contract provisions that may have questionable legal ramifications.

Exclusion of Consequential Damages:
The parties agree that Seller will not be liable for any consequential damages of any nature caused to the business or property of Buyer by any failure, defect, or malfunction of the computer.

Waiver of Statute of Limitations:
The Buyer promises and agrees not to plead the statute of limitations as a defense to any payment that may become due under this contract, and waives the statute of limitations as to any and all claims that may accrue under this contract for the period of seven years.

Disavowal of Extraneous Representations:

The Buyer has read and understands the whole of the above contract, and states that no representation, promise, or agreement not expressed in this contract has been made to induce such party to enter into it.

Severability:

It is understood and agreed by the parties that if any part, term, or provision of this contract is held by the courts to be illegal or in conflict with any law of the state where made, the validity of the remaining portions or provisions shall not be affected, and the rights and obligations of the parties shall be construed and enforced as if the contract did not contain the particular part, term, or provision held to be invalid.

SUMMARY

6.1 The final element in contract formation is legality. A contract can be illegal if it violates a statute or a public policy. Illegal contracts are void and enforceable.

6.2 An illegal agreement is one prohibited by law. A number of activities which violate a statute will render a contract illegal: usury, wagering, Sunday business, and licensing.

6.3 Contracts that violate public policy can also be illegal. Surrogacy contracts have come under attack as violating public policy. Covenants not to compete, incident to the sale of a business or an employment contract, also have come under close scrutiny. An exculpatory clause limits a party's liability. If the parties have unequal bargaining powers, an exculpatory clause may be illegal.

6.4 When the parties are not *in pari delicto*, a court may enforce the contract against the party who is less guilty. If a party repents from a contemplated illegal act, the court will allow recovery in the form of restitution. If a contract is divisible, the illegal portions may be excised and the remaining portions enforced.

REVIEW QUESTIONS

1. Define the term *legality*.
2. What are the two types of illegality upon which a contract may be voided?
3. What is a usury law and what is its function?
4. Define Sunday laws and the reasoning behind their existence.
5. Identify two reasons for having professional licensing laws.
6. Name three types of contracts that violate public policy.
7. When are covenants not to compete permitted to restrict competition?

TERMS

restitution
In both contract and tort, a remedy that restores the status quo. Restitution returns a person who has been wrongfully deprived of something to the position he or she occupied before the wrong occurred; it requires a defendant who has been unjustly enriched at the expense of the plaintiff to make the plaintiff whole, either, as may be appropriate, by returning property unjustly held, by reimbursing the plaintiff, or by paying compensation or indemnification.

divisible contract
A contract whose parts are capable of separate or independent treatment; a contract that is enforceable as to a part which is valid, even though another part is invalied and unenforceable.

8. What is an exculpatory clause?
9. Define *in pari delicto* and *locus poenitentiae.*
10. What is the doctrine of divisibility?

EXERCISES

1. From your daily activities, collect examples of exculpatory clauses, such as on dry cleaning receipts, car parking receipts, theatre ticket receipts, or any others that may disclaim liability for an act. Discuss which exculpatory clauses would be enforceable or unenforceable.

2. Compare *Sirek v. Fairfield Snowbold, Inc.,* 800 P.2d 1291 (Ariz. 1990) and *Weiner v. Mt. Airy Lodge, Inc.,* 719 F. Supp. 342 (M.D. Pa. 1989) and answer the following questions:
   a. What are the facts in *Sirek?* In *Weiner?*
   b. What is the holding in *Sirek?* In *Weiner?*
   c. How can you reconcile these results?
   d. What test did the Pennsylvania court apply in *Weiner* in analyzing exculpatory clauses?

3. Review *In re Adoption of Paul,* 550 N.Y.2d 815 (Fam. Ct. 1990) and answer the following:
   a. How does this case compare to the *Baby M* and *Johnson* cases?
   b. What facts differentiate each case?
   c. Do you agree with each court's analysis? Why or why not?
   d. Does invalidating surrogacy contracts based on public policy grounds seem legally sound? Why or why not?

CHAPTER 7
Proper Form of the Contract: The Writing

OUTLINE

7.1 UNDERSTANDING THE STATUTE OF FRAUDS

Simply complying with all the elements of contract formation may not be sufficient. In some instances, law requires that certain types of contracts be in writing to be enforceable. The statute that sets out this requirement is the **Statute of Frauds**, which dates back to old English law, where the Parliament in 1677 passed the statute known as the Act for Prevention of Fraud and Perjuries because of numerous problems with people attempting to enforce oral contracts. Apparently, allegations of perjury were rampant in England when a contract was oral; to prevent the widespread chaos that was brewing, Parliament passed a statute requiring that certain kinds of contracts be in writing.

The concept established in the English Statute of Frauds crossed over the Atlantic and became part of our law of contracts. Virtually every state, except Louisiana, has adopted some form of the Statute of Frauds, so it has become a basis for challenging the enforceability of contracts. Except for Maryland and New Mexico, which have adopted the statute by judicial decision, the remaining states have passed legislation following the original English version to some degree.

TERMS

Statute of Frauds
A statute, existing in one or another form in every state, that requires certain classes of contracts to be in writing and signed by the parties. Its purpose is to prevent fraud or reduce the opportunities for fraud.

123

The Statute of Frauds states that five types of contracts must be in writing to be enforceable:

1. Contracts not to be performed within one year of the date of their making
2. Contracts to answer for the debt of another
3. The promise of an executor to pay the debt of a decedent's estate
4. Contracts in consideration of marriage
5. Contracts involving real property.

Contracts with subject matter in any of these categories cannot be oral, but must be in writing to have any legal effect.

Realistically, complying with the Statute of Frauds creates another requirement for the enforceability of contracts. Although not technically an element of a valid oral contract, the Statute of Frauds does raise a barrier to enforceability of a seemingly valid contract.

Many states have enumerated additional situations in which a writing is necessary to enforce a contract. Although each states' statutes vary to some degree, most have at minimum accepted the five categories set out in the original English statute. Figure 7-1 shows the California and New York Statutes of Frauds. Compare the similarities and differences.

---

§ 1624. Statute of frauds [California]

The following contracts are invalid, unless they, or some note or memorandum thereof, are in writing and subscribed by the party to be charged or by the party's agent:

(a) An agreement that by its terms is not to be performed within a year from the making thereof.

(b) A special promise to answer for the debt, default, or miscarriage of another, except in the cases provided for in Section 2794.

(c) An agreement for the leasing for a longer period than one year, or for the sale of real property, or of an interest therein; such an agreement, if made by an agent of the party sought to be charged, is invalid, unless the authority of the agent is in writing, subscribed by the party sought to be charged.

(d) An agreement authorizing or employing an agent, broker, or any other person to purchase or sell real estate, or to lease real estate for a longer period than one year, or to procure, introduce, or find a purchaser or seller of real estate or a lessee or lessor of real estate where the lease is for a longer period than one year, for compensation or a commission.

(e) An agreement which by its terms is not to be performed during the lifetime of the promisor.

(f) An agreement by a purchaser of real property to pay an indebtedness secured by a mortgage or deed of trust upon the property purchased, unless assumption of the indebtedness by the purchaser is specifically provided for in the conveyance of the property.

(g) A contract, promise, undertaking, or commitment to loan money or to grant or extend credit, in an amount greater than one hundred thousand dollars ($100,000), not primarily for personal, family, or household purposes, made by a person engaged in the business of lending or arranging for the lending of money or extending credit. For purposes of this section, a contract, promise, undertaking or commitment to loan money secured solely by residential property consisting of one to four dwelling units shall be deemed to be for personal, family, or household purposes.

This section does not apply to leases subject to Division 10 (commencing with Section 10101) of the Commercial Code.

FIGURE 7-1 Sample Statutes of Frauds

---

§ 5-701.   Agreements required to be in writing [New York]

a.   Every agreement, promise or undertaking is void, unless it or some note or memorandum thereof be in writing, and subscribed by the party to be charged therewith, or by his lawful agent, if such agreement, promise or undertaking:

1.   By its terms is not to be performed within one year from the making thereof or the performance of which is not to be completed before the end of a lifetime;

2.   Is a special promise to answer for the debt, default or miscarriage of another person;

3.   Is made in consideration of marriage, except mutual promises to marry;

[4.   Repealed]

5.   Is a subsequent or new promise to pay a debt discharged in bankruptcy;

6.   Notwithstanding section 2-210 of the uniform commercial code, if the goods be sold at public auction, and the auctioneer at the time of the sale, enters in a sale book, a memorandum specifying the nature and price of the property sold, the terms of the sale, the name of the purchaser, and the name of the person on whose account the sale was made, such memorandum is equivalent in effect to a note of the contract or sale, subscribed by the party to be charged therewith;

[7,8.   Repealed]

9.   Is a contract to assign or an assignment, with or without consideration to the promisor, of a life or health or accident insurance policy, or a promise, with or without consideration to the promisor, to name a beneficiary of any such policy. This provision shall not apply to a policy of industrial life or health or accident insurance.

10.   Is a contract to pay compensation for services rendered in negotiating a loan, or in negotiating the purchase, sale, exchange, renting or leasing of any real estate or interest therein, or of a business opportunity, business, its good will, inventory, fixtures or an interest therein, including a majority of the voting stock interest in a corporation and including the creating of a partnership interest. "Negotiating" includes procuring an introduction to a party to the transaction or assisting in the negotiation or consummation of the transaction. This provision shall apply to a contract implied in fact or in law to pay reasonable compensation but shall not apply to a contract to pay compensation to an auctioneer, an attorney at law, or a duly licensed real estate broker or real estate salesman.

FIGURE 7-1   *(Continued)*

This chapter discusses not only the Statute of Frauds, but also the extent of the writing necessary to satisfy the Statute of Frauds and some of the exceptions circumventing that statute. Additionally, rules of interpretation are analyzed to determine the intent of the parties when the contract is in some form of a writing. But first, a thorough discussion of the types of contracts requiring a writing is essential.

7.2   TYPES OF CONTRACTS REQUIRED TO BE IN WRITING

As mentioned, five general categories of contract fall within the Statute of Frauds. Each is discussed in this section.

Contracts Not to Be Performed Within One Year

Contracts that cannot be performed within one year of the date of the agreement must be in writing. This rule suggests that if a contract cannot be fully performed within one year after consummation of the contract, the contract must be in writing. For example, if you agree to teach school on August 15, and your position runs from September 1 through August 31, but you do not begin performance until September 1, under the Statute of Frauds the agreement must be in writing.

This provision of the Statute of Frauds has met with much hostility within the courts, because often it can cause inequitable results. One type of contract that has come under scrutiny is the lifetime contract. A contract for the lifetime of a person suggests that it cannot be performed within one year and thus must be in writing. However, some courts have interpreted this provision to suggest that the possibility exists that a person may die within one year, thereby allowing enforceability of an oral contract without requiring a writing.

Courts ask whether it is *possible* for performance to occur within the one year. If the answer is yes, the courts do not require that the contract be in writing. For example, City Insurance Company orally agrees to insure Mr. Dennison's house for 10 years from losses from natural disasters. A court could determine that , because a hurricane could hit tomorrow, the contract *could* be performable within one year, and thus need not be in writing. Courts interpret this requirement differently and thus each provision should be examined on a case-by-case and state-by-state basis. Examine *Dobson v. Metro Label Corp.*, 786 S.W.2d 63 (Tex. Ct. App.–Dallas 1990, no writ), in which the court had to interpret a one-year provision in an oral contract.

TERMS

surety
A person who promises to pay the debt or to satisfy the obligation of another person (the principal). As opposed to the obligation of a guarantor, the obligation of a surety is both primary and absolute; that is, it does not depend upon a default by the principal.

DOBSON v. METRO LABEL CORPORATION

Court of Appeals of Texas, Dallas
Feb. 27, 1990

Ron Dobson sued Metro Label Corporation for wrongful discharge under an employment contract. According to Dobson's pleadings, Metro Label hired him on July 14, 1987, to be its general manager at a salary of $60,000 a year. Jerome T. Abbott, the sole stockholder and chief executive officer of Metro Label, signed a memorandum stating:

> 7/14/87
> Offer today for General Manager @ $60,000 base salary per year with no bonus arrangement initially.
>   Jerome T. Abbott

After immediately giving notice of resignation to his previous employer, Dobson began work for Metro Label on August 3, 1987. On September 8, 1987, Metro Label terminated Dobson's employment.

First, Metro Label contended that the memorandum does not satisfy the Statute of Frauds and,

therefore, could not form the basis of an enforceable employment contract. Second, Metro Label contended that even if the memorandum is enforceable, Metro Label nonetheless had a right to terminate Dobson's employment at will because Metro Label did not expressly agree in writing to forego this right.

Under Metro Label's first contention, we note that if an employment agreement, either by its terms or by the nature of the required acts, cannot be completed within one year, the Statute of Frauds will apply, and the agreement must meet its requirements. To satisfy the Statute of Frauds, there must be a written memorandum which is complete within itself in every material detail and which contains all of the essential elements of the agreement so that the contract can be ascertained from the writing without resorting to oral testimony. The written memorandum must, within itself or by reference to other writings and without resort to parol evidence, contain all the elements of a valid contract, including an identification of both the subject matter of the contract and the parties to the contract.

The evidence undisputedly establishes that Dobson responded to a newspaper advertisement placed by Abbott who was seeking a general manager for Metro Label's three plants. Abbott and two consultants hired by Abbott interviewed Dobson. Abbott and Dobson discussed salary, bonus, and other benefits several times. Dobson rejected an offer of $50,000 plus bonus as too low to justify leaving his current position which paid $40,000 with an expected $10,000 bonus.

On July 14, 1987, the parties discussed a salary of $60,000 per year and reached an agreement on that basis. To evidence the agreement, Dobson wrote down: "Offer today for general manager at $60,000 base salary per year with no bonus arrangement initially" and asked Abbott to sign it. Abbott signed it. Abbott and Dobson further agreed that Dobson would have the usual benefits such as group health insurance. Also, as agreed, Dobson did not begin to work at Metro Label until August 3, 1987.

The Statute of Frauds requires an agreement to be in writing if it cannot be performed within one year from the date it was made. As alleged by Dobson, his contract covered employment for the term of one year. If Dobson had worked for Metro Label for one year as contemplated by the alleged contract, he would have worked until August 2, 1988. From the making of the contract on July 14, 1987, until the period of employment would have ended August 2, 1988, more than one year would elapse. Thus, since the contract alleged by Dobson could not have been performed within one year from the date of its making, it is subject to the Statute of Frauds.

The Statute of Frauds requires a writing complete within itself in every material detail and containing all essential elements so that resort to oral testimony is not required. Therefore, to satisfy the Statute of Frauds, the written memorandum must contain all the essential elements of the agreement between Dobson and Metro Label. The memorandum signed by Abbott shows only that he made an offer on July 14, 1987, for some unspecified managerial position at a salary of $60,000 per year, with no initial bonus arrangement. Dobson now contends that this writing establishes much more, namely that it was he who was hired, that his employer was Metro Label, that the job he accepted was as general manager of three Metro Label plants, and that the period of employment was for one full year. The memorandum itself, however, cannot be stretched so far. Since resort to oral testimony is necessary to complete the material terms of the contract, we hold that as a matter of law the memorandum does not satisfy the Statute of Frauds.

QUESTIONS FOR ANALYSIS

Identify the facts of the case. What provision of the Statute of Frauds was at issue? What was the court's ruling?

Contracts of a Third Party to Pay the Debt of Another

In most contractual arrangements, two parties are involved and there is an exchange of promises and obligations. Each party is primarily liable for its obligations under the contract. However, occasionally a third party offers assistance in paying the debt of another party. If the primary promisee does not pay, the third party offering to pay is known as a **surety** or **guarantor**. The relationship is called a *suretyship*.

Under the Statute of Frauds, a collateral or secondary promise by a third party to pay the debt of another must be in writing. The reason behind the requirement of a writing in this situation is that ordinarily the third party does not benefit in any way from the contract. Often the third party is

guarantor
A person who makes or gives a guaranty.

only lending his or her name to the transaction for credibility. The third party who is offering to pay the debt of another must be aware of the guaranty of payment—thus the requirement of a writing. Knowledge is critical to the enforceability of a suretyship contract against the surety or guarantor. Assume that Mr. Sutherland walks into a store and says to the salesperson, "Sell my friend Robert a raincoat, and I will pay for it." This situation does not fall within the Statute of Frauds and does not require a writing, because Mr. Sutherland is the primary **obligor** to the transaction, not Robert. However, if Mr. Sutherland says, "Sell Robert a raincoat, and if he does not pay, I will pay you," this type of contract must be in writing. Mr. Sutherland is guaranteeing payment for Robert as surety because Robert, not Mr. Sutherland, is now the primary obligor. Notice that Mr. Sutherland also has knowledge of his promise to pay Robert's debt if Robert defaults.

The most common situation in which a guaranty or surety arrangement arises is in lending money. Typically, a party makes application to a bank for a loan. Sometimes, if a corporation or individual does not have a substantial credit history to ensure payment of the loan, the bank will require a third party to agree to pay the debt in the event that the primary obligor on the debt cannot or does not pay. The third party is, in effect, guaranteeing payment of the original obligation, even though he or she may not benefit in any way from the borrowed money. Because the third party does not benefit from the transaction, the Statute of Frauds requires that this kind of contract be in writing to be enforceable. If this were not so, any person could offer other individuals' names to guarantee payment without those individuals' knowledge, and thus allegedly they could be made responsible for a debt of which they had no knowledge. As protection, to be effective, the obligation must be in writing and signed by the third party.

Main Purpose Rule

The requirement of a writing applies only when the third party intends to be secondarily liable rather than primarily liable. If the party who offers the guarantee is gaining direct advantage or benefit from the transaction, then the writing requirement is inapplicable. The question is whether the surety or guarantor's main purpose is to obtain direct benefits from the contract. If the answer is yes, then the contract need not be in writing. This rule is known as the *main purpose rule* or the **leading object rule**. Under the main purpose rule, the party making the promise must directly benefit from the transaction or gain advantage from the contract. When a court determines that the third party's promise to pay the debt of another is directly linked to that third party's interest, the transaction will not fall within the Statute of Frauds and does not have to be in writing.

As an example, suppose Martin, a house painter, has a contract to paint your house. He has been having financial difficulties and has bad credit. When he goes to the paint store to purchase the paint on credit, the store refuses. The store calls you and asks you to guarantee payment of purchase.

TERMS

obligor
The person who owes an obligation to another; a promisor.

You agree. Does this oral contract have to be in writing? No, because your main purpose is to receive a direct benefit by furthering your economic interest in having your house painted.

When considering whether a promise by a third party must be in writing, determine who benefits from the transaction and to whom the promise is being made. If the third party benefits, and the promise is made directly to the debtor, the contract need not be in writing, thereby circumventing the Statute of Frauds.

Contract Made by Executors and Administrators of Estates

In the **probate** area, it is common for a personal representative to be appointed to administer the interests of the deceased party by distributing the assets of the estate and paying off debts. The **executor** or **administrator**, as such persons are known, is only a representative of the estate and is not responsible for the debts incurred by the **decedent** during his or her lifetime. As a result, the Statute of Frauds requires that any agreement by an executor or an administrator of an estate to pay the debts of the decedent's estate out of the executor's own personal funds be in writing. Under ordinary circumstances, the executor or administrator is not responsible for the debts of the decedent, and forcing the representative to pay the debt would be not only unfair but also unconscionable. To remedy this problem, if an executor or an administrator does agree to pay the debts of the decedent, such agreement must be in writing.

An administrator or executor might desire to pay the debts of the decedent's estate if he or she were representing a relative, parent, or sibling. The representatives may feel a moral obligation to pay the debts of their loved ones, even though they do not have a legal obligation to do so. When this situation arises, a creditor who wants to hold the personal representative responsible for a deceased person's debt must put this obligation in writing for it to be effective and enforceable.

Contracts in Consideration of Marriage

It is unusual for an agreement to marry to be in writing. There is an exception, however, under the Statute of Frauds, which requires that a contract in consideration of marriage coupled with an interest be in writing. This rule suggests that a marriage contract which involves the exchange of money or property must be in writing to be enforceable. For example, suppose the Smith family promises the Jenner family that if the eldest Jenner son marries the eldest Smith daughter, the Smiths will "provide the eldest Jenner with a $500,000 home complete with pool and tennis court." This agreement must be in writing.

In effect, this section of the Statute of Frauds protects **dowry** rights. Dowries played a significant role in the past when marriages occurred more

---

leading object rule (main purpose rule)
The rule that a contract to guarantee the debt of another must be in writing does not apply if the promisor's "leading object" or "main purpose" in giving the guaranty was to benefit himself or herself.

probate
1. The judicial act whereby a will is adjudicated to be valid. 2. A term that describes the functions of the probate court, including the probate of wills and the supervision of the accounts and actions of administrators and executor of decedents' estates.

executor
A person designated by a testator to carry out the directions and requests in the testator's will and to dispose of [the testator's] property according to the provisions of his or her will.

administrator
A person who is appointed by the court to manage the estate of a person either who died without a will or whose will failed to name an executor or named an executor who declined or was ineli- gible to serve. The ad-ministrator of an estate is also referred to as a personal representative.

decedent
A . . . person who has died.

dowry
Under the Code Civil, the property a woman brings to her husband when she marries.

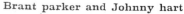

for money and family position than for love. The contract for marriage had to be in writing. We still see this today in some countries where people are promised to each other at birth in exchange for social position and wealth without regard to matters of love or affection. Under the Statute of Frauds, these types of agreements are required to be in writing.

The most common present-day use of this section of the Statute of Frauds involves premarital agreements and cohabitation agreements. Again, such contracts must be in writing to be enforceable.

Contracts for the Transfer of Real Property

Perhaps the most significant and important type of contract that must be in writing under the Statute of Frauds is a contract for the transfer or sale of real property. Virtually any agreement that involves real estate must be in writing. This includes, for example, deeds, mortgages, deeds of trust, leases, and easements. Over the years, the requirement of the writing has become more detailed in order to comply with the Statute of Frauds. Many states have instituted statutes that go beyond the dictates of the Statutes of Fraud to enable and enforce transfers of real property.

There is an exception to the rule that a transfer of real estate must be in writing, however. If an individual promises to sell real estate to another, and the party purchasing the real estate moves onto the real estate, pays part of the purchase price, takes possession of the land, and makes valuable improvements on it, a writing is not necessary. Here, the courts will not penalize the party who has relied to his or her detriment on the promise of another to transfer the real estate. To enforce this type of contract, most courts focus on the *doctrine of detrimental reliance.* Under this doctrine, if a person relied on an oral contract involving real property, and experienced legal detriment by performing obligations under that agreement to the extent that reasonable persons would believe that such a contract (although only oral) existed, there would be an enforceable contract. This exception to the Statute of Frauds eliminates the possibility of injustice resulting from requiring a written contract. This issue was discussed in *Meyer v. Meyer*, 775 S.W.2d 561 (Mo. Ct. App. 1989), in which an oral contract for the transfer of land was at issue. See if you agree with the court's result.

MEYER v. MEYER

Missouri Court of Appeals
Aug. 1, 1989

By warranty deed executed January 8, 1963, plaintiff and her husband, Walter (Gene's father), acquired ownership—by purchase—of the tract in dispute, along with an 85-acre tract immediately east thereof, the two parcels being separated by a county road. Plaintiff and Walter established their "homeplace" on the 85-acre tract.

Gene, who was in military service at the time of the transaction, entered into a verbal agreement with Walter. It provided: (1) Gene and Mary would reside on the 80-acre tract, (2) Gene and Walter would farm both tracts jointly when Gene was released from military service, (3) Gene would take care of Walter and plaintiff, and (4) upon the deaths of Walter and plaintiff, the 80-acre tract would belong to Gene and Mary. Plaintiff and Mary knew about the agreement and assented to it.

After the agreement was made Gene paid Walter and plaintiff $127 per month to apply on the "mortgage payments." According to Gene, he made eight such payments, after which the amount was reduced to $65 per month. He made 16 payments in that amount, terminating them when plaintiff received an "inheritance" enabling her and Walter to make the mortgage payments.

Gene and Mary moved into a house on the 80-acre tract, and Gene and Walter farmed the two tracts together. Because money was "very tight" it was decided by Gene and his parents that Gene would get an outside job. He did so, and he and Mary moved off the 80-acre tract, but they returned each weekend to help with the farming. In June 1966, Gene and Mary moved back onto the 80-acre tract, and Gene and Walter resumed farming together.

The operation continued that way until March 1971, when Walter suffered a heart attack. He was able to do only light work thereafter, so the milking operation was terminated and the dairy cattle were replaced by beef cattle.

Defendants had started their own beef herd in 1970. Their cattle and those owned by Walter and plaintiff were pastured together on both tracts. Hay was cut on both tracts and was stored "anywhere there was an open spot," irrespective of where it had grown. It was fed to all cattle without regard to ownership.

On April 17, 1973, Walter executed a will leaving all his estate to plaintiff on the condition that she survive him by more than 30 days. If she did not, the 80-acre tract was devised to Gene. Plaintiff simultaneously executed a will leaving all her estate to Walter subject to the same survival condition, and alternatively devising the 80-acre tract to Gene.

Walter suffered a stroke January 28, 1978, and was thereafter unable to work. From then on, Gene, aided by Mary and their children, did all the farm work and took care of all the cattle.

Walter died December 6, 1983. Defendants, with their children's help, continued farming both tracts and caring for all cattle. Gene made the decisions with respect to sale of plaintiff's cattle. When any were sold plaintiff would receive the sale bills and checks.

On July 22, 1985, plaintiff wrote Gene this letter:

> I am very disappointed with your attitude. First toward your father and me, now me. Your not coming to see him when he was so ill and dying. At the time I was to [sic] busy taking care of him and at night to [sic] tired to do much thinking. But now I am tired of getting the cold shoulder. The way it seems you think I should be satisfied with all you are doing.

Well, I am tired of being kept in the dark. So I am asking for the whole herd count and how many are mine. Also if there is any change by sales, death, or the like I want to know. Also I want to know ahead of time when you are going to sell any of my cows. I want to see them and know the reason why they are being sold. If they are to be sold you had better saved enough heifers to replace them. You always seem to sell my heifers.

Now if this isn't to your liking, you can cut out my cattle and bring them down here. Also you can bring back all the machinery and all the tools and everything else your father left up there when he had to quit. I have a list of everything. I will have a farm sale and you can just pay cash rent.

Oh! Yes, what about the loafing shed manure? It hasn!t [sic] been cleaned out for two or three years! I want an answer within a week!

s/ Mother

Plaintiff's letter triggered a responsive letter from Mary.

Mary and Gene testified that even after the exchange of letters they continued to do everything they had in the past to fulfill their part of the agreement. Plaintiff conceded that was so.

On October 20, 1985, plaintiff had gates in the perimeter fences of the 85-acre tract padlocked and "no trespassing" signs erected. Asked whether the contract had "worked fine" until then, plaintiff answered, "Yes, I guess so."

Gene acknowledged he performed no work on the 85-acre tract after the gates were locked and the signs went up. He explained, "[W]e figured we were not welcome anymore." Gene avowed he and Mary remain willing and able to do the same farm chores they had done through the years.

On November 25, 1985, plaintiff's lawyer sent defendants a letter making "formal demand" that defendants surrender possession of the 80-acre tract. Defendants refused. Plaintiff commenced this suit November 27, 1985.

Plaintiff had a sale April 19, 1986, at which she sold the cattle Gene had returned, together with farm machinery, household appliances and miscellaneous other items. After the sale she leased the 85-acre tract to a third party for $1,600 per year. At trial plaintiff disclosed she has made a new will

providing that upon her death the 80-acre tract shall be sold. She refused to reveal how the proceeds are to be disbursed.

The trial court found that when defendants moved onto the 80-acre tract in 1966 it was worth $7,000, and that its value at time of trial was $75,000. The trial court further found: (1) defendants had made improvements to the residence they occupy and had constructed outbuildings on the 80-acre tract, spending approximately $23,000 for materials, (2) when plaintiff needed help caring for Walter after his stroke she called Mary, and Mary provided assistance, (3) plaintiff has not asked defendants for any care or assistance for herself since Walter's death, and after receiving Mary's letter plaintiff has not asked defendants to do any work on the 85-acre tract, and (4) if granted the opportunity defendants are willing to continue to farm the 85-acre tract along with the 80-acre tract, and to provide care for plaintiff under the agreement. Plaintiff does not dispute any of those findings.

While it might have been argued that the agreement contemplated defendants' ownership in the 80-acre tract would be vested by deed in which Walter and plaintiff would reserve life estates for themselves, the parties obviously treated the agreement as a contract whereby ownership would be transferred to defendants by will, as evidenced by the wills executed by Walter and plaintiff in 1973.

An oral contract for a devise is unenforceable because of the statute of frauds; however, equity will enforce such a contract where a promisee has performed his part of the bargain and where denial of enforcement would work an equitable fraud on him. Plaintiff concedes the existence of the oral contract and she does not challenge the trial court's findings as to its provisions. Consequently, we need not discuss the requirements for proving an oral contract to make a devise.

Plaintiff also acknowledges that part performance "may take an agreement out of the statute [of frauds]." She cautions, however, that the party seeking enforcement of the contract must have performed as fully as he has been permitted. It is manifest, of course, that defendants cannot fully perform their obligations under the contract so long as plaintiff is alive, as one of defendants' duties is to take care of plaintiff until she dies. Only then will that obligation cease.

Defendants' first breach, says plaintiff, was Mary's letter which, according to plaintiff, revealed that defendants intended "to not provide full service for the plaintiff." We find no breach in the letter. While it was intemperate in tone, it was in response to plaintiff's letter of like tenor. Nowhere in Mary's letter did she say defendants would no longer carry out their contractual duties. The letter did warn plaintiff there would be no further free breeding of her cattle, but the trial court did not find that defendants were obliged to supply their bull for plaintiff's cows at no expense to plaintiff, nor did the trial court find the defendants were required to pay veterinarians' bills for services to plaintiff's cattle.

Defendants' second breach, according to plaintiff's first point, was failing to care for plaintiff. Neither the point nor the argument that follows it identifies any specific deficiency. Plaintiff merely refers us to her testimony that "I don't think they treated me like I was their mother." However, even if defendants failed to exhibit the degree of tenderness and affection plaintiff thought they should, that would not be a violation of the agreement. Plaintiff's claim that defendants breached the contract by failing to care for her is without merit.

If a party's performance substantially complies with a contract, such performance is sufficient to allow him to recover under it. A party's performance is substantial if the deviation from the contract was slight and if the other party received substantially the same benefit it would have from literal performance. Not every breach of a contract authorizes the other party to abandon it and refuse further performance. Defendants' retention of the seven head of plaintiff's cattle in connection with their demand for payment for the hay, when measured against some 20 years of undisputed performance by them, did not release plaintiff from her contractual duty to devise the 80-acre tract to defendants.

It is obvious, of course, that inasmuch as the 85-acre tract has been leased to a third party, defendants have no right to enter it and, consequently, no duty to perform any work on it. The trial court, as noted earlier, found that defendants' right to farm both tracts, as conferred by the contract, was beneficial to them, and that plaintiff's lease of the 85-acre tract to a third party—thereby making it unavailable to defendants—constituted a substantial breach of the contract. Ordinarily a material breach by one party to a bilateral contract has the simple effect of relieving the opposite party from the duty of further performance. Plaintiff has a contractual duty to make the 85-acre tract available to defendants for farming in conjunction with the 80-acre tract. Defendants have the concomitant duties to farm both tracts and to take care of plaintiff for the rest of her life. As plaintiff has breached the contract by making it impossible for defendants to farm the 85-acre tract, defendants are absolved from their contractual obligations while plaintiff's breach continues.

QUESTIONS FOR ANALYSIS

What are the facts of the case? What facts did the court determine were essential in reaching its result? Was the Statute of Frauds applicable in this case? Why or why not? Identify the court's holding.

It is prudent for paralegals to be familiar with their state's Statute of Frauds requirements. Additionally, many states enumerate other situations that require a contract to be in writing. When confronted with an oral contract situation, be sure to examine statutes and case law to determine the enforceability of the contract.

Additional Contracts Requiring Writing

Many jurisdictions require other types of contracts to be in writing. These may include oral one-year leases, consumer transactions, and promises to pay debts when the statute of limitations has run or the debt has been discharged in bankruptcy.

Another contract that may require a writing is one in which a **principal** appoints an **agent** to execute a contract on his behalf and the contract falls within the Statute of Frauds. This type of contract may have to comply with the *equal dignities rule*. Under the equal dignities rule, when a representative is appointed to perform a duty which is required to be in writing, both the appointment and the contract must be in writing. The reason behind this doctrine is that if one transaction requires a writing, to be on equal footing, the contract for the appointment must be in writing as well. If the transaction that the party is being asked to negotiate is not required to be in writing, the equal dignities rule does not apply. California subscribes to the equal dignities rule. A section of the California Statute of Frauds states:

> An agreement for the leasing for a longer period than one year, or for the sale of real property, or an interest therein; and such agreement, if made by an agent of the party sought to be charged, is invalid, unless the authority of the agent is in writing subscribed by the party sought to be charged.

Again, it is important to check state law to determine if the equal dignities rule is followed in your state.

The Uniform Commercial Code's Statute of Frauds

The Statute of Frauds is not limited to the common law of contracts. The Uniform Commercial Code (U.C.C.), which is discussed in the second half of this book, adds another category of contracts that must be in writing. Under § 2-20(1), contracts for the sale of goods over $500 must be in writing to comply with the Statute of Frauds. The U.C.C. thus expands upon the common law rule.

7.3 SATISFYING THE STATUTE OF FRAUDS: THE WRITING

The type of writing necessary to satisfy the Statute of Frauds is not a full-blown, formal, and completed contract document. Nor does the Statute of Frauds suggest that only a typed, formal contract satisfies the Statute of Frauds. In fact, a contract scribbled on a napkin or pieces of scratch paper, a memorandum, and the like could very well satisfy the Statute of Frauds if the writing contains the minimum amount of information necessary. Section 131 of the *Restatement (Second) of Contracts* suggests the following:

> Unless additional requirements are prescribed by the particular statute, a contract within the Statute of Frauds is enforceable if it is evidenced by any writing, signed by or on behalf of the party to be charged, which

(a) reasonably identifies the subject matter of the contract,

(b) is sufficient to indicate that a contract with respect thereto has been made between the parties or offered by the signer to the other party, and

(c) states with reasonable certainty the essential terms of the unperformed promises in the contract.

Consequently, what is required in the writing to satisfy the Statute of Frauds is the identity of the parties; the subject matter of the agreement; the material terms, including the price or the consideration; and the signature of the parties to be charged under the contract.

Identity of the Parties Important to any contract is the identity of the parties to the contract. This information must be clearly indicated in the writing for the Statute of Frauds to be effective. If any doubt arises as to the identity of the parties, it is highly likely that the writing requirement has not been met.

Subject Matter of the Agreement The subject matter of the contract must be identified so as not to raise questions between the parties who have entered into the contract. The subject matter must be specific and clearly noted to satisfy the Statute of Frauds. If the subject matter of the contract is a house, the legal description must be given or a specific street address stated. The contract cannot leave any question as to the subject matter of the contract. If the subject matter is not clearly identified, the contract will not be enforced.

Material Terms There is no specific formula for determining what constitutes the material terms of a contract, but each party must understand the substance of the contract and this information must be identified in the writing between the parties. Such terms as quantity, warranties, size, or color of a product and delivery dates may be considered material terms. A court will look at each case to determine whether this requirement has been fulfilled.

Price or Consideration Another material term, identification of which is essential to satisfy the Statute of Frauds, is the price term or the consideration exchanged to bind the parties to their contract. The amount and terms of payment should be clearly stated in the contract.

Signature of Party to Be Charged with Contract The party against whom enforcement of the contract is being sought must have signed the writing if the contract is to satisfy the Statute of Frauds. To constitute a signature, a party does not have to completely write out his or her name. Rather, a party's mark, initials, typewritten name, or whatever else constitutes a party's mark will suffice.

As a review of the concepts discussed regarding the Statute of Frauds, examine *Pallas v. Black*, 226 Neb. 728, 414 N.W.2d 805 (1987), in which the court had to determine the sufficiency of the writing. Carefully follow

TERMS

principal
In an agency relationship, the person for whom the agent acts and from who the agent receives his or her authority to act. . . . The person for whose debt or default a surety is responsible under a contract of suretyship. . . . The person whose obligation is guaranteed by the guarantor under a contract of guaranty.

agent
One of the parties to an agency relationship, specifically the one who acts for and represents the other party, who is known as the *principal*. The word implies service as well as authority to do something in the name of or on behalf of the principal.

the court's analysis in determining whether the writing was sufficient to satisfy the Statute of Frauds.

PALLAS v. BLACK

Supreme Court of Nebraska
Oct. 30, 1987

The property, commonly known as 2727 Q Street, Omaha, Douglas County, Nebraska, was acquired in equal shares by Thomas Pallas and his brother, James C. Pallas, on October 9, 1946. Thomas died in 1968, leaving his share to his widow, Fania Pallas. On September 21, 1968, Fania transferred her interest by quitclaim deed to her sons, the plaintiffs Gus and George, in equal shares. Subsequently, George either gave his share to Gus or appointed Gus as his representative in the management of the property. In any event, George testified he stood "ready" to execute a deed transferring whatever interest he might have to Black.

On September 9, 1977, James and his wife, Dorothy, executed a nondurable power of attorney appointing James' nephew Gus their attorney in fact for the purpose of handling and taking "care of our financial affairs, and to [sic] all matters pertaining thereto."

James was injured in a fall sometime in 1979, and thereafter resided in a nursing home until his death on April 11, 1982, at the age of 95. Gus and George visited their uncle at the home at least every other day. During some of these visits, James did not understand business questions his nephews tried to discuss, but at other times he did. James' last will and testament, dated March 10, 1977, devised all his property to his wife and named Gus as executor. The will further provided, however, that if Dorothy should die before James, his undivided one-half interest in the subject property was to be inherited by Gus and his wife, Rose. James' will was admitted to probate on May 20, 1982, and Gus was appointed as the personal representative of his uncle's estate. The probate proceeding, by failing to name Dorothy as one of James' heirs at the time of his death, establishes that Dorothy died before her husband and that, as a consequence, title to James' undivided one-half interest in the subject property vested in Gus and Rose.

The parties stipulated that at all times relevant to this litigation, George's wife, Finija, and Gus' wife stood ready, willing, and able, at the request of their respective husbands, to execute any documents reasonably required to effect the transfer of the property to Black. Gus testified that at all times relevant to this litigation, he has been ready, willing, and able to convey the property to Black, both on his own account and on behalf of his Uncle James' estate.

In May 1975, the property was leased for a term of 18 months to Pancho's, Inc., a corporation controlled by Black and on behalf of which corporation Black signed the lease. On September 23, 1977, the property was again leased to Pancho's for a term of 1 year, with two 1-year extension options. Black again signed this lease on behalf of Pancho's.

In the summer of 1980, Black initiated discussions with Gus about buying the real estate. Following those discussions, Black signed and sent the following letter to Gus:

July 9, 1980

Dear Gus,

I hereby agree to pay $20,000.00 for the premises located at 2727 Q Street. The $20,000.00 will be paid as agreed upon with a down payment of $5,800.00. The balance with 11% interest will be paid in monthly payments over 4 years, no payment to be less than $300.00. Also, I will continue to make the monthly rent payments for the duration of the lease which expires October 31, 1980.

A check for $5,800.00 is attached herewith. The final documents will be drawn up by my attorney for your review and approval along with the schedule of payments as soon as possible.

It is my intention to begin removing various items from the building beginning this Friday and continuing until completed.
Very truly yours,
Leon F. Black

Gus testified that this letter expressed the terms of the agreement which had been reached between himself and Black. Accompanying the letter was a $5,800 check, drawn on Black's behalf, payable to Gus' order.

After July 9, 1980, the only key to the building was in Black's possession. The weekend following receipt of the letter of July 9, Gus visited the property and found a crew of laborers removing the "fancy, old-fashioned ceiling" and wall paneling from the property. At a later time, the bar and back bar were removed as well.

After July 9, 1980, plaintiffs made no effort to lease the property to anyone, viewing the property as belonging to Black. Black, however, did take steps to lease the property. On November 29, 1982, he, as "Black & Associates," executed a document captioned "Business Property Lease," purporting to lease the property for a term of 1 year and 11 months to Kathleen Alston Curtis, to be used by her to operate a tavern, for a rental of $150 per month, total rent being $3,450 over the term of the lease. Black testified that he entered into this lease as an accommodation to Gus, but admitted he never informed Gus of that fact. Plaintiffs continued to pay the real estate taxes as they came due through March 27, 1984, a total amount of $842.23.

On August 28, 1980, Black wrote and signed the following letter to Gus:

Dear Gus,

Enclosed herein is a check in the amount of $430.00 for 2 months rent, and also a check in the amount of $600.00, which is the minimum monthly payment we agreed to. This monthly payment for the land contract will be properly computed with a schedule of payments in the near future.

You should be hearing from Roy Breeling, our attorney, to obtain the information he needs to prepare these papers.

Sorry for the delay, but I've been super busy.
Very truly yours,
Leon F. Black
cc: Roy Breeling

A Pancho's, Inc., check in the amount of $430 and a check drawn by Black on the same account as the $5,800 check accompanying the July 9, 1980, letter accompanied this letter. Breeling never produced a writing which, in Gus' opinion, accurately reflected the agreement he and Black had reached. The building was permitted to deteriorate to the point that it was ultimately condemned as a nuisance and torn down by the city of Omaha sometime after 1982.

In connection with the first issue, Black argues that there exists no sufficient written memorandum of the agreement to purchase the property. Every contract for the sale of any lands, shall be void unless the contract or some note or memorandum thereof be in writing and signed by the party by whom the sale is to be made. [To] authorize specific performance under a statute of frauds, only the party to be charged need have signed the memorandum. It is sufficient if the contract or memorandum thereof is signed by the party to be charged, that is, by the vendor. In this case, Black is the party to be charged, and, therefore, it is his signature which is required.

Black also asserts that his letter of July 9, 1980, cannot support an order of specific performance because it does not contain a sufficient statement of the terms of the agreement to serve as an adequate memorandum. A memorandum, in order to make enforceable a contract within the Statute [of Frauds], may be any document or writing, formal or informal, signed by the party to be charged or by his agent actually or apparently authorized thereunto, which states with reasonable certainty, (a) each party to the contract either by his own name, or by such a description as will serve to identify him, or by the name or description of his agent, and (b) the land, goods or other subject-matter to which the contract relates, and (c) the terms and conditions of all the promises constituting the contract and by whom and to whom the promises are made. Black's letter of July 9, 1980, clearly satisfies these requirements.

QUESTIONS FOR ANALYSIS

What elements in the writing were necessary to satisfy the Statute of Frauds? Did the contract satisfy the Statute of Frauds? What was the basis of the court's decision?

7.4 INTERPRETATION OF A CONTRACT

When a contract is reduced to writing, a court must follow certain rules in interpreting the meaning and intentions of the parties to the contract when the contract language is unclear or comes into question. In interpreting a writing, the court focuses on the contract process itself, the meaning of the words, and the intentions the parties had in making their agreement. Interpreting what the parties meant is a difficult task that takes a significant amount of investigation. In determining how to interpret and enforce a contract, it is often hard to ascertain, from what the parties wrote in the contract, what they actually meant.

To alleviate some of these problems, a court will attempt to determine the intentions of the parties by applying the reasonable person standard. Courts will objectively review what the parties' expectations were in making their agreement, what their conduct was in performing the agreement, and what words they chose when writing their agreement.

Rules of Interpretation

Although courts often have difficulty determining the parties' intentions in a contract, courts faced with interpretation problems use some common rules:

1. Examine the contract as a whole
2. Investigate the circumstances surrounding the contract
3. Construe terms more strictly against the drafter
4. Determine the primary purpose of the parties
5. Give common words their plain meanings
6. Give technical words their technical meanings
7. Let negotiated provisions control over standardized ones.

These rules set the parameters for a court when it interprets a contract.

The doctrine that courts apply in interpreting a document is the **strict construction doctrine**, also known as the **four corners** *doctrine*. This doctrine should be the starting place for any analysis.

The Strict Construction Doctrine

The strict construction doctrine states that a contract should be interpreted within its own pages or "four corners" to determine the meaning and intent of the parties to the contract. The doctrine further suggests that this interpretation should not be strained or create an unnatural perversion of the language in the contract. Consequently, the intentions or purpose of the contract should be ascertained from the contract as a whole, not from isolated provisions or sections that may not reveal the parties' real meaning. All parts of the contract, including clauses, paragraphs, sentences, and particular words, should be considered in light of the entire contract.

This doctrine of interpretation places a burden on the drafter of the contract. The rule is that a court will construe a contract more strictly against the person who drafted the contract, because that person chose the wording and presumably knew what was intended.

Plain Meaning

Further, the words chosen in the contract should be given their **plain meanings**. This suggests that a word should be given its generally accepted meaning. Resorting to an extreme or exotic interpretation of a word could frustrate the parties' intentions and the purpose of the contract. Therefore, the rule is that the words used in a contract will be given their ordinary or common meaning, unless it is shown that the parties used them in a different sense.

When technical words are used, they are to be construed in their technical sense. Terms used in the computer industry, for example, sometimes have very specific meanings that differ from their usual (plain) meanings. When this occurs, courts often employ experts to interpret the technical words used.

Arriving at a fair interpretation of commonly used words was the court's task in *Hellenic Investment, Inc. v. Kroger Co.*, 766 S.W.2d 861 (Tex. Ct. App.–Houston 1989, no writ), wherein the court had to interpret the word *nightclub*. This court had a challenge in interpreting the words used in the contract, and the case shows why precision in contract language is critical.

TERMS

strict construction doctrine
As opposed to a broad construction, a narrow or literal construction of written material.

four corners
The face of a document or instrument. The expression generally relates to the act of construing a document based upon the document alone, without recourse to extrinsic evidence.

plain meaning
The rule that in interpreting a contract whose wording is unambiguous, the courts will follow the "plain meaning" of the words used.

HELLENIC INVESTMENT, INC. v. KROGER COMPANY

Court of Appeals of Texas, Houston
March 1, 1989

This is an appeal from a permanent injunction enjoining the operation of a "night club" in a shopping center. Pasadena Associates leased space in the center to the appellee, the Kroger Company, to operate a grocery store. Under the terms of that lease, Pasadena Associates agreed it would not lease any other premises in the center for a "bar," "night club," or "other business of like nature." Pasadena Associates then leased space to appellant, Hellenic Investment, Inc., which opened an establishment named "Hallabaloo." Under the terms of Hellenic's lease agreement, it was permitted to use the lease premises for a "restaurant" or "dining facility" . . . "with the sale of alcoholic beverages, dancing, games, and related facilities and activities." In an "Addendum" to the lease agreement, Hellenic acknowledged that Kroger was the major anchor in the shopping center and that Kroger's lease prohibited

Pasadena Associates from leasing center premises to a "night club"; Hellenic also warranted that it was not a "night club." The Addendum further provided that if Pasadena Associates received any complaints or threats of litigation, Hellenic would either alter its operation to satisfy the complaints or pay any legal fees, expenses, and damages incurred by Pasadena Associates.

In February 1988, Hellenic opened the Hallabaloo as a "supper club," investing approximately $150,000 in renovating the premises. This new business venture was a huge success, and it immediately attracted large crowds of customers. As a result, the shopping center parking lot was often congested with customers' vehicles, particularly on weekends, and sometimes Kroger's customers could not find parking space in the center parking lot. There were also complaints of an "inordinate amount of trash on the parking lot" on weekends, and some complaints of harassment of Kroger's customers by Hellenic's patrons. Both Hellenic and Kroger tried to solve these problems by hiring additional security, valet parking, and clean-up services. But those remedial measures were only partially successful.

In August 1988, after a non-jury trial, the trial court permanently enjoined Hellenic from operating, and Pasadena Associates and Equity Fund from leasing, the leased premises as a "night club." The injunctive order defines the term "night club" as an operation selling "alcoholic beverages while also, in combination, playing loud volume dance music, providing a space for dancing, and allowing its patrons to dance, so long as its gross food sales make up less than 70% of its gross sales of all sources."

Kroger contends that a "night club" has certain characteristics that distinguish it from a restaurant. [Its expert] testified that a "night club" has four key characteristics: (1) food and alcoholic beverages are sold, and entertainment is provided; (2) dancing is the main form of entertainment; (3) special effects, strobe lights, fog-making machines, mirror balls, and bar tables and bar stools; and, (4) alcoholic beverages accounting for more than 75% of gross revenue. By comparison, [the expert] testified that a restaurant's food sales account for more than 80% of its gross sales. [The expert] also testified that the two primary activities at Hallabaloo are dancing and drinking alcoholic beverages. In [the] expert opinion, Hallabaloo was operated as a "night club."

As a general rule, parties are presumed to contract in reference to the usage or custom prevailing in the particular trade or business to which the contract relates, and evidence of custom or usage, which tends to explain the intent of the parties regarding an ambiguous contract term, is generally admissible to assist the factfinder in ascertaining the parties' true intent. The testimony of Dr. Waskey was admissible evidence to explain the meaning of the term "night club" as used in the lease agreement.

Under the terms of the Hellenic lease, Hellenic was permitted to operate a restaurant or dining facility, with attendant liquor and dancing privileged, but was not allowed to operate a "bar" or "night club." Based on the evidence before it, the trial court could properly have found that Hellenic was operating a "night club" facility, as that term is used in the Hellenic lease agreement.

QUESTIONS FOR ANALYSIS

What were the facts of the *Hellenic* case? What points did the court focus upon in reaching the result? Identify the holding.

General versus Specific Terms

Negotiated terms prevail over standardized ones. For example, if a standard provision in a lease is that 30 days' notice will be given upon vacating the premises, but the landlord and tenant negotiate and ultimately change this provision to state a 60-day notice provision, the negotiated provision will prevail over the form. Using the same concept is the rule that handwritten or typed provisions will prevail over a standardized, preprinted form.

Courts do not, however, rely solely on the contract words themselves. They also consider the parties' actions, known as general custom and usage.

General Custom and Usage

People's actions also play a part in contract interpretation. What is general **custom and usage** in a particular community or trade is critical in determining a party's intent and purpose. This suggests that community practices guide a court in interpreting the purpose and intent of a contract. This information is established by presenting evidence of the practice normally accepted by the community (usually by employing experts in a particular field).

Another method of interpreting conduct between parties is through examination of their *course of dealing*, the sequence of previous conduct between the parties to a particular transaction. Thus, course of dealing is the specialized conduct established in private or individualized dealings. For example, a seller and a buyer have always handled their sales relationship by telephone. They make offers via the telephone and communicate acceptances the same way. One day, the seller calls the buyer and offers 50 dresses at $20. The seller waits two days but gets no response. The seller then sells the dresses to someone else. Unbeknownst to the seller, the buyer has communicated the acceptance by mail, which reaches the seller five days later. The buyer sues, arguing that there was a contract. The court would look to the parties' course of dealing to establish whether a contract existed.

The third consideration in a contract interpretation regarding conduct is *course of performance*. This term is directly related to a specific contract. Consequently, *course of performance* refers to the pattern of performance in the existing contract, whereas *course of dealing* focuses on the pattern of performance between the parties in prior contracts.

Summary of Interpretation

When faced with the task of interpreting a contract, use the rules cited in this section as a guide. Remember, case law should always be consulted when a contract meaning is challenged.

The Parol Evidence Rule

A court must not only examine the words chosen and the intentions of the parties, but it must also consider certain other rules which have evolved over the years to preserve the integrity of contracts and their interpretation. The most critical rule for interpretation of a written contract is the **parol evidence rule**. *Parol* means "oral" or "verbal." The parol evidence rule states that a written contract may not be varied, contradicted, or altered by any prior or contemporaneous oral declarations. Once a contract has been reduced

TERMS

custom
Often referred to as *custom and usage*; a practice that has acquired the force of law because it has been done that way for a very long time.

parol evidence rule
Under the parol evidence rule, evidence of prior or contemporaneous oral agreements that would change the terms of a written contract are inadmissible. . . . [T]he intention of the parties, as evidenced by the language of a written contract, cannot be varied by parol proof of a different intention. The presumption is that the written contract incorporated all of the terms of the contract.

TERMS

merge
The combining of one
of anything with another
or others; the absorption
of one thing by another;
a disappearing into
something else.

to a writing that is the final expression of the parties' agreement, the agreement cannot be changed or challenged by any prior oral evidence. This rule prevents parties from changing their agreement after the contract has been finalized. Consequently, all previous oral agreements **merge** into the final written contract, which cannot then be modified or changed by parol evidence. To understand how a court applies the parol evidence rule, review *Jack H. Brown & Co. v. Toys "R" Us, Inc.*, 906 F.2d 169 (5th Cir. 1990).

JACK H. BROWN & COMPANY v. TOYS "R" US, INC.

United States Court of Appeals, Fifth Circuit
July 20, 1990

GOLDBERG, Circuit Judge

For eight or nine years prior to 1985, Signgraphics supplied custom signs for Toys "R" Us retail stores. Typically, Signgraphics and Toys entered into annual contracts under which Signgraphics agreed to build and supervise installation of the signs Toys needed for any new stores opened during the year. After 1983, Toys also began contracting with Signgraphics for the construction of prefabricated "mansards," which are false-front, built-up roofs upon which the signs are mounted.

In 1985 Toys and Signgraphics had two agreements in effect: one for the construction of ten mansards ("the 1984 contract") and one for signs ("the 1985 contract"). Early in 1985, a dispute arose between Signgraphics and Toys over late payment of invoices. Sometime in March, toys requested shipment of one of the completed mansards, but Signgraphics refused to ship the mansard until Toys made some payment on the disputed invoices. In response to Signgraphics' refusal to ship the mansard Toys cancelled both the 1984 and 1985 contracts via telegram on April 1, 1985.

On April 23, 1985, James Markham, Director of Industrial Buying for Toys, along with several other Toys representatives, travelled to Dallas to meet with representatives from Signgraphics. Markham met individually with Jack R. Brown, Signgraphics' owner and president, in an attempt to resolve the conflict between the two parties. As a result of this meeting, Markham and Brown reached an agreement on the various disputes that existed between their respective companies.

On April 29, 1985, Markham sent Brown a letter summarizing the agreement reached during the April 23 meeting. Among other things, the letter indicated that Signgraphics would continue as the sign vendor for ten Toys "R" Us stores. The letter stated that except for these ten stores, the remainder of the 1985 contract was "terminated with no further liability on the part of either party." Markham's letter also indicated that Signgraphics had been paid in full for four mansards, and that any contract for additional mansards was "terminated with no further liability to either party." In closing, Markham wrote, "I trust you will agree that the foregoing accurately reflects our understanding." Brown received the letter, signed and dated a copy as of April 30, 1985, and returned the copy to Markham along with an addendum.

In November 1985, Signgraphics submitted bids for Toys' 1986 sign program. The bids were unsuccessful. Brown wrote to Markham expressing surprise over the fact that Signgraphics had not been selected as a sign vendor for 1986. Specifically, Brown asserted that in exchange for releasing Toys from Signgraphics' lost profits claim, Markham "promised" at the April 23 meeting that Signgraphics "would be a major sign vendor for Toys R Us in 1986, so that [Signgraphics] could recoup these claims in that manner." Because Toys did not select Signgraphics as a sign vendor for 1986, Brown reasserted his earlier claim for lost profits.

In a letter dated March 4, 1986, Markham denied making "any promises, representations or agreements, orally or in writing, that [Signgraphics] would be 'a major sign vendor' or do any sign work for Toys "R" Us in 1986." Maintaining that the April 29, 1985 settlement agreement effectively released Toys from further liability under the 1984 and 1985 contracts, Markham rejected Signgraphics' demand for payment of lost profits.

We are bound in this diversity case to apply the parol evidence rule as a Texas court would. [The] Texas Supreme Court stated that "[w]hen parties have concluded a valid integrated agreement with respect to a particular subject matter, the [parol evidence] rule precludes the enforcement of inconsistent prior or contemporaneous agreements." It is well settled that written agreements are presumed to be integrated. Once the parties have reduced their agreement to writing "they are presumed to have selected from [prior] negotiations only the promises and agreements for which they choose to be bound."

For reasons set out more fully below, [we] hold that parol evidence was improperly admitted in this case.

For a court to determine that a written agreement is incomplete, it must decide: (1) that the writing is facially incomplete and requires extrinsic evidence to clarify, explain or give meaning to its terms; or (2) that when viewed in light of the circumstances surrounding its execution, the writing does not appear to be the complete embodiment of the terms relating to the subject matter of the writing. In either instance, the trial court must make some threshold determination as to the incompleteness of the document before admitting parol evidence. We believe the district court made such a threshold determination in this case.

A finding of incompleteness, however does not end our inquiry. An agreement might be incomplete in some respects but perfectly clear and complete in others. Extrinsic evidence necessary to explain or give meaning to an agreement cannot be admitted to vary or contradict those portions of the agreement that are complete and unambiguous. Therefore, we must look to the particular parol evidence at issue and the purpose for which it was offered to see if it falls within an exception to the parol evidence rule.

Under Texas law, parol evidence is admissible to clarify, explain, or give meaning to a writing that is facially incomplete, but only insofar as the evidence does not vary or contradict those terms of the writing that are complete and unambiguous. Similarly, where the written agreement does not include the entire agreement of the parties parol evidence is admissible to show collateral agreements. Here again, parol evidence is admissible only insofar as it does not vary or contradict the terms of the writing. The district court found, and we agree, that the settlement agreement "unambiguously released [Toys] from further liability on the 1985 sign contracts and from liability on any contracts for mansards." The settlement agreement's release language was not so incomplete that extrinsic evidence was required to give it meaning.

Furthermore, we cannot agree that Toys' alleged oral promise was collateral to the written settlement agreement. With respect to proof and enforcement of collateral agreements:

(1) An oral agreement is not superseded or invalidated by a subsequent or contemporaneous integration, nor a written agreement by a subsequent integration relating to the same subject-matter, if the agreement is not inconsistent with the integrated contract, and

(a) is made for separate consideration, or

(b) is such an agreement as might naturally be made as a separate agreement by parties situated as were the parties to the written contract.

The promise alleged by Signgraphics that Toys would make Signgraphics a "major supplier" in 1986 simply does not meet the standard.

It is also significant that Toys, through Markham's April 29 letter, memorialized the terms of the settlement agreement. Markham's letter contained explicit language releasing Toys from further liability on the 1984 and 1985 contracts. The next day, and just one week after filing a lawsuit against Toys, Signgraphics signed and returned a copy of Markham's letter with only minor modifications. If it wanted to incorporate some reference to the alleged oral promise, Signgraphics could simply have made its acceptance "subject to our understanding on future business." Instead, Signgraphics accepted the terms of Markham's letter without challenging the release language in any way. In light of these circumstances, we find that the alleged oral promise is not one that "might naturally be made as a separate agreement" by parties situated as were Toys and Signgraphics.

Both the parol evidence rule and the doctrine of integration exist so that parties may rely on the enforcement of agreements that have been reduced to writing. If it were not for these established principles, even the most carefully considered written documents could be destroyed by "proof" of other agreements not included in the writing.

In the case at bar, parol evidence of Toys' alleged oral promise does not fall within any of the exceptions. The evidence was not introduced to explain or give meaning to any part of the written settlement agreement. Nor was the promise one that could rightfully be described as collateral to the written settlement agreement. Moreover, the alleged promise was inconsistent with the settlement agreement's clear and unambiguous release language. Therefore, we hold that parol evidence of the alleged oral promise was improperly admitted in this case.

QUESTIONS FOR ANALYSIS

What are the facts in the *Toys "R" Us* case? What determination must a court make in applying the parol evidence rule? What was the court's holding?

Merger Clauses: The Presumption of a Contract

Including a merger clause may prevent a challenge to the final contract. A *merger clause* is a provision in a contract that negates any prior oral agreements. It provides that all prior oral or written agreements have been merged into the written contract and that the contract is the final expression of the parties' agreement. All terms stated in the contract are what the parties agreed to. Any omission of a term or provision from the contract suggests that the parties decided to disregard it in the final contract. Merger clauses are a common tool in drafting and preparing a final contract. Figure 7-2 presents examples of typical merger clauses.

The merger clause gives the presumption that the contract is a totally integrated contract. Whether a contract is integrated will determine how or if the parol evidence rule applies.

Integrated Contracts

An **integrated contract** represents the final expression of the parties' agreement when there are to be no additions or changes. An integrated contract cannot be changed or supplemented by any prior oral evidence. The presumption is that if any other terms were discussed, they were eliminated in preliminary discussions or drafts and thus did not become part of the final contract. The parol evidence rule protects the integrity of written contracts by prohibiting a party from changing an agreement that is final and totally integrated.

No prior evidence can be admitted as evidence if the contract is totally integrated. However, when there is a partially integrated contract, the rule is slightly different.

This instrument contains the entire agreement between the parties relating to the rights herein granted and the obligations herein assumed. Any oral representations or modifications concerning this instrument shall be of no force or effect excepting a subsequent modification in writing, signed by the party to be charged.

Entire Agreement Clause

This agreement supersedes any and all other agreements, either oral or in writing, between the parties hereto with respect to the subject matter hereof and contains all of the covenants and agreements between the parties with respect to said matter. Each party to this agreement acknowledges that no representations, inducements, promises, or agreements, orally or otherwise, have been made by any party, or anyone acting on behalf of any party, which are not embodied herein, and that no other agreement, statement, or promise not contained in this agreement shall be valid or binding.

OR

This contains the entire agreement of the parties with respect to the matters covered by this lease. No other agreement, statement, or promise made by any party, or to any employee, officer, or agent of any party, which is not contained in this lease shall be binding or valid.

OR

This instrument constitutes the sole and only agreement of the parties hereto relating to said project and correctly sets forth the rights, duties, and obligations of each to the other as of its date. Any prior agreements, promises, negotiations, or representations not expressly set forth in this agreement are of no force or effect.

FIGURE 7-2   Typical merger clauses

Partially Integrated Contracts

A *partially integrated* contract is a final expression of the parties' intentions, but is incomplete. Usually a partially integrated contract results when the parties to the contract omit a term. The contract is silent on a term because the parties assumed the term in the contract. If the additional term does not contradict the original contract, oral evidence can be brought in to supplement the contract's missing term.

7.5 EXCEPTIONS TO PAROL EVIDENCE RULE

There are usually exceptions to every rule, and there are a number of important exceptions to the parol evidence rule.

Oral Evidence May Be Used to Clarify But Not Alter   When a writing appears to be a final expression of the parties' intentions, but is incomplete, the contract is said to be partially integrated (as discussed earlier). Oral evidence will be allowed to supplement the contract consistent with the terms and conditions upon which the parties have already agreed. In this situation, oral evidence will be allowed to explain or clarify a contract, but not to change or modify it. What the court looks for is consistency of the agreement and obligations that the parties have made; it allows oral evidence only to clarify the agreement.

TERMS

integrated contract
A written contract that contains all the terms and conditions of the parties' agreement. It must expressly say so. An integrated contract cannot be modified by parol evidence.

Ambiguity   The courts allow oral evidence when the contract language is ambiguous. An ambiguity exists when a word or phrase is reasonably capable of more than one meaning. Under this exception, no new terms are presented to the court; rather, information is given to clarify ambiguous words, phrases, or the intentions of the parties to the contract.

Conditions Precedent   Courts also allow oral evidence to show that a **condition precedent** has not been met, thus rendering the contract void or voidable. (A condition precedent is a contingency found in a contract before it comes into existence; this is discussed in detail in Chapter 8.) In this situation a party must show that, although the contract appears to be final and integrated, certain events have not occurred which are prerequisite to performance of the contract terms. Conditions precedent are commonly found in real estate contracts. For example, a seller will not tender a deed unless the buyer qualifies for financing.

Destruction of Mutual Assent (Contract Defenses)   When allegations of fraud, misrepresentation, mistake, undue influence, duress, violation of public policy, and other types of destruction of mutual assent are raised, the parol evidence rule does not apply. By raising such a defense, a party is claiming that there has been some defect in formation of the contract and suggests that no enforceable contract actually exists between the parties. Again, on its face the contract appears to be fully integrated and complete, but because of some act which was unconscionable or illegal, it may be found to be ineffective and unenforceable. The parol evidence rule is cast aside and any oral evidence showing the invalidity of the contract is admitted. Coupled with this concept is that of violation of public policy.

TERMS

condition precedent
A condition that must first occur for a contractual obligation (or a provision of a will, deed, or the like) to attach.

The key to understanding the parol evidence rule is that it applies only to written final contracts. If some exception can be found, the parol evidence rule will not apply. That is important to remember if the need to admit oral evidence is found. Knowing the exceptions will make the paralegal's task easier. Examine *Adler & Shaykin v. Wachner*, 721 F. Supp. 472 (S.D.N.Y. 1988), which discusses some further applications of the parol evidence rule and its exceptions.

ADLER & SHAYKIN v. WACHNER

United States District Court, S.D. New York
Dec. 12, 1988

Wachner and A & S entered into their first agreement ("the Retention Agreement") on December 14, 1984. By the terms of the Retention Agreement, Wachner was to identify potential acquisitions for

A & S in the beauty market and then head the acquired company. A & S formed the Beauty Acquisition Corporation ("BAC") for that purpose. After several months, BAC agreed to buy Revlon's beauty and fragrances business ("the BAC Transaction"). However, by December of 1985, Wachner's Retention Agreement with A & S had expired; the BAC Transaction had collapsed due to Pantry Pride's acquisition of Revlon; and A & S faced a drawn out litigation against Revlon. The Retention Agreement between the parties had no provision that would entitle Wachner to any share of whatever break-up fees or damages A & S might eventually recover from Revlon. As a result, Wachner and Adler negotiated an agreement dated December 12, 1985 ("the 1985 Agreement"). That agreement addressed various distribution possibilities of any break-up fee received from Revlon.

After several months of litigation, on December 2, 1986, Revlon paid a $23.7 million break-up fee ("the Settlement Amount") to A & S pursuant to the Settlement Agreement negotiated by the parties. A letter agreement between A & S and Wachner, dated December 5, 1986 ("the 1986 Agreement"), addressed her share of that fee. Following an introductory paragraph that refers its readers to the 1985 Agreement as well as other relevant agreements, the 1986 Agreement provides: "In view of the settlement provided in the Settlement Agreement, it is agree as follows . . ." The agreement between A & S and Wachner provides that, in consideration of $2.785 million to Wachner, she would release A & S and related entities from all actions and future demands regarding the Settlement Agreement. The 1986 Agreement also outlined in detail, with several formulae, an agreement between the parties that called for them to share whatever future taxes might be assessed against the Settlement Amount.

According to A & S, at the time of the 1986 Agreement, the parties entered into a separate oral "understanding." The terms of this "understanding" were that

we [A & S] would pay her [Wachner] the amount she was entitled to receive under the formula we had worked out ($2,785,000), based, however, on the planned distribution of $4,600,000 to the Limited Partners [from the aborted BAC Transaction].

In light of the fact that the Limited Partners were objecting to that distribution and might ultimately succeed in causing A & S to increase it, Wachner and I [Adler] further agreed that her share would be recalculated if and when we had to increase the payment to the Limited Partners and she would repay the difference.

Because of his friendship with Wachner, Adler did not feel it was necessary to memorialize his further understanding with Wachner that she might return a portion of her share of the Settlement Amount. He and Wachner had a series of conversations during which she never questioned her obligation to return a portion of the money, but rather only questioned the amount. Wachner told Adler that she wanted to be kept advised of A & S's continued dealings with its Limited Partners. In her own words, she wanted "to see and understand any givebacks" to the "Limited Partners" and "wanted to be a part of it."

Furthermore, Adler felt it was unwise to raise the possibility of additional payments to A & S's limited partners "in a writing [ ] the Limited Partners had every right to view": "Such a provision would have fueled the dispute between A & S and the Limited Partners concerning how much the Limited Partners were to receive."

As it turned out, on April 23, 1987, A & S paid its Limited Partners roughly $9.94 million, not $4.6 million. Based upon the actual distribution, A & S notified Wachner that she owed an additional $810,375. By May of 1987, Shaykin, on behalf of A & S, forwarded to Wachner a "new Agreement prepared for the purpose of superceding [sic] [the 1986 Agreement]."

This May 1987 Agreement is virtually identical to the 1986 Agreement except for the fact that it takes into consideration Wachner's alleged oral agreement to return a portion of her distribution from the Settlement Amount in case A & S had to pay more to its Limited Partners. As a result, it provides for Wachner to return $810,375 to A & S. The May 1987 Agreement states: "Except as expressly set forth herein, the 1986 Letter will remain in full force and effect (including but not limited to the release and tax indemnification provisions thereof)." The May 1987 Agreement, like all the previous agreements between the parties, did not contain a merger or integration clause. Some time after the parties entered into the 1986 Agreement, Wachner repaid a $50,000 loan to A & S. The loan was originally made to cover expenses Wachner had incurred while working in New York for A & S on the proposed BAC Transaction. A & S brought this action to recover that $810,375.

Where the parties have reduced their agreement to an integrated writing, the parol evidence rule operates to exclude evidence of all prior or contemporaneous negotiations or agreements offered to contradict or modify the terms of their writing. The party relying on the rule to bar the admission of evidence must first show that the agreement is integrated, which is to say, that the writing completely and accurately embodies all of the mutual rights and obligations of the parties. And "under New York law a contract which appears complete on its face is an integrated agreement as a matter of law."

However, under New York law, in the absence of a merger clause, the court must determine whether or not there is an integration by reading the writing in the light of surrounding circumstances, and by determining whether or not the agreement was one which the parties would ordinarily be expected to embody in the writing. The New York Court of Appeals long ago provided a guideline for this determination:

> If upon inspection and study of the writing, read, it may be, in the light of surrounding circumstances in order [to determine] to its proper understanding and interpretation, it appears to contain the engagements of the parties, and to define the object and measure the extent of such engagement, it constitutes the contract between them, and is presumed to contain the whole of that contract.

Factors New York courts consider include: whether the document in question refers to the oral agreement, or whether the alleged oral agreement between the parties "is the sort of complex arrangement which is customarily reduced to writing"; whether the parties were represented by experienced counsel when they entered into the agreement; whether the parties and their counsel negotiated during a lengthy period, resulting in a specially drawn out and executed agreement, and whether the condition at issue is fundamental; if the contract, which does not include the standard integration clause, nonetheless contains wording like "[i]n consideration of the mutual promises herein contained, it is agreed and covenanted as follows," and ends by stating that "the foregoing correctly sets forth your understanding of our Agreement."

Having examined both the document itself and the circumstances surrounding it, the Court concludes that the parties intended the 1986 Agreement to contain the mutual promises of the parties with respect to the Settlement Amount. It thus is a valid integrated agreement and the Court will exclude evidence of prior or contemporaneous negotiations or agreements which would vary or be inconsistent with its terms, as would the alleged oral understanding between Adler and Wachner.

Furthermore, the parties were represented and aided by experienced counsel in drafting the agreement at issue. The complex tax indemnification provision in the 1986 Agreement reveals their ability to address a potential recalculation of Wachner's share of the Settlement Amount when the parties so desired. Regardless of whether the oral agreement was made—and, for the purposes of this motion, the Court assumes that it was—the Court concludes that it remains just the sort of complex arrangement customarily reduced to writing and which the parties would ordinarily be expected to embody in the writing. It stretches credulity too far to believe that, after more than a year of work, Wachner would grant A & S what amounts to unlimited discretion to reduce the one thing she had to show for her work: $2.785 million. The surrounding circumstances convince the Court that the oral agreement was "so clearly connected with the principal transaction as to be part and parcel of it."

Under certain circumstances, parol evidence may be admitted even if an agreement *is* integrated. First, parol evidence may come in if the alleged agreement is collateral, that is, one which is separate, independent and complete . . . although relating to the same object. Only where three conditions are met will the Court allow evidence in support of an allegedly collateral agreement.

[B]efore such an oral agreement as the present is received to vary the written contract at least three conditions must exist, (1) the agreement must in form be a collateral one; (2) it must not contradict express or implied provisions of the written contract; (3) it must be one that parties would not ordinarily be expected to embody in the writing . . . [The oral agreement] must not be so clearly connected with the principal transaction as to be part and parcel of it.

The alleged oral understanding at issue here is not collateral. As noted above, it is "part and parcel" of the underlying agreement, precisely the sort of provision "the parties would ordinarily be expected to embody in the writing." Moreover, A & S's explanations of the provision's absence are unconvincing. First, Adler's friendship with Wachner did not prevent him from having her execute at least three highly specific contracts. His friendship did not prevent him from explaining with precise formulae Wachner's exact share of any future taxes that might be levied against the Settlement Amount.

Even if an agreement is integrated, parol evidence may be admitted if the underlying contract is ambiguous. As both sides agree, the traditional view is that the search for ambiguity must be conducted within the four corners of the writing. Under this analysis, it is self-evident that the 1986 Agreement is not ambiguous. There are no words or phrases that appear "susceptible of at least two fairly reasonable meanings." As discussed at length above,

the fact that the agreement contains only a one-way release does not create any ambiguity.

The parol evidence rule has no application in a suit brought to rescind a contract on the ground of fraud. Under New York law, to plead a prima facie case of fraud the plaintiff must allege representation of a material existing fact, falsity, scienter, deception and injury. In short, a contractual promise made with the undisclosed intention not to perform it constitutes fraud and, despite the so-called merger clause, the plaintiff is free to prove that he was induced by false and fraudulent misrepresentation.

> Although proof of fraud can vitiate an agreement, such proof may only be offered to show "the intention of the parties that the entire contract was to be a nullity, not as here that only certain provisions of the agreement were to be enforced." Here the plaintiff is not claiming that no agreement existed. . . . [H]e is not seeking rescission, but enforcement of the contract, albeit upon terms . . . markedly different from those in the writing. . . . Here the plaintiff seeks materially to alter, by introducing prior parol evidence, a single unambiguously expressed item—the terms of compensation—in a comprehensive contract that includes [a merger clause]. To allow him to do so would be to eviscerate the parol evidence rule.

The Court will not allow the plaintiff to introduce parol evidence to alter the unambiguous terms of an integrated agreement.

QUESTIONS FOR ANALYSIS

Identify the facts in *Adler*. In what instances did the court circumvent the parol evidence rule? What was the court's decision?

7.6 PRACTICAL APPLICATIONS

A number of situations require contracts to be reduced to a writing because of the Statute of Frauds. Common contracts which have evolved over the years to deal with the Statute of Frauds issue are prenuptial agreements and guaranty agreements. Figure 7-3 provides examples of each.

Antenuptial Agreement—Each Relinquishing Interest in Other's Property

Agreement made the 25th day of November, 1994, between Leanne Street of Dallas, Texas, and John Callender of Mesquite, Texas.

Whereas, the parties contemplate entering into the marriage relation with each other, and both are severally possessed of real and personal property in his and her own right, and each have children by former marriages, all of said children being of age and possessed of means of support independent of their parents, and it is desired by the parties that their marriage shall not in any way change their legal right, or that of their children and heirs, in the property of each of them.

Therefore, it is agreed:

Husband Releases Rights in Wife's Property

1. John Callender agrees, in case he survives Leanne Street, that he will make no claim to any part of her estate as surviving husband; that in consideration of said marriage he waives and relinquishes all right of curtesy or other right in and to the property, real or personal, which Leanne Street now owns or may hereafter acquire.

Wife Releases Rights in Husband's Property

2. Leanne Street agrees, in case she survives John Callender, that she will make no claim to any part of his estate as surviving wife; that in consideration of said marriage she waives and relinquishes all claims to downer, homestead, widow's award, or other right in and to the property, real or personal, which John Callender now owns or may hereafter acquire.

Intent that Marriage Shall Not Affect Property

3. It is declared that by virtue of said marriage neither one shall have or acquire any right, title, or claim in and to the real or personal estate of the other, but that the estate of each shall descend to his or her heirs at law, legatees, or devisees, as may be prescribed by his or her last will and testament or by the law of state in force, as though no marriage had taken place between them.

Agreement to Join in Conveyances

4. It is agreed that in case either of the parties desires to mortgage, sell, or convey his or her real or personal estate, each one will join in the deed of conveyance or mortgage, as may be necessary to make the same effectual.

Full Disclosure between the Parties

5. It is further agreed that this agreement is entered into with a full knowledge on the part of each party as to the extent and probable value of the estate of the other and of all the rights conferred by law upon each in the estate of the other by virtue of said proposed marriage, but it is their desire that their respective rights to each other's estate shall be fixed by this agreement, which shall be binding upon their respective heirs and legal representatives.

In witness thereof, etc.

_____
John Callender

_____
Leanne Street

Guaranty of Payment

For value received, Marvin Heath hereby guarantees the payment of the within Note at maturity, or at any time thereafter, with interest at the rate of 10 per cent per annum until paid, waving demand, notice of nonpayment, and protest.

_____
Marvin Heath

FIGURE 7-3 Sample antenuptial agreement and guaranty of payment (subject to Statute of Frauds)

Other Statute of Frauds-type contracts that often are reduced to writing are leases, mortgages, and deeds. Figure 7-4 illustrates one of the most important applications of the Statute of Frauds, the real estate transaction.

Mortgage—General Form

This mortgage is made December 20, 1995, between Wendy Raines of 1234 R. Street, City of Cape May, County of Cape May, State of New Jersey, herein referred to as mortgagor, and Robert Wind, of 8029 NBC Street, City of Vineland, County of Cumberland, State of New Jersey, herein referred to as mortgagee.

Mortgagor, by a Note dated December 20, 1995, is indebted to mortgagee in the sum of EIGHTY NINE THOUSAND DOLLARS ($89,000.00), with interest from date at the rate of eight percent (8%) per annum on the unpaid balance until paid, principal and interest to be paid at the office of Don Morgan, at 7568 Preston Road, or at such other place as the holder may designate in writing, delivered or mailed to mortgagor, in monthly installments of SIXTEEN HUNDRED TWENTY THREE DOLLARS AND EIGHTY FIVE CENTS ($1,623.85), beginning January 20, 1996, and continuing on the 20th day of each month thereafter until the indebtedness is fully paid; except that, if not paid sooner, the final payment thereof shall be due and payable on January 20, 2021. The terms of such Note are incorporated herein by reference.

Mortgagor, in consideration of above-stated obligation, hereby mortgages to mortgagee all of the following described property in the County of Cumberland, state of New Jersey: [set forth legal description of property], together with the appurtenances and all the estate and rights of the mortgagor in and to such premises.

Mortgagor covenants and agrees as follows:

1. PAYMENT OF INDEBTEDNESS.   Mortgagor shall pay the indebtedness as hereinbefore provided.

2. WARRANTY OF OWNERSHIP.   Mortgagor warrants that she is lawfully seised of an indefeasible estate in fee in the premises.

3. MAINTENANCE OF INSURANCE.   Mortgagor shall keep the buildings on the premises insured for loss by fire for mortgagee's benefit; mortgagor shall assign and deliver the policies to mortgagee; and mortgagor shall reimburse mortgagee for any insurance premiums paid by mortgagee on mortgagor's default in so insuring the buildings or in so assigning and delivering the policies.

4. TAXES AND ASSESSMENTS.   Mortgagor shall pay all taxes and assessments; in default thereof, mortgagee may pay such taxes and assessments and mortgagor shall reimburse mortgagee therefor.

5. REMOVAL OR DEMOLITION OF BUILDINGS.   No building on the premises shall be removed or demolished without mortgagee's consent.

6. ACCELERATION OF PRINCIPAL AND INTEREST.   The full amount of the principal sum and interest shall became due at the option of mortgagee: After default in the payment of any installment of principal or of interest for 10 days; or after default in the payment of any tax or assessment for 10 days after notice and demand; or after default after notice and demand either in assigning and delivering the policies insuring the buildings against loss by fire or reimbursing mortgagee for premiums paid on such insurance, as provided above; or after failure to furnish a statement of the amount due on the mortgage and of any offsets and/or defenses existing against the mortgaged debt, after such has been requested as provided below.

7. APPOINTMENT OF RECEIVER.   The holder of this mortgage, in any action to foreclose it, shall be entitled to the appointment of a receiver.

8. STATEMENT OF AMOUNT DUE. Mortgagor, within 10 days when requested in person, or within 10 days when requested by mail, shall furnish to mortgagee a duly acknowledged written statement of the amount due on the mortgage and whether any offsets and/or defenses exist against the mortgaged debt.

9. SALE IN ONE PARCEL.   In case of a foreclosure sale, the premises, or so much thereof as may be affected by this mortgage, may be sold in one parcel.

FIGURE 7-4   Sample mortgage (subject to Statute of Frauds)

10. ASSIGNMENT OF RENTALS, ISSUES, AND PROFITS. Mortgagor hereby assigns to mortgagee the rents, issues, and profits of the premises as further security for the payment of the obligations secured hereby, and grants to mortgagee the right to enter on the premises to collect the same, to let the premises or any part thereof, and to apply the moneys received therefrom, after payment of all necessary charges and expenses, to the obligations secured by this mortgage, on default under any of the covenants, conditions, or agreements contained herein. In the event of any such default, mortgagor shall pay to mortgagee or to any receiver appointed to collect the rents, issues, and profits of the premises or of such part thereof as may be in mortgagor's possession; and on default in payment of such rental, to vacate and surrender possession of the premises, or that portion thereof occupied by mortgagor, to mortgagee or the receiver appointed to collect the same.

11. PAYMENT OF EXPENSES. If any action or proceeding is commenced, except an action to foreclose this mortgage or to collect the debt secured hereby, in which it is necessary to defend or assert the lien of this mortgage, whether or not the mortgagee is made or becomes a party to any such action or proceeding, all of mortgagee's expenses incurred in any such action or proceeding to prosecute or defend the rights and lien created by this mortgage, including reasonable counsel fees, shall be paid by mortgagor, and if not so paid promptly on request, shall be added to the debts secured hereby and become a lien on the mortgaged premises, and shall be deemed to be fully secured by this mortgage and to be prior and paramount to any right, title, interest, or claim to or on the premises accruing or attaching subsequent to the lien of this mortgage, and shall bear interest at the rate provided for the obligations secured hereby. This covenant shall not govern or affect any action or proceeding to foreclose this mortgage or to recover or to collect the debt secured hereby, which action or proceeding shall be governed by the provisions of law respecting the recovery of costs, disbursements, and allowances in foreclosure actions.

12. CONDEMNATION OF PREMISES. If the premises or any part thereof shall be condemned and taken under the power of eminent domain, or if any award for any change of grade of streets affecting the premises shall be made, all damages and awards for the property so taken or damaged shall be paid to the holder of this mortgage, up to the amount then unpaid on the indebtedness hereby secured, without regard to whether or not the balance remaining unpaid on the indebtedness may then be due and payable; and the amount so paid shall be credited against the indebtedness and, if it is insufficient to pay the entire amount thereof, it may, at the option of the holder of this mortgage, be applied to the last maturing installments. The balance of such damages and awards, if any, shall be paid to mortgagor. Mortgagee and subsequent holders of this mortgage are hereby given full power, right, and authority to receive and receipt for all such damages and awards.

13. BANKRUPTCY. If mortgagor or any obligor on the [note or bond] secured hereby: (1) files a voluntary petition in bankruptcy under the Bankruptcy Act of the United States, or (2) is adjudicated a bankrupt under such act, or (3) is the subject of a petition filed in federal or state court for the appointment of a trustee or receiver in bankruptcy or insolvency, or (4) makes a general assignment for the benefit of creditors, then and on the occurrence of any such conditions, at the option of mortgagee, the entire balance of the principal sum secured hereby, together with all accrued interest thereon, shall become immediately due and payable.

14. WASTE. Mortgagor shall not commit, suffer, or permit any waste, impairment, or deterioration of the premises or of any improvement thereon and shall maintain the premises and all improvements thereon in good condition and repair. If mortgagor fails or neglects to make any necessary repair or replacement in any improvement for 10 days after notice to do so from mortgagee, mortgagee may effect such repair to replacement and the cost thereof shall be added to the debt secured hereby, shall bear interest at the rate provided in the Note secured hereby, and shall be covered by this mortgage and the lien hereof.

15. COMPLIANCE WITH LAWS AND REGULATIONS. Mortgagor shall comply with all statutes, ordinances, and governmental requirements that affect the premises. If mortgagor neglects or refuses to so comply and such failure or refusal continues for 2 months, then, at mortgagee's option, the entire balance of the principal sum secured hereby, together with all accrued interest, shall become immediately due and payable.

Wherever the sense of this mortgage so requires, the word "mortgagor" shall be construed as if it reads "mortgagors" and the word "mortgagee" shall be construed as if it reads "'mortgagees." The word "holder" shall include any payee of the indebtedness hereby secured or any transferee thereof whether by operation of law or otherwise. Unless otherwise

FIGURE 7-4 *(Continued)*

provided, any notice and demand or request specified in this mortgage may be made in writing and may be served in person or by mail.

In witness whereof, this mortgage has been duly executed by mortgagor the day and year first written above.

_____
Signature

SUBSCRIBED AND SWORN TO this the _____ day of _____, 19____.

_____
Notary Public in and for the
State of New Jersey

FIGURE 7-4 *(Continued)*

Notice in all these examples that the minimum requirements of the Statute of Frauds have been met: (1) identity of the parties; (2) subject matter; (3) material terms; (4) price or consideration; and (5) a place for a signature. These basic requirements should be kept in mind when drafting any contract. Additionally, a common clause which aids the court in contract interpretation is found in Figure 7-5.

If any term, provision, covenant, or condition of this agreement is held by a court of competent jurisdiction to be invalid, void, or unenforceable, the remainder of the provisions shall remain in full force and effect and shall in no way be affected, impaired, or invalidated.

FIGURE 7-5 Sample contract interpretation clause

SUMMARY

7.1   The Statute of Frauds dates back to English common law and requires that certain types of contracts must be in writing to be enforceable. Most states except Louisiana have adopted the Statute of Frauds by statute or case law. The Statute of Frauds can become a barrier to an enforceable contract.

7.2   There are five types of contracts that must be in writing to be enforceable. They are (1) contracts which cannot be performed within one year after making; (2) contracts of a third party to pay the debt of another; (3) contracts made by an executor or administrator of an estate to pay the debts of the decedent's estate; (4) contracts in consideration of marriage; and (5) contracts for the transfer of real property. Specific states may require other types of contracts to be in writing, especially those involving principals and agents.

7.3 A formal contract is not necessary to satisfy the Statute of Frauds, but certain terms must be included in the writing: (1) the identity of the parties, (2) the subject matter, (3) the material terms, (4) the price, and (5) the signatures of the parties.

7.4 When a court interprets a writing, it will look to both the words and the intentions of the parties. One of the rules of construction that the court will use is the strict construction (or four corners) doctrine. The court will also tend to give words their plain meaning and consider general usage and general custom in interpreting the contract. The most important rule for contract interpretation is the parol evidence rule, which states that oral evidence cannot be used to modify or alter a written contract. A merger clause gives the presumption of a final contract. Therefore, to decide whether the parol evidence rule applies, determine whether the contract is integrated or only partially integrated.

7.5 There are a number of exceptions to application of the parol evidence rule. Oral evidence can be used to clarify but not vary a contract. Oral evidence may also be used when there is an ambiguity, a condition precedent, or destruction of mutual assent.

REVIEW QUESTIONS

1. Why was the Statute of Frauds created?
2. What types of contracts does the Statute of Frauds require to be in writing?
3. What is the main purpose rule and where is it applied?
4. When can a real estate transaction be enforceable in oral form?
5. What information in a contract is required to satisfy the Statute of Frauds?
6. What is the equal dignities rule?
7. Define the strict construction doctrine.
8. What are some of the common rules that a court follows in interpreting a writing?
9. What is the parol evidence rule? List the exceptions to the parol evidence rule.
10. Distinguish between an integrated contract and partially integrated contract.

EXERCISES

1. Read *Metropolitan Sports Facilities Commission v. General Mills*, 470 N.W.2d 118 (Minn. 1991) and answer the following questions:
   a. Identify the parties and prior proceedings.
   b. What is the main point in the case?
   c. What rules of contract interpretation did the court apply?

2. Mr. Brown agrees to sell Mr. Blackwell the house at 423 Cherrytree
    Lane for $50,000. They prepare the following document on a piece of
    paper:

    > I, Mr. Brown, agree to sell my house to Mr. Blackwell.
    >
    > Mr. Brown (signed)

    Is this an enforceable contract? Why or why not?

3. Go to your local law library and find your state Statute of Frauds and
    compare it to the Texas or California Statute of Frauds in this Chapter.
    a. Identify the similarities between your state statute and those of Cali-
        fornia or Texas.
    b. Identify the differences between your state statute and those of
        Texas or California.

CHAPTER 8
Performance and Discharge of the Contract

8.1 CONDITIONS TO PERFORMANCE

Formation of the contract is only the beginning of the process. Once the parties agree to their duties and obligations, the next stage is **performance**, which occurs when the parties complete their obligations under the contract. Often, though, conditions are attached to a party's performance, which can either terminate contractual obligations or continue them. Whether the conditions are met will determine the status of the contract.

A condition qualifies the contractual obligation. It acts as a trigger to the promises between the parties. Section 224 of the *Restatement (Second) of Contracts* defines a *condition* as:

> an event, not certain to occur, which must occur, unless its non-occurrence is excused, before performance under a contract becomes due.

Five types of conditions are important in understanding contract law: (1) condition precedent; (2) concurrent condition; (3) condition subsequent;

(4) express condition; and (5) implied condition. Each type of condition bears on a party's contractual obligations.

Condition Precedent

A **condition precedent** is a condition in a contract that qualifies the contractual obligation before it comes into existence. When a condition precedent is part of a contract, the condition must be fulfilled before the contract can come into existence. Words such as *when, if, before, after, on condition that, subject to, provided that, so long as*, and other words of like import create conditions precedent in contracts. When words such as these are used in a contract, the contingency must be performed before the contract will come into existence.

Perhaps the most typical contract with conditions precedent is a real estate contract. One of the most standard conditions on the sale of property is that the buyer must qualify for financing. This is a condition precedent for the buyer's acquiring the right to purchase the property from the seller. Normally, at the time of the contract, the buyer has not qualified for financing, and the seller does not have to sell the house to the buyer unless the seller knows that the buyer can pay the sales price. As a result, sales contracts for the purchase of real estate virtually always have a provision stating that the buyer must qualify for financing *prior to* the sale being consummated. If the buyer does not qualify for financing, neither party has any further obligation to continue the transaction. In *Harmon Cable Communications v. Scope Cable Television,* 237 Neb. 871, 468 N.W.2d 350 (1991), one of the issues before the court was whether a condition precedent existed. Notice how the court makes a clear distinction between a condition precedent and a promise.

TERMS

performance
1. The doing of that which is required by a contract at the time, place, and in the manner stipulated in the contract, that is, according to the terms of the contract.
2. Fulfilling a duty in a manner that leaves nothing more to be done.

condition precedent
A condition that must first occur for a contractual obligation . . . to attach.

HARMON CABLE COMMUNICATIONS OF NEBRASKA v. SCOPE CABLE TELEVISION, INC.

Supreme Court of Nebraska
April 19, 1991

Under separate contracts, plaintiff-appellee, Harmon Cable Communications of Nebraska Limited Partnership, a limited partnership, purchased a cable television system from each of the defendants-appellants, Scope Cable Television, Inc., a corporation, and Scope Cable Television of Nebraska Co., a general partnership. Claiming that each of the sellers failed to deliver the promised number of subscribers and that each had improperly charged for certain accounts receivable, the purchaser brought [this] action.

On June 21, 1985, the purchaser's predecessor in interest and the sellers entered into contracts. By their terms, the contracts were not to be closed until sometime between October 31 and December 31, 1985. As part of its contract, the corporate seller warranted that it would, as of the date of closing, deliver at least 1,200 "basic subscribers," that is, consumers of the basic cable services the seller offered, and 1,160 "pay subscribers," that is, consumers of services in addition to basic services. The partnership seller warranted that it would deliver at least 2,125 basic subscribers and 2,060 pay subscribers.

In August or September 1985, the sellers informed the purchaser's predecessor of potential subscriber shortfalls. On November 5, 1985, the parties entered into a written addendum to their agreements. This document acknowledged that the sellers would be unable to deliver the warranted number of subscribers, and recited that the parties disagreed as to the purchaser's remedies for that failure. The compact noted that the sellers were of the view that the purchaser's sole remedy was to terminate the agreements and receive a refund of all moneys paid, whereas the purchaser maintained that such failure was a breach of the agreements, entitling it to exercise any remedy agreed upon in the contracts, including the instigation of a lawsuit. Having thus covenanted to disagree, the parties nonetheless contracted to close and complete the transactions on November 5, 6, or 7, 1985.

At the November 5, 1985, closing, the purchaser delivered $2,470,000 to the sellers, plus a note in the sum of $5,000 to the corporate seller and a note in the sum of $20,000 to the partnership seller, totaling the agreed-upon purchase price of $2,495,000.

On December 3, 1985, the purchaser sent the sellers a letter notifying them that they had not delivered the warranted number of subscribers, that they had sold accounts receivable which represented past-due balances on disconnected accounts in violation of the purchase agreements, and that unless they cured these failures within 60 days, the purchaser would offset against its damages those amounts otherwise due the sellers under the promissory notes the purchaser had issued. These lawsuits followed.

The number of subscribers actually delivered was undisputed at trial. The corporate seller delivered 1,144 basic and 813 pay subscribers, amounting to a shortfall of 56 basic and 347 pay subscribers. The partnership seller delivered 2,096 basic and 2,085 pay subscribers, amounting to a shortfall of 29 basic subscribers and a surplus of 25 pay subscribers.

On September 8, 1988, the trial court entered its judgments. It awarded the purchaser $106,763 against the corporate seller, $110,800 as determined by the jury for the subscriber shortfall plus $963 in accounts receivable adjustments, less $5,000 due the corporate seller under the promissory note the purchaser had executed. The trial court also awarded the partnership seller $9,146 against the purchaser. It gave the purchaser credit for $9,000 as determined by the jury on the subscriber shortfall, awarded the purchaser $1,854 in accounts receivable adjustments, and found that the partnership seller was entitled to $20,000 on the promissory note the purchaser executed.

The first assignment questions the propriety of granting the purchaser summary judgment on the question of the sellers' liability for the subscriber shortfall. The sellers claim that the purchaser forfeited any right to damages for that failure because it did not comply with the notice provisions of the contracts and, in any event, did not act in good faith.

Each contract contain an indemnification paragraph, which provides:

[Purchaser] shall not assume any debts or other liabilities of Seller. *Seller* hereby covenants and *shall* defend and *indemnify [Purchaser]* and hold harmless [Purchaser] at all times after the Closing Date from and against and *in respect to any and all losses, liabilities, costs (including, without limitation, court costs), damages, expenses (including, without limitation, reasonable attorneys fees) or deficiencies arising out of or due to:*

(a) Any inaccuracy in or breach of any representation, breach of warranty or nonfulfillment of any agreement, covenant or obligation on the part of Seller made in this Agreement;

(b) Any and all liabilities or obligations of Seller of any nature, whether accured [sic], absolute, contingent or otherwise, existing on the Closing Date; and

(c) Any actions, suits,proceedings, costs, expenses and legal fees incident to any of the foregoing items listed under paragraphs (a) and (b) of this paragraph. *[Purchaser] shall assert any claim* or claims for indemnification under the provisions of this paragraph above *by giving written notice* of such claim or claims to Seller within 30 days of discovery, but not later than 18 months from the date of closing. *Each such notice shall set forth* in reasonable detail the factual basis giving rise to the claim or claims and *the amount of the damages and expenses incurred by [Purchaser] as a result of such claim or claims.* Seller agrees that it shall promptly reimburse and pay [Purchaser] for such damages and expenses. If any claim for indemnification is *based upon an action or claim filed or made against [Purchaser] by a third party,* then Seller shall have the right to negotiate a settlement or compromise of any such action or claim or to defend any such action or claim at the sole cost and expense of, and with counsel selected by Seller.

(Emphasis supplied.)

Whether the sellers' contention that the purchaser cannot recover damages resulting from the subscriber shortfall because it failed to comply with the notification provisions of the indemnification paragraphs has merit depends upon whether those provisions are conditional or promissory. Courts have struggled for centuries with differentiating between conditions and promises. A condition has been defined as "an operative fact, one on which the existence of some particular legal relation depends." Another author similarly defines a condition as "(1) Any operative fact that will create some new legal relation, or extinguish an existing relation; or (2) Words or other manifestations that indicate that a fact shall have such operation." The Restatement definition of a condition is also in accord: "A condition is an event, not certain to occur, which must occur, unless its non-occurrence is excused, before performance under a contract becomes due."

A promise, on the other hand, occurs when one "expresses an intention that some future performance will be rendered and gives assurance of its rendition to the promisee." "A promise is a manifestation of intention to act or refrain from acting in a specified way, so made as to justify a promisee in

understanding that a commitment has been made." In the event of nonfulfillment, the distinction between a promise and a condition becomes important. As a general rule, a condition must be exactly fulfilled before liability can arise on the contract. This general rule finds support in the Restatement as well:

(1) Performance of a duty subject to a condition *cannot become due unless the condition occurs* or its non-occurrence is excused.
(2) Unless it has been excused, the non-occurrence of a condition discharges the duty when the condition can no longer occur.

Non-occurrence of a condition is not a breach by a party unless he is under a duty that the condition occur. Nonfulfillment of a promise, however, gives rise to a different remedy. "The non-fulfillment of a promise is called a breach of contract, and *creates in the other party a secondary right to damages;* it is the failure to perform that which was required by a legal duty."

Thus, if the notice requirements of the indemnification paragraphs are deemed to be a condition to the sellers' liability, the purchaser's noncompliance would discharge the sellers' liability. If the notice requirements are deemed to be a promise, then the remedy lies in an action for damages.

Whether contractual language is deemed conditional or promissory generally depends upon the intention of the parties. Terms such as "if," "provided that," "when," "after," "as soon as," "subject to," "on condition that," or some similar phrase are evidence that performance of a contractual provision is a condition. [The] absence of any language indicative of a condition precludes a conclusion that the parties clearly intended the notice requirement to constitute a condition to the creation of the contract. They therefore are promises, the breach of which gives rise to an action for damages.

QUESTIONS FOR ANALYSIS

How did the court define a condition? A promise? What words did the court decide showed a condition precedent? Did the court find that a condition precedent existed? Why or why not?

Concurrent Condition

The more typical contract condition is a *concurrent condition,* a condition that the parties to the contract perform at the same time. Following through with the real estate example, assume that the buyer qualifies for financing. It is now time for the **closing,** where the buyer will be expected to tender a check for the purchase price of the property; at the same time, with the tendering of that check, the seller will be expected to tender the **title** and a **deed** to the buyer. These acts occur concurrently and thus are known as concurrent conditions. Many contracts contain concurrent conditions.

Condition Subsequent

A **condition subsequent** is a condition in a contract that triggers the contractual obligation after the contract comes into existence. In this situation, a specific condition that occurs after the contract has come into existence will terminate the contract. This type of condition relates to performance of future contractual obligations: if it occurs, it will extinguish a party's contractual obligation.

Although conditions subsequent are not as prevalent as conditions precedent, they are often found in insurance policies. For example, most of us purchase car insurance. We pay the premiums but hope that an accident will not occur. As part of the contractual obligations of the parties, if an accident occurs, the insurer will pay on the policy for any damages arising from the accident. However, a condition subsequent in the policy normally states that the insured must notify the insurer within a specified period of time after the accident or loss; otherwise the insurance company need not pay the obligation. This condition of notice is considered a condition subsequent.

Whether a condition subsequent existed was the central issue in *Lindsey v. Clossco,* 642 F. Supp. 250 (C.D. Ariz. 1986). There a basketball coach's contract with a shoe distributor was challenged when the coach's contract with the university was terminated.

TERMS

closing
Completing a transaction, particularly a contract for the sale of real estate.

title
1. The right of an owner with respect to property, real or personal, i.e., possession and the right of possession. 2. A document that evidences the rights of an owner; i.e., ownership rights.

deed
A document by which real property, or an interest in real property, is conveyed from one person to another.

condition subsequent
In a contract, a condition that divests contractual liability that has already attached . . . upon the failure of the other party to the contract . . . to comply with its terms.

LINDSEY v. CLOSSCO

United States District Court, D. Arizona
July 30, 1986

The University of Arizona is a member of the National Collegiate Athletic Association (NCAA) and a participant in the Pacific Ten Conference. Since 1972 Arizona has played its home basketball games in an arena with a seating capacity of fourteen thousand (14,000). Arizona basketball games are broadcast regularly on local television and the program receives extensive coverage in the local and regional media. In addition, the Pacific Ten Conference markets a regional television contract which includes contests between the University of Arizona and its conference opponents.

Defendant Clossco distributes athletic products manufactured by adidas in thirteen western states. Defendants' chief competitors in the athletic shoe market are Nike, Converse and Puma. As part of their advertising efforts, shoe manufacturers and their distributors regularly enter into contracts with professional athletes and coaches at prominent NCAA institutions.

Contract with collegiate coaches provide, expressly or impliedly, that the coach will direct the university's team to wear the manufacturer/distributor's shoes in practices and games. The manufacturers/distributors thereby receive broad exposure of their products and the tacit endorsement of the universities, prominent college basketball teams and the NCAA. Coaches view these shoe endorsement contracts as a method of supplementing the salaries they receive from the universities. Although these contracts virtually ensure that NCAA institutions shall utilize the manufacturers/ distributors' shoes, the universities are not party to the contracts. These contracts routinely include a confidentiality clause, prohibiting disclosure of the terms of such agreements to other persons, necessarily including coaches, the institutions utilizing the shoes, and the NCAA. While the universities are not party to such contracts, representatives of the athletic departments of prominent NCAA institutions regularly exploit the existence of such contracts in negotiating with candidates for coaching positions. Thus some representatives of university athletic departments perceive a benefit to the universities from such agreements.

Plaintiff Ben Lindsey began negotiating to become Head Basketball Coach at the University of Arizona following the conclusion of the 1981–82 season. During those negotiations, Arizona Athletic Director David H. Strack represented that if Lindsey were to accept the position of head basketball coach, he could expect a shoe endorsement contract valued at twenty to thirty thousand dollars ($20,000–30,000) per year.

Lindsey was hired as head basketball coach in April 1982. In May 1982, Clossco representative Phil Vukicevich and Ben Lindsey entered into an oral agreement providing that Clossco pay Lindsey an annual "advisory and consulting" fee of thirty thousand dollars ($30,000) in return for Lindsey's commitment to have the University of Arizona basketball team wear adidas basketball shoes. This oral agreement did not include a provision respecting Clossco's obligation in the event Lindsey should be terminated or resign for any reason.

On May 26, 1982, Clossco president Bill Closs delivered a written agreement memorializing the parties' earlier oral agreement. This agreement referred to plaintiff Ben Lindsey as "Coach Lindsey" and "Ben Lindsey, Head Basketball Coach, University of Arizona." The material terms of this agreement provided [that] Lindsey was to "have the University of Arizona basketball team exclusively in adidas brand basketball shoes." Further, Lindsey was to be available to Clossco/adidas for appearances such as clinics or special events, on behalf of adidas, on such dates as were mutually agreeable. Finally, Lindsey was to be available to adidas, at reasonable times, to advise and consult with adidas relative to the construction, design and playing features of adidas basketball shoes.

In return, Clossco was to pay Lindsey an annual fee of thirty thousand dollars ($30,000), provide Lindsey a clothing allowance of one thousand dollars ($1,000), provide two assistant coaches a clothing allowance of five hundred dollars ($500), provide forty (40) t-shirts for the team, and provide Lindsey one hundred-fifty (150) summer camp t-shirts.

Before the 1982–83 basketball season, Lindsey advised Arizona Athletic Director David H. Strack that he had entered into a shoe endorsement contract. The terms of the contract were not revealed to Strack or any other University officials.

Throughout the 1982–83 basketball season, University of Arizona basketball players, with few exceptions, wore adidas basketball shoes. Don Crenshaw, a Clossco promotion representative, monitored Lindsey's compliance with the shoe endorsement agreement. At various times throughout the season he contacted Lindsey and discussed Lindsey's obligation to encourage and direct use of adidas shoes by all his players. Lindsey recognized this obligation and cooperated throughout the season.

Clossco/adidas never requested that Lindsey make any appearances or consult with them relative to adidas basketball shoes. In January 1983 defendant Clossco paid plaintiff Lindsey a five thousand dollar ($5,000) advance on the second contract year.

The University of Arizona terminated plaintiff Ben Lindsey from the position of head basketball coach in March 1983. Thereafter Lindsey made a demand for further payment under the agreement. That demand was denied by defendant Clossco.

Ben Lindsey's termination as head basketball coach at the University of Arizona operated as a condition subsequent, extinguishing Clossco's obligation to perform. "A condition subsequent is one referring to a future event, upon the happening of which the obligation becomes no longer binding upon the other party, if he chooses to avail himself of the condition." While the intent to create a condition subsequent must appear expressly or by clear implication, no precise words are necessary. It is clear from the nature of the agreement that it was entered into subject to the implied condition subsequent that it should be binding only if Lindsey remained head basketball coach at the University of Arizona. The services to be performed under the agreement, i.e., "encouraging" or promoting by his best efforts the use of adidas basketball shoes by the University of Arizona basketball team, were of such character that they could be performed effectively only if Lindsey retained the position of head basketball coach at the University.

QUESTIONS FOR ANALYSIS

What were the facts of the case? How did the court define *condition subsequent*? What was the court's holding?

Express and Implied Conditions

When a condition is specifically stated in a contract, it is known as an **express condition**. An express condition is normally stated on the face of the contract and is part of the obligations between the parties. Each of the parties knows the obligations to which it is committing and agrees to perform those obligations according to the terms and conditions of the contract.

An **implied condition**, also known as an *implied in fact condition,* is inferred or presumed under the law. The parties understand that the implied condition exists, although it is not specifically stated in the contract.

To avoid injustice, a court may deem a condition to be implied to assure fairness in a contract. This is known as the rule of constructive or implied in law conditions. In this situation, the court will imply a condition, even though neither of the parties expressly or impliedly agreed to it, because the existence of the condition is implied in the parties' respective duties. The rule suggests that one party's performance is a necessary (constructive) condition of another party's responsive performance. Critical to the concept of constructive conditions is that such conditions are not recited in the contract. For a fairly recent treatment of constructive conditions, examine *TPS Freight Distributors, Inc. v. Texas Commerce Bank,* 788 S.W.2d 456 (Tex. Ct. App.–Fort Worth 1990).

TERMS

express condition
A condition that is stated rather than implied.

implied condition (implied in fact condition)
A condition that is not expressed but that is inferred by the law from the acts of the parties.

TPS FREIGHT DISTRIBUTORS, INC. v. TEXAS COMMERCE BANK-DALLAS
Court of Appeals of Texas, Fort Worth
April 18, 1990

On December 16, 1985, TPS ("appellants") purchased the assets of a company called TPS Distributors/Consolidators, Inc. ("Distributors"). The sellers of Distributors had earlier purchased this company from Kenneth Blair, pursuant to which the sellers and Blair executed a contract of sale and a covenant preventing Blair from competing with Distributors. When the sellers failed to fulfill their obligations to Blair under the contract of sale, Blair began running Distributors as, according to Blair, an informal "debtor in possession." After Blair succeeded in returning Distributors to profitability, he proceeded to look for new buyers on behalf of the sellers. At this time, appellants purchased the assets of Distributors from the sellers.

In exchange for purchasing the assets of Distributors, B. Bowlus West, on behalf of TPS, agreed to assume most of the original purchaser's obligations to Blair. On behalf of TPS, West executed a promissory note to Blair, and agreed to pay Blair the sum of $112,000 under a new covenant not to compete. The total amount (assumption note, second note, and covenant sum) was secured by a single letter of credit, but the assumed note and the second note were paid off prior to trial.

The new covenant not to compete was executed by both parties on December 16, 1985, and provided that Blair could not compete with TPS from December 16, 1985 through December 31, 1990. In consideration, TPS agreed to pay Blair twenty-three monthly payments of $1,266.67 beginning February 1, 1986, and then thirty-seven monthly payments of $2,266.67, with the last payment being due January 1, 1991, the day after full performance by Blair. Under the agreement, Blair agreed not compete with TPS, but did not make any affirmative promises or agree to perform any services or provide any advice to TPS. Paragraph seven of the agreement also provides that it "shall . . . inure to the benefit of the respective heirs, successors, assigns and legal representatives of the parties."

TPS made payments to Blair each month through and including September 1987. Blair died on September 10, 1987, after which TPS ceased making voluntary payments on the ground that TPS considered the covenant to have terminated upon Blair's death.

Appellants urge that a covenant not to compete is a personal-services contract because a contract is personal in its character if one party relies upon the skill, character, or credit of the other party. Appellants then note that a personal services contract terminates upon the death of the party whose personal performance or character formed the basis of the contract. Following this reasoning, appellants urge that a covenant not to compete will also terminate upon the death of the covenantor. Appellants admit that there are no Texas cases supporting their theory that a covenant not to compete is a personal services contract.

Appellees argue that a covenant not to compete is *not* a personal services contract. Blair had no obligation to provide any services or advice to appellants, and there was no promise made by Blair remaining unperformed after his death. As appellants' obligation was not conditioned on Blair's survival and was not terminated by his death, appellees say that appellants are ignoring the distinctions "between covenants for personal services . . . and covenants not to compete" recognized by Texas courts.

Appellees further argue that there are no services or advice that appellants will be denied by reason of Blair's death, nor have Blair's heirs and successors, the beneficiaries of the covenant, competed with appellants. Therefore, Blair's premature death does not deprive appellants of any of the benefits for which they agreed to pay the money. Appellees' argument is persuasive.

[A]ppellants argue that the covenant, as a personal services contract, contained a condition implied by law that Blair would survive during its term. In Texas, unless the express terms of the contract state otherwise, or unless the contract's terms show a contrary intent by necessary implication, the continued life of the covenantor in a *personal services contract* is a constructive condition to further obligation of either party to such a contract. Appellants reason tptembercontract, Blair's death during the term of the covenant violated this implied condition and excused appellants' further performance.

As previously noted, Blair did not contract to provide any services or do anything for appellants, instead, he agreed to *refrain* from doing something. Further, Blair's heirs are bound to the covenant by its terms, in that in order to receive the benefits of the covenant, they too must refrain from competing with appellants. Appellants are still getting the bargain for which they contracted. If appellants had wished to reserve the right to pay less than the full sum, in the event of Blair's death, they could have inserted such a condition into the contract. They did not. Having already held that this covenant not to compete is not a personal services contract, we also hold that there was no implied condition in the contract that Blair should survive throughout the term of the contract. Contracts often survive the death of one of the parties involved. When the trial court granted appellees' Motion for Summary Judgment it did not commit error in failing to conclude the contract terminated on Blair's death because of an implied condition therein.

QUESTIONS FOR ANALYSIS

What are the facts of the *TPS Freight* case? How did the court define a constructive condition? Did the court find that a constructive condition existed? Why or why not?

8.2 DISCHARGING CONTRACTUAL OBLIGATIONS

When the conditions in a contract are not performed, the obligations of the parties are normally either discharged or terminated, depending on the circumstances. However, in some circumstances, contractual obligations can be terminated by the happening of certain events. *Termination* implies that the contractual obligations of the parties have ended. Whether the termination has positive or negative results depends on how the performance was discharged.

When **discharge** occurs, a party to a contract is relieved of his or her obligations under the contract. Thus, discharge creates a valid termination of contractual duties. Discharge can occur in many ways: by performance, by agreement, by nonperformance, and by operation of law. Each has its own legal ramifications.

8.3 DISCHARGE BY PERFORMANCE

The most common type of discharge is by complete performance of the contract by the parties. When there is *complete performance*, the parties to the contract have fully performed their duties and obligations to the contract without incident. Then all the legal rights and duties of the parties are extinguished. Expectations have been fulfilled and all the legal obligations have been met. In some instances, when a party's performance of the contract is not fully completed, the issue of whether the contract has been substantially performed must be explored.

Substantial Performance

Sometimes the parties to a contract complete most of their obligations to the contract, but leave some minor areas unfulfilled or incomplete. This is known as **substantial performance** or *substantial compliance*. When substantial performance occurs, one of the parties to the contract has made a minor deviation from full performance of the contract, rendering the contract incomplete. In this situation, the court will determine whether the deviation was minor or material to the contract; that is, the court will ask whether the deviation in the performance is inconsequential or whether it goes to the heart of the contract. If the deviation is minor, the court can enforce the contract and provide reimbursement to the party who suffered loss due to the nonperformance. However, if the court determines that the deviation is material and goes to the heart of the contract, the court will not apply the doctrine of substantial performance. As discussed later in this chapter, the doctrine of substantial performance does not apply when the deviation is material to the contract and thus results in a **breach**.

In considering whether substantial completion exists, a court can consider:

1. Expectation of the nonbreaching party. What was the principal reason for entering into the contract? If that expectation has been met, substantial performance may be found.
2. Compensation to the injured party. If the injured party's loss is easily calculated and the deviation is not material, a court could find substantial performance. When the loss is speculative and virtually cannot be

TERMS

discharge
A release from an obligation (such as a contract, a mortgage, or a note) because of performance or as a matter of grace.

substantial performance
Performance of a contract that, although not full performance, is in good faith and in compliance with the contract except for minor deviations.

breach
A break; a breaking; a violation; the violation of an obligation, engagement, or duty.

calculated, the likelihood diminishes that a court will find substantial performance.

3. Willfulness of the act. When the party's acts are willful, deliberate, and intentional, the excuse of substantial performance will not be afforded. The court looks closely at the actions of the nonperforming party to determine the nature of the acts.

4. Timing of performance or delay. Unless time is crucial to the completion of the contract, a delay or time lag when full performance has otherwise been completed may result in a court finding substantial performance. The courts closely examine the performance and any damage resulting from the delay.

Review *Vincenzi v. Cerro,* 186 Conn. 612, 442 A.2d 1352 (1982), in which the court was faced with the problem of whether a contract had been substantially performed. Pay close attention to the factors the court considered in rendering its decision.

VINCENZI v. CERRO

Supreme Court of Connecticut
Decided April 6, 1982

[O]n October 5, 1976, the parties signed a written contract for the plaintiffs to construct a three-family house on land owned by the defendants in Bridgeport. The contract price was $91,000, to be paid in five installments as various stages of the work were finished. The house was to be completed within 150 days from the date of execution of the contract, which would make the projected completion date March 4, 1977. Except for $2000 withheld for incomplete items, the first four scheduled payments were made. The payments made totaled $67,100, leaving a balance of $23,900 on the contract price. In August 1977, the plaintiffs demanded this balance, but the defendants refused on the ground that the house was not complete and that some work was defective. The court found that the work was not finished at that time because the heating system was not approved until October 1977, and a certificate of occupancy was not issued until November 9, 1977. This date, when the certificate of occupancy was obtained, was deemed by the trial court to be the date when the contract had been substantially performed by the plaintiffs.

The judgment awarded the plaintiffs the balance of the contract price, $23,900, plus certain extras totalling $1118.30, but deducted therefrom $5002.90 for defective or incomplete work and for the loss of rent suffered by the defendants for the period of unjustifiable delay.

The principal claim of the defendants is that the doctrine of substantial performance was inapplicable in this case because the plaintiffs were guilty of a wilful or intentional breach of contract by failing to complete all of the work required. "There is no reason why one who has substantially performed such a contract, but unintentionally failed of strict performance in the matter of minor details, should have imposed upon him as a condition of recovery for that of which the other party has received the benefit, the burden of showing by direct evidence its reasonable value, or why he should be deprived of all benefit of the contract which he has substantially performed." The defendants rely on this articulation of the doctrine of substantial performance, as indicating that a builder who has failed to complete his contract fully may not invoke its benefit unless he was prevented from doing so by some circumstance beyond his control, such as interference by the owner. We have in several cases approved the common statement that a contractor who is guilty of a "wilful" breach cannot maintain an action upon the contract. The contemporary view, however, is that even a conscious and intentional departure from the contract specifications will not necessarily defeat recovery, but may be considered as one of the several factors involved in deciding whether there has been full performance. The pertinent inquiry is not simply whether the breach was "wilful" but whether the behavior of the party in default "comports with standards of good faith and fair dealing." Even an adverse conclusion on this point is not decisive but is to be weighed with other factors, such as the extent to which the owner will be deprived of a reasonably expected benefit and the extent to which the builder

may suffer forfeiture, in deciding whether there has been substantial performance.

The reference to the "wilful default" qualification of the doctrine of substantial performance indicates the court considered this factor as well as others in concluding that the plaintiffs were entitled to recover on the contract. The court allowed the defendants $2060.40 on their claim for defective or incomplete items, $1527 for repairing stress cracks in the foundation walls and $533.40 for five minor items. Upon a contract price of $91,000 the proportion of unperformed work, therefore, was so minimal as to warrant the conclusion of substantial performance drawn by the court. The reliance upon the certificate of occupancy as indicating substantial performance was entirely appropriate, despite the fact that two minor items were still to be performed, installing two electric plates and building a railing for front steps.

QUESTIONS FOR ANALYSIS

How did the court define *substantial performance*? What was the court's decision in this case? State the court's reasoning behind its decision.

8.4 DISCHARGE BY AGREEMENT

A contract may also be discharged by agreement of the parties. In this instance, the parties' agreement to discharge absolves the parties from any future liability under the original contract. This is a very common method of discharge in contract law. Discharge by agreement may occur through rescission, release, novation, accord and satisfaction, or operation of the terms of the contract.

Rescission

Rescission is the voluntary mutual agreement of the parties to discharge their contractual obligations and duties, and thus return to the same position they were in prior to entering into the contract. When both parties agree to voluntarily discharge their contractual obligations, there is *mutual rescission;* both parties agree to cancel the contract. For rescission to be effective, both parties must agree to cancellation of the contract. Unless prohibited by the Statute of Frauds, a rescission may be either written or oral.

TERMS

rescission
The abrogation, annulment, or cancellation of a contract by the act of a party. Rescission may occur by mutual consent of the parties; pursuant to a condition contained in the contract; or for fraud, failure of consideration, material breach, or default. It is also a remedy available to the parties by a judgment or decree of the court. More than mere termination, rescission restores the parties to the status quo existing before the contract was entered into.

Release

Another method to discharge performance by agreement is a **release**, which relieves the parties of their duties and obligations under a contract. Ordinarily, to be valid, a release should be in writing and supported by some form of consideration. When the parties agree to a release, the law will not allow them to pursue any legal action against each other once the agreement has been signed. Figure 8-1 shows a common standard release and mutual release.

Mutual Release on Termination of Contract

Agreement, made this 11th day of March, 1995, between ABC Construction of Chicago, Illinois, hereinafter called the Contractor, and the United States of America, hereinafter called the Government.

Whereas, the Contractor and the Government entered into a certain contract deal dated December 15, 1993, covering the site known as 123 Main Place (hereinafter called the Contract);

Whereas, the parties thereto desire to terminate the Contract;

Whereas, the Contractor is willing to waive unconditionally any claim against the Government by reason of such termination; and

Whereas, such unconditional waiver by the Contractor will expedite settlement of the contract and will otherwise promote the objectives of the Contract Settlement Act.

Now, therefore, the parties hereto agree as follows:

The Contractor hereby unconditionally waives any claim against the Government arising under the terminated portion of the Contract or by reason of its termination, including, without limitation, all obligations of the Government to make further payments or to carry out other undertakings in connection with said terminated portion, and the obligation to perform further work or services or to make further deliveries of articles or materials under the terminated portion of the Contract; provided, however, that nothing herein contained shall impair or affect in any way any other covenants, terms, or conditions of the Contract.

Release of Claim under Contract

Know All Men by These Presents, that Marshall Wright of Memphis, Tennessee, in consideration of the sum of Six Hundred Fifty Dollars ($650.00) to him in hand paid, the receipt of which is by him acknowledged, does hereby, for himself and his heirs, executors, administrators, and personal representatives, release and forever discharge Daryl Brown, his heirs, executors, administrators, and personal representatives, from any and all manner of claims, demands, damages, causes of action, or suits that he might now have or that might subsequently accrue to him by reason of any matter or thing whatsoever, and particularly growing out of or in anyway connected with, directly or indirectly, that certain contract entered into on or about February 7, 1994, covering the repair of a driveway located at 3214 Walnut Street.

Dated May 26, 1995.

FIGURE 8-1 Sample releases

Novation

A common form of discharge by agreement is the formation of a **novation** between the parties. A novation occurs when both parties agree to extinguish or discharge a previously existing contractual obligation and substitute a new contractual obligation for the old agreement. The original parties to the contract are discharged and new parties are substituted under the new contract for the prior obligations. A novation clearly creates new contractual rights and obligations between the parties; through this substitution, it discharges any obligations of the prior parties to the contract. All parties in a novation are required to assent to the terms, and it must be supported by consideration. In effect, a novation acts as a release of the original parties' duties and obligations to the contract. Figure 8-2 lists the necessary components for a valid novation. For a case involving a novation, read *Moffat County State Bank v. Told,* 800 P.2d 1320 (Colo. 1990), which illustrates the necessary components of a valid and enforceable novation.

---

1. Previous enforceable obligation.
2. Mutual assent of parties to old agreement to substitution of new parties in new contract.
3. Intention to eliminate old contractual obligations and substitute new ones.
4. New valid and enforceable obligation between the new parties.

FIGURE 8-2 Elements of a valid novation

TERMS

release
The act of giving up or discharging a claim or right to the person against whom the claim exists or against whom the right is enforceable.

novation
The extinguishment of one obligation by another; a substituted contract that dissolves a previous contractual duty and creates a new one. Novation, which requires the mutual agreement of everyone concerned, replaces a contracting party with a new party who had no rights or obligations under the previous contract.

MOFFAT COUNTY STATE BANK v. TOLD

Supreme Court of Colorado
Nov. 19, 1990

Moffat County State Bank (the Bank) brought this action against Thomas and Molly Told (the Tolds) to obtain a judgment against the Tolds for their failure to honor a $100,000 loan guaranty agreement. The Tolds defended on the ground that their liability on the loan guaranty was discharged by Orin Farnsworth's (Farnsworth) oral agreement with the Bank that he would assume the Tolds' obligation.

On October 13, 1980, Mollie Told and Orin Farnsworth, joint owners of Cowan's Drug, Inc. (Cowan's Drug), entered into an agreement to sell Cowan's Drug to Ronald Batt (Batt). As part of the sale, the Tolds executed a loan guaranty agreement in which the Tolds guaranteed payment to the Bank of obligations of up to $100,000 undertaken by Cowan's Drug. Farnsworth executed an identical loan guaranty. In reliance on the loan guaranties the Bank loaned Batt $450,061.31.

On January 14, 1981, the Bank extended a letter of credit to Cowan's Drug for $3,600, and on March 5, 1981, the Bank extended an additional $60,000 loan to Cowan's Drug. On October 29, 1982, Cowan's Drug defaulted on its loans and the Bank initiated liquidation proceedings. As part of the liquidation proceedings, the Bank sent the Tolds a written notice informing them that a private sale of Cowan's Drug's collateral and accounts receivable would be held after November 8, 1982. On November 30, 1982, the Bank loaned Cowan's Drug an additional $10,000 in the form of payments to cover overdrafts. On December 6, 1982, the Bank informed the Tolds of the upcoming sale of the Batts' private residence and some additional property. The Tolds did not object to these sales and the resulting proceeds were credited to Cowan's Drug's outstanding debt, resulting in a deficiency of $379,535.19.

On January 6, 1983, Farnsworth executed a $200,000 promissory note in favor of the Bank. The note stated on its face that it was for "business—rewrite notes." The Bank applied the $200,000 note to Cowan's Drug's debt. On July 31, 1983, the Bank made demand on Batt for payment on the remaining deficiency. Batt refused to pay and subsequently declared bankruptcy. In March 1984, the Bank made demand on the Tolds for payment of the promissory notes according to the terms of their loan guaranty agreement. The Tolds refused the Bank's request for payment of the loan guaranty. In June 1984, the Bank renewed and extended Farnsworth's $200,000 promissory note. Farnsworth made payments on the note, but later stopped making payments and declared bankruptcy. A balance of $49,108.33 in principal and $33,632.71 in interest remained unpaid on the note. The Bank brought this action in June 1985, alleging that the Tolds had failed to perform under their loan guaranty agreement.

The Bank argues that the Statute of Frauds barred proof of the oral agreement, and rendered any oral modification of the written guaranty void and unenforceable. We disagree and hold that the Statute of Frauds does not bar proof of an oral agreement intended to constitute a novation.

[The] Statute of Frauds provides that "every special promise to answer for the debt, default, or miscarriage of another person" is void unless in writing and signed by the person so charged. The purpose of this section of the statute is to protect third parties from fraudulently being held to answer as a surety for another party's debt. The statute does not bar enforcement of an oral promise that is "original," but does require "collateral" promises to be in writing. A promise is collateral if the leading object of the promise is to become a surety or guarantor for the debt of another. An unconditional promise to pay the debt of another is an original promise and is not within the Statute of Frauds.

The extinguishment of an old contract by the substitution of a new contract or obligation is an original promise known as a novation. A contract of novation has four requisites: a previous valid obligation, an agreement between the parties to abide by the new contract, a valid new contract, and the extinguishment of the old obligation by the substitution of the new one. The pre-existing obligation must be extinguished or there is not a novation. A mere modification will not suffice; anything remaining of the original obligation prevents a novation.

An essential element of novation is that there must be a release of all claims of liability against the original debtor on the old obligation. A creditor's acceptance of a note of a third party who becomes obligated to pay the debt owed by the debtor is not of itself evidence of an agreement to discharge the debtor from his obligation. The parties must have intended the note to discharge the debtor in order to effect a novation.

"While . . . the intention to accomplish a novation need not be by express agreement to that effect, but may be inferred, like any other contract, from the facts, circumstances, and conduct of the parties, in order for a subsequent contract to constitute a novation and discharge of a prior one by implied intention of the parties, ordinarily it must appear that the new contract is so radically different from the old one that it necessarily supersedes it as an entirety."

"Whether there has been a novation is ordinarily a question of fact[,]" and proof of a novation "may be established by evidence of an express understanding to this effect or by circumstances showing such assent."

We hold that there are genuine issues of material fact present in this case and that the Bank was not entitled to summary judgment as a matter of law.

QUESTIONS FOR ANALYSIS

State the facts of the cases. What are the necessary elements of a novation? How did the court define *novation*?

Accord and Satisfaction

When a dispute arises between the parties, the parties can agree to terminate the rights and obligations under the contract and settle any claims and disputes between them through use of an **accord and satisfaction** (also discussed in Chapter 4 under consideration). The new agreement created between the parties is known as the **accord**; when the obligations of that new agreement are complied with by the parties, **satisfaction** occurs. This normally takes the form of a settlement that discharges performance of a contract by agreement of the parties.

Discharge by Contract Terms

Parties to the contract may agree that certain events or happenings will discharge the parties' duties and obligations under a contract. Thus, through the terms of the contract itself, the parties agree that the occurrence of certain events will discharge the contractual obligations. As long as all the parties agree to the terms, this is a valid method of discharging a contract. For example, the parties can agree that if a hurricane or flood devastates the area where the contract is performed, the contract will be discharged.

8.5 DISCHARGE BY NONPERFORMANCE

In certain instances, the parties' obligations and duties under a contract may be discharged due to nonperformance. Discharge by nonperformance may occur through: (1) impossibility of performance; (2) frustration of purpose; (3) failure of a condition; and (4) breach. Discharge by nonperformance can have harsh legal ramifications, especially if a party is in breach. Nonperformance is not a recommended method of discharge!

Impossibility of Performance

Courts routinely allow the discharge of contractual obligations by nonperformance due to impossibility. Impossibility of performance results when some act or event makes it impossible for the contract to be performed under the terms and obligations set forth in the contract. The *Restatement (Second)* focuses on this issue. Section 261 uses the term *impracticability* rather than *impossibility,* but both terms serve the same result—a method of discharge. Section 261 states:

> Where, after a contract is made, a party's performance is made impracticable without his fault by the occurrence of an event the nonoccurrence of which was a basic assumption on which the contract was made, his duty to render that performance is discharged, unless the language or the circumstances indicate the contrary.

TERMS

accord and satisfaction
An agreement between two persons, one of whom has a cause of action against the other, in which the claimant accepts a compromise in full satisfaction of his or her claim.

accord
Agreement; an agreement.

satisfaction
1. The discharge of an obligation by the payment of a debt.
2. The performance of a contract according to its terms.

Common occurrences involving impossibility are destruction of the subject matter (which includes natural disasters), supervening illegality, death, or disability of the party.

Destruction of the Subject Matter When the subject matter of a contract is destroyed through no fault of the parties, the contract is discharged. Events such as hurricanes, tornadoes, floods, bombings, or fires constitute methods of discharging a party's obligations because of a form of impossibility of performance. Generally, any act of God or natural disaster falls under this category. Clauses that address acts out of one's control are known as **force majeure** clauses.

Supervening Illegality When, after a contract has been formed, a law is passed that makes the subject of the contract illegal, a party's performance is discharged. Assume that Mrs. Goodman contracts with Ms. Waite to bear Goodman's baby (a surrogacy contract). Prior to Ms. Waite being impregnated, the state where the parties live passes a statute making surrogate motherhood illegal. The obligations cannot be fulfilled because of the supervening illegality and are thus discharged.

Death Death can be a means of discharging a party's obligations to a contract, as long as the contract involves personal services. Suppose you hire a particular photographer, because of his reputation and knowledge, to take your graduation pictures. Prior to the shoot, the photographer dies in a car accident. The obligation is discharged. However, if your school hires a *company* to photograph each graduating student and the company-assigned photographer dies, the obligation may not be discharged, because one photographer's performance could be replaced by another.

Disability of the Party As with death, if a party suffers a disability, such as an illness or incapacity, the performance will be discharged under the doctrine of impossibility. This method of discharge occurs if the parties' performance was essential to the contract. Review *Parker v. Arthur Murray, Inc.*, 10 Ill. App. 3d 1000, 295 N.E.2d 487 (1973), in which the doctrine of impossibility was applied.

TERMS

force majeure
A force that humans can neither resist, foresee, nor prevent; an act of God. Some contracts contain a force majeure clause, which excuses nonperformance if the contract cannot be performed because of the occurrence of an unforeseeable and irresistible event.

PARKER v. ARTHUR MURRAY, INC.

Appellate Court of Illinois
April 3, 1973

The sole issue raised by defendants is whether the terms of the contracts barred plaintiff from asserting the doctrine of impossibility of performance as the basis for seeking rescision.

The operative facts are not in dispute. In November 1959 plaintiff went to the Arthur Murray Studio in Oak Park to redeem a certificate entitling him to three free dancing lessons. At that time he was a 37 year-old college-educated bachelor who lived alone in a one-room attic apartment in Berwyn, Illinois. During the free lessons the instructor told plaintiff he had "exceptional potential to be a fine and accomplished dancer" and generally encouraged further participation. Plaintiff thereupon signed a contract for 75 hours of lessons at a cost of $1000. At the bottom of the contract were the bold-type words, "NON-CANCELLABLE NEGOTIABLE CONTRACT." This initial encounter set the pattern for the future relationship between the parties. Plaintiff attended lessons regularly. He was praised and encouraged regularly by the instructors, despite his lack of progress. Contract extensions and new contracts for additional instructional hours were executed. Each written extension contained the bold-type words, "NON-CANCELLABLE CONTRACT," and each written contract contained the bold-type words, "NON-CANCELLABLE NEGOTIABLE CONTRACT." Some of the agreements also contained the bold-type statement, "I UNDERSTAND THAT NO REFUNDS WILL BE MADE UNDER THE TERMS OF THIS CONTRACT."

On September 24, 1961 plaintiff was severely injured in an automobile collision, rendering him incapable of continuing his dancing lessons. At that time he had contracted for a total of 2734 hours of lessons, for which he had paid $24,812.80. Despite written demand defendants refused to return any of the money, and this suit in equity ensued.

Plaintiff was granted [rescission] on the ground of impossibility of performance. The applicable legal doctrine is expressed in the Restatement of Contracts, § 459, as follows:

A duty that requires for its performance action that can be rendered only by the promisor or some other particular person is discharged by his death or by such illness as makes the necessary action by him impossible or seriously injurious to his health, unless the contract indicates a contrary intention or there is contributing fault on the part of the person subject to the duty.

Similarly:

(1) Where the existence of a specific thing or person is, either by the terms of a bargain or in the contemplation or both parties, necessary for the performance of a promise in the bargain, a duty to perform the promise . . . (b) is discharged if the thing or person subsequently is not in existence in time for seasonable performance, unless a contrary intention is manifested, or the contributing fault of the promisor causes the nonexistence.

In Illinois impossibility of performance was recognized as a ground for [rescission].

Defendants do not deny that the doctrine of impossibility of performance is generally applicable to the case at bar. Rather they assert that certain contract provisions bring this case within the Restatement's limitation that the doctrine is inapplicable if "the contract indicates a contrary intention." It is contended that such bold type phrases as "NON-CANCELLABLE CONTRACT," "NON- CANCELLABLE NEGOTIABLE CONTRACT" and "I UNDERSTAND THAT NO REFUNDS WILL BE MADE UNDER THE TERMS OF THIS CONTRACT" manifested the parties mutual intent to waive their respective rights to invoke the doctrine of impossibility. This is a construction which we find unacceptable. Courts engage in the construction and interpretation of contracts with the sole aim of determining the intention of the parties. We need rely on no construction aids to conclude that plaintiff never contemplated that by signing a contract with such terms as "NON-CANCELLABLE" and "NO REFUNDS" he was waiving a remedy expressly recognized by Illinois courts. Were we also to refer to established tenets of contractual construction, this conclusion would be equally compelled. An ambiguous contract will be construed most strongly against the party who drafted it. Exceptions or reservations in a contract will, in case of doubt or ambiguity, be construed least favorably to the party claiming the benefit of the exceptions or reservations. Although neither party to a contract should be relieved from performance on the ground that good business judgment was lacking, a court will not place upon language a ridiculous construction. We conclude that plaintiff did not waive his right to assert the doctrine of impossibility.

QUESTIONS FOR ANALYSIS

What facts are critical to the court's finding? What was the rule of law in *Parker*? Set forth the court's rationale in reaching its result.

TERMS

impracticability
1. Legal term unique to the Uniform Commercial Code, from the provision of the UCC that excuses a seller from the obligation to deliver goods when delivery has become unrealistic because of unforeseen circumstances. 2. The state of being unworkable, unrealistic, or not capable of successful or worthwhile accomplishment.

Relaxing the Doctrine of Impossibility: Impracticability of Performance

Directly related to the doctrine of impossibility is a modern development referred to as **impracticability**. In situations where performance will be extremely expensive, inordinately time-consuming, and otherwise impracticable for the one who has to render performance, courts may discharge that party's performance. Here impracticability becomes synonymous with impossibility.

Impracticability is usually applied in the commercial context. The party alleging this defense must show that the burden of performance would be "extreme." This is not an easy standard to meet. A case in which the doctrine of impracticability was tested was *American Trading & Production Corp. v. Shell International Marine, Ltd.*, 453 F.2d 939 (2d Cir. 1972).

AMERICAN TRADING AND PRODUCTION CORPORATION v. SHELL INTERNATIONAL MARINE LTD.

United States Court of Appeals, Second Circuit
Decided Jan. 5, 1972

The owner is a Maryland corporation doing business in New York and the charterer is a United Kingdom corporation. On March 23, 1967 the parties entered into a contract of voyage charter in New York City which provided that the charterer would hire the owner's tank vessel, WASHINGTON TRADER, for a voyage with a full cargo of lube oil from Beaumont/Smiths Bluff, Texas to Bombay, India. On May 15, 1967 the WASHINGTON TRADER departed from Beaumont with a cargo of 16,183.82 long tons of lube oil. The charterer paid the freight at the invoiced sum of $417,327.36 on May 26, 1967.

On May 29th, 1967 the owner advised the WASHINGTON TRADER by radio to take additional bunkers at Ceuta due to possible diversion because of the Suez Canal crisis. The vessel arrived at Ceuta, Spanish Morocco on May 30, bunkered and sailed on May 31st, 1967. On June 5th the owner cabled the ship's master advising him of various reports of trouble in the Canal and suggested delay in entering it pending clarification. On that very day, the Suez Canal was closed due to the state of war which had developed in the Middle East. The owner then communicated with the charterer on June 5th through the broker who had negotiated the charter party, requesting approval for the diversion of the WASHINGTON TRADER which then had proceeded to a point about 84 miles northwest of Port Said, the entrance to the Canal. On June 6th the charterer responded that under the circumstances it was "for owner to decide whether to continue to wait or make the alternative passage via the Cape since Charter Party Obliges them to deliver cargo without qualification." In response the owner replied on the same day that in view of the closing of the Suez, the WASHINGTON TRADER would proceed to Bombay via the Cape of Good Hope and "[w]e [are] reserving all rights for extra compensation." The vessel proceeded westward, back through the Straits of Gibralter and around the Cape and eventually arrived in Bombay on July 15th (some 30 days later than initially expected), traveling a total of 18,055 miles instead of the 9,709 miles which it would have sailed had the Canal been open. The owner billed $131,978.44 as extra compensation which the charterer has refused to pay.

On appeal and below the owner argues that transit of the Suez Canal was the agreed specific means of performance of the voyage charter and that the supervening destruction of this means rendered the contract legally impossible to perform and therefore discharged the owner's unperformed obligation. Consequently, when the WASHINGTON TRADER eventually delivered the oil after journeying around the Cape of Good Hope, a benefit was conferred upon the charterer for which it should respond in *quantum meruit*. The validity of this proposition depends upon a finding that the parties contemplated or agreed that the Suez passage was to be the exclusive method of performance, and indeed it was so argued on appeal. We cannot construe the agreement in such a fashion. The parties contracted for the shipment of the cargo from Texas to India at an agreed rate and the charter party makes absolutely no reference to any fixed route. It is urged that the Suez passage was a condition of performance because the ATRS rate was based on a Suez Canal passage, the invoice contained a specific Suez Canal toll charge and the vessel actually did proceed to a point 84 miles northwest of Port Said. In our view all that this establishes is that both parties contemplated that the Canal would be the probable route. It was the cheapest and shortest, and therefore it was in the interest of both that it be utilized. However, this is not at all equivalent to an agreement that it be the exclusive method of performance. The charter party does not so provide and it seems to have been well understood in the shipping industry that the Cape route is an acceptable alternative in voyages of this character.

This leaves us with the question as to whether the owner was excused from performance on the theory of commercial impracticability. Even though the owner is not excused because of strict impossibility, it is urged that American law recognizes that performance is rendered impossible if it can only be accomplished with extreme and unreasonable difficulty, expense, injury or loss. There is no extreme or unreasonable difficulty apparent here. The alternate route taken was well recognized, and there is no claim that the vessel or crew or the nature of the cargo made the route actually taken unreasonably difficult, dangerous or onerous. The owner's case here essentially rests upon the element of the additional expense involved—$131,978.44. This represents an increase of less than one third over the agreed upon $417,327.36. We find that this increase in expense is not sufficient to constitute commercial impracticability under either American or English authority.

Mere increase in cost alone is not a sufficient excuse for non-performance. It must be an "extreme and unreasonable" expense.

Matters involving impossibility or impracticability of performance of contract are concededly vexing and difficult. On the basis of all of the facts, [and] the pertinent authority, we affirm.

QUESTIONS FOR ANALYSIS

What were the facts in the case? What facts did the court focus on in rendering its decision? How did the court define *impractibility*? What was the court's holding?

Frustration of Purpose

When the purpose of the contract has been defeated by some event occurring after formation, the doctrine of **frustration of purpose** may be applied. This doctrine discharges performance by excusing it because of an unanticipated event the parties could not have contemplated. When frustration of purpose is found, the contract will be discharged.

Courts will not impose this method of discharge readily, especially when parties are simply trying to avoid a bad bargain. For the frustration-of-purpose doctrine to be applied, a party must show that the circumstance frustrating the purpose was unforeseeable and that, because of that unforeseeability, the party will not derive the benefit anticipated by the contract. The party's purpose for contracting must, therefore, be totally frustrated.

This doctrine had its origins in the early 1900s in what is known as the "Coronation Case." In that case, Mr. Henry rented an apartment from Mr. Krell, for a high fee, to view King Edward VII's coronation. The purpose of the rental was only for viewing the coronation. Because the king became ill, the coronation was canceled. Henry wanted his rental money anyway; Krell refused. The court excused Henry's performance based upon frustration of purpose, and awarded no money to Mr. Krell.

Failure of a Condition

Another situation that will discharge a contractual obligation by non-performance is the failure of a condition to a contract. As discussed earlier in this chapter, when a condition has not been satisfactorily performed by the parties to a contract, the parties' obligations will be discharged by nonoccurrence of the condition. This is a common method of terminating a contract.

Breach of Contract

When a party fails to perform its contractual obligations, a *breach* results. A breach occurs when the acts of nonperformance are so material to the transaction that the nonbreaching party can treat the obligation as terminated. The *Restatement (Second)* sets out guidelines for determining whether a breach is material in § 241:

> In determining whether a failure to render or to offer performance is material, the following circumstances are significant:
>
> (a)   the extent to which the injured party will be deprived of the benefit which he reasonably expected;
>
> (b)   the extent to which the injured party can be adequately compensated for the part of that benefit of which he will be deprived;
>
> (c)   the extent to which the party failing to perform or to offer to perform will suffer forfeiture;

(d) the likelihood that the party failing to perform or to offer to perform will cure his failure, taking account of all the circumstances including any reasonable assurances;

(e) the extent to which the behavior of the party failing to perform or to offer to perform comports with standards of good faith and fair dealing.

Although a contract may be terminated, this is not the end of story. The person who has been injured by the breaching party can hold the breaching party to his or her contractual obligations through enforcement of a court action. The law provides certain legal remedies or methods of compensation for the nonbreaching party. These remedies, which may be either monetary or nonmonetary, are discussed in Chapter 9.

The question of breach was brought before the court in *Weiss v. Nurse Midwifery Associates,* 476 N.Y.S.2d 984 (Kings County, N.Y. 1984). Pay close attention to the court's analysis.

TERMS

frustration of purpose
An event that may excuse nonperformance of a contract because it defeats or nullifies the objective in the minds of the parties when they entered into the contract.

WEISS v. NURSE MIDWIFERY ASSOCIATES

Civil Court of the City of New York, Kings County
April 30, 1984

In this action plaintiff seeks recovery for a $750 fee paid to defendant Nurse Midwifery Associates, and further compensatory damages relating to the defendant's alleged dereliction of duties. Plaintiff's principal allegation is that defendant failed to render adequate services, to wit: by dispensing improper and/or incomplete pre-natal advice to plaintiff's wife and by neglecting to provide services during the birth of plaintiff's son.

Testimony adduced at trial indicates that a contractual arrangement was created between the plaintiff and defendant for certain midwifery services. It appears that, for various administrative reasons, no fee was to be charged by defendant for services rendered during childbirth, but that the agreed upon fee was for pre-natal and post-natal care. Nevertheless, this Court believes that the promise of defendant to be present during the childbirth was a material factor for plaintiff to retain the services of defendant and was therefore an important part of the contract. Even so, it does not appear that the defendant's presence at childbirth was unconditionally guaranteed or that, even if it were

guaranteed, defendant was at fault in not attending that event.

In order to establish whether defendant's conduct constituted a breach of contract, this Court will construe the agreement to identify those terms which determine the pertinent obligations of the respective parties.

Plaintiff argues, and this Court agrees, that defendant promised to perform delivery services during the childbirth. However, it is apparent to this Court that such service was an integral part of a *package* of services—preliminary to, during and subsequent to the childbirth. Since defendant was obligated to perform a total package of services, the failure to perform only one facet, the attendance at the childbirth, did not necessarily constitute a material breach of the contract.

The facts indicate that plaintiff received a substantial benefit of the bargain by requesting and accepting the rendition of defendant's pre-natal and post-natal services on approximately one dozen occasions. Although the failure of defendant to attend the childbirth was indeed unfortunate, defendant did expend a significant amount of time, energy and expertise. As a result, it is the Court's opinion that defendant performed a substantial portion of the obligations which arose upon the formation of the contractual relationship and therefore did not materially breach the contract.

Notwithstanding the finding that the alleged failure to act was not a material breach, this Court also holds that defendant's conduct could not, even in a non-material manner, be considered a breach of the contract.

We recognize, at the outset, an implicit understanding between the parties that defendant would make "best efforts" to attend to the delivery of the child. Such interpretation is based upon the fact that the parties were in frequent contact, as per defendant's promise to render services to plaintiff's wife "as needed." Attendance at the childbirth would be an expected part of these services, but would necessarily be dependent upon plaintiff first notifying defendant that the childbirth was imminent.

"In construing the provisions of a contract we should give due consideration to the circumstances surrounding its execution . . . and, if possible, we should give to the agreement a fair and reasonable interpretation." Under the circumstances existing at the time that *this* contract was created, this Court believes that defendant would be obligated to make "best efforts" to attend to the delivery, and that such obligation would arise only after proper notification of this event was relayed to defendant.

The facts indicate that plaintiff's wife contacted the defendant several hours prior to the childbirth and complained of various pains in her stomach and head. However, plaintiff admits that defendant questioned plaintiff's wife extensively and *then,* based upon the answers given, concluded that plaintiff's wife was not experiencing labor pains. Indeed, plaintiff further admits that the pains suffered by his wife immediately prior to the childbirth *were* of a substantially qualitative difference and *were* obviously labor pains. Since the labor pains

did not begin until just a few minutes before the childbirth, proper notification of plaintiff's wife's condition could not be conveyed to defendant. As a result, defendant was not provided an opportunity to exert the best efforts to attend this childbirth.

Stated in a more "legalistic" fashion, defendant should not be liable for breach of contract because the purported breach was directly caused by plaintiff's breach of *his* contractual condition, i.e., the timely notification to defendant of the forthcoming birth. It is not necessary that plaintiff's breach be intentional—a mere failure to perform the condition would be enough to vindicate the defendant. Thus, even if defendant had "guaranteed" to attend the childbirth, plaintiff's inability and resultant failure to notify defendant of the forthcoming birth, relieved defendant of its "guaranteed" obligation.

The general rule [is] that a party to a contract cannot rely on the failure of another to perform where the original party has *frustrated* or *prevented* the occurrence of the condition. [W]here one of the parties to a contract makes performance by the other materially more difficult or expensive, the latter will be discharged." Plaintiff's failure to satisfy the condition precedent—notification of defendant of the impending birth—should relieve this defendant of the obligation to attend that event. Justice dictates that this rule apply even though plaintiff's failure to notify defendant in a timely manner was unintentional and unavoidable. This holding seems clearly to be the most equitable disposition of the instant action, especially in light of the degree of services rendered by defendant, even without attendance at the childbirth.

Based upon the finding that defendant's failure to attend the childbirth did not constitute a breach of its contractual obligations, and that defendant performed in a significant and substantial manner, this Court holds that plaintiff's action to recover payments made to defendant should be dismissed in its entirety.

QUESTIONS FOR ANALYSIS

What significant facts related to the court's holding? What was the court's holding? What rationale did the court rely upon to reach its result?

Anticipatory Breach

In certain instances, one of the parties to a contract will learn that another party, without justification, intends to breach the contract when performance becomes due. When the words and conduct of the parties indicate that performance will not or cannot be rendered, this is referred to as **anticipatory breach** or **anticipatory repudiation**. Here the nonbreaching party believes that the other party will not perform its obligations and, rather than waiting for the actual breach to occur, the nonbreaching party may either substitute performance with another party in anticipation of the breach or immediately bring an action for breach. Insolvency or financial inability is a signal of anticipatory breach. The parties need to be careful in an anticipatory breach situation, though, because if the act by the supposedly breaching party is not unequivocal, the nonbreaching party may wrongfully repudiate the contract and thereby itself cause a breach. Consequently, indications of performance difficulties, unhappiness with the contract, or an uncertainty as to whether performance will be timely are not sufficient to manifest an anticipatory breach. As *Restatement (Second)* § 250 suggests:

> A repudiation is:
>
> [a] a statement by the obligor to the obligee indicating that the obligor will commit a breach that would of itself give the obligee a claim for damages for total breach under § 243, or
>
> [b] a voluntary affirmative act which renders the obligor unable or apparently unable to perform without such a breach.

To reduce the legal uncertainties that anticipatory breach may cause, the nonbreaching party may demand adequate assurances of performance. If such assurances are not given, repudiation is assumed. Section 251 of the *Restatement (Second)* states in part:

> (1) the obligee may demand adequate assurances of due performance and may, if reasonable, suspend any performance for which he has not already received the agreed exchange until he receives such assurance.
>
> (2) The obligee may treat as a repudiation the obligor's failure to provide within a reasonable time such assurance of due performance as is adequate in the circumstances of the particular case.

Wrongful repudiation may result in an award of contractual remedies to the injured party. Suit for anticipatory breach is not encouraged under the law if the act is not clear and unequivocal.

8.6 DISCHARGE BY OPERATION OF LAW

In some instances, contracts can be discharged because of a legal technicality, commonly known as *by operation of law*. Two methods of discharge by operation of law are bankruptcy and statutes of limitations.

TERMS

anticipatory breach (anticipatory repudiation)
The announced intention of a party to a contract that it does not intend to perform its obligations under the contract; an announced intention to commit a breach of contract.

Bankruptcy

When a party files bankruptcy and seeks the court's protection from creditors, contractual obligations may be discharged without providing the creditors much recourse. The Bankruptcy Act, which sets out the circumstances under which contractual obligations can be discharged, is applied by the federal courts. Bankruptcy is a form of discharge by operation of law.

Statute of Limitations

The time period in which a party must file a claim or lawsuit is regulated by state statutes known as **statutes of limitations**. If a party fails to file a lawsuit or claim within the time period set forth in the statute, and the defending party claims running of the statute of limitations as an affirmative defense, the contractual obligation could be discharged.

Discharge by this method can have some inequitable results. For example, if a contractor who is hired to put up a fence leaves in the middle of the job, he or she has breached the contractual obligations. If the statute of limitations for breach is four years and you file after that time period, a court will not enforce the contract even though you have been harmed. The contract is discharged by operation of law.

8.7 CONTRACT MODIFICATION: THREATS OF NONPERFORMANCE

Under proper circumstances, the parties to a contract may agree to change the terms of their original contract. Such a change is referred to as a *contract modification.* For example, unforeseen problems may arise, creating a situation in which continued performance would inflict undue hardship on at least one of the parties. The parties may agree to modify the contract to accommodate the new situation.

However, if a dispute arises, courts closely examine the circumstances surrounding contract modification. They will not enforce a modification made under duress or in bad faith, such as when one party unfairly threatens breach unless the other party accepts modification of the contract. Recall the *Problem Child II* example in Chapter 3. The child actor demanded more than the contracted amount of money to complete a movie. The studio felt compelled to yield to the demand in order to finish the movie. Later the studio filed suit and won. The modification of contract was not valid because it was obtained through duress (improper threats).

However, there are situations when modification of contract following threats of breach will be upheld. The key to enforceability of a modification is set out in § 89 of the *Restatement (Second):*

> A promise modifying a duty under a contract not fully performed on either side is binding:

(a) if the modification is fair and equitable in view of the circumstances not anticipated by the parties when the contract was made; or

(b) to the extent provided by statute; or

(c) to the extent that justice requires enforcement in view of material change of position in reliance on the promise.

Another issue arising under modification is the requirement of consideration. Remember Chapter 4's discussion of the preexisting duty rule? When there is already a duty to perform, a court will not enforce the new contract, because it lacks consideration. Some states find that consideration is necessary to uphold the modification. Others, focusing on the unforeseen difficulties issue, do not require separate consideration for modification.

To help ensure a modification's validity, it should probably be in writing. Consequently, Statute of Frauds requirements should be considered as well. An issue arises, though, when the modification is oral and a party relies to its detriment on the agreement to modify. The court may find that either a **waiver** or an **estoppel** existed. A waiver exists when a party knowingly or voluntarily relinquishes a right or dispenses with the performance of something to which the law entitles him or her. If the modification is oral, a court may find that a waiver existed if reliance is evident. In contrast, a court may impose an estoppel theory to prevent an injustice. Under estoppel principles, a court will determine whether a party's acts or statements induced the other party to act based upon the belief that what was agreed to was true, and whether to find otherwise would cause injustice or hardship.

When nonperformance is threatened, modification can be an effective tool to remedy a possible breach. But modifications are not always enforceable, and courts examine the circumstances surrounding a modification to determine its enforceability. Figure 8-3 sets forth some modification

---

Disavowal of intent to modify earlier contract

It is to be understood that this agreement shall in no way act as a waiver of any of the conditions and obligations imposed on the parties by the earlier contract executed between them, and any rights that either of the parties may have by virtue of such earlier contract are to be considered in full force and effect.

Changes in printed portion of contract

No change, addition, or erasure of any printed portion of this agreement shall be valid or binding on either party.

Agent's right to modify

No agent of either party, unless authorized in writing by the principal, has any authority to waive, alter, or enlarge this contract, or to make any new or substituted or different contracts, representations, or warranties.

Written modification as necessary

There may be no modification of this agreement, except in writing, executed with the same formalities as this instrument.

FIGURE 8-3 Sample modification provisions

TERMS

statutes of limitations
Federal and state statutes prescribing the maximum period of time during which various types of civil actions and criminal prosecutions can be brought after the occurrence of the injury or the offense.

waiver
The intentional relinquishment or renunciation of a right, claim, or privilege a person knows he or she has.

estoppel (estoppel by contract)
A prohibition against denying the validity or significance of acts done in performance of a contract. . . . A person may be estopeed by his or her own acts or representations (that is, not be permitted to deny the truth or significance of what he or she said or did) if another person who was entitled to rely upon those statements or acts did so to his or her detriment.

provisions found in contracts. Consider also *Gross v. Diehl Specialties International, Inc.*, 776 S.W.2d 879 (Mo. Ct. App. 1989), wherein the court analyzed whether a valid modification existed between the parties.

GROSS v. DIEHL SPECIALTIES INTERNATIONAL, INC.
Missouri Court of Appeals
Sept. 7, 1989

Plaintiff was employed under a fifteen-year employment contract originally executed in 1977 between plaintiff and defendant. Defendant, at that time called Dairy Specialties, Inc., was a company in the business of formulating ingredients to produce non-dairy products for use by customers allergic to cow's milk. The owner of the company, Harry Schenberg, had produced such a product but the formulation was unable to withstand pasteurization by the customers to whom it was sold for processing and packaging for retail distribution. Schenberg requested plaintiff's technical assistance in formulating the product, Vitamite, for com- mercial usage. Plaintiff successfully reformulated the product for that usage.

Thereafter, on August 24, 1977, plaintiff and defendant corporation entered into an employment contract employing plaintiff as general manager of defendant for fifteen years. Compensation was established at $14,400 annually plus cost of living increases. In addition, when 10% of defendant's gross profits exceeded the annual salary, plaintiff would receive an additional amount of compensation equal to the difference between his compensation and 10% of the gross profits for such year. On top of that plaintiff was to receive a royalty for the use of each of his inventions and formulae of 1% of the selling price of all of the products produced by defendant using one or more of plaintiff's inventions or formulae during the term of the agreement. That amount was increased to 2% of the selling price following the term of the agreement. The contract further provided that during the term of the agreement the inventions and formulae would be owned equally by plaintiff and defendant and that following the term of the agreement the ownership would revert to plaintiff. During the term of the agreement defendant had exclusive rights to use of the inventions and formulae and after the term of agreement a non-exclusive right of use.

At the time of the execution of the contract, sales had risen from virtually nothing in 1976 to $750,000 annually from sales of Vitamite and a chocolate flavored product formulated by plaintiff called Chocolite. Schenberg was in declining health and in 1982 desired to sell his company. At that time yearly sales were $7,500,000. Schenberg sold the company to the Diehl family enterprises for 3 million dollars.

Prior to sale Diehl insisted that a new contract between plaintiff and defendant be executed or Diehl would substantially reduce the amount to be paid for defendant. A new contract was executed August 24, 1982. It reduced the expressed term of the contract to 10 years, which provided the same expiration date as the prior contract. It maintained the same base salary of $14,400 effective September 1982, thereby eliminating any cost of living increases incurred since the original contract. The 10% of gross profit provision remained the same. The new contract provided that plaintiff's inventions and formulae were exclusively owned by defendant during the term of the contract and after its termination. The 1% royalty during the term of the agreement remained the same, but no royalties were provided for after the term of the agreement. No other changes were made in the agreement. Plaintiff received no compensation for executing the new contract. He was not a party to the sale of the company by Schenberg and received nothing tangible from that sale.

After the sale plaintiff was give the title and responsibilities of president of defendant with additional duties but no additional compensation. In 1983 and 1984 the business of the company declined severely and in October 1984, plaintiff's employment with defendant was terminated by defendant. This suit followed.

We turn now to the court's holding that the 1982 agreement was the operative contract. Plaintiff contends this holding is erroneous because there existed no consideration for the 1982 agreement. We agree. A modification of a contract constitutes the making of a new contract and such new contract must be supported by consideration. Where a contract has not been fully performed at the time of the new agreement, the substitution of a new provision, resulting in a modification of the obligations on *both* sides, for a provision in the old contract still unperformed is sufficient consideration for the new contract. While consideration may consist of either a detriment to the promisee or a benefit to the promisor, a promise to carry out an already existing contractual duty does not constitute consideration.

Under the 1982 contract defendant assumed no detriment it did not already have. The term of the contract expired on the same date under both contracts. Defendant undertook no greater obligations than it already had. Plaintiff on the other hand received less than he had under the original contract. His base pay was reduced back to its amount in 1977 despite the provision in the 1977 contract for cost of living adjustments. He lost his equal ownership in his formulae during the term of the agreement and his exclusive ownership after the termination of the agreement. He lost all royalties after termination of the agreement and the right to use and license the formulae subject to defendant's right to non-exclusive use upon payment of royalties. In exchange for nothing, defendant acquired exclusive ownership of the formulae during and after the agreement, eliminated royalties after the agreement terminated, turned its non-exclusive use after termination into exclusive use and control, and achieved a reduction in plaintiff's base salary. Defendant did no more than promise to carry out an already existing contractual duty. There was no consideration for the 1982 agreement.

Defendant asserts that consideration flowed to plaintiff because the purchase of defendant by the Diehls might not have occurred without the agreement and the purchase provided plaintiff with continued employment and a financially viable employer. There is no evidence to support this contention. Plaintiff had continued employment with the same employer under the 1977 agreement. Nothing in the 1982 agreement provided for any additional financial protection to plaintiff. The essence of defendant's position is that Schenberg received more from his sale of the company because of the new agreement than he would have without it. We have difficulty converting Schenberg's windfall into a benefit to the plaintiff.

QUESTIONS FOR ANALYSIS

How did the court define *modification*? Was a modification found in *Gross*? Why or why not? What was the rule of law in *Gross*?

8.8   PRACTICAL APPLICATIONS

Provisions regarding termination and discharge are common in contracts. These provisions are usually found in the performance sections of a contract. Figure 8-4 illustrates these types of provisions.

In addition, condition provisions are common in contracts as well. Provisions to look for are set forth in Figure 8-5.

Notice of Breach or Demand for Performance

It is agreed between the parties that no claim can be made for breach of this agreement unless notice of the breach, and demand for performance, is made to the other party. Notice of breach under this provision must specify the details of the claimed breach. Demand for performance under this provision must specify the details specific to the demanded performance.

Death or Disability as Terminating Contract

This contract shall terminate on the death or disability of either party from any cause whatsoever.

Payment of Sum as Basis of Right to Terminate

This agreement may be terminated only on notification by registered mail sent to [*name*], and on payment of all obligations then accrued, together with the payment of 10 percent (10%) of the remaining monthly payments, as liquidated damages.

FIGURE 8-4 Sample termination and discharge provisions

Approval of Sale by Corporate Directors or Stockholders

Before the closing date, the execution and delivery of this agreement by seller and the performance of its covenants and obligations under this agreement shall have been duly authorized by all necessary corporate action, whether by the board of directors, the shareholders, or otherwise. Buyer shall receive copies of all resolutions pertaining to that authorization, certified by the secretary of seller.

Filing of Claim as Condition Precedent to Suit

Employee shall not commence any suit against employer in connection with this agreement without first filing a claim with employer, specifying the nature and basis for the claim, and no action shall be instituted until after thirty (30) days from the date of filing of such claim.

Approval of Sale by Tax Authorities

The obligations of seller hereunder are subject to the condition that seller shall have received a ruling or rulings from the United States Internal Revenue Service substantially to the effect that:

(a) For federal income tax purposes, no gain or loss will be recognized to seller on receipt by it of the total purchase price from the sale of assets, properties, and rights sold to buyer, other than assets excluded from the term "property" by I.R.C. § 337(b), provided that within the 12-month period beginning on the day of adoption of the plan of liquidation, seller shall have distributed to its shareholders all assets of seller except for those assets reasonably retained to meet claims and specifically set aside for that purpose.

(b) The day of adoption of the plan will be, for the purposes of determining the 12-month period referred to in I.R.C. § 337, the day on which the stockholders of seller approve resolutions adopting the plan.

Within ten (10) days after the date hereof, seller shall make application for such rulings from the United States Internal Revenue Service, and shall submit to buyer copies of the applications. Within ten (10) days after receipt of a tax ruling, seller will forward a copy of the ruling to buyer. Neither buyer nor seller shall be obligated to close if a ruling is found to be unfavorable to it by its counsel.

FIGURE 8-5 Sample condition provisions

Often a paralegal may be asked to assist in preparation of an accord and satisfaction. Usually, this document relates to settlement of a disputed claim between the parties. Figure 8-6 will guide the paralegal in preparing an accord and satisfaction.

Agreement for Accord and Satisfaction—Disputed Claim for Personal Injuries of Property Damage

Agreement made on June 18, 1995, between Harvey Fields of Alpha County, New Jersey, referred to as claimant, and Ralph Stanton, 1234 Brentwood, Beta County, New Jersey, referred to as obligor.

Obligor agrees to pay, and claimant agrees to accept, the sum of $11,500 in full payment of a disputed claim arising from damages sustained by claimant in an automobile collision that occurred between the parties at Ocean City, New Jersey, on August 18, 1994, for which injuries claimant claims obligor to be legally liable, and which claimed liability obligor expressly denies.

In consideration of the payment by obligor to claimant, claimant releases and forever discharges obligor, his heirs, successors, executors, administrators, and assigns, from any and all actions, causes of action, claims, and demands for or by reason of any damage, loss, injury, or suffering that has been, or that hereafter may be, sustained by claimant as a consequence of such bodily injuries and property damage.

In witness whereof, the parties have executed this agreement at _____ on the date first mentioned above.

FIGURE 8-6 Sample accord and satisfaction

Finally, Figure 8-7 is an illustration of a novation.

Novation Between an Original Contractor, a Substituted Contractor, and a Contractee

Agreement made this 26th day of April, 1995, between ABC Contracting, of Dallas, Texas, and Smith Construction of Arlington, Texas, and Bill Davis, of Dallas, Texas.

Whereas, an agreement dated February 1, 1995, was made between ABC and Davis, and ABC desires to be released and discharged from the contract contained in the agreement, and Davis has agreed to release and discharge ABC therefrom upon the terms of Smith undertaking to perform the said contract and to be bound by its terms;

It is agreed as follows:

1. **Undertaking of Substituted Contractor.** Smith undertakes to perform said contract and to be bound by the terms thereof in all respects as if Smith were a party to said agreement in lieu of ABC.

2. **Release of Original Contractor and Agreements for Acceptance of Substituted Contractor.** Davis releases and discharges ABC from all claims and demands in respect to the agreement, and accepts the liability of Smith upon the agreement in lieu of the liability of ABC, and agrees to be bound by the terms of the agreement in all respects as if Smith were named therein in place of ABC.

In Witness Whereof, the parties have signed this agreement on the day and year first above written.

FIGURE 8-7 Sample novation

SUMMARY

8.1 Conditions may place a contingency on contract performance. Conditions which may qualify performance are conditions precedent, conditions subsequent, and concurrent conditions. Conditions also may be express or implied.

8.2, Discharge relieves a party of contractual obligations. One of the methods of discharge is by performance. Completed performance is the usual method of discharge. If there is a slight deviation in full performance, a contract may be substantially completed. To determine whether substantial completion exists, the court can look to the expectation of a party, compensation, the willfulness of the act, and the timing of performance.

8.4 Contracts also can be discharged by agreement of the parties. Ways to discharge a contract by agreement are through rescission, release, novation, accord and satisfaction, and operation of the terms of the contract.

8.5 Parties can discharge performance by nonperformance. Impossibility of performance is a method of discharge by nonperformance which includes destruction of the subject matter, supervening illegality, death, and disability. Impracticability is related to the doctrine of impossibility. When the main purpose of the contract has been frustrated, discharge can occur. The most common method of discharge of a contract is a breach, when at least one of the parties fails to perform his or her contractual obligations.

8.6 Methods to discharge a contract by operation of law are bankruptcy and statute of limitations. Discharging a contract by these methods can have inequitable results.

8.7 Modification is a method of changing the parties' obligations to a contract. Modification usually occurs when unforeseen circumstances arise or undue hardship would result if the contract were performed.

REVIEW QUESTIONS

1. Define the term *condition*.
2. Distinguish between a condition precedent and a condition subsequent.
3. What are the different ways a contract can be discharged?
4. How do completed performance and substantial performance differ?
5. What can a court consider when determining whether a contract has been substantially completed?
6. Identify the ways a contract can be discharged by agreement.
7. What are the various methods by which a contract can be discharged by nonperformance?

8. List the methods by which a contract can be discharged for impossibility of performance.
9. How can a contract be discharged by operation of law?
10. What are some of the issues raised when a contract is modified?

EXERCISES

1. Find a contract for the sale of a residential house and list the conditions precedent found in the contract.
2. Frederick Houseman and Michael Monterey have been feuding over Michael's performance when putting in Frederick's sprinkler system. In their settlement of this matter, Frederick agreed to pay Michael $5,000 in settlement of all their claims against each other. Your attorney has asked you to draft a mutual release between Frederick and Michael.
3. Review *Chicago College of Osteopathic Medicine v. George A. Fuller Co.,* 776 F.2d 198 (7th Cir. 1985), and answer the following questions:
   a. What are the facts of the case?
   b. Identify the issue and holding.
   c. Set out the court's reasoning in this case.
   d. How did the court define *waiver?*
   e. Was there a valid modification? Explain your response.

CHAPTER 9
Remedies in Contract Law

9.1 DISTINGUISHING BETWEEN LEGAL AND EQUITABLE REMEDIES

When a party fails to perform its obligations under a contract, the injured party may request a court to award compensation for the losses. This compensation is known as a *remedy*. The type of remedy a court can grant will depend upon the kind of injury suffered, but remedies fall into two general categories: legal remedies and equitable remedies. A **legal remedy** is a monetary damage that the party can claim for the loss suffered as a result of the other party's failure to perform contractual obligations. Legal remedies are the type of remedy most commonly awarded in contract lawsuits and are always in the form of money known as **damages**.

The other type of remedy a court can order is a nonmonetary remedy known as **equitable relief** or an *equitable remedy*, awarded when there is no suitable monetary remedy. The court can fashion such a remedy according to the facts of the case.

9.2 LEGAL REMEDIES OR DAMAGES

Courts often determine the appropriate damages to award an injured party by evaluating the extent and severity of the nonperforming party's acts. When damages have been suffered by an injured party, the court will attempt to place that party back in the financial position it would have been in had the contract been fully performed. Consequently, monetary damages are usually awarded when someone has breached his or her contractual obligations and that breach has resulted in damages. The legal remedies that can be awarded by a court can be categorized as compensatory damages, consequential damages, punitive damages, nominal damages, and liquidated damages.

Compensatory Damages

Compensatory damages are the actual sum of money a party has lost as a result of nonperformance by the other party to a contract. Compensatory damages are also known as **actual damages** or *expectation damages.* They are the amount of money that will place the injured party in the same position it would have attained had the contract been fully performed. They are the damages that satisfy a party's expectations under the contract.

Ordinarily, the compensatory damages awarded by a court are not only the actual sum lost, but also the costs foreseeable as a probable result of a breach of the contract. In evaluating the amount to award a party in a damages lawsuit, a court will determine what were the natural and proximate consequences of the acts of the parties that could have been reasonably foreseen or predicted as a result of a breach. If damages were reasonably foreseeable, the court will compensate the injured party for losses that are the direct result of the breach of contract.

When the court is calculating compensatory damages, it may consider and award lost profits, any incidental expenses that resulted from the breach, and the actual amount lost (which is the difference between the actual price of the contract and any loss for substituted performance that the nonbreaching party would incur due to the breach). Review *Brandon & Tibbs v. George Kevorkian Accountancy Corp.*, 226 Cal. App. 3d 442, 277 Cal. Rptr. 40 (1990) for an analysis of compensatory damages. Notice what damages the court considered in determining the compensatory damage award.

TERMS

legal remedy
A remedy available through legal action.

damages
The sum of money that may be recovered in the courts as financial reparation for an injury or wrong suffered as a result of breach of contract or a tortious act.

equitable relief (equitable remedy)
A remedy available in equity rather than at law; generally relief other than money damages.

compensatory damages (actual damages)
Damages recoverable in a lawsuit for loss or injury suffered by the plaintiff as a result of the defendant's conduct. Also called *actual damages*, they may include expenses, loss of time, reduced earning capacity, bodily injury, and mental anguish.

BRANDON & TIBBS v. GEORGE KEVORKIAN ACCOUNTANCY CORPORATION

Court of Appeal, Fifth District
Dec. 19, 1990

In 1981, plaintiff was a professional accounting corporation with offices in Salinas, Monterey, and Watsonville. At that time, plaintiff sought to expand its practice by purchasing an existing accountancy practice in the Fresno area. Historically, plaintiff preferred purchasing existing accounting practices to avoid the expenses of starting up a new accounting practice.

James Brandon, plaintiff's chief executive officer, handled the negotiations of the acquisition of an accounting practice for plaintiff in the Fresno area. George Kevorkian, at that time corporate defendant's sole shareholder, received a letter of interest from Mr. Brandon and responded by indicating that he was interested in selling his accountancy practice.

The two men negotiated in November and December of 1981. Negotiations were then suspended until February of 1982 when Mr. Brandon presented to Mr. Kevorkian a proposal which had been prepared by an attorney at Mr. Brandon's request. The first proposal outlined a purchase of the corporate defendant for $300,000, a $50,000 deposit, and a salary to George Kevorkian for one year at $120,000. Mr. Kevorkian rejected the first proposal and Brandon prepared a second proposal. Neither of these proposals mentioned a joint venture agreement between the parties.

Mr. Kevorkian subsequently arranged to have an attorney, Tim Born, review the second proposal and make various changes in it. Out of concern for the tax liability of his client, Mr. Born suggested that the entity created by the parties be a joint venture; this was discussed and orally agreed to by Brandon and Kevorkian. Several other changes were discussed and incorporated into the final agreement. The buy-out formula was changed to $1.50 per dollar for the first $250,000 of gross revenue in the 12 months preceding the exercise of Mr. Kevorkian's option to sell, which was extended to a 3-year period, and a 75 cent per dollar of gross receipts over that amount. The initial $50,000 payment, originally characterized as a nonrefundable good faith deposit, was stated to be a one-time consulting fee. A $10,000 per month payment was to be made to the corporate defendant for management services and equipment leasing. The final agreement, entitled "Management, Joint Venture, and Sales Agreement," was signed by the parties on May 21, 1982.

Over the course of the joint venture's operation, friction and disagreements increased between Mr.

Kevorkian and Mr. Brandon. Mr. Kevorkian ultimately terminated the joint venture, caused Mr. Brandon's phone to be removed from the joint venture office then occupied by Mr. Brandon, and demanded that he leave the joint venture offices. Mr. Kevorkian caused the locks on the joint venture offices to be changed without informing Mr. Brandon and ordered joint venture staff to refuse to accept telephone calls or to perform services for Mr. Brandon. Mr. Kevorkian further refused to provide records of the joint venture's operations to plaintiff and refused to divide joint venture profits with plaintiff. Mr. Kevorkian transferred money from joint venture accounts to his own accounts without the consent or knowledge of plaintiff.

The trial court concluded that these acts and the "arbitrary" termination of employees furnished by the plaintiff constituted a breach of contract.

In November 1983, plaintiff, acting upon the advice of legal counsel, immediately established a new Fresno branch office by leasing space in the same building in which the former joint venture offices were located. Mr. Brandon, Mr. Bustamente, and another nonprofessional staff person worked in the new offices. Mr. Brandon ceased to function as chief executive officer of plaintiff and became the managing partner of the Fresno branch office. The total loss incurred by plaintiff in operating its Fresno office after corporate defendant's breach of the agreement was $154,292, not including any computation of claimed interest.

It is often said that damages must be "foreseeable" to be recoverable for breach of contract. First, general damages are ordinarily confined to those which would naturally arise from the breach, or which might have been reasonably contemplated or foreseen by both parties, at the time they made the contract, as the probable result of the breach. Second, if special circumstances caused some unusual injury, special damages are not recoverable therefor unless the circumstances were known or should have been known to the breaching party at the time he entered into the contract. The requirement of knowledge or notice as a prerequisite to the recovery of special damages is based on the theory that a party does not and cannot assume limitless responsibility for all consequences of a breach, and that at the time of contracting he must be advised of the facts concerning special harm which might result therefrom, in order that he may determine whether or not to accept the risk of contracting.

Contract cases not involving the sale of goods have not precluded the recovery of lost profits as damages. The objection that lost profits damages are "collateral" or "remote" has been raised and rejected from the time that the earliest cases were decided awarding such damages. The only prerequisite to recovery of lost profits is proximate causation: the lost profits must be the natural and direct consequences of the breach. This rule is to be applied in any action for damages for breach of contract.

The objective of the law is to place the injured party in the same position he would have held were it not for the breach. The only purpose in entering into the "Joint Venture, Management and Sales Agreement" was to ultimately acquire ownership of the corporate defendant's accounting practice and generate profits therefrom. If the contract had not been breached, plaintiff would have complete and sole ownership of the accountancy corporation.

The existing rule requires only reason to foresee, not actual foresight. It does not require that the defendant should have had the resulting injury actually in contemplation or should have promised either impliedly or expressly to pay therefor in case of breach. If, because of his own education, training, and information, he had reason to foresee the probable existence of such circumstances, the judgment for compensatory damages measured by the extent of such injury will be given against him. In such a case the defendant knew or had reason to know of the surrounding circumstances and had such reason to foresee the extent of the resulting injury as would have affected the conduct of the ordinary man and would have prevented him from committing the breach of contract.

It is well settled that "[o]ne whose wrongful conduct has rendered difficult the ascertainment of the damages cannot escape liability because the damages could not be measured with exactness." "[L]oss of prospective profits may nevertheless be recovered if the evidence shows with reasonable certainty *both* their *occurrence* and the *extent* thereof." "[I]t appears to be the general rule that while a plaintiff must show with reasonable certainty that he has suffered damages by reason of the wrongful act of the defendant, once the cause and existence of damages have been so established, recovery will not be denied because the damages are difficult of ascertainment."

An injured party may recover for a breach of contract the amount which will compensate it "for all the detriment proximately caused [by the breach], or which, in the ordinary course of things, would be likely to result [from the breach]." The damages awarded should, insofar as possible, place the injured party in the same position it would have held had the contract properly been performed, but such damage may not exceed the benefit which it would have received had the promisor performed. Damages may be awarded for breach of contract for those losses which naturally arise from the breach, or which might reasonably have been foreseen by the parties at the time they contracted, as the probable result of the breach. Where the injured party shows that, as a reasonable probability, profits would have been earned on the contract except for its breach, the loss of the anticipated profits is compensable. Where business activity has been interrupted by a breach of contract, damages for the loss of prospective profits that otherwise might have been made from its operation are generally recoverable where such damages are shown to have been foreseeable and reasonably certain.

The trial court's decision to award plaintiff lost profit damages is clearly within the doctrine enunciated and we have reversed and remanded for the trial court's error in failing to offset net mitigation profits against plaintiff's net breach of contract damages.

QUESTIONS FOR ANALYSIS

What is the basic theory behind compensatory damages and how they are awarded? Can lost profits be recovered as a compensatory damage? Why or why not? What facts provide the basis for the compensatory damage award?

Consequential Damages

Not only can compensatory damages be awarded when someone has breached a contract, but the injured party may also receive **consequential damages**, those indirect or special damages which are a foreseeable consequence of the breach. Consequential damages are usually awarded in addition to the actual damages.

There has to be some direct causal connection between the breach and the damages resulting from the breach. Mere conjecture is not sufficient. The court is mindful that consequential damages cannot be speculative. **Speculative damages** are damages that depend upon the happening of events. They are improbable and contingent. Did the parties know, or should they have known, that a breach would result in the damages claimed? If the answer to the question is yes, then consequential damages may be awarded. In *Redgrave v. Boston Symphony Orchestra, Inc.*, 855 F.2d 888 (1st Cir. 1988), the court explored in great detail what constitutes consequential damages.

REDGRAVE v. BOSTON SYMPHONY ORCHESTRA, INC.

United States Court of Appeals, First Circuit
Aug. 31, 1988

In March 1982, the Boston Symphony Orchestra (BSO) engaged Vanessa Redgrave to narrate Stravinsky's "Oedipus Rex" in a series of concerts in Boston and New York. Following announcement of the engagement, the BSO received calls from its subscribers and from community members protesting the engagement because of Redgrave's political support for the Palestine Liberation Organization and because of her views regarding the state of Israel. On or about April 1, 1982, the BSO cancelled its contract with Redgrave and its performances of "Oedipus Rex." Redgrave sued the BSO for breach of contract . . . . The BSO argued at trial that the contract rightfully was cancelled because the cancellation was the result of "a cause or causes beyond the reasonable control" of the BSO. Following a sixteen-day trial, the jury found that the BSO wrongfully had breached its contract with Redgrave.

The district court utilized the jury in an advisory capacity on this claim. In response to special interrogatories, the jury found that the BSO did not cancel the contract because of the disagreements of BSO agents with Redgrave's political views. The district court stated that this finding eliminated an "essential factual premise" of Redgrave's primary claim based on the MCRA.

Redgrave's consequential damages claim is based on the proposition that a significant number of movie and theater offers that she would ordinarily have received in the years 1982 and following were in fact not offered to her as a result of the BSO's cancellation in April 1982.

In cases that have analyzed the reasons for disallowing a contract claim for reputation damages, courts have identified two determinative factors. First, courts have observed that attempting to calculated damages for injury to reputation is "unduly speculative." In many cases, the courts have viewed the claims for damages to reputation as analogous to claims for physical or emotional distress and have noted the difficulty in ascertaining such damages for contract purposes. An estimate of injury to reputation "must rest upon a number of imprecise variables," including the causal connection between the breach of contract and the injury to reputation and the amount by which any future earnings would be decreased by causes other than the breach.

The second factor that courts identify is that damages for injury to reputation "cannot reasonably be presumed to have been within the contemplation of the parties when they entered into the contract." [The basic rule] requires that contract damages be of the kind that arise naturally from the breach of a contract or be of a kind that reasonably may have been in the contemplation of the parties when they entered the contract, cannot possibly be met in a claim for general damages to reputation occurring as the result of a breach of contract.

The claim advanced by Redgrave is significantly different, however, from a general claim of damage to reputation. Redgrave is not claiming that her general reputation as a professional actress has been tarnished by the BSO's cancellation. Rather, she claims that a number of specific movie and theater performances that would have been offered to her in the usual course of events were not offered to her as a result of BSO's cancellation. [In] a breach of contract action, injured party receives compensation for any loss that follows as a natural consequence from the breach, was within the contemplation of reasonable parties as a probable result of breach, and may be computed by "rational methods upon a firm basis of facts."

> [I]f plaintiffs proved other employers refused to hire Redgrave after termination of the BSO contract because of that termination (that loss of the other employment "followed as a natural consequence" from the termination of the contract), that this loss of other employment would reasonably have been foreseen by the parties at the time of contracting and at the time of termination, and that damages are rationally calculable, then plaintiffs may be entitled to damages that include monies for loss of the other employment. Although plaintiffs have a heavy burden to carry here, it cannot be said with certainty at this time that they will not be able to meet this burden.

The jury was given appropriate instructions to help it determine whether Redgrave had suffered consequential damages through loss of future professional opportunities. They were told to find that the BSO's cancellation was a proximate cause of harm to Redgrave's professional career only if they determined that "harm would not have occurred but for the cancellation and that the harm was a natural and probable consequence of the cancellation." In addition, they were told that damages should be allowed for consequential harm "only if the harm was a foreseeable consequence within the contemplation of the parties to the contract when it was made." In response to special interrogatories, the jury found that the BSO's cancellation caused consequential harm to Redgrave's career and that the harm was a foreseeable consequence within the contemplation of the parties.

Although we find that Redgrave did not present sufficient evidence to establish that the BSO's cancellation caused consequential harm to her professional career in the amount of $100,000, we hold that a plaintiff may receive consequential damages if the plaintiff proves with sufficient evidence that a breach of contract proximately caused the loss of identifiable professional opportunities. This type of claim is sufficiently different from a nonspecific allegation of damage to reputation that it appropriately falls outside the general rule that reputation damages are not an acceptable form of contract damage.

Most of Redgrave's annual earnings prior to April 1982 were derived from appearances in films and the English theater. Redgrave presented evidence at trial that she earned more than $200,000 on the average since her company's fiscal year 1976, and she testified that she had a constant stream of offers from which she could choose films that had secure financial backing. After the BSO's cancellation in April 1982, Redgrave contended, her career underwent a "startling turnabout." Redgrave testified that she did not work at all for the fourteen months following the cancellation and that the only offers she received during that time were for films with insufficient financial backing.

We have some doubt as to whether Redgrave presented sufficient evidence to prove that the type of film offers she received in the year following the BSO cancellation were radically different from the film offers received before the cancellation. The evidence does not present an effective comparison between the type of film offers received before and after the

BSO cancellation and we are left primarily with Redgrave's allegation that the film offers received in the two time periods were significantly different.

Even if we accept, however, that Redgrave proved she had experienced a drop in the quality of film offers following the BSO cancellation, Redgrave must also prove that the drop was proximately caused by the BSO cancellation and not by other, independent factors. Redgrave failed to carry her burden of presenting evidence sufficient to allow a jury reasonably to infer this causal connection.

Redgrave contends that, as a result of the BSO cancellation, she no longer received offers to appear on Broadway. The evidence presented by Redgrave concerning her drop in Broadway offers after April 1982, is not sufficient to support a finding of consequential damages. In addition, we note that it would be difficult for any assessment of damages resulting from the lack of Broadway theater offers to meet the standard that damages must be "capable of ascertainment by reference to some definite standard, either market value, established experience or direct inference from known circumstances."

A jury reasonably could infer that the BSO's cancellation did more than just highlight the potential problems that hiring Redgrave would cause but was actually a cause of [the no-hire] decision. Because this is a possible inference that a jury could draw from [the] testimony, we defer to that inference. We therefore find that Redgrave presented sufficient evidence to prove consequential damages of $12,000, the fee arrangement contemplated for Redgrave's appearance in *Heartbreak House,* minus expenses she personally would have incurred had she appeared in the play.

The judgment on the contract claim is VACATED *and REMANDED for entry of judgment for consequential damages to the extent approved herein. No costs.*

QUESTIONS FOR ANALYSIS

Did the court award Ms. Redgrave consequential damages? What was the court's reasoning on the consequential damage issue? How did the court define *consequential damages*? Was the result just? Why or why not?

Coupled with the concept of consequential damages is that of *incidental damages*, those which the injured party expends to prevent further loss. Incidental damages can be out-of-pocket expenses or any other expenses incurred to prevent any further loss or injury to the party. Incidental damages can be awarded in addition to compensatory and consequential damages.

Punitive Damages

When the conduct of the nonperforming or breaching party is intentional, deliberate, willful, and in complete disregard of the rights of the injured party, the court may award **punitive** (or **exemplary**) **damages** to compensate the party. These types of damages are sparingly given in contract cases. Because punitive damages act as a punishment or penalty against the breaching party, they are used only in the most extreme circumstances. For example, punitive or exemplary damages might be awarded in a fraud case if the injured party could show the willful nature of the other party's acts. Punitive or exemplary damages are awarded more frequently in **tort** cases than in contract cases. However, courts can award exemplary damages when the conduct is so offensive that public policy would thus be served.

An award of punitive damages is intended to act as a deterrent to future willful conduct. When punitive damages are awarded, statutes generally provide for **treble damages** (three times the amount of actual damages) to make an example of the conduct of that party. The purpose is to discourage such heinous behavior.

Nominal Damages

Nominal damages are token damages awarded when a party has either suffered a minimal amount of loss or cannot prove the substantial loss required for a higher award. When a trial decides a victor in a case, the court can award a small amount to acknowledge the wrongful act and compensate the victor when the damages are not substantial. Nominal damages are really symbolic for the victor. A case in which nominal damages became an issue was *United States Football League v. National Football League*, 842 F.2d 1335 (2d Cir. 1988). There the jury awarded the USFL one dollar as compensation for its antitrust action against the NFL. Review this decision and see why the court agreed with the jury's award.

tort
A wrong involving a breach of duty and resulting in an injury to the person or property of another. A tort is distinguished from a breach of contract in that a tort is a violation of a duty established by law, whereas a breach of contract results from a failure to meet an obligation created by the agreement of the parties. Although the same act may be both a crime and a tort, the crime is an offense against the public which is prose- cuted by the state in a criminal action; the tort is a private wrong that must be pursued by the injured party in a civil action.

UNITED STATES FOOTBALL LEAGUE v. NATIONAL FOOTBALL LEAGUE
United States Court of Appeals, Second Circuit
March 10, 1988

This appeal follows a highly publicized trial and jury verdict of $1.00. The plaintiff is a now-defunct professional football league that began play in this decade; the defendant is a football league founded nearly seventy years ago. The older of the two leagues, the National Football League, is a highly successful entertainment product. Blaming its older competitor for its difficulties, the USFL instituted this litigation. Plans to play in the fall of 1986 were abandoned after the jury's verdict that is the principal subject of this appeal.

The USFL and certain of its member clubs brought this suit in the Southern District of New York against the NFL, its commissioner, Alvin R. "Pete" Rozelle, and twenty-seven of its twenty-eight member clubs. Seeking damages of $1.701 billion and appropriate injunctive relief, the USFL alleged that the NFL violated Sections 1 and 2 of the Sherman Anti-Trust Act, 15 U.S.C. §§ 1 and 2 (1982), and the common law.

After five days of deliberations, the jury found that the NFL had willfully acquired or maintained monopoly power in a market consisting of major-league professional football in the United States. The jury also found that the NFL's unlawful monopolization of professional football had injured the USFL. The jury awarded the USFL only $1.00 in damages, however, an amount that, even when trebled, was no consolation for the USFL.

The jury rejected the remainder of the USFL's claims. It found that the NFL had neither monopolized a relevant television submarket not attempted to do so; that the NFL did not commit any overt act in furtherance of a conspiracy to monopolize; that the NFL did not engage in a conspiracy in restraint of trade; that the NFL's television contracts were not unreasonable restraints of trade; that the NFL did not control access to the three major television networks; and that the NFL did not interfere either with the USFL's ability to obtain a fall television contract or with its spring television contracts. The USFL's common law claims were also rejected.

The USFL contends that it received an award of only $1.00 because of incorrect jury instructions regarding damages. [W]e disagree. Specifically, the USFL challenges the instructions with respect to an antitrust plaintiff's burden of proving the amount of damages and with respect to nominal damages. The jury was given the following nominal damages instruction:

> Just because you have found the fact of some damage resulting from a given unlawful act, that does not mean that you are required to award a dollar amount of damages resulting from that act. You may find, for example, that you are unable to compute the monetary damages resulting from the wrongful act, except by engaging in speculation or guessing, or you find that you cannot separate out the amount of the losses caused by the wrongful act from the amount caused by other factors, including perfectly lawful competitive acts and including business decisions made by the plaintiffs or the plaintiffs' own mismanagement. Or you may find that plaintiffs failed to prove an amount of damages.
>
> You may decline to award damages under such circumstances, or you may award a nominal amount, say $1.

The jury's $1.00 award was consistent with this instruction. The NFL offered much evidence of self-destructive USFL decisions, and the jury's nominal award suggests that it credited this proof, as it was free to do. In awarding only nominal damages, the jury might reasonably have concluded that the USFL had failed to prove any damages.

We also reject the USFL's claim that the award of nominal damages in antitrust cases is somehow "suspect." Other courts routinely approve the award of such damages.

We next consider whether the district court properly instructed the jury with respect to an antitrust plaintiff's burden of proving the amount of damages. To recover treble damages an antitrust plaintiff must prove that its injury was, in fact, caused by the defendant's violation of the antitrust laws. Whatever latitude is afforded antitrust plaintiffs as to proof of damages, however, is limited by the requirement that the damages awarded must be traced to some degree to unlawful acts. That latitude is thus circumscribed by the need for proof of causation. The Supreme Court emphasized this in Bigelow by relaxing the standard for proving amount of damages only after "proof of defendant['s] wrongful acts and their tendency to injure plaintiff['s] business, and from the evidence of the decline in prices, profits and values, *not shown to be attributable to other causes.*"

A plaintiff's proof of amount of damages thus must provide the jury with a reasonable basis upon which to estimate the amount of its losses caused by other factors, such as management problems, a general recession or lawful factors. The Supreme Court's decisions in *Bigelow* and *Story Parchment* thus do not shift the burden of proving the cause of damages from the plaintiff to the defendant. They simply restate the established principle that where damages have been shown to be attributable to the defendant's wrongful conduct, but are uncertain in amount, the defendant bears the risk of those uncertainties.

QUESTIONS FOR ANALYSIS

What are the facts of this case? What was the basis for the court's holding? Why did the court affirm the $1.00 damage award?

Liquidated Damages

When the parties agree in advance to a particular sum that will be awarded upon a breach, that sum is known as **liquidated damages**. Liquidated damages are normally agreed to as a *contractual* provision by which the parties anticipate what the loss might be in the event of a breach; it is an estimate of the probable damages in the event of a breach. Courts look very carefully at liquidated damage clauses to be sure they are not punitive, which would be contrary to generally accepted legal principles. Liquidated damages that would act as a punishment rather than as compensation will not be upheld by a court. The liquidated damages clause must be reasonable and must fairly anticipate the cost of a breach.

The purpose of liquidated damages clauses is to avoid expensive litigation, force a party to perform contractual obligations, or diminish the loss suffered by the breaching party. The court weighs the reasons underlying liquidated damages clauses and closely examines the intent of the clause. If its basis is to extract performance in a coercive manner, the clause will probably be unenforceable. If the clause truly is a reasonable approximation of the future costs that would result from nonperformance, the clause will likely be enforced. Consequently, reasonableness is critical in determining a liquidated damages clause's validity.

In determining whether a liquidated damages clause is reasonable, the court looks to the actual amount of the contract, how much of the contract has been performed, the amount it would cost to litigate the claim, and any other reasonable factors that the parties may have considered in reaching the specific damage amount. It is clear that parties have difficulty accurately calculating the actual amount that could be incurred in the event of a breach. Consequently, when a liquidated damages clause has been challenged, the court examines the contract as a whole and considers the parties' intentions to determine whether the liquidated damages clause is reasonable. *Cad Cam, Inc. v. Underwood* 36 Ohio App. 3d 90, 521 N.E.2d 498 (1987) illustrates a court's analysis.

TERMS

treble damages
Damages in triple the amount of the damages actually incurred. Treble damages are a form of punitive damages or exemplary damages authorized by statute in some circumstances if warranted by the severity of the violation or the seriousness of the wrong.

nominal damages
Damages awarded to a plaintiff in a very small or merely symbolic amount. Such damages are appropriate in a situation where: (1) although a legal right has been violated, no actual damages have been incurred, but the law recognizes the need to vindicate the plaintiff; (2) some compensable injury has been shown, but the amount of that injury has not been proven.

CAD CAM, INC. v. UNDERWOOD

Court of Appeals of Ohio, Montgomery County
March 10, 1987

Cad Cam, Inc., seeks to enforce Section 8 of its employment contract with Edwin Underwood, its employee. From the trial court's judgment in favor of Underwood, Cad Cam appeals. Section 8 of the employment contract reads as follows:

Employee acknowledges that by virtue of his employment with Employer, he will be acquiring certain unique training, skills, and experience. In consideration therefor, and only if Employee becomes employed by another Employer whose services uses, manufactures, or contemplates the service, use or manufacture of computer-aided design equipment or facilities, Employee agrees upon termination of his employment with Employer to pay to Employer the sum of one half of his annual based salary which shall be due within

30 days after the effective date of termination and may be offset by Employer against any amount then due and owing to Employee.

Cad Cam sought judgment for $9,500, being one half of Underwood's annual salary.

It is undisputed that Underwood signed the contract, and that Cad Cam performed its obligations under the contract. It is undisputed that Underwood, at his initiative, left Cad Cam's employ and began immediately to work for "another [e]mployer whose services uses, manufactures, or contemplates the service, use or manufacture of computer-aided design equipment or facilities," within the contemplation of Section 8. Underwood claimed that Section 8 of his contract constituted an illegal restraint of trade and a penalty clause, and was unenforceable. The trial court held that Section 8 was unenforceable because "it is blatantly a penalty clause and has no relationship whatsoever to liquidated damages."

The test for determining whether a contract provision is a liquidated damages provision or a penalty has been articulated as follows:

Where the parties have agreed on the amount of damages, ascertained by estimation and adjustment, and have expressed this agreement in clear and unambiguous terms, the amount so fixed should be treated as liquidated damages and not as a penalty, if the damages would be (1) uncertain as to amount and difficult of proof, and if (2) the contract as a whole is not so manifestly unconscionable, unreasonable, and disproportionate in amount as to justify the conclusion that it does not express the true intention of the parties, and if (3) the contract is consistent with the conclusion that it was the intention of the parties that damages in the amount stated should follow the breach thereof.

In applying this test, a first point of departure is to determine for what injury the specified damages are intended to compensate. Cad Cam argues that the $9,500 is intended to compensate it for its expenses in training the employee, and for the bonuses that it paid to its employee. The difficulty with this analysis of the injury for which the specified damages are intended to compensate is that Cad Cam will have suffered the expenses of training its employee and having paid its employee bonuses in every instance in which the employee leaves Cad Cam's employ, and yet the damages provision is not triggered in every such instance—it is only triggered in those instances in which the former employee is hired by a competitor within the industry. This strongly suggests that the injury for which Section 8 compensates is not the training expenses and bonuses, but is rather the adverse impact, if any, that the hiring of Cad Cam's employee by a competitor would have upon Cad Cam's business.

Opposed to this conclusion is testimony by Cad Cam's president and majority stockholder that Cad Cam wanted to be reimbursed for its employee's training, but only if that training were of benefit to him in subsequent employment in the industry; otherwise, no reimbursement would be paid. That is at least an argument in favor of linking, conceptually, the training expenses to the payment required by Section 8. Based on the whole record, however, we are not prepared to hold that the trial court was required to accept the foregoing rationale offered by Cad Cam as a primary rationale for Section 8, or even as a valid rationale for Section 8. There was evidence in the record that on at least one occasion the same witness had admitted, at a deposition, that one intention of Section 8 was "to advise and warn other companies that in the event they steal * * * [Cad Cam's] employee, they will have to make a token payment for those employees." That admission is more consistent with Section 8 being a penalty to secure enforcement of a covenant not to compete, than with Section 8 being a provision for reimbursing Cad Cam for the expenses of training its employee in the event of the employee's having derived some post-Cad Cam employment benefit from the training.

We conclude that the trial court could reasonably find, from this record, that the purpose of Section 8 was to ensure that Cad Cam's employee did not leave Cad Cam's employ and go to work for a competitor. In that event, the injury to Cad Cam would be the adverse impact, if any, that the hiring of another employee by Cad Cam's competitor would have upon Cad Cam's business.

First, we must determine if the damages to Cad Cam's business resulting from the hiring of a former employee by a competitor were "uncertain as to amount and difficult of proof." It would seem that they would be. It will ordinarily be difficult to determine how much business has been lost to a competitor as a result of any single factor, since a customer's decision with whom to do business is potentially subject to many varied influences.

Second, we must determine if the contract is so manifestly unconscionable, unreasonable, and disproportionate in amount as to justify the conclusion that it does not express the true intent of the parties. Here we conclude that the trial court could reasonably have found that the contract was manifestly unconscionable, unreasonable, and disproportionate in amount.

In the case we decide today, there is a specific contractual undertaking—not to become subsequently employed by a competitor—that corresponds with the specified damages, $9,500. There was sufficient evidence in the record from which the trial court could conclude that the $9,500 damages stipulated in the contract were not reasonably proportionate to any injury to Cad Cam likely to result from Underwood's subsequent employment by a competitor. The training Underwood required at Cad Cam in order to use the Computervision system (which was similar to the system Underwood used when subsequently employed by Cad Cam's competitor) was completed in Underwood's first week on the job, so that it would not have taken Cad Cam's competitor very long to have trained a newly hired employee with comparable innate ability, even if the newly hired employee had not had Underwood's background in the Computervision system. In any event, Underwood did require new training by his subsequent employer. There are many software systems to facilitate the work done by both Cad Cam and its competitor, so that the Computervision and Intergraph system learned by Underwood at Cad Cam were not valuable trade secrets of Cad Cam. In any event, Underwood did not use the Computervision or Intergraph system in his new employment. Finally, the scope of Underwood's job at Cad Cam was essentially limited to copying drawings, not a task in which one would expect there to be much in the way of secret proprietary knowledge of much value to Cad Cam. All of the foregoing evidence would tend to support the trial court's conclusion

that the potential for any adverse impact upon Cad Cam's business resulting from Underwood's going to work for a competitor was quite limited.

The fundamental test for whether a contractual provision is a liquidated damages or a penalty provision has been recently expressed as follows: "[R]easonable compensation for actual damages is the legitimate objective of liquidated damage provisions and where the amount specified is manifestly inequitable and unrealistic, courts will ordinarily regard it as a penalty. Since there is evidence in the record from which the trial court could properly have concluded that any actual damages likely to be sustained by Cad Cam as a result of Underwood's having gone to work for a competitor were negligible, the specification in Section 8 of the contract of one half of Underwood's annual compensation, or $9,500, as the damages for his breach would seem to be unrealistically out of proportion to the actual damages likely to be sustained by Cad Cam. In summary, there was sufficient evidence in the record from which the trial court could conclude that Section 8 of the contract was intended as a penalty clause, rather than as a liquidated damages provision. Accordingly, Cad Cam's third assignment of error is without merit.

Cad Cam [also claims] the trial court erred in not enforcing the employment agreement, because the agreement for reimbursement is a valid and reasonable covenant not to compete. Even if the trial court had found that the covenant not to compete intended to be enforced by Section 8 had reasonable geographical and temporal limits, it could still have properly found that the $9,500 forfeiture provision enforcing Section 8 was a penalty clause, and therefore unenforceable, rather than a liquidated damages provision.

In any event, the covenant not to compete intended to be enforced by Section 8 is unlimited both in area and in time. We have found no cases upholding as reasonable a covenant not to compete unlimited as to both geography and time. It would take an extraordinary showing to establish that an unlimited restriction against competition, anywhere in the world and at any time in the future, was reasonably necessary to protect the covenantee's legitimate business interests, and no such showing has been made. Cad Cam's first assignment of error is without merit.

Cad Cam [further claims that the] trial court erred in not enforcing the reimbursement provision, because the reimbursement provision is a valid promise exchanged for fair consideration and is enforceable independent of the rest of the agreement. If the provision upon which Cad Cam relies was not supported by fair consideration, the lack of fair consideration would have been an independent ground for declining to enforce the provision. It is unnecessary to reach that issue, however, since we conclude that Section 8 was properly found by the trial court to be a penalty clause, intended to compel Underwood's adherence to the non-competition restriction by the deterrent effect of its punitive forfeiture provision, disproportionate to any injury likely to have been done to Cad Cam's business as a result of Underwood's going to work for a competitor. Cad Cam's second assignment of error is without merit.

There remains Cad Cam's fourth assignment of error, which is as follows: "The trial court erred in dismissing the claim because even if the agreement was defective the defect should have been corrected and relief awarded."

It is one thing for a court to determine whether the application of a covenant not to compete to a particular fact pattern is reasonably necessary to protect an employer's legitimate interests; it is quite another for a court to fashion a liquidated damages provision that would be reasonably related to any injury likely to result from a breach. If Cad Cam is asking that the trial court be required to rewrite Section 8 to provide for a reasonable scheme of liquidated damages to cover all future cases of breach, then we conclude that the trial court would be required to wander too far afield from its ordinary adjudicative function. On the other hand, if Cad Cam is asking only that the trial court be required to determine what award of damages would be reasonable given the facts of this particular case, then we are unable to differentiate that exercise from a trial court's ordinary determination and award of compensatory damages.

We do not quarrel with the proposition that a plaintiff may recover proven damages for a breach of contract, even if the damages stipulated in the contract itself are held to be unenforceable as a penalty. Cad Cam's difficulty in this case is that it has not offered sufficient proof of the adverse impact upon its business of Underwood's having left his employment in order to work for a competitor. The trial court was entitled, on the record in this case, to conclude that there had been a failure to prove any injury at all accruing to Cad Cam as a result of Underwood's having gone to work for a competitor. Therefore, the trial court's failure to award damages was not error.

QUESTIONS FOR ANALYSIS

What is the fundamental test to determine the validity of a liquidated damages clause? Was the liquidated damages clause in *Cad Cam* valid? What was the basis for the court's decision?

Mitigation of Damages

TERMS

liquidated damages
A sum agreed upon by the parties at the time of entering into a contract as being payable by way of compensation for loss suffered in the event of a breach of contract; a sum similarly determined by a court in a lawsuit resulting from breach of contract.

Under the common law, there is a general duty, when it is reasonably possible, to minimize the amount of damage caused by a party's nonperformance. This is known as **mitigation of damages**. The party who has been injured must make necessary and reasonable efforts to prevent escalation of the losses brought about by the breach. It is important to note that the duty to mitigate does not require a person to go to extraordinary lengths to minimize the damage. If the high risks and expenses involved would cause undue hardship to a party, there is no duty to mitigate.

A common instance involving a duty to mitigate is when a party breaches a lease. Suppose, for example, that the parties have agreed on a monthly amount to lease commercial space. Due to economics or some other unforeseen situation, the **lessee** determines that it is not feasible to make future payments on the lease agreement. During the night, the lessee quietly moves out. When the landlord discovers that the tenant has moved, there is no doubt that the landlord can sue the tenant for the payments remaining during the lease term. However, the landlord must attempt to mitigate its damages by advertising the commercial space for lease. Generally, the landlord need not go to any other or further lengths to fulfill its obligation to mitigate losses. If the landlord does lease the property, any income from the new lease will be deducted from the prior tenant's obligations. The prior tenant will be responsible for any costs and expenses in acquiring the new tenant and for any unpaid balance on the lease. The landlord would have fulfilled its duty to mitigate its damages.

In contrast, if there is an overabundance of commercial space and the landlord, after reasonable efforts, cannot lease the property, the landlord has still fulfilled its duty to mitigate. Courts do not require parties to go to extraordinary lengths to mitigate their damages, but to do only what is reasonable. The mitigation-of-damages issue was examined in *Nylen v. Park Doral Apartments*, 535 N.E.2d 178 (Ind. Ct. App. 1989), in which the court was faced not only with a mitigation of damages issue, but also a liquidated damages question in a lease.

TERMS

mitigation of damages
Facts that tend to show that the plaintiff is not entitled to as large an amount of damages as would otherwise be recoverable. The law obligates an injured party to mitigate his or her injury, i.e., to do all he or she reasonably can to avoid or lessen the consequences of the other party's wrongful act.

lessee
The person receiving the right of possession of real property, or possession and use of personal property, under a lease. A lessee of real estate is also known as a *tenant*.

NYLEN v. PARK DORAL APARTMENTS
Court of Appeals of Indiana
March 20, 1989

The facts relevant to this appeal may be summarized as follows. Susan Nylen, Elizabeth Lewis and Julie Reed, students at Indiana University, executed a Rental Agreement with Park Doral Apartments for a term from August 26, 1986 until August 19, 1987. Performance of the lease was secured by a deposit in the amount of $420, constituting pre-payment of rent for the last month of the lease term, and by the signatures of Ronald Nylen, Boyd Lewis and Lucy Reed as co-signers.

At the end of the fall semester, Julie Reed moved out of the apartment and in February of 1987, she refused to pay any further rent. Susan Nylen and Elizabeth Lewis remained in possession of the apartment, paying only two-thirds of the total rent due for the month of February. Park Doral Apartments filed

suit for ejectment of the tenants for failure to pay rent in full for the month of February.

While the ejectment proceedings were pending, Susan Nylen and Elizabeth Lewis made a payment of $280 for the rent due in March. Subsequently, on March 10, 1987, the trial court ordered Nylen and Lewis to pay full rent or vacate the premises. They vacated the apartment, pursuant to court order, on March 13, 1987.

A final hearing on the issue of damages was held on September 14, 1987. The trial court awarded delinquent rent owed plus the balance of rent due under the lease from the time of Nylen and Lewis' eviction. The delinquent portion of the rent was $140 per month for February and March, and the balance for the remainder of the lease was $420 per month for April through July. The court also awarded $362 in late fees, $600 in attorney fees and $75.24 in consequential damages. Total relief awarded by the court, set off by the $420 security deposit, was $2,577.24 plus the costs of the action.

The issue raised on appeal concerns whether the lower court erroneously permitted Park Doral Apartments to pursue inconsistent remedies.

> The test of such inconsistency of remedies has its basis in the factual background which constitutes the cause of action. If the assertion of one cause of action involves the repudiation of another, then the modes of redress are inconsistent. If the one cause of action admits a state of facts, and the other denies the same facts, the remedies sought by such actions are inconsistent.

According to the appellants, Park Doral Apartments could not seek both an order of ejectment and recovery of rent for the balance of the lease term. The appellants maintain that the suit for ejectment brought by Park Doral Apartments operated as a denial of the Rental Agreement, thereby barring recovery under the savings clause of the lease. That argument reflects a basic misunderstanding as to the nature of a suit for ejectment.

[The] appellants suggest that the lower court's judgment violates the doctrine of mitigation of damages. The appellants first argue that they were discharged from liability for post-ejectment losses, because the evidence disclosed an exacerbation rather than mitigation of damages. The appellants reason that there was a failure to mitigate damages when Park Doral Apartments sought to evict Susan Nylen and Elizabeth Lewis, instead of permitting them to continue in possession while paying only two-thirds of the rent due per month. There is no authority for the proposition that a landlord must tolerate a breach of lease terms in order to mitigate its damages, and this Court declines to endorse such a premise.

The doctrine of mitigation of damages creates an obligation on the part of the landlord to use such diligence as would be exercised by a reasonably prudent man under similar circumstances to re-let the premises, if possible, in order to mitigate damages resulting from the tenant's breach of lease. The obligation exists even if there is no mandatory re-letting clause in the lease.

In the instant case, there was evidence before the trial court that Park Doral Apartments used due diligence to re-let the premises. The manager of the apartments had placed a series of advertisements in the Indiana Daily Student newspaper. In response to the advertisements, three persons came to view the apartment. Subsequently, the manager reduced the monthly rental rate in an effort to find a tenant. Considering the evidence most favorable to the judgment, this Court holds that the award of future rents based on a savings clause was not contrary to law as a violation of the doctrine of mitigation of damages.

The appellants' next challenge the trial court's award of late fees to Park Doral Apartments. That award was based on a provision of the Rental Agreement which stated:

> 2. The tenant(s) understands and agrees that the rent will be due and payable on the 1st day of each month at the designated address and should said rent not have been paid by the 1st day of the month, the landlord reserves the right to require a $2.00 per day, per person late fee.

The appellants characterize Paragraph 2 of the lease as a penalty, while Park Doral Apartments maintains that the paragraph is a liquidated damages provision. In determining whether a stipulated sum payable on breach of a contract constitutes liquidated damages or a penalty, the facts, the intention of the parties and the reasonableness of the stipulation under the circumstances of the case are all to be considered. Where the nature of the agreement is such that a breach would result in damages which are uncertain and difficult to prove, and where the stipulated sum payable on breach is not greatly disproportionate to the loss likely to occur, then that fixed sum will be accepted as liquidated damages and not as a penalty.

The evidence before the lower court showed that the damages incurred by Park Doral Apartments for late rent were dependent upon several variables: the number of tenants in an apartment, each tenant's share of the rent, the ability to locate the breaching tenant and the lateness of the particular share of rent. According to the manager of the apartments, a tenant's failure to pay rent on time created extra work for the management in sending notices, preparing a weekly rent delinquency report, calling the tenant and using and preparing additional cash journals. There was also testimony concerning loss of interest income when rental payments are delinquent.

The question whether a contractual provision stipulating damages in the event of a breach is a valid liquidated damages clause or a penalty is purely a question of law for the court. The trial court's determination that Paragraph 2 of the Rental Agreement is an enforceable liquidated damages provision cannot be deemed to be contrary to law. Therefore, Park Doral Apartments may recover appellate attorney fees. The preferred procedure, however, is for the trial court to hear the evidence and determine a reasonable fee when the appeal has been concluded.

QUESTIONS FOR ANALYSIS

In *Nylen*, what was required of the landlord to fulfill its mitigation-of-damages responsibilities? Did the court find the liquidated damages clause valid? State the reasons for your answer. Can the liquidated damages issue in *Nylen* be reconciled with *Cad Cam?* Why or why not?

9.3 Equitable Remedies

Monetary remedies often are insufficient to compensate a party for the injuries sustained. When this is so, a party can request a court to award an equitable remedy. An *equitable remedy* is a nonmonetary remedy awarded when legal remedies are either inadequate or inappropriate as a remedy for the injured party. A number of equitable remedies are available in contract law: specific performance, injunctive relief, rescission, reformation, restitution, and reliance. Which equitable remedy is appropriate for the injured party is determined by a court based upon the facts of each case.

Specific Performance

Specific performance is an equitable remedy unique to contract law, whereby a court requires a party who has breached a contractual obligation to perform that which was promised under the original contract. Courts can order specific performance when a legal remedy is insufficient. Specific performance can be granted if it can be shown that the subject matter of the contract is unique or that money damages would not be sufficient to make the nonbreaching party whole again, or that a duplicate or substantial equivalent is impossible. Awarding this remedy is purely within the discretion of a court. Courts will consider the effect and harm created if specific performance is granted; it is not taken lightly, because of its effects.

The remedy of specific performance is most commonly used when real estate is involved. Because of the unique nature of real property, courts generally find that any substituted performance is inadequate to make the person whole again. Thus, when determining whether specific performance should

TERMS

specific performance
The equitable remedy of compelling performance of a contract, as distinguished from an action at law for damages for breach of contract due to nonperformance. Specific performance may be ordered in circumstances where damages are an inadequate remedy.

be awarded, a party must show (1) the uniqueness of the item or act that is the subject of the original contract and (2) that no substituted performance will be appropriate.

For example, assume that you contract with a company to purchase Joan Crawford's Academy Award Oscar statuette. You have tendered the cash to the seller, but after some thought a Crawford family member decides that the sale would be offensive to Ms. Crawford's memory and refuses to sell the Oscar. The court could require specific performance because it is virtually impossible to buy an Oscar. (Anyone who has received one since the 1950s signed an agreement that it would not be sold.) Because the Oscar is considered unique, the court could order specific performance and force the seller to tender the Oscar for the agreed price.

If a party can show that the subject of the contract is not unique, and a substitute product can easily be obtained, the remedy of specific performance is inappropriate. In such instance, money damages would be sufficient to make the party whole again and would probably be the remedy the court would award.

Although contracts for personal services are considered unique, especially when a famous personality is involved (such as a baseball player playing for a team or an actor or actress playing a role), the courts generally will not enforce a contract by ordering specific performance. Courts have viewed this as involuntary servitude, which is offensive to courts and violate civil rights. Recently, Kim Basinger, an actress, was sued for breaching an oral contract to play a role in the movie "Boxing Helena." Ms. Basinger claimed that a contract had not been consummated, but the studio and director promoting the movie claimed that publicity and promotions had begun based upon Ms. Basinger playing the female lead. Ms. Basinger refused to play the role and was then sued. A court could probably not force Ms. Basinger to play the role through specific performance, but she could be, and was, sued for damages. Although Ms. Basinger lost her lawsuit at the trial court and a multimillion dollar award of damages was entered against her an appeals court has reversed the trial court on a legal issue. Another case in which specific performance was at issue was *Madariaga v. Morris*, 639 S.W.2d 709 (Tex. Ct. App.–Tyler 1982, no writ), where a claim for specific performance under a contract for Mexican hot sauce was brought before the court.

MADARIAGA v. MORRIS

Court of Appeals of Texas, Tyler
Sept. 10, 1982

The Madariagas had a business in Kilgore, Texas, for "making, manufacturing and selling 'Albert's Famous Mexican Hot Sauce.' " They owned the formula for this sauce. On or about December 9, 1970, they entered into a written contract whereby they leased said business, including the formula and goodwill of said business, to Morris and his partner James D. Mayfield for a consideration of $54,000.00. Under the contract, Morris and Mayfield were obligated to make rental payments of $500.00 per month with the first payment due on or before the 10th day of January, 1971, and a like payment on the 10th day of each month thereafter until said $54,000.00 had been paid in full.

Paragraph (5) of the contract granted the following option for purchase of the business:

(5) When James D. Mayfield and James R. Morris have paid to Albert Madariaga and Mae Madariaga the sum of $54,000.00 in accordance with the terms and provisions of this lease memorandum, then Albert Madariaga and Mae Madariaga agree to convey said business to James D. Mayfield and James R. Morris, doing business as Mayfield and Morris, or their assigns, *said business, formula and all rights under this lease contract* for a consideration of $1,000.00 cash. (Emphasis added.)

The contract contained the following provision for royalty payments:

(6) *In addition to the payment of said rental payments as above set out,* James D. Mayfield and James R. Morris, a partnership doing business as Mayfield & Morris, agree and obligate themselves to pay to Albert Madariaga and Mae Madariaga 25¢ per case on all sales of Albert's Famous Mexican Hot Sauce as a royalty. This payment shall be made once per month and shall be due and payable on or before the 10th of said month with the first payment being due and payable on or before the 10th day of January, 1971. (Emphasis added.)

Shortly after the execution of the contract, Mayfield on July 30, 1971, assigned all his interest in the contract (including the lease agreement and option) to Morris; the Madariagas joined in and consented to this assignment; and Morris thereby assumed all obligations set out in the contract.

It is undisputed that on December 10, 1979, Morris had made the following payments to the Madariagas as provided in the contract: (1) the sum of $54,000 as consideration for the lease in monthly installments of $500 as due under the contract, (2) all royalty payments called for during the rental payment period, and (3) the sum of $1,000 in cash as consideration for a conveyance of the business under the option granted in the contract. After paying the $1,000, Morris requested that the Madariagas convey him the business. This, they refused to do unless he would continue paying the royalty perpetually.

The equitable remedy of specific performance is not ordinarily available when the complaining party can be fully compensated through the legal remedy of damages. Where, however, the personal property contracted for has a special, peculiar, or unique value or character, and the plaintiff would not be adequately compensated for his loss by an award of money damages, specific performance may be decreed. Similarly, special performance of a contract involving personal property may be granted where the subject matter of the contract is of a special and peculiar nature and value, and damages are not measurable. [It] is provided that specific performance may be decreed where the goods are unique or in other proper circumstances.

Equity will generally decree specific performance at the instance of the buyer of personal property, which property he needs and which is not obtainable elsewhere. The *scarcity* of a chattel has been recognized as an important factor in determining whether specific performance of a contract for its sale will be granted. In the case at bar, we hold that the plaintiff, by the facts brought out in his pleadings and evidence show that he does not have an adequate remedy at law and cannot be adequately compensated in damages. This is apparent from the subject matter of the sale. The business, including the hot sauce formula and goodwill, has a special,

peculiar, unique value or character; it consists of property which Morris needs and could not be obtained elsewhere.

We believe that the plain language of paragraph (6) clearly ties any royalty payments to rental payments, the only provision for royalty under the contract being "In addition to the payment of said rental payments"; and that the Madariagas' right to claim royalty terminated when Morris timely paid to them the total rental consideration of $54,000.00 and the additional sum of $1000.00 in exercise of his option to purchase under paragraph (5). We therefore hold that Morris came with "clean hands" in seeking specific performance, and that the trial court properly disregarded the testimony of Mrs. Madariaga that it was her intention at the time she signed the contract that the royalty payments would continue "as long as hot sauce was on the shelves."

[T]he Madariagas assert that the contract is not sufficiently clear to support a decree of specific performance. We believe that, considering the entire contract from its four corners, the option to purchase granted to Morris in the contract is sufficiently clear, definite and certain for enforcement by specific performance. The terms of the contract are so expressed that the court can determine with reasonable certainty what is the duty of each party and the conditions of each performance. The business to be conveyed under the option was the "making, manufacturing and selling of 'Albert's Famous Mexican Hot Sauce,'" the formula, and all rights (including goodwill) under the lease contract.

The judgment of the trial court is affirmed.

QUESTIONS FOR ANALYSIS

What are the facts of the *Madariaga* case? When did the court deem specific performance an appropriate remedy? Did the court grant specific performance? Why or why not?

In cases that involve services, money damages are often the remedy—or, until a resolution can be accomplished, courts can look to an alternative equitable remedy such as injunctive relief.

Injunctive Relief

A very common type of equitable remedy, used not only in contract law but in virtually all aspects of civil litigation, is the **injunction**. An injunction can be granted when one party can show that money is insufficient compensation, that immediate and irreparable harm and injury is occurring to the party, and that it would serve the party's interests to maintain the status quo until a permanent resolution can be reached.

Injunctive relief normally progresses in three stages. In the first stage, the request is for issuance of a **temporary restraining order**; the party who is suffering immediate, irreparable harm and injury requests a court to have the other party do (or refrain from doing) something that is causing harm. Often a temporary restraining order is granted **ex parte**, and is a very temporary measure, effective anywhere from 10 to 14 days. Usually an informal hearing occurs, during which a court makes a determination as to whether it is appropriate to issue the temporary restraining order. If the order is granted, the party will be restrained from acting until a more extensive hearing is held.

Normally, the next stage is a request for a temporary injunction. A temporary injunction is issued after a hearing and notice to all parties. Here, the injured party is requesting that the other party refrain from doing something (or be required to do something) during the pendency of the action, so that no further injury can occur. A temporary injunction may also be called a **preliminary injunction**. When a court grants the temporary injunction, it is effective only until a final trial on the merits can be had.

The final stage of injunctive relief results in a **permanent injunction**. When a court determines that the activity is one that should be forever prohibited, the court can enter a permanent injunction that absolutely prohibits the party from doing (or refraining from doing) a certain act. Injunctions are commonly used in the contracts areas of covenants not to compete and construction contracts.

Rescission

When parties voluntarily agree to set aside a contract, this is known as *voluntary* **rescission**. Under voluntary rescission, all the parties' obligations are discharged under the contract, with no negative consequences. This form of rescission normally takes place in the early stages, when neither party has begun performance.

However, rescission can also take the form of an involuntary cancellation or termination of the contract due to breach by one of the parties to the contract. This is known as *unilateral rescission.* When this occurs, the injured party may ask the court to cancel the contract and restore to the injured party whatever consideration has been paid. Unilateral rescission is very common in mistake, fraud, and misrepresentation cases.

TERMS

injunction
A court order that commands or prohibits some act or course of conduct. It is preventive in nature and designed to protect a plaintiff from irreparable injury to his or her property or property rights by prohibiting or commanding the doing of certain acts. An injunction is a form of equitable relief.

temporary restraining order (TRO)
Under the Federal Rules of Civil Procedure, injunctive relief that the court is empowered to grant, without notice to the opposing party and pending a hearing on the merits, upon a showing that failure to do so will result in "immediate and irreparable injury, loss or damage." TROs are similarly available under state rules of civil procedure.

ex parte
Means "of a side," i.e., from one side or by one party. The term refers to an application made to the court by one party without notice to the other party.

preliminary injunction
An injunction granted prior to a full hearing on the merits. Its purpose is to preserve the status quo until the final hearing. A preliminary injunction is also referred to as a provisional injunction or temporary injunction.

permanent injunction
An injunction granted after a final hearing on the merits, as distinguished from a temporary injunction granted to provide temporary relief.

As a summation of many of the concepts discussed in this chapter, examine *Ennis v. Interstate Distributors, Inc.*, 598 S.W.2d 903 (Tex. Civ. App.—Dallas 1980), in which the court analyzed not only the rescission issue, but also the distinction between an equitable and a legal remedy.

ENNIS v. INTERSTATE DISTRIBUTORS, INC.

Court of Civil Appeals of Texas, Dallas
April 1, 1980

This appeal is from a judgment granting rescission of a covenant which restricted competition by William B. Ennis with his former employer, Interstate Distributors, Inc. and ordered restitution to Interstate of the consideration paid by it for the restrictive covenant. Ennis was formerly the president of Interstate and owned one-third of its outstanding shares. The judgment is based upon jury findings that after he terminated his employment and sold his stock to Interstate, Ennis materially breached the restrictive covenant by soliciting sales from its customers and otherwise competing with it. Ennis contends that the remedy of rescission was not appropriate because, due to his partial performance, the contract was not wholly executory and the status quo could not be restored. We conclude under the facts of this case that the nature of appellant's breach was such that a return to the status quo was not required as a condition to granting rescission. We therefore hold that rescission was a proper remedy and affirm.

Rescission and restitution were ordered by the trial court because of the material breach of a covenant not to compete. The covenant was part of a purchase agreement whereby appellant Ennis sold, and appellee Interstate acquired, his one-third of the outstanding shares of Interstate, a corporation engaged in the sale and distribution of ice machines and related products. The agreement provided that Ennis would not for a period of three years following his termination, compete with Interstate in the states of Louisiana, Texas, New Mexico, and Mississippi.

The primary purpose of the covenant was to protect Interstate's interest in its Frigidaire account for which it held an exclusive distributorship in all of the restricted area except South Texas and the Texas Panhandle. The covenant was initially formulated in August 1973, as a part of Ennis' contract of employment. It was subsequently adopted and by reference made a part of the purchase contract on August 31, 1975. While the term of the covenant was for three years commencing August 31, 1975, and ending August 31, 1978, its practical effect was a tem of two and one-half years ending August 31, 1978, because Ennis did not finally terminate his employment with Interstate until February 1976.

The record reflects that before his termination, but after signing the purchase contract, Ennis solicited the representation of Sani-Serv, one of Interstate's manufacturers, for his individual account. He commenced to represent this account actively in December 1976. In February 1976, upon his termination from Interstate, Ennis accepted employment with La Beaume and Company, a manufacturer's representative engaged in the sale of Frigidaire equipment as well as other lines of related equipment which were in direct competition with those represented by Interstate. This employment continued until July 1976. During the period from August 1976 until December 1976, Ennis was engaged in an unrelated business or was unemployed. Commencing in December 1976, he became a representative of Sani-Serv and, in February 1977, became a sales agent for Savoy Industries, a manufacturer of product lines which competed with Interstate. This employment continued until June 1977 when Ennis became associated with with American Ice Machines, a wholesale distributor of equipment which competed with the Frigidaire product distributed by interstate. This employment continued beyond the term of the covenant, August 31, 1978, and through the date of trial, February 1979. The documentary evidence, as well as his own testimony, confirm that Ennis called upon and made sales to Interstate's customers, solicited business with its manufacturers and distributors, and engaged in other acts which the jury could reasonably infer were in violation of his duty not to disclose the confidential information prohibited by the covenant.

This evidence supports the jury finding of a material breach. We conclude that the breach, or more precisely stated, the failure to perform the obligations of the covenant, was of such a nature as to warrant its rescission and require restitution of the consideration paid.

Rescission is authorized if there is a breach of a contract in a material part. The breach need not be total but a partial breach may be sufficient if it goes to the essence of the contract. Ordinarily, however, rescission will be denied when full relief at law can be provided. While there is authority for the proposition that rescission may not be granted unless in so doing the parties may be restored to the status quo which existed prior to the breach, restoration is not indispensable. Rather, inability to return the parties to their former position is an element to be considered in determining whether, under a particular state of facts, rescission would be inequitable. [T]he right to restitution rests upon equitable grounds such as a failure of consideration.

Interstate could not prove with certainty the damage flowing from the sales. The material injury shown by the proof was the loss of the consideration paid for a covenant which Ennis failed to perform.

QUESTIONS FOR ANALYSIS

When is rescission an appropriate equitable remedy? Did the court find that rescission was warranted in the *Ennis* case? Explain what facts supported a finding of rescission.

Reformation

Reformation is another form of equitable remedy. To avoid an injustice, a court may "rewrite" or modify a contract to reflect the true agreement of the parties. Through the rewriting process, the court can reflect the parties' true intentions and meanings, so that injustice is avoided. This is a very common method of avoiding unfairness, and is often used in mistake cases.

9.4 RESTITUTION AND RELIANCE AS A REMEDY

Equity attempts to avoid injustices that may occur in the legal process. Injustices are sometimes remedied by either *restitution* or *reliance* damages.

Restitution

Restitution damages prevent another party from being unjustly enriched because of a breach by a party's acts. Restitution focuses on the value of the benefit received by a party that was unjustly obtained. Restitution can be awarded in a breach of contract claim or a quasi-contract claim.

When a party has breached a contract, the nonbreaching party has the option of suing for restitution or damages. However, the nonbreaching party can request restitution damages only if there has not been full performance

TERMS

rescission
The abrogation, annulment, or cancellation of a contract by the act of a party. Rescission may occur by mutual consent of the parties, pursuant to a condition contained in the contract, or for fraud, failure of consideration, material breach, or default. It is also a remedy available to the parties by a judgment or decree of the court. More than mere termination, rescission restores the parties to the status quo existing before the contract was entered into.

of the contract. If full performance has not occurred, the nonbreaching party can request recovery for the amount of enrichment received by the breaching party, even if the restitution damages exceed the original contract price. The rationale behind such a result is that the wrongdoer should not profit from its wrongful act. Consequently, courts may not limit restitution recovery to the actual contract price.

When considering whether restitution is the appropriate choice of remedies, courts pose the following questions:

1. Was the breach material?
2. Was there partial performance by the nonbreaching party?
3. Did the breaching party receive any benefit from the partial performance?

If the answers to these three questions are yes, a party has the option of requesting compensation for the reasonable value of the benefit received. Courts will then evaluate the benefit received to determine the appropriate award to the nonbreaching party. What is critical to the analysis is that full performance has not been rendered; otherwise, the appropriate remedy is compensatory damages.

Quasi Contract Chapter 1 discussed the concept of quasi contract, under which the court, to prevent unjust enrichment, will find a contract. This is also known as **quantum meruit**. Under the doctrine of quantum meruit (as much as one had earned), a court can award a specific amount to a party who has been damaged because of an unjust benefit to another party. Ordinarily, the court will not allow one party to benefit at the expense of another. Even if a contract was not mutually agreed upon, when a party has derived benefits from a contractual relationship through an implied in law contract, the court will allow an amount of damages to compensate the claiming party for the benefit bestowed. This is a form of restitution damages. An example of restitution in quasi-contract cases is when a doctor performs emergency medical treatment on a patient without formal agreement. Restitution in the form of payment for the services would be appropriate.

Reliance Damages

The focus of reliance damages is the detrimental **reliance** of the non-breaching party. Because one party has changed its position in reliance that the other party would perform under the contract, a court can award damages for the amount expended in reliance upon performance. The court thus looks to returning the nonbreaching party to the same position it was in prior to entering into the contract. Section 139 of the *Restatement* sets out when reliance damages are appropriate:

> (1) A promise which the promisor should reasonably expect to induce action or forbearance on the part of the promisee or a third person and which does induce the action or forbearance is enforceable notwithstanding the Statute of Frauds if injustice can be avoided only by

TERMS

reformation
An equitable remedy available to a party to a contract provided he or she can prove that the contract does not reflect the real agreement, i.e., the actual intention, of the parties.

enforcement of the promise. The remedy granted for breach is to be limited as justice requires.

(2)   In determining whether injustice can be avoided only by enforcement of the promise, the following circumstances are significant:

(a)   the availability and adequacy of other remedies, particularly cancellation and restitution;
(b)   the definite and substantial character of the action or forbearance in relation to the remedy sought;
(c)   the extent to which the action or forbearance corroborates evidence of the making and terms of the promise, or the making and terms are otherwise established by clear and convincing evidence;
(d)   the reasonableness of the action or forbearance;
(e)   the extent to which the action or forbearance was foreseeable by the promisor.

Normally, in a reliance case, one of the parties who promised to perform fails to do so and the party who relied on the promise expends money and time in reliance on the promise to perform.

9.5   ELECTION OF REMEDIES

When two or more available remedies for a breach of contract action exist, but are inconsistent, a party may be required to make an **election of remedy**. Under this doctrine, when remedies are mutually exclusive, a party elects one remedy or another and is bound by the remedy chosen. After choosing one remedy over another, the party cannot go back and request another remedy hoping for a better result. Once the election is made, the choice is absolute.

Remedies that are mutually exclusive are compensatory damages and restitution damages. A party cannot ask for both, as this may result in a prohibited double recovery. Consequently, when analyzing a remedy, the following questions should be asked:

1. Has performance begun?
2. If so, has the performance been completed?
3. Does the client require a legal remedy or an equitable remedy?
4. If a legal remedy, what type of damages has the party suffered?
5. If an equitable remedy is appropriate, which one?
6. Are the remedies chosen mutually exclusive? If so, which remedy should be elected?

9.6   PRACTICAL APPLICATIONS

Paralegals will find many different types of remedy clauses in contracts. One type of clause that must be carefully analyzed is a liquidation clause, as it cannot appear to act as a penalty. Careful drafting can avoid the pitfalls that may accompany a liquidated damages clause. Remember, the

restitution
In both contract and tort, a remedy that restores the status quo. Restitution returns a person who has been wrongfully deprived of something to the position he or she occupied before the wrong occurred; it requires a defendant who has been unjustly enriched at the expense of the plaintiff to make the plaintiff whole, either, as may be appropri-ate, by returning property unjustly held, by reim-bursing the plaintiff, or by paying compen- sation or indemnification.

quantum meruit
Means "as much as is merited" or "as much as is deserved." The doctrine of quantum meruit makes a person liable to pay for services or goods that he or she accepts while knowing that the other party expects to be paid, even if there is no express contract, to avoid unjust enrichment.

reliance
Trust; confidence; dependence.

election of remedy
1. A requirement often present in the law that a party to a lawsuit must choose between two or more different types of relief allowed by law on the same set of facts. The adoption of one has the effect of barring use of the others. 2. The act of choosing between two or more different types of relief allowed by law on the same set

amount of the liquidated damages clause can dictate its validity. Consequently, consideration of a client's situation is critical. Figure 9-1 illustrates some helpful language.

Liquidated Damages

In the event either party should breach this contract, the parties agree that the breaching party shall pay to the other party the sum of _____ dollars ($____) as liquidated damages.

Liquidated Damages for Violation of Covenant Not to Compete

Employee agrees that in the event of violation by employee of the agreement against competition contained in this agreement, employee will pay as liquidated damages to employer the sum of _____ dollars ($____) per day, for each day or part thereof that employee continues to so breach such agreement. It is recognized and agreed that damages in such event would be difficult or impossible to ascertain, though great and irreparable, and that this agreement with respect to liquidated damages shall in no event disentitle employer to injunctive relief.

Delay in Completion of Contract—Liquidated Damages

For each and every day that the work contemplated in this agreement remains uncompleted beyond the time set for its completion, [first party] shall pay to [second party] the sum of _____ dollars ($____), as liquidated damages and not as a penalty.

The sum stated in the immediately preceding paragraph may be deducted from money due or to become due to [first party] as compensation under this agreement.

FIGURE 9-1 Sample liquidated damages clauses

In addition, many contracts set forth general provisions for remedy in the event of a breach. Some examples of these provisions are found in Figure 9-2.

Remedies for Breach of Employment Contract

Any breach or evasion of any term of this agreement by either party will cause immediate and irreparable injury to the other party and will authorize recourse by such party to injunction and/or specific performance, as well as to all other legal or equitable remedies to which such party may be entitled under the provisions of this agreement.

Remedies as Cumulative

All remedies transferred to either party by this agreement shall be deemed cumulative of any remedy otherwise allowed by law.

**Breach of Contract—No Liability by Seller for
Incidental or Consequential Damages**

In no event shall seller be liable for incidental or consequential damages nor shall seller's liability for any claims or damage arising out of or connected with this agreement or the manufacture, sale, delivery, or use of the products with which this agreement is concerned exceed the purchase price of such products.

FIGURE 9-2 Sample remedy provisions

SUMMARY

9.1   There are two general types of remedies: legal and equitable. A legal remedy is a monetary remedy, whereas an equitable remedy is a non-monetary remedy. The type of injury will dictate the type of remedy.

9.2   Legal remedies are known as damages. Damages may be compensatory, consequential, punitive, nominal, or liquidated. Compensatory damages are the actual amount lost by the injured party. Consequential damages are the damages that are a direct consequence of the breach. Damages that are rarely awarded in contract cases are punitive or exemplary damages; these are punishment or penalty damages. Nominal damages are token damages and are awarded when the actual amount of damages is not proved. Liquidated damages are agreed to in the contract, but must not be excessive. In any damage case, the injured persons are required to mitigate their damages.

9.3   Equitable remedies are nonmonetary remedies which include specific performance, injunctive relief, rescission, reformation, restitution, and reliance. Specific performance is forced performance on a contract. Injunctive relief acts to restrain a party from doing something or to require that something be done. There are three stages: temporary restraining order, temporary injunction, and permanent injunction. Rescission is when parties agree to set aside their contract. Reformation is when a court corrects a contract.

9.4   Restitution is another remedy which prevents another party from being unjustly enriched as a result of a party's act. Restitution is awarded in breach-of-contract cases and quasi-contract cases. Reliance damages award a party money when a change of position occurs in reliance that another party will perform on a contract, but the performance does not occur.

9.5   Parties are required to elect a remedy when more than one remedy is available but they are mutually exclusive. Compensatory and restitution damages are mutually exclusive; therefore, one must be chosen over the other.

REVIEW QUESTIONS

1. What is the difference between a legal remedy and an equitable remedy?
2. What are the various types of legal remedies?
3. Define compensatory damages.
4. Distinguish between compensatory damages and consequential damages.
5. When are exemplary damages awarded in contract law?

6. What is the doctrine of mitigation of damages?
7. Identify the equitable remedies.
8. Define specific performance and explain when it may be awarded by a court.
9. What are the general stages for injunctive relief?
10. When can restitution be elected as an equitable remedy?

EXERCISES

1. Joe Valentine, an avid baseball card collector, went to purchase a Nolan Ryan rookie card at Sports Card World in Arlington, Texas. After browsing awhile, he found the Nolan Ryan card he was looking for. A young clerk asked Mr. Valentine if he could be of assistance. Mr. Valentine pointed to the Ryan card. The clerk quickly looked at the price and said that the card was $100. Valentine was surprised at the low price, as he was prepared to go up to $900. Wasting no time, Valentine wrote Sports Card World a check and basked in his find. A day later, Mr. Valentine received a telephone call from the owner of Sports Card World. The owner was very upset that the clerk had misread the price and the real price for the card was $1,100, not $100. The store owner stated he would refund Valentine's $100 and apologized. Mr. Valentine refused the refund and stated that they had a contract. Sports Card World sued Mr. Valentine. Discuss all issues and remedies the court would consider.

2. Your attorney has just been retained by a new client, Cannon Construction Company. It appears that Cannon entered into a contract with Speedy Lumber Company whereby Speedy was to supply the lumber for Cannon's construction project with the City of Dallas. The contract was for $50,000, with delivery to be June 15, 1992. Time was important to Cannon. The contract had a liquidated damages clause for $60,000 in the event either party breached. Speedy had problems with its supplier in Washington State and called Cannon, stating that they couldn't ship the lumber until June 30, 1992. Cannon was furious. What rights and remedies does Cannon have against Speedy?

3. Paul is a wealthy collector of rare stones. It has recently come to his attention that the famous "Faith diamond" is for sale. The Faith diamond is a magnificent 15-carat stone which has been in the possession of the Vanderweigh family for generations; however, the Vanderweighs have decided to sell the Faith diamond to raise enough money to pay certain vexatious creditors. The eldest son, KiKi, is the family's representative for the purpose of selling the Faith diamond for the best possible price.

   Paul contacted KiKi and offered him $2 million for the precious stone. KiKi accepted Paul's offer. Paul then immediately sent KiKi the following letter via telecopy:

May 19, 1992

VIA: TELECOPY AND REGULAR MAIL
FACSIMILE NO. 123-456-7890

Your Highness KiKi
The Vanderweigh Mansion
900 Britain Way
London, England B98ENG89

Re: Sale of Faith Diamond

Dear KiKi:

    The purpose of this letter is to confirm our conversation regarding the sale of the Faith Diamond (the "Diamond").
    I have agreed to tender the sum of $2,000,000 in the form of a certified check (the "Check") to you within ten (10) days from the date of this letter, and you having the authority to do so, on behalf of your family have agreed to deliver the Diamond to me within five (5) days after receiving my check. The Diamond will be delivered to the address printed on this letterhead.
    Please contact me if you believe the above terms do not accurately represent our conversation.
    Of course, if you have any other comments or questions regarding the foregoing, please do not hesitate to call.

                    Very truly yours,

                    Paul

Two days later, KiKi agreed to sell the diamond to an Arab sheik for $4 million. The sheik knew that $4 million was well above the fair market value, but as he explained, "What do I care, it's only money." The sheik paid KiKi in full immediately. According to the terms of the agreement between KiKi and the sheik, the diamond was to be delivered within 21 days from the date of payment.

Of course, as a matter of courtesy, KiKi informed Paul that the diamond has been sold to someone else. Paul, who incidentally has a genuine love and admiration for this precious stone, is disappointed. Paul appeals to KiKi's sense of decency and asks KiKi to honor the agreement between them. KiKi apologetically declines.

Paul comes to you for advice. Describe to Paul his remedies, if any, against KiKi, the Vanderweighs, or the Arab sheik.

CHAPTER 10
Third-Party Contracts

10.1 DEFINING THE RELATIONSHIP
IN THIRD-PARTY CONTRACTS

In the definition of contracts, the law focuses on an exchange between two parties, the promisor and the promisee. The contract sets out each party's duties and obligations, with performance being the final phase of completion of the contract. There are situations, though, when the promisor and the promisee intend for a third party, who is not directly involved in the contract, to reap advantages from the contractual relationship. This situation involves what is known as a **third-party beneficiary contract**. A third-party beneficiary contract requires an original agreement between the promisor, the promisee, and a third party who benefits from the original contract. The person who benefits from the contract, who is known as a **beneficiary**, is a person or entity who will receive benefits from a contract. The beneficiary may or may not know of the benefits to be received.

The law categorizes beneficiaries into two groups: intended beneficiaries (which include donee beneficiaries and creditor beneficiaries) and incidental beneficiaries. The *Restatement (Second) of Contracts* § 302 describes intended and incidental beneficiaries as follows:

> (1) Unless otherwise agreed between promisor and promisee, a beneficiary of a promise is an intended beneficiary if recognition of a right to performance in the beneficiary is appropriate to effectuate the intention of the parties, and either
>   (a) the performance of the promise will satisfy an obligation of the promisee to pay money to the beneficiary; or
>   (b) the circumstances indicate that the promisee intends to give the beneficiary the benefit of the promised performance.
> (2) An incidental beneficiary is a beneficiary who is not an intended beneficiary.

Note that the definition of an incidental beneficiary is by exclusion. Although the *Restatement* blurs the distinction between the various intended beneficiary categories, the most widely recognized are donee and creditor beneficiaries.

Intended Beneficiary

If when contracting the parties intend a specific third party to benefit, that party is an *intended beneficiary*. The intended beneficiary is not directly involved in the contracting process, yet the process will affect his or her rights. To determine whether a third party is an intended beneficiary, ask three basic questions:

1. Did the promisee *intend* the third party to benefit from the contract?
2. Did the beneficiary *rely* on the contractual rights conferred?
3. Did the performance run directly from the promisor to the third-party beneficiary?

If any of these questions are answered yes, the third party is probably an intended beneficiary of the contract. Figure 10-1 illustrates a third-party intended beneficiary situation.

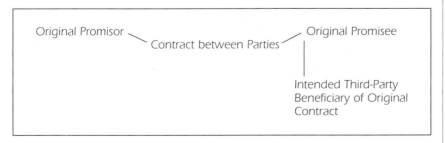

FIGURE 10-1 Third-party intended beneficiary relationship

TERMS

third-party beneficiary contract
  A contract made for the benefit of a third person.
beneficiary
  1. A person who receives a benefit. . . .
  4. A person who is entitled to the proceeds of a life insurance policy when the insured dies.

Donee Beneficiary

A type of intended beneficiary is a **donee beneficiary**. In this circumstance, a promisee makes a gift to the third-party **donee**, who will benefit in some way from the contractual relationship between the original promisor and promisee.

The most common donee beneficiary situation involves life insurance policies. One person agrees to purchase insurance on his or her own life, or the life of another person, and names a third person as beneficiary. If the insured person dies, the beneficiary receives the proceeds of the life insurance policy. The promisor is the insurance company and the promisee is the insured, who may be a spouse, for example. The survivor, often a spouse, is the intended donee beneficiary. As this situation suggests, in a donee beneficiary situation, the benefit flowing from the contract is a gift. Consequently, a person may choose to change the intended beneficiary without obtaining the agreement of that intended beneficiary. This is often done using a change of beneficiary form provided by the insurance company. Figure 10-2 is a sample change of beneficiary form.

Election of Change of Beneficiary of Life Insurance Policy

In accordance with the provisions of Policy No. _____, I hereby elect to change the beneficiary as follows:

_____
(Name)   (Date of Birth)   (Relationship to Insured)

_____
(Name)   (Date of Birth)   (Relationship to Insured)

_____
(Name)   (Date of Birth)   (Relationship to Insured)

I request that this change be endorsed on the policy. By this election I hereby revoke all other and former designations. I make this election subject to all of the conditions and provisions of said policy as well as any existing assignment and, unless otherwise provided by me in this application for change of beneficiary, I expressly reserve the full and absolute right to make other and further changes at any time I may elect. It is understood and agreed that all decisions upon questions of fact in determining any unnamed beneficiaries herein designated, made by the Company in good faith, based on proof by affidavit or other written evidence satisfactory to it, shall be conclusive and fully protect the Company in acting in reliance thereon.

I represent and certify that no insolvency or bankruptcy proceedings are now pending against me.

Upon endorsement of the change of beneficiary as above requested, the policy should be returned to (name of insurance company) at (address).

It Witness Whereof, I have hereunto set may hand and seal, this _____ day of _____, 19____.

_____
Owner of Policy

_____
Acknowledgment or Witness

FIGURE 10-2 Sample change of beneficiary form

One issue that often arises is whether the donee beneficiary has a right under the contract to the benefits, once promised. If the beneficiary has a vested right in the contract, the designation of beneficiary may be irrevocable unless the beneficiary consents to any changes in the contractual arrangement. Whether the donee beneficiary has a vested interest in the contract is determined by a court.

Creditor Beneficiary

A **creditor beneficiary** is a third party to whom the promisee owes a legal duty and obligation. This relationship often arises out of a debt. The creditor beneficiary benefits from a contractual arrangement between the promisor and promisee, whereby the promisee will pay the third-party creditor beneficiary an amount due and owing by the promisor. In this situation, the creditor beneficiary has the right to enforce the original contract in the event of a breach. Review *Galvan v. Jackson Park Hospital,* 187 Ill. App. 3d 774, 543 N.E. 2d 822 (1989), which distinguished between a donee beneficiary and a creditor beneficiary.

TERMS

donee beneficiary
Same as third-party beneficiary. The benefit a donee beneficiary receives from the contract between two other persons is a gift.

donee
A person to whom a gift is made.

creditor beneficiary
A creditor who is the beneficiary of a contract made between the debtor and a third person.

GALVAN v. JACKSON PARK HOSPITAL
Appellate court of Illinois
Aug. 17, 1989

Justice JOHNSON

William T. Galvan, Sr. was admitted to Jackson Park Hospital on January 16, 1981, for medical and psychiatric treatment. Dr. Dayon, defendant, was Galvan's treating physician. Several days after Galvan was admitted, he attempted to hang himself. The attempted suicide rendered Galvan comatose until his death on April 17, 1982.

Prior to Galvan's death, plaintiffs had begun negotiations with Jackson Park Hospital to dispose of all claims plaintiffs may have against the hospital and its various affiliates and employees including, arguably, defendants, for the attempted suicide. As part of the proposed agreement the hospital was to pay $675,000 to Galvan's estate to cover expenses that were not reimbursed for Galvan's medical and convalescent care and to oversee such care for the remainder of his natural life.

In consideration of these undertakings the guardians were to "release and forever discharge any and all persons and entities, including but not limited to [Jackson Park Hospital], its affiliated doctors, directors, officers, employees, agents, assigns, successors, subsidiaries and affiliates, from any and all manner of action, cause and causes of action, claims and demands, whatsoever, in law or equity, which they now have or hereafter can, or shall have whatsoever."Galvan's ex-wife and sons declared in the agreement that they "release[d] and forever discharge[d] any and all persons and entities including but not limited to [Jackson Park Hospital], its affiliated doctors, directors, officers, employees, agents, assigns, successors, subsidiaries and affiliates of and from any and all claims." On March 12, 1982, the guardians, Galvan's ex-wife, and his sons signed the release. The release was then delivered to the hospital's legal representatives for signature on March 15, 1982. Galvan died on April 17, 1982. The release was never signed by the hospital. On May 17, 1982, one of the hospital's representatives informed plaintiff's attorney that the settlement offer of $675,000 was withdrawn. Notwithstanding the withdrawal of the offer, plaintiffs' attorney proceeded to probate court to present the proposed release and settlement for court approval of its terms.

The first issue presented for review is whether defendants as third-party beneficiaries had enforceable rights to an agreement that was subsequently breached. We find that a donee beneficiary has no vested interest in an agreement that was subsequently breached or repudiated when the $675,000 settlement monies were not paid.

A donee beneficiary, as distinguished from a creditor beneficiary, is a third party to whom the benefit comes without cost, such as a donation or gift. A creditor beneficiary is a third party to whom a preexisting duty or liability is owed. Defendants' counsel admitted at oral argument that defendants would be categorized as donee beneficiaries. We agree. Further, "[w]here the donee beneficiary's right is contingent upon the occurrence of certain events, [such right] does not vest until the occurrence of these events." A creditor beneficiary's rights vest at the time the contract is executed. Since defendants' rights, as donee beneficiaries, were contingent upon the hospital's performance, which never occurred, defendants' rights never vested.

It will not be necessary to address the second issue raised as we find that, as donee beneficiaries, defendants acquired no vested rights in the 1982 settlement agreement which would allow defendants to preclude the parties from entering into the subsequent covenant. The rights of a third party beneficiary, prior to vesting, may be altered, rescinded, or revoked by the parties to the agreement.

For the foregoing reasons, the orders of the circuit court are reversed and remanded.

QUESTIONS FOR ANALYSIS

What are the facts of *Galvan*? What distinguishes a creditor beneficiary from a donee beneficiary? How did the court hold? Were the results just? Explain your answer.

Incidental Beneficiary

A party who will benefit only indirectly from a contract is an **incidental beneficiary**. The benefit conferred is not intentional. Therefore, this beneficiary has no rights of enforcement against either the promisor or promisee to the original contract. *Baldwin v. Leach,* 115 Idaho 713, 769 P.2d 590 (Ct. App. 1989), sets out the distinction between incidental and intended beneficiaries.

BALDWIN v. LEACH

Court of Appeals of Idaho
Feb. 16, 1989

BURNETT, Judge.

In 1974, the Baldwins, the Leaches, and another married couple formed a corporation known as 5MM, Inc. The corporation operated the "Main and Fifth" grocery market in Boise. In 1980, the Baldwins withdrew from the business and entered into an agreement for the corporation to redeem their stock at a total price of $85,000. The money was paid through Idaho First National Bank, an escrow holder, in installments of $919.40 per month. In 1981, the Leaches also withdrew and—although the record is not clear—they apparently relinquished their stock. The corporation owed the Leaches approximately $75,000 for cash advanced at the time of their withdrawal.

After the withdrawal of the Baldwins and Leaches, the remaining officers and shareholders of the corporation transferred its real property to a partnership known as G-P Properties. Upon learning of this transfer, the Baldwins and Leaches filed separate lawsuits asserting that the corporation was indebted to them and seeking to have the transfer set aside as a fraudulent conveyance. This led to a series of negotiations among all the interested parties. At the conclusion of these negotiations the lawsuits were dropped, the corporation's real property was transferred to the Leaches in satisfaction of the debt owed to them, and the corporation agreed to lease certain personal property to the Leaches. The lease instrument also contained an assignment to the Baldwins of the corporation's right to $919.40 from each rental payment. Thus, the assignment was equal to the installments of $919.40 per month which the Baldwins formerly had been receiving under the redemption agreement. The Baldwins gave notice of this assignment to potential creditors or other interested parties by filing a UCC-1 form with the Ada County Recorder.

The Leaches made the assigned payments, which were directed to the Baldwins' escrow account, for about a year and a half. At the time the corporation and Mr. Leach executed an "addendum" to the lease, transferring ownership of the leased property from the corporation to the Leaches. Consequently, the Leaches owned outright the real and personal property that once belonged to the corporation. The corporation subsequently was dissolved. Although the Leaches were no longer leasing from the corporation, they continued for some time to make monthly payments of $919.40 to the escrow holder. This practice ceased in December, 1985.

On appeal the Leaches have argued that the Baldwins were not third party beneficiaries but were merely creditors with a security interest in the lease payments. This argument presents a mixed issue of fact and law.

Under Idaho law, if a party can demonstrate that a contract was made expressly for his benefit, he may enforce that contract, at any time prior to rescission, as a third party beneficiary. The test for determining a party's status as a third party beneficiary, is whether the transaction reflects an intent to benefit the party. The party must show that the contract was made for his direct benefit and that he is not merely an incidental beneficiary.

Here, the district court noted that the lease was a product of multi-party negotiations resulting, in part, from the Baldwins' suit alleging a fraudulent conveyance. The court further noted that the lease contained the assignment of payments to the Baldwins, and that the lease required the Leaches to continue making payments even if the corporation failed to do so. Accordingly, the court determined that although the lease contained some references to the Baldwins as secured parties, the transaction was intended to benefit the Baldwins directly. We hold that the district court properly applied the law to the facts in concluding the Baldwins were third party beneficiaries.

It has long been held that after a contract for the benefit of a third person has been accepted or acted upon by that person, it cannot be rescinded without his consent.

In the case at hand, the Baldwins arguably accepted and relied upon their rights under the lease. However, we need only discuss their acceptance. The Baldwins manifested such acceptance by recording the UCC-1 financing statement, giving notice of their right to the assigned lease payments. Thereafter, they received and retained such payments for nearly two years. Finally, they filed this suit to enforce the lease when the monthly payments ceased. We hold, upon these undisputed facts, that the Baldwins accepted the contract. Accordingly, we conclude that the rescission was invalid and that the Baldwins were entitled to enforce the lease.

The district court's judgment is affirmed.

QUESTIONS FOR ANALYSIS

Identify the issue that was before the court. What is the test for determining third-party beneficiary status? What was the court's decision in *Baldwin*?

10.2 THE PRIVITY PROBLEM

TERMS

incidental beneficiary
A person to whom the benefits of a contract between two other people accrue merely as a matter of happenstance. An incidental beneficiary may not sue to enforce such a contract.

A promisor and a promisee are in a direct contractual relationship known as **privity**. Under traditional notions of contract law, only those parties who had a direct relationship could sue when a breach or other legal problem arose. The issue of privity thus is raised when the right of a third-party beneficiary is violated. Could the third party sue the promisor, even if the third party was not in privity? Case decisions have answered this question in the affirmative and have allowed third-party beneficiaries to sue in their own right. See Figure 10-3 for a diagram of privity in contracts. Review *Galie v. Ram Associates Management Services, Inc.* 757 P.2d 176 (Colo. Ct. App. 1988), in which privity was the issue in a third-party beneficiary situation.

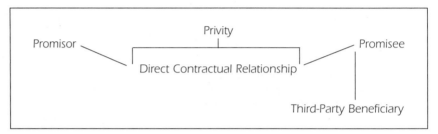

FIGURE 10-3 Privity relationships

GALIE v. RAM ASSOCIATES MANAGEMENT SERVICES, INC.

Colorado Court of Appeals
May 19, 1988

PIERCE, Judge.

Plaintiff, Thomas Galie, appeals the judgment of the trial court granting a motion for directed verdict in favor of defendants, RAM Associates Management Services Inc. (RAM), P.J. Collins (Collins), and Larry Bear (Bear). We reverse and remand.

Plaintiff entered into an agreement with Business Buyers of Colorado (BBC), wherein BBC agreed to arrange for the purchase of a business. BBC also agreed to obtain financing for plaintiff in order to facilitate the acquisition. BBC then hired RAM to obtain the financing for plaintiff's business.

RAM located Levine Family Holds, Inc., d/b/a Jesse C. Levine and Company (Levine). Levine agreed to provide the financing for plaintiff's acquisition. Thereafter, Collins, president of RAM, informed Bear, president of BBC, that the financing had been obtained and the money would be available within 60 days. This information was communicated by BBC to plaintiff.

After Levine failed to provide the financing, plaintiff brought this action against Levine, BBC, and RAM. Plaintiff also sought damages against Collins and Bear, in their individual capacity, complaining that expenses had been incurred in reliance upon the promises that financing had been obtained. Default judgment eventually was entered against Levine and BBC.

Plaintiff contends that the trial court improperly dismissed his claim for negligent misrepresentation against RAM. Specifically, plaintiff claims error in the trial court's holding that because there was no privity between RAM and plaintiff, the claim could not succeed. We agree that this was error. We also agree with plaintiff that the trial court erred in concluding that he could not prevail on his breach of contract claim against RAM because there was no privity of contract. " '[O]ne may enforce a contractual obligation made for his benefit although he was not a party to the agreement.' " There is no requirement that privity of contract exist in order to prevail on a third-party beneficiary claim.

In this case, the trial court dismissed plaintiff's claim upon an incorrect legal conclusion. Therefore, because the court did not address any of the factual issues concerning RAM's alleged breach of the contract, we must remand that claim for further proceedings.

QUESTIONS FOR ANALYSIS

What facts were important to the court's decision? Was privity a requisite on a third-party beneficiary contract? What was the court's reasoning?

10.3   DISTINGUISHING BETWEEN ASSIGNMENTS AND DELEGATIONS

When third parties agree to accept rights and obligations under a contract, another type of third-party relationship is involved. This relationship may be either an **assignment**, which is a present transfer of a contract right; or a **delegation**, which is the transfer of a contract duty. Under either an assignment or a delegation, the contract has already been created, and rights or obligations are transferred after the contract is executed.

In understanding assignments and delegations, some critical distinctions must be made. First, an assignment transfers *rights,* whereas a delegation transfers *duties*. This is significant because duties cannot be assigned. Second, rights are personal and are those which one ought to have or receive from another person, whereas duties are something that are owed to another person. They are not personal and can be freely delegated. Finally, assignments may extinguish the assignor's rights, whereas delegation of duties does not completely remove the liability of the original party to a contract.

10.4   ASSIGNMENTS

An assignment is a transfer of a contractual right to a third party. The individual who is making the transfer is known as the **assignor** and the person who is receiving the contractual right transferred is known as the **assignee**. Upon completion of the assignment, the assignee acquires the rights the assignor had. All performance required from the assignor under the contract is now the responsibility of the assignee.

Assignments commonly arise in lease situations. For example, Mr. Turner is a landlord who leases his house to Ms. Peterson, a tenant. The rental is for one year at $500 a month, payable on the first of each month.

privity
An identity of interest between persons, so that the legal interest of one person is measured by the same legal right as the other; continuity of interest; successive relationships to the same rights of property.

assignment
1. A transfer of property, or a right in property, from one person to another. 2. A designation or appointment.

delegation
The act of conferring authority upon, or transferring it to, another.

assignor
A person who assigns a right.

assignee
A person to whom a right is assigned.

"I've reassigned my homework to Holmes."

After six months, Ms. Peterson gets a new job and moves out of town. She does not want to breach the lease, so she transfers her rights under the lease to her friend, Ms. Stewart. Now Ms. Stewart, who is the assignee, has all the responsibilities under the lease including the obligation to pay the rent. Ordinarily, the formal lease agreement between the parties contains a provision dealing with assignments. Some typical types of assignment provisions are shown in Figure 10-4.

Assignment

1. Sam Connor shall have the right to sell, assign, and transfer this agreement with all his right, title, and interest herein to any person, firm, or corporation at any time during the term of this agreement, and any such assignee shall acquire the rights and assume all of the obligations of Sam Connor under this agreement.

2. This agreement may be assigned by Sam Connor only upon condition that he give Michael Old notice of such assignment in writing by personal service or registered mail to Michael Old.

Conditional Assignment

The duties and obligations of performance under this agreement may be assigned by Michael Old provided that the assignee shall be capable of performing such duties and obligations in a manner satisfactory to Sam Connor.

Assignment to Corporation

In the event that Sam Connor desires to conduct business as a corporation, Michael Old shall, upon Sam Connor's compliance with such requirements as may from time to time be prescribed by Michael Old, consent to an assignment of this agreement to such corporation.

FIGURE 10-4 Sample assignment provisions

Notice that in these provisions, no specific language is used for the assignment. What is important in vesting the rights to the assignee is that the assignor indicate a present intent to vest the rights and to transfer those contractual obligations to the assignee. Although a writing is not a requirement for an assignment, unless it comes under the Statute of Frauds, the assignment should indicate the rights to be assigned and transferred, to avoid any confusion between the parties. This formally memorializes the transfer of rights.

Although consideration is not required to perfect an assignment, in most business contexts consideration is present between the parties. This helps ensure the validity of the assignment. Figure 10-5 is a diagram of an assignment.

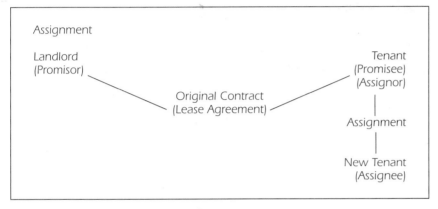

FIGURE 10-5 Assignment relationships

Perfecting the Assignment

There are no specific requirements necessary to perfect an assignment. However, it is good business practice to give notice of any assignment to the original promisor in the contract. This preserves the assignee's rights under the transfer from the assignor. Notice is appropriate because usually the original promisor to the contract now has to tender performance to or receive performance from a different party. If notice is not given to the original promisor, the required performance may still be tendered to the assignor (the original promisee); this may make the assignor liable to the assignee. But if the original promisor does not have notice of the transfer, the original promisor will not be held responsible for any legal injury to the assignee. Consequently, it is a good idea to formalize any transfer or assignments of rights and obligations by a notice of assignment to affected parties.

In addition, problems often arise when notice is not properly given and the assignor attempts to assign its rights twice. In effect, the assignor is improperly benefiting twice from the assignment. Courts can follow two approaches to determine who can recover when a subsequent assignment is made by the assignor. Most states follow the rule that the first person to receive the assignment has superior rights over any later assignee, even after notice is given to the original party to the contract. This is known as the *American Rule* and generally produces fair results. In a minority of states, the rule is that the assignee who first gives notice of the assignment to the original promisor has a superior right, even over those who claim prior benefits. This is known as the *English Rule* and often produces unfair results. Check your state for the rule followed.

When an assignment is completed, the assignee assumes the position of the original party to the contract, with all the rights, duties, and benefits of the contract as well as the obligations. In effect, the assignee is now substituted for the original party to the contract, and is treated as though he or she was the original contracting party.

Assumption of Rights and Obligations Under an Assignment

The assignor warrants to the assignee that the assignor has a valid legal right to transfer the right assigned and that no valid defenses can be raised against that assigned right. In return, the assignee warrants that it will perform as required under the original contract and will do so in a complete and satisfactory manner. These **warranties** are both **express** and **implied** and protect the parties to the contract and the assignment. If either party to the assignment breaches any obligation, the injured party may sue.

10.5 NONASSIGNABLE CONTRACT RIGHTS

An assignment is not an unbridled contract right that can go unchecked or unchallenged by the original parties to the contract. *Restatement (Second)* § 317(2) suggests when contract rights cannot be assigned:

(2) A contractual right can be assigned unless
   (a) the substitution of a right of the assignee for the right of the assignor would materially change the duty of the obligor, or materially increase the burden or risk imposed on him by his contract, or materially impair his chance of obtaining return performance, or materially reduce its value to him, or
   (b) the assignment is forbidden by statute or is otherwise inoperative on grounds of public policy, or
   (c) assignment is validly precluded by contract.

Contracts often attempt to limit the right of assignment. Clauses such as "no assignment shall be made," or "no assignments shall be made without the prior written consent of the promisor," are representative of wording parties may draft to prohibit or limit assignment. Sometimes parties to a contract use language that tries to void *any* assignment, with phrases such as "all assignments made under this contract shall be void" or "any attempt by any party to this contract to assign any rights and duties shall be hence further null and void," thus limiting the parties' right to transfer. However, courts narrowly interpret these provisions to prohibit assignments and often allow assignments even when they violate a contractual provision. Courts view the provision as a promise not to assign, but not as a prohibition against it. Apparently, no language will absolutely prevent assignments. However, Figure 10-6 provides some suggested language.

Covenant Not to Assign

It is agreed by the parties that there will be no assignment or transfer of this contract, nor of any interest in this contract.

Assignment—Notice by Registered Mail

This agreement and the payments to be made hereunder may be assigned by Sam Connor, on condition, however, that such party gives notice in writing by registered mail to Michael Old.

Nonassignability Clause—General Provision

This agreement shall not be assigned by either party without the prior written consent of the other party.

Assignment—Consent to Assignment of Pecuniary Interest

This agreement shall not be assignable without the consent of both parties; but this provision shall not prevent either party from selling, assigning, or transferring a pecuniary interest in any specific property acquired pursuant to this agreement.

FIGURE 10-6 Sample language prohibiting assignments

When assignments do not require notice or approval by the parties to a contract, a party may challenge an assignment on the ground that there will be either a material change of a duty and obligation under the contract or an increased burden on the party who is required to perform under the contract. Courts look closely at these arguments, but usually uphold the assignments. If the contract involves a unique duty and is substantially different from the original agreement, the court will not enforce the assignment. However, if the rights involved are not unique and assignment will not impair the performance of the parties, the court will usually enforce the assignment even over the objections of one of the original parties to the contract.

There are exceptions to assignment where the duties are personal or professional in nature. When the person involved has been hired specifically because of talent, expertise, or profession, assignment often is not permitted. Persons such as actors, artists, attorneys, and physicians fall under this category. Such persons are selected because of their special attributes, and assigning those duties to someone else generally violates the spirit of the contract. If the service required can be performed by anybody in a particular trade, a court will allow the assignment of a personal professional service contract. A court will analyze this on a case-by-case basis. *Evening News*

TERMS

warranty
Generally, an agreement to be responsible for all damages arising from the falsity of a statement or the failure of an assurance.

express
Stated; declared; clear; explicit; not left to implication.

implied
Something intended although not expressed, or not expressed in words.

Association v. Peterson, 477 F. Supp. 77 (D.D.C. 1979), illustrates how an assignment of a personal services contract was questioned.

EVENING NEWS ASSOCIATION v. PETERSON

United States District Court, District of Columbia
Sept. 7, 1979

BARRINGTON D. PARKER, District Judge:

The question presented in this litigation is whether a contract of employment between an employee and the owner and licensee of a television station, providing for the employee's services as a newscaster-anchorman, was assigned when the station was sold and acquired by a new owner and licensee.

The defendant was employed by Post-Newsweek Stations, Inc. from 1969 to 1978. During that period he negotiated several employment contracts. Post-Newsweek had a license to operate television station WTOP-TV (Channel 9) in the District of Columbia. In June of 1978, following approval by the Federal Communications Commission, Post-Newsweek sold its operating license to Evening News and Channel 9 was then designated WDVM-TV. A June 26, 1978, Bill of Sale and Assignment and Instrument of Assumption and Indemnity between the two provided in pertinent part:

> PNS has granted, bargained, sold, conveyed and assigned to ENA, . . . all the property of PNS . . . including, . . . all right, title and interest, legal or equitable, of PNS in, to and under all agreements, contracts and commitments listed in Schedule A hereto.

When Evening News acquired the station, Peterson's Post-Newsweek employment contract, dated July 1, 1977, was included in the Bill of Sale and Assignment. The contract was for a three-year term ending June 30, 1980, and could be extended for two additional one-year terms, at the option of Post-Newsweek. As compensation the defendant was to receive a designated salary which increased each year from 1977 through the fifth (option) year. Post-Newsweek was also obligated to provide additional benefits.

There was no express provision in the 1977 contract concerning its assignability or nonassignability. However, it contained the following integration clause:

> This agreement contains the entire understanding of the parties . . . and this agreement cannot be altered or modified except in a writing signed by both parties.

The defendant's duties, obligations and performance under the 1977 contract did not change in any significant way after the Evening News' acquisition. In addition, the Evening News met all of its required contract obligations to the defendant and its performance after acquisition in June, 1978, was not materially different from that of Post-Newsweek. According to Mr. Peterson, the close relationship and rapport which existed between him and them was an important factor as he viewed the contract; these relationships made the contract in his view nonassignable and indeed their absence at the Evening News prevented defendant from contributing his full efforts. Even if Mr. Peterson's contentions are accepted, it should be noted that he contracted with the Post-Newsweek corporation and not with the News Director and Executive Producer of that corporation. The Court cannot find that Peterson contracted with Post-Newsweek in 1977 to work with particular individuals or because of a special policy-making role he had been selected to perform in the newsroom. Finally, the Court does not find that Post-Newsweek contracted with Peterson because of any peculiarly unique qualities or because of a relationship of personal confidence with him.

In summary, the Court finds that the performance required of Mr. Peterson under the 1977 contract was (1) not based upon a personal relationship or one of special confidence between him and Post-Newsweek or its employees, and (2) was not changed in any material way by the assignment to the Evening News.

The distinction between the assignment of a right to receive services and the obligation to provide them is critical in this proceeding. This is so because duties under a personal services contract involving special skill or ability are generally not delegable by the one obligated to perform, absent the consent of the other party. The issue, however, is not whether the personal services Peterson is to perform are delegable but whether Post-Newsweek's right to receive them is assignable.

Contract rights as a general rule are assignable. This rule, however, is subject to exception where the assignment would vary materially the duty of the obligor, increase materially the burden of risk imposed by the contract, or impair materially the obligor's chance of obtaining return performance. There has been no showing, however, that the services required of Peterson by the Post-Newsweek contract have changed in any material way since the Evening News entered the picture. Both before and after, he anchored the same news programs. Similarly he has had essentially the same number of special assignments since the transfer as before. Any additional policy-making role that he formerly enjoyed and is now denied was neither a condition of his contract nor factually supported by other than his own subjective testimony.

The general rule of assignability is also subject to exception where the contract calls for the rendition of personal services based on a relationship of confidence between the parties. In almost all cases where a "contract" is said to be non-assignable because it is "personal," what is meant is not that the contractor's right is not assignable, but that the performance required by his duty is a personal performance and that an attempt to perform by a substituted person would not discharge the contractor's duty.

Given the silence of the contract on assignability, its merger clause, and the usual rule that contract rights are assignable, the Court cannot but conclude on the facts of this case that defendant's contract was assignable. Defendant's employer was a corporation, and it was for Post-Newsweek Stations, Inc. that he contracted to perform. The corporation's duties under the contract did not involve the rendition of personal services to defendant; essentially they were to compensate him.

Plaintiff's argument that defendant has waived any objection to the assignment by accepting the contract benefits and continuing to perform for the Evening News for over a year has perhaps some merit. If defendant has doubts about assignability, he should have voiced them when he learned of the planned transfer or at least at the time of transfer. His continued performance without reservation followed by the unanticipated tender of his resignation did disadvantage Evening News in terms of finding a possible replacement for him and possibly in lost revenues. The court, however, concludes that the contract was assignable in the first instance and thus it is not necessary to determine whether defendant's continued performance constitutes a waiver of objection to the assignment.

QUESTIONS FOR ANALYSIS

What are the facts of the *Peterson* case? Did the court find a valid assignment? Why or why not? What was the court's holding?

10.6   DELEGATION IN CONTRACTS

Assignments and delegations are different. An assignment involves rights, whereas a delegation involves duties. Under a delegation, the original promisor finds a new promisor or a substitute to perform the original duties under the contract. The *delegator* is the original promisor and the *delegatee* is the new promisor, the person who will perform the delegated duties. Figure 10-7 illustrates a delegation.

FIGURE 10-7 Delegation relationships

For a delegation to occur, the duty cannot be unique and it must be one that is assumed by the delegatee. The *Restatement (Second)* sets out a position on delegations in § 318:

> (1) An obligor can properly delegate the performance of his duty to another unless the delegation is contrary to public policy or the terms of his promise.
>
> (2) Unless otherwise agreed, a promise requires performance by a particular person only to the extent that the obligee has a substantial interest in having that person perform or control the acts promised.
>
> (3) Unless the obligee agrees otherwise, neither delegation of performance nor a contract to assume the duty made with the obligor by the person delegated discharges any duty or liability of the delegating obligor.

As with assignments, delegations may be prohibited contractually. The contracting parties may state that "there shall be no delegations under this contract and any delegations attempted under this contract shall be void." Courts normally enforce this type of provision in a contract.

Delegations have different legal ramifications than assignments. Unlike an assignment, the delegator of a duty remains liable on the original contract. In fact, if a delegator denies that the obligation to perform exists, this denial may constitute a repudiation of the contract for which the delegator can be sued. Therefore, in a delegation, the delegator is not relieved of liability under the original contract.

As with assignments, certain types of duties are not delegable. When specific skills or talents of a particular party are involved, these duties are not delegable. Examples of such duties are those of an attorney, artist, dancer or actor. The skills or talents of the persons in this example are unique, and delegating a duty would be a burden to the original promisee.

However, if the skill contracted for is not particularized or unique, the duty may be delegated even over the objection of the original promisor. Assume that you are a house painter and you have been hired to paint the

Mitchell house. On the day you are to paint the Mitchell house, you are also scheduled to paint the McGee house, so you delegate your contract to another house painter. In this case, the delegation would probably be valid. However, if you hired a famous artist to paint your portrait, and he or she attempted to delegate that duty to an unknown painter, the delegation would probably be prohibited.

When issues arise as to whether a duty is delegable, the court looks to see how personalized the duty is. If the performance is too personalized or unique, the party to whom performance is to be rendered can refuse to accept performance from the delegatee and may hold the original party liable. But if the recipient of performance takes a wait-and-see approach when the performance is delegated, the right to object may be cut off. Here silence may imply assent and thus waive the right to enforce performance against the delegator.

An assignment and a delegation may occur simultaneously. A party can assign rights and the recipient of those rights can also assume the duties under the contract. The presumption in the law is that when there is an assignment, there is usually an implied delegation as well. Unless there is a clear intention to the contrary, the assumption will be that if an assignment occurs, the delegation is implied. This is the position set out in *Restatement (Second)* § 318. Figure 10-8 is an example of assignment and delegation language.

No assignment of this agreement or of any duty or obligation of performance hereunder shall be made in whole or in part by Sam Conner without the prior written consent of Michael Old.

FIGURE 10-8 Sample assignment and delegation language

Review *Buckeye Ag-Center, Inc. v. Babchuk,* 533 N.E.2d 179 (Ind. Ct. App. 1989), in which a delegation was challenged. Determine if the court's decision was equitable and focus on analysis of the court's reasoning.

BUCKEYE AG-CENTER, INC. v. BABCHUK
Court of Appeals of Indiana
Jan. 30, 1989

HOFFMAN, Judge.

The facts indicate that on December 9, 1985, B & H Poultry entered into a sales contract with Central Soya. B & H Poultry agreed to buy 30,000 bushels of #2 yellow corn between October 15, 1986 and November 15, 1986 at $2.29 per bushel from Central Soya's Winamac facility.

On August 15, 1986 Buckeye Ag-Center acquired Central Soya's Winamac facility. Central Soya delegated the contractual duties of the facility to Buckeye Ag-Center. B & H Poultry refused to honor the sales contract because delegation of the sellers' contractual duty was made without B & H Poultry's consent. Buckeye Ag-Center brought suit for damages caused by the repudiation of the sales contract. The trial court granted summary judgment in favor of B & H Poultry. The trial court ruled that B & H Poultry had a substantial interest in not being required to do business with Buckeye Ag-Center.

Buckeye Ag-Center argues that the trial court misapplied [state law] which states:

> "A party may perform his duty through a delegate unless otherwise agreed or unless the other party has a substantial interest in having his original promisor perform or control the acts required by the contract. No delegation of performance relieves the party delegating of any duty to perform or any liability for breach."

The general rule is that absent a provision to the contrary a party may delegate its duties under a contract. An exception is made if the duty is of a personal nature and performance by an assignee would vary materially from performance by the obligor. The test is whether performance by the original obligor has been bargained for and is of the essence of the contract. If the contract is premised on a personal relationship, unique skill or discretion, the duty is not delegable.

In the present case, the parties bargained for the sale of #2 yellow corn. The seller's contractual duty did not involve a personal relationship, unique skill or discretion. The seller's contractual duty to supply a quantity of #2 yellow corn was delegable without the consent of the buyer. The trial court erred in granting summary judgment in favor of B & H Poultry.

QUESTIONS FOR ANALYSIS

Identify the facts of the *Buckeye* case. Was the duty delegable? Explain your answer. What is the basis of the court's decision?

10.7 NOVATION DISTINGUISHED

Another type of third-party contract (discussed in Chapter 8) is a **novation**, a substitution of a new contract for an old one. Three parties are involved in this situation. As you will recall, you have the two original parties to the contract—the promisor and the promisee—and now a new third party who is going to contract with the original promisor. The parties are agreeing to replace the original contract with a new one, invalidating the prior contract and, in effect, releasing the original promisee.

There are significant differences between a novation and an assignment or delegation. In a novation, all parties must mutually agree to the new contract, because the novation releases the prior parties from their obligations, whereas an assignment or delegation does not. In an assignment or delegation, the rights and obligations are exact, where the assignee (delegatee) is replacing the assignor (delegator) as the primary party responsible on the contract. In a novation, a new contract with differing terms may exist, with new rights and responsibilities.

To determine whether a delegation can be a novation, review *Brooks v. Hayes,* 133 Wis. 2d 228, 395 N.W.2d 167 (1986), where the court had to distinguish between a delegation and a novation.

TERMS

novation
The extinguishment of one obligation by another; a substituted contract that dissolves a previous contractual duty and creates a new one. Novation, which requires the mutual agreement of everyone concerned, replaces a contracting party with a new party who had no rights or obligations under the previous contract.

BROOKS v. HAYES
Supreme Court of Wisconsin
Oct. 29, 1986

SHIRLEY S. ABRAHAMSON, Justice.

The issue is whether a general contractor who hires an independent contractor to perform services under the general contractor's agreement with a landowner to "provide all necessary labor and materials and perform all work of every nature whatsoever to be done in the erection of a residence" is liable to the landowners for damage to their property caused by the independent contractor's negligent construction. We hold that a general contractor who has a contractual duty of due care in performing the construction contract may be liable to the owner for damages when an independent contractor hired by the general contractor negligently performs under the construction contract and causes property damage to the owner.

In May of 1978, John and Judith Brooks, hereafter plaintiff-owners, contracted with Wayne Hayes, doing business as Wayne Hayes Real Estate, to construct a Windsor Home, a "package, predesigned, precut" home, on a lot they owned. While Hayes was primarily a real estate broker, he also sold Windsor Homes.

The construction contract required Hayes to "provide all necessary labor and materials and perform all work of every nature whatsoever to be done in the erection of a residence for" the plaintiff-owners. The circuit court found that the plaintiff-owners and Hayes contemplated that subcontractors hired by Hayes would perform much of the home construction work and Hayes would not control the method of construction. The circuit court further found that Hayes had no personal experience in construction.

During construction, the plaintiff-owners requested that a "heatilator" be installed as "an extra" to increase the efficiency of the fireplace. Claude Marr, who had been hired by Hayes to do the masonry work, including the fireplace, installed the heatilator.

The plaintiff-owners moved into the house in the winter of 1978. When the plaintiff-owners used

the fireplace they smelled smoke in areas of the house remote from the fireplace. In response to their complaints, Maasz of Hayes Realty inspected the fireplace system, once with Marr and once with a different mason. The plaintiff-owners also hired a mason to inspect the fireplace system. None of these three masons could detect the cause of the problem.

The plaintiff-owners used the fireplace with some frequency until November 1, 1980, when a fire in the home caused structural damage around the fireplace and smoke damage both to the house and to personal belongings, including clothes and furniture. The circuit court found, and the parties do not dispute this finding, that the mason's negligence in installing the heatilator caused the fire.

The plaintiff-owners contend that although the construction contract was silent with regard to the level of performance or standard of care required by Hayes or the subcontractors, the contract implicitly imposes on Hayes the duty to perform with due care. We agree with the plaintiff-owners' interpretation of the contract and, for purposes of this review, Hayes has not disputed this interpretation of the construction contract. Accompanying every contract is a common-law duty to perform with care, skill, reasonable expediency and faithfulness the thing they agreed to be done, and a negligent failure to observe any of these conditions is a tort, as well as a breach of contract.

Although Hayes assumed a contractual duty to the plaintiff-owners to perform the construction contract with skill and due care, Hayes delegated the performance of the contract to others. The question then is whether the delegation of performance of the masonry work relieved Hayes of liability for breach of contract when the mason, an independent contractor, negligently performed that part of Hayes' contractual obligation.

The plaintiff-owners assert that Hayes may not avoid responsibility to them for his failure to perform his contractual duty of due care merely by hiring an independent contractor. We agree with this assertion. The hornbook principle of contract law is that the delegation of the performance of a contract does not, unless the obligee agrees otherwise, discharge the liability of the delegating obligor to the obligee for breach of contract.

[A] general contractor is liable to the owner for breach of the contractual duty of due care when an independent contractor negligently performs the general contractor's work under the contract. Hayes has confused delegation of the performance of an obligation with delegation of responsibility for the performance of an obligation. The rule for delegation of the performance of a contractual obligation is that the obligor may delegate a contractual duty without the obligee's consent unless the duty is "personal." The rule for delegation of responsibility is that if the obligor delegates the performance of an obligation, the obligor is not relieved of responsibility for fulfilling that obligation or of liability in the event of a breach. The obligor under the contract is treated as having rendered the performance even when an independent contractor has rendered it, and the obligor

remains the party liable for that performance if the performance proves to be in breach of the contract.

Where the obligee consents to the delegation, the consent itself does not release the obligor from liability for breach of contract. More than the obligee's consent to a delegation of performance is needed to release the obligor from liability for breach of contract. For the obligor to be released from liability, the obligee must agree to the release. If there is an agreement between the obligor, obligee and a third party by which the third party agrees to be substituted for the obligor and the obligee assents thereto, the obligor is released from liability and the third person takes the place of the obligor. Such an agreement is known as a novation.

If Hayes is asserting that he and the plaintiff-owners modified the contract to release Hayes from liability for the performance of the independent contractor or that there was a novation by which he, the plaintiff-owners and the mason agreed to substitute the mason as obligor in place of Hayes, the circuit court made no such findings. This court cannot make such findings on this record.

QUESTIONS FOR ANALYSIS

What is the *Brooks* court's position on the liability of the original delagator (obligor)? When is a delegation prohibited? Distinguish between a delegation and novation. What is the court's holding?

10.8 PRACTICAL APPLICATION

Drafting is important in creating an effective assignment or delegation clause. A number of examples have already been set forth in this chapter. However, a paralegal may be asked to draft an assignment with the corresponding acceptance of assignment. To assist the paralegal in this task, Figure 10-9 gives some guidance.

Assignment

(1) For $10.00, I hereby assign to Andrew Marcus all my right, title, and interest in and to the contract dated September 15, 1995, between Albert Charles and myself on the lease for my sailboat, a copy of which is attached to this assignment.

Dated this ____ day of _____, 19____.

_____

Assignor

OR

(2) By this assignment dated this 18th day of October, 1995, I hereby delegate to David Stevens all of my duties and obligations of performance under a contract dated July 15, 1993, between Kevin Hampton and myself concerning the senior class photography pictures.

By accepting this assignment, David Stevens agrees to assume and perform all duties and obligations that I have under said contract and to hold me harmless from any liability for performance or nonperformance of such obligation.

_____

Assignor

Acceptance

In consideration of the right, title, and interest that are being assigned to me, I hereby accept the foregoing assignment, and agree if the foregoing assignment is consented to by Harvey Childs, I will assume and perform all the duties and obligations previously to be performed by Kevin Hampton under the contract referred to in the foregoing assignment as if I had been an original party to the contract, and agree to indemnify and hold Kevin Hampton harmless for any liability for performance or nonperformance of the duties and obligations assumed by me.

Dated this ____ day of _____, 1995.

_____

Assignee

Assignment

I hereby assign to David Stevens my claim and demand against Marvin Todd for $10,571 arising out of the judgment dated November 1, 1995, for purposes of collection; and hereby grant to David Stevens the full power to collect, sue for, or in any other manner enforce collection thereof in his name or otherwise.

Dated this ____ day of _____, 1995.

_____

Assignor

FIGURE 10-9 Sample assignment with acceptance

SUMMARY

10.1 Although contracts normally have two parties, a promisor and a promisee, sometimes a third party, known as a third-party beneficiary, reaps advantages from a contract. There are intended beneficiaries, donee beneficiaries, creditor beneficiaries, and incidental beneficiaries.

10.2 A third-party beneficiary contract does not require privity between the parties. Third-party beneficiary contracts do not require a direct contractual relationship for the third party to have rights against the original promisor and promisee.

10.3 An assignment is a present transfer of a contractual right, whereas a delegation is a present transfer of a contractual duty to another party.

10.4 Assignments transfer the contract rights from an assignor to an assignee. No specific requirements are necessary to perfect an assignment, but written notice is normally appropriate. When an assignment is effectuated, the assignee assumes the obligations and rights of the assignor.

10.5 Certain contract rights are nonassignable. Often parties contractually agree that rights are not assignable, but courts closely interpret such restrictions. When the duties are unique or are personal or professional in nature, assignment will often be prohibited.

10.6 A delegation involves duties between the parties. Unlike assignments, prohibitions against delegations are ordinarily enforced by the courts. Duties which require specific skills are not delegatable, but general skills or tasks can be delegated even over the objection of a party. Assignments and delegations often occur simultaneously.

10.7 A novation is a type of third-party contract in which a new contract is substituted for an old one. In a novation, all parties must agree, and the rights and obligations of the original contract may be changed in the novation.

REVIEW QUESTIONS

1. Define how a third-party beneficiary contract is created.
2. What is an intended beneficiary?
3. Name the categories of intended beneficiaries and cite their differences.
4. How is privity of contract defined?
5. What is an assignment? A delegation?
6. Identify the key distinction between an assignment and a delegation.
7. What approaches do courts follow when two assignments have been made for the same transaction?
8. When are contract rights nonassignable?
9. Define delegator and delegatee.
10. When can duties not be assigned under a contract?

EXERCISES

1. Your attorney has asked you to draft a Notice of Assignment and Assignment of a lease dated July 15, 1993, between Harry Crawford, Landlord, and Lyle Morgan, Tenant. Lyle wants to assign his rights to Molly Riley. The assignment is for the property located at 11863 Main Avenue, Hartford, Connecticut, and is effective the date the assignment is drafted. Draft both the Notice of Assignment and the Assignment.

2. Brief *In re Ashford,* 73 B.R. 37 (Bankr. N.D. Tex. 1987) and answer the following questions.
   a. What are the facts of *Ashford?*
   b. What is the holding?
   c. How did the court define *assignment?*
   d. What is the court's rationale for its holding?

3. Contact three insurance companies and ask for a change of beneficiary form from each. Compare the forms and list the similarities and differences between the forms.

PART II

An Introduction to the Uniform Commercial Code

CHAPTER 11
Sales: Article 2 of the Uniform Commercial Code

11.1 UNDERSTANDING THE UNIFORM COMMERCIAL CODE

As the common law of contracts lagged behind the needs of the commercial world, statutes were passed to regulate commercial transactions. These general statutes adopted by some states cured the problem for a while, but the need arose for a uniform system of laws to govern commercial transactions. Therefore, the National Conference of Commissioners on Uniform State Laws began developing what we now know today as the **Uniform Commercial Code** (U.C.C. or Code). Although the Code received a lukewarm reception in the early 1950s, by 1968 all the states except Louisiana had adopted or amended the Code as proposed by the Conference. The general intent of the U.C.C., as stated in Article 1-102, is to simplify, clarify and modernize the law governing commercial transactions; (b) to permit the continued expansion of commercial practices through custom, usage and agreement of the parties; and (c) to make uniform the law among the various jurisdictions.

Article 1-102 of the U. C. C. thus set the stage for this statute to govern transactions between merchants and nonmerchants in the United States.

The U.C.C. has now been adopted, in whole or in part, by all 50 states, including Louisiana in the late 1980s, making it state law throughout the United States. This allows uniformity for parties who are entering into commercial transactions and thus removes some of the mystery and contusion from standard commercial dealings.

The Uniform Commercial Code has developed into nine articles and two new subarticles governing various stages of commercial transactions. For assistance in understanding how to interpret and apply the various Code sections, the Conference included "official comments" appended to each section of the text of the Code. These comments have guided courts and lawyers in interpretation of Code sections. Figure 11-1 sets out the general articles of the U.C.C.

Article 1:	General Provisions
Article 2:	Sales
Article 2A:	Leases (new addition)
Article 3:	Negotiable Instruments
Article 4:	Bank Deposits and Collections
Article 4A:	Fund Transfers
Article 5:	Letters of Credit
Article 6:	Revised Bulk Sales
Article 7:	Warehouse Receipts, Bills of Lading, and other Documents of Title
Article 8:	Investment Securities
Article 9:	Secured Transaction

FIGURE 11-1   Articles of the U.C.C.

Detailing all the articles is beyond the scope of this text; therefore, the focus of this book's second part is on Article 2 of the U.C.C., Sales. Article 2 complements the common law of contracts. Article 2 has seven parts:

Part One: General Construction and Subject Matter
Explanation: This section sets out the general scope of Article 2 and specifies important definitions used in sales transactions.
Part Two: Form, Formation, and Readjustment of the Contract
Explanation: This section focuses on general formation of the sales contract, including offer and acceptance. It sets out some of the guidelines for formation of a contract, including requirements under the Statute of Frauds.

TERMS

Uniform Commercial Code
One of the Uniform Laws, which has been adopted in much the same form in every state. It governs most aspects of commercial transactions, including sales, leases, negotiable instruments, deposits and collections, letters of credit, bulk sales, warehouse receipts, bills of lading and other documents of title, investment securities, and secured transactions.

Part Three: General Obligations and Construction of Contracts

Explanation: This section deals with interpretation of terms and expressly focuses on the various warranties provided under the U.C.C. It also defines legal requirements for delivery terms in connection with a sale.

Part Four: Title, Creditors, and Good Faith Purchasers

Explanation: This article deals with the passing of title from seller to buyer, and the ramifications when title is questioned.

Part Five: Title Performance

Explanation: This section focuses on the rights of seller and buyer when performance is tendered.

Part Six: Breach, Repudiation, and Excuse

Explanation: This section focuses primarily on the buyer's rights when the seller has not tendered goods that have been purchased. This section explores the situations between buyer and seller when performance is not perfect.

Part Seven: Remedies

Explanation: The last section focuses on the remedies seller and buyer have when one of the parties fails in performance of a commercial transaction.

Although Article 2 focuses exclusively on sales of goods, it is incumbent upon anyone who is analyzing a sales transaction to also pay close attention to the general definition section in Article 1-201. This section defines approximately 46 terms which are used exclusively in commercial transactions and specifies how those definitions are applied under the U.C.C.

11.2 THE SCOPE OF ARTICLE 2

Certain basic rules must be understood prior to any study of Article 2. Article 2 deals with the sale of goods, and both the words **sale** and **goods** are specifically defined in the article.

A *sale* is defined in § 2-106, which states that a sale "consists in the passing of title from the seller to the buyer for a price." Article 2 covers both present or future sales of goods, and defines a *present sale* as "a sale which is accomplished by the making of a contract."

The next important definition under Article 2 is of the term *goods*. As identified in § 2-105, *goods* are "things which are movable at the time of identification to the contract for sale." This Code section further states that goods may be the "unborn young of animals and growing crops and other identified things attached to realty, if they are not attached to the land at the time of the sale." Thus, to determine whether Article 2 applies to a transaction, ask whether a sale has been consummated and whether the sale is of goods as defined under Article 2.

One area that has been hotly litigated is the sale of blood. With the onset of the AIDS crisis, questions arose as to whether the sale of blood fell

---

TERMS

sale
A transfer of title to property for money or its equivalent. Both real property and personal property (tangible as well as intangible) may be the subject of a sale. A sale may be executory or executed. A sale does not always result in an absolute transfer of title.

goods
A term of variable meaning, sometimes signifying all personal property or movables, sometimes limited to merchandise held for sale or in storage, sometimes meaning tangible property only, and sometimes including intangible property such as securities. Securities, money, and things in action, however, are not "goods" within the definition of the Uniform Commercial Code; commodities, including futures and fungibles, are.

within the U.C.C. A case addressing this issue is *McKinstrie v. Henry Ford Hospital,* 55 Mich. App. 659, 223 N.W.2d 114 (1979).

McKINSTRIE v. HENRY FORD HOSPITAL

Court of Appeals of Michigan
Sept. 25, 1974

On November 11, 1970, plaintiff Betty McKinstrie was operated on at Henry Ford Hospital. During the operation she received two units of blood, which was supplied to the hospital by defendant Midwest Blood Service, Inc. Mrs. McKinstrie was released, but readmitted on January 1, 1971 with serum hepatitis. Plaintiffs then brought this action claiming that serum hepatitis is a disease which comes from blood and that the blood transfusion given by defendant hospital was the proximate cause of Mrs. McKinstrie's illness. Defendants contend that because of the blood banking and transfusion act, they are not liable to plaintiffs absent a showing of negligence. This act provides:

> "The procurement, processing, storage, distribution or use of whole blood, plasma, blood products, and blood derivatives, for the purpose of injecting or transfusing them, or any of them, into the human body for any purposes whatsoever where there is no medical test to determine the fitness of such whole blood, plasma, blood products, or blood derivatives, is the rendering

of a service and does not constitute a sale by any person participating therein, whether or not any remuneration is paid therefor."

The effect of this statute is to make what would otherwise be a sale—and, therefore, subject to the implied warranty provisions of the Uniform Commercial Code—a service, and, therefore, exempt from those provisions.

First, plaintiffs contend that the blood banking and transfusion act is an unconstitutional delegation of legislative power. They argue that the language delegates to unknown persons the power to determine whether or not there exists a "medical test to determine the fitness" of blood. We think this position is without merit.

There is no delegation of power in this statute. It simply provides that if "there is no medical test to determine the fitness of * * * blood", the transfusion of that blood will be considered a service, not a sale. We recognize that in a suit such as this, the fact finder must take the facts, apply them to the statute and decide whether such a test of "fitness" exists.

QUESTIONS FOR ANALYSIS

What are the facts of *McKinstrie*? What criteria did the court use to determine whether a blood transfusion is a "sale" within the meaning of the U.C.C.? Do you agree with the court's holding? Why or why not?

When it has been determined that a transaction falls under Article 2 of the U.C.C., the analysis turns to determining who are the parties to the sale. Article 2 requires that a sale be between a **seller**, who provides the product, and a **buyer**, who agrees to purchase the product. Article 2, however, makes a distinction between sales between merchants and nonmerchants. A **merchant** is defined in § 2-104:

(1) "merchant" means a person who deals in goods of the kind or otherwise by his occupation holds himself out as having knowledge or skill peculiar to the practices or goods involved in the transaction or to whom such knowledge or skill may be attributed by his employment of an agent or broker or other intermediary by who his occupation holds himself out as having such knowledge or skill.

If the transaction is between two merchants—a seller merchant and a buyer merchant—the parties are held to a higher standard of dealing than *non-merchants* (persons who are not in the business of selling a product). The Code requires that parties who are merchants to a sales transaction must act in good faith and in a commercially reasonable manner. This means that the parties must act fairly in their dealings and according to acceptable standards of common conduct for persons in that particular industry.

When nonmerchants are involved, the U.C.C. requires only that the nonmerchants act in good faith in their dealings. This is a lower standard than for merchants. No matter what the other's status, each party must act within the confines of the U.C.C. When a merchant deals with a nonmerchant, the merchant is held to a higher standard than the nonmerchant and will be judged by that higher standard in the course of dealing. The U.C.C. sets out all these relationships and how they are applied.

11.3 FORMATION OF THE CONTRACT: DEPARTURE FROM COMMON LAW

Under the Code, contracts are formed in the same manner as under common law. The parties must indicate an offer and a corresponding acceptance. However, the rules with respect to offer and acceptance have been greatly relaxed under the U.C.C. to accommodate the realities of the commercial business world. In fact, these rules have been relaxed to such an extent that often terms are left open, quantities are uncertain, and even the time of agreement is unclear. Under the U.C.C., lack of definiteness in the offer often is not a barrier to formation of the contract. (Recall from Chapter 2 that, under common law, indefiniteness means the terms are not sufficient to constitute an offer. Not so in the formation of a contract under the U.C.C.) Specifically, § 2-204 sets out the principles required for formation:

(1) A contract for sale of goods may be made in any manner sufficient to show agreement, including conduct by both parties which recognizes the existence of such a contract.

(2) An agreement sufficient to constitute a contract for sale may be found even though the moment of its making is undetermined.

(3) Even though one or more terms are left open, a contract for sale does not fail for indefiniteness if the parties have intended to make a contract and there is a reasonably certain basis for giving an appropriate remedy.

Thus, if the parties intend for a contract to exist, the Code often allows the court to find one. Even when terms are indefinite, missing, or later supplied, decisions under the Code often find that a contract existed between the parties if the conduct of the parties indicates that one was intended.

Another major departure from the common law is § 2-206, relating to the effectiveness of an offer and acceptance. Recall that, in the common law, an offer by fax may require an acceptance by fax. This is clearly not the case under the sales provisions of the U.C.C. Section 2-206 states:

(1) Unless otherwise unambiguously indicated by the language or circumstances

(a) an offer to make a contract shall be construed as inviting acceptance in any manner and by any medium reasonable in the circumstances;

(b) an order or other offer to buy goods for prompt or current shipment shall be construed as inviting acceptance either by a prompt promise to ship or by the prompt or current shipment of conforming or non-conforming goods, but such a shipment of non-conforming goods does not constitute an acceptance if the seller seasonably notifies the buyer that the shipment is offered only as an accommodation to the buyer.

(2) Where the beginning of a requested performance is a reasonable mode of acceptance an offeror who is not notified of acceptance within a reasonable time may treat the offer as having lapsed before acceptance.

This section of the Code clearly departs from the common law principles examined in previous chapters. Let us first look at § 2-206(1)(a). When an offer specified a mode of acceptance, the common law required that acceptance be by that specific mode, without any deviation. The Code relaxes this requirement by allowing the seller to accept by the means set out in the offer *or* any other medium that is reasonable under the circumstances. Thus, acceptance can occur by shipping goods rather than communicating the acceptance back to a party, as set out in § 2-206(1)(b). For example, the party can accept by communicating the acceptance through the same form of communication, or the party can accept by shipping conforming goods.

The Code also allows a party to ship nonconforming goods as an **accommodation** to the party requiring the goods. When nonconforming goods are sent as a prompt shipment, the Code does not treat this as an acceptance of the offer. The buyer then has the opportunity to either accept or reject the nonconforming goods; if they are rejected, the buyer may return them at the seller's expense.

Accepting by prompt shipment of goods can cause many problems and unnecessary expense, however. The person to whom the goods were shipped generally does not have any responsibility for the shipment of nonconforming goods, and thus the entire responsibility for the act falls on the party who did the shipping. Nevertheless, this practice is commonplace in the commercial context.

TERMS

seller
A person who sells property he or she owns; a person who contracts for the sale of property, real or personal; a vendor.

buyer
One who makes a purchase.

merchant
1. A person who regularly trades in a particular type of goods.
2. Under the Uniform Commercial Code, "a person who deals in goods of the kind or otherwise by his occupation holds himself out as having knowledge or skill peculiar to ... the ... goods involved in the transaction." The law holds a merchant to a higher standard than it imposes upon a casual seller; his or her transactions may carry with them an implied warranty of merchantability.

accommodation
An obligation undertaken, without consideration, on behalf of another person; a favor.

Not only does the Code make it easier for a contract to be formed, but it also makes it more difficult for **firm offers** to be revoked. Section 2-205 modifies the common law once again and provides:

An offer by a merchant to buy or sell goods in a signed writing which by its terms gives assurance that it will be held open is not revocable, for lack of consideration, during the time stated, or, if no time is stated for a reasonable time, but in no event may such period of irrevocability exceed three months; but any such term of assurance on a form supplied by the offeree must be separately signed by the offeror.

The Code does require that an offer be in writing, but does not require consideration to keep an offer open. The firm offer rule under the U.C.C. does not require any consideration to keep the offer open for an agreed period of time. If a merchant makes an offer in writing for specific goods and for a specific amount of time, and signs the writing, the Code treats this as a firm offer. This offer is irrevocable for a "reasonable" period of time, which the Code has interpreted as not to exceed three months. Figure 11-2 shows come examples of firm offers.

**Firm Offer for Sale Agreement—By Merchant
—Open for Less than Three Months**

Ms. Patsy Ruben   June 1, 1995
1234 Field Street
Dallas, Texas 76543

Dear Ms. Ruben:

I, Suzanne Stuckey, of 2345 Brentwood, Wichita Falls, Texas, hereby offer to [buy or sell] 100 round tables for Twelve Thousand Dollars and No Cents ($12,000.00) on the following terms:

This offer shall be kept open until September 1, 1995, which is ninety days from the date of this offer.

Very truly yours,

Suzanne Stuckey

**Firm Offer for Sale Agreement—Specifications of Manner of Acceptance—
Offer Revocable if Acceptance Not Received by Specified Date**

Ms. Debbi Gray   November 1, 1995
1234 Old Mill Road
Burbank, California 12345

Dear Ms. Gray:

I, Catherine Zorra, of 5678 West 18th Street, Burbank, California, am making the following firm offer which I assure will be held open for your acceptance from November 15, 1995, until December 15, 1995.

FIGURE 11-2 Sample firm offers for sale

TERMS

firm offers
Under the Uniform Commercial Code, an offer to buy or sell goods made in a signed writing which, by its terms, gives assurance that it will be held open. A firm offer is not revocable for want of prosecution during the time it states it will be held open, or, if no time is stated, for up to three months.

The subject of this offer, and the conditions under which this offer is made, are as follows: Fiory Dresses for $25.00 each, cash on delivery. The dresses will be delivered to your place of business within thirty (30) days of ordering.

Your acceptance must be received not later than the close of business on December 15, 1995, at 5678 West 18th Street, Burbank, California. The offer is revocable if your acceptance is not received by the above-specified date.

Very truly yours,

Catherine Zorra

Firm Offer for Sale Agreement—Acceptance on Offeree's Form

Mr. Harry Zachary   December 1, 1995
Exercise, Inc.
1700 Main Street
Dallas, Texas 76543

Dear Mr. Zachary:

In accordance with our telephone conversation of November 28, 1995, it is understood that I shall have until December 31, 1995, to accept your offer to [buy or sell] 100 stairsteppers for Four Thousand Dollars ($4,000.00), on the following terms:

[state each term]

Please indicate your agreement with this statement by countersigning the enclosed copy of this offer and returning it to me by December 15, 1995.

Very truly yours,

Joseph Andrews

I agree to this offer as stated.

By: _____
      Harry Zachary, President of
      Exercise, Inc.

_____
Date

FIGURE 11-2 *(Continued)*

A case that interpreted § 2-205 is *Ivey's Plumbing & Electric Co. v. Petrochem Maintenance, Inc.*, 463 F. Supp. 543 (N.D. Miss. 1978).

IVEY'S PLUMBING & ELECTRIC COMPANY INC.
v. PETROCHEM MAINTENANCE, INC.

United States District Court, N. D. Mississippi
Dec. 19, 1978

KEADY, Chief Judge.

Prior to September 13, 1977, Ivey's became interested in submitting a bid as subcontractor for the mechanical portion of a construction project designated as the Maintenance and Repair Facility, Naval Construction Battalion Facility, at Gulfport, Mississippi. In order to submit a bid it was necessary for Ivey's to receive quotations on five air compressors called for by the project specifications. Petrochem supplied a quotation orally on September 13; its quotation for $89,073.62 being the lowest for these components, Ivey's used it in making its bid, which was that day accepted by the prime contractor. The day before, Petrochem had obtained an oral quotation from [Gardner-Denver Company] G–D's agent, Robert Theriot, who gave Petrochem an estimate sheet listing two of the air compressors with accessory equipment, orally indicating they could supply three more compressors at the same unit price. This document, entitled "Estimate Sheet" was dated September 12 and signed by Theriot.

Shortly after Ivey's made its successful bid as mechanical contractor, Wright, Petrochem's branch manager, learned that other suppliers were quoting five compressors of like character with equipment for a reported $144,000, or approximately $64,000 more than Petrochem's quotation to Ivey's and so advised G–D. G–D's agents, Theriot and Geers, visited Petrochem's office to review the project's plans and specifications which were in Petrochem's possession. On September 26, G–D issued a revised quotation for the compressors and equipment called for by the plans and specifications for approximately $113,000. Petrochem, ignoring this revised quotation, issued a purchase order on October 24 to G–D for the lump sum price of $80,366.24, which was the amount of the original oral quotation by G–D. On November 4, Wright forwarded a letter to G–D advising that Petrochem

had not received notice of G–D's intention to fulfill the purchase order of October 24 and stated that "should we fail to receive notice by November 7 we shall be compelled to assume that you do not intend to fulfill the contract." By letter dated November 7, G–D advised that it did not intend to furnish equipment as per their original quotation but only in accordance with their revised quotation of September 26.

Meanwhile, Ivey's had become apprised of the quotation problems connected with Petrochem's supplying the air compressors and equipment at the originally quoted price. On October 6, Wright and Beeson, representing Petrochem, met at Ivey's office with Hayes, Ivey's vice-president and senior project manager. At this meeting, Hayes delivered a purchase order to Wright for the compressor equipment in the amount of $89,073.62. Immediately prior to the issuance of the purchase order, certain discussions took place regarding problems associated with the quotation on the air compressors.

On November 1, Ivey's wrote Petrochem advising that it had received notice of the latter's attempt to fulfill the October 6 purchase order, and stating that unless Petrochem notified Ivey's by November 4 the subcontractor would have no alternative but to purchase air compressors elsewhere. Upon Petrochem's failure to supply the equipment, Ivey's purchased the compressors from Ingersoll-Rand for a price of $121,000. Ivey's thus seeks to recover nearly $32,000 as the difference between the original quotation which it received from Petrochem and the amount it was required to pay to the other supplier for the identical equipment.

The basic question is whether a quotation or estimate by a seller is irrevocable for a reasonable period of time or whether it is simply an offer to sell which is subject to revocation by the seller at any time prior to the buyer's acceptance. The pertinence of this question is made clear when it appears, without contradiction, that prior to Petrochem's acceptance of the original quotation, G–D, on September 26, 1977, following telephone conversations with Petrochem concerning the mistake which it purportedly made in its original quotation, issued a revised written quotation, No. 231-97, at a substantially higher price. This revised quotation can be viewed only as a withdrawal, or revocation, of its original offer to sell at the lower price. It is settled by explicit provision of Uniform Commercial Code that a merchant's quotation, or estimate, or other offer, to be irrevocable for a reasonable length of time, must *by its terms give assurance that it will be held open.* Otherwise, a mere offer lacking such assurance is subject to revocation by the seller at any time prior to the buyer's acceptance. [T]his section reverses the common law rule that any offer not supported by a consideration may be revoked at any time prior to acceptance. Theriot's written estimate contains no assurance, or signification of any kind, that the quotation would be held open for any period of time. It constitutes, at best, a mere

offer subject to revocation at the will of the seller, unless previously accepted by the buyer.

Thus, Petrochem was fully advised that G–D's original quotation offer, which was not firm by its terms, had been effectively withdrawn prior to any attempt by Petrochem to place a purchase order with G–D. The record shows without contradiction that it was not until after Petrochem received a purchase order from Ivey's on October 6, that it attempted, on October 24, 1977, to submit to G–D a purchase order based on the original but withdrawn quotation. At this point, G–D by letter returned Petrochem's purchase order stating "we cannot accept this purchase order since it is not conformative with our quotation No. 231-97 dated September 26, 1977." Petrochem thereafter appealed to G–D for some adjustment or to seek an accommodation with the prime contractor or the job manager of the project but this proved to be unavailing. In summary, the "writing" which Petrochem claims to be "sufficient to indicate a that a contract of sale has been made between the parties [G–D and Petrochem]" was at best a mere offer which had been effectually revoked by G–D at a time when it had the lawful right to do so.

QUESTIONS FOR ANALYSIS

What are the facts of *Ivey*? How is § 2-205 defined? What was the court's holding?

11.4 MODIFYING THE MIRROR IMAGE RULE

Recall that, under the common law, an offer and acceptance must be exact and that any deviation is a counteroffer. The common law is very strict in its interpretation of the mirror image rule and does not allow any change in the terms of the offer and the acceptance. This rule was substantially changed under the U.C.C. The Code does not treat the new or different terms as a rejection of the offer or even as a counteroffer, but rather interprets these terms as an additional proposal to an existing contract. The Code specifically states in § 2-207:

(1) A definite and seasonable expression of acceptance or a written confirmation which is sent within a reasonable time operates as an acceptance even though it states terms additional to or different from those offered or agreed upon, unless acceptance is expressly made conditional on assent to the additional or different terms.

Although the Code does set out specific limitations for an acceptance, the Code leans toward finding a contract between the parties. This is completely opposite to the view of the common law. Section 2-207 continues:

> (2) The additional terms are to be construed as proposals for addition to the contract. Between merchants such terms become part of the contract unless:
>
> (a) the offer expressly limits acceptance to the term of the offer;
> (b) they materially alter it; or
> (c) notification of the objection to them has already been given or is given within a reasonable time after notice of them is received.

Section 2-207(3) takes contract formation a step further. This section suggests that when the parties *act* as though they have a contract under Article 2, they do in fact have a contract. Section 2-207(3) provides:

> (3) Conduct by both parties which recognizes the existence of a contract is sufficient to establish a contract for sale although the writings of the parties do not otherwise establish a contract. In such case, the terms of the particular contract consist of those terms on which the writings of the parties agree, together with any supplementary terms incorporated under any other provisions of this Act.

Consequently, Article 2 is more broadly interpreted to favor formation of a contract compared to the strict requirements under the common law. This can cause problems for courts, but more so for seller and buyer. Caution should be used when contracting under the U.C.C.; whether seller or buyer, the best advice is to bargain for the terms and clearly set forth the intent.

Courts have had a difficult time interpreting § 2-207. Consequently, case results are in conflict among jurisdictions. Carefully review your state's version of the U.C.C. and judicial decisions interpreting § 2-207.

Missing and Open Terms

A contract can be formulated between the parties even if terms are missing or have not been agreed to. The U.C.C. focuses on the parties' intent: if the parties intended a contract, a contract will be found. For example, most of us would think that if the parties failed to agree on a price, there would be no contract. Not so under the U.C.C. Section 2-305 provides that:

> (1) The parties if they so intend can conclude a contract for sale even though the price is not settled. In such a case the price is a reasonable price at the time for delivery if
>
> (a) nothing is said as to price; or
> (b) the price is left to be agreed by the parties and they fail to agree; or
> (c) the price is to be fixed in terms of some agreed market or other standard as set or recorded by a third person or agency and it is not so set or recorded.

(2) A price to be fixed by the seller or by the buyer means a price for him to fix in good faith.

(3) When a price left to be fixed otherwise than by agreement of the parties fails to be fixed through fault of one party the other may at his option treat the contract as canceled or himself fix a reasonable price.

(4) Where, however, the parties intend not to be bound unless the price be fixed or agreed and it is not fixed or agreed there is no contract. In such a case the buyer must return any goods already received or if unable so to do, must pay their reasonable value at the time of delivery and the seller must return any portion of the price paid on account.

Consequently, leaving open even a critical term such as the price will not defeat the contracting process. This is a major deviation from the common law.

In addition to leaving price terms open, delivery terms can also be omitted and the Code may still find a contract between the parties. Under the Code, delivery is to be in one shipment (§ 2-307) at the seller's place of business (§ 2-308), at a reasonable time (§ 2-309). Illogical as it may seem, the Code fills in the omitted terms as though they were part of the parties' communications.

Finally, if the method of payment is omitted, the Code provides the answer to the payment problem. Section 2-310 states:

Unless otherwise agreed

(a) payment is due at the time and place at which the buyer is to receive the goods even though the place of shipment is the place of delivery; and

(b) if the seller is authorized to send the goods he may ship them under reservation, and may tender the documents of title, but the buyer may inspect the goods after their arrival before payment is due unless such inspection is inconsistent with the terms of the contract (Section 2-513); and

(c) if delivery is authorized and made by way of documents of title otherwise than by subsection (b) then payment is due at the time and place at which the buyer is to receive the documents regardless of where the goods are to be received; and

(d) where the seller is required or authorized to ship the goods on credit the credit period runs from the time of shipment but postdating the invoice or delaying its dispatch will correspondingly delay the starting of the credit period.

Additional Consistent Terms

Unlike the common law, when the offeree proposes additional terms to the original offer, a contract can still be formed. As long as those terms are consistent with the basis of the contract, a contract is found. Granted, a party can condition its acceptance upon acceptance of the additional or different terms, but unconditional additions will constitute an acceptance.

Of course, there are exceptions to this rule. If the additional or different terms materially alter the contract, a contract will not be formed. Further, if the party to whom the changes are directed objects to the additional or different terms within a reasonable period of time, there is no contract. Finally, the offeror can specifically limit acceptance to only these terms and provisions in the offer, thereby avoiding any possibly objectional deviations. Some provisions to alleviate problems when the seller does not want additional terms to be part of the offer are:

---

(1) This offer may be accepted only on the exact terms set forth in this offer, and no additional terms or modifications shall be accepted.

(2) This order supersedes and cancels all prior communications between the parties, except as specifically shown on the face of this order. No conditions in the acceptance by seller and no subsequent agreements or communications in any way modifying the provisions of this order or increasing charges under this offer shall be binding unless made in writing and signed by the authorized representative of buyer.

The buyer may nevertheless propose additional terms, as shown in Figure 11-3. The seller may then send a letter either confirming acceptance of the additional terms or rejecting them. Figure 11-4 provides drafting assistance.

Notice to Seller—Acceptance Demanding Additional Terms

Ms. Joanne Lacey   December 1, 1995
1234 West Main Street
Austin, Texas 76543

Dear Ms. Lacey:

Your offer of November 15, 1995, for 25 wicker chairs for Eighteen Hundred Dollars and No cents ($1,800.00) is hereby accepted. But, in lieu of shipment being made on or before January 31, 1996, I must have an earlier delivery date, with shipment to be completed on or before January 15, 1996. It is also necessary that the following additional terms apply to the order:

[state each additional term]

This notice is not to be construed as an acceptance of your offer unless the additional terms set forth in this notice are agreed to by you.

Very truly yours,

David J. Thompson

FIGURE 11-3 Buyer's proposal of additional terms

**Notice to Seller—Transaction Between Merchants—
Limitation of Time for Rejection of Additional Terms**

Ms. Joanne Lacey   December 2, 1995
1234 West Main Street
Austin, Texas 76543

Dear Ms. Lacey:

You are hereby notified that unless I receive, on or before January 15, 1996, notice of your rejection of the terms that modify your offer of November 27, 1995, the new terms shall become part of the agreement between us.

Very truly yours,

David J. Thompson

FIGURE 11-3 *(Continued)*

Seller's Acceptance of Modified Terms

Mr. David J. Thompson   December 5, 1995
5678 East Street
Austin, Texas 76543

Dear Mr. Thompson:

I hereby consider your letter of December 1, 1995 as an acceptance of the offer for 25 wicker chairs for $1800.00. I agree to the additional terms specifically requiring an earlier shipment date of January 15, 1996.

Sincerely,

Ms. Lacey

Seller's Rejection of Modified Terms

Mr. David J. Thompson   December 5, 1995
5678 East Street
Austin, Texas 76543

Dear Mr. Thompson:

Your letter of December 1, 1995 is received as an acceptance of my letter dated November 15, 1995, relating to the purchase of 25 wicker chairs.

I regret that I cannot accept the additional terms that you propose, and therefore insist that the agreement operate exclusively on the basis of my original letter to you without modification.

Sincerely,

Ms. Lacey

FIGURE 11-4 Seller's acceptance or rejection of modified terms

Examine *Mace Industries, Inc. v. Paddock Pool Equipment Co.,* 339 S.E.2d 527 (S.C. Ct. App. 1986), which addressed the condditional acceptance issue and § 2-207(3) of the Code.

MACE INDUSTRIES, INC. v. PADDOCK POOL EQUIPMENT COMPANY, INC.

Court of Appeals of South Carolina
Jan. 21, 1986

CURETON, Judge.

The facts are basically undisputed. The parties' business relationship commenced in October 1981 when Mace sent a quotation to Paddock for the equipment. The quotation was in the form of a sales agreement which contained the terms and conditions on which Mace proposed to sell the equipment to Paddock. Among other things, the sales agreement contained a provision that all invoices must be paid within the time specified on the invoices; that any balance 30 days overdue would be subject to a delinquency charge; and that Paddock would be required to reimburse Mace for any collection costs and attorneys' fees incurred in collecting any past due debts. Finally, the sales agreement provided for a limited warranty and disclaimed all other warranties.

Upon receipt of Mace's quotation, Paddock responded with a purchase order which referred to the quotation. The reverse side of the purchase order contained certain terms and conditions. These terms did not include provisions for attorneys' fees, delinquency charges, collection costs or a warranty. Mace promptly acknowledged receipt of Paddock's purchase order and excepted to two conditions on the reverse of the purchase order. The purchase order, as did the quotation, contained a provision that the document constituted the entire agreement of the parties which could be modified only by written agreement of the parties. Paddock claims the purchase order was a counteroffer to purchase the equipment on the terms and conditions contained in the purchase order, while Mace characterizes the purchase order as an acceptance of its offer.

The crux of the parties' dispute is what warranties are applicable to the equipment. Mace argues that the limited warranty contained in the sales agreement is the only applicable warranty. Paddock argues that since the purchase order contains no warranties, the implied warranties provided for in the Uniform Commercial Code cover the equipment. Another aspect of the parties' dispute is whether delinquency charges, collection costs and attorneys' fees are recoverable.

Close analysis must be made of section 36-2-207, 1976 Code of Laws of South Carolina in order to determine what constitutes the contract of the parties in view of the language in the purchase order. Section 36-2-207 provides in part:

Additional terms in acceptance or confirmation

(1) A definite and seasonable expression of acceptance or a written confirmation which is sent within a reasonable time operates as an acceptance even though it states terms additional to or different from those offered or agreed upon, unless acceptance is expressly made conditional on assent to the additional or different terms.

(2) The additional terms are to be construed as proposals for addition to the contract. Between merchants such terms become part of the contract unless:

(a) the offer expressly limits acceptance to the terms of the offer;

(b) they materially alter it; or

(c) notification of objection to them has already been given or is given within a reasonable time after notice of them is received.

Prior to enactment of the Uniform Commercial Code, a purported acceptance containing terms that did not "mirror" those of the offer operated as a rejection thereof and amounted to a counterclaim.

Uniform Commercial Code Section 2-207(1) was designed to abrogate two "rather severe common-law concepts, the so called 'mirror image' rule and its 'last shot' consequence." Under this code section an expression of acceptance of an offer creates a contract on the offered terms despite additional or different terms contained in the acceptance unless the acceptance is expressly made conditional on assent to the additional or different terms. "In other words, the result of the offeree making his acceptance expressly conditional on the offeror's assent is the transformation of the offeree's document into a traditional counter-offer."

The dispositive question in this appeal is whether Paddock made its acceptance expressly conditional on Mace's assent to the terms and conditions contained in the purchase order. [To] convert an acceptance into a counteroffer under Section 2-207(1), the conditional nature of the acceptance must be clearly expressed in a manner sufficient to notify the offeror that the offeree is unwilling to proceed with the transaction unless the additional or different terms are included in the contract. We discern no indication from the sales agreement and purchase order that Paddock so conditioned its acceptance.

Paddock argues that because its purchase order was specifically accepted by Mace and because the purchase order also contained on its reverse side (1) a notice that "THE SELLER AGREES TO ALL OF THE FOLLOWING TERMS AND CONDITIONS" and (2) a provision that the order form shall constitute the entire agreement of the parties, these requirements made its acceptance expressly conditional upon Mace's acceptance of the terms contained in the purchase order. We disagree. The courts have held that an acceptance does not fall within the proviso in Section 2-207(1) unless the acceptance clearly reveals that the offeree is unwilling to proceed with the transaction unless he is assured of the offeror's assent to the new terms. The fact that Paddock followed through with the purchase even though Mace in its acknowledgment of receipt of the purchase order expressly rejected two provisions contained on the reverse of the purchase order amply demonstrates to us that Paddock was willing to proceed with the purchase of the equipment even though Mace did not assent to all the terms contained in the purchase order.

Under the provisions of Section 36-2-207(2) the additional terms of the purchase order are to be construed as proposals for additions to the contract. We hold that the additional terms became a part of the contract between the parties inasmuch as (1) both parties are merchants, (2) Mace's offer did not expressly limit acceptance to the terms of its offer, and (3) the additional terms did not materially alter the proposed contract between the parties. Therefore, regarding the main issue in controversy, we hold that the provision contained in the sales agreement concerning the limited warranties shall control.

Affirmed.

QUESTIONS FOR ANALYSIS

Identify the facts of *Mace Industries*. Did the court determine that the additional terms to the offer became part of the contract? Why or why not? What was the court's holding in *Mace Industries*?

Output and Requirements Contracts

Contracts which provide that a seller will sell to the buyer "all goods we produce" are known as *output contracts*. This type of contract was not favored under the common law, because of the indefiniteness of the amount the buyer was purchasing.

Contracts that allow a buyer to purchase "as much as we need" from a seller are known as *requirements contracts*. As with an output contract, the common law disfavors requirements contracts.

The U.C.C. changes all that. Section 2-306 suggests:

(1) A term which measures the quantity by the output of the seller or the requirements of the buyer means such actual output or requirements as may occur in good faith, except that no quantity unreasonably disproportionate to any stated estimate or in the absence of a stated estimate to any normal or otherwise comparable prior output or requirements may be tendered or demanded.

(2) A lawful agreement by either the seller or the buyer for exclusive dealing in the kind of goods concerned imposes unless otherwise agreed an obligation by the seller to use best efforts to supply the goods and by the buyer to use best efforts to promote their sale.

Output and requirements contracts are acceptable under the U.C.C. as long as the parties deal in good faith and adhere to standards of reasonableness. Again, this is a major deviation from the common law approach to contracts. For an illustration of a court faced with analyzing a requirements contract, review *Fashion House, Inc. v. K-Mart Corp.*, 892 F.2d 1076 (1st Cir. 1989).

FASHION HOUSE, INC. v. K MART CORPORATION

United States Court of Appeals, First Circuit
Dec. 19, 1989

SELYA, Circuit Judge.

K mart is one of the nation's largest retailers, operating an extensive chain of discount stores. During the early 1980s, K mart was experiencing a decline in earnings. It entered into a flirtation with FHI, a young but highly successful jobber. Under their written memorandum of understanding, FHI was to act as a buying agent for K mart. Evidently, both parties were pleased by the results of the experiment: on June 30, 1983, they executed a long-term agreement (Agreement).

In general, subject to various conditions, exceptions, and qualifications, defendant agreed to purchase through plaintiff 85% of its overall requirements of "recognized designer and national brand name fashion and fashion-related apparel merchandise" and to award plaintiff a 5% commission on the net prices paid for the merchandise.

On January 21, 1986, FHI wrote to K mart, articulating suspicions about K mart's commission accounting under the Agreement. Plaintiff demanded access to K mart's financial data for verification purposes. K mart denied that it owed additional commissions, but refused to open its books and records. On February 6, it sent FHI a letter purporting to order a large but unspecified amount of apparel under particular brand names and labels then unavailable to FHI. Plaintiff broke the news that it had sued to obtain access to defendant's ledgers and to recover commissions earned but unpaid. K mart immediately terminated the Agreement (which at that juncture had over 18 months to run), claiming breach.

Terms of the Agreement. In general, the Agreement obligated K mart to purchase 85% of its merchandise requirements through FHI. "Merchandise" and "Requirements" were contractually defined terms.

[Section 2] "Merchandise" shall mean men's, women's, boys', girls', infants' and toddlers' recognized designer and national brand name fashion and fashion-related apparel merchandise; but not (a) products with names or labels owned or used by or licensed or exclusive to K mart or any of its Affiliates including products such as "Jonathan Logan" and "Esquire" and (b) products with names or labels originated by or for K mart or any of its Affiliates. The parties recognize that the definition of Merchandise is, of necessity, imprecise. *Therefore, as may be required from time to time, whether particular products are included in or excluded from the definition of Merchandise shall be determined by mutual agreement between Fashion House and K mart.*

[Section 3.1] "Requirements" shall mean Merchandise requirements for resale during the term of this Agreement in stores operated by K mart and its Subsidiaries in the United States, provided, however, that it shall not include (i) stores, departments or merchandise lines which are not within the current operations of K mart and its presently-existing Subsidiaries, (ii) "Wrangler" and "Sasson" products, and (iii) Merchandise for which orders or commitments were given by K mart or any of its Subsidiaries to third parties prior to the [effective] date [of the Agreement].

This asseveration depends upon the premise that, if the agreeing-to-agree proviso applies to items obviously apparel, then no such items are "Merchandise" unless and until K mart assents to their inclusion. But, the premise is flawed. The district court found, and K mart does not now dispute, that the contract was a requirements contract. As such, K mart had an enduring duty to determine the extent of its requirements in good faith. A [contract] term which measures the quantity by . . . the requirements of the buyer means such actual . . . requirements as may occur in good faith. Certainly, a blanket determination by K mart that all purchases for which it abjured commission payments were not "Merchandise requirements" would transgress this obligation.

Indeed, interpreting the agreeing-to-agree proviso as encompassing apparel does not suffocate, but breathes life into, the specific exceptions. Rather than being surplusage, as under the district court's reading, those sections would exclude from a good-faith determination of "Merchandise requirements" items—presumably, apparel items—that might otherwise be subject to inclusion. Instead of being redundant, as the district court feared, the provisions would serve to explicate the required good faith. Outside of the specifically mentioned brand name exclusions, the characteristics enumerated in sections 2 and 3.1 regain their relevance as foci of the definitional disputes foreseen by the parties. In this instance, the agreeing-to-agree proviso extends to items obviously apparel.

The "Brand Name" Exclusion. The court's reading of section 3.1 construed § 3.1(iii) to exclude from "Requirements" only in-the-pipeline orders, *i.e.,* those placed before the Agreement became effective. K mart exhorts that the parties intended clause (iii) to sweep more broadly and exclude future purchases of goods bearing brand name merchandise labels ordered by K mart at any time in the past. But, if this is so, the language chosen, *which makes no mention of labels or brand names,* is an extremely awkward locution, not fairly expressive of the intent which K mart, after the fact, assigns to it. We are wary about crediting what seems to be an obvious *post hoc* rationalization. Certainly, K mart knew the brands it had previously ordered, and could have excluded them by name. That defendant took no such step is a reliable indication that, other than "Wrangler" and "Sasson," brands purchased in the past were not meant to enjoy a blanket exclusion for purposes of calculating defendant's "Requirements."

K mart further complains that the trial court's interpretation of the requirements section makes no "logical business sense" because K mart would wind up paying commissions for items previously purchased commission-free. The remonstrance is true, but largely beside the point. While under Michigan law contracts ought not to be interpreted to impose absurd results, the result reached here is neither chimerical nor illogical. The total picture may well eclipse any seeming inequity: K mart might have thought FHI was positioned to negotiate lower prices or more attractive terms (thus saving K mart money even after commission costs); or K mart may have believed that internal economies would counterbalance commissions; or K mart may have been willing to accept an extra burden in order to obtain the perceived benefit of an across-the-board relationship with a well-credentialed jobber. In addition, it bears remembering that K mart reserved 15% of "Merchandise requirements" for itself, which it might have considered enough to cover all purchases of name brands to which it previously enjoyed access. We need not speculate. It is the very possibility that a buyer may be disadvantageously bound to a seller which supplies the consideration that makes requirements contracts enforceable. We agree with the district court's interpretation of section 3.1 of the Agreement and do not believe that such a reading produces an absurd result.

Taking Inventory. In our estimation, the lower court's use of an erroneous definition of "Merchandise" not only improperly colored the jury's determination of damages, but also influenced—indeed, effectively removed from the jury's province—a salient question of liability. Under the court's construction of the Agreement, no question could ever arise as to whether any apparel items were "Merchandise." At trial, therefore, evidentiary proffers in that vein were ruled irrelevant, and reflexively excluded. Combined with the sanction order and the fact that FHI's commission claims related exclusively to apparel, K mart was effectively blocked from offering evidence of apparel purchases form various vendors *on any issue.* As the court stated: "The amount of purchases by K mart from all of those different vendors is irrelevant on any issue, except damages, in this case." That pronouncement may have been so under the district court's construction of the Agreement; but, under a proper construction, the dollar amounts were plainly relevant to liability.

The twin facts which the district court deemed determinative—that this was a requirements contract and that K mart purchased labeled apparel (aside from the 15% exclusion) without paying commissions—did not necessarily establish liability. If

defendant could demonstrate that the difference between the dollar amount of all its labeled apparel purchases and the dollar amount of the purchases on which FHI was paid commissions consisted of labeled apparel purchases which were not "Merchandise requirements" within the Agreement's contemplation, or that any excess was within the 15% exclusion, defendant would not be liable for unpaid commissions. The proof that some labeled apparel purchases were not includable in the category of "Merchandise requirements" would, to be relevant, necessarily include evidence of the dollar amount of those purchases. In that way, total exclusion of such evidence improperly removed a potential issue of liability from the jury's consideration.

In fine, the lower court's ban of dollar amount evidence for all purposes was reversible error. Concededly, the jury found K mart liable for commissions in addition to those calculated by using the preclusory order—but the talesmen's determination was tainted by the court's evidentiary rulings and instructions on liability. We see no alternative but to remand for a new trial to permit the questions of liability and damages to be ascertained in accordance with law.

Under section 1.1 of the Agreement, FHI was obligated to "acquire (or cause to be acquired)" only such "Merchandise" as K mart "ordered." The Agreement further provided that "Fashion House will acquire Merchandise ordered hereunder only pursuant to authorization from and on terms approved by K mart in writing. . . ." Orders were to be placed and processed "based on samples . . . or as otherwise mutually agreed between the parties, and within guidelines mutually agreed between the parties."

In practice, a regular course of conduct soon developed. FHI would bring garment samples to K mart. Regardless of whether the samples came from manufacturers, diverters, or middlemen, K mart's buyers would inspect them and then determine whether to test the mercantile waters. If the decision was affirmative, K mart personnel would give FHI what amounted to an order, that is, particulars as to quantities, prices, sizes, and the like. It was only after K mart staffers set the specifications that FHI executed orders on K mart's behalf.

Based on this historical record, the district court determined that the Agreement required "very specific orders" from K mart before FHI could be expected to procure goods to K mart's behoof. We agree entirely with this interpretation: an unbroken skein of custom and usage demonstrated beyond cavil that the parties had "mutually agreed" on the nature of the ordering process and their relative duties within that process. Once FHI secured samples, it was up to K mart to determine which merchandise would be ordered. And it was pellucid that only K mart could authorize a purchase under the Agreement.

QUESTIONS FOR ANALYSIS

What are the facts of the *Fashion House* case? What duties did the court delineate for the parties to a requirements contract? Is the holding a just result? Why or why not?

11.5 UNCONSCIONABILITY IN SALES CONTRACTS

Contracts that are too one-sided or too harsh can be considered unconscionable as a matter of law. As with the common law, the U.C.C. provides a specific section on unconscionability. Section 2-302 sets out the available legal options:

FARCUS

© 1994 Farcus Cartoons/Distributed by Universal Press Syndicate   WAISBLASS/COULTHART   2-11

"What small print? All our fees are clearly stated in this contract."

(1) If the court as a matter of law finds the contract or any clause of the contract to have been unconscionable at the time it was made the court may refuse to enforce the contract, or it may enforce the remainder of the contract without the unconscionable clause, or it may so limit the application of any unconscionable clause as to avoid any unconscionable result.

(2) When it is claimed or appears to the court that the contract or any clause thereof may be unconscionable the parties shall be afforded a reasonable opportunity to present evidence as to its commercial setting, purpose and effect to aid the court in making the determination.

All states have guidelines for determining whether a contract is unconscionable. Most use § 2-302 as a guide, but others, such as California and Louisiana, use case law to determine what constitutes an unconscionable contract. When the issue of unconscionability is raised, the contract is usually between a merchant seller and a nonmerchant buyer (the consumer). Nonmerchant buyers are acknowledged to have less skill, experience, and bargaining power than merchants. Thus, the nonmerchant may be successful when alleging that a contract is invalid on grounds of unconscionability. However, because there is usually no great disparity in the bargaining power of two merchants, their contracts are not likely to be deemed unconscionable. There are two general types of unconscionability: procedural and substantive.

Procedural Unconscionability

Lack of meaningful choice is usually associated with procedural unconscionability. Here the process of negotiation and formation of the contract is examined. Procedural unconscionability usually consists of consumer ignorance balanced against the finesse of the skilled seller in a "take-it-or-leave-it" contract. In this situation, the consumer has no meaningful bargaining powers and can often be duped into signing an offensive contract.

In a procedural unconscionability case, educational and intelligence levels are considered by the courts. Courts evaluate a person's background to determine whether lack of skills and general knowledge contributed to the unconscionable contract. Consequently, two people can sign the same contract but, because of skills and education, procedural unconscionability may be found in one case but not another.

Substantive Unconscionability

Substantive unconscionability focuses on the terms set forth in the contract. Overly harsh terms that are not negotiable and lean heavily toward the seller's interest are substantively unconscionable. Courts must evaluate the terms of the contract to determine whether they are excessive and too lopsided. Courts have had difficulties in determining substantive unconscionability because there is no definitive test. They can consider the return of profit or the price charged by other sellers, but those standards are not dispositive. For example, a person whose command of the English language is limited purchases a refrigerator for $900. The refrigerator cost the seller $300. Add to that cost $300 in finance charges, and you probably have a good case of substantive unconscionability.

In addition to § 2-302, the Code suggests two other areas in which substantive unconscionability becomes an issue. Addressing liquidated damages clauses, § 2-718(1) states that "[a] term fixing unreasonably large liquidated damages is void as a penalty." Section 2-719(3) deals with consequential damages and provides:

> Consequential damages may be limited or excluded unless the limitation or exclusion is unconscionable. Limitation of consequential damages for injury to the person in the case of consumer goods is prima facie unconscionable but limitation of damages where the loss is commercial is not.

When sellers attempt to unduly increase their available remedies and substantially decrease or erase a consumer buyer's remedies, unconscionability has been found. Examine *Frank's Maintenance & Engineering, Inc. v. C.A. Roberts Co.*, 86 Ill. App. 3d 980, 408 N.E.2d 403 (1980), which dealt with the distinction between procedural and substantive unconscionability.

FRANK'S MAINTENANCE & ENGINEERING, INC. v. C. A. ROBERTS CO.

Appellate Court of Illinois
July 24, 1980

The plaintiff, Frank's Maintenance & Engineering, Inc., manufactures motorcycle front fork tubes. On February 1, 1974 the plaintiff orally ordered some steel tubing from the defendant C. A. Roberts Co. (Roberts). Roberts sent a written acknowledgment. The record does not disclose whether there was an oral contract or merely an oral offer and a subsequent acceptance in the form of an acknowledgment from Roberts. On the back of this acknowledgment were various conditions including the following paragraph 11:

> Seller shall not be liable for consequential damages, and except as provided in paragraph 10 hereof, Seller's liability for any and all losses and damages sustained by Buyer and others, rising out of or by reason of this contract, shall not exceed the sum of the transportation charges paid by Buyer, mill or warehouse price and

extras, applicable to that portion of the products upon which liability is founded. Claims for defective products must be promptly made upon receipt thereof and Seller given ample opportunity to investigate; whereupon Seller may, at its option, replace those products proven defective or allow credit for an amount not exceeding the sum of the transportation charges, mill or warehouse price and extras, applicable thereto.

While several paragraphs on the front of the acknowledgment informed the plaintiff that the order had been entered with Roberts' mill and advised plaintiff to compare the acknowledgment with the original order and to advise Roberts of any error, nothing on the face of the acknowledgment advised plaintiff of the conditions on the back. To the contrary, the printed legend "conditions of sale on reverse side" had been stamped over and rendered practically illegible. Indeed, at first glance that box appears to read "No conditions of sale on reverse side." The terms of limitation were not discussed by Roberts and the plaintiff and were first brought to the attention of plaintiff's president after the commencement of the suit. Roberts ordered the steel from the other defendant, Leland Tube Company, Inc. (Leland), and directed it to send the steel directly to the plaintiff, which it did. Although the steel was supposed to be shipped in July, it was not shipped until December 1974.

The occurrence of cracks or other defects in steel tubing of the nature ordered is highly unusual. However, they can occur and such defects may be invisible to the naked eye particularly if they originate on the inside surface of the tube and do not reach the outer surface. The outer surface of the tube is covered with oxide which conceal marks which would otherwise be visible. Plaintiff had no testing equipment for such defects, the quality control procedure of manufacturers usually making such testing unnecessary.

When processing was begun on the first part of the shipment in the summer of 1975 it was discovered that the steel was pitted and corroded beyond the point where it could be reclaimed by grinding; the steel was cracked, useless and dangerous for the high-stress purposes for which it was ordered. Contrary to the express terms of the contract, the steel was welded rather than seamless. Plaintiff gave notice to Roberts of these defects on August 25, 1975, informed Roberts that it was revoking its acceptance of the goods and that it would hold the goods for thirty days for Roberts and after that time the steel would be sold and any amount received deducted from plaintiff's claim. In fact, after some sixty days had elapsed, and Roberts failed to respond in any way the plaintiff scrapped the entire lot of steel, allegedly because it was worthless.

Procedural unconscionability consists of some impropriety during the process of forming the contract depriving a party of a meaningful choice. Factors to be considered are all the circumstances surrounding the transaction including the manner in which the contract was entered into, whether each party had a reasonable opportunity to understand the terms of the contract, and whether important terms were hidden in a maze of fine print; both the conspicuousness of the clause and the negotiations relating to it are important, albeit not conclusive factors in determining the issue of unconscionability. To be a part of the bargain, a provision limiting the defendant's liability must, unless incorporated into the contract through prior course of dealings or trade usage, have been bargained for, brought to the purchaser's attention or be conspicuous. If not, the seller has no reasonable expectation that the remedy was being so restricted and the restriction cannot be said to be part of the agreement of the parties. Nor does the mere fact that both parties are businessmen justify the utilization of unfair surprise to the detriment of one of the parties since the Code specifically provides for the recovery of consequential damages and an individual should be able to rely on their existence in the absence of being informed to the contrary either directly or constructively through prior course of dealings or trade usage. This requirement that the seller obtain the knowing assent of the buyer "does not detract from the freedom to contract, unless that phrase denotes the freedom to impose the onerous terms of one's carefully-drawn printed document on an unsuspecting contractual partner. Rather, freedom to contract is enhanced by a requirement that both parties be aware of the burdens they are assuming. The notion of free will has little meaning as applied to one who is ignorant of the consequences of his acts."

Substantive unconscionability concerns the question whether the terms themselves are commercially reasonable. While the Code permits the limitation of remedies, it must be remembered that it disfavors them and specifically provides for their deletion if they would act to deprive a contracting party of reasonable protection against a breach. [The Code] specifically provides that the remedies provided by it shall be liberally construed to the end that the aggrieved party may be put in as good a position as if the other party had fully performed. And as specifically stated in Comment 1 to section 2-719, if the parties intend to conclude a contract for sale within the scope of the Uniform Commercial Code-Sales, they must accept the legal consequence that there be at least a fair quantum of remedy for breach of the obligations or duties outlined in the contract.

Reasonable agreements which limit or modify remedies will be given effect but the parties are not free to shape their remedies in an unreasonable or unconscionable way.

Courts have tended to strike down clauses barring the recovery of consequential damages or otherwise limiting recovery when the defect was latent.

In the present case, the evidence produced by the plaintiff discloses that the limiting clause was not conspicuous and was not known to the plaintiff at the time the contract was made. Indeed, the clause directing the plaintiff's attention to conditions on the reverse side of the acknowledgment was stamped over, indicating that legend was irrelevant. In addition, the plaintiff was directed to check to see if the order as acknowledged conformed to

the terms of the order as the seller otherwise could not be responsible for mistakes in the execution of the order. Thus by implication plaintiff was informed that there was nothing else in the acknowledgment to be checked. Furthermore the defects in the steel allegedly were latent. Absent evidence produced by the defendants tending to refute this evidence or tending to show the paragraph had been negotiated by the parties and agreed to, or that prior contracts between the parties had established a consistently adhered to policy of excluding consequential damages, or whether a recognized trade practice, reasonable as applied to the plaintiff, had established such a policy, we do not believe that the court could reasonably find the clause to be conscionable.

QUESTIONS FOR ANALYSIS

What are the facts in the *Frank's* case? Was the court's reasoning justified? Identify the court's holding. Distinguish between procedural and substantive unconscionability.

11.6 WRITING REQUIREMENTS UNDER ARTICLE 2: THE STATUTE OF FRAUDS

As with the common law, Article 2 of the U.C.C. requires that, under certain circumstances, a contract be in writing to be enforceable; the contract must therefore satisfy the Statute of Frauds. The U.C.C., in § 2-201, provides that contracts for the sale of goods for over $500 must be in writing. The U.C.C. also requires that the contract be "signed by the party against whom enforcement is sought or by his authorized agent or broker." Again, the writing requirement has been relaxed under § 2-201(1), which states that:

> [A] writing is not insufficient because it omits or incorrectly states a term agreed upon but the contract is not enforceable under this paragraph beyond the quantity of goods shown in such writing.

Consequently, lack of price or quantity terms may not defeat allegations that a contract was formed.

The Code has additional requirements for contracts between merchants in complying with the Statute of Frauds. When there is a communication by one party to another, unless the merchant objects to the communication in writing within 10 days after receiving it, the merchant may be bound to a contract for failure to object even if there was no intent to contract. This places an important responsibility on a merchant to pay attention to the communications that are being transmitted.

The writing requirement can be circumvented in three instances, however. Section 2-201(3) indicates that a writing is not required (1) for specially manufactured goods; (2) when a party admits in a court that an oral contract existed; or (3) if the goods have been delivered and accepted or paid for and accepted. In these instances, the U.C.C. does not require that a writing exist in order to find an enforceable contract. Again, we see a relaxation of the restrictions imposed under the common law. Take a look at *R.S. Bennett & Co. v. Economy Mechanical Industries, Inc.*, 606 F.2d 182 (7th Cir. 1979) for a court's interpretation of the U.C.C. Statute of Frauds.

R.S. BENNETT & CO., INC. v. ECONOMY MECHANICAL INDUSTRIES, INC.

United States Court of Appeals, Seventh Circuit
Sept. 19, 1979

PELL, Circuit Judge.

The major issues are, first, whether the defendants are entitled to the protection of the UCC sales statute of frauds, and second, whether, under Illinois law, the statute of frauds defense raised here precludes recovery on either a promissory or equitable estoppel theory.

The plaintiff's claims arise from the bidding on the O'Hare Water Reclamation Plant project owned by the Metropolitan Sanitary District of Greater Chicago. Three parties bid on the contract. The plaintiff is a supplier and servicer of sewage pumps and was at this time seeking to be supplier of the large pumps called for by the general contract.

The defendants formed a joint venture for the purpose of obtaining the mechanical subcontract work from the Paschen joint venture. To accomplish this the defendants orally agreed to work with the Paschen joint venture on the pricing of the mechanical work, and if the Paschen joint venture was successful in obtaining the general contract, the defendants would receive a subcontract for a portion of the mechanical work.

Final bids were due May 6, 1976, at 10:30 a.m. On April 30, the plaintiff sent a scope letter on the large pumps required by the contract to the three general contractors bidding on the contract. The letter did not include a price term. On May 5 the plaintiff provided the defendant, who was representing the Paschen joint venture, with a firm price on the

pumps of $3,295.00. On the same day, the plaintiff provided the same price to the other two general contractors.

On the morning of May 6, only 45 minutes before the close of the bidding, the plaintiff notified each of the three general contractors of its offer to reduce the pump price substantially on the condition that the contractor promise to give the large pump subcontract to the plaintiff if: 1) the general contractor was awarded the job; 2) the plaintiff's price was used in the bid; and 3) the plaintiff's price was the lowest on large pumps. The defendants made this promise to the plaintiff and received the plaintiff's new price, which was used in their bid. The defendants' bid was incorporated in the Paschen joint venture general contract bid. The other general contractors likewise agreed to the terms and received the plaintiff's low price. The Paschen joint venture's final bid was $76,000 lower than the Foster joint venture's bid, however, and Paschen was therefore awarded the contract. The defendants called the plaintiff at 11:50 a.m. on May 6, to inform it of the successful bid and acknowledged that the plaintiff's bid helped them get the job.

In mid-June the parties met to discuss certain modifications to the credit terms. In July 1976, however, the defendants entered a contract with another pump dealer.

The plaintiff's first basis for recovery is breach of contract. The defendants have raised the Uniform

Commercial Code statute of frauds applicable to sales of goods as an affirmative defense to the alleged oral contract. In rebuttal the plaintiff relies on section 2-201(2), which provides that the use by merchants of confirmatory memoranda will, under some circumstances, satisfy the writing requirement of section 2-201(1):

> Between merchants if within a reasonable time a writing in confirmation of the contract and sufficient against the sender is received and the party receiving it has reason to know of its contents, it satisfies the requirements of subsection (1) against such party unless written notice of objection to its contents is given within 10 days after it is received.

The plaintiff has offered two letters to satisfy the section 2-201(2) requirement of a confirmation. It is undisputed that the defendants did not reply to the letters.

The first letter submitted by the plaintiff to satisfy section 2-201(2) was sent on May 6, 1976, after plaintiff heard that the Paschen joint venture had been awarded the contract. It is in form and wording identical to the April 30 general scope letter, except for a price term of "$2,940,000" typed in on the second page. The introductory phrase of the May 6 letter says, "The R.S. Bennett & Company, Inc. is pleased to offer for your consideration its equipment proposal as specified below." The remainder of the 2½ page letter is a fairly detailed list of terms and specifications, including a notation that "pricing [is] firm for 60 days after the bid date."

The other letter relied on by the plaintiffs is dated June 18, 1976. The letter opens with this statement:

> The R.S. Bennett & Company, Inc. is pleased to confirm the following modifications and clarifications to our original equipment offering of May 6, 1976 and our meeting of June 15, 1976.

This statement is followed by a description of terms. The terms listed were followed by this statement:

> As an alternate to the above terms we also offer for your consideration the following.

The rest of the letter described these alternative terms and closed with an invitation to contact Bennett if more information was needed.

The language of these letters quite clearly indicates that the writings are offers and are not "in confirmation of a contract and sufficient against the sender" within the meaning of the plain language of section 2-201(2).

The clear purpose of section 2-201(2) is to make memos of a contract that would be binding on the sender under 2-201(1) equally binding on the party receiving the memo in the absence of objection. In this way the drafters of the Code sought to prevent section 2-201(1) from unfairly becoming an instrument of fraud used to bind the signer of a writing against whom enforcement is sought under that section, while the other party remains free for an unlimited period to continue to shop for a better bargain.

Nothing in these letters indicates that the parties have already made a deal or reached an agreement, or in other words, "evidences a contract," so that the plaintiff, as its sender, would lose the defense of the statute of frauds under section 2-201(1). While we recognize that a firm offer is binding on the sender in the sense that a contract might come into existence if the offer is timely accepted before it is withdrawn, we do not regard this as being the sense of the statutory reference to sufficiency which, in our opinion means sufficient as a contract, not as an executory offer. It thus follows that neither of the letters is a "writing in confirmation of the contract sufficient against the sender" within the meaning of section 2-201(2). We therefore affirm the summary judgment in favor of the defendants on the contract claim.

QUESTIONS FOR ANALYSIS

What facts were important to the court's decision? What did the court cite as the purpose of § 2-201 of the U.C.C.? Identify the court's holding.

Parol Evidence Rule

The Code provides for a parol evidence rule under § 2-202. When an agreement is a final expression of the parties' intention, the parol evidence rule will apply, in that any prior oral statements made to alter or contradict the contract will be excluded. The rule does, however, allow for extrinsic evidence to explain, clarify, or supplement the parties' understanding of the contract. Section 2-202 states:

> Terms with respect to which the confirmatory memoranda of the parties agree or which are otherwise set forth in a writing intended by the parties as a final expression of their agreement with respect to such terms as are included therein may not be contradicted by evidence of any prior agreement or of a contemporaneous oral agreement but may be explained or supplemented
>
> (a) by course of dealing or usage of trade (Section 1-205) or by course of performance (Section 2-208); and
> (b) by evidence of consistent additional terms unless the court finds the writing to have been intended also as a complete and exclusive statement of the terms of the agreement.

The Code thus provides that terms can be explained by course of dealing, usage of trade, and course of performance.

Course of Dealing

Prior actions and conduct have legal significance when determining whether a contract exists between the parties. Section 1-205(1) governs how the parties' course of dealing is interpreted:

> A course of dealing is a sequence of previous conduct between the parties to a particular transaction which is fairly to be regarded as establishing a common basis of understanding for interpreting their expressions and other conduct.

As the Code section suggests, the conduct is personal to the parties and may be different between different sellers and buyers.

Usage of Trade

Commonly accepted industry standards and practices are the basis of **usage of trade**. The Code provides guidance in § 1-205(2):

> A usage of trade is any practice or method of dealing having such regularity of observance in a place, vocation or trade as to justify an expectation that it will be observed with respect to the transaction in question. If it is established that such a usage is embodied in a written trade code or similar writing, the interpretation of the writing is for the court.

Course of Performance

The repeated acts of performance by the parties to the contract are construed as a *course of performance.* This concept encompasses the parties' habits; that is, the parties' past performance with each other. The Code provides in § 2-208(1):

> Where the contract for sale involves repeated occasions for performance by either party with knowledge of the nature of the performance and opportunity for objection to it by the other, any course of performance accepted or acquiesced in without objection shall be relevant to determine the meaning of the agreement.

How to interpret the conduct of the parties was an issue in *Blalock Machinery & Equipment Co. v. Iowa Manufacturing Co.,* 576 F. Supp. 774 (N.D. Ga. 1983). Review this case and see if the conclusion is fair.

TERMS

usage of trade
Under the Uniform Commercial Code, "Any practice or method of dealing having such regularity of observance in a place, vocation, or trade as to justify an expectation that it will be observed with respect to the transaction in question." Trade usage is also referred to as usage of trade.

BLALOCK MACHINERY AND EQUIPMENT COMPANY, INC. v. IOWA MANUFACTURING COMPANY

United States District Court, N.D. Georgia
July 5, 1983

The parties entered into a distributorship contract on January 2, 1960 which was a confirmation of an earlier agreement between the parties. The defendant is a manufacturer of heavy equipment, and the plaintiff was one of its dealers for over 27 years. Under the contract the plaintiff received a "protected area"—the entire state of Georgia. It further appears to the court that during the life of the contract, plaintiff sold no products of competitors of the defendant, hired personnel to sell and handle defendant's products, and maintained a stock of defendant's products and replacement parts.

Paragraph XVIII of the distributorship contract states in pertinent part that the agreement is deemed to be executed and entered into in the State of Iowa and that it shall be construed, enforced and performed in accordance with the laws of the State of Iowa.

Paragraph XV(1) of the distributorship contract states that the agreement shall continue until terminated as provided in the agreement.

Paragraph XV(2) of the distributorship contract states that "either party may terminate this contract

at any time by notice in writing of an election to do so, transmitted by United States registered mail or by telegram addressed to the other party at the address herein indicated. Any such cancellation shall become effective thirty (30) days from the date of transmittal of such notice, subject to the rights and obligations of the parties then existing."

On August 10, 1981, written notice of termination of the distributorship contract by Iowa Manufacturing was forwarded to Blalock by United States registered mail. The termination of the distributorship contract became effective 30 days from the date of the written notice.

The court recognizes that the good faith obligation of the UCC has been adopted by Iowa and is applicable to distributorship contracts; however, the parties have not cited and the court has not found any cases applying Iowa law that hold that the good faith obligation overrides the express terms of the contract. [T]he court declines to conclude that the UCC prohibits arbitrary termination of distributorship contracts. The express terms of the contract state that either party may terminate the contract at any time. There is no specific language in the termination clause which states that such termination may only be made with cause. Absent such language, it is logically inferred and may be concluded that either party may terminate the contract at any time without cause, and the court believes the parties to have "understood" the termination clause to mean such.

Plaintiff contends that even if the language in the termination clause of the contract could be interpreted to permit an unrestricted and arbitrary termination, this result is not supported by the parties' course of dealing and course of performance. Plaintiff directs the court's attention to Iowa Code Ann. § 554.2202 which provides that the "parties' course of dealing or course of performance may explain or supplement the contract."

The court recognizes that the course of dealing and course of performance may supplement the express terms of the contract. [It] appears to the court that the parties had a business relationship for approximately 27 years, and that due to the continuous dealings between the parties and the continuous performance of both parties, both the plaintiff and the defendant may have created a reasonable expectation in the other that neither would terminate the distributorship contract without cause, although the contract expressly gave both of them the right to do so.

As previously stated, the plaintiff attempted to construe the express terms of the termination clause to mean that either party could terminate the contract only upon a showing of cause. The court has ruled that the express terms in the termination clause of the contract cannot be construed as such, and therefore concludes that these express contract terms must control over any conflicting course of dealing or course of performance.

QUESTIONS FOR ANALYSIS

What are the facts of *Blalock*? Did the court consider the parties' conduct in its decision? Why or why not? What was the court's holding?

11.7 A NEW ADDITION: ARTICLE 2A ON LEASES

Leasing of goods has been common in the United States for quite some time. However, in interpreting the parties' rights under **leases**, the courts often looked to Articles 2 and 9 of the Uniform Commercial Code. This did not solve everyone's problems and, as a result, Article 2A was drafted by the National Conference of Commissioners on Uniform State Laws beginning in 1985. After some adjustments and amendments, the official version that was adopted and approved by the commissioners is what we now recognize as the 1990 version. More than 31 states have, since December 1, 1992, adopted Article 2A in its present or revised form. Consequently, it is an important addition to understanding current commercial transactions. See Figure 11-5 for states adopting Article 2A.

As with the previous articles under the Code, Article 2A is divided into sections, which are structured as shown in Figure 11-6. These sections govern the performance of the parties to a lease agreement and guide the courts in determining a person's rights or responsibilities under a lease.

Article 2A regulates transactions for the lease of goods between a lessor and a lessee. A *lease* is defined in § 2A-103 as a transfer of the right

TERMS

lease
A contract for the possession of real estate in consideration of payment of rent, ordinarily for term of years or months, but sometimes at will. The person making the conveyance is the landlord or lessor; the person receiving the right of possession is the tenant or lessee.

Alabama	Maine	Pennsylvania
Arizona	Michigan	Rhode Island
California	Minnesota	South Dakota
Colorado	Missouri	Utah
Delaware	Montana	Virginia
District of Columbia	Nebraska	Wisconsin
Florida	Nevada	Wyoming
Hawaii	New Mexico	
Illinois	North Dakota	
Indiana	Ohio	
Kansas	Oklahoma	
Kentucky	Oregon	

FIGURE 11-5   States that have adopted U.C.C. Article 2A

Part 1:   General Provisions

Explanation: Includes the scope of Article 2A, definitions that apply in Article 2A, and which laws govern such transactions.

Part 2:   Formation and Construction of Lease Contract

Explanation: General discussion of offer and acceptance. Included is a very detailed explanation of warranties given in lease arrangements, as well as some important risk-of-loss provisions, and the effect when goods identified to the contract are damaged or destroyed.

Part 3:   Effect of the Lease Contract

Explanation: Deals with the effect of the lease on the performance and transfer of rights as well as any subsequent leases by the parties. Also deals with the priority of rights under liens when goods become fixtures or are seized.

Part 4:   Performance of Lease Contract: Repudiated, Substituted, and Excused

Explanation: Explains the legal ramifications when performance is either not given or is legally excused.

Part 5:   Default

Explanation: Divided into three subsections. The first, "General," deals with general provisions regarding default of a party. The second part, "Default by Lessor," sets forth a *lessee*'s rights and remedies upon a lessor's default. The third subsection deals with default by the lessee; it also deals with the rights and remedies of the lessor and the legal ramifications when the lessee fails to perform under the lease.

FIGURE 11-6   Parts of U.C.C. Article 2A

to possession and use of goods for a term in return for consideration. The big question under Article 2A is whether the transaction between the parties creates a "true lease": Is the lease between the parties in fact a security interest and not a lease? This answer determines whether Article 2A or Article 9 governs the transaction. This determination is made under § 1-201(37), which states that:

> [W]hether a transaction creates a lease or security interest is determined by the facts of each case; however, a transaction creates a security interest if the consideration the lessee is to pay the lessor for the right to possession and use of the goods is an obligation for the term of the lease and not subject to termination by the lessee, and
>
> (a) the original term of the lease is equal to or greater than the remaining economic life of the goods,
> (b) the lessee is bound to renew the lease for the remaining economic life of the goods or is bound to become the owner of the goods,
> (c) the lessee has an option to renew the lease for the remaining economic life of the goods for no additional consideration or nominal additional consideration upon compliance with the lease agreement, or
> (d) the lessee has the option to become the owner of the goods for no additional consideration or nominal consideration upon compliance with the lease agreement.

This section provides guidance in determining which article is to govern, but much confusion and uneasiness still remain because Article 2A is relatively new and has not been interpreted in many cases.

In addition to defining a true lease, Article 2A governs consumer leases and finance leases. This again gives some assistance to courts in interpreting the governing principles of leases.

In determining what rules apply to leases, it is important to review U.C.C. Article 2's sections on formation of a contract (which include offer and acceptance, course of performance, the parol evidence rule, and the Statute of Frauds). Virtually all provisions discussed in Article 2 have a corresponding provision in Article 2A specifically dealing with leases. However, there are some restrictions under Article 2A that are not found in Article 2. Specifically, the freedom of contract is restricted in dealing with consumer leases. Article 2A reduces the restrictions on warranties and, in effect, extends the statute of limitations on the filing of cases. Article 2 establishes a four-year statute of limitations on sale of goods. Although Article 2A does have a four-year statute of limitations, the statute begins to run on discovery of the defect rather than when the goods are provided. This is a major difference between Article 2A and Article 2.

The rights and remedies afforded to parties in a lease arrangement are similar to those in Article 2. In addition, parties can agree to provisions regarding remedies. The remedies provided a lessor and a lessee upon default are extensively treated in part 5 of Article 2A and are similar to those in Article 2.

It is incumbent upon the paralegal to determine whether Article 2A has been adopted in a state where a lease is in dispute. This will show which case law and statutes will determine the rights and responsibilities of the parties.

11.8 PRACTICAL APPLICATIONS

As a paralegal, you will probably be asked to draft standard bills of sale. When drafting a bill of sale, be sure to include the names of the seller and buyer, the date, the amount paid and the description of the goods sold. Figure 11-7 illustrates a typical bill of sale.

Bill of Sale

Know All Men by These Presents that Wayne Morrison, of 2200 Burkdale, Oklahoma City, Oklahoma, in consideration of Ten Thousand Dollars ($10,000.00) paid and delivered by Jonathan Ramos of 22 East 10th Street, Oklahoma City, Oklahoma, the receipt of which is hereby acknowledged, does hereby sell, assign, convey, transfer, and deliver to Jonathan Ramos the following goods:

650 pairs of roller skates

To have and to hold the same unto the said buyer and the heirs, executors, administrators, successors, and assigns of the said buyer forever.

Dated this the 21st day of November, 1995.

_____
Wayne Morrison

FIGURE 11-7 Sample bill of sale

Often, a contract which forms the basis of the sale is part of the sales transaction. How detailed the contract must be depends entirely on the transaction and the parties' requirements. Figure 11-8 is an example of a general contract for the sale of goods.

General Contract for Sale of Goods

Jason Jones of 223 10th Street, Boston, Massachusetts (seller), agrees to sell and Cynthia Day of 123 ABC Street, Boston, Massachusetts (buyer), agrees to buy [describe or identify goods] at $ [price] per ton to be delivered by Jason Jones to Cynthia Day on or before June 1, 1995. In consideration of the promises and of the mutual benefits to each party, it is further agreed as follows:

1. *Description.* The goods which are the subject of this sale and which seller shall deliver to buyer and for which buyer shall pay shall conform to the following specifications: [insert terms].

2. *Warranty.* Seller warrants that the goods shall meet the specifications described herein. The foregoing warranty is exclusive and is in lieu of all other warranties, whether

---

FIGURE 11-8 Sample general contract for sale of goods

written, oral, or implied, including the warranty of merchantability and the warranty of fitness for a particular purpose.

3. *Delivery.* Delivery shall be on or before [date] and shall be to buyer at seller's place of business. Seller agrees to furnish the facilities and at its cost to load the goods on trucks furnished by buyer.

4. *Packaging.* Buyer shall give seller instructions for the packaging of the goods not less than 48 hours prior to the date of delivery, and the reasonable cost of such packaging shall be charged to buyer.

5. *Title.* Title shall remain with seller until delivery and actual receipt thereof by buyer.

6. *Risk of Loss.* Identification shall take place on the packaging of the goods, and the risk of loss shall pass on such identification.

7. *Price and Time of Payment.* The price of the goods shall be $[amount], and shall be paid at the time and place of delivery by bank draft or cashier's check or certified check.

8. *Inspection.* Inspection shall be made by buyer at the time and place of delivery.

9. *Claims.* Buyer's failure to give notice of any claim within [number] days from the date of delivery shall constitute an unqualified acceptance of the goods and a waiver by buyer of all claims with respect thereto.

10. *Remedies.* Buyer's exclusive remedy and seller's limit of liability for any and all losses or damages resulting from defective goods or from any other cause shall be for the purchase price of the particular delivery with respect to which losses or damages are claimed plus any transportation charges actually paid by buyer.

11. *Assignment.* Buyer may not assign its rights or delegate its performance hereunder without the prior written consent of seller, and any attempted assignment or delegation without such consent shall be void.

12. *Construction.* This contract is to be construed according to the laws of, and under the Uniform Commercial Code as adopted by, the State of Massachusetts. This document constitutes the full understanding of the parties, and no terms of this document shall be binding unless hereafter made in writing and signed by the party to be bound.

Signed and sealed in triplicate this 3d day of May, 1995.

_____   _____
Buyer   Seller

FIGURE 11-8 *(Continued)*

On occasion, the paralegal may be asked to draft an output or requirements contract. Figure 11-9 provides an example of each.

Contract by Manufacturer to Sell Entire Output

1. *Parties.* This contract is executed November 1, 1995, between James Woods, of 123 Dee Street, Branson, Missouri, herein called "seller," and Thomas James, of 987 Lily Street, Branson, Missouri, herein called "buyer."

2. *Agreement of Sale.* Seller agrees to sell and buyer agrees to buy all [identify goods], herein called "goods," manufactured by seller in its place of business at 1200 Elm Street, Branson, Missouri, from November 1, 1995 to December 1, 1995, at the following prices: [set forth price schedules].

3. *Delivery and Payment.* Seller agrees to deliver promptly to buyer, at the place of business of buyer, all goods manufactured by it; and buyer agrees to pay on Saturday at each week for all goods delivered at the prices above specified.

4. *Exclusive Dealings.* Seller covenants and agrees that it will not sell or give away the goods manufactured by it to any person or persons, firm or firms, corporation or corporations,

FIGURE 11-9 Sample output and requirements contracts

other than buyer, during the term of this agreement, and in case of a violation of this covenant on the part of seller, buyer shall have, in addition to such remedy or remedies as it may be entitled by law to pursue, the right to refuse to accept and pay for any goods thereafter manufactured by seller under the terms of this agreement.

5. *Nonpayment.* If buyer fails to make payment, as herein provided, for goods delivered, seller shall have, in addition to such remedy or remedies as it may be entitled by law to pursue, the right to rescind and cancel this contract, or at its option, to defer further deliveries until all goods delivered have been paid for.

6. *Excuse for Nonperformance.* Seller shall not be responsible for delay in deliveries, or for failure to make deliveries, caused by fire, strike, or any other contingency beyond its control.

By: _____   By: _____

_____ [Title]   _____ [Title]
[Seller]   [Buyer]

Requirements Contract

1. *Parties.* This contract is executed by Matthew Chandler, of 8209 Chesham Drive, Rowlett, Texas, herein called "seller," and Lori Bugsby, of 2003 Walnut Street, Rowlett, Texas, herein called "buyer."

2. *Requirements of Buyer.* Seller agrees to supply to buyer its requirements of petroleum products for a period of three years and thereafter until termination of this agreement.

3. *Price.* The price of the products, consisting of [describe product], to be delivered to buyer shall be based on seller's tank wagon market price in effect at the time of delivery less the following deductions or discounts: [specify discounts].

4. *Termination upon Notice.* Either party hereto may terminate this agreement by giving to the other 120 days' notice in writing before the end of any yearly period.

_____   _____
Matthew Chandler   Lori Bugsby

FIGURE 11-9 *(Continued)*

The paralegal may be given the task of drafting a lease or related lease documents that conform to Article 2A requirements. Sometimes, in the negotiation process, one party may make an offer in writing to lease. Figure 11-10 is a sample of such an offer.

Offer to Lease Personal Property

To: Janet Donally, 821 Main Street, Cedar Rapids, Iowa

I, D & J Leasing Co., offer to lease to you, Janet Donally, the following goods: Four (4) 486X Computers and Printers for monthly payments of Two Hundred Fifty Dollars ($250.00). The terms of this offer to lease are to be negotiated. This offer to lease is made pursuant to Article 2A of the Uniform Commercial Code.

This offer remains open until March 31, 1995. You may accept this offer by mailing a written notice of acceptance on or before the date indicated above. However, this offer may be accepted only on the terms set forth in this instrument.

FIGURE 11-10 Sample offer to lease personal property

The paralegal also may be asked to draft a personal property lease. There are a number of forms that can be followed, but Figure 11-11 is an example of a basic personal property lease. Some provisions to consider when drafting a lease are as follows. In some form, these provisions should be included in any lease.

Personal Property Lease

1. DESCRIPTION OF PARTIES AND PROPERTY LEASED. Discovery Computers, Inc., of 1234 East Lake Road, City of Las Vegas, State of Nevada, addressed as lessor in this agreement, leases to Jon M. Vaughn, 5678 Lake Pine Drive, City of Las Vegas, State of Nevada, addressed as lessee in this agreement, and lessee hires from lessor, the following described personal property: [computer equipment to be installed at] 2345 Main Street, Las Vegas, Nevada.

2. TERMS OF LEASE. The term of this lease shall be 12 months, such term to commence on June 1, 1995, and to terminate on May 30, 1996, unless otherwise terminated as provided in this lease.

3. RENT. In consideration for leasing of the above-described property, lessee agrees to pay lessor as rent for such property the sum of Two Hundred Fifty Dollars and No Cents ($250.00) per month, the first payment of which rent is due on or before June 1, 1995, and each subsequent payment of which is payable on or before the first day of each month thereafter, during the entire term of the lease. Such payments shall be made at lessor's address as set out in § 1 if this lease.

4. MAINTENANCE AND REPAIR. Lessee shall exercise due care in the use and maintenance of the leased property, keeping it in good repair and in a condition equivalent in all respects to that in which it was received by lessee, normal wear and tear excepted.

5. ASSIGNMENT OR SUBLEASE. Lessee will not assign this lease or sublet the leased property unless the written consent of lessor to such assignment or sublease is first obtained.

6. DEFAULT. If lessee shall be in default of any of the rental payments, when the payments shall become due and payable as provided in this agreement, or shall remove or attempt to remove the leased property from 2345 Main Street, Las Vegas, Nevada, without first obtaining the written consent of lessor, lessor shall, at his or her option, terminate this lease and lessee's right to possession of the leased property, and lessor shall then without demand on or notice to lessee take possession of such leased property.

7. INSPECTION BY LESSOR. Lessor shall at all times during lessee's business hours have the right to enter on the premises where the leased property is located for the purpose of inspecting the property.

8. INDEMNITY. Lessee will indemnify lessor against, and hold lessor harmless from, all claims, actions, proceedings, damages, and liabilities, including attorney fees, arising from or connected with lessee's possession, use, and return of the leased property.

9. APPLICABLE LAW. This lease and the construction of this lease will be governed by the laws of the State of Nevada.

10. NOTICES. Any notices to be given under this lease shall be given by mailing the notices to lessor at 1234 East Lake Road, City of Las Vegas, State of Nevada, and to lessee at 5678 Lake Pine Drive, City of Las Vegas, State of Nevada.

Dated _____.

_____
Discovery Computers, Inc., Lessor

_____
Jon M. Vaughn, Lessee

FIGURE 11-11 Sample personal property lease

- Applicable law
- Applicable judicial forum
- Modification of agreement—Signed writing required
- Transferability of rights clause authorizing transfer or transferability of rights clause prohibiting transfer
- Disclaimer of implied warranties
- Renewal clause (automatic or optional renewal)

Typical contractual provisions relate to notice of renewal of the lease and notice of default. Usually these types of letters are in direct response to a lease's contractual provisions. Figure 11-12 illustrates each type of notice letter.

Notice by Lessee of Intention to Renew Lease

You are notified pursuant to Section _____ of the lease executed on December 14, 1995, between Geyser, Inc., as lessor, and Hamilton Corporation, as lessee, that the undersigned, as lessee, elects to renew the lease for an additional period of two years (2) beginning January 14, 1996, on the termination of the lease, pursuant to the same terms and same rental as contained in the lease and pursuant to the terms of such lease.

Dated:_____

_____
Geyser, Inc., Lessor

_____
Hamilton Corporation, Lessee

Notice by Lessor of Termination of Lease Due to Default in Rental

Geyser, Inc.   October 31, 1996
14550 Dallas Parkway
Dallas, Texas 75240

Notice is given that under the lease agreement between Geyser, Inc. and Hamilton Corporation, dated December 14, 1995, whereby Geyser, Inc. leased from Hamilton Corporation hospital beds, the sum of Ten Thousand Five Hundred Dollars ($10,500.00), rent payment for the period of October 1, 1996 through November 31, 1996, is unpaid and in default.

Notice is given that Hamilton Corporation, pursuant to the terms of such agreement, elects to terminate the lease by reason of such default, and to take immediate possession of the personal property that is the subject of the lease.

You are hereby required to deliver to Hamilton Corporation all of the leased property, at the premises of Hamilton Corporation on receipt of this notice, in accordance with the terms of the lease agreement.

Very truly yours,
Hamilton Corporation

FIGURE 11-12 Sample lease renewal notices

SUMMARY

11.1 The Uniform Commercial Code is a statute that regulates commercial transactions. It has been adopted in some form in all 50 states and provides uniformity for parties entering into commercial transactions. The U.C.C. developed into nine articles.

11.2 A sale transfers title from seller to buyer for a price. Article 2 relates to the sale of goods between merchants and nonmerchants. Sales between merchants are subject to higher standards of good faith and reasonableness than for nonmerchants. The sale between parties must be a sale of goods.

11.3 Rules of contract formation have been relaxed under the U.C.C. Contracts may be enforceable even if they are indefinite, lack terms, and are incomplete. The Code will allow nonconforming goods to be shipped as an accommodation, although the buyer's right to accept or reject the goods is unchanged. Additionally, consideration is not necessary to hold an offer open under the U.C.C.

11.4 The mirror image rule is completely modified under the Code. An offer and acceptance need not be exact. Even if terms are missing or left open, a contract may be formed between the parties. Further, delivery and price terms can be left open. New terms can be added to the offer if they are consistent with the contract. Output and requirements contracts are allowed under the U.C.C. and will not be held invalid for indefiniteness.

11.5 As with the common law, contracts cannot be unconscionable. Unconscionability falls into two categories: procedural and substantive. Procedural unconscionability is when the contract lacks meaningful choice. Substantive unconscionability focuses on the terms of the contract itself. Two important areas of substantive unconscionability focus on liquidated damage clauses and remedy provisions.

11.6 The U.C.C. has a Statute of Frauds and a parol evidence rule provision. Both of these rules have been relaxed under the U.C.C. Lack of a writing containing all the material terms will not defeat a contract. Under the parol evidence rule, course of dealing, usage of trade, and course of performance are used to interpret the conduct of the parties.

11.7 Because leasing of goods is a common method of doing business, a new U.C.C. article, known as Article 2A, was developed to govern transactions between lessors and lessees. Article 2A has five parts. In addition, different types of leases are analyzed, as are remedies for breach of a lease.

REVIEW QUESTIONS

1. Is the U.C.C. a successful statute? Why or why not?
2. How many articles are found in the U.C.C., and what are their titles?
3. How does Article 2 define *sale* and *good*?
4. Distinguish between a merchant and a nonmerchant.
5. List three main departures that the U.C.C. made from the common law of contracts.
6. How is the mirror image rule modified under the Code?
7. Distinguish a requirements contract from an output contract.
8. What is the difference between procedural and substantive unconscionability?
9. When can the Statute of Frauds be circumvented in a sale-of-goods transaction?
10. Identify the different sections under Article 2A and why Article 2A was developed.

EXERCISES

1. Mr. Michael Andrews wants to lease his computer with laser printer to Ms. Emily Browning for a one-year term beginning April 8, 1995, until April 8, 1996. The lease payment is $300 per month due on the 8th day of each month. The parties have agreed to have two renewals at the same payment and for the same terms. Draft the personal property lease between the parties.
2. After some thought, Ms. Browning decides to buy her own computer and laser printer from Computers America. The computer costs $1,500 and the laser printer costs $939. Draft the bill of sale for this transaction.
3. Ms. Browning has met with some financial difficulties and she has missed her August and September payments. Mr. Andrews wants to terminate the computer lease and give notice to Ms. Browning that she is in default. Draft the default letter to Ms. Browning.

CHAPTER 12
Performance under Article 2: Seller and Buyer Duties

12.1 GENERAL OBLIGATIONS

When a contract for the sale of goods has been created between a buyer and a seller, the parties have certain basic duties. Section 2-301 of the Uniform Commercial Code sets out the general obligations of the parties to a sale-of-goods contract:

> The obligation of the seller is to transfer and deliver and that of the buyer is to accept and pay in accordance with the contract.

Thus, the seller simply has to deliver goods that conform to the terms of the contract and deliver those goods in accordance with the agreement or in accordance with the Code; the buyer has the responsibility to pay for those goods upon delivery. Once these acts have occurred, the sales transaction is complete.

There are variations on this simple rule that goods must be tendered and payment must be made under the U.C.C. This chapter explores the

U.C.C. provisions for when the seller's and buyer's duties are not specifically stated.

12.2 SELLER'S DUTIES AND OBLIGATIONS

The basic duties of a seller in a sales contract are to tender and deliver goods to the buyer. One question that may arise is whether a proper tender of the goods has been made. The U.C.C. states, in § 2-503, that:

> [T]ender of delivery requires that the seller put and hold conforming goods at the buyer's disposition and give the buyer any notification reasonably necessary to enable him to take delivery.

Section 2-503 also specifies the manner, time, and place for the tender of goods. The Code specifically states that tender must be made at a reasonable hour and that the buyer must furnish facilities to accept the goods in the contract.

There are variations under § 2-503, which affect when the goods are to be shipped by means of a common carrier, when the goods are in the hands of a bailee, and when the goods are being delivered through a document of title. Therefore, when the seller delivers conforming goods, no matter what the method of delivery, the buyer must accept the goods and pay for them.

Delivery by Common Carrier

Although delivery to a **common carrier** is a frequent requirement in sales transactions, additional considerations arise between the parties. First, the seller must deliver the goods to the common carrier, such as a ship, truck, or train. There will usually be documents that instruct the carrier as to the method of shipment and liability of the parties while the goods are in transit. (This becomes important with respect to the title issues discussed in Chapter 13.) Second, the goods must be properly loaded and transported by the common carrier. A concern by the seller is that the goods arrive to the buyer undamaged. This can be a problem, because once the goods are placed on the carrier, the seller loses control over the goods. Third, once the goods arrive, the buyer must accept them and pay for them. If the goods reach the buyer unharmed, the sales contract is completed when all parties perform their obligations. But, as will be seen later in this chapter, complications may arise.

Delivery to a Bailee

Goods can be delivered to a third party known as a **bailee**. The bailee holds the goods on behalf of the **bailor** until instructions are given as to disposition of the goods. Normally, the instructions for delivery are found in a **document of title**, which tells the bailee who owns the goods and to whom

TERMS

common carrier
A person or company that represents itself as engaged in the business of transporting persons or property from place to place, for compensation, offering its services to the public generally.

bailee
The person to whom property is entrusted in a bailment.

bailor
The person who entrusts property to another in a bailment.

document of title
Any document which in the regular course of business is treated as evidencing that the person in possession of it is entitled to receive, hold, and dispose of the document and the goods to which it pertains.

BLONDIE

DEAN YOUNG

title is to be transferred upon delivery. Section 2-503(4)(a) and (b) provide guidance in a bailment situation:

> (4) Where goods are in the possession of a bailee and are to be delivered without being moved
>
>   (a) tender requires that the seller either tender a negotiable document of title covering such goods or procure acknowledg-ment by the bailee of the buyer's right to possession of the goods; but
>
>   (b) tender to the buyer of a non-negotiable document of title or of a written direction to the bailee to deliver is sufficient tender unless the buyer seasonably objects, and receipt by the bailee of notification of the buyer's rights fixes those rights as against the bailee and all third persons; but risk of loss of the goods and of any failure by the bailee to honor the non-negotiable document of title or to obey the direction remains on the seller until the buyer has had a reasonable time to present the document or direction, and a refusal by the bailee to honor the document or to obey the direction defeats the tender.

In a sense, the transfer is done on paper, without physical delivery of the goods to the buyer. This is a common method of delivery in the commercial world (see Figure 12-1).

Bailor
(transfers goods and title) ——————————— Bailee
holds goods until
instructed to transfer

Buyer (third party)
gains title to goods

FIGURE 12-1   Delivery by bailment

Figure 12-2 shows some provisions to use when goods are delivered to a bailee.

Tender of Delivery When Goods in Possession of Bailee to Be Delivered Without Being Moved—Negotiable Document

At the time of executing this contract, the goods are located in the [name of warehouse] at [address]. Seller shall deliver the documents necessary for buyer to obtain the goods from the warehouseman to the buyer at [address]. Delivery of documents shall satisfy seller's obligations hereunder.

OR

The goods which are the subject of this agreement are presently in the possession of [identify warehouseman] at [address]. Delivery will be made by negotiable documents covering the goods by seller to buyer.

Tender of Delivery When Goods in Possession of Bailee to Be Delivered Without Being Moved—Procure Acknowledgment

The goods which are the subject of this agreement are presently in the possession of [identify carrier or warehouseman]. Delivery will be made by seller to buyer when seller obtains and delivers to buyer an acknowledgment from the bailee of the buyer's right to possession of the goods.

FIGURE 12-2   Sample delivery clauses for bailments

Delivery by Document of Title

When a document of title is used to effectuate delivery, the inquiry goes beyond Article 2. A document of title can be a bill of lading, a warehouse receipt, or any other document that transfers ownership. Article 7 of the Code, entitled "Warehouse Receipts, Bills of Lading, and other Documents of Title," governs documents of title and sets out the rights of the parties handling documents of title. Consequently, Article 2 and Article 7 may have to be reviewed together if documents of title are used as a means of delivery of goods.

Delivery of the Goods: No Delivery Place

When a contract does not specifically state a place for delivery, § 2-308(a) sets forth how delivery should be made. Delivery is proper at the seller's place of business or, if there is no place of business, at the seller's residence. This suggests that the buyer has a responsibility to pick up the goods and that the seller has only to notify the buyer that the goods are ready and provide a reasonable time to pick them up. This is logical. Think about when you purchase a television or VCR: you, the buyer, go to the seller's place of business to pick up the product and, in effect, there is a tender of delivery.

However, § 2-308(b) suggests that the proper place of delivery for identified goods, when the goods are at a location other than the seller's residence or place of business, is where the goods are located. The Code is specific in its guidance when a place for delivery is not identified. Familiarity with these Code sections is important in determining whether proper tender of delivery has occurred between the parties.

12.3 SHIPMENT CONTRACTS: PARTIES' RIGHTS AND RESPONSIBILITIES

When the goods which are the subject of the contract have to be transported, the U.C.C. provides direction as to the proper means of delivery. Any contract under which the goods must be shipped to the buyer is either a shipment contract or a destination contract. In a *shipment contract,* the seller contracts with a carrier for shipment of the goods and releases those goods to the carrier. When the goods are surrendered to the carrier, the buyer technically owns the goods. Under a shipment contract, tender of performance occurs when the goods are surrendered to the carrier. Thus, the buyer is thereafter responsible for the goods as the owner.

In contrast, under a *destination contract,* the seller tenders the goods to the carrier, but the buyer neither becomes responsible for the goods nor has ownership of the goods until the carrier tenders the goods directly to the buyer. However, the buyer agrees to accept delivery when the goods arrive. Tender is not complete until the goods reach the buyer's destination. If the parties have not agreed to the type of delivery contract, the Code provides that a shipment contract, rather than a destination contract, will be implied.

A seller is required to perform certain obligations to accomplish proper tender of the goods. Under § 2-504, a seller must:

(a) put the goods in the possession of such a carrier and make such a contract for the transportation as may be reasonable having regard to the nature of the goods and other circumstances of the case; and

(b) obtain and promptly deliver or tender in due form any documents necessary to enable the buyer to obtain possession of the goods or otherwise required by the agreement or by usage of trade; and

(c) promptly notify the buyer of the shipment.

These provisions must be carefully met, or the seller may be found not to have properly tendered delivery. Lack of proper tender of delivery may allow the buyer to reject the goods, which the seller undoubtedly does not desire.

Note, however, that a destination contract is very specific as to the method of transport. It not only requires shipment from a particular place but also delivery at a particular destination. For example, a seller located in Boston contracts to sell and deliver goods to a buyer in New York at the buyer's warehouse in New York. The delivery is not complete until the goods are delivered to the buyer's warehouse, after notice to the buyer that the goods have been shipped and delivery is forthcoming.

The Code, as well as custom and usage, determine the type of contract between the parties through the use of certain *mercantile terms.* These terms are important in determining who has responsibility for the shipment and when ownership rights pass to the buyer.

F.O.B. The term F.O.B. means "free on board." In the shipping of goods, "F.O.B. place of origin" or "F.O.B. place of destination" are used to determine title, liability, and shipping costs. Therefore, understanding the term *F.O.B.* is essential to determining the seller's and buyer's responsibilities under the contract. For example, assume that the seller's place of business is St. Louis and the seller is shipping goods from St. Louis to Miami, F.O.B. St. Louis. That means that once the seller has loaded the goods on the carrier, the buyer becomes responsible for the goods. "F.O.B. place of origin" indicates a shipment contract.

If, however, the seller was in St. Louis, the buyer was in Miami, and the contract was F.O.B. Miami, the seller would be responsible for the goods until they reached their destination. Thus, "F.O.B. place of destination" creates a destination contract.

F.A.S. The term *F.A.S.* means "free along side" and is used primarily when goods are shipped on a seagoing vessel. When the term *F.A.S.* is used, the price quoted will include all costs and shipping expenses to get the goods to the buyer's place of business or named destination. Consequently, if the seller is in Miami and the buyer is in New York, a contract stating "F.A.S. Miami" means that the buyer is responsible for the goods the moment they are loaded on the ship. Once the seller transports the goods to the ship at the port of departure, the seller has technically delivered the goods and is relieved of further responsibility. The buyer is responsible for the goods in transit from the point of departure, at Miami, to New York.

Sometimes sellers will interchange the term *F.A.S.* with *F.O.B.* The results and responsibilities are the same. If there is any question as to when a party's responsibility begins and ends, ask. Do not let lack of experience cause undue costs to a client or customer. Provisions that might be included when the contract calls for F.O.B. or F.A.S. shipment are in Figure 12-3.

C.I.F. and C & F The terms *C.I.F.* and *C & F* are related shipment terms. *C.I.F.* means cost, insurance, and freight, whereas *C & F* means only cost and freight. The price of the goods includes the freight costs and insurance costs under a C.I.F. contract. C.I.F. and C & F are normally used in conjunction with a shipment contract, where the seller's responsibilities cease when the goods are loaded onto the carrier. Figure 12-4 shows some common C.I.F. and C & F provisions in shipment contracts.

Ex-Ship The term *Ex-Ship* refers to a contract under which the goods are shipped by sea. Like an F.O.B. destination contract to the buyer's place of business, ex-ship indicates a destination contract where the seller pays all

---

Provision of Sales Agreement—F.O.B. and F.A.S. as price terms

The terms F.O.B. and F.A.S. as used in this agreement are price terms only and impose no duty on seller apart from guaranteeing the price at which the goods are to be sold.

Provision of Sales Agreement—F.O.B. and F.A.S. as delivery terms modified as to risk

Any F.O.B. or F.A.S. term used in this agreement shall be construed as a delivery term, but seller shall have the risk of loss until the goods covered by this agreement have been delivered to the facility of buyer and are approved after inspection by buyer.

Provision of Sales Agreement—F.O.B. and F.A.S. as delivery terms modified as to expenses

Any F.O.B. or F.A.S. term used in this agreement shall be construed as a delivery term, but expenses incurred by seller in moving the goods from the place of business of seller, and in loading, shipping, or delivering the goods, shall be charged to buyer.

FIGURE 12-3 Sample clauses for F.O.B. or F.A.S. shipment

costs and expenses, including unloading the goods at the buyer's named destination. The seller is not relieved of any responsibility until the goods reach the specified destination and are unloaded. Some ex-ship provisions used in shipment contracts are shown in Figure 12-5.

No Arrival, No Sale When goods are placed in transit and arrive either damaged, destroyed, or not at all, the seller may be responsible. In a **no arrival, no sale** contract, the seller bears the risk of transit. Critical to a no arrival, no sale contract is determining who is responsible for the damaged or destroyed goods. If the seller can show proper performance under the contract,

---

Provision of Sales Agreement—Insurance requirements

On shipment of goods by [type of carrier] to [address], seller shall purchase for the account of and at the expense of buyer sufficient insurance to cover the costs of the goods to buyer plus _____ percent [____%] of such costs. The insurance policy shall be a [form of policy]. In the discretion of seller or at the request of buyer, seller shall obtain additional insurance for the account of buyer to cover the following risks: [set out specific risks].

Provision of Sales Agreement—Expansion of C.I.F. and C & F terms

In addition to the duties imposed on the parties to this agreement by [cite applicable Uniform Commercial Code section] in effect in [state] relating to C.I.F. and C & F terms, buyer shall perform the following additional duties: [state duties].

Mercantile Terms—Clause postponing until tender of goods in F.O.B. or F.A.S. vessel shipment

Buyer shall not be required to make payment for any goods shipped F.O.B. vessel or F.A.S. vessel until tender of documents after arrival of the goods at destination.

FIGURE 12-4 Sample clauses for C.I.F. or C & F shipment

Provision of Sales Agreement—Delivery "Ex-Ship"

Seller is required under this contract to deliver the goods EX-SHIP from the carrying vessel at [destination], in a manner and at a place that is appropriate. The risk of loss shall not pass to buyer until the goods leave the ship's tackle or are otherwise properly delivered, and seller shall furnish buyer with a direction that puts the carrier under a duty to deliver the goods. Seller must discharge all liens arising out of the carriage.

Provision of Sales Agreement—Delivery "Ex-Ship," option of buyer when goods subject to lien

In the event the goods on the ship are subject to any lien, buyer shall have the option to discharge the lien and receive the goods, or may refuse to accept the goods and treat the agreement as a breach by seller. Payment by buyer in discharge of any liens shall be chargeable to seller. In no case shall the payment of the amount of any liens be deemed a waiver by buyer of any right to damages for the breach by seller.

Mercantile Terms—Clause relating to meaning of term requiring delivery "ex-ship"

Under an "ex-ship" term in this agreement, seller is required to ship the goods on the [name of ship] operated by [name the operator of the ship] and the goods must be discharged at the destination port at [name the exact location at the destination port where the goods are to be unloaded].

FIGURE 12-5 Sample ex-ship clauses

the seller may be absolved from liability. However, if it can be shown that the seller caused the damage, the seller will be responsible. Figure 12-6 shows sample contracts used in shipping goods.

Provision of Sales Agreement—No arrival, no sale, buyer to determine nonconformity

This agreement shall be subject to no arrival, no sale terms, but on arrival buyer shall be the sole judge of whether the goods have so deteriorated as to no longer conform to the agreement.

Provision of Sales Agreement—No arrival, no sale, avoidance for deterioration of goods

This agreement shall be subject to no arrival, no sale terms, but on arrival buyer may treat any deterioration of the goods as entitling buyer to the rights resulting from a casualty to identified goods without regard to whether there has been sufficient deterioration so that the goods no longer conform to this agreement.

FIGURE 12-6 Sample no arrival, no sale clauses

12.4 BUYER'S DUTIES AND RESPONSIBILITIES

After the goods have been tendered by the seller, the buyer's responsibilities develop. Section 2-606 sets out the rules for the buyer's acceptance of goods. According to § 2-606(1):

TERMS

no arrival, no sale
A term in a contract for sale of goods, which means that if the goods do not arrive at their destination, title does not pass to the buyer and he or she is not liable for the purchase price.

(1) acceptance of the goods occurs when the buyer
    (a) after a reasonable opportunity to inspect the goods signifies to the seller that the goods are conforming or that he will take or retain them in spite of their nonconformity; or
    (b) fails to make an effective rejection [§ 2-602(1)] but such acceptance does not occur until the buyer has had a reasonable opportunity to inspect them; or
    (c) does any act inconsistent with the seller's ownership; but if such act is wrongful as against the seller it is an acceptance only if ratified by him.
(2) Acceptance of a part of a commercial unit is acceptance of the entire unit.

Common sense suggests that, prior to making payment for goods, the buyer should have the opportunity to inspect the goods to determine whether they conform or are an improper tender. Consequently, prior to acceptance of the goods, a buyer has the right of inspection to determine if the goods conform to the contract.

Right to Inspect

Section 2-513 provides for the buyer's inspection rights as to goods tendered:

(1) Unless otherwise agreed and subject to subsection (3), where goods are tendered or delivered or identified to the contract for sale, the buyer has a right before payment or acceptance to inspect them at any reasonable place and time and in any reasonable manner. When the seller is required or authorized to send the goods to the buyer, the inspection may be after their arrival.
(2) Expenses of inspection must be borne by the buyer but may be recovered from the seller if the goods do not conform and are rejected.
(3) Unless otherwise agreed and subject to the provisions of this Article . . . , the buyer is not entitled to inspect the goods before payment of the price when the contract provides:
    (a) for delivery "C.O.D." or on other like terms; or
    (b) for payments against documents of title, except where such payment is due only after the goods are to become available for inspection.
(4) A place or method of inspection fixed by the parties is presumed to be exclusive but unless otherwise expressly agreed it does not postpone identification or shift the place for delivery or for passing the risk of loss. If compliance becomes impossible, inspection shall be as provided in this section unless the place or method fixed was clearly intended as an indispensable condition failure of which avoids the contract.

Oddly enough, under the Code the expenses for inspection are borne by the buyer and not the seller. The reasoning is that the buyer will be more conscientious in inspection when it is the one paying for the inspection.

However, the Code further states that if the inspection shows that the goods do not conform and thus are rejected by the buyer, then the seller is responsible for the cost of that inspection. In this situation, the buyer has not paid for the goods prior to the inspection.

Exceptions to the payment-after-inspection rule are set out in § 2-513(3). When the contract calls for delivery against documents, or if the delivery is C.O.D. (cash on delivery), inspection follows delivery. In this circumstance, the payment is tendered prior to inspection. This does not waive a buyer's right to inspection, nor does it waive the buyer's right to reject the goods if they are nonconforming, but, because of the terms of the shipment contract, payment must be tendered prior to any inspection.

The inspection must occur at the time the goods are delivered. If the buyer fails to exercise its right to inspect, the buyer will not have a later opportunity to inspect the goods and reject them. The Code is very specific that, unless a reasonable inspection is made when delivery is tendered, the buyer waives any rights to any future inspections. Once the opportunity has come and gone, the assumption is that the goods are conforming and that the buyer has accepted them and will pay for them. Figure 12-7 shows a Notice of Inspection Demand by a Buyer.

Notice by Buyer to Seller—Demand for inspection

To: Elliott Pate Freeman
     Imports International
     431 Chestnut Street
     Philadelphia, Pennsylvania 01234

Dear Mr. Freeman:

Please be advised that we have received your notification that the goods sold pursuant to our "no arrival, no sale" contract dated April 20, 1995, regarding the following goods: 80 lawn chairs and 20 tables, have not yet arrived or arrived in partially deteriorated state.

Pursuant to Section 2-324 and 2-613 of the U.C.C., we hereby demand that you allow us to inspect the goods within a reasonable time so that we may exercise our option either to avoid the contract or to accept the [late or partially deteriorated] goods with due allowances.

Please advise us of a reasonable date and time at which we can inspect the goods.

_____

Edna Parrish

FIGURE 12-7   Sample notice of inspection demand by buyer

There is an exception to the inspection rule, however. When the inspection does not reveal a hidden defect, and it would be unreasonable to expect a buyer to find the defect at the time of inspection, the Code allows rejection of the goods at a later date. In this instance, the buyer must notify the seller of the hidden defect and make a determination as to how the parties will proceed, as the goods are now nonconforming. When the goods are nonconforming, the seller can offer to remedy the defect by shipping conforming goods. This is known as the *opportunity to cure.*

There is a caveat to the seller's right to cure. Under § 2-508(1), the Code suggests that when goods are nonconforming, the seller may cure *if* the time for performance has not passed. This means that the right to cure exists only within the specified time period allotted in the original contract. Unless the buyer permits, the Code does not provide an extension of time for cure.

However, when a seller ships nonconforming goods which the seller had reasonable grounds to believe the buyer would accept, and the buyer rejects those nonconforming goods, the Code provides a reasonable time period to substitute conforming goods without creating a breach of contract. This exception is based on the prior dealings of the parties in that nonconforming goods had been shipped in the past and accepted. Because the seller is working under a prior course of dealings between the parties, the Code relaxes the strict standard that performance must occur within the time specified under the contract. Some provisions to limit the acceptance of nonconforming goods appear in Figure 12-8.

Provision of Offer for Sales Agreement—Acceptance by shipment of nonconforming goods excluded

This order may be accepted only by shipment of goods that conform to the specifications provided in the offer. The shipment of nonconforming goods shall be considered a rejection of the offer.

Provision of Offer for Sales Agreement—Acceptance by shipment of nonconforming goods excluded—Instruction not to ship goods for accommodation if goods cannot be supplied as ordered

This offer to purchase [quantity] [type of goods] may be accepted in writing addressed to [name] at [complete mailing address] or by prompt shipment of the specified goods by seller. In the latter event, the goods as specified must be shipped to [specify complete shipping sddress and any other terms for shipment].

In the event you elect to accept this offer to purchase by prompt shipment of the goods specified, you are instructed that you must not ship any goods for accommodation if you cannot supply the goods as ordered. Any such shipment will not be considered acceptance of the offer to purchase, and any nonconforming goods so shipped will be totally at your risk and cost and will be refused by the offeror.

Provision of Offer for Sales Agreement—Efforts of buyer to correct defects not considered acceptance

Efforts of the buyer to correct any of the goods delivered in a defective or nonworking condition shall not constitute an acceptance of such goods where commercially reasonable in extent and cost, so that the buyer may revoke acceptance and reject the goods when the attempt to correct such defect has proved unsuccessful.

FIGURE 12-8 Sample provisions to limit acceptance of nonconforming goods

Corinthian Pharmaceutical Systems, Inc. v. Lederle Laboratories, 724 F. Supp. 605 (S.D. Ind. 1989), deals with the issue of a seller shipping nonconforming goods. The court went into great detail regarding offers and acceptance under the Code.

CORINTHIAN PHARMACEUTICAL SYSTEMS, INC. v. LEDERLE LABORATORIES

United States District Court, S.D. Indiana
Oct. 30, 1989

McKINNEY, District Judge.

Defendant Lederle Laboratories is a pharmaceutical manufacturer and distributor that makes a number of drugs, including the DTP vaccine. Plaintiff Corinthian Pharmaceutical is a distributor of drugs that purchases supplies from manufacturers such as Lederle Labs and then resells the product to physicians and other providers. One of the products that Corinthian buys and distributes with some regularity is the DTP vaccine.

In 1984, Corinthian and Lederle became entangled in litigation when Corinthian ordered more than 6,000 vials of DTP and Lederle refused to fill the order. That lawsuit was settled by written agreement whereby Lederle agreed to sell a specified amount of vaccine to Corinthian at specified times. One of the conditions of the settlement was that Corinthian "may order additional vials of [vaccine] from Lederle at the market price and under the terms and conditions of sale in effect as of the date of the order."

After that litigation was settled Lederle continued to manufacture and sell the vaccine, and Corinthian continued to buy it from Lederle and other sources. Lederle periodically issued a price list to its customers for all of its products. Each price list stated that all orders were subject to acceptance by Lederle at its home office, and indicated that the prices shown "were in effect at the time of publication but are submitted without offer and are subject to change without notice." The price list further stated that changes in price "take immediate effect and unfilled current orders and back orders will be invoiced at the price in effect at the time shipment is made."

From 1985 through early 1986, Corinthian made a number of purchases of the vaccine from Lederle Labs. During this period of time, the largest single order ever placed by Corinthian with Lederle was for 100 vials. When Lederle Labs filled an order it sent an invoice to Corinthian. The one page, double-sided invoice contained the specifics of the transaction on the front, along with form statement at the bottom that the transaction "is governed by seller's standard terms and conditions of sale set forth on back hereof, notwithstanding any provisions submitted by buyer. Acceptance of the order is expressly conditioned on buyer's assent to seller's terms and conditions."

On the back of the seller's form, the above language was repeated, with the addition that the "[s]eller specifically rejects any different or additional terms and conditions and neither seller's performance nor receipt of payment shall constitute an acceptance of them." The reverse side also stated that prices are subject to change without notice at any time prior to shipment, and that the seller would not be liable for failure to perform the contract if the materials reasonably available to the seller were less than the needs of the buyer.

Lederle concluded that a substantial increase in the price of the vaccine would be necessary. In order to communicate the price change to its own sales people, Lederle's Price Manager prepared "PRICE LETTER No. E-48." This document was dated May 19, 1986, and indicated that effective May 20, 1986, the price of the DTP vaccine would be raised from $51.00 to $171.00 per vial. Price letters such as these were routinely sent to Lederle's sales force, but did not go to customers. Corinthian somehow gained knowledge of this letter on May 19, 1986, the date before the price increase was to take effect. In response to the knowledge of the impending price increase, Corinthian immediately ordered 1,000 vials of DTP vaccine from Lederle. Corinthian placed its order on May 19, 1986, by calling Lederle's "Telgo" system, a telephone computer ordering system that allows customers to place orders over the phone by communicating with a computer. After Corinthian placed its order with the Telgo system, the computer gave Corinthian a tracking number for its order. On the same date, Corinthian sent Lederle two written confirmations of its order. On each form Corinthian stated that this "order is to receive the $64.32 per vial price."

On June 3, 1986, Lederle sent invoice 1771 to Corinthian for 50 vials of DTP vaccine priced at $64.32 per vial. The invoice contained the standard Lederle conditions noted above. The 50 vials were sent to Corinthian and were accepted. At the same time, Lederle sent its customers, including Corinthian, a letter regarding DTP vaccine pricing and orders. This letter stated that the "enclosed represents a partial shipment of the order for DTP vaccine, which you placed with Lederle on May 19, 1986." The letter stated that under Lederle's standard terms and conditions of sale the normal policy would be to invoice the order at the price when shipment was made. However, in light of the magnitude of the price increase, Lederle had decided to make an exception to its terms and conditions and ship a portion of the order at the lower price. The letter further stated that the balance would be priced at $171.00, and that shipment would be made during the week of June 16. The letter closed, "If for any reason you wish to cancel the balance of your order, please contact [us] . . . on or before June 13."

Based on these facts, plaintiff Corinthian Pharmaceutical brings this action seeking specific performance for the 950 vials of DTP vaccine that Lederle Labs chose not to deliver.

The fundatmental question is whether Lederle Labs agreed to sell Corinthian Pharmaceuticals 1,000 vials of DTP vaccine at $64.32 per vial.

Initially, it should be noted that this is a sale of goods covered by the Uniform Commercial Code, and that both parties are merchants under the Code.

The starting point in this analysis is where did the first offer originate. An offer is "the manifestation of willingness to enter into a bargain, so made as to justify another person in understanding that his assent to that bargain is invited and will conclude it." The only possible conclusion in this case

is that Corinthian's "order" of May 19, 1986, for 1,000 vials at $64.32 was the first offer. Nothing that the seller had done prior to this point can be interpreted as an offer.

First, the price lists distributed by Lederle to its customers did not constitute offers. It is well settled that quotations are mere invitations to make an offer, particularly where, as here, the price lists specifically stated that prices were subject to change without notice and that all orders were subject to acceptance by Lederle.

Second, neither Lederle's internal price memorandum nor its letter to customers dated May 20, 1986, can be construed as an offer to sell 1,000 vials at the lower price. There is no evidence that Lederle intended Corinthian to receive the internal price memorandum, nor is there anything in the record to support the conclusion that the May 20, 1986, letter was an offer to sell 1,000 vials to Corinthian at the lower price. If anything, the evidence shows that Corinthian was not supposed to receive this letter until after the price increase had taken place. Moreover, the letter, just like the price lists, was a mere quotation (i.e., an invitation to submit an offer) sent to all customers. Thus, as a matter of law, the first offer was made by Corinthian when it phoned in and subsequently confirmed its order for 1,000 vials at the lower price. The next question, then, is whether Lederle ever accepted that offer.

Under the Code, an acceptance need not be the mirror-image of the offer. However, the offeree must still do some act that manifests the intention to accept the offer and make a contract. Under § 2-206, an offer to make a contract shall be construed as inviting acceptance in any manner and by any medium reasonable in the circumstances. The first question regarding acceptance, therefore, is whether Lederle accepted the offer prior to sending the 50 vials of vaccine.

The record is clear that Lederle did not communicate or do any act prior to shipping the 50 vials that could support the finding of an acceptance. When Corinthian placed its order, it merely received a tracking number from the Telgo computer. Such an automated, ministerial act cannot constitute an acceptance. Thus, there was no acceptance of Corinthian's offer prior to the delivery of 50 vials.

The next question, then, is what is to be made of the shipment of 50 vials and the accompanying letter. Section 2-206(b) of the Code speaks to this issue:

[A]n order or other offer to buy goods for prompt or current shipment shall be construed as inviting acceptance either by a prompt promise to ship or by the prompt or current shipment of conforming or non-conforming goods, *but such a shipment of non-conforming goods does not constitute an acceptance if the seller seasonably notifies the buyer that the shipment is offered only as an accommodation to the buyer.*

Thus, under the Code a seller accepts the offer by shipping goods, whether they are conforming or not, but if the seller ships non-conforming goods *and* seasonably notifies the buyer that the shipment is a mere accommodation, then the seller has not, in fact, accepted the buyer's offer.

In this case, the offer made by Corinthian was for 1,000 vials at $64.32. In response, Lederle Labs shipped only 50 vials at $64.32 per vial, and wrote Corinthian indicating that the balance of the order would be priced at $171.00 per vial and would be shipped during the week of June 16. The letter further indicated that the buyer could cancel its order by calling Lederle Labs. Clearly, Lederle's shipment was non-conforming, for it was for only $\frac{1}{20}$ th of the quantity desired by the buyer. The narrow issue, then, is whether Lederle's response to the offer was a shipment of non-conforming goods not constituting an acceptance because it was offered only as an accommodation under § 2-206.

An accommodation is an arrangement or engagement made as a favor to another. The term implies no consideration. In this case, then, even taking all inferences favorably for the buyer, the only possible conclusion is that Lederle Labs' shipment of 50 vials was offered merely as an accommodation. The accommodation letter, which Corinthian is sure it received, clearly stated that the 50 vials were being sent at the lower price as an exception to Lederle's general policy, and that the balance of the offer would be invoiced at the higher price. The letter further indicated that Lederle's proposal to ship the balance of the order at the higher price could be rejected by the buyer. Moreover, the standard terms of Lederle's invoice stated that acceptance of the order was expressly conditioned upon buyer's assent to the seller's terms.

Under these undisputed facts, § 2-206(1)(b) was satisfied. Where, as here, the notification is properly made, the shipment of nonconforming goods is treated as a counteroffer just as at common law, and the buyer may accept or reject the counteroffer under normal contract rules.

Thus, the end result of this analysis is that Lederle Lab's price quotations were mere invitations to make an offer, that by placing its order Corinthian made an offer to buy 1,000 vials at the low price, that by shipping 50 vials at the low price Lederle's response was non-conforming, but the non-conforming response was a mere accommodation and thus constituted a counteroffer.

QUESTIONS FOR ANALYSIS

What are the facts in *Corinthian Pharmaceutical?* How did the court address the issue of the seller's nonconformity? What was the court's holding?

The Code further requires that if there are commercial units in the shipment, shipment of a commercial unit is acceptance of the entire commercial unit. Consequently, the buyer cannot accept part of a shipment and reject part.

Once the rights of inspection have passed, or the seller's opportunity to cure has passed as well, the buyer has a duty to accept and pay for the tendered goods.

12.5 PAYMENT

After the prerequisites of acceptance have been completed, such as inspections and any other contingencies in the contract, the buyer has a duty to pay the seller. Ordinarily, the duty to pay arises after acceptance of the goods and after an opportunity to inspect, but this is not always so. There are instances when payment will be made prior to acceptance, but this does not impair a buyer's rights to reject nonconforming goods.

The manner of payment is normally that which the parties have used in the past. This can be accomplished by check, a letter of credit, or against a document of title.

Payment by Check

Payment by a check or a **draft** is common. Upon the buyer's tender of the check to the seller and the seller's presentment of the check to the bank, all obligations of payment are fulfilled. If the check is not paid by the bank (dishonored), however, the buyer's obligations are not discharged and the seller can exercise any available remedies.

When a party's credit rights have been questioned, the seller may demand cash at the time of the delivery. In this situation, the Code allows a reasonable extension of time after the delivery to obtain the cash.

Letters of Credit

A typical method of payment in a sales transaction is by **letter of credit**. Governed by Article 5 of the U.C.C., a *letter of credit* is a written negotiable instrument that authorizes one party (normally a bank) to advance money or give credit to another person (usually the customer) in accordance with the terms and conditions of the transaction. Upon the advice of the customer, the bank will honor demands for payment for the goods which are the subject of the letter of credit. Letters of credit can be irrevocable or revocable. An **irrevocable** letter of credit is a guarantee by the bank that the credit will not be withdrawn or canceled, whereas a **revocable** letter of credit allows the bank to cancel or withdraw the credit, normally upon notice to its customer. The process of buying goods under a letter of credit generally works as follows:

1. Buyer approaches bank for credit to purchase goods.
2. Assuming buyer has good credit, bank agrees to issue the credit to buyer to purchase the goods. Seller is the beneficiary (receiver of the money) of the letter of credit.
3. Letter of credit is issued by bank.
4. Buyer agrees to repay bank for extension of credit.
5. Bank notifies seller of letter of credit.
6. Seller ships goods with appropriate invoices and supporting documents.

7. Goods arrive.
8. After inspection, goods determined to be conforming.
9. Bank pays seller for goods shipped based on letter of credit.

Payment Against a Document of Title

Payment can also be made against a document of title. Documents such as bills of lading, warehouse receipts, and other similar documents are used to transfer ownership of goods. This is a method of payment by the holder of the document. If the document is negotiable, it is akin to the payment of money through a check, and the holder has the right to pay under the document of title. When the goods have been accepted and payment has been tendered, for all practical purposes the contract for the sale of goods is complete. At this stage, there are no further obligations between the parties.

12.6 SPECIAL TYPES OF SALES UNDER ARTICLE 2

The standard methods of selling goods between parties have undergone some changes lately. In an effort to acknowledge these changing methods of doing business, the Code has recognized conditional sales known as "sale on approval" and "sale or return." Some believe that these new styles of sales are a passing fad, but often they are simply a new way of acquiring business and revenue. Article 2 also covers auction sales, discussed later in this section.

Sale on Approval

A *sale on approval* occurs when a buyer purchases goods from a seller with the understanding that the buyer can return the goods without any recourse. Under this type of sale, the buyer is given a reasonable time to try out the goods and determine if the goods conform to its needs. Such a sale is at the seller's risk. Until the buyer actually accepts the goods, by either signifying acceptance, not returning them, or using them in an unreasonable manner, the buyer does not take ownership or assume any risk of loss if the goods are returned. Suppose that you purchase a knife from one of those television advertisers that state "10-day free trial for use of the product and can be returned for a complete refund." You use the knife for a week and determine, for whatever reason, that you do not want it. You send it back and request a refund of the purchase price. The company is obligated to return your money because it was a sale on approval. Check Figure 12-9 for some contract language regarding sales on approval. A case that dealt with the acceptance issue as well as the sale on approval issue was *Gold'n Plump Poultry, Inc. v. Simmons Engineering Co.*, 805 F.2d 12 (8th Cir. 1986).

TERMS

draft
1. An order in writing by one person on another (commonly a bank) to pay a specified sum of money to a third person on demand or at a stated future time. 2. Compulsory military service. 3. A preliminary version of a document or plan. 4. To make a preliminary version of a document. 5. In the case of the Selective Service System, to require a person to perform military service.

letter of credit
A written promise, generally by a bank, that it will honor drafts made upon it by a specified customer so long as the conditions described in the letter are complied with; a document which states in legal form that the bank has extended credit to the owner of the letter and will pay his bills. Transactions involving letters of credit are governed by the Uniform Commercial Code.

irrevocable
That which cannot be abrogated, annulled, or withdrawn; not revocable.

revocable
That which can be abrogated, annulled, or withdrawn.

Provision of Sales Agreement—Sale on approval

The transaction between the parties to this agreement is a sale on approval.

Provision of Sales Agreement—Sale on approval—After trial period

Seller guarantees buyer complete satisfaction, and will allow buyer to determine whether the goods fulfill all descriptions, guarantees, and expectations of buyer.

Buyer shall have a 10-day trial period in which to determine whether the goods are entirely satisfactory, the trial period to run at the option of seller either from the date of receipt of the goods by buyer or from a date two weeks after arrival of the goods at the place designated as the point to which shipment is to be made. The goods must prove entirely satisfactory to buyer, or the buyer shall repackage the goods in the same condition as received, ordinary wear and tear excepted, and return to seller F.O.B. carrier at [designated delivery point].

When the goods are returned as directed above, billed to any point designated by seller, are received at that point, and on immediate examination are shown to be in good condition, ordinary wear and tear excepted, seller shall immediately return to buyer all money and any notes transferred for the goods to seller by buyer. The return of the goods and the return to buyer of all notes and money transferred to seller shall cancel and void this agreement, and shall terminate any and all liability of either party to the other.

**Provision of Sales Agreement—Sale on approval—
Right to return goods if unsatisfied**

Seller guarantees that the goods delivered to buyer will be entirely satisfactory to buyer, and buyer shall be the sole judge of such satisfaction. Buyer shall be allowed ten days from the time buyer receives the goods at the buyer's place of business to ascertain whether the goods are satisfactory. If for any reason buyer is not entirely satisfied with the goods, the buyer shall write seller for the shipping instructions for return of the goods, and seller shall furnish buyer with shipping instructions within five days. On return of the goods, seller shall return to buyer within ten days the purchase price of the goods without question.

FIGURE 12-9 Sample sale on approval clauses

GOLD'N PLUMP POULTRY, INC. v. SIMMONS ENGINEERING CO.

United States Court of Appeals, Eighth Circuit
Nov. 24, 1986

In the fall of 1982, Armour Food Company (Armour) entered into negotiations with Simmons Engineering Company (Simmons) of Georgia for the purchase of two "venter opener" chicken processing machines for Armour's Cold Spring, Minnesota plant. During the two years prior to purchase, Armour's profits from the Cold Spring plant had suffered because its chickens were oversized (up to five pounds and over). The standard average industry size was three and one-half pounds, and processing equipment was generally designed for average sized chickens, with tolerance up to approximately four pounds. Armour sought to become more efficient in processing and to decrease chicken size.

Armour based its decision to purchase Simmons' machines on the results of an extensive two-year investigation of venter opener machines. Before final selection, Armour solicited information from various plants throughout the country using Simmons' machines, including quality control reports with information on the effectiveness of processing relative to chicken *size*.

In October 1982, Theis requested a price quote from Simmons and it responded by letter of October 13, 1982:

In response to your request, we quote as follows:
One Simmons Venter/Opener (SVO-1011) $54,000.00 FOB Cold Spring, MN with Simmons installation supervision. Delivery would be 3–4 weeks A.R.O.

We feel we have used the best engineering materials available, however, only time will prove us right. With this in mind, Mr. Simmons has instructed us to provide you with spare parts and service, at no charge, for six months, just as we have done for the other plants that have this equipment.

This was the only written document evidencing the sale. Theis agreed to the terms of sale for Armour and ordered two machines. The full purchase price was $113,400, which included tax.

The first machine was installed at Cold Spring over the weekend of December 4 and 5, 1982. Processing began on Monday, December 6, 1982. Problems arose immediately because of the large size of Armour's five and one-half pound chickens. The evidence discloses Armour was aware of the size problem. Its former chief engineer testified: "[T]he birds were excessively sized for what the machine was *purchased* and designed for." Simmons advised Armour not to install the second machine because of the size problem and was willing to take back the first machine. However, Armour insisted that Simmons attempt to modify the machines while it worked on decreasing chicken size.

Simmons' terms of sale were that Armour pay cash within ten working days from the date of installation. More than two months after the sale Armour still had not paid Simmons, however. To obtain payment, Simmons issued a letter to Armour dated February 14, 1983:

* * * [I]n the event our venter openers do not function within reasonable tolerance;

we will refund all monies paid to us for this equipment.

We reserve the right to make such modifications as we deem proper in an attempt to attain a satisfactory machine.

This letter prompted Armour's full payment of the purchase price of $113,400 to Simmons. On March 2, Armour received approval of the formal purchase order from its Phoenix home office. The only written terms of the purchase order were "as agreed."

On April 1, 1983, Armour sold its entire Cold Spring plant, including the disputed machines, to Gold'n Plump. Gold'n Plump had been created at this time by its parent, JFC, Inc., to own and operate the Armour Cold Spring processing facility. Despite Gold'n Plump's full knowledge of the size problem, the plant sale agreement provided for transfer of the machines to Gold'n Plump "as is" and with an express warranty disclaimer.

Gold'n Plump did not purchase the disputed machines unwittingly. Theis, the plant manager, who had negotiated the machine purchase from Simmons in December, transferred to the same position with Gold'n Plump. Gold'n Plump's vice president of finance and administration testified that Gold'n Plump insisted upon purchasing the entire plant with clear title and under "a clean deal." He testified that were it not for Gold'n Plump's insistence, the plant purchase documents could have been changed and the disputed machines purchased without Armour having paid Simmons before the plant sale. Under the plant sale agreement, Gold'n Plump paid Armour "net book value" for the two Simmons machines. This was $113,400 or the full purchase price which Armour had paid Simmons, despite testimony that the machines were worthless.

Gold'n Plump contends that it is entitled to return the machines for a full refund because the sale was on approval. According to Gold'n Plump, Simmons' conduct and representations manifested a sale for use on a trial basis. Gold'n Plump cites Simmons' promises to Armour to modify the machines, provide free service and spare parts for a six-month period, and refund the purchase price if the machines malfunctioned.

A sale is on approval only if the parties agree that the proposed buyer may return the goods even though they conform to the sales contract. The general presumption runs against a delivery to a consumer being a sale on approval, however. The district court held that Gold'n Plump failed to

establish a sale on approval. Accordingly, we affirm that judgment of the district court denying relief to Gold'n Plump.

QUESTIONS FOR ANALYSIS

State the pertinent facts of *Gold'n Plump*. Did the court find a sale on approval? What was the court's rationale for its findings?

Sale or Return

When a party purchases goods for resale and can return the unsold goods to the seller without any legal ramifications, this is known as a *sale or return*. In this instance, the buyer assumes the risk of breakage or theft and thus must pay the seller for any items broken or stolen. However, if the buyer determines that the goods cannot be sold, the buyer can return the goods to the seller without any legal consequences. A sale or return is similar to a **consignment**, which occurs when a party accepts goods and does not pay for them. If the goods do not sell, the party can return them without recourse. A consignment sale is really a sale or return contract. Figure 12-10 provides some language for drafting a sale or return provision.

Provision of Sales Agreement—Sale or return

The transaction between the parties to this agreement is a sale or return.

Provision of Sales Agreement—Sale or return

Buyer shall have the right to return the goods sold under this agreement to seller at any time within five days after receipt of the goods for the following reasons: defective goods or damaged. Any return of goods by buyer under this provision shall be at the expense of buyer.

Buyer shall be deemed to have accepted the goods if seller has not received the goods within the five-day period.

Provision of Sales Agreement—Sale or return—Goods subject to inspection and approval by buyer with right to return after inspection

All goods ordered shall be subject to final inspection and approval at the facility of buyer. Any goods that do not conform to the order of buyer or that contain defective material or workmanship may be rejected by buyer regardless of date of payment of the goods. Buyer may hold any goods rejected for cause pending instructions from seller, or buyer may return the goods to seller at seller's expense.

FIGURE 12-10 Sample sale or return provisions

Auction Sales

Sales of goods may be by **auction**. In an auction, a person known as an *auctioneer* offers goods for sale to members of the public, who make offers known as **bids** on the goods. Ordinarily, the person who bids the highest is entitled to the goods once the auctioneer acknowledges the sale, usually by calling out the word "sold."

Auction sales are conducted *with reserve* or *without reserve*. These terms are critical, as the auctioneers can have leverage in accepting or rejecting bids. When an auction is conducted with reserve, the auctioneers can withdraw an item for sale at their discretion. This usually occurs when an item is not receiving high enough bids and the auctioneers have been instructed to withdraw the item if the minimum bid is not reached. When an auction is conducted without reserve, once the bidding begins, the auctioneer cannot withdraw the item, no matter how low the bid. Section 2-328 governs auction sales.

12.7 BULK SALES AND TRANSFERS

Any transfer of a major part of a seller's materials, supplies, merchandise, or other inventory is known as a **bulk** *sales transfer.* Bulk sales transfers normally are governed by Article 6 of the U.C.C.

The U.C.C. sets forth certain requirements that a seller and buyer must follow for a valid bulk sales transfer. In the past, though, Article 6 has come under heavy criticism. In response, the National Conference of Commissions on Uniform State Laws revised Article 6 in 1989. The National Conference offered two alternatives: Alternate A in effect repealed Article 6 and suggested other Code articles which should govern bulk sales; Alternate B better deals with the realities of transfers involving all or substantially all of a seller's assets. The revised Article 6 is organized as follows:

6-101: Short Title
6-102: Definitions
6-103: Applicability of Article
6-104: Obligations of Buyer
6-105: Notice to Claimants
6-106: Schedule of Distribution
6-107: Liability for Noncompliance
6-108: Bulk Sales by Auction
6-109: Filing Requirements
6-110: Limitations of Action

The following section sets out the requirements to complete a bulk sales transfer. Once the requirements are met, the buyer can retain possession of the goods or inventory without legal consequences.

TERMS

consignment
The entrusting of goods either to a carrier for delivery to a consignee or to a consignee who is to sell the goods for the consignor.

auction
A sale of property to the highest bidder.

bid
An offer, especially one made at the letting of a contract, an auction, or a judicial sale. To invite; to make an offer, particularly at an auction or a judicial sale, or to secure a contract.

bulk
1. A quantity of unpackaged goods or cargo. 2. Unbroker packages. 3. The greater part; the largest or principal portion.

1. *Prepare list of creditors.* Under new § 6-104, the buyer must obtain a list of any existing creditors, with their addresses and the amounts due and owing. This list reflects those whom the seller knows to be creditors. To heighten the legal assurances to the buyer, the Code requires this list to be in writing. The revised Article 6 requires, under § 6-109, that the list of creditors be filed with the Secretary of State, where it is kept on file for two years.

2. *Prepare list of items to be transferred.* A list is prepared by the seller (with the buyer's participation, if necessary) of the items or property to be transferred. The list must be specific enough that the items are easily identifiable by such information as model numbers, weight, color, brand, and quantity to be transferred.

3. *Give notice of transfer to creditors.* All creditors are entitled to at least 30 or 45 days' notice, depending on the circumstances of the impending transfer. This gives the creditor the option to demand payment for the goods. Notice should be given by certified mail, as creditors who do not receive notice of the sale can ignore the sale and exercise any rights they may have under the U.C.C. or law. Article 6 gives very specific suggestions for the notice to a creditor (see Figure 12-11).

A person who buys at a bulk sale by auction or conducted by a liquidator need not comply with the requirements of § 6-104(1) and is not

---

Notice of Sale

Jonathan Day, whose address is 1234 Dee Street, Chicago, Illinois, is described in this notice as the "seller."

Timothy Bridges, whose address is 5678 Common Lane, Chicago, Illinois, is described in this notice as the "buyer."

The seller has disclosed to the buyer that within the past three years the seller has used other business names, operated at other addresses, or both, as follows: _____.

The seller and the buyer have entered into an agreement dated December 28, 1995, for a sale that may constitute a bulk sale under the laws of the State of Illinois.

The date on or after which more than 10 percent of the assets that are the subject of the sale were or will be transferred is January 15, 1996, and [if not stated in the schedule of distribution] the date on or after which more than 10 percent of the net contract price was or will be paid is January 31, 1996.

The following assets are the subject of the sale:

4 fork lifts	5 computers
8 racks	3 printers
4 desks	4000 cases of liquor other than wine or beer

[If applicable] The buyer will make available to claimants of the seller a list of the seller's claimants in the following manner: _____.

[If applicable] The sale is to satisfy $5,000 of an antecedent debt owed by the seller to ABC Distributors, Inc.

A copy of the schedule of distribution of the net contract price accompanies this notice.

FIGURE 12-11 Sample Article 6 notice to creditor (bulk sale)

Notice of Sale (Auction)

Jonathan Day, whose address is 1234 Dee Street, Chicago, Illinois, is described in this notice as the "seller."

Timothy Bridges, whose address is 5678 Common Lane, Chicago, Illinois, is described in this notice as the "auctioneer" or "liquidator."

The seller has disclosed to the auctioneer or liquidator that within the past three years the seller has used other business names, operated at other addresses, or both, as follows: _____.

The seller and the auctioneer or liquidator have entered into an agreement dated December 24, 1995, for auction or liquidation services that may constitute an agreement to make a bulk sale under the laws of the State of Illinois.

The date on or after which the auction began or will begin or the date on or after which the liquidator began or will begin to sell assets on the seller's behalf is January 15, 1996, and [if not stated in the schedule of distribution] the date on or after which more than 10 percent of the net proceeds of the sale were or will be paid is January 31, 1996.

The following assets are the subject of the sale: _____.

[If applicable] The auctioneer or liquidator will make available to claimants of the seller a list of the seller's claimants in the following manner: _____.

[If applicable] The sale is to satisfy $5,000 of an antecedent debt owed by the seller to ABC Distributors, Inc.

A copy of the schedule of distribution of the net proceeds accompanies this notice.

FIGURE 12-11 *(Continued)*

liable for the failure of an auctioneer or liquidator to comply with the requirements of that section.

4. *Pay debts.* The new Article 6 proposes a distribution schedule of the net contract price. This payment may be made entirely to either the seller or a creditor. Failure to comply with Article 6 results in liability for the buyer to the seller's creditors. Section 6-107 does set ceilings as to a buyer's liability, but the liability exists nevertheless.

12.8 PRACTICAL APPLICATION

The paralegal may be asked to draft a number of documents when a sale of goods is involved. On occasion, the paralegal may also have to draft a consignment sale contract. A complete consignment contract is shown in Figure 12-12. This contract incorporates many of the provisions discussed in this chapter.

Contract for Sale of Goods—Sale on Consignment

Agreement made on August 31, 1995, between Jonathan Day, of 1234 Dee Street, Chicago, Illinois, referred to as consignor, and Mary Ann Pooh, of 5678 Bell Street, Chicago, Illinois, referred to as consignee.

FIGURE 12-12 Sample consignment contract

In consideration of their mutual covenants, the parties agree as follows:

1. Delivery of Merchandise. Consignor agrees to deliver, from time to time, such goods, wares, and merchandise as it, in its judgment, sees fit, and consignee agrees to accept possession of such goods, wares, and merchandise on the terms and conditions set forth in this agreement.

2. Acceptance of Merchandise; Title. Consignee agrees to accept possession of the goods, wares, and merchandise from consignor, and to hold and care for the same as the property of consignor, it being agreed that the title to the merchandise, or its proceeds, is always vested in consignor, and such merchandise shall be at all times subject to and under the direction and control of consignor. The title to the merchandise shall pass directly from consignor to such person or persons to whom the same shall be sold in the manner and on the terms contained in this agreement.

3. Insurance of Merchandise. Consignee agrees to keep the merchandise fully insured for the benefit of and in the name of consignor in fire insurance companies approved by consignor.

4. Sale of Merchandise by Consignee; Proceeds. Consignee agrees to sell such merchandise to such persons as it shall judge to be of good credit and business standing, and to collect for and in behalf of consignor all bills and accounts for the merchandise so sold, and to immediately pay to consignor any amount collected as mentioned above immediately on collection, minus, however, the difference between the price at which the merchandise so collected for has been invoiced to consignee and the price at which the merchandise has been sold as mentioned above by consignee.

5. Consignee's Guarantee of Payment. Consignee hereby guarantees the payment of all bills and accounts for merchandise, possession of which is delivered under this agreement, and hereby agrees, in case any merchandise delivered under the provisions of this agreement by consignor to consignee is not accounted for to consignee under the provisions of Section Four of this agreement, to pay to consignor the invoiced price of the merchandise, and on such payment title to the merchandise, or to the proceeds thereof, so paid for shall pass to consignee and shall be exempted from the provisions of this agreement.

6. Trade Discounts. The invoices sent by consignor to consignee are subject to the usual trade discounts of [enumerate].

7. Restrictions on Merchandising by Consignee. Consignee agrees that except in [enumerate exception], it will not, during the continuance of this agreement, engage in the merchandising, in any manner, of any [name of product], except as provided in this agreement.

8. Duration: Return of Merchandise on Termination. This agreement shall continue for _____ years from the date of its execution, until [date]. If, for any reason, this agreement terminates, all of the merchandise, possession of which is held by consignee under this agreement, shall at the termination be immediately returned to the possession of consignor.

9. Further Documentation. Consignee agrees to execute any and all other documents that consignor shall deem advisable in order to carry out the purpose of this agreement.

10. Effect of Breach. Any breach on the part of consignee of any of the agreements contained in this consignment agreement shall, at the option of consignor, be cause for its termination.

In witness whereof, the parties have executed this agreement at the offices of [firm] the day and year first above written.

_____
Jonathan Day

_____
Mary Ann Poolman

FIGURE 12-12 *(Continued)*

SUMMARY

12.1   The basic duties under a sales contract are for the seller to tender the goods and for the buyer to accept and pay for them. With few exceptions, once these acts of the parties have occurred, the transaction is complete.

12.2   Tender of delivery occurs when the seller holds conforming goods for the buyer's delivery after ratification. Variations of this rule apply when the goods are delivered to a common carrier, a bailee, or through a document of title. When the place for delivery is not specified in the contract, delivery at a seller's place of business is proper. When one of these methods of delivery is used, the Code sets out the procedures.

12.3   Determining the type of shipment contract is important. Under the shipment contract, the buyer is responsible for the goods when placed with the carrier, whereas in a destination contract, the buyer is responsible when the goods are received. Certain terms are used to designate the parties' duties and obligations: F.O.B., F.A.S., C.I.F., C & F, ex-ship, and no arrival, no sale.

12.4   Upon receipt of the goods, the buyer has the opportunity to inspect them to make sure they conform to the terms of the contract. Under certain circumstances, if the goods do not conform, the seller may have an opportunity to cure. Unless the goods are C.O.D. or delivered against documents, payment is not tendered until after inspection.

12.5   After all inspections are complete, the buyer's duty to pay arises. Payment is proper by check, letter of credit, or against a document of title. A letter of credit may be revocable or irrevocable.

12.6   There are other types of sales than the "standard" sale of goods in the U.C.C. Sales terms may be sale on approval, sale or return, or auction sales. An auction sale may be conducted with reserve or without reserve.

12.7   When all or substantially all of a seller's merchandise or inventory is being sold, a bulk sale occurs. The U.C.C. provisions for bulk sales were revised in a new Article 6. Some states have adopted the revised Article 6, which protects creditors more than the old version of Article 6.

REVIEW QUESTIONS

1. What are the general obligations of the seller and the buyer in a sales contract?
2. When is a proper tender completed in a sales transaction?
3. How is a proper delivery to a common carrier consummated?

4. What is the distinction between a shipment contract and a destination contract?
5. Define the terms *F.O.B.*, *F.A.S.*, *C.I.F.*, and *C & F.*
6. When goods are properly tendered, what are the buyer's duties under a sales contract?
7. When does the opportunity to cure arise in a sales contract?
8. What various methods of payment may a buyer use in paying for goods?
9. What is a sale on approval?
10. What is the difference between an action conducted "with reserve" or "without reserve"?

EXERCISES

1. Brief *Warrior Tombigbee Transportation v. 5,775.674 Net Tons of Coal,* 570 F. Supp. 1405 (S.D. Ala. 1983) and answer the following questions:
   a. Identify the facts.
   b. State the disposition and holding.
   c. Determine the court's reasoning.
   d. Set forth your opinion as to whether the court's opinion is valid.
2. Find an irrevocable letter of credit and a revocable letter of credit. Review each document and set forth the distinguishing characteristic and language in each.
3. Locate your state's bulk sales transfer act.
   a. Identify the steps necessary to create a valid bulk sales transfer in your state.
   b. Has your state adopted the new U.C.C. version of Article 6?

Chapter 13
Title, Risk of Loss, and Warranties

OUTLINE

13.1 GENERAL RULES OF PASSAGE OF TITLE AND RISK OF LOSS

Determining who owns goods involved in a transaction is important to the law of sales, because with ownership comes certain rights and obligations. In any analysis under Article 2 of the Uniform Commercial Code, one of the first questions is who has title to the goods. **Title** is equivalent to legal ownership. The person who owns the goods has legal ownership and, therefore, title to the goods. In most sales transactions, the seller retains title to the goods until they are sold to the buyer.

TERMS

title
1. The right of an owner with respect to property, real or personal, i.e., possession and the right of possession. 2. A document that evidences the rights of an owner; i.e., ownership rights.

303

Coupled with title is *risk of loss,* which refers to the financial responsibility for goods that are damaged, lost, or destroyed. Whether the risk of loss is on the buyer or the seller is determined by the type of contract the seller and the buyer have entered. Is the contract a shipment contract or a destination contract? When is the buyer's acceptance effective? What was the parties' agreement with regard to risk of loss? The answers to these questions determine who bears the risk of loss.

Because title and risk of loss are closely related, one of the biggest issues under sales is when the title passes. When does ownership transfer from the seller to the buyer, and when does the buyer assume the obligations of ownership of the goods, including risk of loss? To determine when title passes, the goods first must be identified; then the goods must be delivered to the buyer for title to pass, together with the assumption of risk of loss.

13.2   PASSAGE OF TITLE: SHIPMENT CONTRACTS

Under a *shipment contract,* the buyer and the seller agree to place the goods with a carrier for delivery to the buyer. Recall from Chapter 12 that the buyer's responsibility begins when the goods are placed on the carrier. In a shipment contract, at the moment the goods are delivered to the carrier, title—and all its consequences—vest in the buyer. Thus, both title to the goods and the risk of loss pass to the buyer when the goods are placed on the carrier at the seller's origin. From that moment on, the seller is free from any responsibility regarding shipment of the goods, and the buyer assumes title and risk of loss and thus all responsibility for the goods. For example, if a contract is F.O.B. Dallas, Texas, and the goods are being shipped to San Juan, Puerto Rico, the title to the goods is at the buyer's place of shipment, or where the shipment originates, not the final destination. Thus, title passes to the buyer in Dallas and not San Juan. The risk of loss also passes to the buyer in Dallas and not San Juan. Consequently, title and risk of loss pass simultaneously in a shipment contract.

13.3   PASSAGE OF TITLE: DESTINATION CONTRACTS

In a *destination contract,* the title and risk of loss pass to the buyer when the goods arrive at the destination on which the seller and buyer have agreed. In this type of contract, title does not pass, nor is the risk of loss assumed by the buyer, until the buyer has received the goods at the agreed destination. If a carrier is used, the seller pays for all costs of transportation and takes all responsibility for shipment of the goods to the destination. Recall that destination contracts also use the term *F.O.B.;* to distinguish a shipment contract from a destination contract, though, check the place of destination—that agreement will determine the parties' responsibilities.

Using the previous example, if the contract is F.O.B. San Juan and the goods originate and are loaded in Dallas, title and risk of loss pass when the goods are delivered in San Juan. To pass title and the risk of loss to the buyer, the goods must arrive at the destination, with notice of the arrival to the buyer and a reasonable time period for pickup of the goods. Only then do title and risk of loss pass to the buyer.

13.4 PASSAGE OF TITLE: OTHER CONSIDERATIONS

No Delivery Requirement in Contract

When the parties to the sales contract do not require shipment or delivery of the goods to a destination other than the seller's place of business, title to the goods passes when the contract is made with the buyer. In this situation, delivery occurs when the buyer picks up of the goods at the seller's place of business. Risk of loss is a different problem altogether. If the seller is a merchant, the risk of loss passes upon receipt of the goods by the buyer. If the seller is a nonmerchant, the risk of loss passes when the seller tenders the goods to the buyer.

Documents of Title

In some instances, goods are not delivered directly to the buyer, but are delivered through transfer of a **document of title**. When the goods are not to be delivered to any specified destination, nor moved to the buyer's place of business or a designated delivery place, title and risk of loss pass when the seller gives a document of title to the buyer. Provisions to consider for a sales contract when title and risk of loss are at issue are found in Figure 13-1.

On Identification of Goods to Agreement

Title to the [type of goods] sold under this agreement shall pass to buyer at the time that seller identifies the goods subject to this agreement.

At Time and Place of Shipment of Goods

Title to the [type of goods] sold under this agreement shall not pass to buyer at the time the goods are identified in the agreement, but shall pass only at the time of and place from which shipment of the goods is made by seller to buyer.

On Execution of Sales Agreement

Title to the [type of goods] sold under this agreement shall pass to buyer at the time of execution of this sales agreement.

FIGURE 13-1 Sample clauses on title and risk of loss

By Agreement of the Parties

The parties can contractually agree to other title and risk-of-loss arrangements. If they do so, title and risk of loss will pass at the agreed time and place.

TERMS

document of title
Any document which in the regular course of business is treated as evidencing that the person in possession of it is entitled to receive, hold, and dispose of the document and the goods to which it pertains.

Sale on Approval

When goods are sold "on approval," title and risk of loss do not pass to the buyer until the goods are accepted. To have title and risk of loss pass, the buyer must consent to the sale, either orally or in writing, or use the goods in a reckless manner. A sale on approval presents some unique problems, and Figure 13-2 offers some suggestions on contract language.

Seller to Retain Title until Goods Approved by Buyer

The following goods are sent by seller to buyer for examination, but are to remain the property of seller and are to be returned to seller on demand: [describe goods and quantity]. The sale shall take effect from the date of approval by buyer, and until then the goods are to be held subject to the order of seller.

Risk of Loss and Title Passing to Buyer Immediately

The risk of loss and title to the goods shall pass to buyer immediately upon execution of this agreement.

Acceptance of Part of Goods Not Acceptance of Entire Quantity

The acceptance by buyer of a specifically designated quantity of the total goods ordered, or the acceptance of a single installment, shall operate as an acceptance of that specific quantity or installment only, and shall not operate as an acceptance of the balance of the goods to be delivered or not specifically accepted. Each partial quantity or installment shall be subject to separate acceptance by buyer.

FIGURE 13-2 Sample sale on approval clauses

Revesting of Title

When a buyer rejects goods that have been delivered by the seller, title reverts to the seller and is said to *revest*. Revesting of title shifts title, and often the risk of loss, from the buyer back to the seller. Thus, the seller retains all its previously held rights and interests in the goods. Under the U.C.C., a buyer does not have to rightfully reject goods for title to revest in the seller, nor does the rejection have to be justified for the title to revest in the seller. Section 2-401(4) states:

> A rejection or other refusal by the buyer to receive or retain the goods, whether or not justified, or a justified revocation of acceptance revests title to the goods in the seller. Such revesting occurs by operation of law and is not a "sale."

Nonconforming goods contracts present a different problem. If nonconforming goods are shipped and rejected, title and risk of loss remain with the seller. A unique problem arises when insurance is involved. When goods are shipped and accepted by the buyer, but later rejected because of a defect, assumption of the risk of loss depends on insurance coverage. If the buyer is insured, the risk of loss remains with the buyer. If not, the risk of loss reverts to the seller. The following example is a provision to use in an agreement when revesting of title is required.

Revesting of Title in Seller:

Title to the [type of goods] sold under this agreement shall revest in seller if buyer shall either reject the goods or refuse to accept the goods.

13.5 VOID AND VOIDABLE TITLE

In a sales transaction, the seller can transfer only the same quality title as the seller retains. If the selling individual or entity has **valid** title and is the rightful owner of the goods, upon sale the seller can pass good and valid title to the buyer, and the buyer will then enjoy all the rights and title that have been transferred from the seller.

Sometimes, however, a party that does not have valid title attempts to sell goods to a buyer. The person who does not have valid title to goods is said to have **void** title; any transfer from a seller who has void title transfers only void (and therefore worthless) title to that buyer. This situation may arise when a person attempts to transfer stolen goods to an unsuspecting buyer. Even if the buyer purchases the goods in good faith, not knowing that the goods are stolen, the original owner of the goods retains the right to repossess the goods. Thus, any transfer of the goods from a party when void title is involved transfers only void title. A buyer who purchases goods with a void title will never have clear title to the goods, but will always hold the goods subject to the superior rights of the original and rightful owner.

For example, a friend offers you a 1994 Camaro for $5,000. You jump on this good deal, of course. Unbeknownst to you, the Camaro was stolen from a man in Philadelphia by an international auto theft ring. If they track the stolen Camaro back to you, the authorities could (and would) take the car back from you without returning your $5,000, even though you had no idea that the car was stolen. Your only recourse is to locate your "friend."

When a person obtains *voidable title* to goods, title can legally transfer from that person to another person. In fact, the rights possessed by the person who has voidable title are better than those of the original owner. Voidable title situations usually arise when a person has gained access to goods through fraud, misrepresentation, mistake, undue influence, or duress. Titles transferred by minors and persons who are mentally incompetent are also voidable. If persons purchase goods without knowledge that the title was voidable, they have valid title to the goods. What is critical to transforming voidable title into valid title is that the person purchasing the goods be a good faith purchaser for value (money) who has no knowledge of any prior transaction that would harm the title.

The person who acquired the goods through improper means can attempt to reclaim the goods prior to sale to a good faith purchaser. See

TERMS

valid
Effective; sufficient in law; legal; lawful; not void; in effect.

void
Null; without legal effect.

Charles Evans BMW, Inc. v. Williams, 196 Ga. App. 230, 395 S.E.2d 650 (1990), which deals with the voidable title issue.

CHARLES EVANS BMW, INC. v. WILLIAMS
Court of Appeals of Georgia
July 3, 1990

Appellee-defendant agreed to sell his car to an individual named Hodge and he accepted a cashier's check from Hodge as payment. With no indication on the certificate of title that Hodge was the purchaser, appellee signed the title in his capacity as seller and then delivered that document and the car to Hodge. The next day, Hodge, representing himself to be appellee, offered to sell the automobile to appellant-plaintiff. When a price was agreed upon, Hodge presented to appellant the certificate of title bearing appellee's signature as seller and appellant gave Hodge a check which named appellee as the payee. The check was cashed at a local bank when Hodge produced as identification a Kentucky driver's license bearing the same number of the Kentucky driver's license that had been issued to appellee. After the car had been purchased by appellant from Hodge, appellee was notified that the cashier's check he had accepted from Hodge was a forgery. By the time that appellant was made aware of the fact that it had not actually purchased the car from appellee but from Hodge representing himself to be appellee, it had already resold the car. At the direction of the local police authorities, however, the car and the certificate of title were returned to appellant and the purchase price was refunded by appellant. Thereafter, appellant was further required to return the car to appellee. However, appellant retained the certificate of title and initiated this trover action against appellee.

[State U.C.C. § 2–403(1) provides, in relevant part, that "[a] purchaser of goods acquires all title which his transferor had or had power to transfer. . . . A person with voidable title has power to transfer a good title to a good faith purchaser for value. When goods have been *delivered under a transaction of purchase* the purchaser has such power even though: (a) The transferor was deceived as to the identity of the purchaser; or (b) The delivery was in exchange for a check which is later dishonored; or . . . (d) The delivery was procured through fraud punishable as larcenous under the criminal law." (Emphasis supplied.) Appellee was not deprived of his car by a physical taking of which he was unaware. The undisputed evidence of record shows that appellee *delivered his car under a transaction of purchase* procured by the perpetration of a criminal fraud whereby he was deceived as to the identity of the purchaser who gave him a check which was later dishonored. In these circumstances, appellee conveyed *voidable title* to Hodge and Hodge, having voidable rather than void title, had the power to transfer *good title* to a good faith purchaser for value. § 2–403(1) empowers a purchaser with a voidable title to confer good title upon a good faith purchaser for value where the good[s] were procured through fraud punishable as larcenous under the criminal law. The distinction between *theft* and *fraud* in this context is found in the statutory definitions of "delivery" and "purchase." Delivery concerns a voluntary transfer of possession, and purchase refers to a voluntary transaction creating an interest in property. In the present case, [appellee] voluntarily relinquished possession to [Hodge]. As one commentator has pointed out, "[a] thief who wrongfully takes goods is not a purchaser . . . but a swindler who fraudulently induces the victim to voluntarily deliver them is a purchaser."

It follows that, if appellant was a good faith purchaser for value, it acquired good title to the car from Hodge.

" 'Good faith' means honesty in fact in the conduct or transaction concerned." § 1–201(19). " 'Good faith' in the case of a merchant means honesty in fact and the observance of reasonable commercial standards of fair dealing in the trade." § 2–103(1)(b). There is ample evidence of appellant's "good faith" in its transaction with Hodge. Appellant's agent who actually negotiated the purchase neither knew nor had reason to know that Hodge's representations were false. When appellant's agent noticed an error on the registration form, Hodge was told that he would have to obtain a corrected registration form from the county. When Hodge left and returned with the corrected form, this gave additional credence to his representations that he was appellee and the owner of the car. Hodge also presented a certificate of title which bore appellee's unforged signature as seller. The price that appellant agreed to pay for the car was not nominal. Appellant gave Hodge a check made out to appellee and Hodge was successful in cashing that check by using a driver's license bearing the same number of the license that had actually been issued to appellee. Thus, Hodge's scheme to impersonate appellee not only duped appellant, but was also successful against the county and the bank.

Judgment reversed.

QUESTIONS FOR ANALYSIS

State the facts of *Williams*. What type of title did the appellee transfer? What is the difference between void and voidable title? What is the holding in *Williams*?

Entrustment of Goods

An entrustment presents unique problems in the sale of goods. An *entrustment* occurs when a person (the entruster) gives goods to a merchant who normally deals in those types of goods. This often happens when you take an appliance for repairs or have a computer cleaned at a repair shop. In this situation, the merchant takes possession of the goods with the understanding that the entruster will get them back. However, sometimes the merchant attempts to sell the goods without the entruster's knowledge. Although the merchant does not have title to the goods, if it transfers the goods to a good faith purchaser, the good faith purchaser receives valid title to the goods even to the exclusion of the original owner. In this situation, the entruster would have a cause of action against the merchant for money damages; unfortunately, though, that does not bring the goods back to the original owner. *Canterra Petroleum, Inc. v. Western Drilling & Mining Supply,* 418 N.W.2d 267 (N.D. 1987) reviewed the entrustment issue. Pay close attention to the court's analysis.

CANTERRA PETROLEUM, INC. v. WESTERN DRILLING & MINING SUPPLY

Supreme Court of North Dakota
Dec. 29, 1987

This multi-party litigation arises out of various transactions involving a certain quantity of oilfield pipe. The pipe was originally owned by Mitchell Energy Corporation ["Mitchell"]. In late 1981, Mitchell entrusted the pipe to Port Pipe Terminal, Inc. ["Port Pipe"] for storage.

Through paper transactions, two high-ranking employees of Port Pipe succeeded in fraudulently transferring apparent ownership of the pipe to Pharoah, Inc. ["Pharoah"], a "dummy" corporation which they had created to facilitate the fraudulent sale of merchandise stored at Port Pipe's facilities. On March 3, 1982, Pharoah sold the pipe owned by Mitchell to Nickel Supply Company, Inc. ["Nickel"]. On that same date, Nickel sold the pipe to Yamin Oil Supply ["Yamin"]. Five days later Yamin sold the pipe to NorthStar. On March 23, 1982, NorthStar sold it to Western, which a few days later sold it to Canterra Petroleum, Inc. ["Canterra"].

All of these intervening transactions, culminating in the sale to Canterra, were paper transactions only. The pipe never left Port Pipe's storage facility in Houston, Texas, until Canterra had it delivered to Getter Trucking in Dickinson sometime after its purchase in March 1982. The pipe remained stored at Getter Trucking until December 1983, when Canterra relinquished the pipe to Mitchell upon being informed by law enforcement agencies that the pipe was owned by Mitchell.

Canterra sued Western for breach of warranty of title seeking damages of $201,014.39, the price Canterra had paid for the pipe, plus interest. Western commenced a third-party action against North-Star for breach of warranty of title, and NorthStar commenced a fourth-party action against Yamin.

NorthStar contends that this case falls within the entrustment provision of the Uniform Commercial Code, codified at U.C.C. § 2–403:

> 2. Any entrusting of possession of goods to a merchant who deals in goods of that kind gives him power to transfer all rights of the entruster to a buyer in ordinary course of business.

In essence, this statute contains three elements: (1) an entrustment of goods, (2) to a merchant who deals in goods of the kind, (3) followed by a sale to a buyer in the ordinary course of business. If all three elements are present, the rights of the entruster are transferred to the buyer in ordinary course of business. Port Pipe was merely a storage facility and not a merchant which dealt in pipe. "Merchant" is defined in U.C.C. § 2–104:

> 3. 'Merchant' means a person who deals in goods of the kind or otherwise by his occupation holds himself out as having

knowledge or skill peculiar to the practices or goods involved in the transaction or to whom such knowledge or skill may be attributed by his employment of an agent or broker or other intermediary who by his occupation holds himself out as having such knowledge or skill.

Although this definition provides several ways by which a party may acquire "merchant" status, the entrustment statute applies only to a "merchant who deals in goods" of the kind entrusted. U.C.C. § 2–403. The entrustment statute requires that goods be entrusted to a "merchant who deals in goods of that kind." [U.C.C. § 2-403]. The requirement that the party "deals in goods" has been construed to mean one who is engaged regularly in selling goods of the kind.

The relevant factual inquiry is whether Port Pipe was regularly engaged in selling pipe. Viewing [evidence] in the light most favorable to NorthStar, we conclude that it does raise an inference that Port Pipe regularly sold pipe. Chisholm admits that Port Pipe did sell pipe "from time to time." It will be for the factfinder, after presentation of further evidence regarding the frequency and quantity of Port Pipe's sales of pipe, to determine whether Port Pipe regularly engaged in the sale of pipe and therefore was a merchant which dealt in pipe.

In this case, it is undisputed that Mitchell entrusted the pipe to Port Pipe for storage. In this case, there is intervention by two high-ranking employees of Port Pipe, the entrustee, who allegedly sold the pipe through their dummy corporation, Pharoah, to a buyer in the ordinary course of business. Section 2–403 was intended to determine the priorities between two innocent parties: (1) the original owner who parts with his goods through fraudulent conduct of another and (2) an innocent third party who gives value for the goods to the perpetrator of the fraud without knowledge of the fraud. By favoring the innocent third party, the Uniform Commercial Code endeavors to promote the flow of commerce by placing the burden of ascertaining and preventing fraudulent transactions on the one in the best position to prevent them, the original seller.

We believe this policy also supports application of the entrustment doctrine to a situation where employees of the entrustee transfer the entrusted goods to their sham corporation, which in turn sells the goods to a buyer in the ordinary course of business. As between the two innocent parties in this case [Mitchell, which entrusted the pipe to Port Pipe, and Nickel, which bought the pipe in the ordinary course of business from Pharoah], the policy of the Code places the risk of the entrustee's employees fraudulently diverting and selling the goods upon the entruster, Mitchell, which had the opportunity to select its entrustee. Applying the doctrine to this case, Nickel would acquire the title of the entruster, Mitchell, and title would have passed on to the subsequent purchasers of the pipe.

We conclude that the trial court erred in holding that, as a matter of law, Port Pipe was not a "merchant" and that the entrustment doctrine was therefore inapplicable. Material issues of fact remain which require resolution upon trial.

U.C.C. § 2–714 sets forth the measure of the buyer's damage for breach of the warranty of title:

2. The measure of damages for breach of warranty is the difference at the time and place of acceptance between the value of the goods accepted and the value they would have had if they had been as warranted,

unless special circumstances show proximate damages of a different amount.

NorthStar contends on appeal that "special circumstances" exist which take this case out of the general rule. Special circumstances exist when there has been a breach of warranty of title but the purchaser has enjoyed the use and possession of the goods for a substantial period of time. In such cases, the appropriate measure of damages is the value of the goods at the time the purchaser loses possession and use. "Special circumstances" exist in that situation because it would be unjust to allow the purchaser unfettered use and possession of the goods for a substantial period of time and then allow recovery of the full purchase price paid for the goods.

In this case there clearly was no "use" of the goods by any of the purchasers. Thus, there was no actual "use" of the pipe which would constitute "special circumstances." We therefore conclude that the general rule was applicable, and the appropriate measure of damages for a breach of the warranty of title, if any, in this case will be the difference at the time of sale between the value of the goods accepted and the value they would have had if they had been as warranted.

QUESTIONS FOR ANALYSIS

What facts are critical to the court's analysis? How did the court define *entrustment*? Did the court find that an entrustment existed? Why or why not?

13.6 SPECIAL PROBLEMS IN RISK-OF-LOSS SITUATIONS

To protect goods or property, it is likely that a person will take out insurance on those goods or property. An **insurable interest** is the value placed on property by the insured. A seller retains an insurable interest in a good until title passes, and can have a continuous insurable interest if the risk of loss has not passed. Buyers can have an insurable interest the moment the goods to a contract are identified.

Sending nonconforming goods presents a different problem relating to insurable interests. When the seller sends nonconforming goods to the buyer, the risk of loss remains with the seller. Because a nonconforming shipment is considered a breach by the seller, the buyer will not assume responsibility for it. U.C.C. § 2-510 suggests that if a buyer later discovers a defect

TERMS

insurable interest
An interest from whose existence the owner derives a benefit and whose nonexistence will cause him or her to suffer a loss. The presence of an insurable interest is essential to the validity and enforceability of an insurance policy because it removes it from the category of a gambling contract.

in the goods and revokes the acceptance, the risk of loss remains with the buyer, but there is a caveat: the buyer's exposure to loss is limited to the buyer's insurance coverage. Any loss that exceeds the insurance is borne by the seller.

13.7 WARRANTIES AND SALES

Once title passes to the buyer, the buyer owns the goods and seemingly has no recourse against a seller who tenders a good that does not conform to the standards promised. This is not the case, however. Once the good leaves the seller's hands, the seller warrants that the good will be in a certain condition and form suitable for the use for which the product was intended and for which the buyer purchased it. A promise or guarantee that the product or good is of a certain type, quality, and condition is known as a **warranty**. Warranties are implicit in the sale of any product and are normally categorized as either express or implied warranties.

Express Warranties

When goods are sold, certain guarantees, known as warranties, come with the goods. An **express warranty** may be an oral or written statement that makes certain representations about the quality of the product. Under the U.C.C., there are three basic types of express warranties. Section 2-313(1) provides that express warranties by the seller are created as follows:

(a) Any affirmation of fact or promise made by the seller to the buyer which relates to the goods and becomes part of the basis of the bargain creates an express warranty that the goods shall conform to the affirmation or promise.

(b) Any description of the goods which is made part of the basis of the bargain creates an express warranty that the goods shall conform to the description.

(c) Any sample or model which is made part of the basis of the bargain creates an express warranty that the whole of the goods shall conform to the sample or model.

If the seller makes any of these representations, an express warranty is created.

Statement of Fact or Promise to Buyer

Any specific fact that a seller states about a good is considered an express warranty. Ordinarily, any statement upon which the buyer relies becomes part of the basis of the bargain and is an express warranty. The statement itself is considered a representation or a guarantee of the product.

The issue that frequently arises in express warranty cases is whether the statement was a fact or an opinion, which the law refers to as **puffing**. Puffing is the "big talk" a salesperson often gives to get a customer interested in a product. An example of puffing is a salesperson's saying, "This boat is the greatest boat this side of the Mississippi." Most of us would know that is sales talk. But if the salesperson says to you, "This boat comes with a two-year free maintenance guarantee," that is a statement of fact or promise to you, the buyer. The distinction that has to be made is whether the seller is stating a specific fact or merely giving an opinion. Sellers who are attempting to convince a buyer to purchase their goods often use language to encourage or entice the buyer into purchasing the goods. Courts are called upon to make the distinction as to whether a seller is communicating a fact upon which the buyer relies (in which case an express warranty is created), or whether puffing or mere opinion was being communicated to the seller. This has been a difficult area of law for the courts, as there are no specific guidelines for determining the distinction between fact and opinion. Case law will guide the determination of whether a salesperson's words are fact or opinion.

The U.C.C. does not require that certain language or words be used to create an express warranty. It is the representation or the intent to make a warranty that creates the express warranty, not the language.

Description of the Goods

A description of the goods by a merchant or salesperson can also create an express warranty. If the description of the good induces a buyer to purchase the good, the buyer can claim an express warranty for that product. Assume that Martha sees an advertisement for a microwave that has a turntable in it. She orders the microwave. When it arrives, Martha finds a glass plate inside the oven, but no revolving turntable. Martha would have an action against the seller for breach of express warranty, because the microwave was not as represented in the advertisement, either as pictured or as described. Language that can be used in sales contracts for an express warranty based on description of the goods is provided in Figure 13-3.

Declaration of Warranty—Specifications

The specifications set forth in Section _____ of this agreement constitute express warranties by seller that the goods covered by this agreement shall conform to those specifications.

Declaration of Warranty—Based on Description

Seller warrants that the goods when delivered shall conform to the description in Section _____ of this agreement.

FIGURE 13-3 Sample express warranties

TERMS

warranty
1. Generally, an agreement to be responsible for all damages arising from the falsity of a statement or the failure of an assurance. 2. With respect to a contract for sale of goods, a promise, either express or implied by law, with respect to the fitness or merchantability of the article that is the subject of the contract.

express warranty
A warranty created by the seller in a contract for sale of goods, in which the seller, orally or in writing, makes representations regarding the quality or condition of the goods.

puffing
Exaggerating. A seller who "talks up" what he or she is selling by praising it is not guilty of fraudulent misrepresentation so long as he or she confines himself or herself to his or her own opinion and does not misrepresent a material fact. Such salesmanship is "mere puffing."

Sample or Model

A common sales technique is to show a buyer a sample or model of the product offered. When a buyer is shown a sample or model, it becomes part of the purchase contract and thus an express warranty. Implicit in the showing of the sample or model is that any good sold and delivered to the buyer will be of the same type and quality as the sample or model. If this is not so, the buyer will have an action against the seller for breach of an express warranty. Provisions to consider when the express warranty is based upon a sample or model are found in Figure 13-4.

Declaration of Warranty—Based on Sample or Model

Seller warrants that the goods when delivered shall conform to the [sample or model] that was [exhibited or demonstrated] to buyer on February 1, 1995, by Shay Cullivan, the sales representative of seller, at 1234 19th Street, New York, New York.

Identity of Sample or Model Used as Basis of Warranty

This sale has been made on the basis of a [sample or model] of the goods that is marked for identification purposes in the following manner: _____. The [sample or model] is in the possession of William Payne Johnson, of 12th and 85th Streets, New York, New York.

Effect of Damage or Destruction of Sample or Model Used as Basis of Warranty

If the [sample or model] identified in Section _____ of this agreement is damaged or destroyed in any manner or by any cause, the party to this agreement not responsible for the damage or destruction shall have the option of canceling this agreement.

FIGURE 13-4 Express warranties based on sample or model

Implied Warranties

In addition to imposing standards for express warranties upon sellers, the U.C.C. also imposes standards for implied warranties. An **implied warranty** is a warranty imposed by law that is *implicit* (understood, but not expressed) as the basis of the bargain. Implied warranties set out certain standard business dealings and are designed to protect the consumer or buyer. The U.C.C. cites four basic types of implied warranties: (1) warranty of title, (2) warranty against infringement, (3) warranty of merchantability, and (4) warranty of fitness for a particular purpose. The type of contractual arrangement of the parties will control which warranties, if any, are implied in the contract.

Warranty of Title

In any sale of a good, a **warranty of title** is deemed to exist. Warranty of title ensures that the goods purchased are free of any liens or

TERMS

implied warranty
In the sale of personal property, a warranty by the seller, inferred by law (whether or not the seller intended to create the warranty), as to the quality or condition of the goods sold. Under the Uniform Commercial Code, the most important implied warranties are the implied warranty of merchantability and the implied warranty of fitness for a particular purpose. In any sale of goods, a warranty of merchantability (fitness for general or customary purposes) is implied if the seller normally sells such goods. An implied warranty of fitness for a particular purpose exists when the seller has reason to know the purpose for which the buyer wants the goods and the buyer is relying on the seller to furnish goods suited to that purpose.

encumbrances of which the seller has knowledge. Unless excluded by the seller, the warranty of title guarantees that the transfer of the goods from the seller to the buyer is proper. The seller warrants to hold the buyer harmless from any possible title issues or claims from third parties that might affect the buyer's ownership interest in the good. U.C.C. § 2-312 provides:

(1) Subject to subsection (2) there is in a contract for sale a warranty by the seller that
   (a) the title conveyed shall be good, and its transfer rightful; and
   (b) the goods shall be delivered free from any security interest or other lien or encumbrance of which the buyer at the time of contracting has no knowledge.
(2) A warranty under subsection (1) will be excluded or modified only by specific language or by circumstances which give the buyer reason to know that the person selling does not claim title in himself or that he is purporting to sell only such right or title as he or a third person may have.
(3) Unless otherwise agreed, a seller who is a merchant regularly dealing in goods of the kind warrants that the goods shall be delivered free of the rightful claim of any third person by way of infringement or the like but a buyer who furnishes specifications to the seller must hold the seller harmless against any such claim which arises out of compliance with the specifications.

To establish a case for breach of the warranty of title, the buyer must show that: (1) the title acquired was not valid; or (2) the transfer of title was improper; or (3) the goods transferred are subject to another's rights of which the buyer had no knowledge. Warranty of title was an issue in *Jefferson v. Jones,* 408 A.2d 1036 (Md. 1979). For examples of provisions that could be considered in drafting warranty-of-title language, review Figure 13-5.

> **warranty of title**
> With respect to the sale of goods, a warranty by the seller, implied by law, that he or she has title to the goods.

JEFFERSON v. JONES
Court of Appeals of Maryland
Dec. 14, 1979

In the present case, we are called upon to decide an issue arising under the Maryland Uniform Commercial Code—whether a purchaser of goods must prove that a third party has a superior or paramount title to those goods in order to substantiate a claim that a seller's warranty of title as established by section 2–312 has been breached.

The genesis of this dispute was the sale of a Honda motorcycle by appellee Lawrence V. Jones to appellant Thomas N. Jefferson in July 1975.

At the time of sale, although appellant received immediate possession of the cycle, the seller retained the title certificate as security for the unpaid portion of the agreed purchase price. Upon receipt of the balance due, Jones executed an assignment of the certificate to Jefferson, which was then reissued in the new owner's name by the Maryland Motor Vehicle Administration. Approximately two years later, while Jefferson was having the motorcycle repaired at a garage in the District of Columbia, he was asked by the D.C. police, for reasons not apparent in the record, to prove his entitlement to the vehicle. In an effort to establish his ownership, Jefferson produced his title certificate, but when the identification number listed on it did not correspond to the one embossed on the frame of the vehicle, the police became suspicious and seized the motorcycle. Following the denial of his demand that possession of the motorcycle be relinquished to him, Jefferson instituted an action in the Superior Court of the District of Columbia against the police in replevin and for conversion. Before trial, the matter was settled and the motorcycle was returned to Jefferson. He then asked Jones to indemnify him for the legal expenses which he had incurred in retrieving the vehicle, and when Jones refused, the appellant file the present breach of warranty action.

Section 2–312 of the Maryland Uniform Commercial Code sets forth the warranty of title, relevant here, that is inherent in every sale of goods in this State:

Warranty of Title . . .
(1) Subject to subsection (2) there is in a contract for sale a warranty by the seller that
    (a) The title conveyed shall be good, and its transfer rightful; and
    (b) The goods shall be delivered free from any security interest or other lien or encumbrance of which the buyer at the time of contracting has no knowledge.
(2) A warranty under subsection (1) will be excluded or modified only by specific language or by circumstances which give the buyer reason to know that the person selling does not claim title in himself or that he is purporting to sell only such right or title as he or a third person may have.

Of primary concern in this case is the requirement imposed upon the seller by subsection (1)(a) that a good title be rightfully transferred. In analyzing its meaning we mention that the term "good title" is not one of art with a fixed significance in the law of property, nor is it in any way defined by the provisions of the Commercial Law Article.

Although we are directed by the General Assembly to construe the Uniform Commercial Code in a manner which "make[s] uniform the law among the various [states]" adopting it, we nonetheless utilize, in interpreting the Code, the same principles of statutory construction that we would apply in determining the meaning of any other legislative enactment.

A seller transfers to his purchaser "a good, clean title . . . in a rightful manner [when he does] *so that [the buyer] will not be exposed to a lawsuit in order to protect it.*" Thus, in the absence of any indication, express or otherwise, that the General Assembly intended anything to the contrary, we hold that the U.C.C.'s warranty of title requirement is to protect a vendee from legal claims which may arise concerning his ownership of the purchased goods. The type or nature, however, of a third party's claim of title or right to possession giving rise to a breach of the warranty is not further delineated by the statute. However, it is our view that the legislature intended, that the Code's warranty of title would provide a buyer with greater protection than its common law counterpart. Our determination in this regard here is amply supported by the statement in the comments that "[d]isturbance of quiet possession . . . [which at common law required interference by a holder of a superior or paramount title before a breach was declared] is one way, *among many,* in which the breach of the warranty of title may be established." Again, finding nothing to the contrary, we therefore conclude that section 2–312's protection, unless waived by the purchaser, applies to third party claims of title no matter whether eventually determined to be inferior or superior to the buyer's ownership.

Our holding here, that proof of a superior title is not necessary, does not mean, however, that all claims, no matter how unfounded, which may be made against the buyer's title should result in a breach of the warranty. "Good title" is "usually taken to mean that the title which the seller gives to the buyer is 'free from reasonable doubt, that is, not only a valid title in fact, but [also] one that can again be sold to a reasonable purchaser or mortgaged to a person of reasonable prudence.' " As such, "there is some point at which [a] third party's claim against the goods becomes so attenuated that we should not regard it as an interference against which the seller has warranted." All that a purchaser should expect from a seller of property is that he be protected from colorable claims against his title and not from all claims. Spurious title claims can be made by anyone at any time. Thus, before a third party's claim against the title of another will result in a breach of the warranty of title, the claim must be colorable, nonspurious and of such a nature as to produce a reasonable doubt as to the title's validity.

When we examine the facts of the case no before us, we conclude that, as a matter or law, a warranty of title has been breached here. An undisputed aspect of possessing good title is that a purchaser be "enable[d] . . . to hold the [property] in peace and, if he wishes to sell it, to be reasonably certain that no flaw will appear to disturb its market value." Whenever the title to personal property is evidenced by a document which is an aid to proving ownership, as is true in the case of motor vehicles, any substantial defect in that document necessarily creates a reasonable doubt as to that ownership. If problems do arise, as in this case, the seller is responsible for any damages caused. A breach of the warranty of title occurs whenever a seller of a motor vehicle fails to provide his purchaser with adequate proof of ownership because of the reasonable doubts which faulty documentation raise as to the validity of the buyer's title.

QUESTIONS FOR ANALYSIS

Identify the relevant facts in *Jefferson*. How does the court determine when a possessor has "good title"? What is the court's reasoning for its decision?

Warranty of Title

Seller warrants and represents that seller has absolute and good title to and full right to dispose of the [type of goods], and that there are no liens, claims, or encumbrances of any kind against the goods.

Right of Agent to Transfer Title

Seller warrants that Bud Johnson of 8900 Walnut Street, Dallas, Dallas County, Texas, is the owner of the goods covered by this agreement, and that seller is the authorized agent of the owner and has authority to transfer the title to goods to buyer.

Right of Pledge to Transfer Title

Seller is a pledgee of the goods covered by this agreement, which goods were pledged with seller on March 17, 1994, by Collin Casperson, of 1813 West Buckingham Drive, Ft. Lauderdale, Florida, as pledgor. On March 17, 1994, and at all times thereafter, pledgor was in default under the terms of the agreement of pledge and this sale is made by seller as pledgee under that agreement of pledge and is made in accordance with the rights of seller under that agreement. Seller warrants that the sale by seller is authorized and rightful with respect to pledgor.

FIGURE 13-5   Sample warranty-of-title language

Warranty of Infringement

The warranty of infringement relates to **patent, copyright**, and **trademark** rights. This warranty applies only to a merchant who is selling goods which are part of the normal stock or inventory of the merchant. Although the warranty of infringement has not received much attention over the past years, new applications are being tested in the courts. Much attention has been given to unofficial ("bootleg") copies of compact discs (CDs), cassette tapes, and videos. Individuals who make unauthorized copies and attempt to sell them to the unsuspecting public as the real thing, are engaged in *pirating,* a practice that has cost the entertainment industry untold millions of dollars over the years. Those who make and sell the unauthorized copies violate the warranty against infringement. Illustrations of contractual provisions that may be used in a contract for warranty against infringement appear in Figure 13-6.

Warranty of Seller Against Patent and Trademark Infringement

Seller warrants that the goods shall be delivered free of the rightful claim of any person arising from patent or trademark infringement.

Warranty of Seller Against Patent and Trademark Infringement—Indemnification of Buyer

Seller shall indemnify buyer or the customers of buyer against any liability arising from claims of patent or trademark infringement on account of any composition, process, invention, article, or appliance used or furnished by seller in the performance of this agreement, including, but not limited to, patents or processes for the manufacturing, sale, and delivery of the goods. Seller shall defend any actions brought against buyer for any such claim, and shall bear all the costs, expenses, and attorney fees of buyer in the defense of any action, and seller shall pay any judgment that may be awarded against buyer. Seller shall have the right to participate in or take over the defense of any such claim or action.

Exclusion of Warranty Against Infringement by Seller

Seller makes no warranty, and no warranty shall be deemed to exist, that buyer holds the goods free of the claim of any third person that may arise from patent or trademark infringement.

FIGURE 13-6 Sample warranties against infringement

Warranty of Merchantability

From a buyer's perspective, the implied warranty of merchantability is perhaps the most valuable. This warranty attaches when there is a sale of a good by a merchant, manufacturer, wholesaler, or retailer. Implicit in the sale of the product is that the product will be free from defects and fit for the purpose for which it was intended. For example, when foreign objects such as worms or mice are found in a food product, needless to say, the product will be deemed unmerchantable. The six elements of warranty of merchantability are set forth in U.C.C. § 2-314(2):

Goods to be merchantable must be at least such as

(a) pass without objection in the trade under the contract description; and

(b) in the case of fungible goods, are of fair average quality within the description; and

(c) are fit for the ordinary purposes for which such goods are used; and

(d) run, within the variations permitted by the agreement, of even kind, quality and quantity within each unit and among all units involved; and

(e) are adequately contained, packaged, and labeled as the agreement may require; and

(f) conform to the promises or affirmations of fact made on the container or label if any.

When a product fails to conform to the standards in § 2-314(2), a breach of warranty may be found.

Food Products The warranty of merchantability has been challenged in court in many food cases, which range from chemical contamination to foods containing foreign objects. Because of the volume of disputes about food, the courts have developed two general approaches to these cases: the foreign–natural test and the reasonable expectation test.

Under the *foreign–natural test*, substances that are considered natural to a product do not violate the warranty of merchantability. For example, an unshelled nut in a can of mixed nuts is natural to the product; a fish bone found in fish chowder is natural to the product. These examples are from actual cases in which courts decided issues of warranty of merchantability. Review *Coffer v. Standard Brands, Inc.*, 30 N.C. App. 134, 226 S.E.2d 534 (1976).

copyright
The right of an author, granted by federal statute, to exclusively control the reproduction, distribution, and sale of his or her literary, artistic, or intellectual productions for the period of the copyright's existence. Copyright protection extends to written work, music, films, sound recordings, photographs, paintings, sculpture, and some computer programs and chips.

trademark
A mark, design, title, logo, or motto used in the sale or advertising of products to identify them and distinguish them from the products of others. A trademark is the property of its owner and, when registered under the Trademark Act, is reserved for the exclusive use of its owner.

COFFER v. STANDARD BRANDS, INC.

Court of Appeals of North Carolina
July 21, 1976

Defendant is a New York corporation, registered in North Carolina "for the general manufacturing of its products"; and "defendant does on a daily and regular basis manufacture and sell its products in the State of North Carolina". On or about 1 April 1974 plaintiff purchased a bottle of "Planters Dry Roasted Mixed Nuts", a product manufactured by defendant and sold and distributed by it in North Carolina. Plaintiff purchased the product in its original and unopened container from a food store in Greensboro. Thereafter, plaintiff opened the bottle and, as he was eating some of the nuts therefrom, he bit down on a nut that had not been shelled, resulting in damage to his teeth. He suffered great pain as a result of the incident and has incurred considerable expense in getting his teeth repaired. Defendant is liable to plaintiff on theories of negligence, breach of express warranty, breach of implied warranty, and strict liability in tort. At the close of the evidence defendant's motion for directed verdict was allowed and from judgment dismissing the action, plaintiff appealed.

Plaintiff contends that defendant breached an express warranty that the mixed nuts were all shelled. The evidence does not support this position. The only language appearing on the label of the container is as follows:

> "PLANTERS
> Dry Roasted
> MIXED NUTS
> no oils or sugar
> used in processing"

Nowhere does there appear a representation that the nuts contained in the jar were shelled. The Uniform Commercial Code mandates that in order for an express warranty to be effective, a manufacturer's representations must be a part of the basis of the bargain. We feel that use of the jar, while revealing shelled nuts, was a mere passive marking tool. It was not an affirmative representation and as such was insufficient to give rise to an express warranty.

First, we consider plaintiff's claim in the light of the Uniform Commercial Code and defendant's implied warranty of merchantability under § 2–314(1). Unless excluded or modified pursuant to 2–316, this warranty arises as a matter of law where the seller is a merchant with respect to the goods in question under 2–104(1). Some basis for determining the merchantability of goods is provided in 2–314(2).

We feel that the goods were impliedly warranted to be nuts, a natural incident of which were the shells. As such they were fit for the ordinary purposes under 2–314(2)(c). The argument could be made that the clear glass jar revealing only shelled nuts was a "promise or affirmation of fact" as provided in 2–314(2)(f). However, we feel that this approach is inconsistent with the nature of the goods at issue and 2–314(2)(c).

While there appear to be no standards governing the permissible limits for presence of unshelled filberts in a lot of otherwise shelled nuts, such standards do exist for peanuts. We find these figures highly persuasive in establishing merchantability under 2–314(2)(a). They indicate that in the context of the peanut industry as a regulated trade, there is some tolerance for unshelled nuts in a lot of shelled nuts.

Since mixed nuts are subject to the same standards as individual varieties, it logically follows that as in case of peanuts there is some tolerance in the trade for unshelled filberts as well. Thus the mixed nuts marketed by defendant were merchantable notwithstanding the presence of an unshelled filbert, since the presence of limited quantities of unshelled nuts does not render shelled nuts objectionable in the trade within the meaning of 2–314(2)(a).

2–314(2)(c) provides that goods are merchantable when they are fit for ordinary purposes. As a food, defendant's mixed nuts are subject to various state and federal regulatory acts dealing with the quality of food goods. [State statute] dealing with adulterated foods is instructive.

> A food shall be deemed to be adulterated:
> (1) a. If it bears or contains any poisonous or deleterious substance which may render it injurious to health; *but in case the substance is not an added substance* the food shall not be considered adulterated under this paragraph if the quantity of such substance in such food does not ordinarily render it injurious to health (emphasis added).

Thus, it appears by statute and regulation that a certain limited amount of naturally occurring unshelled filberts is permissible without rendering the food goods adulterated. As such they are fit for ordinary purposes and merchantable under 2–314(2)(c).

Plaintiff can find no comfort in the foreign substance doctrine as the unshelled filbert was not a foreign substance. It is well recognized in this and other jurisdictions passing on the question that the presence of natural impurities is no basis for liability. Since the impurity complained of in this case was a natural incident of the goods in question, we feel that there was no breach of the implied warranty of merchantability.

QUESTIONS FOR ANALYSIS

What are the facts of *Coffer*? Did the court hold that there was a breach of the warranty of merchantability? Why or why not? What was the court's reasoning?

Under the *reasonable expectations* test, the court inquires as to what a reasonable person would expect to find in the product. Undoubtedly, one does not expect to find bits of glass or an insect in food, or a syringe in soda. Having such foreign objects in a food product is unreasonable.

Cars and Trucks Another area in which the warranty of merchantability has been challenged is in the use and manufacture of cars and trucks. This issue received national attention when the Ford Pinto's merchantability came into question (several Pintos exploded on impact due to the gas tank design). More recently, a truck design was litigated (because of the placement of side gasoline tanks, when hit, the trucks often exploded). In each case, one of the bases for challenge was warranty of merchantability.

Cigarettes Courts have had the difficult task of determining whether cigarettes are merchantable because they cause cancer. To date, the courts have taken the "no-worse-than-anybody else" approach. Unless contaminated by some foreign substance, a cigarette is merchantable, because the product as intended is free from defects, even though it may cause cancer. Many disagree with that analysis, and the case law is sure to develop rapidly in this area as new cases are decided.

Warranty of Fitness for a Particular Purpose

Sometimes a seller knows that the buyer is relying on the seller's expertise and judgment in the purchase of goods. When this occurs, the warranty of fitness for a particular purpose comes into play. Under U.C.C. § 2-315:

> Where the seller at the time of contracting has reason to know any particular purpose for which the goods are required and that the buyer is relying on the seller's skill or judgment to select or furnish suitable goods, there is unless excluded or modified an implied warranty that the goods shall be fit for such purpose.

The critical question is whether the product is fit for a particular purpose, not whether the product is fit for an ordinary purpose. Fitness for a particular purpose is more specific and defined than fitness for ordinary purpose, which is considered a merchantability issue. When a buyer communicates to a seller the particular needs of that buyer, and relies on the skill and judgment of the seller, the warranty of fitness for a particular purpose is breached if the product fails to meet those specific needs and expectations However, the respective expertise of the parties will be considered in determining whether the buyer relied on the seller's skill and knowledge of the product. *Royal Business Machines, Inc. v. Lorraine Corp.,* 633 F.2d 34 (7th Cir. 1980) illustrates this point.

ROYAL BUSINESS MACHINES, INC. v. LORRAINE CORP.

United States Court of Appeals, Seventh Circuit
Oct. 7, 1980

The case arose from commercial transactions extending over a period of 18 months between Royal and Booher in which Royal sold and Booher purchased 114 RBC I and 14 RBC II plain paper copying machines.

Paraphrasing U.C.C. § 2–313 as adopted in Indiana, an express warranty is made up of the following elements: (a) an affirmation of fact or promise, (b) that relates to the goods, and (c) becomes a part of the basis of the bargain between the parties. When each of these three elements is present, a warranty is created that the goods shall conform to the affirmation of fact or to the promise.

The decisive test for whether a given representation is a warranty or merely an expression of the seller's opinion is whether the seller asserts a fact of which the buyer is ignorant or merely states an opinion or judgment on a matter of which the seller has no special knowledge and on which the buyer may be expected also to have an opinion and to exercise his judgment. General statements to the effect that goods are "the best," or are "of good quality," or will "last a lifetime" and be "in perfect conditions," are generally regarded as expressions of the seller's opinion or "the puffing of his wares" and do not create an express warranty.

No express warranty was created by Royal's affirmation that both RBC machine models and their component parts were of high quality. This was a statement of the seller's opinion, the kind of "puffing" to be expected in any sales transaction, rather than a positive averment of fact describing a product's capabilities to which an express warranty could attach. Similarly, the representations by Royal that experience and testing had shown that the frequency of repair was "very low" and would remain so lack the specificity of an affirmation of fact upon which a warranty could be predicated. These representations were statements of the seller's opinion.

On the other hand, the assertion that the machines could not cause fires is an assertion of fact relating to the goods, and substantial evidence in the record supports the trial judge's findings that the assertion was made by Royal to Booher. The same may be said for the assertion that the machines were tested and ready to be marketed.

This case is complicated by the fact that it involved a series of sales transactions between the same parties over approximately an 18-month period and concerned two different machines. The situations of the parties, their knowledge and reliance, may be expected to change in light of their experience during that time. An affirmation of fact which the buyer from his experience knows to be untrue cannot form a part of the basis of the bargain. Therefore, as to each purchase, Booher's expanding knowledge of the capacities of the copying machines would have to be considered in deciding whether Royal's representations were part of the basis of the bargain.

A warranty of merchantability is implied by law in any sale where the seller is a merchant of the goods. To be merchantable, goods must, *inter alia,* pass without objection in the trade under the contract description, be of fair average quality, and be fit for the ordinary purposes for which such goods are used. They must "conform to ordinary standards, and . . . be of the same average grade, quality and value as similar goods sold under similar circumstances."

An implied warranty of fitness for a particular purpose arises where a seller has reason to know a particular purpose for which the goods are required and the buyer relies on the seller's skill or judgment to select or furnish suitable goods. The court found that Royal knew the particular purpose for which all the RBC machines were to be used and, in fact, that Royal had taken affirmative steps to persuade Booher to become its dealer and that occasionally its employees even accompanied Booher on calls to customers. For the foregoing reasons the judgment of the district court is reversed, and the cause is remanded for a new trial.

QUESTIONS FOR ANALYSIS

What are the facts of *Royal Business Machines?* What is the test for determining whether a warranty is given or is the seller's opinion? What types of statements constitute puffing? What was the court's holding?

FARCUS

WAISGLASS/COULTHART

13.8 GENERAL WARRANTY OF PROTECTION: MAGNUSON-MOSS ACT

Buyers and consumers have had many problems with companies attempting to disclaim warranties without the buyers' knowledge and attempting to circumvent their responsibilities under contracts. Buyers and consumers were left with little protection under the law and were literally helpless. However, in 1975, Congress passed the "Consumer Protection Warranty Act," also known as the Magnuson-Moss Act (15 U.S.C. § 45 *et seq.*), which created new protections for consumers against sellers.

No longer could sellers hide warranties in the fine print or exclude warranties of which the buyer had no knowledge. The Act required that sellers or manufacturers provide presale warranty information; it also set forth procedures to assist consumers in having their claims heard.

According to the Act, when goods are sold for more than $10:

1. The warranty has to be available prior to the purchase
2. The warranty must be presented in easily understood English
3. The warranty must state whether it is full or limited.

Unless these basic statutory requirements are followed, the seller may be subject to certain civil penalties.

One of the Act's most notable requirements is that the seller/manufacturer must designate whether a warranty is full or limited. The Act provides four basic requirements for a **full warranty**:

1. Defects will be remedied within a reasonable period of time
2. Any exclusions or limitations of consequential damages must be conspicuously set forth
3. An implied warranty cannot be limited as to time
4. If a product is defective and the defects cannot be remedied, the buyer has the right to a refund or a replacement item.

In addition, a full warranty must state its duration. For example, if the warranty is for 90 days, it must state in a conspicuous manner "Ninety-Day Warranty." Most products today have full warranties. For example, a hair dryer is usually sold with a printed warranty setting out in specific language the rights and responsibilities of both the seller and the buyer.

A **limited warranty** is any warranty that does not fulfill all the requirements of a full warranty. In a sense, a limited warranty is created by exclusion. Many of the requirements for creating a full warranty are not met in a limited warranty; thus, the rights of the party who is purchasing the item are limited. Figure 13-7 shows a sample combined full warranty and limited warranty.

AUTOMATIC WASHER WARRANTY
Full One-Year Warranty

For one (1) year from the date of original retail purchase, any part which fails in normal home use will be repaired or replaced free of charge. This warranty applies when the appliance is located in the United States or Canada. Appliances located elsewhere are covered by the limited warranty, including parts which fail during the first year.

Limited Parts Warranty

After the first year from the date of original retail purchase, through the time periods listed below, the designated parts which fail in normal home use will be repaired or replaced free of charge for the part itself, with the owner paying all other costs, including labor.
    Second Year—all parts; **Third through Fifth Year**—all parts of the transmission assembly (as illustrated).

Additional Limited Warranty Against Rust

Should an exterior cabinet, including the top and lid, rust during the five year period starting from the date of retail purchase, repair or replacement will be made free of charge during the first year. After the first and through the fifth year, repair or replacement will be made free of charge for the part itself, with the owner paying all other costs, including labor.

How and Where to Receive Warranty Service

Call or write the authorized dealer from whom the appliance was purchased or the authorized service firm designated by it.
    If the owner moves from the selling dealer's servicing area after purchase, call or write any authorized dealer or authorized service firm in or near the new location.
    Should the owner not receive satisfactory warranty service from one of the above, call or write Service Department.

This Warranty gives you specific legal rights, and you may also have other rights which vary from state to state.

FIGURE 13-7 Sample combined full and limited warranty

13.9 THE RIGHT TO EXCLUDE WARRANTIES

Sellers may exclude warranties on the products they sell, but the exclusion must be readily apparent so that the consumer or buyer is not misled when purchasing the product. U.C.C. § 2-316(1) discusses when express warranties can be excluded. In part, this section states that:

> Words or conduct relevant to the creation of an express warranty in words or conduct intending to negate or limit warranty shall be construed whenever reasonable as consistent with each other.

If the warranty and the exclusion are inconsistent with each other, the warranty will supersede the exclusion. Thus, the warranty will be interpreted in favor of the buyer.

The Code provides specific methods of excluding implied warranties, which must be strictly met. Section 2-316(2) states how certain implied warranties can be excluded:

> To exclude or modify the implied warranty of merchantability or any part of it, the language must mention merchantability and in case of a

TERMS

full warranty
    A warranty that is not confined to specified defects and that covers labor as well as materials.

limited warranty
    1. A warranty that is limited in duration or confined to specified defects. 2. A warranty providing less than a full warranty provides.

writing must be conspicuous, and to exclude or modify any implied warranties of fitness, the exclusion must be a writing and conspicuous.

Language which excludes all implied warranties of fitness is sufficient if it states, for example, that "There are no warranties which extend beyond the description on the face hereof."

Notice that under § 2-316(2), all the exclusions of implied warranties must be written and **conspicuous**. This means that the language must either be underlined, or in boldface print, or in capital letters, so that the buyer can easily see that the exclusion exists. Language that does not comply with the requirements of § 2-316(2) will not exclude the implied warranty.

Further, § 2-316(3) provides a method of exclusion for implied warranties of quality:

(a) unless the circumstances indicate otherwise, all implied warranties are excluded by expressions like "as is", "with all faults" or other language which in common understanding calls the buyers' attention to the exclusion of warranties and makes plain there is no implied warranty; and

(b) when the buyer before entering into the contract has examined the goods or the sample or model as fully as he desired or has refused to examine the goods, there is no implied warranty with regard to defects which an examination ought in the circumstances to have revealed to him; and

(c) An implied warranty can also be excluded or modified by course of dealing or course of performance or usage of trade.

The key to warranty exclusion is notice to the buyer. Be sure the notice is clear, unambiguous, and easily understood. Figure 13-8 provides examples of warranty exclusions.

Exclusion of Warranties of Merchantability and Fitness for Any Purpose

SELLER MAKES NO WARRANTY OF MERCHANTABILITY OF THE GOODS OR OF THE FITNESS OF THE GOODS FOR ANY PURPOSE.

Exclusion of Warranties of Merchantability and Fitness for Any Purpose

Except for the warranty of title, NO WARRANTY OF MERCHANTABILITY, FITNESS, OR OTHER WARRANTY (WHETHER EXPRESSED, OR IMPLIED, OR STATUTORY) IS MADE BY SELLER, except that seller warrants the goods to be free from defects in materials and workmanship in normal use and service.

Exclusion of Warranty of Fitness for Any Purpose

THE GOODS SUBJECT TO THIS CONTRACT ARE NOT WARRANTED AS SUITABLE FOR ANY PURPOSE PARTICULAR TO BUYER. THE SUITABILITY OF GOODS FOR ANY PURPOSE PARTICULAR TO BUYER IS FOR BUYER, IN BUYER'S SOLE JUDGMENT, TO DETERMINE. SELLER ASSUMES NO RESPONSIBILITY FOR THE SELECTION OR FURNISHING OF GOODS SUITABLE TO THE INDIVIDUAL NEEDS AND PURPOSES OF ANY PARTICULAR BUYER.

FIGURE 13-8 Sample warranty exclusions

Alternative A: Seller's warranty, whether express or implied, extends to any natural person who is in the family or household of the buyer or who is a guest in his home, if it is reasonable to expect that such person may use, consume, or be affected by the goods and who is injured in person by breach of the warranty. Seller may not exclude or limit the operation of this section.

Alternative B: Seller's warranty, whether express or implied, extends to any natural person who may reasonably be expected to use, consume, or be affected by the goods who is injured in person by breach of the warranty. A seller may not exclude or limit the operation of this section.

Alternative C: A seller's warranty, whether express or implied, extends to any person who may reasonably be expected to use, consume, or be affected by the goods and who is injured by breach of the warranty. A seller may not exclude or limit the operation of this section with respect to injury to the person of an individual to whom the warranty extends.

FIGURE 13-9 U.C.C. warranty alternatives (§ 2-318)

13.10 PERSONS COVERED UNDER WARRANTIES

Under § 2-318, the U.C.C. extends warranties to the persons who benefit from the product and who may use the product. This suggests that **privity**, a direct contractual relationship between the buyer and seller, is unnecessary. If a person uses a product and is injured by it, the injured party has a cause of action against the appropriate parties. Privity is not an issue.

The Code presents three alternatives (see Figure 13-9) for state adoption on the issue of who is included in a warranty. A number of states have adopted one of these various alternatives; others have created their own versions to deal with the extended warranty problem. Check Figure 13-10 to determine individual state policy.

Alternate A	Alternate B	Alternate C
Alaska	Alabama	Hawaii
Arizona	Colorado	Iowa
Arkansas	Delaware	Minnesota
Connecticut	Kansas	North Dakota
District of Columbia	South Dakota	Utah
Florida	Vermont	
Georgia	Wyoming	
Idaho		
Illinois		
Indiana		
Kentucky		
Maryland		

FIGURE 13-10 State adoption of warranty language

TERMS

conspicuous
Clearly visible; easily seen.

privity
An identity of interest between persons, so that the legal interest of one person is measured by the same legal right as the other; continuity of interest; successive relationships to the same rights of property.

Alternate A	Alternate B	Alternate C
Michigan		
Mississippi		
Missouri		
Montana		
Nebraska		
Nevada		
New Jersey		
New Mexico		
North Carolina		
Ohio		
Oklahoma		
Oregon		
Pennsylvania		
South Carolina		
Tennessee		
Washington		
West Virginia		
Wisconsin		

Own Version	None
Maine	California
Massachusetts	Louisiana
New Hampshire	
New York	
Rhode Island	
Texas	
Virginia	

FIGURE 13-10 *(Continued)*

13.11 REMEDIES FOR BREACH OF WARRANTY

A prerequisite for any action involving a breach of warranty is the plaintiff's notice to the seller of the defect in the product. The notice must occur within a reasonable time period after discovery of the defect or after the defect should have been discovered. Unless notice has been properly given, recovery for damages will be difficult. Figure 13-11 is an example of a notice letter for breach of warranty.

The damage provisions for breach of warranty situations are found in § 2-714(1) and (2), which state:

> (1) Where the buyer has accepted goods and given notification (subsection (3) of Section 2-607), he may recover as damages for any non-conformity of tender the loss resulting in the ordinary course of events from the seller's breach as determined in any manner which is reasonable.

Mr. Conrad Holmes   May 15, 1994
1234 Elm Street
Dallas, Texas 76543

Dear Mr. Holmes:

   Please take notice that on July 15, 1994, the warranty of merchantability given by you in
our agreement of July 10, 1994, for the sale of 45 vacuum cleaners was breached by you in
that within fifteen (15) days of receiving the goods, seven (7) customers have brought back
their vacuums because of defective motors.
   The warranty is based on Section 14 of our agreement, which provided as follows: [set
forth agreement].
   Unless you remedy this problem within ten (10) days of receipt of this letter, I will take
the appropriate legal action.
   Your prompt attention to this matter is advised.

                              Very truly yours,

                              Andrew Davids

FIGURE 13-11   Sample notice letter for breach of warranty

(2) The measure of damages for breach of warranty is the difference
at the time and place of acceptance between the value of the goods
accepted and the value they would have had if they had been as
warranted, unless special circumstances show proximate damages
of a different amount.

Notice that incidental and consequential damages are recoverable in a breach
of warranty case.
   However, contract law is not the only method of recovery for breach of
warranty or a defective product. Tort law now allows consumers to file actions against sellers, manufacturers, suppliers, and retailers when a product
causes injury. When a consumer is injured by a product, products liability
law offers remedies based upon **negligence** or **strict liability**.

Negligence

   A common method of recovery for an injury suffered from the purchase
of a product is a negligence action. Under present legal theories, an injured
party can sue the manufacturer, supplier, and/or retailer for damages caused
by a product held out for sale to the public. Based upon public policy arguments, entities that put unsafe products in the stream of commerce are held
responsible for injuries resulting from defective products. For a consumer to
be successful in a negligence action, it must be shown that:

TERMS

negligence
   The failure to do something that a reasonable
person would do in the
same circumstances, or
the doing of something
a reasonable person
would not do. Negli-
gence is a wrong gene-
rally characterized by
carelessness, inatten-
tiveness, and neglect-
fulness rather than by a
positive intent to cause
injury.

strict liability
   Liability for an injury
whether or not there is
fault or negligence;
absolute liability. The
law imposes strict
liability in product
liability cases.

1. The consumer's injuries were proximately caused by normal use of the product
2. The manufacturer, supplier, or retailer owed a duty of care to the consumer
3. That duty of care was breached
4. The consumer suffered damages.

If all four elements can be proven, a consumer could recover damages for injuries caused by the product.

A negligence case may require knowledge of the unsafe nature of the product by the manufacturer, supplier, or retailer as a necessary element. Sometimes proving such knowledge can be difficult. Consequently, another theory of recovery, known as strict liability, has developed.

Strict Liability

The strict liability theory of recovery for injury makes it easier for consumers to recover for injuries suffered. Under strict liability, the seller must engage in the selling of the product and the defect in the product that caused the injury must be shown to be unreasonably dangerous. Further, no privity of contract is required. The guide for strict liability cases has been *Restatement (Second) of Torts* § 402(A), which states:

(1) One who sells any product in a defective condition unreasonably dangerous to the user or customer or to his property is subject to liability for physical harm thereby caused to the ultimate user or consumer, or to his property if:
   (a) the seller is engaged in the business of selling such a product, and
   (b) it is expected to and does reach the user or consumer without substantial change in the condition in which it is sold.
(2) The rule stated in Subsection (1) applies although
   (a) the seller has exercised all possible care in the preparation and sale of his product, and
   (b) the user or consumer has not bought the product from or entered into any contractual relation with the seller.

Many states have adopted 402A in either their case law or by statute.

Strict liability in tort law has given consumers the means to recover for unsafe products. In fact, recovery under tort theories, rather than contract theories, may be less restrictive for the consumer. Normally, no notice to the seller is required when an injury or defect occurs. Further, contractual disclaimers and exclusions are usually ineffective because the theory of recovery is based in tort law, not contract law.

Parties sustaining injuries due to a defective product usually sue on both tort theories, thus maximizing the legal options available. *Toney v. Kawasaki Heavy Industries, Ltd.*, 763 F. Supp. 1356 (S.D. Miss. 1991) provides some insight into tort law when negligence and strict liability issues are raised in product liability cases.

TONEY v. KAWASAKI HEAVY INDUSTRIES, LTD.

United States District Court, S.D. Mississippi
May 15, 1991

On August 16, 1985, Plaintiff purchased a used Kawasaki KZ 750 motorcycle from Henry Banks. That motorcycle was designed and manufactured by Defendant Kawasaki Heavy Industries, Ltd. ("KHI"), a Japanese corporation. On August 17, 1985, one day after purchasing the motorcycle, Plaintiff was operating the motorcycle on an open highway when he was struck from the side by a truck. Plaintiff suffered severe injuries in the collision which later necessitated the amputation of his left leg.

In order to recover on a theory of strict liability under Mississippi law, it must be established that: (1) the defendant placed a product on the market that was in a defective condition and unreasonably dangerous for its intended use; (2) the plaintiff was using the product in a manner that was reasonably foreseeable; and (3) the defective condition was the proximate cause of the injury to the plaintiff.

The existence of a product defect must be established before recovery may be had in strict liability. In determining whether a product is defective so as to be considered unreasonably dangerous, Mississippi applies the consumer expectation test. In order to recover in strict liability where the consumer expectation test is applied, plaintiff must establish that the product at issue was "dangerous to an extent beyond that which would be contemplated by the ordinary consumer who purchases it, with the ordinary knowledge common to the community as to its characteristics."

Numerous cases construing Mississippi law and its adoption of the consumer expectation test have concluded that, where the danger associated with an alleged defect in the design of a product was open and obvious, a claim in strict liability cannot be maintained. Thus, a "manufacturer is under no duty to warn or adopt alternate designs when the danger associated with the use of the product is open and obvious to the user."

Applying the consumer expectation test to the facts of the instant case, the Court concludes that the dangers associated with motorcycles which are not equipped with leg guards or other leg protection features are so open and obvious that, as a matter of law, Plaintiff's strict liabilty claim is precluded. The Court finds that, under the objective standard of the consumer expectation test, the risks associated with the operation of the motorcycle at issue here would be patently obvious to any ordinary consumer.

In addition to strict liability claims, Plaintiff also asserts that Defendants are liable for breach of warranties regarding the condition and safety of the motorcycle. In order to recover under a theory of breach of warranty, plaintiff must prove, among other elements, that the goods were unfit for their normal use at the time of sale and that plaintiff incurred injuries that were proximately caused by the defective nature of the goods. Just as in strict liability cases, a manufacturer cannot be held liable under breach of warranty for defects that create an open and obvious hazard.

[A] general warranty does not extend to open and visible defects in the quality or condition of goods sold, although they are inconsistent with the warranty. As has been stated, an express warranty does not survive acceptance with knowledge of the defects. It has been stated that neither a general nor an implied warranty covers external and visible defects which are plain and obvious to the purchaser upon mere inspection with the eye.

In the instant action, Plaintiff has predicated his breach of warranty claims upon the alleged defects relating to the lack of leg protection features. Because this Court has found that the lack of leg protection features created an open and obvious danger, a breach of warranty action cannot be maintained on these grounds as a matter of law.

13.12 PRACTICAL APPLICATION

Throughout this chapter, there are examples of provisions to assist in drafting tasks. Remember that all states have adopted U.C.C. Article 2 (Sales) in some form. As a result, you can often locate applicable sales and warranty provisions in state statutes. Many states provide forms which guide the attorney or paralegal who is searching for appropriate language. Consequently, consult state statutes as well as formbooks when presented with a drafting task. Figure 13-12 shows two contacts that address the warranty, title, and risk-of-loss issues.

Contract for Manufacture and Sale of Machinery

This Agreement of Sale made this 10th day of September, 1995, between Misti Rainey, Seller, of 1234 Beach Drive, West Palm Beach, Florida, and Karen Simpson, Buyer, of 5678 Ocean Drive, West Palm Beach, Florida.

1. Subject Matter of Contract. Subject to the terms and conditions hereof, Seller agrees to manufacture and sell to Buyer the following described machinery: [specify machinery and set forth specifications, such as "specifications attached" or "Seller's standard specifications are set forth in its catalog of certain date"], hereafter called "Machinery."

2. Payment. Buyer agrees to pay therefor as follows: One-fourth down within five days after execution of contract; one-half within ten days after Seller notifies Buyer of opportunity to inspect and Seller's intent to make delivery at expiration of ten days from notice; one-fourth upon delivery, installation, and readiness for commercial operations upon Buyer's designated premises. If Seller should regard its prospect of receiving the last payment as insecure, it may demand payment prior to delivery.

3. Delivery Schedule. Seller shall commence to manufacture within two weeks following receipt of Buyer's initial deposit. Subject to the provisions of paragraph 5, Seller will complete such manufacturing and make the Machinery available for inspection at Seller's plant not later than September 31, 1995. In the event that Buyer's inspection discloses defects or need for adjustments, Seller shall have a reasonable time to correct such defects and make such adjustments as are necessary. Buyer shall thereafter have an opportunity to make a final shipment inspection. Seller shall within five days of inspection cause the Machinery to be appropriately packaged and shipped to the designation specified by Buyer. Seller shall pay all expenses of packaging and preparations for shipment and Buyer shall pay all costs of shipment, including insurance on both Seller's and Buyer's respective interests therein.

4. Installation. Within ten business days after receipt of notice of arrival at Buyer's destination, Seller shall cause such machinery to be assembled and installed at Buyer's plant. Seller will furnish one master mechanic for such purpose and pay his wages, and Buyer shall pay all other costs of assembly and installation, including the master mechanic's reasonable travel to and living expenses while at Buyer's plant, and the cost of any other laborers or workers needed by the master mechanic for assistance in such assembly and installation.

FIGURE 13-12 Sample sales contracts

5. Excuse for Nonperformance. Seller's obligations hereunder are accepted subject to strikes, labor troubles (including strikes or labor troubles affecting any suppliers of Seller), floods, fires, accidents, delays, shortage of cars, contingencies of transportation, and other causes of like or different character beyond the control of Seller. Impossibility of performance by reason of any legislative, executive, or judicial act of any governmental authority shall excuse performance or delay in performance of this agreement.

6. Warranties and Limitations Thereof. Seller warrants that the machinery shall be delivered free of the rightful claim of any third person by way of patent infringement, and if Buyer receives notice of any claim of such infringement, it shall, within ten days, notify Seller of such claim. If Buyer fails to forward such notice to Seller, it shall be deemed to have released Seller from this warranty as to such claim.

There are NO WARRANTIES OF MERCHANTABILITY and NO WARRANTIES WHICH EXTEND BEYOND THE DESCRIPTION ON THE FACE HEREOF.

Seller further agrees that it will replace without charge any part which proves defective in material or workmanship within the first 2,000 hours of operation or a period of one year from date of delivery to Buyer, whichever shall occur first.

7. Entire Contract. The parties agree that this constitutes the entire agreement and there are no further items or provisions, oral or otherwise. Buyer agrees that it has not relied upon any representations of Seller as to prospective performance of the Machinery, but has relied upon its own inspection and investigation of the subject matter.

8. Inspection of Machinery by Seller. Buyer agrees to permit Seller, its agents or employees, or any independent experts or their agents or employees to inspect such Machinery and observe its performance at reasonable times and after reasonable notice. Buyer further agrees to permit Seller, its agents or employees, and its independent manufacturer's agents to show such machines while in operation to persons who are prospective purchasers of comparable machinery and notwithstanding that such prospective purchasers are competitors or potential competitors of Buyer.

In Witness Whereof, Seller and Buyer have signed their names and caused their corporate seals to be affixed as of the day, month, and year aforesaid.

Misti Rainey

By:_____

President of D&D Corporation

Attest:

_____

Corporate Seal

Karen Simpson

By:_____

President of H&B Corporation

Attest:

_____

Corporate Seal

General Form of Contract to Sell in Future

This Contract made this 27th day of September, 1995, between Misti Rainey, Seller, of 1234 Beach Drive, West Palm Beach, Florida, and Karen Simpson, Buyer, of 5678 Ocean Drive, West Palm Beach, Florida.

WITNESSETH

1. Description of Goods. Seller agrees to sell and Buyer agrees to buy on the 10th day of October, 1995, the following described goods: [specifically describe goods]. Until such date, the goods shall remain the property of Seller and Seller shall be free to make normal use of such goods in and about the operation of its business.

2. Delivery. Seller shall deliver the said goods to Buyer at 5678 Ocean Drive, West Palm Beach, Florida, on or before the 10th day of October, 1995.

FIGURE 13-12 *(Continued)*

3. Price. Buyer shall pay to Seller on day of delivery the sum of Twenty-Eight Thousand Dollars ($28,000.00), with appropriate adjustments, if any, under paragraph 4 hereof.

4. Condition of Goods; Risk of Loss. Buyer has inspected such goods and agrees to purchase such goods AS IS, including normal wear and tear to date of delivery. Except as expressly set forth herein, there are NO WARRANTIES OF MERCHANTABILITY OR OF FITNESS OR OTHERWISE. Seller does warrant that on date of delivery, the goods will be in equally good condition as of the date of this Contract, excepting only normal wear and tear occurring after such date. Until delivery, all risk of loss shall be on Seller. In the event of damage, destruction, or deterioration to or of such goods (other than normal wear and tear), there shall be an appropriate adjustment in the purchase price to reflect any diminution in value as a result thereof.

FIGURE 13-12 *(Continued)*

SUMMARY

13.1   Determining ownership to goods is important. Title is equivalent to legal ownership. Risk of loss, often associated with title, refers to the assumption of financial responsibility when goods are damaged, lost, or destroyed.

13.2–
13.4   In a shipment contract, title and risk of loss pass when the goods are placed on a carrier. In a destination contract, title and risk of loss do not pass until the buyer receives the goods at the agreed destination. When delivery is not required, title and risk of loss pass when the contract is made. In addition, if a buyer rejects goods, title may revest in the seller.

13.5   Void title is not a valid title. If persons with a void title attempt to transfer title, they transfer only a void title. Voidable title is different. If a person who has voidable title transfers title to a good faith purchaser, the transferred title is valid.

13.6   An insurable interest is the value placed on the property by the insured. Depending on the circumstances, a seller usually retains an insurable interest up to the point when title passes, and the buyer has an insurable interest when the goods are identified.

13.7   Warranties can be either express or implied. An express warranty may be oral or written. An express warranty can be created (1) by a statement of fact or promise to the buyer, (2) through description of the goods, or (3) through a sample or model.

Implied warranties are imposed by law. They are implicit in the bargain. The implied warranties are the warranty of title, warranty against infringement, warranty of merchantability, and warranty of fitness for a particular purpose.

13.8   The Magnuson-Moss Act establishes general warranty protection for consumers. The Act establishes two types of warranties: full and limited. A full warranty must comply with certain statutory requirements, whereas a limited warranty is created by exclusion.

13.9 Sellers may exclude warranties. To be effective, the exclusion should be in writing, mention merchantability, and be conspicuous.

13.10 Persons need not be in privity with the seller to be included under warranty provisions.

13.11 The Code provides statutory remedies when a warranty has been breached. However, contract law is not the only avenue a consumer has for recovery. A consumer may also sue in tort law under theories of negligence and strict liability.

QUESTIONS

1. Define the concepts of title and risk of loss.
2. When do title and risk of loss pass in a shipment contract? In a destination contract?
3. Under what circumstances will title revest in the seller?
4. Distinguish between void and voidable title and give one example of each.
5. When does risk of loss pass when a good is insured? What special problems are presented when the buyer revokes an acceptance?
6. What is an express warranty and under what circumstances is it created?
7. Identify the four types of implied warranties.
8. Distinguish between a full warranty and a limited warranty.
9. How can warranties be properly excluded under the law?
10. What remedies are available when warranties have been breached?

EXERCISES

1. Review some warranties given for products you have bought. Using the Code, determine if the warranties comply with the requirements set forth in the U.C.C.
2. Using the examples in this chapter, draft an enforceable warranty clause that excludes the warranty of merchantability and is sold without guaranteeing title.
3. Ms. Charlene Thomas has purchased a car from ABC Motors. She drives it home and for a week the car is fine. After one week, the engine goes dead and the radiator begins to leak. The contract she signed excludes the warranty of fitness for a particular purpose. Prepare a notice letter setting forth the reasons why the exclusion is ineffective and demanding the return of the car and all monies tendered to the car dealer.

CHAPTER 14
Seller and Buyer Remedies

OUTLINE

"Mr. Hobbs, your supplying a bottle of aspirin will not be considered a remedy for nonperformance."

14.1   OVERVIEW OF THE AVAILABLE REMEDIES

When one of the parties to a commercial sales contract fails to perform, certain remedies are available to the injured party under Part 7 of the Uniform Commercial Code. The two sections in U.C.C. concerning available remedies are § 2-703 for the seller and § 2-711 for the buyer. These sections should be interpreted in conjunction with other provisions in the Code, but each is a good starting point for determining the available remedies.

Because different remedies are available when a seller has been injured than when a buyer has been injured, one of the first questions to be addressed is who is seeking the remedy. The next question is whether the injury occurred prior to acceptance or after acceptance of the goods.

14.2   REMEDIES AVAILABLE TO SELLER

The general remedies available to a seller are set out in § 2-703 of the U.C.C., which states:

> Where the buyer wrongfully rejects or revokes acceptance of goods or fails to make a payment due on or before delivery or repudiates with respect to a part or a whole, then with respect to any goods directly affected and, if the breach is of the whole contract, then also with respect to the whole undelivered balance, the aggrieved seller may
>
> (a)   withhold delivery of such goods;
> (b)   stop delivery by any bailee as hereinafter provided [§ 2-705];
> (c)   proceed under the next section respecting goods still unidentified to the contract;
> (d)   resale and recover damages as herein provided (2-706);
> (e)   recover damages for nonacceptance or in a proper case the price (2-709);
> (f)   cancel.

Understanding which remedy may be appropriate is important. Often a variety of remedies will be available to the seller upon a breach, and the appropriate remedy is a matter of choice for the injured party.

Withhold Delivery of Goods

When a buyer breaches a sales contract, the seller has the right to withhold delivery of the goods under § 2-703 of the Code. When the seller learns in advance of the buyer's intention to breach, the seller is not under an obligation to perform under the contract.

Furthermore, § 2-702(1) addresses a common problem—that of the insolvent buyer. Section 2-702(1) states:

> (1) Where the seller discovers the buyer to be insolvent he may refuse delivery except for cash including payment for all goods theretofore

delivered under the contract, and stop delivery under this Article (Section 2-705).

This provision allows the seller to refuse delivery to the buyer unless paid in cash at the time of delivery. Some provisions to include in a contract when insolvency is an issue are illustrated in Figure 14-1. In addition, the paralegal may be asked to draft a notice letter (see Figure 14-2) to the buyer when an insolvency is discovered.

---

(1) "Insolvent" for the purpose of this agreement means being unable to pay one's debts in the ordinary course of business.

(2) In the event of bankruptcy or insolvency of buyer, or in the event any proceeding is brought by or against buyer under the bankruptcy or insolvency laws, seller shall be entitled to cancel any order then outstanding and shall receive reimbursement for the reasonable and proper cancellation charges accrued by seller.

(3) In the event of insolvency as defined by the Uniform Commercial Code in effect in [state], any act of bankruptcy, whether voluntary or involuntary, or any insolvency proceeding instituted by or against buyer, seller may refuse delivery of the goods covered by this sales agreement except for cash, including payment for all goods theretofore delivered under the agreement, and seller may stop delivery of goods in transit.

FIGURE 14-1 Sample clauses treating insolvency

Lamps Unlimited
7321 Grove Street
Sonoma, California 12345

Dear Walter:

I have learned from reliable sources that you are now insolvent within the meaning of U.C.C. Section 2-702. I accordingly suspend the credit term under our agreement dated January 4, 1993, for the sale of lampshades and will not make deliveries to you except on payment by cash or cashier's check received by me in advance of shipment to you of any goods.

I hope that your difficulties are only temporary, and I will be pleased to return to a credit basis as soon as your solvency is restored.

Very truly yours,
Arthur Howell

[OR]

Lamps Unlimited
7321 Grove Street
Sonoma, California 12345

Dear Walter:

I have learned from reliable sources that you are now insolvent within the meaning of U.C.C. Section 2-702. For this reason, I must notify you that I shall refuse to deliver the goods pursuant to our sales agreement dated January 4, 1993, except for cash or cashier's check, including payment for all goods previously delivered to you.

FIGURE 14-2 Sample notice letters to insolvent buyer

To date you owe me the amount of Two Thousand Three Hundred Twenty One Dollars and Eighty Six Cents ($2,321.86) for deliveries already made. The balance of the purchase price is due on delivery.

I therefore ask you to pay for the goods on September 3, 1994, the date of delivery, in cash or cashier's check made payable to Arthur Howell, Inc. in the amount of Two Thousand One Hundred Dollars and No Cents ($2,100.00).

I hope that your difficulties are only temporary, and I will be pleased to return to a credit basis as soon as your solvency is restored.

Very truly yours,
Arthur Howell

[OR]

Lamps Unlimited
7321 Grove Street
Sonoma, California 12345

Dear Walter:

Pursuant to U.C.C. Section 2-702, I revoke the credit term of our agreement dated January 4, 1993, with respect to the goods delivered to you on September 3, 1994, consisting of lampshades, and demand immediate return of the goods to me because of your insolvency.

I also call to your attention the financial statement you furnished to me on August 11, 1994, which misrepresents that you are solvent when in fact you are not.

Very truly yours,
Arthur Howell

FIGURE 14-2 *(Continued)*

Stoppage of Delivery in Transit

Section 2-705 of the Code also provides another method of withholding delivery, known as **stoppage in transit**. Under this method, the seller may stop delivery of the goods when the buyer is insolvent or repudiates the contract. Section 2-705(1) provides:

(1) The seller may stop delivery of goods in the possession of a carrier or another bailee when he discovers the buyer to be insolvent (Section 2-702) and may stop delivery of carload, truckload, planeload or larger shipments of express or freight when the buyer repudiates or fails to make a payment due before delivery or if for any other reason the seller has a right to withhold or reclaim the goods.

There is a caveat about using this remedy. The goods must be in the possession of a third party, such as a common carrier, and must not have reached the final destination.

When communicating to the common carrier that the buyer is insolvent, the seller can instruct the carrier not to continue delivery. Unfortunately, this may put a burden on the seller, as the responsibility for any costs incurred by the carrier for not completing the contract, or any damages suffered in the

TERMS

stoppage in transit
A right that a seller of goods on credit has to retake them while they are in the possession of a carrier or other intermediary, upon discovering that the buyer is insolvent.

event that the stoppage was improper, must be borne by the seller. Use care when choosing this remedy! If the seller elects stoppage in transit, Figure 14-3 provides a sample letter to follow.

Mr. Oscar H. White
486 Industrial Park, #301
St. Paul, Minnesota 23456

Dear Mr. White:

    Demand is hereby made pursuant to U.C.C. Section 2-705(1) that delivery of goods at present in your possession be stopped forthwith and held by you at the disposition of the undersigned seller for delivery in accordance with subsequent instructions of the undersigned.
    This STOP ORDER is made with reference to the following goods: 80 twin mattresses. The goods were consigned by B.K. Beds, Inc. of 821 Stately Drive, St. Paul, Minnesota, as consignor, to Beds Limited, of 246 Main Street, St. Paul, Minnesota, as consignee, on November 1, 1994, for which goods you issued a negotiable warehouse receipt No. 4861 dated November 1, 1994.
    The undersigned seller is in rightful possession of the above-described negotiable document of title and herewith surrenders it to assure prompt execution of this stop order and warrants that this stop order is made in accordance with Section 2-705, in that the buyer is insolvent as defined in U.C.C. Section 1-201(23).
    The undersigned agrees (1) to pay all charges for storage and shipment of the goods; (2) to reimburse you for any expenses, costs and attorney fees that may be incurred by you by reason of this stop order; and (3) to indemnify and hold you harmless against any claims or demands that may be made against you by any person in connection with the execution of this stop order.
    Dated and dispatched on:_____.

                            Very truly yours,
                            Abe Standsfield

FIGURE 14-3   Sample stoppage-in-transit letter

Note that § 2-705 also provides that a seller may stop the delivery of goods when a buyer breaches the contract prior to delivery, if the delivery is by carload, truckload, or planeload or larger shipments of express freight. This situation presents some problems if delivery has been by a document of title and the buyer has received the transfer of the document of title. At that juncture, delivery cannot be stopped and the seller will have to use an alternate method against the buyer's breach.

Resale of Goods

When goods are still in the possession of the seller and the buyer intends to breach, the seller may resell the goods to recoup as much as possible, and minimize its damages. The resale must be in good faith and done in a commercially reasonable manner. Once the resale is completed, the injured seller may sue the nonperforming party for the difference between the contract price and the resale price, adding any expenses and consequential damages that the seller incurred due to the breach.

Code § 2-706(4) specifies what type of sale is acceptable when there has been a breach by the buyer. Section 2-706 distinguishes between a public and a private sale:

> (2) Except as otherwise provided in subsection (3) or unless otherwise agreed resale may be at public or private sale including sale by way of one or more contracts to sell or of identification to an existing contract of the seller. Sale may be as a unit or in parcels and at any time and place and on any terms but every aspect of the sale, including the method, manner, time, place and terms must be commercially reasonable. The resale must be reasonably identified as referring to the broken contract, but it is not necessary that the goods be in existence or that any or all of them have been identified to the contract before the breach.
>
> (3) Where the resale is at private sale the seller must give the buyer reasonable notification of his intention to resell.
>
> (4) Where the resale is at public sale
>
>   (a) only identified goods can be sold except where there is a recognized market for a public sale of futures in goods of the kind; and
>
>   (b) it must be made at a usual place or market for public sale if one is reasonably available and except in the case of goods which are perishable or threaten to decline in value speedily, the seller must give the buyer reasonable notice of the time and place of the resale; and
>
>   (c) if the goods are not to be within the view of those attending the sale, the notification of sale must state the place where the goods are located and provide for their reasonable inspection by prospective bidders; and
>
>   (d) the seller may buy.

If the sale is a private one, the seller must comply with certain restrictions to meet its obligations under the Code. The seller must give the buyer reasonable notice of the sale, to give the buyer an opportunity to cure the breach. However, in a public sale, not only must notice be given to the buyer, but the sale must also occur in what is considered the normal, customary procedure for those types of public sales. The method, time, place, and any other conditions must be commercially reasonable. If these conditions are not met, the buyer may question the validity of the sale, and may have rights to invalidate it. Figure 14-4 shows sample notice letters for a private and a public sale.

Persons who buy at such a sale are considered purchasers in good faith. As a result, they take the goods free from any claims of the previous buyer; the previous buyer cannot come back to the good faith purchaser and reclaim the goods. If the seller profits from the public or private sale of the goods (which is unusual), the seller may retain the profit without any benefits to the breaching buyer. If the goods are not identified, § 2-704 governs.

Mr. Ben Harley
Beds Unlimited
989 Bed Parkway
Detroit, Michigan 01234

Dear Mr. Harley:

    I hereby declare that you are in default under our agreement dated August 15, 1994, for the sale to you of 80 twin mattresses, due to your breach of the agreement on November 1, 1994, by failing to make payment on the goods purchased.

    In exercise of my authority under U.C.C. Section 2-706, I shall make a private sale of the goods, which have been identified to our agreement, to James Woods Bedding, 2223 18th Street, Detroit, Michigan, for a purchase price of Ten Thousand Four Hundred Fifty Dollars and No Cents ($10,450.00). I shall hold you liable for the loss sustained by me on the resale to the extent authorized by the Uniform Commercial Code.

    Dated December 20, 1994.

Very truly yours,
Abe Stansfield

[OR]

Mr. Ben Harely
Beds Unlimited
989 Bed Parkway
Detroit, Michigan 01234

Dear Mr. Harley:

    I hereby notify you that I will hold a public auction sale without reservation at 10:00 o'clock a.m. on November 15, 1994, at my place of business, of those goods identified to our agreement dated August 15, 1994. The goods consist of 80 twin mattresses and may be examined at the location on any weekday between 9:00 o'clock a.m. and 5:00 o'clock p.m.

    I shall hold you liable for any loss sustained by me on the public resale to the extent authorized by the Uniform Commercial Code.

    Dated November 1, 1994.

Very truly yours,
Abe Standsfield

FIGURE 14-4   Sample notice-of-sale letters

Consequently, if the seller identifies the goods after a breach, the seller can proceed under § 2-706 and resell the goods. *Apex Oil Co. v. Belcher Co.*, 855 F.2d 997 (2d Cir. 1988) illustrates the remedy of resale when a buyer has breached.

APEX OIL COMPANY v. BELCHER COMPANY OF NEW YORK, INC.

United States Court of Appeals, Second Circuit
Aug. 30, 1988

Apex buys, sells, refines and transports petroleum products of various sorts, including No. 2 heating oil, commonly known as home heating oil. Belcher also buys and sells petroleum products, including No. 2 heating oil. In February 1982, both firms were trading futures contracts for No. 2 heating oil on the New York Mercantile Exchange ("Merc"). In particular, both were trading Merc contracts for February 1982 No. 2 heating oil—i.e., contracts for the delivery of that commodity in New York Harbor during that delivery month in accordance with Merc's rules. As a result of that trading, Apex was short 315 contracts, and Belcher was long by the same amount. Being "short" one contract for oil means that the trader has contracted to deliver one thousand barrels at some point in the future, and being "long" means just the opposite—that the trader has contracted to purchase that amount of oil.

Apex was matched with Belcher by the Merc, and thus became bound to produce 315,000 barrels of No. 2 heating oil meeting Merc specifications in New York Harbor. Those specifications required that oil delivered in New York Harbor have a sulfur content no higher than 0.20%. Apex asked Belcher whether Belcher would take delivery of 190,000 barrels of oil in Boston Harbor in satisfaction of 190 contracts, and Belcher agreed. At trial, the parties did not dispute that, under this [exchange for physicals (EFP)], Apex promised it would deliver the No. 2 heating oil for the same price as that in the original contract—89.70 cents per gallon—and that the oil would be lifted from the vessel *Bordeaux*. The parties did dispute, and vigorously so, the requisite maximum sulfur content. At trial, Belcher sought to prove that the oil had to meet the New York standard of 0.20%, while Apex asserted tht the oil had to meet only the specifications for Boston Harbor of not more than 0.30% sulfur.

Later in the evening of February 10, after fifty or sixty thousand barrels had been offloaded, an independent petroleum inspector told Belcher that tests showed the oil on board the *Bordeaux* contained 0.28% sulfur, in excess of the New York Harbor specification. Belcher nevertheless continued to lift oil from the ship until eleven o'clock the next morning, February 11, when 141,535 barrels

had been pumped into Belcher's terminal. After pumping had stopped, a second test indicated that the oil contained 0.22% sulfur—a figure within the accepted range of tolerance for oil containing 0.20% sulfur. (Apex did not learn of the second test until shortly before trial.) Nevertheless, Belcher refused to resume pumping, claiming that the oil did not conform to specifications.

After Belcher ordered the *Bordeaux* to leave its terminal, Apex immediately contacted Cities Service. Apex was scheduled to deliver heating oil to Cities Service later in the month and accordingly asked if it could satisfy that obligation by immediately delivering the oil on the *Bordeaux*. Cities Service agreed, and that oil was delivered to Cities Service in Boston Harbor on February 12, one day after the oil had been rejected by Belcher. Apex did not give notice to Belcher that the oil had been delivered to Cities Service.

Belcher refused to pay Apex the contract price of $5,322,200.27 for the oil it had accepted, and it demanded that Apex produce the remaining 48,000 barrels of oil owing under the contract. On February 17, Apex agreed to tender the 48,000 barrels if Belcher would both make partial payment for the oil actually accepted and agree to negotiate as to the price ultimately to be paid for that oil. Belcher agreed and sent Apex a check for $5,034,997.12, a sum reflecting a discount of five cents per gallon from the contract price.

Belcher had sold the 142,000 barrels and did not have an equivalent amount of No. 2 oil in its entire Boston terminal. Instead of admitting that it did not have the oil, Belcher told Apex that a dock for the *Mersault* was unavailable. Belcher also demanded that Apex either remove the oil *and* pay terminalling and storage fees, or accept payment for the oil at a discount of five cents per gallon. Apex refused to do either. On the next day, Belcher and Apex finally reached a settlement under which Belcher agreed to pay for the oil discharged from the *Bordeaux* at a discount of 2.5 cents per gallon. The settlement agreement also resolved an unrelated dispute between an Apex subsidiary and a subsidiary or Belcher's parent firm, The Coastal Corporation. It is this agreement that Apex now claims was procured by fraud.

The Uniform Commercial Code, adopted by New York in 1964, provides various remedies to sellers for default by buyers. An aggrieved seller may, for example, withhold delivery of goods, cancel the contract, recover the unpaid price of accepted goods, or recover damages for nonaccepted or repudiated goods based on their market price. In addition, a seller may, as Apex seeks to do, fix its damages by reselling the goods and recovering from the buyer the difference between the resale price and the contract price.

Resolving the instant dispute requires us to survey various provisions of the Uniform Commercial Code. The first such provision is section 2-501, which defines "identification" and states in pertinent part:

(1) The buyer obtains a special property and an insurable interest in goods by identification of existing goods as goods to which the contract refers even though the goods so identified are non-conforming and he has an option to return or reject them. Such identification can be made at any time and in any manner explicitly agreed to by the parties. *In the absence of explicit agreement identification occurs*

(a) when the contract is made if it is for the sale of goods already existing and identified;

(b) if the contract is for the sale of future goods other than those described in paragraph (c) [crops and livestock], *when goods are shipped, marked or otherwise designated by the seller as goods to which the contract refers.*

Finding no clear guidance in the language of the Code, we turn to the only decision concerning the identification of fungible goods under Section 2-706. We agree that fungible goods resold pursuant to Section 2-706 must be goods identified to the contract, but need not always be those *originally* identified to the contract. In other words, at least where fungible goods are concerned, identification is not always an irrevocable act and does not foreclose the possibility of substitution.

Here it would make no sense to hold that such replacement (that is, reidentification) can never occur after breach. For example, it serves no purpose of the Code to force an aggrieved seller to segregate goods originally identified to the contract when doing so is more costly than mixing them with other identical goods. To give a concrete example, suppose that Apex had been unable to find someone to take the *Bordeaux* oil immediately after the oil was rejected by Belcher and that the only storage tank available to Apex in Boston was already half-full of No. 2 heating oil. To mix the *Bordeaux* oil with the oil in the only available tank and to identify the first 48,000 gallons sold to the contract is the only sensible thing to do. Doing so, of course, bases the damage award on resales of different oil from that previously identified to the contract. Under a rule that prevents any reidentification of goods to a contract, Apex would be forced in the hypothetical to choose between its resale remedy and a costly diversion of the *Bordeaux*. Yet for the purpose of the resale remedy—which is simply to fix the price of 48,000 barrels of fungible No. 2 oil—resale of any such quantity of conforming oil would do.

Thus Section 2-706 should not be construed as always proscribing the resale of goods other than those originally identified to the broken contract. Nevertheless, as that section expressly states, "[t]he resale must be *reasonably* identified as referring to the broken contract," and "every aspect of the sale including the method, manner, time, place and terms must be commercially reasonable." Moreover, because the purpose of remedies under the Code is to put "the aggrieved party . . . in as good a position as if the other party had fully performed," the reasonableness of the identification and of the resale must be determined by examining whether the market value of, and the price received for, the resold goods "accurately reflects the market value of the goods which are the subject of the contract."

The most pertinent aspect of reasonableness with regard to identification and resale involves timing.

[T]he object of the resale is simply to determine exactly the seller's damages. These damages are the difference between the contract price and the market price at the time and place when performance should have been made by the buyer. The object of the resale . . . is to determine what the market price in fact was. *Unless the resale is made at about the time when performance was due it will be of slight probative value, especially if the goods are of a kind which fluctuate rapidly in value.* If no reasonable market existed at this time, no doubt a delay may be proper and a subsequent sale may furnish the best test, though confessedly not a perfectly exact one, of the seller's damage. The issue of delay between breach and resale has previously been addressed only in the context of determining commercial reasonableness where the goods resold are the goods originally identified to the broken contract. However, the principles announced in that context apply here as well:

What is . . . a reasonable time [for resale] depends upon the nature of the goods, the condition of the market and other circumstances

of the case; its length cannot be measured by any legal yardstick or divided into degrees. Where a seller contemplating resale receives a demand from the buyer for inspection under the section of [sic] preserving evidence of goods in dispute, the time for resale may be appropriately lengthened.

Here, Apex's delay of nearly six weeks between the breach on February 11, 1982 and the purported resale on March 23 was clearly unreasonable, even if the transfer to Cities Service had not occurred.

The rule that a "resale should be made as soon as practicable after . . . breach," should be stringently applied where, as here, the resold goods are not those originally identified to the contract. Because the sale of the oil identified to the contract to Cities Service on the next day fixed the value of the goods refused as a matter of law, the judgment on the breach-of-contract claim must be reversed.

QUESTIONS FOR ANALYSIS

What are the facts of *Apex Oil?* What factors did the court identify to determine the reasonableness of the resale of goods? How did the court hold? Why?

In addition, the following provisions may be useful when resale is elected:

No resale of goods may be made by seller in the event of breach of this agreement by buyer unless seller shall have given buyer not less than ten (10) days' written notice of seller's intention to effect a resale.

In the event of breach of the agreement by buyer, no private sale may be made of any goods intended for or identified to this agreement. Any resale must be made at a public sale.

Lawsuit for Damages

When a buyer has breached a sales contract, the seller always has the option to sue the buyer for damages. In this type of lawsuit, the damages will include not only the actual damages, but also any consequential damages, lost profits, expenses, or any other damages which are a direct result of the buyer's breach. The formula used to determine the amount of damages to which a seller is entitled is the difference between the actual contract price and the market price at the time the buyer breached the contract, plus any incidental damages that are a direct or indirect result of the buyer's breach. Review *National Controls Corp. v. National Semiconductor Corp.*, 833 F.2d 491 (3d Cir. 1987), in which the cause of the damages was at issue.

NATIONAL CONTROLS CORPORATION
v. NATIONAL SEMICONDUCTOR CORPORATION

United States Court of Appeals, Third Circuit
November 23, 1987

NCC is a small Pennsylvania company involved in the design and production of control systems and electrical devices for its various customers. It also was participating in the development of a new or "SNAP" type of telephone for MCI, a national telephone company exclusively engaged in providing long distance service. This "SNAP" telephone would allow consumers direct access to MCI's long distance telephone services by automatically dialing the MCI code numbers and would also reach the rotary market.

NCC also participated in the pretest phase of the project. MCI ordered 200 test telephones from NCC in December of 1982 for a total price of $27,400. Purchase orders for additional quantities were to be authorized "only after the 200 sets are tested, approved and accepted." Dissatisfied with the small quantity of telephones ordered, NCC sought to gain MCI's commitment to an order for 60,000 telephone units. MCI was unwilling to place such a large order and, after further negotiations, MCI issued a final purchase order on February 7, 1983, for an aggregate of 450 test telephone units at a total price of $55,400. MCI's purchase order specifically limited its purchase commitment to the 450 telephones.

NCC planned to use NSC's chips to produce the phones. Late in 1982, NCC entered into a contract with NSC, through NSC's agent CAM/RPC, in which it ordered a total of 1,200 microprocessor units from NSC. NSC breached its contract and its warranties of merchantability and fitness for a particular purpose with respect to this order by

delivering only a small number of defective microcontroller units. As a consequence, NCC supplied only 126 of the first 200 test telephone sets, and some of those failed because of the poor quality of the microprocessors supplied by NSC.

Notwithstanding the failure to make the required delivery for the 450 test telephones, MCI ordered 6,000 units from NCC in May of 1983 in anticipation of the third, or pilot test, phase of the SNAP phone project. The total purchase price of the order was $38,580. NCC in turn ordered 6,100 microcontroller units from the defendant for a purchase price of $35,014. In addition, NCC sent MCI a price quotation for 5,000 telephones for this pilot test phase of the project, but MCI never issued a purchase order accepting that quotation.

NSC failed to deliver any of the 6,100 chips ordered by NCC and MCI eventually cancelled the purchase order it had placed with NCC. Some five months later, MCI terminated the SNAP phone project in its entirety.

It is undisputed that Pennsylvania law governs the jury's consideration of damages in this action. Pennsylvania has adopted the Uniform Commercial Code (UCC) and permits recovery of consequential damages resulting from breach of warranty or contract by a seller. Such consequential damages may include "any loss resulting from general or particular requirements and needs of which the seller at the time of contracting had reason to know and which could not reasonably be prevented by cover or otherwise." Lost profits are recoverable as consequential damages in a proper case, such as where a seller knows or has reason to know that a buyer is purchasing a good for resale. The award of such damages, however, pits the plaintiff's right to the bargain of his contract against the need to prevent jury verdicts based on speculation rather than proper proof.

Under Pennsylvania law, lost profits are recoverable when they are "lost on a particular sale or contract for the performance of which the goods in question were purchased." In contrast, a breach of contract or warranty may lead to non-recoverable loss of good will where the defendant's breach causes customer dissatisfaction with the plaintiff which is then translated into a loss of expected profits. The bar to recovery of damages for loss of good will, including proof of such damages, is a matter of law in Pennsylvania, thus precluding the plaintiff from attempting to show that in his case the damages would not be speculative.

Even where the plaintiff's claim truly represents a claim for lost profits, rather than loss of good will, it may be rejected as speculative and unrecoverable. This is particularly true where the claim of lost profits is made in the context of a new and untried business venture. To sustain a damages award, NCC must have provided sufficient evidence from which the jury could have found that its lost profits were proximately caused by the defendant's breach. The damages sought must be a proximate consequence of the breach, not merely remote or possible.

The element of causation defines the range of socially and economically desirable recovery and requires not only "but-for" causation in fact but also that the conduct be a "substantial factor" in bringing about the harm." Where the losses cannot be allocated between those caused by the defendant's breach and those not, an entire claim may be rejected. NCC thus had to prove that any lost profits were proximately caused by NSC's breach, and not through some other cause. In essence, the proximate causation requirement demands that the plaintiff prove that the defendant's breach was a substantial factor in causing some harm. Two types of proof will thus be relevant: evidence of MCI's commitments to NCC and evidence of a causal relationship between the defendant's breaches and the alleged repudiation.

The evidence clearly showed that NCC had a purchase order for 450 telephones from MCI. Further, the evidence was sufficient to show that NSC breached its contract to produce the microchips that NCC had planned to use to build the 450 phones. As a result, only 126 phones were delivered, and some of those were defective.

The plaintiff thus presented sufficient evidence from which the jury could have readily found that NSC's breaches were the proximate cause of some damage to NCC. Unfortunately, the plaintiff does not point to any evidence, and we have not been able to find any, to show that it lost money on this order or that it was not paid by MCI for its purchase order of February 7, 1983. The claim for lost profits on this contract must therefore be rejected.

As to the alleged loss of profits for the 5,000 teleset telephones it expected to produce on the basis of the purchase order from MCI for 6,000 microcomputer chips, NCC is correct in stating that it sent MCI a price quotation for 5,000 telephones expected to be used in connection with the pilot test phase of the project. However, there is no evidence that MCI ever accepted the quotation. Therefore the claim for this item must also be rejected.

On March 28, 1983, MCI had requested that the plaintiff obtain mass production scheduling from NSC for high volume production quantities of the microprocessor, and MCI had internally projected the sale of a minimum of 800,000 telephones for the first year. NSC's microprocessor failed both merchantability standards and its use for the particular purposes, the plaintiff asserts, and NSC also breached its contract with respect to the original order. It delivered only 126 microprocessors, some of which were flawed. NCC never was able, the plaintiff argues, to deliver any portion of the balance of the 60,000 units scheduled because of defendant's repeated breaches. Thus, plaintiff contends, "The first generation teleset project was cancelled."

The problem with the plaintiff's argument, however, is that the record fails to sustain it. An award of lost profits required speculation by the jury on the likelihood that, absent NSC's breaches, MCI would have proceeded with the project and on the likelihood that MCI would have chosen NCC as a supplier of some portion of the telephones produced. The plaintiff failed to present evidence sufficient to transform the jury's speculation on these two probabilities into the reasoned assessment necessary to support a damage award.

The total of the evidence supporting any further agreement between MCI and MCC consists of inquiries by MCI regarding NCC's production capacity and the statement by MCI in a Request For Proposal (RFP) to suppliers for production of computerized single line telesets that MCI already had contracted for the production of a first generation telephone. The statements in the RFP do not contradict the written terms of MCI's purchase orders limiting its purchases to 450 telephones.

Nor do MCI's inquiries as to NCC's ability to produce large quantities of telephones indicate that NCC had been given a contract for such production. There is no evidence to show that there were any other contracts or that MCI cancelled any other commitments because of NSC's breaches. In its initial pleadings and its arguments in the district court, NCC recognized that it had no contract for the production of the thousands of telephones for which it claimed lost profits. NCC's belated argument in this court that its contract with MCI included commitments for later orders of such phones is without support in the record.

Even if such commitments were made and provide a sufficient basis upon which to award lost profits, the plaintiff still failed to show that the commitments were lost because of NSC's breaches.

In summary, the trial court should have entered judgment N.O.V. in favor of National Semiconductor Corporation because of the plaintiff's failure to prove that NSC's breaches were the proximate cause of its alleged loss of profits and because of the lack of evidence to sustain its claims for losses on existing contracts or expenses allegedly incurred in connection with potential contracts.

QUESTIONS FOR ANALYSIS

State the facts of *National Controls*. Were the lost profits recoverable? Why or why not? What was the court's reasoning for its decision?

Another type of damage suit that a seller can institute against the buyer is a suit for the contract price. A lawsuit on the price occurs when the seller is unable to resell the goods that have been identified to the contract. This is not the best possible route for an injured seller, because there are heavy responsibilities on the seller in this type of action. Section 2-709 suggests:

(1) When the buyer fails to pay the price as it becomes due the seller may recover, together with any incidental damages under the next section, the price
   (a) of goods accepted or of conforming goods lost or damaged within a commercially reasonable time after risk of their loss has passed to the buyer; and
   (b) of goods identified to the contract if the seller is unable after reasonable effort to resell them at a reasonable price or the circumstances reasonably indicate that such effort will be unavailing.
(2) Where the seller sues for the price he must hold for the buyer any goods which have been identified to the contract and are still in

his control except that if resale becomes possible he may resell them at any time prior to the collection of the judgment. The net proceeds of any such resale must be credited to the buyer and payment of the judgment entitles him to any goods not resold.

(3) After the buyer has wrongfully rejected or revoked acceptance of the goods or has failed to make a payment due or has repudiated (Section 2-610), a seller who is held not entitled to the price under this section shall nevertheless be awarded damages for nonacceptance under the preceding section.

In an action for the price, the seller must hold for the buyer any goods that are under the seller's control. However, if there is any future sale, any proceeds from such a sale must be credited to the buyer, and any goods not sold can be retained by the buyer if a judgment is paid off. The burdens shouldered by the seller that uses this remedy are enormous. Some general provisions to consider including in a sales contract are presented in Figure 14-5.

If buyer refuses to accept or repudiates delivery of the goods sold to buyer under this agreement, seller shall be entitled to damages based on the difference between the market price for the goods at the time and place tender of the goods is made under this agreement, and the unpaid sales price, together with any incidental damages authorized by U.C.C. Section 2-710, if applicable, but less expenses saved due to the breach by buyer.

If the measure of damages suffered by seller is inadequate when based on difference in price on the refusal to accept, or repudiation of delivery by buyer, seller shall be entitled to damages based on the profit seller would have received had buyer performed in full, together with any incidental damages authorized by U.C.C. Section 2-710, if applicable, plus due allowances for costs reasonably incurred and due credit for payment of proceeds of resale.

If buyer refuses to accept or repudiates delivery of goods sold to buyer under this agreement, seller's extent of recovery and buyer's extent of liability are limited to the difference between the contract price and the market price at the time and place of tender. In no event shall the seller be entitled to lost profits or incidental or consequential damages as defined in the Uniform Commercial Code.

FIGURE 14-5 Sample damages provisions

Cancellation of the Contract

Upon notification of a breach, the seller can cancel the contract and proceed directly to a lawsuit for damages. When a seller cancels a contract due to the buyer's breach, the seller's ability to elect damages is not impeded by the act of cancellation.

Reclamation of Goods

When a buyer has accepted goods and it comes to the seller's attention that the buyer is now insolvent, under § 2-702(2) the seller can reclaim the goods. There are certain restrictions on this remedy, however. To reclaim the goods, the seller must show that: (1) the buyer received the goods on credit while insolvent; and (2) the seller demanded the return of the goods within 10 days of delivery. If misrepresentation of solvency was made to the particular seller in writing within three months before delivery, the ten-day limitation does not apply (§ 2-702(2)).

Practical application of this rule can create major headaches for the injured seller, especially because the courts are divided in interpreting what constitutes a misrepresentation. The seller is probably better served by choosing another remedy. However, in *Burk v. Emmick*, 637 F.2d 1172 (8th Cir. 1980), the court was faced with interpreting the reclamation provision.

BURK v. EMMICK

United States Court of Appeals, Eighth Circuit
Nov. 13, 1980

This appeal arises out of a transaction in which plaintiff Willard Burk contracted to sell approximately 950 head of yearling steers to defendant Bob Emmick, d/b/a Emmick Cattle Company. The terms of the sales contract provided that the buyer would make a $15,000 down payment and tender the balance upon delivery. The contract was amended, postponing the delivery date and modifying the manner in which payment would be made. The amended agreement called for a payment of a major portion of the purchase price at delivery by sight draft drawn upon the codefendant, Northwestern National Bank of Sioux City. The balance of the purchase price was to be covered by the buyer's personal note. Just prior to delivery, the defendant Bank orally guaranteed to the seller that funds were available to cover the sight draft so that delivery could be made. The seller made delivery, but the sight draft was not accepted by the Bank and the buyer's personal note was never honored. Subsequent to these transactions, the seller reclaimed the cattle and resold them for less than the original contract price. Thereafter, the seller sued the buyer.

[U.C.C.] 2-403 gives a transferor power to pass good title to certain transferees even though the transferor does not possess good title. This section contemplates the situation in which a cash seller delivers goods to a buyer who pays by a draft that is subsequently dishonored, and then transfers title to a good faith purchaser. In such a situation, as between the good faith purchaser and the unpaid seller, the former's claim is clearly superior.

Furthermore, § 2-403 does not limit the power of transferor to pass good title only through sales transactions. The language of the Code specifically provides that "purchasers" may take good title from transferors. The term *purchaser* is broadly defined in the Code to include an Article IX secured party. Here, if the Bank had acted in good faith, its interest in the cattle would be superior to the aggrieved seller. However, as the district court noted, the issue was properly submitted to the jury and the jury determined that the Bank did not exercise good faith. Accordingly, the Bank does not quality as a good faith purchaser under 2-403. As between the seller and the Bank, the seller's interest in the cattle is superior.

Section 2-507(2) gave the seller in this case the right to reclaim the cattle which were sold and not paid for. The buyer's main contention is that once the seller had successfully reclaimed the goods, he could not also seek a deficiency judgment. The buyer asserts the election remedies provision in 2-702(3) is applicable to a cash seller's 2-507 right of reclamation. We do not agree. There is nothing in the language of the Code or the Comments to suggest that the election of remedies provision applies to a cash seller's reclamation under 2-507.

They buyer also asserts that the seller failed to demand reclamation within ten days of delivery of the cattle. Some courts have decided that a cash seller's reclamation right is subject to the ten-day limitation provision covering credit sale transactions involving insolvent buyers under 2-702, but those decisions are factually dissimilar. The courts that have imposed the ten-day limitation have concerned the respective rights of a good faith purchaser or trustee in bankruptcy and an unpaid seller. But here, a good faith purchaser is not involved. Nor are we faced with the conflicting interests of an unpaid seller and a trustee in bankruptcy representing the interests of a bankrupt's creditors. Rather, the conflict is between the unpaid cash seller and the breaching buyer, and the question is whether the seller may reclaim and recover a deficiency judgment from that buyer.

Our holding is quite limited. We determine that as between the seller and the buyer, where a cash seller reclaims goods sold to a breaching buyer, the only limitation imposed upon the seller's right is a reasonableness requirement. Since we determine that the buyer was not prejudiced by the seller's delay in reclaiming the cattle, we find the seller's reclamation was not unreasonable.

Furthermore, the district court was correct in determining that 2-702 did not properly apply to the instant case. By its very terms, that section applies when the seller discovers the buyer to be insolvent *and* when the underlying transaction is a credit sale. The transaction that gave rise to this lawsuit was a cash sale. As the district court reasoned, the fact that payment was made by a draft that was subsequently dishonored does not alter the nature of the underlying transaction.

The district court properly determined that 2-703 controls this case. This section declares the right of the aggrieved seller to: (1) withhold delivery; (2) stop delivery by any bailee; (3) proceed under section 2-704; (4) *resell and recover damages as provided in section 2-706;* (5) recover damages for nonacceptance or the price; or (6) cancel. In this case, the seller properly chose the fourth alternative. This section's applicability to this case is highlighted by Official Comment 3, which provides: "In addition to the typical case of refusal to pay or default in payment, the language in the preamble, 'fails to make a payment due,' is intended to cover the dishonor of a check on due presentment, or the non-acceptance of a draft."

In this case, when the draft was not accepted by the Bank, the seller chose to reclaim the cattle pursuant to 2-507 and resell them. Section 2-703(d) allows the seller to recover a deficiency judgment upon a reasonable resale.

QUESTIONS FOR ANALYSIS

What were the facts of *Burk?* Upon what sections of the U.C.C. did the court rely in making its decision? Was the court's decision fair? Why or why not?

14.3 BUYER'S REMEDIES

When a seller breaches a sales contract, the buyer has a number of remedies to compensate for the loss. The buyer's election of remedy is guided by the circumstances producing the breach.

Lawsuit for Damages

The most common buyer's remedy is a suit for the damages caused by the seller's breach. Section 2-713 of the U.C.C. provides the method of recovery under a suit for damages; the formula used in determining the damages is the excess of the market price over the contract price at the time of the breach and at the place of delivery. Added to this amount are any incidental or consequential damages incurred due to the breach. Each is defined in § 2-715:

(1) Incidental damages resulting from the seller's breach include expenses reasonably incurred in inspection, receipt, transportation and care and custody of goods rightfully rejected, any commercially reasonable charges, expenses or commissions in connection with effecting cover and any other reasonable expense incident to the delay or other breach.

(2) Consequential damages resulting from the seller's breach include

(a) any loss resulting from general or particular requirements and needs of which the seller at the time of contracting had reason to know and which could not reasonably be prevented by cover or otherwise; and

(b) injury to person or property proximately resulting from any breach of warranty.

This method of recovery is often the best avenue for the buyer. Some contract damage provisions to consider, which benefit the buyer, are shown in Figure 14-6.

> If seller fails to deliver the goods required by this agreement or repudiates the entire agreement, buyer shall be entitled to damages based on the difference between the market price of the goods at the time when buyer learns of the breach and the contract price, together with any incidental or consequential damages authorized by Section 2-715 of the U.C.C., if applicable, but less expenses saved in consequence of the breach of seller.
>
> Buyer shall be entitled to all incidental damages resulting from a breach by seller, including, but not limited to, all expenses reasonably incurred in inspection, receipt, transportation, and care and custody of goods rightfully rejected, any commercially reasonable charges, expenses, or commissions incurred in effecting cover, and any other reasonable expense incident to a delay or breach by seller.
>
> Buyer shall be entitled to consequential damages resulting from a breach by seller for any loss resulting from general or particular requirements and needs of buyer of which seller is aware at the time of executing this agreement, and that reasonably cannot be prevented by cover or otherwise, and damages sustained by buyer from any injury to person or property proximately resulting from any breach of warranty by seller.

FIGURE 14-6 Sample contract damages clauses

Cover the Sale

Under § 2-712, an injured buyer may use the remedy known as **cover.** Cover occurs when the buyer has substituted goods from another seller to minimize the loss incurred because of the original seller's breach. If a buyer has to pay more than the original contract price for the substitute goods, the buyer has a right to sue the seller for the difference between the original contract price and the cost of the cover and any incidental expenses related to the cover. Section 2-712 guides the buyer as follows:

(1) After a breach within the preceding section the buyer may "cover" by making in good faith and without unreasonable delay any reasonable purchase of or contract to purchase goods in substitution for those due from the seller.

(2) The buyer may recover from the seller as damages the difference between the cost of cover and the contract price together with any incidental or consequential damages as hereinafter defined (Section 2-715), but less expenses saved in consequence of the seller's breach.

(3) Failure of the buyer to effect cover within this section does not bar him from any other remedy.

A case dealing with the buyer's remedy of cover is *Kanzmeier v. McCoppin,* 398 N.W.2d 826 (Iowa 1987). After revising the case, provisions to consider when drafting a provision on a buyer's right to cover are set out in Figure 14-7.

TERMS

cover
Under the Uniform Commercial Code, "cover" relates to the right of a buyer, if the seller has breached a contract of sale to purchase the goods elsewhere (the "cover") and hold the seller liable for the difference between the cost of the cover and the original contract price.

KANZMEIER v. McCOPPIN

Supreme Court of Iowa
Jan. 14, 1987

On December 2, 1983, two livestock order buyers contacted defendant Charles McCoppin to determine whether McCoppin was interested in selling any of his cattle. The three men discussed the price of cattle sold at a local sale barn earlier that day. As a result of this discussion, defendant stated that he would be willing to sell 360 head of cattle for $60 per hundred weight.

That evening one of the order buyers called plaintiff Bill Kanzmeier, a cattle feeder with whom the buyer had dealt for several years. Kanzmeier had previously told the order buyer that he was interested in buying cattle of this type. After being advised of the price, Kanzmeier agreed to buy the cattle and to pay the order buyer a commission of $.50 per hundred weight. Kanzmeier suggested that the cattle be picked up by truck on December 8, when he would have room available for them. The order buyer then called defendant and accepted his offer, finalizing the delivery date on which the cattle were to be picked up by plaintiff.

The next day the defendant learned that some cattle had been sold at a sale barn on December 2 for $62 per hundred weight. He maintains that the order buyer advised him concerning the sale prices of cattle at that particular sale barn, but neglected to mention that some cattle brought $62 per hundred weight. On December 5 defendant called the order buyer and told him he was not quite ready to sell the cattle. On December 6 defendant told the order buyer he did not want to sell his cattle. Plaintiff went to defendant's farm on December 7 and learned that the cattle had been sold that morning to another party for $62 per hundred weight. Plaintiff subsequently filed a petition seeking damages for the breach of oral contract entered into by defendant and the plaintiff's agent, the order buyer.

To fully understand the issues concerning the validity of the contract, it may be helpful to trace the contentions of the parties. In his petition claiming breach of contract, plaintiff alleged that the order buyer, as a duly authorized agent, entered into an oral agreement with defendant, whereby plaintiff and defendant agreed to the contract in question. Because the order buyer approached defendant as broker, rather than agent of the plaintiff, defendant urges that plaintiff never was a party to the contract. The trial court did not accept this contention and made findings of fact that the "buyers were representing . . . the plaintiff" and "that there was in fact a contract between the plaintiff and defendant to sell 360 head of steers." The trier of fact could determine from [the] evidence that the order buyer acted on behalf of the plaintiff and was subject to his control and consent with regard to the purchase of the steers in question.

On appeal defendant maintains that the trial court erred in the method used in calculating damages. The trial court adopted the "cover" method of determining damages. The court awarded damages based on the difference between the sale price agreed upon by the parties and the hundred weight price of 358 replacement cattle multiplied against the weight of the replacement cattle. This resulted in a judgment of $19,458.07. On appeal, defendant concedes that the trial court should not have allowed a recovery of consequential damages for loss of profits, but also maintains that the "cover" price method was inappropriate. Plaintiff purchased cattle on four occasions between December 21, 1983, and February 6, 1984, for various prices. These cattle weighed approximately 135 pounds less apiece than defendant's cattle. Defendant urges that the court erred in finding that 60 days was a reasonable time within which to replace the cattle with cattle of lesser weight, and that the court did not consider testimony that the cattle could have been replaced immediately at a price similar to the price of defendant's cattle. Although defendant relies primarily on the time period, we believe there is a more serious problem in determining whether these cattle were in fact a proper cover.

The Uniform Commercial Code provides that the buyer has several options as to remedy when the seller repudiates or fails to make delivery. The buyer may "cover" and recover damages equal to the difference between the cost of cover and contract price, plus incidental and consequential damages. Alternatively, the buyer may recover damages equal to the difference between the market price (at the time the buyer learned of the breach) and the contract price, plus incidental and consequential damages.

Certain principles concerning "cover" are applicable here. The buyer may choose to cover by making "in good faith and without unreasonable delay any reasonable purchase of or contract to purchase goods in substitution for those due from the seller." Furthermore, the goods must be a likekind substitute. Consequently, there is no cover if the buyer does not purchase like goods but rather purchases goods substantially different. This is not to say that the goods must be identical with those contract for, but the cover goods must be commercial usable as reasonable substitutes under the circumstances of the particular case. Whether an item was a cover in fact is for the trier of fact to decide. We will not interfere with the trial court's finding of fact if it is supported by substantial evidence. In applying these principles, it is basic that the remedies are to be liberally administered to put the aggrieved party in as good a position as if the other party had fully performed.

After reviewing the record we must agree with the defendant that there is not substantial evidence that the 358 cattle purchased were a reasonable substitute for the cattle promised under the contract. Thus, those purchases did not qualify as cover. Plaintiff testified that he purchased about 2000 cattle a year. He was selling cattle and wished to replace them with "big steers" so that he could hit an early April market. Defendant's cattle were big steers that had been fed corn and would not require a feeding break-in period. They were local cattle, out of one group, and would not be prone to sickness. The 358 cattle purchased over a period of 60 days could not be ready for market until almost two months later than defendant's cattle because of their weight and time of purchase.

The remaining evidence showed that these lighter cattle could not substitute for the purpose for which he had purchased the defendant's cattle. There was no evidence that the price of lighter cattle was similar to heavier cattle at the time they were purchased. Consequently, the finder of fact would have no way of determining whether the higher price paid for the lighter cattle was the result of the differences in the weight or of the rise in the market. As we do not believe there was substantial evidence in the record to substantiate the trial court's determination of cover, we hold that, as a matter of law, this was not a proper cover.

This matter must be remanded to the trial court to redetermine damages on the record made before

it. The measure of damages must be the difference between the contract price and the market price at the time the plaintiff learned of the breach, plus incidental and consequential damages.

QUESTIONS FOR ANALYSIS

Identify the facts of *Kanzmeier.* How can damages be calculated under the theory of "cover"? What was the court's reasoning?

On any breach of this sales agreement by seller, due to either a failure by seller to deliver the goods specified in this agreement or a repudiation of the entire agreement by seller, buyer shall have the right to effect cover by purchasing or agreeing to purchase substitute goods in the open market. The purchase or agreement to purchase substitute goods must be reasonable and effected without unreasonable delay.

Buyer shall be entitled to recover from seller any damages buyer incurs as a result of being required to effect cover due to either the repudiation of this agreement or the refusal by seller to deliver the goods specified in this agreement.

If seller either fails to deliver the goods required by this agreement or repudiates this agreement entirely, buyer shall not be required to effect cover. The failure of buyer to effect cover will not affect any remedy buyer has for the breach of this agreement by seller, except the remedy granted by Uniform Commercial Code Section 2-712(2) to claim damages on effecting cover.

FIGURE 14-7 Sample clauses on buyer's right to cover

Specific Performance

If the buyer cannot locate suitable substitute goods, the buyer can request a court to order **specific performance** of the contract under U.C.C. § 2-716(1) and (2). Recall that this is an equitable remedy. Normally, a court will not order specific performance unless the buyer has unsuccessfully attempted to cover. In addition, the buyer must show that the goods were unique and that the buyer cannot find the goods at any other place; thus, the buyer can reasonably request the court to order that the seller perform in accordance with the original contract.

Replevin

Replevin is another equitable remedy that is available to the buyer under § 2-716(3) of the U.C.C., when cover is not appropriate. This remedy can be used when a legal one is inappropriate. Replevin occurs when a court orders that the seller turn the goods over to the buyer in accordance with the contract. When the goods have been identified under the contract

TERMS

specific performance
1. The equitable remedy of compelling performance of a contract, as distinguished from an action at law for damages for breach of contract due to nonperformance. Specific performance may be ordered in circumstances where damages are an inadequate remedy. 2. The actual accomplishment of a contract by the party bound to fulfill it.

replevin
An action by which the owner of personal property taken or detained by another may recover possession of it.

and reasonable but unsuccessful efforts have been made to find a suitable substitute, replevin is appropriate. Equitable remedy provisions to include in a sales contract are suggested in Figure 14-8.

---

(1) Buyer shall have the right to bring an action against seller for specific performance of this agreement if the goods covered by this sales agreement are unique.

(2) It is hereby agreed by both buyer and seller that the goods that are the subject matter of this sales agreement are unique. Consequently, if seller breaches this sales agreement, buyer shall have the right to specific performance as an alternative to any other remedy available to buyer at buyer's option. Such option by buyer shall not limit buyer's right to incidental or consequential damages caused by seller's breach of this sales agreement.

(3) Buyer shall have the right to bring a replevin action against seller where the goods required to be sold under this agreement have been identified to the agreement and buyer is unable to effect cover, or the goods have been shipped under a security reservation that has been satisfied or tendered.

FIGURE 14-8 Sample equitable remedy provisions

Buyer's Resale of the Goods

If the seller ships nonconforming goods, after notice to the seller of rejection of the nonconforming goods, the buyer may attempt to resell the goods to collect any damages incurred due to the nonconforming tender. As in any sale, the sale must be in a reasonable manner and time. Oddly enough, in this type of resale, if any excess results from the sale, the buyer cannot claim the excess, but must return the overage to the seller.

Cancellation

Upon a breach, the buyer has a right to cancel the contract and sue for damages. This is a very common buyer's remedy under the Code.

Revocation of Acceptance

When the buyer has accepted the goods and has determined that there are defects in the goods, the buyer may elect to revoke acceptance if the defect "substantially impairs" the value of the goods to the buyer. A revocation of acceptance is considered a rejection, and thus the buyer can use any remedy that is deemed appropriate under the U.C.C. The section that provides guidance regarding this type of remedy is § 2-608, which states:

(1) The buyer may revoke his acceptance of a lot or commercial unit whose nonconformity substantially impairs its value to him if he has accepted it

(a) on the reasonable assumption that its non-conformity would be cured and it has not been seasonably cured; or

(b) without discovery of such non-conformity if his acceptance was reasonably induced either by the difficulty of discovery before acceptance or by the seller's assurances.

(2) Revocation of acceptance must occur within a reasonable time after the buyer discovers or should have discovered the ground for it and before any substantial change in condition of the goods which is not caused by their own defects. It is not effective until the buyer notifies the seller of it.

(3) A buyer who so revokes has the same rights and duties with regard to the goods involved as if he had rejected them.

Figure 14-9 is an example of a letter rejecting a revocation of acceptance.

Dresses Unlimited   August 1, 1994
414 State Street
Boston, Massachusetts 12345

Dear Mr. McCoy:

    Please take notice that I have received your notice of revocation of acceptance of the dresses shipped to you by me under our agreement dated June 12, 1994.

    It was provided in Section 2 of our sales agreement that any notice of revocation must be submitted by you not later than ten (10) days after your receipt and inspection of the goods. In your notice, you stated the goods were received and inspected on July 1, 1994. This notice was given more than twenty (20) days after your receipt and inspection of the goods.

    Your notice of revocation of acceptance is untimely and, therefore, unacceptable. I hereby refuse your revocation of acceptance.

                                    Very truly yours,
                                    Thomas McKay

FIGURE 14-9   Sample letter rejecting revocation of acceptance

    A court decision that analyzed a buyer's right of revocation of acceptance is *Kessner v. Lancaster*, 378 S.E.2d 649 (W. Va. 1989). Pay attention to what the court considers as "substantially impairing the value of goods."

KESNER v. LANCASTER

Supreme Court of Appeals of West Virginia
Feb. 17, 1989

    On or about September 13, 1985, the seller advertised a 1974 John Deere tractor-loader for sale in a local newspaper. The buyer responded to the advertisement and arranged to see the machine the following day at the seller's home near Keyser, Mineral County.

    The buyer inspected the two-track loader and noted that it was freshly painted and that the undercarriage was in good condition. The seller started the motor, and the buyer observed that the engine ran well. When the buyer told the seller that he needed to use the loader immediately to dig a ditch for a septic system and inquired about its condition, the seller assured him that the equipment was in fine shape. The buyer asked to operate the machine, but was discouraged from doing so by the seller because attachments would have to be changed.

On Monday, September 16, 1985, the buyer arranged to consummate the sale at the seller's residence. The parties again discussed the condition of the loader, and, according to the buyer, the seller again assured him that there was nothing wrong with the machine. The buyer paid for the loader with a personal check of $9,000, drove the machine onto a low-boy trailer, and hauled it away. There was no written contract.

The next day the buyer transported the loader to Reese Mill Road, where he was going to install the septic system. At the work site, the buyer drove the loader from the trailer and began removing the topsoil. Within minutes, the machine stopped and would not move. The buyer testified he could tell from the way the machine was operating that one of the steering clutches was defective.

The buyer decided to fix the steering clutch himself. He removed the seats to obtain access to the clutch and noticed that the transmission had pulled away from its housing. When the buyer removed the floorboards to get a closer look, he noticed that the bolts securing the transmission in its housing were rusted and stripped. Upon further investigation, the buyer discovered that the bolts at the bottom of the housing were also rusted and stripped [and] that the transmission and frame rails had cracked and been welded together and that several bolts to the A-frame were missing.

A mechanic for the buyer estimated that repairs to the transmission mounting bolts, the frame rails, and the steering clutch would take a minimum of thirty-six hours at $20.00 per hour, or $720. The mechanic also stated, however, that he would have to disassemble the transmission to see if there was any internal damage and could not estimate the cost of any additional repairs.

Convinced that major repairs were necessary, the buyer called the seller and told him that he wanted to return the loader and get his money back. The seller refused.

The right of the buyer to rescind a contract for the purchase of goods is long established. Where a purchaser of chattels has right to rescind the contract, for breach of it, the breach must be in a material matter. In addition to a material breach, our case law required a buyer who sought rescission or revocation of a sales contract to provide "[c]lear and unambiguous notice" of the fact to the seller promptly or within a reasonable time after the purchase or sale.

These principles permit the buyer to revoke acceptance of goods for nonconformity to the contract of sale. In general, this [West Virginia U.C.C.] section requires several conditions to be met before the buyer may revoke his acceptance: (1) the nonconformity must have substantially impaired the value of the goods to the buyer; (2) the goods must have been accepted on the reasonable assumption that the nonconformity would be cured, and it was not, or accepted without discovery of the nonconformity, either because of the difficulty of discovery or because of the seller's assurances; (3) the revocation must have occurred within a reasonable time after discovery of the defect and before any substantial change in the condition of the goods; and (4) the revocation is not effective until the buyer has notified the seller. A buyer making a revocation after acceptance on these terms has the same rights and duties under the UCC as one who had rejected the goods originally.

In this case, the parties raise the issues of whether the loader was substantially impaired and whether the defects should have been reasonably discovered. An additional and more fundamental issue is whether the UCC applies to an isolated sale.

The UCC applies to the sale of any goods. It makes a distinction between the general term "seller" and the more specific term "merchant." A seller is "a person who sells or contracts to sell goods." A "merchant" is defined as one "having knowledge or skill peculiar to the practices or goods involved in the transaction[.]" The official commentary indicates that casual sellers are covered, and this has led courts to conclude that the sales provisions of the UCC apply to isolated sales of goods by persons who are not merchants. Thus, the sale in the present case is within the ambit of the UCC.

Even though this transaction is subject to the revocation provision of the UCC, the seller argues that the buyer did not present a prima facie case. He contends that since the cost of repairs was much less than the purchase price, the value of the loader was not substantially impaired by the defects. This Court has not spoken in any detail to the substantial impairment language. The official commentary explains that in assessing substantial impairment, "the question is whether the nonconformity is such as will in fact cause a substantial impairment of value to the buyer though the seller had no advance knowledge as to the buyer's particular circumstances."

Most commentators and courts agree that there ar both subjective and objective aspects to the determination of whether a defect "substantially impairs" the value of goods so as to enable a buyer to revoke his acceptance of them. The subjective component of the test takes into consideration the buyer's needs and expectations. The objective element focuses on the actual defects, which must not be trivial or insubstantial.

This section, therefore, creates a subjective test in the sense that the needs and circumstances of the particular buyer must be examined. This determination is not, however, made by reference to he buyer's personal belief as to the reduced value of the goods in question. The trier of fact must make an objective determination that the value of the goods to the buyer has in fact been substantially impaired.

In the present case, there was sufficient evidence for the jury to find that the value of the loader had been substantially impaired within the meaning of the statute. The loader was inoperable and needed major repairs. The mechanic's estimate of $720 did not include the cost of disassembling the transmission nor the repair of any internal damage. From the time he purchased the loader, the buyer has been unable to use it. From an objective standpoint, the machine's value has been substantially impaired. In light of the evidence presented, we find that the jury's determination that the value of the loader was substantially impaired was not clearly erroneous.

The seller also argues that the buyer accepted the goods when the nonconformity could reasonably have been discovered prior to acceptance. As we have already noted, to be entitled to revocation under the UCC, the buyer must show that his acceptance of the goods without discovery of the nonconformity was either due to the difficulty of discovering the defect or induced by the assurances of the seller. A buyer need only prove one of these factors.

Courts have generally concluded that unless a defect is reasonably apparent or the buyer has some special expertise, a buyer who has made a reasonable inspection of goods and failed to find the defect has satisfied the "difficulty of discovery" test. Here, both parties testified that the buyer visually inspected the equipment prior to purchasing it. The buyer noted that the machine had been freshly painted, the undercarriage was in good condition, and the engine ran well. It was not until the machine stopped running, and the buyer removed the seats, floorboard, and belly pan that the defects were discovered. We believe there was sufficient evidence to carry the question to the jury.

It is also clear that this is not a case where the buyer purchased the goods after disclosure by the seller of the defects. Where this occurs, or where the defects were sufficiently obvious that the buyer is charged with knowledge of them, he is foreclosed from revoking his prior acceptance of the goods. "Acceptance of goods by the buyer precludes rejection of the goods accepted and if made with knowledge of a nonconformity cannot be revoked because of it unless the acceptance was on the reasonable assumption that the nonconformity would be seasonably cured but acceptance does not of itself impair any other remedy provided by this article for nonconformity. Affirmed.

QUESTIONS FOR ANALYSIS

State the facts of *Kessner.* How did the court define *substantially impairs* the value of the goods to the buyer? What was the court's holding?

Retain Goods with Adjustment

When a seller has tendered nonconforming goods, the buyer has the option to keep the goods and ask for an adjustment based on the nonconformity. Section 2-714(2) provides guidance in this circumstance. If the seller refuses to make any adjustments on the nonconforming goods, the buyer has the option of suing for the difference between the value of the goods contracted for and the value of the goods received. This is the basis for another form of damages lawsuit.

14.4 CONTRACTUAL REMEDIES

The Code is not the exclusive guide for remedies when a problem arises between the parties in a sales contract. Contracting parties can agree to additional remedies or remedies other than in those found in the U.C.C. Basically, the choice rests with the parties involved. Section 2-719(1)(a) and (b) state:

(1) Subject to the provisions of subsections (2) and (3) of this section and of the preceding section on liquidation and limitation of damages,

    (a) the agreement may provide for remedies in addition to or in substitution for those provided in this Article and may limit or alter the measure of damages recoverable under this Article, as by limiting the buyer's remedies to return of the goods and repayment of the price or to repair and replacement of non-conforming goods or parts; and

    (b) resort to a remedy as provided is optional unless the remedy is expressly agreed to be exclusive, in which case it is the sole remedy.

One of the remedies that courts closely scrutinize is liquidated damages, discussed in § 2-718(1):

(1) Damages for breach by either party may be liquidated in the agreement but only at an amount which is reasonable in the light of the anticipated or actual harm caused by the breach, the difficulties of proof of loss, and the inconvenience or non-feasibility of otherwise obtaining an adequate remedy. A term fixing unreasonably large liquidated damages is void as a penalty.

Recall from Chapter 9 that the liquidated damages provision must be reasonable in light of the circumstances, or the court will not enforce it. The parties should pay close attention in estimating the damages when a liquidated sum is desired. Some suggested language for liquidated damages provisions is found in Figure 14-10.

---

(1) It is understood that buyer is relying on delivery of the goods on [date],and that delay in delivery will result in serious losses to buyer. It is agreed, therefore, that for any delay in delivery of the goods, regardless of cause and regardless of whether seller had any control over the cause that resulted in delay, seller shall pay to buyer, or buyer may deduct from the price, as the case may be, the sum of Three Hundred Dollars and No Cents ($300.00) per day as liquidated damages to compensate for losses incident to delay. The assessment of such sums shall terminate on delivery of the goods or the effective realization of cover by buyer pursuant to U.C.C. Section 2-712 and, in no event, shall exceed Five Hundred Dollars and No Cents ($500.00). The damages here liquidated are confined to losses resulting from delay in delivery and shall not affect such other rights and remedies as buyer may have under law, including, but not limited to, the Uniform Commercial Code as enacted in [state].

(2) If seller fails to make delivery or repudiates, or buyer rightfully rejects or justifiably revokes acceptance, then, with respect to any goods involved, seller shall pay to buyer the sum of Eight Hundred Dollars and No Cents ($800.00) as liquidated damages, which sum shall include both incidental and consequential damages.

(3) In no event shall seller be liable for consequential damages except where there is injury to the person in a sale of consumer goods.

(4) If, for any reason, buyer fails to accept and settle for the goods, buyer will, if seller so elects and demands, pay to seller, in lieu of the enforcement of this agreement, as liquidated damages, a sum equal to ten percent (10%) of the list price of the goods, and, if shipment has been made, freight from the facility of seller and return, demurrage, cartage, loading and unloading expense, and all other similar expenses actually incurred by reason of the shipment and attempted delivery of the goods. If suit is commenced to enforce performance of any part of this agreement, buyer shall pay to seller reasonable attorney's fees.

FIGURE 14-10 Sample language for liquidated damages provisions

Other damages provisions that have come under close court scrutiny are those for consequential damages. Recall from Chapter 9 that consequential damages result from a direct or indirect consequence of the breach. Section 2-719(3) is illustrative:

> Consequential damages may be limited or excluded unless the limitation or exclusion is unconscionable. Limitation of consequential damages for injury to the person in the case of consumer goods is prima facie unconscionable but limitation of damages where the loss is commercial is not.

But § 2-715(a) and (b) state:

> Consequential damages arising from the seller's breach include:
>
> (a) any loss resulting from general or particular requirements and needs of which the seller at the time of contracting had reason to know and which could not reasonably be prevented by cover or otherwise; and
>
> (b) injury to person or property proximately resulting from any breach of warranty.

The parties must set a consequential damages provision that is reasonable and not unconscionable.

14.5 ANTICIPATORY REPUDIATION

Sometimes parties, either directly or indirectly, indicate their intention to repudiate a contract prior to the time performance is required. If repudiation by one party substantially impairs the contract for the other party, § 2-610 guides the injured party:

> When either party repudiates the contract with respect to a performance not yet due, the loss of which will substantially impair the value of the contract to the other, the aggrieved party may
>
> (a) for a commercially reasonable time await performance by the repudiating party; or
> (b) resort to any remedy for breach (Section 2-703 or Section 2-711), even though he has notified the repudiating party that he would await the latter's performance and has urged retraction; and
> (c) in either case suspend his own performance or proceed in accordance with the provisions of this Article on the seller's right to identify goods to the contract notwithstanding breach or to salvage unfinished goods (Section 2-704).

The Code goes on to say, in § 2-611, that a party may retract the repudiation under certain conditions. Section 2-611 sets forth those conditions:

> (1) Until the repudiating party's next performance is due, he can retract his repudiation unless the aggrieved party has, since the repudiation, canceled or materially changed his position or otherwise indicated that he considers the repudiation final.
> (2) Retraction may be by any method which clearly indicates to the aggrieved party that the repudiating party intends to perform, but must include any assurance justifiably demanded under the provisions of this Article (Section 2-609).
> (3) Retraction reinstates the repudiating party's rights under the contract with due excuse and allowance to the aggrieved party for any delay occasioned by the repudiation.

The Code appears to give each party the opportunity to perform the obligations under the contract unless there is a material change in position by the nonbreaching party. Review *Design for Business Interiors, Inc. v. Herson's, Inc.*, 659 F. Supp. 1103 (D.D.C. 1987), which dealt with anticipatory repudiation.

DESIGN FOR BUSINESS INTERIORS, INC. v. HERSON'S, INC.

United States District Court, District of Columbia
Dec. 2, 1986

This case began as an action on a series of contracts for furniture and other supplies between plaintiff, Design for Business Interiors, Inc. ("DBI") and defendant, Herson's Inc. ("Herson's"). Herson's had entered into these and other contracts in the process of decorating its new automobile showroom in Rockville, Maryland. Plaintiff DBI was formerly an unincorporated division of Commercial Office Environments, Inc. ("COE"), but became a separate entity under a sales agreement of January 23, 1985. Pursuant to the agreement, DBI contracts were allocated between COE and DBI based on the date when an order was placed with a manufacturer: if placed before December 1, 1985, COE retained ownership; if placed after December 1, 1985, ownership was transferred to DBI under the sales agreement. DBI agreed to make "reasonable efforts" to collect payments due under the COE contracts in exchange for a 2% commission on payments collected.

However, on November 25, 1985, long after Herson's had stopped making payments under its contracts, DBI and COE entered into a second agreement, wherein COE assigned to DBI its five contracts with Herson's. DBI agreed to pay any monies received under these five contracts to COE, and the two parties agreed to divide the costs of the litigation equally, including attorneys' fees.

Herson's focuses on the following language in the November 25, 1986 agreement:

COE and DBI have agreed that DBI should institute . . . legal proceedings against Herson for the benefit of itself and COE. Accordingly, in order to permit DBI to institute and maintain such legal proceedings in its own name, COE has and shall deliver to DBI certain assignments . . . of the COE-Herson contracts to DBI *for the sole purpose of permitting DBI to institute such legal proceedings* on behalf of itself and COE.

When reasonable grounds for insecurity arise with respect to the performance of either party the other may in writing demand adequate assurance of due performance and until he receives such assurance may if commercially reasonable suspend any performance for which he has not already received the agreed return.

(2) Between merchants the reasonableness of grounds for insecurity and the adequacy of any assurance offered shall be determined according to commercial standards.

The issue of whether grounds for insecurity are "reasonable" is clearly an issue of fact which would ordinarily preclude summary judgment.

The relevant portion of the February 6, 1985 letter reads:

This account has an overdue balance of $23,153.69. As you are aware, our terms are payment within (10) days from the date of invoice.

All future deliveries on the Herson's account will be held in the warehouse until the account is brought current. Once the account is brought to a current status, *all deliveries for Herson Honda will now be performed on a proforma* [sic] *basis.*

This is not a request for assurance, but is instead a unilateral alteration of the contract's terms, as well as an express refusal to render performance due under the terms of the original agreement—that invoices and payment were to follow, not precede, delivery.

DBI's letter of February 6, 1985, clearly impaired the value of the contract to Herson's within the meaning of [the] definition of anticipatory repudiation. A buyer who has contracted for the right to receive and inspect goods at his premises before making payment, and who is then told that he must pay in advance of delivery as to all performances still owed by the seller, has suffered substantial impairment of the contract.

Moreover, it is clear from the language that even had Herson's paid the amount which DBI erroneously believed was due, bringing the account "current", as the DBI letter puts it, DBI would still have continued to refuse performance except on "pro forma" terms. This is precisely the situation described in the Restatement, Second, of Contracts as an anticipatory repudiation:

where a party states that he will not perform at all unless the other party consents to a modification of his contract rights, the statement is a repudiation even though the concession that he seeks is a minor one, because the breach that he threatens in order to exact it is a complete refusal of performance.

DBI erroneously stated the amount owing, demanded immediate payment of that amount (although it was owing no on its own contracts but on those retained by COE), and then took the opportunity of Herson's supposed "delinquency" to refuse to perform except on terms that altered the contract significantly. This is precisely the type of conduct which UCC § 2-609 seeks to avoid: rather than having a party guess or suppose that the other party is in breach, as DBI did here, the UCC provides that the doubting party ask for and receive "assurance of performance" prior to acting in a way that would constitute anticipatory repudiation. DBI did not avail itself of 2-609. There is no genuine issue of material fact as to this.

Where a party anticipatorily repudiates a contract, as DBI did here, the other party may:

(a) for a commercially reasonable time await performance by the repudiating party; or

(b) resort to any remedy for breach . . .; and

(c) in either case suspend his own performance . . .

Thus, under the Code, Herson's conduct upon receipt of the February 6, 1985 letter was perfectly justified.

QUESTIONS FOR ANALYSIS

State the facts of the *Herson* case. Did the court find anticipatory repudiation? Why or why not? What was the court's holding?

If a party allows retraction of a repudiation, but still remains uncomfortable about a party's performance, the Code, in § 2-609, gives the insecure party the right to *adequate assurances* of performance.

(1) A contract for sale imposes an obligation on each party that the other's expectation of receiving due performance will not be impaired. When reasonable grounds for insecurity arise with respect to the performance of either party, the other may in writing demand adequate assurances of due performance and until he receives such assurance may, if commercially reasonable, suspend any performance for which he has not already received the agreed return.

(2) Between merchants the reasonableness of grounds for insecurity and the adequacy of any assurance offered shall be determined according to commercial standards.

(3) Acceptance of any improper delivery or payment does not prejudice the aggrieved party's right to demand adequate assurance of future performance.

4) After receipt of a justified demand, failure to provide within a reasonable time not exceeding thirty days such assurance of due performance as is adequate under the circumstances of the particular case is a repudiation of the contract.

If the insecure party makes a written demand for assurance of performance, and the assurance is not given within 30 days, this is treated as repudiation. Figure 14-11 is an example of a request for adequate assurances by the buyer. (Note that a seller can also require adequate assurance.)

Ms. Marla Coffee   October 10, 1994
Dresses, Inc.
2118 Broadway
New York, New York

Dear Marla:

   Please be advised that I have not yet received the dresses that, under our agreement
dated September 1, 1994, were to be delivered to me at 8212 Main Street, Greenwich, Connecticut, on October 1, 1994. I have not received any reply to the letter dated October 5,
1994, inquiring as to the missing goods.
   In accordance with Section 2-609 of the U.C.C., I demand that within ten (10) days
from your receipt of this letter you furnish me with adequate assurance that you will make
due performance of your obligation to deliver the goods on or before the date to be specified by you.

                                           Very truly yours,
                                           Anthony Finelli

FIGURE 14-11   Sample request for adequate assurances (buyer)

   In addition, the parties can contractually agree to the time for adequate
assurances. Three sample provisions are found in Figure 14-12.

   (1)   Assurance may not be demanded under authority of Section 2-609 of the U.C.C.,
unless the written demand is sent or dispatched to the other party within ten (10) days after the
demanding party learns of the facts giving rise to a right to demand assurance. The expiration
of this period of time shall not bar a demand for assurance when additional grounds, considered alone, might not be sufficient to cause insecurity of the demanding party.
   (2)   Seller shall be deemed insecure when buyer delays making payment for any installment for more than ten (10) days after payment is due, without cause related to performance by seller.
   Buyer shall be deemed insecure when there is any strike or threat of a strike at the
manufacturing facility or plant of seller.
   Grounds for insecurity in this section of the agreement are not exclusive, but are in additional to any other proper grounds for insecurity.
   (3)   In the event that assurance of performance is rightfully demanded by either party, the
party on whom the demand is made shall deliver to the demanding party within ten (10) days
thereafter a bond of an indemnity company acceptable to the demanding party in the amount
of two (2) times the value of the performance remaining to be performed by that party, conditioned to indemnify the demanding party for any loss the demanding party may sustain
by the failure of the other party to perform that party's obligations under this agreement.

FIGURE 14-12   Sample clauses setting time for adequate assurances

14.6   THE DOCTRINE OF IMPRACTICABILITY

   The doctrines of impracticability of performance and commercial impracticability (previously discussed in Chapter 9) hold that a party's performance is excused on the occurence of certain intervening events that were

unanticipated in the contract. As in the common law, the U.C.C. deals with nonperformance due to impracticability. Section 2-615 states that:

(a) Delay in delivery or non-delivery in whole or in part by a seller who complies with paragraphs (b) and (c) is not a breach of his duty under a contract for sale if performance as agreed has been made impracticable by the occurrence of a contingency the non-occurrence of which was a basic assumption on which the contract was made or by compliance in good faith with any applicable foreign or domestic governmental regulation or order, whether or not it later proves to be invalid.

(b) Where the causes mentioned in paragraph (a) affect only a part of the seller's capacity to perform, he must allocate production and deliveries among his customers, but may at his option include regular customers not then under contract as well as his own requirements for further manufacture. He may so allocate in any manner which is fair and reasonable.

However, when a party fails to perform an obligation because of impracticability, the Code sets forth the procedure for notification to the buyer. Section 2-615(c) states:

(c) The seller must notify the buyer seasonably that there will be delay or non-delivery and, when allocation is required under paragraph (b), of the estimated quota thus made available for the buyer.

Once notification is "seasonably" made, the buyer may terminate or modify the contract. This procedure is described in § 2-616:

(1) Where the buyer receives notification of a material or indefinite delay or an allocation justified under the preceding section, he may by written notification to the seller as to any delivery concerned, and where the prospective deficiency substantially impairs the value of the whole contract under the provisions of this Article relating to breach of installment contracts (Section 2-612), then also as to the whole,

    (a) terminate and thereby discharge any unexecuted portion of the contract; or

    (b) modify the contract by agreeing to take his available quota in substitution.

(2) If after receipt of such notification from the seller the buyer fails so to modify the contract, within a reasonable time not exceeding thirty days, the contract lapses with respect to any deliveries affected.

(3) The provisions of this section may not be negated by agreement except in so far as the seller has assumed a greater obligation under the preceding section.

Undoubtedly, familiarity with the Code is important in understanding the rights of the parties. Simply follow the general section headings for guidelines as to Article 2's content.

14.7 STATUTE OF LIMITATIONS

As with any lawsuit, there is a certain time period within which an injured party must file an action with a court. Section 2-725 provides that a lawsuit for breach of a sales contract must be filed within four years of the date of the breach. The parties can contractually agree on a shorter time, but the Code provides that the time period cannot be shorter than one year. Statutes of limitations can always present a problem if a lawsuit is not timely filed, so it is important for both buyer and seller in a sales contract to pay close attention to their rights and responsibilities under the sales contract, and to perform their obligations appropriately to maximize their interests. Language to consider when drafting a statute-of-limitations provision is illustrated in Figure 14-13.

(1) If either party desires to bring an action against the other party for breach of this agreement, the time within which the action shall be commenced shall be governed by the statute of limitations provided by the Uniform Commercial Code Section 2-725.

(2) If either party desires to bring an action against the other party for breach of this agreement, the time within which the action shall be commenced shall be one year after the accrual of the cause of action. This reduced statute of limitations period is established by mutual agreement of the parties.

(3) A cause of action for the breach of this sales agreement shall accrue when the breach occurs, whether or not the parties are aware of the breach at that time.

FIGURE 14-13 Sample statute-of-limitations provisions

14.8 PRACTICAL APPLICATION

Giving a seller or buyer proper remedies under a sales contract is crucial. Some examples of general remedy provisions appear in Figure 14-14.

On default by buyer, seller shall have the option of refusing to perform further under this and any other existing agreement between the parties that seller may elect, and seller may rescind any agreements between the parties and hold buyer responsible for all damages and losses occasioned thereby; or of reselling, at public or private sale, undelivered goods covered by this and any other existing agreement between the parties that seller may elect. Seller shall not be liable to buyer for any profit on any resale, but buyer shall remain liable to seller for the difference between (1) the agreement price of the goods, plus all expenses and charges for the account of buyer specified in this agreement and all expenses of storage and resale, and (2) the resale price of the goods.

In any action brought in any court by seller, any assignee of seller, or buyer concerning this agreement or the goods, the rights and remedies of seller may be enforced successively or concurrently and the adoption of one or more rights or remedies shall not operate to prevent seller from exercising any other or further remedy given to seller under this agreement.

FIGURE 14-14 Sample general remedy provisions

Be sure not to draft a remedy provision that may be considered offensive, a penalty, or unconscionable. A balance of remedies between the parties will give better assurance of enforceability.

SUMMARY

14.1 Part 7 of the Code focuses on the remedies available to seller and buyer in the event of a breach or nonperformance. The Code gives guidance for remedies in § 2-703 for the seller and in § 2-711 for the buyer.

14.2 Section 2-703 sets forth the remedies available to a seller: (1) withholding delivery of the goods, (2) stoppage of the goods in transit, (3) resale of the goods, (4) lawsuit for damages, (5) cancellation, and (6) reclamation of the goods. Depending upon the facts, the seller has the right to elect any appropriate and available remedy.

14.3 A buyer has a number of remedies available when the seller breaches. The typical remedy is a lawsuit for damages, in which the buyer can request actual damages as well as consequential and incidental damages. Additional remedies are (1) cover, (2) specific performance, (3) replevin, (4) resale of the goods, (5) cancellation, (6) revocation of acceptance, and (7) retention of the goods with adjustments.

14.4 Parties can also agree to contractual remedies. The most common contractual remedy is a liquidated damages clause, which must be fair and not a penalty. Additionally, the parties can agree to consequential damages.

14.5 Sometimes parties indicate their intent to repudiate a contract. Section 2-610 is the guide. If a retraction of the repudiation occurs, the insecure party has a right to demand adequate assurance of performance of the contract. This demand should occur within 30 days of the retraction.

14.6 As with the common law, the Code excuses nonperformance due to impracticability. Sections 2-615 and 2-616 set forth the procedure for excuse by impracticability. Once notice is seasonably given, the contract may be terminated.

14.7 The Code has a statute of limitations for filing lawsuits. The time period cannot be shorter than one year, but suit must normally be filed within four years of the breach, unless the contract provides otherwise.

REVIEW QUESTIONS

1. What two U.C.C. sections give guidance as to the remedies available for seller and buyer?

2. List three remedies available to the seller when a buyer breaches a contract.

3. How does the Code distinguish between a private and a public sale of goods when the buyer has breached?

4. When can a lawsuit for the contract price be instituted against a buyer?

5. Under what circumstances can a seller reclaim goods in the sales contract?

6. What is the most common remedy for a buyer and why?

7. When is the remedy of cover available to a buyer?

8. What equitable remedies are available to a buyer when a seller has breached?

9. What is required by a seller who is anticipating a buyer's repudiation?

10. When circumstances render a contract impracticable, what procedures must a seller follow?

EXERCISES

1. Ocean Supplies Company is in the business of selling scuba diving equipment. Scuba Dive, Inc. ordered 500 tanks to be delivered F.O.B. seller's place of business. The goods were loaded in Miami for shipment to Newport, Rhode Island. During transit of the goods by ocean liner, Ocean Supplies finds that Scuba Dive is unable to pay for all the tanks. What remedies does Ocean Supplies have against Scuba Dive?

2. American Furniture, Inc. has agreed to buy from Chairs and Sofa, Ltd. 50 chairs for $30 apiece and 20 sofas for $200 apiece. The parties determined that in the event either party breaches the contract, the defaulting party shall pay the nondefaulting party $10,000 as liquidated damages. Is the provision enforceable? Discuss all issues.

3. Imports of America, Inc. has contracted to purchase from Liquors of the World 900 cases of 1991 Chardonnay at $45 per case. Imports prepaid the shipment of the wine. En route to its final destination in California, the ship carrying the wine sinks due to a storm at sea. What rights and remedies does Imports of America have against Liquors of the World?

PART III

Drafting Contracts

CHAPTER 15
Drafting a Contract: The Essentials

15.1 PREDRAFTING CONSIDERATIONS

Learning how to draft a contract, or any legal document, is essential to the effectiveness of any paralegal. Drafting may seem tedious, but it will be satisfying if the paralegal understands what needs to be accomplished and appreciates the value of good wordcraft. What does the client require? Are all the facts known? Are multiple parties involved? Have the parties agreed to the final contract terms? Before the drafting process can begin, the paralegal must know what the client wants and must develop a plan of organization.

Knowing What the Client Wants

In the normal course of business, clients come to an attorney's office and discuss their legal problems with the attorney and the paralegal. During the initial conference, the attorney and paralegal ask questions about the clients' needs and what the clients hope to accomplish by retaining the attorney. When a contract is involved, it is imperative that the attorney and paralegal ferret out as much information as possible regarding its terms and conditions. It is always important to determine who the parties to the contract are, how long the contract is to last, the subject matter, the general terms and conditions, any warranties of the parties, termination provisions, and any other provisions that might be important to the clients' objectives.

During the initial conference, the paralegal should take copious notes—and not rely upon memory—while determining what the clients' objectives are and recording what was communicated. Memories fade and details blur as days pass, so take comprehensive and accurate notes.

If the paralegal has some idea in advance as to the clients' needs and the purpose of the meeting, it may be prudent to do some preliminary research, such as finding a checklist of questions to be addressed or doing some background legal reading on the topic. For example, assume that you know a client is coming in to discuss setting up a new business, and one area of concern is the preparation of a confidentiality and nondisclosure agreement. Your preliminary checklist could include the following:

1. Names of parties
2. Objectives of client
3. Purpose of agreement
4. State of employment
5. Geographical restrictions
6. Period of nondisclosure
7. Information not to be disclosed.

Many reference books contain legal checklists, some of which are state-specific. Transactional guides such as *American Jurisprudence Forms, West Legal Forms,* or Rabkin and Johnson's *Corporate Forms* assist attorneys in ensuring that all the significant points that should be in the contract are covered.

It is also important for the attorney to discuss any legal ramifications that might arise from the contract provisions and to assist the client in understanding the scope of the contract. When these legal consequences are not discussed with the client and problems later arise, the attorney may inadvertently end up in a compromising situation. It is important that both attorney and paralegal be as honest as possible with respect to the legal effect of the contract by explaining the client's various options for the contract.

Knowing what the client wants and expects can minimize contract drafting problems. The initial step for effective drafting is communication and openness with the client.

15.2 DEVELOP A PLAN OF ORGANIZATION

Once both attorney and paralegal understand the client's needs, the paralegal may assist in outlining the general terms to be included in the contract. This does not necessarily mean preparing a formal outline; often the task is simply to gather general notes of guidance to ensure that all the client's needs are covered. However, it is probably a good idea, for a more complicated project, to prepare a formal outline to use as a guide in drafting. By outlining, the paralegal can set out the basic components of the contract and minimize unintentional omissions and errors. A well-structured outline can be invaluable when the contract is complex. Your outline should focus on the following points:

1. The purpose
2. The parties
3. The subject matter of the agreement
4. The terms of the agreement
5. The legal ramifications of the agreement
6. The effective date

After these general points have been set forth and applied to the client's particular needs, some general structural considerations of the instrument must be dealt with. You will normally have general provisions at the beginning of your document, followed by any special provisions between the parties. Here is a good list to follow for contract organization:

1. Title, if any
2. Statement of purpose or policy, if any
3. Definitions
4. Statement as to whom or to what the instrument applies
5. Most significant general provisions and special provisions
6. Subordinate provisions and exceptions (usually these are important enough to be stated in a separate section)
7. Default provisions, if any

8. Specific provisions relating to amendments
9. Severability clauses, if any
10. Expiration date, if any
11. Effective date, if different from the date of execution

This checklist for organization will help you avoid missing any important sections.

Once you have made your checklist, the next step is to organize the provisions in a logical sequence. For example, you would not want a definitions section in the middle of the document and termination provisions at the beginning. Logical development and presentation of the contract are important. Consequently, think about the importance and use of each section and where it should logically be placed in the contract.

15.3 CHOOSE A MODEL OR FORM

As much as attorneys would like to take credit for all the elegant and seemingly perfect language in a contract, it is well known that most attorneys and paralegals use *models* or **forms** to assist them in drafting. Many of us, without a model or form, would be lost on even begining the task of drafting. Consequently, the first thing a paralegal should do in preparing to draft a contract is locate any models or samples that the attorney may have drafted dealing with a situation similar to the present assignment. Models and samples may be drawn from old client files, and many offices also compile generic form banks containing examples of the different documents a law firm has drafted. Using models and samples will prevent the waste of valuable time.

The paralegal may also want to find some examples in what are known as *form books.* A form book has many samples of documents containing what are considered standard provisions, together with general structural guidance for arranging such documents. Often these forms have blanks to be filled in, but form contracts should always be modified to meet the specific needs of the client. Remember that these form books are only a guide; they are not carved in stone, but are designed to be flexible, so that they can be modified and adapted to any particular client's needs. Form books do, however, give the paralegal a good starting point and a good basis for assisting the attorney in drafting the contract to suit a specific client's objectives and needs.

Virtually all states have their own form books that reflect state law requirements. First examine your state-specific form books before venturing into general form books, which may not comply with your state's regulations for the particular transaction that you are to reduce to writing. Figure 15-1 lists general form books that a paralegal may want to investigate as a guide for drafting a contract.

Do not think that referring to a form book is "cheating" or an underhanded, dishonest method of drafting a contract. All attorneys use form

TERMS

form
  A printed instrument with blank spaces for the insertion of such details as may be required to make it a complete document.

American Jurisprudence Legal Forms 2d (Lawyers Coop. 1971). 25 vols. with updates.

Modern Legal Forms (West 1972). 17 vols. with updates.

Jacob Rabkin & Mark H. Johnson, et al. Current Legal Forms with Tax Analysis (Matthew Bender 1948). 22 vols. looseleaf with updates.

West Legal Forms (2d ed. 1981). 13 vols. and pocket parts.

FIGURE 15-1 Commonly used general form books

books to draft contracts and most other legal documents. Do not, however, get caught in the trap of using wording from form books or models that does not pertain to your client's needs. Your attorney and the form book authors intended that the model forms would be tailored to specific needs. Such samples were never meant to be used solely in their present forms.

15.4 LANGUAGE IN THE CONTRACT

Lawyers are notorious for using complicated, confusing, and unintelligible language in drafting documents. This **legalese** is unnecessarily complex and sometimes uses archaic language, such as "henceforth," "heretofore," "herewith," and "hereinabove." Legalese also refers to the stilted or overly formal construction of sentences, such as:

The said party is intending to purchase the said property hereforth.

This sentence is awful! It says almost nothing and does so in a needlessly complex, obscure way.

Some legal professionals nevertheless persist in using such language and construction. This habit is based partly on tradition; in very old English law, certain specific wording had to appear in a document for it to have legal effect. Those who did not use the proper "magic" phrases often lost, regardless of intent or equity.

Fortunately, such formalistic law has evolved to reflect modern attitudes and needs, and today a new method of contract drafting, known as the "plain English" movement, is gaining momentum and attention. Writing in plain English requires contract drafters to replace complex, incomprehensible legalese with simple, straightforward, understandable language.

In keeping with this trend, a number of states require that consumer contracts be written in plain English. Such states as New York, Connecticut, New Jersey, and Massachusetts have passed legislation requiring that legal documents be simplified to eliminate consumer confusion as to meaning. Figure 15-2 reproduces excerpts from the New York and Connecticut plain English law.

TERMS

legalese
The use by lawyers of specialized words or phrases, rather than plain talk, when it serves no purpose; legal jargon.

NEW YORK PLAIN ENGLISH LAW

§ 5–702. Requirements for Use of Plain Language in Consumer Transactions

a. Every written agreement entered into after November first, nineteen hundred seventy-eight, for the lease of space to be occupied for residential purposes, or to which a consumer is a party and the money, property or service which is the subject of the transaction is primarily for personal, family or household purposes must be:

1. Written in a clear and coherent manner using words with common and every day meanings;

2. Appropriately divided and captioned by its various sections.

Any creditor, seller or lessor who fails to comply with this subdivision shall be liable to a consumer who is a party to a written agreement governed by this subdivision in an amount equal to any actual damages sustained plus a penalty of fifty dollars. The total class action penalty against any such creditor, seller or lessor shall not exceed ten thousand dollars in any class action or series of class actions arising out of the use by a creditor, seller or lessor of an agreement which fails to comply with this subdivision. No action under this subdivision may be brought after both parties to the agreement have fully performed their obligation under such agreement, nor shall any creditor, seller or lessor who attempts in good faith to comply with this subdivision be liable for such penalties. This subdivision shall not apply to agreements involving amounts in excess of fifty thousand dollars nor prohibit the use of words or phrases or forms of agreement required by state or federal law, rule or regulation or by a governmental instrumentality.

b. A violation of the provisions of subdivision a of this section shall not render any such agreement void or voidable nor shall it constitute:

1. A defense to any action or proceeding to enforce such agreement; or

2. A defense to any action or proceeding for breach of such agreement.

CONNECTICUT PLAIN ENGLISH LAW

Sec. 2. (a) Every consumer contract entered into after June 30, 1980, shall be written in plain language. A consumer contract is written in plain language if it meets either the plain language tests of subsection (b) or the alternate objective tests of subsection (c). A consumer contract need not meet the tests of both subsections.

(b) A consumer contract is written in plain language if it substantially complies with all of the following tests:

(1) It uses short sentences and paragraphs; and

(2) It uses everyday words; and

(3) It uses personal pronouns, the actual or shortened names of the parties to the contract, or both, when referring to those parties; and

(4) It uses simple and active verb forms; and

(5) It uses type of readable size; and

(6) It uses ink which contrasts with the paper; and

(7) It heads sections and other subdivisions with captions which are in boldface type or which otherwise stand out significantly from the text; and

(8) It uses layout and spacing which separate the paragraphs and sections of the contract from each other and from the borders of the paper; and

(9) It is written and organized in a clear and coherent manner.

(c) A consumer contract is also written in plain language if it fully meets all of the following tests, using the procedures described in section 8 of this act:

(1) The average number of words per sentence is less than twenty-two; and

(2) No sentence in the contract exceeds fifty words; and

(3) The average number of words per paragraph is less than seventy-five; and

(4) No paragraph in the contract exceeds one hundred fifty words; and

(5) The average number of syllables per word is less than 1.55; and

(6) It uses personal pronouns, the actual or shortened names of the parties to the contract, or both, when referring to those parties; and

(7) It uses no typeface of less than eight points in size; and

(8) It allows at least three sixteenths of an inch of blank space between each paragraph and section; and

FIGURE 15-2 New York and Connecticut "plain English" laws (excerpts)

(9)   It allows at least one-half of an inch of blank space at all borders of each page; and

(10)   If the contract is printed, each section is captioned in boldface type at least ten points in size. If the contract is typewritten, each section is captioned and the captions are underlined; and

(11)   It uses an average length of line of no more than sixty-five characters.

Sec. 3.   (a) This act shall apply to all consumer contracts made, entered into or signed by the consumer in this state after June 30, 1980.

(b)   Mortgages, deeds of real estate, insurance policies and documents relating to securities transactions are not consumer contracts.

Sec. 6. (a)   The use of specific language expressly required or authorized by court decision, statute, regulation or governmental agency shall not be a violation of this act.

(b)   The use of a legal description of real property shall not be a violation of this act.

Sec. 7. (a)   A consumer contract shall remain enforceable, even though it violates this act.

Sec. 8.   Use the following procedures to determine compliance with subsection (c) of section 2 of this act:

(a)   To count the number or words in the contract, proceed as follows:

(1)   Count every word used in the text of the contract.

(2)   Do not count words or numerals used in headings, captions, signature lines, graphs or charts.

(3)   Do not count single words or phrases used to identify the information required in a fill-in section of a contract, such as "Name" or "Address."

(4)   Count as one word a contraction, hyphenated word, numeral, symbol, or abbreviation.

(5)   Do not count words which are exempt under section 6.

(b)   A sequence of words is a "sentence," if:

(1)   It expresses a complete thought, and

(2)   It contains a subject and a verb, including the implied subject "you"; and

(3)   It ends with a period. If it is an item in a list, it may end with a semi-colon. If it is an introduction to a list, it may end with a colon.

(c)   A "syllable" is a unit of spoken language consisting of one or more letters of a word, as the word is divided by any dictionary. To count the number of syllables, proceed as follows:

(1)   If there is more than one acceptable pronunciation for a word, use the one having fewer syllables.

(2)   Count abbreviations, numerals, and symbols as one-syllable words.

(d)   A sequence of words is a "paragraph," if:

(1)   It consists of one or more sentences; and

(2)   It starts on a new line; and

(3)   It is separated by at least three sixteenths of an inch of blank space from the text immediately preceding and following it.

(e)   A sequence of words is a "list," if:

(1)   Each item in the sequence is introduced by a numeral or letter; and

(2)   Each item in the sequence starts on a new line.

(f)(1)   A printed text line does not exceed sixty-five characters if the distance between the inside left and inside right margins does not exceed the width of two and one-half alphabets of the type face being used.

(2)   A text line typed at ten characters per inch does not exceed sixty-five characters if the length of the line does not exceed six and one-half inches.

(3)   A text line typed at twelve characters per inch does not exceed sixty-five characters if the length of the line does not exceed five and one-half inches.

(g)   Count the total number of words and sentences in the contract as described in this section. Then divide the number of words by the number of sentences. The result is the average number of words per sentence.

(h)   Count the total number of words and paragraphs in the contract, as described in this section. Then divide the number of words by the number of paragraphs. The result is the average number of words per paragraph.

(i)   Count the total number of syllables and words in the contract, as described in this section. Then divide the number of syllables by the number of words. The result is the average number of syllables per word.

FIGURE 15-2   *(Continued)*

(j) To count sentences and paragraphs if a list format is used, proceed as follows:

(1) Examine the introduction to the list and each item in the list to see if it is a sentence or a paragraph.

(2) Do not count as part of any sentence the words "and," "or," "if," "if and only if," or "then," if they are used to link the items of the list to each other or to the introduction.

(3) If each item in the list is a sentence, count each as a sentence. If any item is not a sentence, count the entire list as part of the sentence and paragraph containing the introduction. Do not count an item in a list as either a sentence or a paragraph if the subject or verb appears in the introduction.

(4) If each item in the list is a sentence but the introduction is not, count the introduction as part of the sentence containing the first item in the list.

(5) If each item in the list is a sentence and, in addition, each item is separated by at least three sixteenths of an inch of blank space from the sentences immediately preceding and following it, count each item as a paragraph.

FIGURE 15-2 *(Continued)*

Unfortunately, many lawyers do not use the plain English approach, and still write with technical language, convoluted sentence structure, and formal tone. When drafting, try to keep in mind that the persons who will read the contract may not be schooled in law, and may not understand the terms of the agreement if the contract is poorly drafted. Therefore, it is good practice to write in language that is understandable and straightforward. It may prevent later legal disputes.

15.5 WORD CHOICE

Words are an important component of any contract and should be chosen with care. Many people still believe that the more complicated the word, the more legal-sounding it becomes. This is clearly wrong. Legal terms often cannot be avoided; however, they can be used so that they can be understood within the context of the sentence in which they occur. It is not necessary to use a formal legal term when a simple word will suffice. Figure 15-3 contains examples of straightforward terms to substitute for traditional legalese.

Term	Substitute Term
Assist or assistance	Help
Endeavor	Try
Forthwith	Immediately
Institute	Begin or Start
Subsequent or subsequently	Later
Utilize	Use

FIGURE 15-3 Substitute terms for legalese

These are just a few examples of how a simple word can be substituted for a technical term.

Remember, though, that legal words sometimes have specific and necessary meanings and that any substitute may change the meaning of the sentence or document. Such words are known as **terms of art**. When a word is used as a term of art, it should not be changed, but perhaps it should be explained in the context in which it is used or a definitions section. The following are some frequently used terms of art.

life estate	laches	duces tecum
quiet title	sua sponte	habeas corpus
domicile		

Other words that should be avoided as legal gobbledygook are very formal words that have little or no legal significance or are really only an affectation. The following words can almost always be avoided without consequence:

abovementioned	aforementioned	aforesaid	henceforth
hereinafter	hereunto	said	thereunto
wheresoever	whosoever	within-named	

Another bad habit legal professionals have is using two words when one is sufficient. The use of such words is redundant and can be avoided without changing the meaning of the document. Common redundancies in legal drafting include:

assumes and agrees	bind and obligate
for and in behalf of	each and every
kind and character	

Again, these word combinations are commonly seen in legal documents, but they really should be replaced by single words when drafting. By paying attention to these combinations, redundancy can be eliminated and the contract made easier to understand.

Ambiguity

When writing, be sure your intent is being conveyed clearly. *Say what you mean.* Vague or unclear phrases and words create *ambiguity,* which means that a reader can interpret the sentence or word in more than one way. Ambiguous writing lacks clarity and precision and results in confusion. Precise writing is important, especially when drafting contracts. If a person is to assume an obligation, say so. Do not dance around the subject with words that create uncertainty. Ambiguous drafting may even result in a lawsuit, which would have been unnecessary had the contract been more carefully drafted.

Contractions

In formal writing, contractions are inappropriate. Although use of a contraction may seem more familiar, legal drafting has not gotten to the point where the informality of contractions is acceptable. Stay away from them.

Neutralizing Terminology: Bias-Free Writing

The use of the word *he,* although traditionally neutral, has now come under attack as sexist. Using *he* to refer generally to a person such as a lawyer, judge, or doctor is seen as reinforcing gender-specific stereotypes. Therefore, to avoid inappropriate or offensive pronouns, try one of these methods: (1) pluralize; (2) use "he or she"; (3) specify.

Using the plural form avoids any gender-specific references. For example:

> *Biased:*   Before a judge signs an order, he reviews it.
> *Neutral:*   Before judges sign orders, they review them.

An alternative to pluralizing is using the construction "he or she." Some object to the awkwardness of this phrasing, but it is currently widely accepted and used.

A better option, particularly when drafting a contract, is to specify. If a party to the contract is a male, *he* is perfectly acceptable. A group or corporation has no gender, so use short references such as "the Company," "ABC Co.," or simply "it." Such specificity often avoids not only biased writing but also ambiguity.

15.6 GRAMMATICAL STRUCTURES IN THE CONTRACT

When the word *grammar* is mentioned, we tend to think of the grade-school horrors we suffered when the subject was introduced. But proper grammar is a necessary component of drafting any documents, including contracts. Proper sentence structure, verb tenses, and punctuation are critical, so a brief review of some general grammar points is necessary.

Sentence Structure

The nucleus of any legal document is the sentences created by the writer. Sentences are the lifeline of communication. They are built from the basic subject, verb, and object format. Recall that the subject is the actor, the verb is the action, and the object is the recipient or focus of the action. Keep subject and verb close together for clarity. Too many words confuse the reader and cause ambiguity problems. However, when writing, do not use only the subject/verb/object construction. Words can also modify or explain. Such words are *adjectives* and *adverbs.* More complex sentence construction employs clauses to describe the subject of the sentence or create compound sentences. The choice is yours as long as your communication is clear.

TERMS

term of art
Technical words; words or expressions that have a particular meaning in a particular science or profession.

Voice and Tense

Related to sentence structure is the verb tense or *voice*. The general rule is to write in the active voice rather than the passive voice. To maintain the active voice, have the subject of the sentence do the action, rather than receive the action. Ask who did what, rather than what was done by whom. Figure 15-4 provides illustrations.

Active Voice	Passive Voice
The court decided to rule.	The decision to rule was made by the court.
The defendant presented the evidence.	The evidence was presented by the defendant.
The jury deliberated the fate of the defendant.	The fate of the defendant was deliberated by the jury.

FIGURE 15-4 Active versus passive voice

Parallel Construction

Another grammatical rule that we all have violated at one time or another is the requirement of parallel construction. When making a list of items, the following occurs:

Today I ran to the court, started finishing final drafts, and began to draft a new lawsuit.

This example lacks parallelism because the verbs are all in different tenses. To have parallel structure, the sentence should read:

Today I ran to the court, finished final drafts, and drafted a new lawsuit.

All the verbs are in the same tense—they are parallel. Adhere to parallel structures in your drafting, especially when creating lists.

Run-On Sentences and Sentence Fragments

Run-on sentences have too many components, whereas a sentence fragment has too few. Although long sentences can be grammatically correct, they tend to be difficult to follow. If a sentence goes on for four or five lines, break it into two. It will be clearer and less likely to contain grammatical errors. A fragment, in contrast, does not complete a thought. The omission and imprecision usually result in an ambiguity.

Punctuation

Knowing how to use and where to place commas, semicolons and other punctuation marks is critical to drafting any contract or other legal document.

Commas A comma is one of the most important tools of punctuation. Commas are used to separate thoughts, create pauses, and set off a series or transitional phrase. Some basic rules for the use of commas are:

1. In a series of three or more terms, use a comma after each term except the last.
2. Use a comma before a conjunction such as *because, while,* or *since.*
3. Use a comma to set off a transitional word or phrase, such as *therefore, however, consequently, furthermore.*
4. Commas should precede and follow abbreviations such as *Esq., Jr.,* and the like.
5. A comma should precede abbreviations such as *Ltd., Co.,* and *Inc.*

Apostrophes The apostrophe is used to show possessives and contractions. When showing a possessive for a singular noun, add an apostrophe followed by an *s.* Although there are some exceptions with plural names, the general rule is simply to add an apostrophe.

The apostrophe is also used in contractions, to take the place of omitted letters. In formal legal writing, contractions should not be used. However, the most notable error is committed with the contraction *it's.* Too many students confuse the possessive pronoun *its* with the contraction *it's* (it is). The best way to avoid this embarrassing error is to try substituting "it is" in the sentence where *its* or *it's* is used. If the sentence makes no sense when you substitute "it is," then the word to use is the possessive pronoun—omit the apostrophe. For example, look at the sentence: "The court abused its discretion." If the contraction *it's* were used, the sentence would read, "The court abused it is [it's] discretion." Now that sentence makes no sense. Therefore, no apostrophe should be used.

Semicolons Semicolons are often used to join the clauses of a *compound sentence.* If two sentences could stand alone but are related, a semicolon can be used.

Colons Colons are used to introduce information, such as an explanation, list, or quotation. Words like "the following" or "as follows" usually take a colon preceding the next text item.

Parentheses Parentheses are used to set off an explanation or comment that refers to but is not part of the preceding sentence. Parentheses are also used to introduce acronyms or shortened references for a name or position.

Hyphens Hyphens are used to connect two words to form a single word. In some terms which once were hyphenated, the hyphen is now eliminated. Check a dictionary to determine appropriate modern practice.

Stay away from using hyphens with the prefixes *anti, co, inter, multi, non, para, post, pre, re, semi,* and *super.* If the second word is capitalized, then a hyphen can be used.

Incorrect	Correct
Para-legal	Paralegal
Post-mortem	Postmortem
Semi-annual	Semiannual
Multi-purpose	Multipurpose

Capitalization Another common problem in writing is when to capitalize a word. The obvious ones we all know, such as proper names, street addresses, cities, and the days of the week. But there are times when we are not sure whether to capitalize a name or word. You should:

1. Capitalize names of governmental bodies when referring to a specific unit by its full name.
2. Capitalize counties and administrative divisions.
3. Capitalize words used in association with a governmental act.

Brady Bill	Senate Resolution 4321
the Freedom of Information Act	the Warren Commission Report

15.7 EDITING AND REWRITING

Editing is an element of drafting any document. It is important to critically evaluate your work product to make it better. Editing often requires rewriting. Sections of the contract may have to be reworked, rewritten, and changed before the draft can be finalized. Many of us, in high school or college, wrote papers and then went directly to the typewriter to transcribe them. It never entered our minds to change a word or modify any part of a first draft. Your thinking needs to change. Editing and revising are crucial parts of the drafting process. It is virtually impossible for any legal document to be prepared in one draft, and may require three, four, or more drafts.

When editing, look for substantive accuracy and errors in grammar, punctuation, spelling, and sentence structure. Also be sure that your language is clear, precise, and, most importantly, understandable. Ensure that all the headings and subheadings flow logically and that each numbered section is in sequential order. When appropriate, use plain English; unless you are using terms of art that cannot be changed, stay away from legalese. Use the active voice whenever possible, and be consistent with verb tenses. Most importantly, when you are editing, *edit!* Cut out language that is unnecessary; be as precise and concise in your presentation as possible. Editing and rewriting must be taken seriously and accounted for in the time alloted to a project. Figure 15-5 shows some editing marks that will assist word processors or typists in making appropriate changes.

do not change; leave as is	(stet), ...	hyphen	‿ = ‿
		en dash	$\frac{1}{N}$
insert	∧	em dash	$\frac{1}{M}$
delete	ℐ	semicolon	⨀
delete and close up	ℐ︵	colon	⨀
close up	‿	quotation marks	ˇˇ
paragraph	¶	apostrophe	ˇ
no paragraph	no ¶	insert space	#∧
move up	⊓	superscript	ˇ
move down	⊔	caps	(caps), ≡
move left	⊏	lowercase	(lc), /
move right	⊐	small caps	(sc), =
center	⊐ ⊏	bold face	(bf), ⌇
transpose	(tr), ∪	italic	(ital), ___
period	⊙	roman	(rom)
comma	∧	wrong font	(wf)

FIGURE 15-5 Common editing/proofreading marks

15.8 PRACTICAL APPLICATION

There are no hard and fast rules to follow when drafting a contract, but following certain steps helps. Here is a checklist:

1. Write down the client's goals and objectives
2. Prepare a detailed outline
3. Find a form or model to follow
4. Review the form or model and modify it to satisfy the client's needs
5. Review the form or model for legalese; eliminate it if possible
6. Explain or define terms of art and legal terms
7. Avoid awkward construction
8. Check for proper grammar
9. Check for punctuation
10. Edit
11. Review
12. Re-edit
13. Submit final product for review by attorney.

If these steps are followed, the paralegal's task will be accomplished with more ease and precision.

SUMMARY

15.1 In drafting a contract, it is important to determine the client's needs. Seek out all the pertinent information to complete the contract; this may include doing some research. Creating a checklist is helpful to be sure all necessary points are covered in the contract.

15.2 Proper organization is critical to any contract. In more complicated transactions, a detailed outline may be appropriate, with specific provisions set forth. After you have created the outline, organize the provisions in a logical order.

15.3 Often a paralegal will use a guide to draft a contract. The best legal guides are form books or models. Both models and forms should be adapted to the needs of the current client. Be flexible in using forms or models.

15.4 Legal jargon is known as legalese. Avoid legalese if plain English can be used. Plain English is more understandable and is mandated in some states for consumer contracts.

15.5 Choose words carefully when drafting a contract. Stay away from formal legal words when simple ones will suffice. When a legal word has to be used, such as a term of art, try to explain its meaning in the context in which it is used. Also, avoid using redundant word combinations when one word will communicate your intention. Watch for ambiguity and sexist or biased writing, and avoid the use of contractions in contract drafting.

15.6 Sentences should be created so that they are understandable. Most sentences are built from the subject/verb/object format. Watch for nonparallel construction and run-on or fragmented sentences. In addition, pay close attention to punctuation and capitalization.

15.7 Editing is part of writing. It is a necessary prerequisite in preparing any contract. When editing, look for substantive accuracy, and errors in grammar, punctuation, spelling, and sentence structure. Use plain English when possible and write in the active voice.

REVIEW QUESTIONS

1. What information should a legal professional obtain from the client before drafting a contract?
2. Identify what should be included in a preliminary checklist for an employment contract.
3. List some of the points that should be considered when drafting a contract.
4. When drafting a contract, what sources can you use to assist in completing your task?
5. Define the term *legalese.*
6. What is a term of art?
7. Identify some writing traps to avoid.
8. Which tense should a paralegal write in and why?
9. Distinguish between a run-on sentence and a sentence fragment.
10. What is the most commonly misused contraction and why?

EXERCISES

1. Find a sample contract (you can use one from a form book, a model from a lawyer's office, or even one previously used in a legal transaction). Identify all the legalese and then rewrite those provisions in plain English.
2. Determine the errors and correct the following:
   a. The court will announce it's findings in due time.
   b. Prior to the attorney presenting his argument, he began to review his notes, doing some legal research, preparing his presentation and practiced his argument.
   c. One of the tasks of a paralegal is to take proficient notes while in a conference and reviewing the notes with the attorney and then to assist the attorney in drafting the final product for the client's review.

    d. Finding many of the objectives impossible to achieve because of the complexity of the project.

3. Edit the following paragraph:

    The buyer agrees purchased that certain parcel of land herein located on the northwest corner of Sycamore Street with said parcel of land being located therein the within City of Manchester, state of New Hampshire. The said stated purchase price between the specified parties having agreed at $450,000 to be paid under the following terms and conditions which is hereby acknowledged.

CHAPTER 16

Drafting a Contract: Specific Provisions

OUTLINE

16.1 THE GENERAL CONTRACTUAL AGREEMENT

Certain provisions are commonly included in a final contract. These provisions include identification of the parties, definitions of terms, representations, conditions, duration, termination, payment, guarantees and indemnities, limitations of liability, time of the essence, liquidated damages, restrictive covenants, arbitration, release of liability, merger or integration, choice of governing law, choice of forum, assignability, and notice. All these are discussed in this chapter, to give the paralegal guidance as to some of the basic provisions to consider when drafting a contract.

Identity of the Parties

The introductory paragraph identifies the correct names and capacities of the persons or entities that are parties to the contract. This section is important because an individual has different liability than a corporation, and a corporate officer acting as an agent of the corporation has different liability than that same person acting as an individual. It is incumbent upon the paralegal to clearly identify the parties in their proper legal capacities.

After the parties are formally identified, it is often appropriate to use shorthand references for them. This is usually done in a parenthetical that identifies the parties as "seller" or "buyer," or by their last names only. An acronym is often used to shorten a long name. It is important to clearly state any shorthand name used for easy identification throughout the contract. Figure 16-1 gives examples of typical party identifications as used in contracts.

INTRODUCTORY PARAGRAPH

AGREEMENT made this 12th day of December, 1995, between ABC Corporation, a Delaware corporation qualified to transact business in Texas, having its principal place of business at 5560 Wind Street, Harris County, Texas (hereinafter referred to as the Company) and John Smith, residing at 4739 West Seventh Street, Fort Worth, Tarrant County, Texas (hereinafter called Smith).

METHODS OF DESCRIBING PARTIES

Individual: Richard Rye, residing at 2200 Harrison Street, Wichita Falls, Wichita County, Texas

Sole Proprietor: Richard Rye, doing business under the assumed name of Pets Galore or as Richard Rye's Pets Galore

General or Limited Partnership: Pets Galore, Ltd., a Texas limited partnership doing business under the firm name and style of _____ or composed of _____ and _____

Corporation: Pets Galore Corp., a Texas corporation [if foreign, add: qualified to transact business in Texas]

FIGURE 16-1 Sample party identifications

Definitions Section

Defining terms in the contract can be important for clarity. If terms are defined, little is left open to question by the parties. Most definitions sections are tailored to the specific contract, but some general words that often are defined are given in Figure 16-2.

---

1. Where _____ the [word or term or phrase] _____ appears in this contract it shall be construed to mean _____.

2. Unless otherwise provided in this agreement, the word "year" shall be construed to mean a calendar year of 365 days, the word "month" shall be construed to mean a calendar month, the word "week" shall be construed to mean a calendar week of 7 days, and the word "day" shall be construed to mean a period of 24 hours running from midnight to midnight.

3. The use of the singular form of expression shall be construed to include the plural when the meaning so requires.

4. Feminine or neuter pronouns shall be substituted for those of masculine form or vice versa, and the plural shall be substituted for the single number or vice versa in any place or places in which the context may require such substitution.

5. The use of the masculine gender shall be construed to include the feminine gender.

6. The clause headings appearing in this agreement have been inserted for the purpose of convenience and ready reference. They do not purport to and shall not be deemed to define, limit, or extend the scope or intent of the clauses to which they appertain.

FIGURE 16-2 Common general definitions

Representations and Conditions

Any material facts or representations that the client is relying upon to enter into the contract should be set forth in a section entitled "Representations and Conditions." This provides a basis for the parties' understanding of the contract and shows what facts they are relying upon in entering the contract. This section has important legal ramifications. For example, if issues such as fraud or misrepresentation arise, it may provide a basis for substantiating or negating those allegations.

Representations are often conditioned upon a certain event happening before final execution of the contract. If this is the case, it is important to use language to create conditions, such as those discussed in Chapter 8. Remember that terms such as *if, when, after, on condition that, provided that, subject to, unless,* and *until* suggest that an event must happen before the contract comes into effect. The language chosen for a condition can greatly affect the extent of a party's liability, whether past, present, or future.

Duration

The time period for which the contract will last—its *duration*—should be specifically stated so that the parties know and understand the term of the contract. Omission can pose serious problems. For example, if the contract is intended to last for only one year, that should be clearly stated within the contract. If this provision is left out, the length of the contract might be determined by what is "reasonable," or it could be considered terminable at the will of either party. Similarly, any provisions whereby the parties agree to extend the time of the contract should be expressly noted in the contract as well. This often occurs in lease agreements. For instance, a contract is made for five years and the parties are given an option to renew or extend the lease for another period of five years.

When automatic renewals are included in a contract, it is important to determine the length of the term and how the option or automatic renewal is to be implemented. Often this can be done by one party giving notice of the decision to exercise the renewal or to not exercise the option within a certain period of time prior to the original contract's expiration. Figure 16-3 provides illustrations.

---

(1) Unless either party notifies the other by registered mail, at least 60 days before the expiration of this agreement, of its intention not to renew and continue the agreement, such term shall be automatically extended for a period of one year. In such event, all the terms and provisions of the agreement shall remain in full force and effect during the extension period, except that there shall be no automatic renewal after the expiration of the extension period.

(2) Unless terminated on notice, the rights and privileges granted, together with all other provisions of this contract, shall continue in full force and effect for an additional term of one year from the date of expiration, unless either party, at least 60 days prior to the date of expiration, shall notify the other party in writing that it does not desire the contract to be extended for such additional period.

FIGURE 16-3 Sample renewal and expiration clauses

Termination Provisions

Certain contingencies that arise during the term of a contract often afford a party the right to end the contract. Sometimes situations simply do not work out and, therefore, the parties desire to terminate the contract. This right should be stated in the contract. Typically there will be a provision allowing either party to terminate the contract upon 30 days' notice to the other party (or some other time period). Additionally, there are a number of events that might give rise to the right to terminate, such as insolvency, bankruptcy, or death of one of the parties, as well as nonperformance by one of the parties. There are a myriad of different provisions that set out the various contingencies for termination. These should be examined closely, as this could be one of the most important provisions of a contract. Figure 16-4 sets forth some drafting alternatives.

Performance

A contract must set forth the rights and obligations of the parties with respect to the performance that is required of each of them under the

Termination upon Notice. This agreement may be terminated by either party by giving [specify time requirement, if any, e.g., thirty (30) days] written notice thereof to the other party.

Termination for Unsatisfactory Performance. If [party to whom performance is due] at any time shall become dissatisfied with the performance of [party rendering performance] under this agreement, he or she shall have the right to terminate this agreement by giving written notice thereof to [party rendering performance].

Termination upon Happening of Event. In the event that [specify event, e.g., renewal financing is not obtained], [party] may terminate this agreement by giving notification thereof by registered or certified mail to [other party].

Termination upon Payment of Stipulated Sum. This agreement may be terminated [specify time period, e.g., at any time during the first year] by either of the parties hereto by the payment of [amount] to the other party as compensation for relinquishing its rights hereunder.

Automatic Termination. This agreement shall remain in full force and effect for a period of [time period, e.g., five (5) years], and shall terminate automatically at the end of such period unless [specify condition of renewal, e.g., (party) shall give written notice of its intention to renew the agreement for a like period to (other party), such notice to be given at least ninety (90) days prior to the expiration of such initial term].

Termination upon Failure to Cure Default. If [obligor] shall default in the performance of any of the terms or conditions of this agreement, he or she shall have [specify time period, e.g., ten (10) days] after delivery of written notice of such default within which to cure such default. If he or she fails to cure the default within such period of time, then [obligee] shall have the right without further notice to terminate this agreement.

Termination for Default. If [obligor] defaults in the performance of this agreement or materially breaches any of its provisions, [obligee] shall have the option to terminate this agreement by giving written notification thereof by registered or certified mail to [obligor]. For the purposes hereof, the following actions shall constitute material breaches of this agreement: [specify].

FIGURE 16-4 Sample termination clauses

contract. Specifically enumerating these obligations, not leaving anything to chance, is important to the parties' participation in the contract.

Time for Performance

In many instances, the contract will require a specific time for performance. This may be critical, as a delay in performance could be damaging to one of the parties. The best approach when the time of performance is critical is to set out any contingencies related to the performance itself. It is important to distinguish such things as strikes, earthquakes, flood, fire, and governmental regulation, which are unavoidable but may negatively affect performance, without creating liability for default. Standard provisions are given in Figure 16-5.

Payment

For some, the most important provision of the contract concerns payment. The person to whom payment is due, the time due, the amount, and

> **Force Majeure.** In the event that [party] shall be prevented from completing performance of its obligations by an act of God or any other occurrence whatsoever which is beyond the control of the parties hereto, then [party] shall be excused from any further performance of its obligations and undertakings hereunder.
>
> OR
>
> In the event that performance by [party] of any of its obligations or undertakings hereunder shall be interrupted or delayed by any occurrence not occasioned by the conduct of either party hereto, whether such occurrence be an act of God or the common enemy or the result of war, riot, civil commotion, sovereign conduct, or the act or conduct of any person or persons not party or privy hereto, then [party] shall be excused from such performance for such period of time as is reasonably necessary after such occurrence to remedy the effects thereof.

FIGURE 16-5 Sample time of performance and force majeure clauses

any conditions for payment must be set forth. One typical payment schedule is an **installment** contract, under which payments are made incrementally until the agreed balance is paid. If payments are missed, it is appropriate to provide an **acceleration clause** requiring immediate payment of the remaining balance together with any interest or charges due. It is also common to include a provision for opportunity to cure the default after notice, typically 10 to 45 days after notice has been sent to the person in default. Depending on how the provision is drafted, the notice period can begin either upon receipt or as of the date of the notice. This is negotiable: determine what is best for your client.

Another payment consideration, which favors the debtor, is a provision that does not penalize the debtor for early payment of the amount due or prepayment of interest. Illustrations of payment provisions are shown in Figure 16-6.

> **Payment Due.** Contractor will pay subcontractor, on or before [date], the sum of [amount] which, at the option of subcontractor, shall be a condition precedent to the performance of the contract.
> **Time for Payment.** Payment of [amount] under this contract shall be made at subcontractor's place of business on or before [date].
> **Time for Payment—Installment Payments.** Contractor agrees to pay to subcontractor the sum of [amount], on or before [date], and the sum of [amount] thereafter as follows: monthly at [amount] per month until paid.
> It is further agreed that in case of failure of contractor to make any of the mentioned payments, or to perform any of the mentioned covenants on such party's part to be made and performed, then subcontractor may declare this contract null and void, and all payments already made by contractor shall be retained by subcontractor; or subcontractor, on performing the covenants and agreements on such party's part to be performed, shall be entitled to recover the sums as above set forth from contractor, and all costs and expenses, as well as interest from the time the above payments shall have become due and payable.

FIGURE 16-6 Sample payment provisions

Indemnification

An **indemnification** clause, or "hold harmless" clause, is an essential provision that can benefit both parties. Indemnification provisions allow for reimbursement of funds, expenses, and attorney fees when there is a loss or the potential for loss. When drafting an indemnification provision, consider your objective. As a general rule, draft the clause as broadly as possible to cover any possible contingency.

If the indemnification is triggered, a party may have to expend monies in defending a lawsuit. It is prudent to include a notice provision telling the **indemnitor** that if a third party raises a claim, the indemnitor will have the opportunity to defend or participate in the defense as deemed appropriate. Some indemnity provisions are given in Figure 16-7.

Indemnity. Indemnitor shall indemnify and save harmless indemnitee and its agents and employees from all suits, actions, or claims of any character, type, or description brought or made for or on account of any injuries or damages received or sustained by any person, persons, or property, arising out of or occasioned by the negligent acts of indemnitor or its agents or employees, in the execution or performance of this contract.

OR

[When the parties intend that the indemnification shall be unlimited]

[Indemnitee] shall not be liable or responsible for and shall be saved and held harmless by indemnitor from and against any and all claims and damages of every kind, for injury to or death of any person or persons and for damage to or loss of property, arising out of or attributed, directly or indirectly, to the operations or performance of indemnitor under this agreement.

FIGURE 16-7 Sample indemnity clauses

Limitation of Liability

The occurrence of certain events may limit the performance of the parties to a contract. As with termination, limitations of liability are often found in **force majeure** clauses, which limit or completely excuse performance of a contract due to acts of God, such as floods, hurricanes, and earthquakes, or events such as war and strikes.

To provide complete limitation and exoneration from unforeseen events, an **exculpatory clause** is advisable. Here, parties are relieved from liability for events out of their control, including fires, mechanical breakdowns, lockouts, riots, and other unpredictable events.

Liability limitations can also be drafted for damages, such as consequential damages or negligence. If a limitation is appropriate, it should be drafted into the contract.

TERMS

installment
A payment of money due, the balance of which is to be paid at other agreed-upon times.

acceleration clause
A clause in a note, mortgage, or other contract which provides that the entire debt will become due if payment is not made on time or if other conditions of the agreement are not met.

indemnification
1. The act of indemnifying or being indemnified. 2. Payment made by way of compensation for a loss.

indemnitor
A person who indemnifies another.

force majeure
A force that humans can neither resist, foresee, nor prevent; an act of God. Some contracts contain a force majeure clause which excuses nonperformance if the contract cannot be performed because of the occurrence of an unforeseeable and irresistible event.

exculpatory clause
A clause in a contract or other legal document excusing a party from liability for his or her wrongful act.

Time of the Essence

Time-of-the-essence provisions have not been strictly enforced by courts. Although such a statement may be clear, the tendency of courts is to forgo enforcement of these provisions, especially if the delay in performance was not essential to the purposes of the contract. Therefore, determine whether time is of the essence for your client; if it is, be sure to include such a specific provision. If this condition is essential to performance of the contract, it is important to include that as well. That way, if performance is not accomplished by the time specified in the contract, the injured party will have the right to cancel and/or pursue its rights in a court of law. See Figure 16-8 for an example.

---

(1) **Time is of Essence—Option.** It is understood and agreed that time is of the essence in this option agreement, and that the option set out must be exercised on or before [date]. If the option is not exercised before the expiration of such time, all rights to exercise it shall cease.

(2) Time is of the essence in this contract; and in case either party shall fail to perform the agreements on such party's part to be performed at the time fixed for performance by the terms of this contract, the other party may elect to terminate the contract.

FIGURE 16-8 Sample time-of-essence provisions

Liquidated Damages

When the parties to a contract are uncertain about the amount of possible damages, or damage amounts are difficult to ascertain, it is not unusual for the parties to agree in advance to a specific damage amount in the hope of avoiding a lawsuit. What is important in determining whether a liquidated damages clause is valid is the reasonableness of the estimate of the liquidated damages. If the liquidated damages clause is grossly disproportionate to the possible damage that could occur between the parties, it is highly unlikely that a court will enforce it. Courts will not enforce a liquidated damage clause that is really a punishment or penalty. Careful drafting of liquidated damages clauses is thus very important. Some illustrations are provided in Figure 16-9 (see also Chapter 9).

---

(1) **Liquidated Damages Provision** [General Liquidated Damages Clause]. It is agreed by the parties that the actual damages which might be sustained by [obligee] by reason of the breach by [obligor] of its promise to [specify performance, e.g., make delivery within ninety (90) days] are uncertain and would be difficult to ascertain. It is further agreed that the sum of [specify amount, e.g., $1,000 or $10 for each day that delivery is overdue] would be reasonable and just compensation for such breach. Therefore, [obligor]

FIGURE 16-9 Sample liquidated damages clauses

hereby promises to pay and [obligee] hereby agrees to accept such sum as liquidated damages, and not as a penalty, in the event of such breach.

(2) [Liquidated Damages Provision for Delay in Performance of Construction Contract]. It is understood and agreed that, if said project is not completed within the time specified in the Contract plus any extensions of time allowed pursuant thereto, the actual damages sustained by the Owner because of any such delay will be uncertain and difficult to ascertain. It is agreed that the reasonable foreseeable value of the use of said project by the Owner would be the sum of [amount] per day; and therefore the Contractor shall pay as liquidated damages to the Owner the sum of [amount] per day for each day's delay in fully completing said project beyond the time specified in the Contract and any extensions of such time allowed thereunder.

FIGURE 16-9 *(Continued)*

Restrictive Covenants

The buyer of a business often wants to restrict the seller's right to carry on or participate in the same business for a certain period of time and in a specific geographic area. The paralegal must determine what the state laws are regarding restrictive covenants. Many states have set out guidelines regarding what length of time and what areas will be considered reasonable. Case law is very specific, and if a covenant is drafted too broadly, it is very possible that it could be declared void.

It is also possible that a restrictive covenant would be needed in an employment contract. Normally the same standards apply with regard to employment covenants: they must be reasonable with respect to time and geographic limitation. Again, it is important for the paralegal to check state law with respect to the extent of any restrictive covenant.

Arbitration

Arbitration has become a common means of settling disputes, as parties attempt to resolve their differences without resorting to the courtroom. Arbitration is sanctioned under the Federal Arbitration Act. If arbitration is desired, determine whether your state recognizes arbitration by statute or case law, and whether it is an enforceable method of dispute resolution.

In certain contracts, arbitration is agreed to be the exclusive remedy. If this is the case, the American Arbitration Association suggests the following language:

> Any controversy or claim arising out of or relating to this contract, or the breach thereof, shall be settled by arbitration in accordance with the rules of the American Arbitration Association, and judgment upon the award rendered by the arbitrator(s) may be entered in any court having jurisdiction thereof.

This provision can be modified according to the needs of the parties and the requirements of a particular industry. Additional examples are in Figure 16-10.

TERMS

arbitration
A method of settling disputes by submitting a disagreement to a person (an arbitrator) or a group of individuals (an arbitration panel) for decision instead of going to court. If the parties are required to comply with the decision of the arbitrator, the process is called binding arbitration; if there is no such obligation, the arbitration is referred to as nonbinding arbitration. Compulsory arbitration is required by law, most notably in labor disputes.

> (1) Any controversy or claim arising out of or relating to this contract, or the breach thereof, except [specify exceptions, e.g., controversies involving less than $1,000] shall be settled by arbitration in accordance with the rules of the American Arbitration Association, and judgment upon the award rendered by the arbitrators may be entered in any court having jurisdiction thereof.
>
> (2) **Short Form—Texas General Arbitration Act.** As concluded by the parties hereto upon the advice of counsel, and as evidenced by the signatures of the parties hereto and the signatures of their respective attorneys, any controversy between the parties hereto involving the construction or application of any of the terms, covenants, or conditions of this agreement, shall be submitted to arbitration on the written request of one party served upon the other, and such arbitration shall comply with and be governed by the provisions of the Texas General Arbitration Act.

FIGURE 16-10   Sample arbitration provisions

Merger Clauses

A provision that appears in virtually all contracts is a *merger* or *integration clause*. A merger clause states that everything in the agreement is what the parties finally agreed to and anything that contradicts the agreement was not a part of the agreement and therefore is not part of the contract.

Usually, as part of the merger provisions, there is a provision regarding modification. It is best to require that any modification of a contract be written rather than oral. Oral modification is likely to pose enforceability problems, especially if one party challenges whether the modification actually took place. Figure 16-11 exhibits some merger clauses.

> **Disavowal of intent to modify earlier contract.**   It is understood that this agreement shall in no way act as a waiver of any of the conditions and obligations imposed on the parties by the earlier contract executed between them, and any rights that either of the parties may have by virtue of such earlier contract are to be considered as in full force and effect.
>
> **Changes in printed portion of contract.**   No change, addition, or erasure of any printed portion of this agreement shall be valid or binding on either party.
>
> ### Integration
>
> 1. The documents that constitute the agreement between the parties are attached hereto and made a part of this agreement and consist of the following:
>   (a) This document, numbering _____ pages
>   (b) Exhibits to this agreement, numbering _____ through _____.
>   (c) Other _____.
> 2. This instrument embodies the whole agreement of the parties. There are no promises, terms, conditions, or obligations other than those contained herein; and this contract shall supersede all previous communications, representations, or agreements, either verbal or written, between the parties.

FIGURE 16-11   Sample modification and integration clauses

Choice of Governing Law and Choice of Forum

A standard contract provision is the one determining which state's law will govern if any disputes arise between the parties. As part of the contract, the parties name the jurisdiction in which a lawsuit or dispute is to be filed, unless some case law otherwise governs. Such provisions are usually enforced.

The parties can determine not only what laws will apply, but also where suit may be filed (known as **venue**). Ordinarily, such a clause states where a lawsuit is to be filed and which laws will govern. Figure 16-12 sets forth some choice-of-law provisions.

Venue.   The obligations and undertakings of each of the parties to this agreement shall be performable at [specify place such as state or county].

Choice of Law.   This agreement shall be governed and construed in accordance with the laws of [state].

OR

The validity of this agreement, and of any of its terms or provisions, as well as the rights and duties of the parties hereunder, shall be interpreted and construed pursuant to, and in accordance with, the laws of [state].

OR

It is expressly agreed and stipulated that this contract shall be deemed to have been made and to be performable in [specify jurisdiction, e.g., the state of Texas], and all questions concerning the validity, interpretation, or performance of any of its terms or provisions, or of any rights or obligations of the parties hereto, shall be governed by and resolved in accordance with the laws of [state or country].

FIGURE 16-12   Sample choice-of-law provisions

Assignability

It is normally important for the parties to determine whether the type of contract they are making can be assigned to another party. Ordinarily, contracts involving personal services are not assignable. If the parties determine that notice and opportunity to approve of the **assignee** are necessary, then that should be designated in the assignment clause. Typical assignment provisions are found in Chapter 10.

Notice

Contracts frequently require that the parties give notice to each other upon the happening of certain events. These provisions are very important because they dictate when a default has occurred and may trigger the right to an opportunity to cure. The notice must be specific as to when it is effective, such as on the date of mailing or upon the date of receipt. It is also important to set forth the manner or method of giving notice—for example, delivery by

TERMS

venue
    The county or judicial district in which a case is to be tried. In civil cases, venue may be based on where the events giving rise to the cause of action took place or where the parties live or work. . . . Venue is distinguishable from jurisdiction because it is an issue only if jurisdiction already exists and because, unlike jurisdiction, it can be waived or changed by consent of the parties.

assignee
    A person to whom a right is assigned.

registered or certified mail or, if appropriate, by hand. Often, notice is also sent to the attorneys of record or any other persons who may have an interest in the contract. Be complete and accurate with your designations. Figure 16-13 gives some examples.

---

    (1) Any notice to be given hereunder by either party to the other shall be in writing and may be effected by [personal delivery in writing or registered or certified mail, return receipt requested]. Notice to [name of party] shall be sufficient if made or addressed to [specify address], and to [other party] at [address]. Each party may change the address for notice by giving notice of such change in accordance with the provisions of this paragraph.

    (2) Whenever in this agreement it shall be required or permitted that notice be given by either party to the other, such notice must be in writing and must be given personally or by certified mail addressed as follows: [specify].

Time of Notice. Every notice under this agreement shall be deemed to have been given at the time it is deposited in the United States mail, as determined by the postmark.

FIGURE 16-13 Sample notice provisions

Signatures of Parties and Date

One of the most important parts of the contract is the signature section showing the parties' assent to the contract. Be sure that the signature block for the parties is appropriate to their capacities. If they are signing as individuals, the contract should so state. If a party is signing in a corporate capacity, that should also be noted. In addition, often it is required that the document be signed before a **notary public**, an official who attests to the genuineness of documents. The need for notarization is normally determined by the parties to the contract.

The contract must be dated. This date normally determines the effective date of the contract, so any legal ramifications flow from the date of signing. Be sure that there is no question as to the date.

Sometimes contracts require that they be witnessed. It is important that these sections be specifically designated and entitled "Witness." Witnesses usually have to be disinterested parties, that is, persons who have no interest in the contract. Figure 16-14 provides some illustrations of signature blocks.

Execution

[General format where all parties sign at the same time and place]

Executed in [specify the number of executed copies, e.g., triplicate] on December 24, 1995, at Dallas, Texas.

                                         _____

                                         Robert P. Jones

                                         _____

                                         Glen W. Smith

FIGURE 16-14 Sample signature blocks

OR

Executed by the parties hereto on the day and year first above written.

_____
Robert P. Jones

_____
Glen W. Smith

OR

Witness our hands at Arlington, Texas, on this 24th day of December, 1995.

_____
Robert P. Jones

_____
Glen W. Smith

[General format where parties are signing at different times]

Executed on December 14, 1995, at Arlington, Texas.

_____
Robert P. Jones

FIGURE 16-14 *(Continued)*

Sample Contract

The final product should reflect the needs, objectives, and intentions of the parties to the contract, tailored to the client's situation, Figure 16-15 provides a typical sample contract for an independent contractor.

AGREEMENT made between Homes of Florida (the "Company"), 1234 Ninth Street, West Palm Beach, Florida, and ABC Concrete Company, (the "Contractor"), 5678 West Fruit Street, Tampa, Florida.

IN CONSIDERATION of the mutual promises made herein, and for other good and valuable consideration, the parties hereby agree as follows:

1. **Scope of Work.** The Company engages the Contractor to furnish the work described in the Schedule attached to this Agreement at the times specified in that Schedule, and the Contractor agrees to furnish the work at the times specified in the Schedule.

2. **Price and Payment.** The Company agrees to pay the Contractor in accordance with the price and payment terms set forth in the Schedule attached to this Agreement, and the Contractor agrees to accept such amounts as full payment for its work and to sign such waivers of lien, affidavits, and receipts as the Company shall request in order to acknowledge payment.

3. **Independent Contractor Relationship.** The Contractor is an independent contractor and is not an employee, servant, agent, partner, or joint venturer of the Company. The Company shall determine the work to be done by the Contractor, but the Contractor shall determine the means by which it accomplishes the work specified by the Company. The Company is not responsible for withholding, and shall not withhold, FICA or taxes of any kind from any payments which it owes the Contractor. Neither the Contractor nor its employees shall be entitled to receive any benefits which employees of the Company are entitled to receive and shall not be entitled to workers' compensation, unemployment compensation, medical insurance, life insurance, paid vacations, paid holidays, pension, profit sharing, or Social Security on account of their work for the Company.

FIGURE 16-15 Sample contract (independent contractor)

TERMS

notary public
A public officer whose function is to attest to the genuineness of documents and to administer oaths.

4. **Business of Contractor.** The Contractor is engaged in the business of doing the work specified in the attached Schedule. Copies of the following documents verifying the Contractor's established business shall be attached to this Agreement:

(a) Current occupational licenses issued by the counties and municipalities in which the work is to be performed.

(b) Articles of incorporation, if the Contractor is a corporation.

(c) Partnership or joint venture agreement, if the Contractor is a partnership or joint venture.

(d) Acknowledgment of sole proprietorship, if the Contractor is a sole proprietor.

(e) Federal Employer Tax Identification Number.

5. **Employees of Contractor.** The Contractor shall be solely responsible for paying its employees. The Contractor shall be solely responsible for paying any and all taxes, FICA, workers' compensation, unemployment compensation, medical insurance, life insurance, paid vacations, paid holidays, pension, profit sharing, and other benefits for the Contractor and its employees, servants, and agents.

6. **Insurance.** The Contractor shall furnish the Company with current certificates of coverage of the Contractor, and proof of payment by the Contractor, for workers' compensation insurance, general liability insurance, motor vehicle insurance, and such other insurance as the Company may require from time to time. If the Contractor is not required by the [state] Workers' Compensation Law to provide workers' compensation to its employees, the Contractor shall waive its exemption or exclusion from that law and shall purchase workers' compensation insurance and furnish the Company with a current certificate of coverage and proof of payment. The Contractor shall maintain all such insurance coverage in full force during the term of this contract and shall furnish the Company with certificates of renewal coverage and proofs of premium payments. If the Contractor fails to pay a premium for insurance required by this paragraph before it becomes due, the Company may pay the premium and deduct the amount paid from any payments due the Contractor and recover the balance from the Contractor directly.

7. **Risk.** The Contractor shall perform the work at its own risk. The Contractor assumes all responsibility for the condition of tools, equipment, material, and job site. The Contractor shall indemnify and hold harmless the Company from any claim, demand, loss, liability, damage, or expense arising in any way from the Contractor's work.

8. **Assignment.** The Company may assign any or all of its rights and duties under this Agreement at any time and from time to time without the consent of the Contractor. The Contractor may not assign any of its rights or duties under this Agreement without the prior written consent of the Company.

9. **Termination.** This agreement may be terminated for any reason by either party by giving thirty (30) days notice, and may be terminated for cause at any time upon notice.

10. **Term.** This Agreement is effective as of [date] and shall continue for one year.

11. **Law.** This Agreement shall be governed and construed in accordance with [state] law.

IN WITNESS WHEREOF, the parties have executed this Agreement on the dates shown below.

_____
(Date)

_____
Homes of Florida

_____
(Date)

_____
ABC Concrete Company

FIGURE 16-15 *(Continued)*

16.2 THE SALES CONTRACT

With the advent of the Uniform Commercial Code, the common law of contracts has been substantially modified. Under the U.C.C., a contract can be formed even though certain key terms are missing. The certainty and definiteness that are the cornerstone of common law contracts are unnecessary under the Code. The U.C.C. relaxes many of the traditional rules of contract formation and writing requirements, making it easier to create a contract between parties. As a result, when drafting a sales contract, it is important to set out all the particulars that the parties desire, so as to avoid clients' becoming bound by terms to which they did not agree.

In preparing any sales agreement, be sure the terms are set forth in an understandable manner, and be sure that they are conspicuous, so that there can be no claims that parties did not know that certain terms were present or that they did not understand a particular provision. If terms are to be set forth on the back side of a printed form, specific and conspicuous reference should be made to the reverse side of the form, so that the parties to the contract will know that those terms are present.

In addition, pay close attention to the federal and state administrative regulations that may govern sales transactions. In many instances restrictions are placed on contract terms concerning pricing, advertising, labeling, and other such areas. Many states also require parties to obtain permits or licenses before they transact business. It is imperative that, as part of the sales contract, the requisite licenses be made a condition of the transaction. Clearly state the conditions that are necessary to meet the contractual obligation, so that neither party inadvertently violates state or federal law.

The rest of this section contains suggestions as to general provisions that may or should be included in a sales contract. Although some of the restrictions have been relaxed under the U.C.C., specificity can avoid problems in sales transactions.

Description of Goods

The goods that are the subject of the sales agreement should be adequately described. Different grades, sizes, styles, or any other particulars should be specifically stated in the contract so that there is no dispute or question as to what is the subject of the contract. Properly identifying the goods to the contract will avoid future problems.

Often the parties to the sales contract are ordering different sizes and styles. If you are representing the seller, draft provisions for normal deviations in style, size, color, weight, texture, and pattern, so there will not be an undue burden on the seller in filling the order.

Quantity

Quantity is an important term in the contract and should be stated with as much specificity as possible. Although the Code does relax some of the requirements for definiteness, be as specific as possible in delineating the minimum and maximum quantities which are the subject of the contract.

If the contract requires a specific quantity, different sizes, styles, colors, or patterns, state those requirements in clear and specific language. If you represent a buyer that will need additional quantities of the same goods in the future, it is especially important to include such conditions in the purchase contract.

When dealing with output and requirements contracts, it is incumbent upon the parties to be flexible as to price. Because output and requirements contracts are indefinite by nature, try to set fixed minimum and maximum quantity standards or a formula therefor. In this section it may be appropriate to set out the conditions of notice to the seller of the buyer's requirements and the subsequent delivery schedule by the seller when the goods are ordered. Careful drafting is critical when lack of specificity is an integral and unavoidable part of the contract.

Price

Although the U.C.C. does not require that a specific price be set forth in the contract, it is probably a better practice, if at all possible, to do so. When the price is not stated in the contract, a contract could still exist under the Code; under § 2-305, price is the reasonable value at the time of delivery. If nothing specific is stated as to price, it is left to be agreed by the parties. There is much flexibility in the price term standards in sales contracts and this should be recognized by the person doing the drafting.

Once the parties set the price, payment is normally required. If the parties agree to a certain method of payment, that should be clearly stated in the contract so there is no question as to what is required. For example, if the parties require a cashier's check or C.O.D., that should be specified as a condition of payment and ultimate delivery.

In addition, certain sales include excise taxes. If the tax is included in the price, specifically so state. If the price does not include the taxes, say so. If any other items (such as packing and labeling) are included in a price, state them as well in the contract.

When payment must be tendered is important. Unless this is specifically stated in the contract, the U.C.C. provides that the price is normally payable either upon delivery of the goods or according to custom and usage and prior dealings between the parties. Consequently, if the intent is to have different payment terms, it is incumbent upon the drafter to clearly set forth those payment requirements.

If the payment is due in installments, this should be specifically stated, and any conditions to payment should be stated as well. How a default is to be remedied should also be a part of the price terms or included in a separate section entitled "Default." When installment payments are agreed to, a grace period is often granted, and written notice of any default required, before it becomes effective.

Payment can also be conditioned upon an inspection. This is the buyer's right under the Code, but if possible, it should be specifically stated so that there is no confusion as to when payment is due and the conditions of such payment.

Title

The U.C.C. specifies the manner in which title passes to the parties in a sales contract. If the parties desire any variations with respect to transfer of title, they should be so stated in a title provision.

In addition to the specifics of passing title under the Code, documents of title may also be required in a sales contract. Governed by Article 7 of the Code, such documents may include warehouse receipts, bills of lading, or delivery orders. If title documents were part of the transaction, the terms and conditions with respect to the passage of title should be stated in the sales contract. This section should also set forth whether the documents of title are **negotiable** or **nonnegotiable**, so there is no question as to the manner in which the documents must be transferred. Being specific as to such requirements is important when documents of title are involved.

Delivery

Specifying the time, place, and manner of delivery are essential elements in any sales contract. Failure to state these terms may make the contract unenforceable, as certain rights and obligations arise with respect to delivery terms. Unless specifically stated in the contract, the presumption under the law is that the party will pay for the goods upon delivery. If this is not the intention of the parties, it should be stated in a delivery provision.

Setting forth a specific place of delivery is critical. Where goods are delivered has a direct bearing on when title is transferred and who bears the risk of loss. As stated earlier (Chapter 12), such terms as F.O.B., F.A.S., and C.I.F. have specific legal ramifications. It is important to specify the legal responsibilities of the parties in this regard—otherwise, the U.C.C. will control.

Furthermore, the general rule is that if there is a slight delay or deviation in the terms of delivery, performance will be excused under the contract. Consequently, if time is of the essence between the parties, that should be specifically stated. Otherwise, the Code will not treat minor deviations as a breach or a waiver of the buyer's claims based on delivery delays.

Another consideration when drafting a delivery provision is the occurrence of events that are out of the control of the parties. Exculpatory clauses will excuse performance without legal ramifications if properly drafted. Such provisions can be important and should be drafted according to the needs of the contracting parties.

TERMS

negotiable
1. Transferable by indorsement or delivery.
2. Subject to negotiation; bargainable.

non-negotiable
1. A document or instrument not transferable by indorsement or delivery. 2. Not subject to negotiation; not bargainable.

Warranties

The Code allows for a variety of provisions regarding express and implied warranties. If the parties intend to exclude certain warranties in the sales contract, the exclusions must be specifically identified in the sales contract. If the warranty of merchantability is to be excluded, it must be stated in conspicuous language the word *merchantability* specifically used in the exclusion. This exclusion must be in writing and must be conspicuously set with boldface print, underlining, or some other method that sets it apart from the rest of the language of the contract.

If the parties want to exclude implied warranties of fitness, it is sufficient to state that "there are no warranties which extend beyond the description on the face hereof." In addition, if the buyer is purchasing the goods as presented, language such as "as is" and "with all faults" or other commonly used phrases is sufficient to draw to the buyer's attention that all warranties are being excluded from the sales agreement. The more specific the disclaimers, the more likely that the party attempting to exclude the warranty will succeed in enforcing the exclusions.

If the seller is not warranting title, and is therefore attempting to exclude or modify that which it is transferring to the buyer, such exclusion or modification of the warranty of title must be specifically stated. Also, include additional language indicating that the buyer knows the seller is not warranting the title. Transfer of title is important and provisions affecting it should be clearly drafted.

If you are representing the buyer, you should ensure that certain express warranties are included as the basis of the bargain. It is incumbent upon the buyer to include language which states that the seller is warranting the product for the particular purpose for which it was intended. This will place the burden upon the seller to be sure that the goods are warranted for the purposes for which they are being purchased.

A seller may want to limit the time period in which a buyer can return defective goods. Or, the seller may want to include provisions stating that, in the event that the goods are defective, the seller can repair or make substitutions within a specified period of time without any recourse by the buyer. Think about your client's needs and include them in your contract.

On a different front, it may be appropriate for the person who is drafting on behalf of the seller to attempt to limit the amount or types of damages that the other party can recover for breach of warranty. In this section, the seller may want to exclude any special, incidental or consequential damages, or add any other limitations it deems appropriate.

Credit

Many sales transactions are made on credit. Consider including a credit clause stating that no credit will be extended until approved in writing by the appropriate party and then communicated back to the seller.

One of the problems that arises with credit is that circumstances may change and the buyer may become insolvent. The U.C.C. leaves little remedy for the seller, but a seller can contractually protect itself by reserving the right to revoke credit, and insisting upon cash payment prior to actual shipment of the goods, if it determines that the buyer's financial situation has materially changed. This provision should leave no question as to the seller's rights and obligations against the buyer in the event that credit terms are no longer desirable.

Remedies Provided to the Parties

The U.C.C. presents a number of options for buyer and seller in the event of a breach by either party. Nevertheless, a contract should specifically set out the parties' rights and obligations after a breach, even though these rights are specified in the Code. It is always a good idea to set forth in writing the remedies for breach, so that there is no question as to what is available to the parties. However, if you are representing the buyer, it may be appropriate to include not only the damages granted under the Code, but also any special or consequential damages incurred because of the breach. If you are working with the seller, a provision regarding limitation of liability may be appropriate, including limiting all incidental, special, and consequential damages as a result of the breach.

Miscellaneous Standard Provisions

As with other standard contracts, sales contracts usually include miscellaneous standard provisions, such as those on governing law, merger, assignability, notice, and signature. Follow the basic guidelines set forth earlier in this chapter to draft these provisions. Sales contracts usually differ from each other, but an example of a typical sales contract is given in Figure 16-16.

Agreement made April 20, 1995, between Imports, Inc. of Atlanta, Georgia, in this agreement referred to as "seller," and Wines, Inc. of Des Moines, Iowa, in this agreement referred to as "buyer."

1.   SALE OF GOODS. Seller shall sell, transfer, and deliver to buyer on or before May 20, 1995, 900 cases of Australian Shiraz.

2.   CONSIDERATION. Buyer shall accept the goods and pay Fifty Four Thousand Dollars ($54,000.00) for the goods.

3.   IDENTIFICATION OF GOODS. Identification of the goods to this agreement shall not be deemed to have been made until buyer and seller have specified that the goods are appropriate to the performance of this agreement.

4.   PAYMENT ON RECEIPT.   Buyer shall make payment for the goods at the time when, and at the place where, the goods are received by buyer.

FIGURE 16-16   Sample sales contract

5. RECEIPT CONSTRUED AS DELIVERY. Goods shall be deemed received by buyer when delivered to buyer at 187 Main Street, Des Moines, Iowa.

6. RISK OF LOSS. The risk of loss from any casualty to the goods, regardless of the cause, shall be on seller until the goods have been accepted by buyer.

7. WARRANTY OF NO ENCUMBRANCES. Seller warrants that the goods are now free, and that at the time of delivery shall be free, from any security interest or other lien or encumbrance.

8. WARRANTY OF TITLE. Furthermore, seller warrants that at the time of signing this agreement, seller neither knows nor has reason to know of the existence of any outstanding title or claim of title hostile to the rights of seller in the goods.

9. RIGHT OF INSPECTION. Buyer shall have the right to inspect the goods on arrival. Within ten (10) business days after delivery, buyer must give notice to seller of any claim for damages on account of condition, quality, or grade of the goods, and buyer must specify in detail the basis of its claim. The failure of buyer to comply with these conditions shall constitute irrevocable acceptance of the goods by buyer.

IN WITNESS WHEREOF, the parties have executed this agreement at [designate place of execution] the day and year first above written.

_____
Imports, Inc.

_____
Wines, Inc.

FIGURE 16-16 *(Continued)*

16.3 PRACTICAL APPLICATION

Drafting a contract can be an involved process. As a result, this chapter can only act as a guide, but does not include every possible contract provision nor every type of contract. Two types of contracts that paralegals often encounter, which include many of the provisions previously discussed, are employment agreements and contracts for the sale of a business. Specific provisions should be included in each.

Employment Agreement

When drafting an employment agreement, consider the following:

1. *Terms of Employment.* Set forth the contractual term between the employer and the employee. Within this paragraph, it is appropriate to include any automatic renewals and the conditions for renewal.
2. *Compensation.* Clearly state the compensation to be paid to the employee and how it will be paid (e.g., monthly, bimonthly, or weekly).
3. *Duties and Responsibilities.* An employee should know what is required for satisfactory performance. If there are any special duties or responsibilities, describe them in the contract.
4. *Vacation and Sick Leave.* It is customary for employers to provide vacation and sick days. Specifically set forth the conditions of vacation and sick leave. Must the employee work a certain period of time before

receiving paid vacation? Is sick leave paid or not? These provisions can be a source of controversy and consternation; therefore, be specific.

5. *Termination of Employment.*   In this section, make the distinction between termination with cause and without cause. If notice is desired by either party for termination with cause, identify the time period required for each party to notify the other of the termination. If termination-with-cause provisions are needed, be as detailed as possible.

6. *Modification.*   Most contracts require modifications to be in writing and approved by all parties. This requirement is standard

7. *Covenants against Competition.*   Covenants not to compete have come under close scrutiny by the courts. Most states have either statutes or case law which identifies the necessary elements for a legally effective noncompetition provision. Check your state laws and draft accordingly. Usually the law requires that the covenant be reasonable in time, place, and manner.

8. *Nondisclosure of Trade Secrets.*   Coupled with the noncompetition clause is usually a nondisclosure agreement by which the employee agrees not to disclose the confidential, proprietary information and trade secrets of its employer. This provision is important because the employer does not want employees misappropriating information that the employer deems valuable.

9. *Miscellaneous Provisions.*   Include the miscellaneous provisions, such as governing law, assignability, merger, and notice, at the end of the contract.

10. *Signatures.*   End your document with the appropriate signatures and dates to make the agreement effective.

Figure 16-17 is a sample employment agreement.

Sample Employment Agreement

    This contract, dated November 1, 1995, is made between Benjamin Wright, referred to as the "Associate," and XYZ Law Firm, P.C., referred to as the "Law Firm."

    1. **Parties.**   The Associate is duly admitted to the practice of law in [state]. The Law Firm is engaged in the practice of law in [state].

    2. **Term of Employment.**   The Law Firm shall employ the Associate for a period of one (1) year for the purpose of providing legal services on behalf of the Law Firm to such members of the general public as are and as become accepted as clients by the Law Firm. The initial term may be extended from year to year.

    3. **Compensation.**   The Law Firm agrees to pay the Associate the salary of $48,000.00 per year, payable monthly at the rate of $4,000.00 on the first of each month (for the prior month). Salary increases may be made from time to time at the discretion of the Law Firm.

    4. **Bonus.**   The Law Firm may at its sole discretion pay to the Associate a year-end bonus. The Law Firm shall determine the amount, if any, of such bonus considering in part the services rendered to the Law Firm by the Associate.

    5. **Clients.**   All clients are to be considered clients of the Law Firm and not the clients of any particular member of the firm.

FIGURE 16-17   Sample employment agreement (with modification)

6. **Vacation.** The Associate shall be entitled each year to a paid vacation of three (3) weeks, which must be approved by the Law Firm not less than two (2) months prior to the vacation leave.

7. **Medical Insurance.** The Law Firm maintains policies of insurance covering certain hospital and medical expenses incurred by its employees and their families. The Associate shall become eligible to participate in these insurance plans upon the completion of ninety (90) days of employment. The cost of such insurance for the Associate alone shall be paid by the Law Firm, with the Associate paying for all of the additional cost required to provide family coverage. The Law Firm reserves the right to change carriers or plans.

8. **Disability.** If the Associate shall become unable to perform his duties fully by reason of illness or incapacity of any kind, the Law Firm may, in its sole discretion, reduce or terminate all salary payments. Full salary shall be reinstated upon the return of the Associate to full-time employment and full discharge of the duties of employment.

9. **Life Insurance.** The Law Firm provides group life insurance for its employees. The general purpose of this plan is to provide to the beneficiaries the equivalent of twice the employee's annual salary as a death benefit. The Law Firm pays the cost of this insurance. Upon completion of ninety (90) days satisfactory employment, the Associate will be furnished a policy contract indicating the coverage under the plan. The Law Firm reserves the right to change plans and carriers in its sole discretion.

10. **Nonliability of the Law Firm.** All matters of eligibility for coverage or benefits under any insurance provided by the Law Firm shall be determined in accordance with the provisions of the insurance policies. The Law Firm shall not be liable to the Associate, or his heirs, family, executors, or beneficiaries, for any payment payable or claimed to be payable under any plan of insurance.

11. **Duties of Employment.** The Associate shall devote his full business time and attention to the practice of law on behalf of the Law Firm and to the furtherance of the best interest of the Law Firm. The Associate shall not engage in the practice of law except as an employee of the Law Firm. The Law Firm shall have exclusive authority and power to determine the matters to be assigned to the Associate, including the specific duties and standards of performance.

The Law Firm shall have the following powers:

(a) To assign clients and cases to the Associate;
(b) To review all work performed by the Associate and to modify, cancel, or require the Associate to revise the work or work product;
(c) To determine the time and manner of performance of all work; and
(d) To determine standards of performance and, within reason, necessary hours of work.

12. **Authority to Bind the Law Firm.** The Associate is not authorized to enter into any contracts which would bind the Law Firm, or to create any obligations on the part of the Law Firm, except as shall be specifically authorized by the Law Firm.

13. **Professional Standards.** The Associate agrees to abide by and perform his duties in accordance with the ethics of the legal profession and all federal, state, and local laws, regulations, and ordinances regulating the practice of law.

14. **Assistance.** The Law Firm shall make available to the Associate a private office, secretarial assistance, paralegal research aides, and such other facilities and services as are customary, consistent with the position and adequate for the proper performance of the duties of the Associate.

15. **Expense Reimbursement.** The Law Firm shall reimburse the Associate for all expenses reasonably and necessarily incurred in the performance of his duties. Such reimbursable expense shall include but not be limited to the following: (a) travel expenses; (b) automobile expenses; (c) expenses for entertainment for the promotion of the Law Firm; (d) professional and other dues; (e) attendance at lectures, forums, and other meetings conducted for the continuing education of members of the profession.

16. **Accounting for Services.** The Associate shall keep an accurate record, as required by the Law Firm, of all billable time spent on clients' matters and affairs. Such records shall be submitted to the Law Firm as the law requires, together with any special

FIGURE 16-17 *(Continued)*

billing instructions that apply to the matter. All client billings shall be made by the Law Firm and the Law Firm shall have the exclusive authority to fix the fees to be charged to all clients. All fees, compensation, and other monies or things of value received or realized as a result of services provided by the Law Firm shall be strictly accounted for upon demand and turned over to the Law Firm upon receipt thereof. This includes all income generated by the Associate, including but not limited to fees and compensation received for services rendered as executor, administrator, trustee, guardian, and the like, and all income generated by the Associate.

17. **Termination of Employment.** Either party may give written notice to the other, at least sixty (60) days prior to the end of any such term of employment, that the employment is to terminate. No cause is required for termination.

The Associate will also be automatically and immediately terminated if for any reason the Associate becomes disqualified to practice law in this state or otherwise violates the terms of this agreement to provide services to this Law Firm without a conflict of interest with other employment.

The Law Firm may also immediately terminate the Associate upon the occurrence of any of the following events:

(a) the Associate fails or refuses to comply with the policies, standards, and regulations of the Law Firm reasonably established from time to time; or
(b) the Associate's fraud, dishonesty, or other misconduct in the performance of legal services on behalf of the Law Firm; or
(c) the Associate's failure to faithfully or diligently perform the provisions of this agreement or the usual and customary duties of his employment; or
(d) if the Law Firm discontinues the practice of law.

18. **Waiver of Breach.** The waiver by either party to this agreement of a breach of any of its provisions shall not operate or be construed to be a waiver of any subsequent breach of the same or any other provision of this agreement.

19. **Notices.** Any notice to be given under this agreement may be deemed sufficient if made in writing to the party and sent by mail to the address provided in the beginning of this agreement or to such other address provided by the Associate as his new address.

20. **Governing Law.** This agreement shall be governed by the laws of [state].

21. **Binding Effect.** This agreement shall be binding upon the parties hereto and shall inure to the benefit of their respective successors and assigns and to the estate, beneficiaries, and heirs of the Associate.

22. **Signatures.** Both the Law Firm and Associate agree to the above.

LAW FIRM:

By: _____   _____
                                          Name of Associate

Modification of Employment Agreement

AGREEMENT made this 31st day of November, 1995, between the Law Firm, a Maine corporation, hereinafter called "Employer," and Benjamin Wright, hereinafter called "Employee."

The parties hereby agree that the Employment Agreement dated November 1, 1995, between the Law Firm and Benjamin Wright is hereby modified and amended by changing § 3 to read as follows:

3. **COMPENSATION.**

a. **Base Salary.** In consideration of services rendered under this agreement from and after the date hereof, Employee shall receive a base salary per annum of Sixty Thousand Dollars ($60,000.00), payable at Five Thousand Dollars ($5,000.00) a month. The base salary may be changed by mutual agreement of the parties at any time.

In all other respects, the Employment Agreement shall remain as it existed prior to this Modification.

FIGURE 16-17 *(Continued)*

IN WITNESS WHEREOF, the parties or their authorized representatives have signed this Modification as of the day and year first above written.

EMPLOYER: _____

By: _____
       President

EMPLOYEE: _____

_____

FIGURE 16-17 *(Continued)*

Sale of Business Contract

When drafting a contract for the sale of a business, consider:

1. *General Introduction.* This section introduces the parties and the places where the parties reside or have their principal places of business.
2. *Sale and Purchase Provision.* In this section, specify the business purchased and what the sale includes, such as inventory, fixtures, and goodwill of the business.
3. *Purchase Price.* Set forth the purchase price and how it will be allocated. (This usually has tax implications.)
4. *Inspection of Inventory.* The purchaser usually has the right to inspect the inventory prior to any purchase. The inventory verifies what the purchaser is buying.
5. *Accounts Receivable.* The seller of a business often has continuing accounts payable to the business. The issue arises as to who is entitled to this money. A specific date should be identified so that there is no question as to which party is entitled to money received thereafter. The sale need not include the accounts receivable, though; this provision must be negotiated by the parties.
6. *Payment of the Purchase Price.* In this provision, specify how the purchase price is to be tendered to the seller. If the payment is in installments, say so. If the seller is going to lend the purchaser the money and a promissory note is needed, this should also be stated in the contract.
7. *Documents at Closing.* Any documents to transfer title must be identified. Any other corresponding documents should also be noted in this section.
8. *Seller and Buyer Representations.* As part of the sale, seller and buyer make certain representations to each other. The seller represents that there is good title, taxes are paid, no judgments or liens exist, and no contracts have been entered into that affect the business. The buyer represents that an inventory has been taken, books and records have been inspected, and the buyer is satisfied that everything properly

reflects the status of the business. This is standard and a very important provision in such a contract.

9. *Compliance with Bulk Sales Law.* Under Article 7 of the U.C.C., when all or substantially all of the assets of a business are sold, notice shall be given to creditors. If notice is not sent, both seller and buyer will be responsible for the debts. Sometimes the parties agree to waive compliance with the bulk sales law, but if that occurs, the seller will be legally responsible for any consequences.

10. *Restrictive Covenant.* It is customary for the buyer to insist that the seller not compete with the buyer for a period of time within a specific geographic area. If the buyer does not include this provision, the seller could set up a similar business next door. Undoubtedly, the buyer does not want this to occur. Therefore, a restrictive covenant should be in the contract.

11. *Time and Place of Closing.* Specify where and when the closing is to take place.

12. *Notices.* Because letters may have to be sent to the parties because of a problem with the contract, each party's mailing address should be stated.

13. *Miscellaneous Provisions.* Include the general miscellaneous provisions, such as choice-of-law, assignability, and merger clauses.

14. *Signature of Parties and Date.* Set forth a signature block for all parties who intend to sign the contract. Be sure to date the contract. Figure 16-18 is a sample complete sale of business contract.

SALE AND PURCHASE AGREEMENT

This SALE AND PURCHASE AGREEMENT ("AGREEMENT") is made and entered into effective the 1st day of October, 1995, at Dallas, Dallas County, Texas, between Ray Charleston ("Seller"), and Dustin Mancini ("Purchaser").

WITNESSETH:

WHEREAS, Purchaser desires to purchase Seller's interest in the business being conducted under the name of "ABC Cleaners" located at 11800 Dallas Parkway, Dallas, Texas 75245 and assets pertaining thereto, as more particularly described herein, upon terms and conditions hereinafter set forth; and

WHEREAS, the parties agree that the subject of the Sale and Purchase Agreement is the pick-up store located at 11800 Dallas Parkway and NOT any other businesses operating under the name of ABC Cleaners; and

WHEREAS, Seller desires to sell his interest in only the pick-up store business being conducted under the name "ABC Cleaners," located at 11800 Dallas Parkway, Dallas, Texas 75245, and assets thereto, as more particularly described herein, upon the terms and conditions hereinafter set forth;

NOW, THEREFORE, in consideration of the premises, TEN AND NO/100 DOLLARS ($10.00) and other good and valuable consideration, and the mutual promises and agreements of the parties hereto, one to the other, receipt and sufficiency of which are hereby acknowledged by each of said parties, and expressing their intent to be legally bound, the parties hereto agree as follows:

FIGURE 16-18 Sample sale of business contract (sale and purchase agreement with bill of sale

1. PURCHASE AND SALE. Seller shall sell to Purchaser and Purchaser shall purchase from Seller upon the terms and conditions hereinafter set forth in this Agreement, the items set forth in Exhibit "A", attached hereto and incorporated herein by reference for all purposes ("Assets"), and more particularly described as:

(a) all the stock in trade and merchandise of the pick-up dry cleaning store business only;

(b) all the fixtures, equipment, and other tangible assets of the pick-up store business;

(c) all the trade, goodwill, and other intangible assets of the pick-up store business; and

(d) all leases, licenses, and permits of the business.

2. PURCHASE PRICE. The total purchase price (herein called "Purchase Price") to be paid by Purchaser for all the Assets described in Exhibit "A" to this Agreement shall be FIFTEEN THOUSAND DOLLARS ($15,000.00).

3. ALLOCATION OF PURCHASE PRICE. Purchase Price shall be allocated as required by Section 1060 of the Internal Revenue Code of 1986, as amended from time to time.

(a) The Seller and Purchaser further agree that $1,000.00 has been paid to Seller prior to the closing.

(b) The remaining balance of $14,000.00 shall be tendered to Seller in a certified or cashier's check at the time of closing.

4. WARRANTIES AND REPRESENTATIONS. As a material inducement to Purchaser to enter into this Agreement, and to close the contemplated transaction, Seller represents, warrants, and covenants to Purchaser that the following are true and correct as of when made, and will be true and correct through the Closing, as if made on that date:

(a) Seller has taken, or will take, prior to the Closing Date, all action necessary to perform his obligation hereunder. Upon execution and delivery of this Agreement, this Agreement will be the legal, valid, and binding obligation of the Seller enforceable in accordance with its terms.

(b) Neither the execution nor performance of this Agreement, nor the other agreements contemplated hereby, nor the consummation of the transactions contemplated hereby or thereby, will (i) conflict with, or result in a breach of the terms, conditions, and provisions of, or constitute a default under any agreement to which Seller is a party or under which Seller is obligated in any matter whatsoever, or (ii) violate or conflict with any judgment, decree, order, statute, rule, or regulation of any court or any public, governmental, or regulatory agency or body having jurisdiction over Seller or the properties or assets of Seller.

(c) The financial records of the Seller have been reviewed by Purchaser and are a complete and actual record and account of the financial affairs of the Seller for the periods indicated, are in accordance with the books and records of the Seller, present an account of the financial affairs of Seller for the periods indicated, the present financial condition of Seller at such dates and the results of its operations for the periods therein specified, and truthfully set forth all liabilities, assets, and other matters pertaining to the fiscal and financial condition of the business through September 30, 1995, subject to year-end adjustments consistent with generally accepted accounting principles with respect to the statements.

(d) There have not been material changes in Seller's business that adversely affect the business.

(e) No litigation, actions, or proceedings, legal, equitable, or administrative, through arbitration or otherwise ("disputes"), are pending or threatened which might adversely affect the value of the Assets of Seller's business.

(f) Seller owes no obligations and has contracted no liabilities affecting his business or which might adversely affect the value of the Assets or the consummation of the purchase and sale.

(g) All assets listed in Exhibit "A" which are being sold pursuant to this Agreement are in good condition and repair, reasonable wear and tear excepted, and none of the equipment being sold is obsolete or no longer marketable. Seller shall execute and deliver to Purchaser such Bills of Sale with General Warranty and other instruments reasonably

FIGURE 16-18 *(Continued)*

necessary or convenient to transfer to Purchaser all the Assets being sold pursuant to this Agreement, free and clear from all debts, obligations, liens, and encumbrances.

(h)   Seller is operating under the assumed name "ABC Cleaners," which is located at 11800 Dallas Parkway, Dallas, Texas 75245.

(i)   Seller is not a party to any contracts, written or oral, concerning the ownership and the Assets being sold pursuant to this Agreement.

(j)   The Assets sold under this Agreement are not subject to community property rights or the assignment of community property rights, or a lien to secure community property rights, judgment rights, or any other community property rights.

(k)   Neither Seller nor any party acting on Seller's behalf has agreed to pay any party a commission, finder's fee, or similar payment concerning this matter or any matter related hereto, or has taken any action on which a claim for any such payment could be based.

(l)   Seller has duly filed tax returns required to be filed and has paid all federal, state, and local taxes required to be paid with respect to the periods covered by such returns. All taxes, including but not limited to sales taxes, liquor taxes, personal property taxes, withholding, and FICA, FUTA, and SUTA, owing, and which, with the passage of time, will become due and owing, and which are unpaid and would have any material adverse effect on the Assets, shall be paid by the Seller when due.

(m)   There are no governmental licenses, federal, state, or local, or any other licenses required to own and/or operate the business of the Seller that could have any material adverse effect on the value of the Assets.

(n)   No representation, written or oral, warranty or statement of Seller, whether in this Agreement or in any document or exhibit furnished or made to Purchaser, contains or omits a material fact which makes the representation, warranty, or statements misleading. All such representations, warranties, or statements of the Seller are based upon current, accurate, and complete information as of the time of the making of this Agreement, as is available to the Seller.

(o)   "Goodwill" is not an asset of the business for purposes of this agrement.

5. **ACCOUNTS RECEIVABLES.**   Purchaser shall be entitled to all cash receipts and accounts receivable after September 30, 1995, and Seller shall be divested of any rights or entitlement to any cash receipts or receivables. However, the parties agree that all inventory receipts in the pick-up store prior to October 1, 1995, shall be divided equally between the parties. As a condition to closing, Purchaser shall pay to Seller one-half of the receipts of the inventory as of the close of business on September 30, 1995.

6. **COMPLIANCE WITH BULK SALES ACT.**   Seller and Purchaser do not waive compliance with the Bulk Sales Act.

7. **CLOSING.**   The term "Closing," as used in this Agreement, shall mean the consummation of the sale of the Assets and items set forth in this Agreement. The Closing shall take place at such time, date, and place as may be agreed upon by the parties ("the Closing Date").

8. **THE LEASE.**   Purchaser acknowledges that the premises are leased. Seller agrees to assign any and all rights under its lease agreements to Purchaser. Attached hereto as Exhibit "B" is a copy of the Assignment of Lease. The parties acknowledge that Seller is still primarily liable on the original lease between Bonjour Limited Partnership, a Texas limited partnership, and Raymond Charleston, and has not been released by the landlord. In the event Purchaser fails to make a lease payment by the 10th of the month, Seller has the right to enter the premises and reclaim possession of the business without recourse from the Purchaser. In such event, Purchaser shall be divested of all rights, title, and interest in the pick-up store and will waive any rights to any monies from the business located at 11800 Dallas Parkway, Dallas, Texas 75245, and Purchaser acknowledges that he is not entitled to any reimbursement of the purchase price from Seller. Nonpayment of the rent is considered an event of default whereby Seller can exercise any and all rights he has by law.

9. **COSTS AND EXPENSES.**   All costs and expenses incurred in the purchase and sale described in this Agreement in the manner prescribed by this Agreement shall be borne by Purchaser and Seller in the following manner:

(a)   Each party shall pay his own attorney expenses related to this matter.

FIGURE 16-18   *(Continued)*

(b)   All other closing costs and expenses shall be borne by the parties in equal proportions.

(c)   All taxes related to the business and the premises shall be paid by Purchaser from the date of closing and any tax statements received which accrued before the date of closing shall be borne by Seller and prorated accordingly.

(d)   All sales taxes arising because of the sale pursuant to this Agreement of the fixtures and equipment of said business to Purchaser shall be paid by Purchaser.

10. **INDEMNITY AGREEMENT BY PURCHASER.**   Purchaser shall indemnify and hold Seller (including the Assets of the Seller's business) harmless from any and all claims, losses, damages, injuries, and liabilities arising from or concerning the operation of said business by Purchaser after the Closing or ownership of any Assets of said business.

11. **INDEMNITY AGREEMENT BY SELLER.**   Seller shall indemnify and hold Purchaser (including the Assets of Purchaser's business) harmless from all claims, losses, damages, injuries and liabilities arising from or concerning the operation or ownership of any Assets of said business by Seller prior to Closing.

12. **NONCOMPETITION PROVISION.**   There is NO noncompetition provision between the parties. Purchaser acknowledges that Seller can freely compete in the dry cleaning business or related business. There are no geographical or time restrictions between the parties.

13. **MISCELLANEOUS.**   The following miscellaneous provisions apply:

(a)   This agreement is intended to be performed within the State of Texas and the County of Dallas and shall be governed by and construed and enforced in accordance with the laws of the State of Texas. The agreement shall be deemed to have been executed at Dallas County, Texas, and its performance is deemed to have been called for in Dallas County, Texas. To the extent permitted by law, exclusive venue shall be in Dallas, Dallas County, Texas, in any dispute concerning this agreement [Note: Some states require this notice provision to be printed in all capital letters.].

(b)   This agreement may be amended only by a written instrument signed by each party hereto. From and after the closing date, the parties agree to execute any additional instruments and to take such actions as may be reasonably necessary to effectuate the transaction herein described. Further, the parties agree to cooperate in fulfillment of the post-closing agreements required hereunder.

(c)   All notices required to be given pursuant to this Agreement shall be deemed given when given in person, or when mailed certified mail, return receipt requested, to the following at the following addresses:

PURCHASER: Dustin Mancini
                                    1719 Palm Street
                                    Garland, Texas 75040

SELLER: Raymond Charleston
                                    11800 Dallas Parkway
                                    Dallas, Texas 75245

WITH COPY TO: Jane Attorney
                                    Attorney at Law
                                    500 Main Street
                                    Dallas, Texas 75202

(d)   Each party acknowledges that he has carefully read this instrument and fully understands it. Each party further acknowledges that this Agreement is fair, just, and equitable; that the Agreement is being entered into freely and voluntarily, and that each party has had the opportunity to seek the advice of counsel concerning the terms and conditions of this Agreement before executing the same.

(e)   This Agreement shall be binding upon and shall inure to the parties and their respective successors, assigns, legal representatives, heirs, and executors.

(f)   If any provision of this Agreement shall be adjudicated to be invalid or unenforceable in any action or proceeding in which Purchaser and the Seller are parties, then such

FIGURE 16-18   *(Continued)*

provision shall be deemed to be rewritten to the maximum extent permitted by law, so that any invalid or unenforceable provision shall be valid and enforceable to the extent that any such invalid or unenforceable provision shall be deemed deleted or amended, as the case may be, from this Agreement in order to render the remainder of the paragraph, subparagraph or part of such paragraph or subparagraph as both valid and enforceable.

(g) Time is of the essence.

(h) Should any litigation be commenced between the parties to this Agreement, the prevailing party in such litigation shall be entitled, in addition to such other relief as may be granted, to a reasonable sum as attorney fees which shall be determined by the court in such litigation, or in a separate action brought for that purpose.

(i) This Agreement constitutes the entire agreement between the parties respecting the matters set forth in this Agreement.

(j) Whenever the context requires herein, the gender of all words used herein shall include the masculine, feminine, and neuter, and the number of all words shall include the singular and plural.

(k) All titles and/or subtitles in this Agreement are for the convenience of the parties only, and are not substantive in nature.

(l) All Exhibits attached to this Agreement are incorporated into this Agreement as if fully set out in writing in this Agreement.

(m) This Agreement shall be governed by and construed in accordance with the laws of the State of Texas.

14. **COUNTERPARTS.** This Agreement may be executed in one or more counterparts, each of which shall be deemed an original, and all of which together shall constitute the same instrument.

IN WITNESS WHEREOF, the parties hereto have duly executed this Agreement as of the date first above written.

SELLER:

By: _____
Ray Charleston

PURCHASER:

By: _____
Dustin Mancini

BILL OF SALE

KNOW ALL MEN BY THESE PRESENTS:

The undersigned (Seller) does hereby sell, transfer, and deliver unto Dustin Mancini (Buyer) his right, title, and interest in and to the following described: See Schedule "A". The Buyer of said equipment is responsible for all unbilled personal property taxes to the Seller on said equipment. The said Seller hereby warrants that he is the lawful owner of said equipment; that he has the right to sell the same and that it is free from all liens and encumbrances except lien in favor of: None.

Signed this 5th day of October, 1995.

ABC Cleaners

By: _____
Ray Charleston, Owner

ACKNOWLEDGMENT

STATE OF TEXAS   )
)
COUNTY OF DALLAS   )

On this 5th day of October, 1995, before the undersigned, a Notary Public, personally appeared Ray Charleston, the owner of ABC Cleaners, known to me to be the person whose

FIGURE 16-18 *(Continued)*

name is subscribed to the within instrument, and acknowledged that he executed the foregoing Sale and Purchase Agreement on behalf of said corporation as his voluntary act and deed, and under authority duly granted by the coporation for him to so act.

IN WITNESS WHEREOF, I hereunto set my hand and official seal.

_____
Notary Public

_____
My Commission Expires

FIGURE 16-18 *(Continued)*

SUMMARY

16.1 A general contractual agreement should contain certain basic provisions: identity of the parties, definitions, representations and conditions, duration, termination, performance, time of performance, payment, indemnification, limitation of liability, time of the essence, liquidated damages, restrictive covenants, arbitration, merger, choice of law, assignability, notice, signatures of the parties, and date.

16.2 A sales contract is used in the purchase and sale of goods. Some general provisions to consider are description of goods, quantity, price, payment, title, delivery, warranties, credit, remedies, and the miscellaneous standard provisions. When provisions are omitted, the U.C.C. will usually provide for them under the rule of law.

16.3 Some often-encountered general contracts are employment contracts and contracts for the sale of a business. Some provisions to include in an employment contract are term of employment, compensation, duties and responsibilities, vacation, sick leave, termination, covenants against competition, nondisclosure of trade secrets, modification, miscellaneous provisions, and signatures. In a contract for the sale of a business, include such items as the purchase price, warranties, accounts receivable, bulk sales compliance, closing date, indemnification, noncompetition covenants, general miscellaneous provisions, and signatures.

REVIEW QUESTIONS

1. What general provisions should be included in a contract?
2. Why is the representations section important?
3. What is an option in a contract and in what provision will it be found?
4. What is an indemnification clause?
5. What elements should a restrictive covenant include?

6. What is the purpose of a merger clause?
7. What general provisions should be included in a sales contract?
8. List some of the conditions that may be included in a payment provision.
9. How can a warranty be excluded in a sales contract?
10. What are the general provisions in an employment contract? In a contract for the sale of a business?

EXERCISES

1. Mr. St. Johns wanted to hire Harvey Charles as an employee. Harvey was to work for one year with two weeks vacation and five sick days. His compensation is to be $30,000, paid the 15th and last day of each month. The contract is renewable by the employer with 30 days notice to Harvey. Draft the employment contract between the parties.
2. Your attorney has just been retained by a large computer company. One of the client's concerns is employees using important information after they leave employment with the company. Your attorney has asked you to draft nondisclosure and noncompetition provisions for review.
3. Sports Company U.S.A. wants to purchase 500 T-shirts of the following types:

100	Chicago Bulls
200	Super Bowl Champions
100	Yankees
50	Dodgers
10	L.A. Lakers
10	San Francisco 49ers
10	Detroit Lions
10	Philadelphia Phillies
10	Boston Red Sox

Delivery is to be made 30 days after confirmation of the order. An inspection must occur within 24 hours of receipt of the T-shirts, upon which payment of $1,000 has to be tendered to All Around T-Shirts, Inc. Draft the sales contract between the parties.

GLOSSARY

acceleration clause A clause in a note, mortgage, or other contract which provides that the entire debt will become due if payment is not made on time or if other conditions of the agreement are not met.

acceptance [T]he assent by the person to whom an offer is made to the offer as made by the person making it. Acceptance is a fundamental element of a binding contract. . . . In general terms, the receipt and retention of that which is offered. . . . Unspoken consent to or concurrence in a transaction by virtue of failure to reject it. . . . Agreement; approval; assent.

accommodation An obligation undertaken, without consideration, on behalf of another person; a favor.

accord Agreement; an agreement.

accord and satisfaction An agreement between two persons, one of whom has a cause of action against the other, in which the claimant accepts a compromise in full satisfaction of his or her claim.

adhesion contract A contract prepared by the dominant party (usually a form contract) and presented on a take-it-or-leave-it basis to the weaker party, who has no real opportunity to bargain about its terms.

administrator A person who is appointed by the court to manage the estate of a person either who died without a will or whose will failed to name an executor or named an executor who declined or was ineligible to serve. The administrator of an estate is also referred to as a personal representative.

affiant A person who makes a sworn written statement or affidavit.

affidavit Any voluntary statement reduced to writing and sworn to or affirmed before a person legally authorized to administer an oath or affirmation; a sworn statement.

agent One of the parties to an agency relationship, specifically the one who acts for and represents the other party, who is known as the *principal*. The word implies service as well as authority to do something in the name of or on behalf of the principal.

alien Any person present within the borders of the United States who is not a U.S. citizen. . . . Any foreigner.

anticipatory breach (anticipatory repudiation) The announced intention of a party to a contract that it does not intend to perform its obligations under the contract; an announced intention to commit a breach of contract.

arbitration A method of settling disputes by submitting a disagreement to a person (an arbitrator) or a group of individuals (an arbitration panel) for decision instead of going to court. If the parties are required to comply with the decision of the arbitrator, the process is called binding arbitration; if there is no such obligation, the arbitration is referred to as nonbinding arbitration. Compulsory arbitration is required by law, most notably in labor disputes.

assignee A person to whom a right is assigned.

assignment 1. A transfer of property, or a right in property, from one person to another. 2. A designation or appointment.

assignor A person who assigns a right.

auction   A sale of property to the highest bidder.

bailee   The person to whom property is entrusted in a bailment.

bailor   The person who entrusts property to another in a bailment.

bait and switch   A form of fraud in which a merchant advertises an item at a low price to entice customers into the store and then, claiming that the advertised article is no longer in stock, attempts to persuade the customer to purchase a higher priced item. Most states have made this practice a criminal offense.

beneficiary   1. A person who receives a benefit. . . . 4. A person who is entitled to the proceeds of a life insurance policy when the insured dies.

benefit   Anything that adds to the advantage or security of another.

bid   An offer, especially one made at the letting of a contract, an auction, or a judicial sale. To invite; to make an offer, particularly at an auction or a judicial sale, or to secure a contract.

bilateral   1. Involving two interests. 2. Having two sides.

bilateral contract   A contract in which each party promises performance to the other, the promise by the one furnishing the consideration for the promise from the other.

black-letter law   Fundamental and well-established rules of law.

boilerplate   Language common to all legal documents of the same type. Attorneys maintain files of such standardized language for use where appropriate.

breach   A break; a breaking; a violation; the violation of an obligation, engagement, or duty.

bulk   1. A quantity of unpackaged goods or cargo. 2. Unbroker packages. 3. The greater part; the largest or principal portion.

buyer   One who makes a purchase.

capacity   1. Competency in law. 2. A person's ability to understand the nature and effect of the act in which he or she is engaged.

cause of action   Circumstances that give a person the right to bring a lawsuit and to receive relief from a court.

closing   Completing a transaction, particularly a contract for the sale of real estate.

common carrier   A person or company that represents itself as engaged in the business of transporting persons or property from place to place, for compensation, offering its services to the public generally.

common law   Law found in the decisions of the courts rather than in statutes; judge-made law.

compensatory damages (actual damages)   Damages recoverable in a lawsuit for loss or injury suffered by the plaintiff as a result of the defendant's conduct. Also called *actual damages*, they may include expenses, loss of time, reduced earning capacity, bodily injury, and mental anguish.

complaint   The initial pleading in a civil action, in which the plaintiff alleges a cause of action and asks that the wrong done be remedied by the court.

compromise and settlement agreement   An agreement to settle a dispute, followed by performance of the promises contained in the agreement.

condition precedent   A condition that must first occur for a contractual obligation (or a provision of a will, deed, or the like) to attach.

condition subsequent   In a contract, a condition that divests contractual liability that has already attached . . . upon the failure of the other party to the contract . . . to comply with its terms.

consequential damages   Indirect losses; damages that do not result from the wrongful act itself, but from the result or the aftermath of the wrongful act.

consideration   The reason a person enters into a contract; that which is given in exchange for performance or the promise to perform; the price bargained and paid; the inducement. Consideration is an essential element of a valid and enforceable contract. A promise to refrain from doing something one is entitled to do also constitutes consideration.

consignment   The entrusting of goods either to a carrier for delivery to a consignee or to a consignee who is to sell the goods for the consignor.

conspicuous   Clearly visible; easily seen.

copyright The right of an author, granted by federal statute, to exclusively control the reproduction, distribution, and sale of his or her literary, artistic, or intellectual productions for the period of the copyright's existence. Copyright protection extends to written work, music, films, sound recordings, photographs, paintings, sculpture, and some computer programs and chips.

counteroffer A position taken in response to an offer, proposing a different deal.

covenant not to compete (restrictive covenant) A provision in an employment contract in which the employee promises that, upon leaving the employer he or she will not engage in the same business, as an employee or otherwise, in competition with the former employer. Such a covenant, which is also found in partnership agreements and agreements for the sale of a business, must be reasonable with respect to its duration and geographical scope.

cover Under the Uniform Commercial Code, "cover" relates to the right of a buyer, if the seller has breached a contract of sale to purchase the goods elsewhere (the "cover") and hold the seller liable for the difference between the cost of the cover and the original contract price.

creditor beneficiary A creditor who is the beneficiary of a contract made between the debtor and a third person.

custom Often referred to as *custom and usage*; a practice that has acquired the force of law because it has been done that way for a very long time.

damages The sum of money that may be recovered in the courts as financial reparation for an injury or wrong suffered as a result of breach of contract or a tortious act.

decedent A . . . person who has died.

deed A document by which real property, or an interest in real property, is conveyed from one person to another.

defendant The person against whom an action is brought.

delegation The act of conferring authority upon, or transferring it to, another.

detriment Consideration for a contract, in the form not of something given, such as money or other thing of value, but rather in undertaking some responsibility one is not legally bound to undertake or in refraining from exercising some right one would otherwise have been entitled to exercise.

disaffirmance 1. The refusal to fulfill a voidable contract. 2. Disclaimer; repudiation; disavowal; renunciation.

discharge A release from an obligation (such as a contract, a mortgage, or a note) because of performance or as a matter of grace.

divisible contract A contract whose parts are capable of separate or independent treatment; a contract that is enforceable as to a part which is valid, even though another part is invalied and unenforceable.

document of title Any document which in the regular course of business is treated as evidencing that the person in possession of it is entitled to receive, hold, and dispose of the document and the goods to which it pertains.

donee A person to whom a gift is made.

donee beneficiary Same as third-party beneficiary. The benefit a donee beneficiary receives from the contract between two other persons is a gift.

dowry Under the Code Civil, the property a woman brings to her husband when she marries.

draft 1. An order in writing by one person on another (commonly a bank) to pay a specified sum of money to a third person on demand or at a stated future time. 2. Compulsory military service. 3. A preliminary version of a document or plan. 4. To make a preliminary version of a document. 5. In the case of the Selective Service System, to require a person to perform military service.

duress Coercion applied for the purpose of compelling a person to do, or to refrain from doing, some act.

election of remedy 1. A requirement often present in the law that a party to a lawsuit must choose between two or more different types of relief allowed by law on the same set of facts. The adoption of one has the effect of barring use of the others. 2. The act of choosing between two or more different types of relief allowed by law on the same set of facts.

equitable relief (equitable remedy) A remedy available in equity rather than at law; generally relief other than money damages.

estoppel (estoppel by contract) A prohibition against denying the validity or significance of acts done in performance of a contract. . . . A person may be estopeed by his or her own acts or representations (that is, not be permitted to deny the truth or significance of what he or she said or did) if another person who was entitled to rely upon those statements or acts did so to his or her detriment.

exculpatory clause A clause in a contract or other legal document excusing a party from liability for his or her wrongful act.

executed contract A contract whose terms have been fully performed.

executor A person designated by a testator to carry out the directions and requests in the testator's will and to dispose of [the testator's] property according to the provisions of his or her will.

executory contract A contract yet to be performed, each party having bound himself or herself to do or not to do a particular thing.

ex parte Means "of a side," i.e., from one side or by one party. The term refers to an application made to the court by one party without notice to the other party.

express Stated; declared; clear; explicit; not left to implication.

express condition A condition that is stated rather than implied.

express contract A contract whose terms are stated by the parties.

express warranty A warranty created by the seller in a contract for sale of goods, in which the seller, orally or in writing, makes representations regarding the quality or condition of the goods.

fiduciary relationship A relationship between two persons in which one is obligated to act with the utmost good faith, honesty, and loyalty on behalf of the other.

firm offers Under the Uniform Commercial Code, an offer to buy or sell goods made in a signed writing which, by its terms, gives assurance that it will be held open. A firm offer is not revocable for want of prosecution during the time it states it will be held open, or, if no time is stated, for up to three months.

force majeure A force that humans can neither resist, foresee, nor prevent; an act of God. Some contracts contain a force majeure clause, which excuses nonperformance if the contract cannot be performed because of the occurrence of an unforeseeable and irresistible event.

form A printed instrument with blank spaces for the insertion of such details as may be required to make it a complete document.

formal contract 1. A signed, written contract, as opposed to an oral contract. 2. A contract that must be in a certain form to be valid.

four corners The face of a document or instrument. The expression generally relates to the act of construing a document based upon the document alone, without recourse to extrinsic evidence.

fraud Deceit, deception, or trickery that is intended to induce, and does induce, another to part with anything of value or surrender some legal right.

frustration of purpose An event that may excuse nonperformance of a contract because it defeats or nullifies the objective in the minds of the parties when they entered into the contract.

full warranty A warranty that is not confined to specified defects and that covers labor as well as materials.

gift A voluntary transfer of property by one person to another without any consideration or compensation.

goods A term of variable meaning, sometimes signifying all personal property or movables, sometimes limited to merchandise held for sale or in storage, sometimes meaning tangible property only, and sometimes including intangible property such as securities. Securities, money, and things in action, however, are not "goods" within the definition of the Uniform Commercial Code; commodities, including futures and fungibles, are.

guarantor A person who makes or gives a guaranty.

guardian A person empowered by the law to care for another who, by virtue of age or lack of mental capacity, is legally unable to care for himself or herself.

Guardianship may also involve the duty of managing the estate of the incompetent person.

illusory promise A promise whose performance is completely up to the promisor. Because the carrying out of such a promise is optional, there is no mutuality, and therefore the promise cannot form the basis of a valid contract.

implied Something intended although not expressed, or not expressed in words.

implied condition (implied in fact condition) A condition that is not expressed but that is inferred by the law from the acts of the parties.

implied in fact contracts [Contracts which the] law infers from the circumstances, conduct, acts, or relationship of the parties rather than from their spoken words.

implied in law contracts Quasi contracts or constructive contracts imposed by the law, usually to prevent unjust enrichment.

implied warranty In the sale of personal property, a warranty by the seller, inferred by law (whether or not the seller intended to create the warranty), as to the quality or condition of the goods sold. Under the Uniform Commercial Code, the most important implied warranties are the implied warranty of merchantability and the implied warranty of fitness for a particular purpose. In any sale of goods, a warranty of merchantability (fitness for general or customary purposes) is implied if the seller normally sells such goods. An implied warranty of fitness for a particular purpose exists when the seller has reason to know the purpose for which the buyer wants the goods and the buyer is relying on the seller to furnish goods suited to that purpose.

impracticability 1. Legal term unique to the Uniform Commercial Code, from the provision of the UCC that excuses a seller from the obligation to deliver goods when delivery has become unrealistic because of unforeseen circumstances. 2. The state of being unworkable, unrealistic, or not capable of successful or worthwhile accomplishment.

incidental beneficiary A person to whom the benefits of a contract between two other people accrue merely as a matter of happenstance. An incidental beneficiary may not sue to enforce such a contract.

indemnification 1. The act of indemnifying or being indemnified. 2. Payment made by way of compensation for a loss.

indemnitor A person who indemnifies another.

informal contract A contract not in the customary form, often an oral contract.

injunction A court order that commands or prohibits some act or course of conduct. It is preventive in nature and designed to protect a plaintiff from irreparable injury to his or her property or property rights by prohibiting or commanding the doing of certain acts. An injunction is a form of equitable relief.

installment A payment of money due, the balance of which is to be paid at other agreed-upon times.

installment contract A contract that requires or authorizes the delivery of goods in separate lots.

insurable interest An interest from whose existence the owner derives a benefit and whose nonexistence will cause him or her to suffer a loss. The presence of an insurable interest is essential to the validity and enforceability of an insurance policy because it removes it from the category of a gambling contract.

integrated contract A written contract that contains all the terms and conditions of the parties' agreement. It must expressly say so. An integrated contract cannot be modified by parol evidence.

irrevocable That which cannot be abrogated, annulled, or withdrawn; not revocable.

irrevocable offer Under the Uniform Commercial Code, an offer to buy or sell goods made in a signed writing which, by its terms, gives assurance that it will be held open. A firm offer is not revocable for want of consideration during the time it states it will be held open, or, if no time is state, for up to three months.

leading object rule (main purpose rule) The rule that a contract to guarantee the debt of another must be in writing does not apply if the promisor's "leading object" or "main purpose" in giving the guaranty was to benefit himself or herself.

lease A contract for the possession of real estate in consideration of payment of rent, ordinarily for term of years or months, but sometimes at will. The person making the conveyance is the landlord or lessor; the person receiving the right of possession is the tenant or lessee.

legalese   The use by lawyers of specialized words or phrases, rather than plain talk, when it serves no purpose; legal jargon.

legality   The condition of conformity with the law; lawfulness.

legal remedy   A remedy available through legal action.

lessee   The person receiving the right of possession of real property, or possession and use of personal property, under a lease. A lessee of real estate is also known as a *tenant*.

letter of credit   A written promise, generally by a bank, that it will honor drafts made upon it by a specified customer so long as the conditions described in the letter are complied with; a document which states in legal form that the bank has extended credit to the owner of the letter and will pay his bills. Transactions involving letters of credit are governed by the Uniform Commercial Code.

limited warranty   1. A warranty that is limited in duration or confined to specified defects. 2. A warranty providing less than a full warranty provides.

liquidated claim   A claim the amount of which is agreed upon by the parties or which can be determined by applying rules of law or by mathematical calculation.

liquidated damages   A sum agreed upon by the parties at the time of entering into a contract as being payable by way of compensation for loss suffered in the event of a breach of contract; a sum similarly determined by a court in a lawsuit resulting from breach of contract.

mailbox rule   Rule in contract law that acceptance of an offer is effective upon dispatch (i.e., mailing) by the offeree and not upon receipt by the offeror. Sometimes called the implied agency rule because the Post Office is deemed to be the agent of the offeror. This rule applies to the acceptance of an offer, but not to the making, rejection, or revocation of an offer.

merchant   1. A person who regularly trades in a particular type of goods. 2. Under the Uniform Commercial Code, "a person who deals in goods of the kind or otherwise by his occupation holds himself out as having knowledge or skill peculiar to . . . the . . . goods involved in the transaction." The law holds a merchant to a higher standard than it imposes upon a casual seller; his or her transactions may carry with them an implied warranty of merchantability.

merge   The combining of one of anything with another or others; the absorption of one thing by another; a disappearing into something else.

minor   A person who has not yet attained his or her majority; a person who has not reached legal age; a person who has not acquired the capacity to contract.

misrepresentation   The statement of an untruth; a misstatement of fact designed to lead one to believe that something is other than it is; a false statement of fact designed to deceive.

mistake   1. An erroneous mental conception that influences a person to act or to decline to act; an unintentional act, omission, or error arising from ignorance, surprise, imposition, or misplaced confidence. "Mistake" is a legal concept especially significant in contract law because, depending upon the circumstances, it may warrant reformation or rescission of a contract. 2. An error, a misunderstanding; an inaccuracy.

mitigation of damages   Facts that tend to show that the plaintiff is not entitled to as large an amount of damages as would otherwise be recoverable. The law obligates an injured party to mitigate his or her injury, i.e., to do all he or she reasonably can to avoid or lessen the consequences of the other party's wrongful act.

motion   An application made to a court for the purpose of obtaining an order or rule directing something to be done in favor of the applicant. The types of motions available to litigants, as well as their form and the matters they appropriately address, are set forth in detail in the Federal Rules of Civil Procedure and the rules of civil procedure of the various states, as well as in the Federal Rules of Criminal Procedure and the various states' rules of criminal procedure. Motions may be written or oral, depending on the type of relief sought and on the court in which they are made.

mutual assent   A meeting of the minds; consent; agreement.

mutuality   Two persons having the same relationship toward each other with respect to a particular right, obligation, burden, or benefit; the condition of being mutual. Mutuality is essential to the existence of a binding contract.

mutual mistake   A mistake of fact that is reciprocal and common to both parties to an agreement, each laboring under the same misconception with respect to a material fact. Such a mistake will justify reformation of the contract, and may warrant its rescission.

necessaries (necessities)   Things reasonably necessary for maintaining a person in accordance with his or her position in life. Thus, depending upon the person's economic circumstances, "necessaries" may not be limited simply to those things required to maintain existence, i.e., shelter, food, clothing, and medical care.

negligence   The failure to do something that a reasonable person would do in the same circumstances, or the doing of something a reasonable person would not do. Negligence is a wrong generally characterized by carelessness, inattentiveness, and neglectfulness rather than by a positive intent to cause injury.

negotiable   1. Transferable by indorsement or delivery. 2. Subject to negotiation; bargainable.

no arrival, no sale   A term in a contract for sale of goods, which means that if the goods do not arrive at their destination, title does not pass to the buyer and he or she is not liable for the purchase price.

nominal damages   Damages awarded to a plaintiff in a very small or merely symbolic amount. Such damages are appropriate in a situation where: (1) although a legal right has been violated, no actual damages have been incurred, but the law recognizes the need to vindicate the plaintiff; (2) some compensable injury has been shown, but the amount of that injury has not been proven.

non-negotiable   1. A document or instrument not transferable by indorsement or delivery. 2. Not subject to negotiation; not bargainable.

notary public   A public officer whose function is to attest to the genuineness of documents and to administer oaths.

novation   The extinguishment of one obligation by another; a substituted contract that dissolves a previous contractual duty and creates a new one. Novation, which requires the mutual agreement of everyone concerned, replaces a contracting party with a new party who had no rights or obligations under the previous contract.

obligor   The person who owes an obligation to another; a promisor.

offer   A proposal made with the purpose of obtaining an acceptance, thereby creating a contract. 2. A tender of performance. 3. A statement of intention or willingness to do something.

offeree   A person to whom an offer is made.

offeror   A person who makes an offer.

option contract   1. An offer, combined with an agreement supported by consideration not to revoke the offer for a specified period of time; a future contract in which one of the parties has the right to insist on compliance with the contract, or to cancel it, at his or her election.

overreaching   Taking unfair advantage in bargaining.

parol evidence rule   Under the parol evidence rule, evidence of prior or contemporaneous oral agreements that would change the terms of a written contract are inadmissible. . . . [T]he intention of the parties, as evidenced by the language of a written contract, cannot be varied by parol proof of a different intention. The presumption is that the written contract incorporated all of the terms of the contract.

past consideration   Consideration given prior to entering into a contract. Past consideration is not sufficient consideration to support a contract.

patent   The exclusive right of manufacture, sale, or use granted by the federal government to a peson who invents or discovers a device or process that is new and useful.

performance   1. The doing of that which is required by a contract at the time, place, and in the manner stipulated in the contract, that is, according to the terms of the contract. 2. Fulfilling a duty in a manner that leaves nothing more to be done.

permanent injunction   An injunction granted after a final hearing on the merits, as distinguished from a temporary injunction granted to provide temporary relief.

plain meaning   The rule that in interpreting a contract whose wording is unambiguous, the courts will follow the "plain meaning" of the words used.

plaintiff   A person who brings a lawsuit.

pleadings   Formal statements by the parties to an action setting forth their claims or defenses. The various kinds of pleadings, and the rules governing them, are set forth in detail in the Federal Rules of Civil Procedure and, with respect to pleading in state courts, by the rules of civil procedure of the several states.

precedent   Prior decisions of the same court, or a higher court, which a judge must follow in deciding a subsequent case presenting similar facts and the same legal problem, even though different parties are involved and many years have elapsed.

preliminary injunction   An injunction granted prior to a full hearing on the merits. Its purpose is to preserve the status quo until the final hearing. A preliminary injunction is also referred to as a provisional injunction or temporary injunction.

principal   In an agency relationship, the person for whom the agent acts and from who the agent receives his or her authority to act. . . . The person for whose debt or default a surety is responsible under a contract of suretyship. . . . The person whose obligation is guaranteed by the guarantor under a contract of guaranty.

privity   An identity of interest between persons, so that the legal interest of one person is measured by the same legal right as the other; continuity of interest; successive relationships to the same rights of property.

probate   1. The judicial act whereby a will is adjudicated to be valid. 2. A term that describes the functions of the probate court, including the probate of wills and the supervision of the accounts and actions of administrators and executor of decedents' estates.

promisee   A person to whom a promise is made.

promisor   A person who makes a promise.

promissory estoppel   The principle that a promisor will be bound to a promise (that is, estopped to deny the promise), even though it is without consideration, if he or she intended that the promise should be

relied upon and it was in fact relied upon, and if a refusal to enforce the promise would result in an injustice.

puffing   Exaggerating. A seller who "talks up" what he or she is selling by praising it is not guilty of fraudulent misrepresentation so long as he or she confines himself or herself to his or her own opinion and does not misrepresent a material fact. Such salesmanship is "mere puffing."

punitive (exemplary) damages   Damages that are awarded over and above compensatory damages . . . because of the wanton, reckless, or malicious nature of the wrong done by the plaintiff. Such damages bear no relation to the plaintiff's actual loss and are often called exemplary damages, because their purpose is to make an example of the plaintiff to discourage others from engaging in the same kind of conduct in the future.

quantum meruit   Means "as much as is merited" or "as much as is deserved." The doctrine of quantum meruit makes a person liable to pay for services or goods that he or she accepts while knowing that the other party expects to be paid, even if there is no express contract, to avoid unjust enrichment.

quasi contract   An obligation imposed by law to achieve equity, usually to prevent unjust enrichment. A quasi contract is a legal fiction that a contract exists where there has been no express contract.

ratification   The act of giving one's approval to a previous act, whether one's own or someone else's, which, without such confirmation, would be nonbinding. A person may ratify a contract by expressly promising to be bound by it. Ratification may be implied from a person's conduct; it may also take place as a result of accepting the benefits of a transaction. Ratification is the confirmation of an act that has already been performed, as opposed to the authorization of an act that is yet to be performed.

reformation   An equitable remedy available to a party to a contract provided he or she can prove that the contract does not reflect the real agreement, i.e., the actual intention, of the parties.

rejection   Any act or word of an offeree, communicated to an offeror, conveying his or her refusal of an offer.

release The act of giving up or discharging a claim or right to the person against whom the claim exists or against whom the right is enforceable.

reliance Trust; confidence; dependence.

replevin An action by which the owner of personal property taken or detained by another may recover possession of it.

rescission The abrogation, annulment, or cancellation of a contract by the act of a party. Rescission may occur by mutual consent of the parties, pursuant to a condition contained in the contract, or for fraud, failure of consideration, material breach, or default. It is also a remedy available to parties by a judgment or decree of the court. More than mere termination, rescission restores the parties to the status quo existing before the contract was entered into.

restitution In both contract and tort, a remedy that restores the status quo. Restitution returns a person who has been wrongfully deprived of something to the position he or she occupied before the wrong occurred; it requires a defendant who has been unjustly enriched at the expense of the plaintiff to make the plaintiff whole, either, as may be appropriate, by returning property unjustly held, by reimbursing the plaintiff, or by paying compensation or indemnification.

revocable That which can be abrogated, annulled, or withdrawn.

revocation A nullification, cancellation, or withdrawal of a power, privilege, or act.

sale A transfer of title to property for money or its equivalent. Both real property and personal property (tangible as well as intangible) may be the subject of a sale. A sale may be executory or executed. A sale does not always result in an absolute transfer of title.

satisfaction 1. The discharge of an obligation by the payment of a debt. 2. The performance of a contract according to its terms.

seal An imprint made upon an instrument by a device such as an engraved metallic plate, or upon wax affixed to the instrument. The seal symbolizes authority or authenticity. Modern law does not commonly require that instruments be under seal. In instances where it does, the abbreviation "LS" is universally accepted as a legal seal.

seller A person who sells property he or she owns; a person who contracts for the sale of property, real or personal; a vendor.

simple contract 1. A parol contract. 2. At common law, any contract not under seal.

solicitation Invitation of a business transaction.

specific performance 1. The equitable remedy of compelling performance of a contract, as distinguished from an action at law for damages for breach of contract due to nonperformance. Specific performance may be ordered in circumstances where damages are an inadequate remedy. 2. The actual accomplishment of a contract by the party bound to fulfull it.

speculative damages Damages that have yet to occur and whose occurrence is doubtful. However, damages are not speculative merely because they cannot be computed with exactness.

Statute of Frauds A statute, existing in one or another form in every state, that requires certain classes of contracts to be in writing and signed by the parties. Its purpose is to prevent fraud or reduce the opportunities for fraud.

statutes of limitations Federal and state statutes prescribing the maximum period of time during which various types of civil actions and criminal prosecutions can be brought after the occurrence of the injury or the offense.

stipulation A mandate; a requirement; a condition.

stoppage in transit A right that a seller of goods on credit has to retake them while they are in the possession of a carrier or other intermediary, upon discovering that the buyer is insolvent.

strict construction doctrine As opposed to a broad construction, a narrow or literal construction of written material.

strict liability Liability for an injury whether or not there is fault or negligence; absolute liability. The law imposes strict liability in product liability cases.

substantial performance Performance of a contract that, although not full performance, is in good faith and in compliance with the contract except for minor deviations.

surety A person who promises to pay the debt or to satisfy the obligation of another person (the principal).

As opposed to the obligation of a guarantor, the obligation of a surety is both primary and absolute; that is, it does not depend upon a default by the principal.

surrogate motherhood   The status of a woman who "hosts" the fertilized egg of another woman in her womb or who is artificially inseminated with the sperm of a man who is married to someone else and to whom (with his wife) she has agreed to assign her parental rights if the child is delivered.

temporary restraining order (TRO)   Under the Federal Rules of Civil Procedure, injunctive relief that the court is empowered to grant, without notice to the opposing party and pending a hearing on the merits, upon a showing that failure to do so will result in "immediate and irreparable injury, loss or damage." TROs are similarly available under state rules of civil procedure.

term of art   Technical words; words or expressions that have a particular meaning in a particular science or profession.

third-party beneficiary contract   A contract made for the benefit of a third person.

title   1. The right of an owner with respect to property, real or personal, i.e., possession and the right of possession. 2. A document that evidences the rights of an owner; i.e., ownership rights.

tort   A wrong involving a breach of duty and resulting in an injury to the person or property of another. A tort is distinguished from a breach of contract in that a tort is a violation of a duty established by law, whereas a breach of contract results from a failure to meet an obligation created by the agreement of the parties. Although the same act may be both a crime and a tort, the crime is an offense against the public which is prosecuted by the state in a criminal action; the tort is a private wrong that must be pursued by the injured party in a civil action.

trademark   A mark, design, title, logo, or motto used in the sale or advertising of products to identify them and distinguish them from the products of others. A trademark is the property of its owner and, when registered under the Trademark Act, is reserved for the exclusive use of its owner.

treble damages   Damages in triple the amount of the damages actually incurred. Treble damages are a form of punitive damages or exemplary damages authorized by statute in some circumstances if warranted by the severity of the violation or the seriousness of the wrong.

unconditional   Without conditions; without restrictions; absolute.

unconscionable   Morally offensive, reprehensible, or repugnant. An unconscionable contract is a contract in which a dominant party has taken unfair advantage of a weaker party, who has little or no bargaining power, and has imposed terms and conditions that are unreasonable and one-sided. A court may refuse to enforce an unconscionable contract. What is or is not "unconscionable" often depends upon the contract's commercial setting.

undue influence   Inappropriate pressure exerted on a person for the purpose of causing him or her to substitute his or her will for he will or wishes of another. Undue influence is a form of coercion to which the aged or infirm are particularly vulnerable, especially at the hands of a person whom they feel they have reason to trust.

Uniform Commercial Code   One of the Uniform Laws, which has been adopted in much the same form in every state. It governs most aspects of commercial transactions, including sales, leases, negotiable instruments, deposits and collections, letters of credit, bulk sales, warehouse receipts, bills of lading and other documents of title, investment securities, and secured transactions.

unilateral   1. Affecting the interests of only one party or one side. 2. One-sided; having only one side.

unilateral contract   A contract in which there is a promise on one side only, the consideration being an act or something other than another promise. . . . [A] unilateral contract is an offer that is accepted not by another promise, but by performance.

unilateral mistake   A misconception by one, but not both, parties to a contract with respect to the terms of the contract.

unjust enrichment   The equitable doctrine that a person who unjustly receives property, money, or other benefits that belong to another may not retain them and is obligated to return them. The remedy of restitution is based upon the principle that equity will not permit unjust enrichment.

unliquidated claim A claim whose existence or amount is not agreed upon by the parties; a claim whose amount cannot be determined by applying rules of law or by mathematical calculation.

usage of trade Under the Uniform Commercial Code, "Any practice or method of dealing having such regularity of observance in a place, vocation, or trade as to justify an expectation that it will be observed with respect to the transaction in question." Trade usage is also referred to as usage of trade.

usury Charging a rate of interest that exceeds the rate permitted by law.

valid Effective; sufficient in law; legal; lawful; not void; in effect.

value 1. Monetary worth. 2. The worth of a thing in money, material, services, or other things for which it may be exchanged. 3. Estimated worth. 4. Valuable consideration; adequate consideration; fair consideration; legal consideration.

venue The county or judicial district in which a case is to be tried. In civil cases, venue may be based on where the events giving rise to the cause of action took place or where the parties live or work. . . . Venue is distinguishable from jurisdiction because it

is an issue only if jurisdiction already exists and because, unlike jurisdiction, it can be waived or changed by consent of the parties.

void Null; without legal effect. . . . [A] transaction that is void is a transaction that, in law, never happened.

voidable Avoidable; subject to disaffirmance; defective but not invalid unless disaffirmed by the person entitled to disaffirm.

waiver The intentional relinquishment or renunciation of a right, claim, or privilege a person knows he or she has.

warranty 1. Generally, an agreement to be responsible for all damages arising from the falsity of a statement or the failure of an assurance. 2. With respect to a contract for sale of goods, a promise, either express or implied by law, with respect to the fitness or merchantability of the article that is the subject of the contract.

warranty of title With respect to the sale of goods, a warranty by the seller, implied by law, that he or she has title to the goods.

will 1. An instrument by which a person (the testator) makes a disposition of his or her property, to take effect after his or her death. A will is ambulatory and revocable during the testator's lifetime.

INDEX

A

Ability to pay, 89
Acceleration clauses, 377
Acceptance, 7, 26–32
  conditional, 251–54
  forms, sample, 36–38, 253
  partial, 291
  revocation of, 356–57
  under U.C.C., 244–45, 249–54,
    285–86
Accommodation, 245
Accord, 82, 171
Accord and satisfaction, 82,
  171, 185
Act of God, 36
Actual damages. *See* Compensatory
  damages
Adequate assurance. *See* Assurance
  of performance
Adhesion contracts, 61–62, 115
Administrators, 129
Advertisements, 24–27
Affiant, 100, 101
Affidavits, 99–100
Agency contracts, 134
Agent, 134, 135
ALI. *See* American Law Institute
Aliens, 98
Ambiguity, 146, 380
American Law Institute (ALI), 3
American Rule, 226
Antenuptial agreements. *See*
  Prenuptial agreements
Anticipatory breach, 179, 362–65
Anticipatory repudiation. *See*
  Anticipatory breach
Arbitration, 380–81

Article 2, 241–42. *See also* Uniform
  Commercial Code
  acceptance, 244–45, 249–54,
    285–86
  bulk sales, 297–99
  buyer's duties, 285–93
  buyer's remedies, 351–60
  contract formation under, 244–59,
    385–86
  parol evidence rule under,
    266–68
  payment, 292–93
  performance, 278–79
  repudiation, 362–65
  risk of loss, 304–12
  sales contract provisions,
    385–91
  scope of, 242–44
  seller's duties, 279–82
  seller's remedies, 337–51
  shipment contracts, 282–85,
    304–5
  special sale types, 293–97
  title to goods, 303–11
  unconscionability under, 259–63
  warranties. *See* Warranties
  writing requirements, 263–68,
    386. *See also* Statute of Frauds
Assent, mutual. *See* Mutual assent
Assignee, 223, 382, 383
Assignment, 223–26, 231,235, 382
  nonassignable rights, 226–29
  prohibition of, 227
Assignor, 223
Assurance of performance, 179, 364–
  65
Auctions, 297, 298

B

Bad faith, 180
Bailee, 279
Bailment, 279–81
Bailor, 279
Bait and switch, 26, 27
Bankruptcy, 81, 134, 180. *See also*
  Insolvency
Bargained-for exchange, 67–69, 73,
  75, 260
Beneficiary, 216–21
  change of, 218
  creditor, 219
  donee, 218–19
  incidental, 217, 220, 222
  intended, 217
  reliance by, 217
  third-party, 217
Benefit, 68, 127–29
Bids, 297
Bilateral, 33
Bilateral contracts, 9–10, 32, 68
Bill of sale, 271
Black-letter law, 3
Blood, sale of, 242–43
Blue laws, 107
Boilerplate, 61
Breach, 165, 176–79, 203, 209–10,
  337, 351
  anticipatory, 179, 362–65
  damages for, 189, 345–49
  threats of, 180
  of warranty, 328–32, 389
Bulk, 297
Bulk sales and transfers, 297–99
Buyer, 243, 245